AT THE OCEAN'S EDC

A History of Nova Scotia to Confederation

At the Ocean's Edge offers a vibrant account of Nova Scotia's colonial history, situating it in an early and dramatic chapter in the expansion of Europe. Between 1450 and 1850, various processes – sometimes violent, often judicial, rarely conclusive – transferred power first from Indigenous societies to the French and British empires, and then to European settlers and their descendants who claimed the land as their own.

This book not only brings Nova Scotia's struggles into sharp focus but also unpacks the intellectual and social values that took root in the region. By the time that Nova Scotia became a province of the Dominion of Canada in 1867, its multicultural peoples, including Mi'kmaq, Acadian, African, and British, had come to a grudging, unequal, and often contested accommodation among themselves. Written in accessible and spirited prose, the narrative follows larger trends through the experiences of colourful individuals who grappled with expulsion, genocide, and war to establish the institutions, relationships, and values that still shape Nova Scotia's identity.

(Studies in Atlantic Canada History)

MARGARET CONRAD is professor emerita in the History Department at University of New Brunswick.

STUDIES IN ATLANTIC CANADA HISTORY

Editors: John G. Reid and Peter L. Twohig

This monograph series focuses on the history of Atlantic Canada, inter-preting the scope of this field in a way that is deliberately inclusive and accommodating. As well as studies that deal wholly with any aspect of the history of the Atlantic region (or part thereof), the series extends to neighbouring geographical areas that are considered in conjunction with or in parallel with a portion of Atlantic Canada. Atlantic Canada's oceanic or global relationships are also included, and studies from any thematic or historiographical perspective are welcome.

At the Ocean's Edge

A History of Nova Scotia to Confederation

MARGARET CONRAD

UNIVERSITY OF TORONTO PRESS
Toronto Buffalo London

© University of Toronto Press 2020
Toronto Buffalo London
utorontopress.com
Printed in Canada

ISBN 978-1-4875-3548-3 (cloth)   ISBN 978-1-4875-3269-7 (EPUB)
ISBN 978-1-4875-2395-4 (paper)   ISBN 978-1-4875-3268-0 (PDF)

Library and Archives Canada Cataloguing in Publication

Title: At the ocean's edge : a history of Nova Scotia to Confederation /
   Margaret Conrad.
Names: Conrad, Margaret, author.
Series: Studies in Atlantic Canada history.
Description: Series statement: Studies in Atlantic Canada history
Identifiers: Canadiana (print) 20190236078 | Canadiana (ebook) 20190236086
   | ISBN 9781487535483 (cloth) | ISBN 9781487523954 (paper) | ISBN
   9781487532697 (EPUB) | ISBN 9781487532680 (PDF)
Subjects: CSH: Nova Scotia – History – To 1784. | CSH: Nova Scotia –
   History – 1784–1867. | CSH: Nova Scotia – Social conditions – To 1867. |
   CSH: Nova Scotia – Economic conditions – To 1867.
Classification: LCC FC2321 .C66 2020 | DDC 971.6/01 – dc23

University of Toronto Press acknowledges the financial assistance to its
publishing program of the Canada Council for the Arts and the Ontario Arts
Council, an agency of the Government of Ontario.

Canada Council   **Conseil des Arts**
for the Arts   **du Canada**

ONTARIO ARTS COUNCIL
CONSEIL DES ARTS DE L'ONTARIO
an Ontario government agency
un organisme du gouvernement de l'Ontario

Funded by the   Financé par le
Government   gouvernement
of Canada   du Canada   **Canadä**

Contents

Figures, Maps, and Tables

Figures

Maps

Tables

Acknowledgments

I am indebted to a great many historians whose research made this book possible. In particular, I want to thank Raymond Blake, Phillip Buckner, Gregory Kealey, Linda Kealey, Edward MacDonald, and Ged Martin for reading an earlier draft of the concluding chapter, and James Hiller, who, as co-author of four editions of *Atlantic Canada: A History*, has helped enormously in shaping my thinking on the Atlantic region. Marion Beyea, Susan Blair, Alvin Finkel, Donald Fyson, Julian Gwyn, Sylvia D. Hamilton, Barbara LeBlanc, and Elizabeth Mancke kindly helped to clarify my thinking on specific topics that befuddled me. Above all, I am grateful to John Reid, who checked the English translations of French texts, offered sage advice on two versions of the manuscript, and graciously accepted it as a volume in his Studies in Atlantic Canada series for the University of Toronto Press. The press waited two decades for the manuscript for this book, and in the end I offered only half what was bargained for, offering a good opportunity for another historian to carry Nova Scotia's story into the twenty-first century. Len Husband, acquisitions editor at UTP, managed the publication process with generosity and patience, two virtues, he will no doubt concede, that I need to improve upon. Editorial assistant Alexandra Grieve tracked down permissions for photos and maps with impressive efficiency. Freelance editor Barry Norris saved me from a number of embarrassing gaffs, and was as eager as I to bring consistency to the manuscript. Any failures to achieve that end are entirely my fault. I am also grateful to Leah Connor for preparing the manuscript for publication and to Nancy Wills for sparing me the burden of creating an index.

Keep On Keepin' On...

Nova Scotia Nova Scotia

People elsewhere
often ask where I come from
I answer Nova Scotia.

They say:
But you don't have an accent.
So where are you really from?
Your parents?
and your grand parents?
your great, great grand parents?

I'm Nova Scotian
As Nova Scotian as the mayflowers
the Black Refugee women picked.

As the evergreens they shaped into wreaths
As the maple stripped bare for market baskets
As the coal mined by Maurice Ruddick
As the salmon smoked by Willy Krauch
As the stories collected by Helen Creighton.

As tart, or as sweet as Annapolis Valley apples
As grand as Grand Pré sunsets
As steady as Sable Island horses.
As reliable as Beechville blueberries
As breathtaking as the Cabot Trail
As thick as Yarmouth fog

As old as Citadel Hill.
As strong as Fortress Louisbourg
As mysterious as Oak Island
As elegant as the Bluenose.

As beautiful as the souls of our ancestors.
You see, we didn't just get off the boat
And we keep on, keeping on
being Nova Scotian.

Map 0.1. Counties of Nova Scotia, 1867.

Sylvia D. Hamilton, written as an acceptance speech for the Portia White Prize in 2002, and used as a narration in the in the short film *Keep On, Keepin' On* (Maroon Films Inc., 2004). © This poem is published with the permission of Sylvia D. Hamilton and may not be republished without her consent.

Introduction

As Sylvia D. Hamilton's poem "Keep On Keepin' On" implies, the name "Nova Scotia" invokes images of fish, flowers, fog, forests, and deeply rooted folk. Her ancestors were among the enslaved Africans who achieved their freedom by fleeing their owners and joining the British side against the United States during the War of 1812. Although they continued to battle racism when they moved to Nova Scotia, the Black Refugees managed to "keep on, keepin' on." My own ancestors – a mix of German-speaking Protestants, New England Planters, and American Loyalists, all of whom arrived in the second half of the eighteenth century – also experienced Nova Scotia as a place of opportunity and refuge.

Despite their claims as "founding" families, our ambitious forebears were johnny-come-latelies. They were superimposed upon a population of French-speaking Acadians who survived a brutal ethnic cleansing in the mid-eighteenth century and Mi'kmaq who have lived in the Maritime region for millennia. As John G. Reid and Thomas Peace explain in their discussion of what scholars call "settler colonialism," Nova Scotia was redefined between 1450 and 1850 by processes – sometimes violent, often judicial, rarely conclusive – that transferred power first from Indigenous societies to the French and British empires, and then to European settlers and their descendants who claimed the land as their own.[1] By the time Nova Scotia became a province of the Dominion of Canada in 1867, its multicultural peoples, including a substantial infusion of English, Irish, Scots, and Welsh in the first half of the nineteenth century, had made a grudging and unequal accommodation among themselves. They subsequently adjusted to later arrivals, whose numbers enriched but never overwhelmed Nova Scotia's cultural fabric, which had been woven into a sturdy warp and woof by the mid-nineteenth century.

My goal in this volume is to explore the evolution of Nova Scotia before it became a province of Canada in 1867. In recent decades, the outpouring of new scholarship on Nova Scotia's pre-Confederation past offers exciting, if troubling, new perspectives that call into question long-held assumptions about what happened in this European colony perched on the western edge of the Atlantic Ocean.[2] A timely re-evaluation of where Nova Scotia fits in the expansion of Europe serves as essential knowledge for anyone hoping to respond creatively to current challenges. As the historian Jerry Bannister reminds us, people living in the Atlantic region of Canada are neither peripheral nor irrelevant to the human story, and they "deserve a history that engages with the present to explain the past."[3] The concluding chapter of this volume, labelled "Afterwards," pursues selected themes explored in the previous chapters through Nova Scotia's post-Confederation experience to demonstrate that history is never dead or even past. Whether we know it or not, it animates our lives, for good or ill, on a daily basis.

An awkward geographical space, Nova Scotia has been imagined in myriad ways. Its irregular coastline drawn on a map gives the impression of a great lobster stuck off the northeastern coast of North America. For those who have spent time in the area, its various regions – the Annapolis Valley, Cape Breton, Halifax, and the Eastern, Northumberland, and South Shores – each conjure up distinct geographies. Identities are often so finely calibrated that anyone without a clear understanding of the history embodied in Nova Scotia's eighteen county names, among them Inverness, Lunenburg, and Pictou, lacks a social as well as a directional compass. In other regions of Canada, Nova Scotia inspires thoughts of a friendly people – on first meeting at least – at home with themselves and their conservative, community-conscious ways. This view raises the hackles of many Nova Scotians, including mine, but it contains a grain of truth that warrants examination. While no fictional creation is identified with Nova Scotia to the same degree that Anne of Green Gables is associated with Prince Edward Island, two imagined characters, Evangeline and Sam Slick, both pre-Confederation imaginaries, signify dramatic developments – the expulsion of the Acadians and Nova Scotia's adjustment to the industrial order – that are central to understanding this Canadian province. And despite an overlay of Christian values introduced by European settlers, Klu'skap, a god of the Mi'kmaq, remains an iconic figure in Nova Scotia's cultural imagination.

Writing the history of Nova Scotia, John G. Reid argues, is a risky undertaking, requiring the author to decide at the outset how to frame the narrative.[4] Does one focus on the current boundaries or on the shape-shifting geography that at various times carried the name Nova

Scotia? I decided to explore Nova Scotia in its several guises, which include the larger region known variously as Mi'kma'ki, Acadie, and the Maritimes. New Brunswickers and Prince Edward Islanders, who also share these designations, no doubt will complain that this is yet another example of Nova Scotia's aspiration for imperial dominance. It must be ever thus. Nova Scotia has been central to defining the Maritimes and, in turn, the larger regional context has defined Nova Scotia.

All historians make choices about which topics to pursue in crafting their narrative. The political space called Nova Scotia inevitably shapes the selection process, but my particular goal has been to explore how the people living in that space sustained themselves economically and socially over time and what values inspired their choices. With the arrival of European settlers beginning in the seventeenth century, agricultural pursuits were imposed on the fishing, hunting, and gathering economies of the Mi'kmaq, and both were transformed by the Industrial Revolution, which, along with its economic and technological impact, inspired new ways of thinking about the world. By the nineteenth century, the tenets of liberalism – individual initiative, democratic accountability, civil liberties, the rule of law, property rights, capitalist enterprise, and separation of church and state – had triumphed, but older aristocratic, communal, and spiritual values continued to evolve and inspire loyalty. Notions of class, ethnic, gender, and religious differences managed to survive even the most disruptive transformations, and so, too, did practices relating to caring for others and sheer cussedness, none of which translated into narrow cost-calculating analyses.[5] Since liberalism is a grand but elusive idea, the details of its unfolding in specific landscapes such as Nova Scotia require careful scrutiny.

In 1987 British Prime Minister Margaret Thatcher famously asserted that "there is no such thing as society. There are individual men and women, and families."[6] Families and individuals figure prominently in what follows – indeed, I argue that Nova Scotia's identity coalesced at a time when possessive individualism was in ascendance – but I also attend to the richly textured society that families and individuals created through their associational efforts. These include political structures that range broadly from the loosely organized Grand Council of the Mi'kmaq to elected legislative assemblies. Between the political and the private spheres, a dazzling array of voluntary alliances – among them chambers of commerce, churches, cooperatives, civil rights organizations, ethnic associations, fraternal orders, mechanics' institutes, reading clubs, sports teams, temperance societies, labour unions, and women's auxiliaries – flourished in the public sphere by the mid-nineteenth century, complementing both the state and the individual.

None of the trends outlined above is unique to Nova Scotia, whose peoples share an Atlantic culture with Europe, Africa, and the Americas. For more than half a millennium, Nova Scotians have been making adjustments within this broad and ever-changing template, which is now global in scope. Neoliberals might well believe that the Maritime provinces, buffered by transfer payments from the federal government and bedevilled by outmigration, are failed states in waiting, but they still enjoy with other Canadian provinces the luxury of what by world standards are relatively peaceful and self-sustaining societies. This outcome is largely due to the complicated evolution of Nova Scotia and the institutions its peoples nurtured before Confederation, enabling them to "keep on, keepin' on" into the twenty-first century.

Margaret Conrad
April 2020

AT THE OCEAN'S EDGE

A History of Nova Scotia to Confederation

Chapter One

Ancient History

Some 10,600 years ago small bands of big-game hunters camped near what is now Debert, in Colchester County, Nova Scotia. Most organic materials from this site have dissolved over time, but some of the distinctive stone tools survived. Discovered in 1948 near a Second World War military base, these artefacts document the earliest humans in the Maritime region. Scholars labelled them Paleo-Indians. In the 1960s archaeologists from the National Museum of Canada recovered 4,500 spear points, knives, scrapers, and other tools from the site (Figure 1.1). This evidence suggests that it was a seasonal camp located near a caribou run or calving ground.[1] Since the excavations at Debert, other similar sites have been discovered at nearby Belmont and elsewhere in the Maritimes. The climate in Nova Scotia more than ten millennia ago was much colder than it is today, and the landscape, dominated by stunted spruce and tundra, would be unrecognizable to the modern eye. Because Nova Scotia's evolution as a geological place is both fascinating and relevant to the human story, it is important to begin with a brief overview of the province's ancient history, which has come into sharper focus only in recent decades.

Geological Beginnings

The origin of Earth and its inhabitants has long perplexed human beings, who have developed comforting explanations to account for their presence. According to stories told by the Mi'kmaq, Kji-kinap made the world and breathed life into a large, flat stone that he named Klu'skap (Glooscap). With the help of a young man and a young woman, Klu'skap cleaned out the silt-choked river beds, made the trees grow, summoned birds and animals from the Sky World, and shaped various geological features in the Maritimes.[2] Christians, Jews, and

Figure 1.1. Artefacts from the National Historic Sites at Debert and Belmont. These distinctive fluted spear points, typical of the Clovis Big-Game Hunting tradition, are among the many stone implements discovered at sites in Debert and Belmont, Nova Scotia.
Canadian Museum of Civilization.

Muslims, meanwhile, subscribed to Old Testament interpretations in which God created Earth and its inhabitants in six days, but the details of the narrative are sketchy, and no mention is made of Nova Scotia.

By the nineteenth century, mythical accounts were supplemented by research in the emerging fields of geology and paleontology. People and places in Nova Scotia played a prominent role in the new scientific explanations of Earth's evolution. In the 1830s, two Nova Scotians, Abraham Gesner and J. William Dawson, began examining coal deposits in the Maritime region, and became intrigued with fossils exposed by the high tide in the Bay of Fundy. Their findings drew the attention of Charles Lyell, the British founder of modern geology. While exploring the cliffs around Joggins on Chignecto Bay in 1852, Lyell and Dawson found the remains of tetrapods (vertebrate animals with four limbs) trapped in a hollow fossil tree. This and later discoveries by Dawson of fossilized reptiles at Joggins spurred further scientific thinking on the development of Earth and the life it supported.

A long stretch of Nova Scotia's ancient history can be read in the Joggins Fossil Cliffs, declared a UNESCO World Heritage site in 2008.[3] Described as the "coal age Galápagos" due to its wealth of fossils from the Carboniferous period (286 to 360 million years ago), the site is home to the earliest representatives of amniotes, a group of animals that includes reptiles, dinosaurs, birds, and mammals. Dinosaurs thrived in the region for nearly 200 million years until they suddenly became extinct due to an enormous asteroid that hit Earth in what is now Mexico nearly 66 million years ago.

Although it was still unclear to nineteenth-century scientists exactly how continents took shape, Joggins provided crucial evidence on which to build now widely accepted geological and evolutionary principles. Dawson's *Acadian Geology*, published in 1855, brought him international acclaim and influenced his famous contemporary Charles Darwin, whose book, *On the Origin of Species by Means of Natural Selection*, appeared in 1859. Meanwhile, Abraham Gesner, who had published *Remarks on the Geology and Mineralogy of Nova Scotia* in 1836, put his knowledge to practical use by developing processes for distilling bituminous materials. One of his most successful products was "coal oil," which he called kerosene. In 1861 Gesner published *A Practical Treatise on Coal, Petroleum and Other Distilled Oils*, signalling the advent of the modern fossil fuels industry.[4]

By the 1960s the theory of plate tectonics offered a compelling explanation for the geological forces that gave birth to the cliffs in Joggins.[5] This theory holds that continents are in constant movement, colliding and breaking apart as they float on the planet's soft, molten interior. When a supercontinent breaks into smaller continents, oceans form between them; when the continents collide, Earth's crust buckles to form mountain chains, while pieces of ocean crust, arcs of volcanic islands, and continental fragments are scattered helter-skelter. Nova Scotia is made up of a variety of these scattered "terranes," welded to each other during more than a billion years of continental movement. The oldest terrane in the Maritime region, an outlier of the Canadian Shield, can be found near the northern tip of the Cape Breton Highlands. Called the Blair River Complex, it is a fragment of ancient rock from a mountain-building collision that developed when the supercontinent Rodinia dominated the planet 1.1 billion to 750 million years ago. The Cape Breton Highlands have their origins in a tectonic collision nearly 500 million years ago that gave birth to the Appalachian Mountains running from Newfoundland to Alabama. By this time, life forms with hard skeletons had become common on land.

Older terranes were cobbled to the rest of Nova Scotia as it began to take shape at the heart of another supercontinent, Pangaea, which formed 350 to 200 million years ago. Located near the equator, its tropical forests, drowned over the course of various continental upheavals, laid the foundations for the rich coal fields of Cape Breton, Inverness, Pictou, and Cumberland counties and for the fossilized plants and animals that caught the attention of Dawson and Lyell. When the plates that had formed Pangaea began to separate 200 million years ago, the space between them was filled by the Atlantic Ocean, which becomes a few centimetres wider each year as the plates continue to drift apart. The coastline stretching from Africa to Scandinavia fits neatly into the eastern shores of the Americas because they were once part of the same supercontinent. In the middle of the Atlantic, a chain of relatively young, mostly submerged mountains hosts periodic eruptions, spreading molten rock along the ocean floor, creating new islands, and slowly increasing the landmass of Iceland, which sits astride what is known as the Mid-Atlantic Ridge.

In the 200 million years since Pangaea divided and North America began shifting northward, adjustments of the earth's crust and the forces of erosion have eaten away the Appalachian chain, whose mountains were once as impressive as the relatively youthful Rockies. This process also built up the continental shelf, with its rich reserves of oil and natural gas, and the undersea banks, which until recently supported an abundance of fish (Map 1.1). Sable Island, a crescent-shaped sandbar 160 kilometres southeast of Canso, serves as a sea-level reminder that the submerged Scotian Shelf, 120 to 249 kilometres wide, is as much a part of the Maritimes as current land formations.

In some circumstances, plates grind past each other, creating what geologists call transform faults. The Cobequid-Chedabucto Fault running across peninsular Nova Scotia from Cape Chignecto to Canso documents the boundary between two ancient terranes, which collided about 390 million years ago, and was once as active as the San Andreas Fault in California is today. It was along this fault line that a rift valley system similar to the Great Rift Valley in the Middle East and Africa developed near the present-day Bay of Fundy. As the lakes that formed in the basin dried up, salt and gypsum deposits were left behind. Active volcanoes around the basin produced the North Mountain, extending from Cape Blomidon to Brier Island. The amethyst, agate, and stilbite (Nova Scotia's provincial mineral) found in the Bay of Fundy region were created when holes in the frothy lava flows filled with minerals from seeping ground water.

More valuable than these semi-precious stones are the ongoing fossil discoveries found along the Fundy shores. In the mid-1980s,

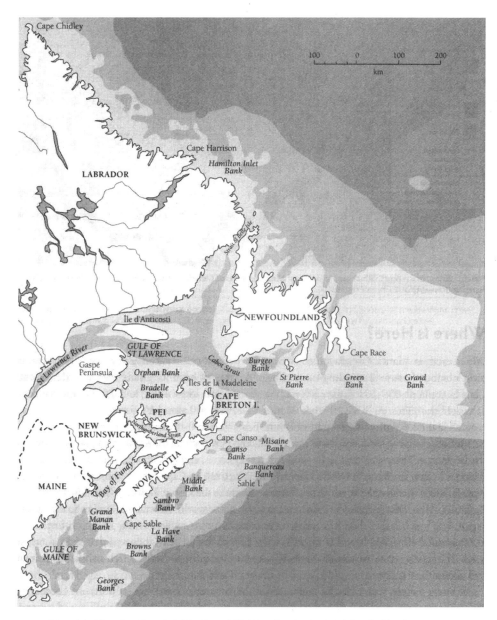

Map 1.1. The Continental Shelf and Fishing Banks in the Atlantic Region.
Adapted from H.A. Innis, *The Cod Fisheries: The History of an International Economy* (New Haven, CT: Yale University Press, 1940), 7, and Margaret R. Conrad and James K. Hiller, *Atlantic Canada: A History*, 3rd ed. (Don Mills, ON: Oxford University Press, 2015), 6.

paleontologists Paul Olsen, Neil Shubin, and Hans-Dieter Sues explored a cache of fossils at Wasson Bluff near Parrsboro. They collected three tonnes of evidence from the site, which documents a variety of species, among them small dinosaurs that survived a mass extinction at the beginning of the Jurassic period about 200 million years ago. Fossil remains of some of Canada's oldest dinosaurs have been recovered at Burntcoat Head in Hants County, a community that also boasts the world's highest tides. Reaching as high as sixteen metres, they are the result of 100 billion tonnes of water funnelling twice a day into the Minas Basin, at the end of the Bay of Fundy.

The final shaping of the Maritimes occurred during the last Ice Age, which gripped the continent from 2 million to 10,000 years ago. Over that period, glacial episodes and intervening warmer temperatures wrought havoc with the landscape. Ice, sometimes more than a kilometre thick, advanced and retreated, cutting deep valleys and fiords and leaving behind boulders, gravel, and fine sand. During one of the most aggressive glacial advances, a giant flow of ice from the interior of the continent carved out the Gulf of St Lawrence and the Cabot Strait. Chunks of debris known as erratics, dropped by the moving ice, still litter the Nova Scotia landscape, most dramatically along the road to Peggys Cove. In a few places, such as Citadel Hill in Halifax, glaciers left deposits of fertile sediment known as drumlins, which provide much of the agricultural land on the otherwise rocky soil of Nova Scotia's South Shore. The Annapolis-Cornwallis Valley, unusual in that it drains into basins at both ends, contains some of the best agricultural land in the province. Endowed with fertile marshlands along its tidal rivers, the Valley is blessed with ancient sediment deep enough to cover the underlying bedrock.[6]

The ice from the last glaciation – the Wisconsinan (75,000 to 10,000 years ago) – reached its maximum extent about 20,000 years ago.[7] As the ice retreated and the land rebounded from the weight of the glaciers, the sea level rose, fell, and rose again. In periods when ice built up and the sea level was low, sections of the continental shelf and the floors of the Bay of Fundy and the Northumberland Strait lay exposed. During warmer periods, peninsular Nova Scotia was an island and the Bras d'Or Lakes joined the Atlantic Ocean. Scientists believe that we are currently experiencing an interglacial episode, rather than the end of the last Ice Age.

Nova Scotia took the geological form we recognize today as recently as 3,000 years ago, but it remains subject to changes in climate and geography. Beginning in the thirteenth century, for example, a Little Ice Age brought cooling temperatures that perhaps help to account for the disappearance of the Norse who ranged throughout the North Atlantic a millennium ago.[8] Anyone living close to the Nova Scotia's coasts knows that they change their shape, sometimes at an alarming rate, as the ocean takes its toll. The sea level has been rising for several thousand years, but its pace has recently increased due to global warming. If polar icecaps continue to melt at the current rate, sea levels will rise dramatically, drowning low-lying coastal areas.[9]

First Peoples

The caribou hunters who ventured into the Maritime region more than 10,000 years ago were testing the northeastern frontiers of human survival as the glacial ice receded. Where did these people come from?[10] Oral tradition among the Mi'kmaq holds they have been here "since the world began," that they are *of* the land and did not come to it. Such a position sits uneasily with recent scientific arguments based on DNA evidence that humans fanned across the world from their homeland in Africa. According to this theory, the Americas were among the last areas of Earth to be occupied by humans.

Until recently, the most commonly held scientific theory posited that the first peoples in North America crossed the Bering land bridge from Asia to Alaska some 13,000 years ago, when the sea levels were lower. Hunting species such as mammoths, mastodons, and longhorn bison, they moved rapidly along an ice-free corridor through central-western Canada and then spread across the Americas, adapting to the changing climate, animal species, and vegetation.[11] This theory has now been called into question. Although people almost certainly arrived this way, earlier migrants from northeast Asia likely moved by watercraft along the western edges of ice-bound North America, setting down on outer islands until they reached more temperate climates. Some scholars argue that human occupation of the Americas dates back 20,000, 40,000, even 110,000 years, and that people might have arrived by multiple routes: sailing from island to island across the Pacific, reaching the east coast of North America via Iceland and Greenland, and even moving along a North Atlantic ice bridge that once connected exposed continental shelves on both sides of the Atlantic.[12]

Whatever their ancestry, the caribou hunters stopped coming to Debert after a few hundred years. It is not clear why, although fluctuating temperatures might have been the cause. Sea levels are estimated to have been sixty metres below current levels 10,600 years ago, rising dramatically for the next 5,000 years before stabilizing.[13] With dense forests increasingly threatening the survival of large terrestrial animals, the caribou moved away, and people might have moved along with them. They might also have adapted to the resources at hand, relying for their livelihood on smaller prey, such as deer and beaver, and on marine life, which included an abundance of seals, swordfish, and walruses.

Elsewhere in North America, hunting societies based on chipped stone technology gave way to a sequence of what are termed Archaic (or Pre-ceramic) cultures. They are distinguished from their predecessors by the sophistication of their stone tools, which were ground and polished. Although scholars believe that people of the Early and Middle Archaic cultures identified in New England also lived in the Maritime region from 10,000 to 2,500 years ago, very little is known about the first 5,000 years of their occupation. Most of the archaeological evidence we have from this period has been found near lakes and rivers and dredged from drowned coastal sites in the Bay of Fundy and elsewhere. This seems to support the hypothesis that rising sea levels submerged the coastal communities where most people would have lived.[14]

By the Late Archaic period beginning about 5,000 years ago, two distinct cultures seem to have taken root in the Maritimes. The Interior Late Archaic peoples represented an eastern version of the Laurentian tradition that extended from the Great Lakes to New Brunswick. Relying primarily on inland resources, they differed from the Coastal Late Archaic peoples, who were more dependent on marine life. According to the archaeologist James Tuck, this culture, which he calls Maritime Archaic, emerged along the coasts from Maine to northern Labrador, and might well reflect a continuous occupation from the great game hunters to European settlement.[15] There has been considerable debate around this interpretation. First, existing sites in the Maritimes seem to follow more closely traditions identified for New England, rather than the Gulf of St Lawrence and Labrador. Second, it raises the question of whether peoples in the Maritime region adapted over time, borrowing practices and technology from their neighbours, or were displaced by incoming populations. The notion of cultural borrowing and adaptation would allow for more continuous human occupation of the region than has hitherto been considered likely.[16]

Although the record is largely silent on the matter of population movements, the region's Indigenous peoples are probably the result of both adaptation and immigration. B.J. Bourque has identified Late Archaic peoples in the southwestern Maritimes and Maine who, he believes, represent a separate Moorehead cultural tradition.[17] People belonging to the Broad Point (or Susquehanna) culture, first defined in what are now the Mid-Atlantic states, also seem to have moved into Maine and the southwestern extremes of the Maritimes about 3,800 years ago. What made them distinct, apart from the broad points of their surviving artefacts, was their practice of cremating their dead and burying their ashes and bone fragments in pits. The Broad Point peoples seem not to have penetrated much beyond southwestern New Brunswick and the Yarmouth–Tusket region of Nova Scotia.

Whatever their specific traditions, all Archaic cultures depended – as had the peoples before them – on some combination of fishing, hunting, and gathering. Their highly mobile communities consisted of bands made up of a few related families, thirty to fifty people on average, who came together on a seasonal basis with neighbouring bands to exploit particular resources, to seek marriage partners, and to engage in trade, diplomacy, ceremony, and conviviality. Adept at crafting stone and bone, they developed an impressive array of tools to ensure survival, including toggling harpoons; lances tipped with bone and slate points; needles crafted from antlers and the bones of small animals; and pots made of hollowed-out stone. Ground and polished axes, adzes, and gouges were used to create hunting equipment, wooden bowls, dugout canoes, house frames, and small decorative objects. Although Archaic peoples established territorial jurisdictions for hunting purposes, interaction between the sea-based and interior peoples was common. The discovery in Archaic sites throughout the Maritime region of tools made of much-prized stone such as chert from Labrador and rhyolite from Ingonish Island in Cape Breton suggest that trading networks operated far and wide.[18]

Archaic peoples had highly developed spiritual beliefs, burying their dead, along with tools, weapons, and decorative objects, in cemeteries. Few burial sites from this period have been found in the Maritimes, but significant among them is one at Cow Point, on the thoroughfare between Grand Lake and Maquapit Lake in New Brunswick. When excavated in the early 1970s, it yielded sixty graves and four thousand artefacts, all covered in red ochre. Radiocarbon dating suggests that the last burials were 3,800 years old, and seem to reflect the Moorehead tradition. The most intriguing artefacts recovered from the late Archaic period are what look like a bayonet. Usually made from slate or bone, they are often decorated on one or both sides. What they represented and whether they had utilitarian or only ceremonial purposes is unknown.[19]

About 3,500 years ago, dramatic developments, perhaps relating to the changing climate, began to transform the Maritime region. Rising sea levels and cooling temperatures encouraged greater reliance on shellfish and fur-bearing animals. Absorbing influences and perhaps immigrants from the south and west,[20] Archaic peoples entered what is called the Woodland (or Ceramic) period. Modern Mi'kmaq, Wolastoqiyik, and Passamaquoddy are almost certainly descended from the Eastern Woodland peoples who predominated in the Maritimes from at least 2,500 years ago until the arrival of Europeans and, if we accept Tuck's hypothesis, whose ancestors had lived in the region for more than ten millennia.

The early Woodland period is characterized by clay pots embellished with cord impressions. One of several varieties of what is known as Vinette pottery, the decorations were made by wrapping a stick with cord and pressing it into the soft clay. The Archaic peoples in the Maritimes likely borrowed this technology from adjacent cultures in New England and the St Lawrence region, a theory supported by burial mound sites found at Red Bank (Metepenagiag) in New Brunswick and at Esson and Whites Lake (Skora), near Halifax. Dating back more than 2,000 years, these sites are similar to those associated with the Adena in Ohio, suggesting either that people from the interior of the continent moved through the region or that Maritime Archaic people had learned – perhaps through trade networks or a visiting shaman – new ways to inter their dead relatives. The burial goods at these sites included not only artefacts of local manufacture such as chipped and ground adze blades, but also beads made from Great Lakes copper and tubular pipes that appear to come from the Ohio region. What is especially unusual about these sites is that the bodies and sometimes also the grave goods were cremated before more objects were placed in the same grave and the whole covered with earth.[21]

In coastal communities, where most of the Woodland peoples lived, the calcium in shell middens – accumulations of discarded shells of clams, quahogs, mussels, scallops, and oysters – helped to preserve bone and other organic materials that were elsewhere destroyed by the region's acidic soils. Remains from nearly the entire span of the Woodland period have survived in a midden site at Sellar's Cove, on the shores of St Margaret's Bay. The evidence suggests that pottery techniques declined, perhaps because people were becoming more mobile. By the time of European contact, both semi-permanent dwellings along the coast and pottery had disappeared, for reasons that have yet to be fully explained.

Mobility was enhanced by the use of birchbark to make canoes, containers, and housing. Light and easily carried, canoes were primarily for river and coastal travel, but they also enabled the Woodland peoples to navigate the Northumberland Strait, the Strait of Canso, and perhaps the Cabot Strait as well. Watertight containers made from birchbark stitched with spruce roots and sealed with spruce gum were used to cook meat and fish. By heating stones in the fire and placing them in the pot filled with water, the contents eventually boiled. Poles covered with bark and lined with spruce bows served as mobile housing for people constantly on the move during the seasonal round. Snowshoes, which enabled men to speed along on top of the snow, increased the chances of success in the winter hunt. If the snow was not too deep, domesticated dogs participated in the chase. Heavy loads were hauled by sleds made of wide flat planks split from rock maple trees or bound to the back by a leather strap worn across the forehead or chest.

Before the arrival of Europeans, the region's Indigenous peoples had adopted the bow and arrow. The weapon's origins are unclear, but the general consensus is that it was first introduced into North America by the Tuniit, a group of Asian migrants who spread rapidly cross the Arctic, reaching Labrador nearly 4,000 years ago.[22] Evidence suggests that people in the Maritime region adopted this technology as recently as 1,000 years ago, but the exact timing is uncertain. There is no uncertainty, though, about the efficacy of the bow and arrow for hunting and warfare. With this new technology, hunters had greater range and accuracy than with the spear throwers it replaced, and it was also relatively easy to manufacture.

Although pre-contact societies in New England and the Great Lakes regions cultivated beans, maize, squash, and tobacco – the staple crops of the Mesoamerican civilizations – it has been widely held that people living in the Maritime region remained primarily fishers, hunters, and gatherers. Jason Hall has questioned this assumption, arguing that the inhabitants of the St John River Valley grew maize and other crops before the arrival of Europeans. Although the Little Ice Age made agricultural pursuits more precarious in the Maritimes before European contact, farming might have persisted in areas with warmer microclimates.[23] Whatever the outcome of this debate, Indigenous peoples in the region almost certainly had access to agricultural products through trade with their southern neighbours. Whether people living in the Maritimes in 1500 would have heard tales of the great city of Cahokia, which rose to prominence a millennium ago in the Mississippi River Valley, remains open to speculation.[24]

The larger context of pre-contact America is essential to understanding the Indigenous people of Nova Scotia on the eve of European contact. Five hundred years ago, there was a rough equivalence in the populations of the Americas and Europe, and major cities in the Americas were as large as any found across the Atlantic. Pre-contact peoples in the Americas shared complex spiritual traditions, calculated the movement of the sun and stars, and understood the medicinal properties of plants. As in Europe, the cycle of empire building, conquest, and destruction prevailed in the more populated areas of what are now Mexico and Central and South America. The small numbers of people on the frontiers of settlement inevitably lived with less elaborate institutional structures and often with more cooperative social arrangements. Because of its rugged terrain and cold winters, the area of present-day Canada was one of those frontiers of settlement.[25] Northern North America nevertheless was home to more than fifty distinct cultures. Scholars have also identified twelve linguistic groups, by far the most widespread of which were the Algonkian peoples who lived in the territory stretching from Atlantic to the foothills of the Rockies. The Mi'kmaq, Wolastoqiyik, and Passamaquoddy who currently live in the Maritime provinces are three of these Algonkian cultures.

The story of how Nova Scotia became a trailing edge of a westward drifting continent stretches the imagination. Even more imagination is required to grasp the relationship of people to the changing landscape. Although it is now possible to trace the main outlines of more than 10,000 years of human occupation in the Maritimes, the details of social life and strategies for adapting to dramatic climatic changes remain elusive. The arrival of Europeans five hundred years ago opens a larger window on how Indigenous peoples in the region experienced their environment and responded to newcomers bringing disruptively new cultural practices.

Chapter Two

Mi'kma'ki

Europeans began visiting the shores of the Americas on a regular basis in the early sixteenth century. Intrigued by what for them was a
"new world," a few literate intruders wrote detailed descriptions of
the peoples they encountered. Even with this additional information,
it is a challenge for anyone in the twenty-first century to understand
how life was experienced in pre-contact North American societies. We
can recover material culture, document historical memory, and reflect
on the comments of early foreign observers, but we strain to grasp the
mentalities of Indigenous peoples before Europeans introduced their
institutions, practices, and values. It is nevertheless important that we
try to understand these long-ago societies and to consider why their
life-worlds remain relevant today. By drawing upon early European
commentators, it is possible to bring more texture to what we have
learned from archaeological evidence and oral history about Nova
Scotia's first peoples (Map 2.1).

What's in a Name?

Before proceeding, it is necessary to interrogate the comments quoted
in this chapter to describe Indigenous peoples. The earliest European
sojourners in the region – men such as Jacques Cartier, Samuel de
Champlain, Marc Lescarbot, Pierre Biard, Nicolas Denys, and Chrétien
Le Clercq – were French colonizers and missionaries whose worldview shaped how they perceived foreign peoples. Confident that their
Christian "civilization" was superior to all others, the French referred
to Indigenous peoples as *les sauvages* and then named various groups
according to an imperfect knowledge of local culture.

In general terms, the Mi'kmaq sometimes referred to themselves
as "Lnu'k," meaning "the people," a term commonly used by North

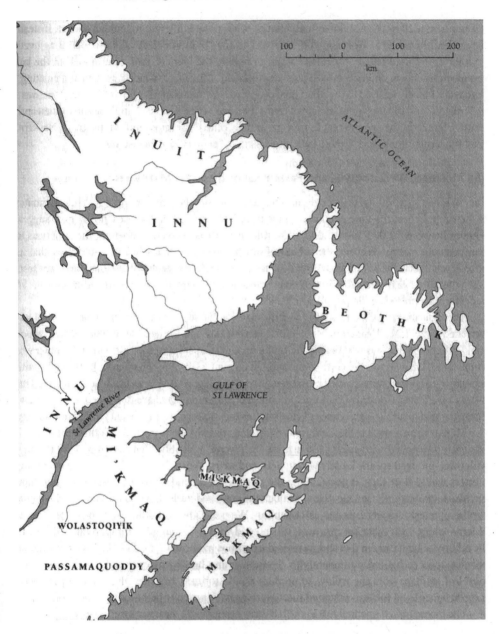

Map 2.1. Mi'kma'ki in the Sixteenth Century.
Adapted from Margaret R. Conrad and James K. Hiller, *Atlantic Canada: A History*,
3rd ed. (Don Mills, ON: Oxford University Press, 2015), 15.

Americans to distinguish themselves from other occupants of Earth. Most Indigenous peoples identified with their kinship relations and a locality – a river or a bay, for example – rather than by a specific linguistic group or nation, both being concepts introduced by Europeans. It is highly unlikely that the people dwelling along what is now the St John River in New Brunswick called themselves "Maliseet." Meaning "broken speakers," it was a derogatory term used by the Mi'kmaq to describe their nearest neighbours, who spoke a different dialect of a common Eastern Algonkian language.

When Champlain and Lescarbot became involved in founding the French colony of Acadie in the first decade of the seventeenth century, they labelled the peoples living there "Souriquois" and "Etchemin." The territorial domain of these two groups conformed roughly to the locations of the Mi'kmaq, Wolastoqiyik, Passamaquoddy, and eastern Abenaki today. In the late seventeenth century, the names "Micmac" and "Malicite" – variously spelled – began to appear on maps and in documents, sometimes referring to a part, rather than the whole, of the group. After the French cavalierly ceded Acadie to the British by the Treaty of Utrecht in 1713, the new names came into common usage. The term "Mi'kmaq" might be derived from "nikmaq," a word meaning "my kin," which was sometimes used as a greeting. In the late twentieth century, Indigenous peoples began to adopt earlier names and spellings that reflect their own language structures, rather than the versions imposed by Europeans. "Micmac" then became "Mi'kmaq." "Malecite" is now spelled "Maliseet" and commonly replaced by "Wolastoqiyik," referring to "the beautiful river" that defines their territory. "Passamaquoddy" is now "Peskotomuhkati."[1]

The documents on which we rely to supplement archaeological evidence and oral testimony must be treated with caution. Although they are thick with details, most were written a century or more after first contact. It is impossible to track with any precision the changes that occurred in the intervening period, including the initial impact of European diseases on population numbers and the adjustments to cultural practices that occurred as European trade goods became more widely available.[2] Communication between the Mi'kmaq and newcomers might also have led to misunderstandings. Since most European observers rarely had more than a rudimentary knowledge of local languages, much could be muddled in any exchange of information. Moreover, the early European documents on which we rely were written exclusively by men, so their comments with respect to women must be assessed with gender bias in mind. And each European writer described different areas of Mi'kma'ki: Cartier and Le Clercq interacted with Mi'kmaq living along the Gulf of St Lawrence; Denys had trading posts there and also on the South Shore of Nova Scotia and in Cape Breton; Champlain, Lescarbot, and Biard were based in the Bay of Fundy region. Although all Mi'kmaq shared a common language and culture, regional variations might well have been relevant. Finally, more than half a century separates the colonization experiences of Champlain on the Bay of Fundy in the early 1600s and Le Clercq's missionary activities in the Gaspé in the 1670s. Over that time, much had changed in Mi'kma'ki.

A depiction of the Mi'kmaq in the wake of European contact is thus, at best, a patchwork of disparate elements sewn together by a fragile thread of imagination. Because the comments of early Europeans in the Americas are as interesting for what they say about the colonizer as about the colonized, this chapter includes a greater number of direct quotations (further filtered by an English translation)[3] than is normally the case in historical narratives. Readers can then see for themselves how early Europeans, able to perceive the world only through their own cultural lenses, struggled to find words to describe societies they encountered.

Mi'kma'ki

The Mi'kmaq are the Indigenous people of Nova Scotia. By the early seventeenth century, their territory encompassed the Maritimes east of the St John River and included the Gaspé region of what is now the province of Quebec. Evidence suggests that, in the century following John Cabot's voyage in 1497, the Mi'kmaq expanded their range to participate in trade with European fishermen who soon became frequent summer visitors to the region. At some point in the sixteenth century, the Iroquoian peoples living along the St Lawrence when Jacques Cartier arrived there in the 1530s had either died out or retreated into the interior. Mi'kmaq and other Algonkian peoples, who were fishers, hunters, and gatherers rather than farmers, replaced them. One or more explanations could account for the disappearance of the St Lawrence Iroquoians. They might have been defeated by their aggressive Algonkian, Inuit, and Iroquoian neighbours in the competition for European trade goods; a pandemic might have swept through the region that was particularly devastating to sedentary agricultural communities; or the Little Ice Age might have prompted them to seek a warmer climate where their crops of beans, corn, and squash would be less endangered by the shorter growing season.[4]

Equally puzzling is the number of Mi'kmaq living in the Maritime region at the time of European contact. Although estimates range widely, from 3,500 to 200,000, the scholarly consensus suggests a figure of about

12,000–15,000.[5] The role of diseases in opening the Americas to European occupation has been the subject of much debate among scholars, but most agree that the impact was catastrophic. Summarizing decades of research, the geographer Cole Harris concludes that mortality rates among populations with no previous exposure to smallpox "were characteristically in the order of 50 to 75 percent, sometimes higher." In addition, he notes: "Growing evidence from around the western hemisphere suggests that a hundred years after the first epidemics reached a certain area, it seldom had more than 10 percent of its pre-epidemic population."[6] If Harris's findings are applied to the Mi'kmaq, their numbers at the time of contact would tilt towards much higher estimates.

The clearest statement concerning the impact of European diseases on the Mi'kmaq was reported by Pierre Biard, a Jesuit missionary who lived at Port-Royal from 1611 to 1613: "They are astonished and often complain that, since the French mingle with and carry on trade with them, they are dying fast and the population is thinning out." Moreover, he reported, "they assert that before this association and intercourse, all their countries were very populous, and they tell how one by one the different coasts, according as they have begun to traffic with us, have been more reduced by disease."[7] In his reflections on the cause of the "sparseness" of the population in Acadie, which he estimated to be about 3,500, Biard explained that the French sometimes tried to poison Indigenous people and that traders sold them spoiled food, which caused dysentery and sometimes death. He nevertheless attributed the overall decline in population not to "these detestable murders" but to other causes: the failure to lay away enough food for the winter; the excessive use of alcohol during the summer months when the European ships arrived; the likelihood of physical accidents in a lifestyle "so irregular, so necessitous and so painful"; and the heavy work undertaken by women, who nursed their children for three years or more, reducing frequent pregnancies. Although sometimes misguided, such thoughtful comments lift the curtain on the most intimate aspects of Mi'kmaw society in the early years of contact.

Upon first meeting the Mi'kmaq, Europeans were impressed by their robust physique. Biard claimed, no doubt with some exaggeration: "You do not encounter a big bellied, hunchbacked, or deformed person among them: those who are leperous, gouty, affected with gravel, or insane are unknown to them."[8] Men were reported as having little facial hair and, if any sprouted, they were inclined to pull it out. Knotting their long hair at the crown or back of the head, men wove into it bird feathers, shell beads, dyed moose hair, or porcupine quills. Unmarried women wore their hair long, gathering it into a tail at the back of the head. And fashion mattered. Made of fur and leather, their clothes were often highly decorated with paint, dyed moose hair, and porcupine quills. Both men and women wore bracelets and necklaces made from shells, and pierced their ears to hold pendants of carved birds, animals, and fish.[9] As was the case with most Indigenous peoples of the Americas, the Mi'kmaq painted their faces on special occasions and when going into battle. French fur trader Nicolas Denys, who spent several decades in the Maritime region beginning in 1632, was impressed: "Even their faces, when they go to ceremonies with their fine clothes, are painted in red and violet," he reported, "or else they make long and short rays of colour, according to fancy, on the nose, over the eyes, and along the cheeks, and they grease the hair with oil to make it shine. Those who are finest among them look like a masquerade."[10]

The extended family, sometimes supplemented by a few unrelated individuals, was the basic unit of Mi'kmaw society. Headed by a chief (*sakamow* or *sagamore*), each kinship band joined other bands in summer villages that could number up to three hundred people. Europeans, who lived in rigidly hierarchical societies, often remarked on the egalitarianism practised by the Mi'kmaq. "They are in no wise ungrateful to each other," Biard observed, "and share everything. No one would dare to refuse the request of another, nor to eat without giving him a part of what he has." Although chiefs had authority, it was exercised only with the approval of the band and shared with spiritual leaders and the most successful hunters. In Biard's experience:

> The sagamore is the eldest son of some powerful family, and consequently also its chief and leader. All the young people of the family are at his table and in his retinue; it is also his duty to provide dogs for the chase, canoes for transportation, provisions and reserves for bad weather and expeditions. The young people flatter him, hunt, and serve their apprenticeship under him, not being allowed to have anything before they are married, for then only can they have a dog and a bag; that is, have something of their own, and do for themselves.[11]

The increase in trade prompted by the arrival of Europeans enhanced the power of chiefs and seems to have contributed to more cohesive political arrangements. By the eighteenth century, Mi'kma'ki was divided into seven districts governed by chiefs who came together in a council of chiefs from each district's communities. The Grand Council might have developed only in response to European trade, but it almost certainly had antecedents in the pre-contact period. In the early seventeenth century, Biard explained that, in summer, "they pay visits and hold their State Councils," consulting "among themselves about peace and war, treaties of friendship and treaties for the common good." If there were major issues to consider "that their neighbors wish to make war upon them, or that they have killed someone, or that they must renew the alliance ... then messengers fly from all parts to make up the more general assembly."[12]

Both oral history and early European records suggest that the Mi'kmaq waged war on their neighbours.[13] Consisting mostly of hit-and-run raids to avenge perceived wrongdoing, military campaigns nevertheless required the careful coordination of otherwise dispersed manpower. When Chief Membertou's band at Port-Royal set out to take revenge against the Armouchiquois living in the area of present-day Maine for the murder of a kinsmen, they drew participants for a force of several hundred warriors from as far away as the Gaspé. Lescarbot was impressed that the Gaspésians took only six days to make the arduous journey to the south shore of the Bay of Fundy.[14] Masters of the region's forests and shores, the Mi'kmaq had clear mental maps of their territories. Chrétien Le Clercq, a Récollet missionary who served in the Gaspé region from 1675 to 1678, reported that they showed "much ingenuity in drawing upon bark a kind of map which marks exactly all the rivers and streams of a country of which they wish to make a representation." Distances, he noted, were calculated by "the number of nights which they are obliged to sleep on the way." Only when the sun was hidden by clouds or the terrain transformed by forest fires caused by lightening or runaway campfires, did their sense of direction fail them.[15]

According to Biard, their wars were "always" characterized "by deceit and treachery." He explained: "They have the bow and the shield, or buckler, but they never place themselves in a line of battle ... And, in truth, they are by nature fearful and cowardly, although they are always boasting, and do all they can to be renowned and to have the name of "Great-heart," which "among them is the crowning virtue."[16] As Europeans would soon discover, the "cowardly" tactics of the Mi'kmaq and other Indigenous peoples in North America – eventually labelled *la petite guerre* by the French – often proved highly effective against formal military strategies.

The goal of most attacks was to take prisoners and scalps. Although the victors often incorporated captive women and children into their communities, enemy warriors were less fortunate. Their treatment ran the gamut from humiliation – making them do women's work, for example – to execution. According to Le Clercq, a crack on the head with an axe or club was the method usually employed to dispatch a murderer among the Mi'kmaq, but various forms of torture were practised on an enemy. The Gaspésians, he noted, took scalps and feasted on the blood of their foes after a successful campaign on the North Shore of the St Lawrence.[17] If a female captive was guilty of treachery, then women sometimes performed the execution. Lescarbot reported that "a young maid of eighteen years of age, plump and fair," delivered the first knife stroke to the neck of an Armouchiquois woman who had helped a fellow captive escape from their village.[18] Lest we see the Mi'kamq as an unusually violent people, it must be remembered that contemporary Europeans had their own cruel and unusual punishments, among them burning people at the stake and "breaking" them on a rack.

The cruelties Mi'kmaq inflicted on their enemies contrasted sharply with their efforts to preserve good relations within the community, where mutual aid prevailed. "They live in great harmony," Le Clercq declared. "There is continual joy in their wigwams."[19] Since expressions of anger were frowned upon, discipline was achieved through ridicule, shaming, and shunning. Le Clercq suggested that the ravages of a Maritime winter, which he claimed reduced some people to cannibalism, put this idyllic life in jeopardy, but the general conclusion of most European observers was that the Mi'kmaq were well adapted to their environment and saw little need to change their practices to accommodate the newcomers. "Which of these two is the wisest and happiest," a chief living in the Gaspé region is reported to have asked, "he who labours without ceasing and only obtains, and that with great trouble, enough to live on, or he who rests in comfort and finds all that he needs in the pleasure of hunting and fishing?"[20]

Making a Living

As primarily fishers, hunters, and gatherers, the Mi'kmaq followed a seasonal rhythm that allowed them to make the most effective use of available resources. Biard reported that in January, "they have the seal hunting" and "in the month of February and until the middle of March, is the great hunt for Beavers, otters, moose, bears (which are very good), and for the caribou." By the "middle of March, fish begin to spawn, and to come up from the sea into certain streams, often so abundantly that everything swarms with them." He noted that "the smelt is the first" and then "the herring at the end of April." Meanwhile, "bustards [Canada geese], which are large ducks, double the size of ours, come from the South and eagerly make their nests upon the Islands ... At the same time come the sturgeon, and salmon, and the great search through the Islets for eggs, as the waterfowl, which are there in great numbers, lay their eggs then, and often cover the Islets with their nests." Spring and summer brought abundance. "From the month of May up to the middle of September, they are free from all anxiety about their food; for the cod are upon the coast, and all kinds of fish and shellfish." In addition, "at certain times birds of passage, like bustards and grey and white geese," along with "gray partridges," and "a great many wild pigeons, which come to eat raspberries in the month of July," brought variety to the diet, as did "birds of prey and some rabbits and hares." In the middle of September, Biard observed, "they withdraw from the sea, beyond the reach of the tide, to the little rivers, where the eels spawn, of which they lay in a supply; they are good and fat. In October and November comes the second hunt for elks and beavers; and then in December (wonderful providence of God) comes a fish called by them *Ponamo* [tomcod], which spawns under the ice. Also then the turtles bear little ones."[21]

The Mi'kmaq had expert knowledge of the flora available to them. In the spring, they tapped the maple trees to produce sugar and gathered the curled fronds of ferns, known today as fiddleheads, which would have brought welcome nourishment after the long winter. Other greens, nuts, roots and tubers (what we now call Jerusalem artichokes, for example), and wild fruit (including blueberries, cherries, gooseberries, raspberries, strawberries, and teaberries) added important nutrients to the otherwise high-protein diet and provided the ingredients for various medicinal remedies.[22]

As the largest terrestrial animal, the moose had pride of place in the pre-contact economy. Every part of the animal contributed to survival and well-being. Its meat was eaten fresh and dried. Moose bones, pounded into a powder and boiled, rendered a highly nutritious butter called *cacamos*. Hides were converted into clothing, moccasins, carrying bags, and snowshoe webbing; antlers and bones became tools, weapons, and needles. Moose brains were used in tanning skins, dew-claws became noisy rattles, shin bones were carved into dice for games, tendons served as thread, and hair was used in embroidery.[23] Although moose were killed throughout the year – cows were fattest in the winter, bulls in the summer – they were most easily caught when deep snow impeded their escape from hunters speeding along on snowshoes. The hunters had dogs to help them track down their prey, which were then dispatched with spears and arrows.

The capture of a moose was a cause for celebration. According to Le Clercq:

> If by good luck it happens that a hunter kills a female in winter, or a male in the summer, there is then the greatest rejoicing in all the neighbouring wigwams, because of the expectation and hope that each one has of

eating delectably some fat of the moose. But they redouble their joy, with cries and songs of gladness, when the hunter, all victorious from the chase, enters into the wigwam, and throws upon the ground, with gravity and pride as though he has triumphed over a redoubtable enemy, the load he has carried upon his shoulders, in which are enwrapped the heart, the kidney, the tongue, the entrails, and the most delicate fat. On these parts his friends and all his family begin forthwith to regale themselves, whilst the girls and women, with a thousand demonstrations of joy, and always singing and dancing, go to fetch upon their sledges the remainder of the meat of the moose, which this proud hunter has left very neatly buried in the snow.[24]

Given the significance assigned to moose, it is not surprising that the animal appeared in iconography. Upon his arrival at Canso in the spring of 1606, Lescarbot reported that the ship was met by two longboats, one manned by Mi'kmaq, "who had a moose on their sail."[25]

Dogs were greatly prized. According to Denys, each hunter worthy of the name had seven or eight dogs. So greatly did they value these animals that women, he claimed, were obliged to suckle the litter if its mother had no milk. Dogs were not fed on bones, beaver meat, or eels for fear of bringing bad luck to hunters in search of this prey. In respect for the animal, their bones were burned, buried, or thrown in the water. "Their wealth was in proportion to their Dogs," Denys maintained, "and, as a testimony to a friend of esteem in which they held him, they gave him that dog to eat which they valued most."[26]

Gender Roles

Gender roles among the Mi'kmaq were carefully defined. While men were hunters, leaders, toolmakers, and warriors, women were responsible for the wigwam, prepared and preserved the carcasses of animals, cared for the young, ill, and elderly, and made the warm clothing on which survival in a cold climate crucially depended. European men, who also conformed to strict gender roles, paid close attention to such matters.

By all accounts, most men were great hunters and warriors. European commentators were universally impressed by their ability to stand upright in moving canoes while spearing fish, to shoot an arrow through a bird on the wing, and, according to Le Clercq, to lay in wait ten to fifteen days behind some tree "all in order to find opportunity to surprise, fight, and vanquish their enemies."[27] One hunting technique drew particular attention. To make a good catch of migrating ducks and geese, hunters floated their canoes among a flock under the cover of darkness and then lit birchbark torches. When the birds circled the light, they were easily knocked down with long poles. Salmon also succumbed to these pyrotechnics, but most fish were caught with three-pronged spears, loosely woven nets, and weirs.

In Biard's opinion, Mi'kmaw women worked especially hard. "These poor creatures," he reported, "endure all the misfortunes and hardships of life; they prepare and erect the houses, or cabins, furnishing them with fire, wood, and water; prepare the food, preserve the meat and other provisions, that is, dry them in the smoke to preserve them; go to bring the game from the place where it has been killed; sew and repair the canoes, mend and stretch the skins, curry them, and make clothes and shoes of them for the whole family; they go fishing and do the rowing; in short, undertake all the work except that alone of the grand chase, besides having the care and so weakening nourishment of their children."[28]

In practice, the roles of men and women were complementary: men caught the large animals, women fetched and dressed them; men made the snowshoe frames, women wove the webbing; men built the wooden structure of the canoe, women stitched the bark and chewed the spruce gum for caulking. There is little doubt, however, that repeatedly setting up and dismantling camp in the seasonal round gave women plenty of work to do. Biard described the process:

> Arrived at a certain place, the first thing they do is to build a fire and arrange their camp, which they have finished in an hour or two; often in half an hour. The women go to the woods and bring back some poles which are stuck into the ground in a circle around the fire, and at the top are interlaced, in the form of a pyramid so that they come together directly over the fire, for there is the chimney. Upon the poles they throw some skins, matting or bark. At the foot of the poles, under the skins, they put their baggage. All the space around the fire is strewn with leaves of the fir tree, so they will not feel the dampness of the ground; over these leaves are often thrown some mats, or sealskins as soft as velvet; upon this they stretch themselves around the fire with their heads resting upon their baggage; And, what no one would believe, they are very warm in there around · that little fire, even in the greatest rigors of the Winter. They do not camp except near some good water, and in an attractive location.[29]

Biard noted that in summer the shape of their houses was "broad and long, that they may have more air; then they nearly always cover them with bark, or mats made of tender reeds, finer and more delicate than ours made of straw, and so skilfully woven that when they are hung up the water runs along their surface without penetrating them." According to Le Clercq, the walls of their dwellings were decorated with images of birds, beaver, moose, and otters.[30]

In courtship, a young man lived with the intended bride's relatives for a year or more, all the while bringing them products of the hunt, building the frames for canoes and snowshoes, and generally proving to be a worthy provider. The object of his affection meanwhile busied herself, according to le Clercq, "making snowshoes, sewing canoes, preparing skins of moose or of beaver, drawing the sled." Once a proposal was accepted, the young man laid in provisions for a community feast that formalized the marriage.[31] The couple then lived in the husband's household.

As well as being patrilocal, the Mi'kmaq were patriarchal, subordinating women and younger men to the authority of adult men. Le Clercq observed: "The women have no command among the Indians. They must needs obey the orders of their husbands. They have no rights in councils, nor in the public feasts. It is the same, as to this, with the young men who have not yet killed any moose, the death of which opens the portal to the honours of the Gaspesian nation, and gives to the young men the right to assist at public and private assemblies. One is always a young man, that is to say, one has no more rights than the children, the women, and the girls, as long as he has not killed a moose."[32] Women experiencing menstruation were considered unclean, required to eat separately from the band, and forbidden to eat beaver meat. According to Le Clercq, the Mi'kmaq were convinced that "the beaver, which has sense, would no longer allow itself to be taken ... if it had been eaten by their unclean daughters."[33] Widows were not permitted to eat the meat from animals caught by young men. Instead, the chief and other older men were responsible for the well-being of widows and orphans.

The Mi'kmaq practised polygamy, and marriages were easily dissolved, especially when no children were involved. According to Biard, a chief was the most likely to have more than one wife, for two reasons: "One is, in order to retain their authority and power by having a number of children; for in that lies the strength of the house, in the great number of allies and connections; the second reason is their entertainment and service, which is great and laborious, since they have large families and a great number of followers, and therefore require a number of servants and housewives; now they have no other servants, slaves, or mechanics but the women."[34]

Le Clercq reported that women sometimes gave birth almost literally in their stride, stopping briefly in the woods to deliver their baby and then moving on. The accuracy of such an assessment coming from a priest may well be called into question, but there is little doubt that women had little time for repose unless experiencing a particularly difficult birth. In that case, Le Clercq claimed, her arms were stretched to a pole, her nose, ears, and mouth stopped up, and her sides pressed. If this intervention failed, the spiritual leader of the band was summoned to perform rituals, including what today would be called a smudging ceremony, using sweetgrass, wild sage, pukeweed, and other plants, to hasten the delivery. As with most Europeans, Le Clercq was intrigued by the method of carrying infants: "in place of a cradle, they make the children rest upon a little board, which they cover with skins of beaver, or with some other furs." Both the cradleboard and the infant's clothing were adorned with beadwork, porcupine quills, and painted designs, which Le Clercq explained were used "to beautify it, and to render it just so much the finer in proportion as they love their children."[35]

According to one report, the chief's wives served as keepers of the fire, which took some effort to rekindle on dry moss or rotted wood by striking two stones or rubbing sticks together. Chief Arguimaut (L'kimu), living on what is now Prince Edward Island, described the following fire ritual to the Roman Catholic missionary Abbé Pierre Maillard in the 1740s:

> To preserve the fire, especially in winter, we would entrust it to the care of our war-chief's women, who took turns to preserve the spark, using half-rotten pine wood covered with ash. Sometimes this fire lasted up to three moons. When it lasted the span of three moons, the fire became sacred and magical to us, and we showered with a thousand praises the chief's woman who had been the fire's guardian during the last days of the third moon. We would all gather together and, so that no member of the families which had camped there since the autumn should be absent, we sent out young men to fetch those who were missing. Then, when our numbers were complete, we would gather round and, without regard to age or rank, light our pipes at the fire. We would suck in the smoke and keep it in our mouths, and one by one we would puff it into the face of the woman who had last preserved the spark, telling her that she was worthy above all to share in the benign influence of the Father of Light, the Sun, because she had so skilfully preserved his emanations.[36]

Lifeways

Biard concluded that the Mi'kmaq remained healthy because they used "hot rooms," "sweat boxes," baths, and massages, and rubbed their bodies with seal oil. The latter practice had a variety of purposes, including warding off mosquitoes, which tormented native and new-comer alike. So successful were the Gaspésians in curing ills with herbal remedies that Le Clercq declared them "all by nature physicians, apoth-ecaries, and doctors."[37] Although herbal medicines were undoubtedly more effective than European practices of purging and bleeding, the rituals designed to release the evil spirits that caused the disease from the afflicted person were reviled by European missionaries, who had their own methods for exorcising demons.

Obliged to live among the Mi'kmaq for extended periods of time to achieve their goals, missionaries were often appalled by Indigenous standards of hygiene. Le Clercq was clear on this point:

> They are filthy and vile in their wigwams, of which the approaches are filled with excrement, feathers, chips, shreds of skin, and very often the entrails of the animals or the fishes ... In their eating they wash their meat only very superficially before putting it on the fire and they never clean the kettle except the first time that they use it. Their clothes are all filthy, both outside and inside, and soaked with oil and grease, of which the stink often produces sickness of the stomach. They hunt for vermin before everybody, without turning aside even a little. They make it walk for fun upon their hands, and they eat it as if it were something good. They find the use of our handkerchiefs ridiculous; they mock at us and say that it is placing excrements in our pockets. Finally, however calm it may be out-side the wigwam, there always prevails inside a very inconvenient wind, since [they] let it go very freely, especially when they have eaten much moose.[38]

It is unlikely that contemporary European dwellings, which for peas-ants often included the close proximity of their domesticated animals, were any more hygienic, but then Catholic priests rarely lived in such conditions.

Most European observers commented on the artistic expression that graced canoes, clothing, cradle boards, and wigwams. In addition to images of animals, birds, and fish, the sun, moon, and stars figured prominently.[39] Denys considered the *peschipotys* – leather bags fash-ioned by women skilled in sewing, weaving, embroidery, and design – to be especially beautiful. Used for holding tobacco and other valued items, these bags, he reported, often displayed "fantastic ornamentation, which they call *matachiez*," consisting of "porcupine quills, white, red, and violet," and sometimes "wampum," made from shells. Ethnologist Ruth Holmes Whitehead has determined that there were five different decorative techniques involving dyed and flattened porcupine quills:

weaving, wrapping, plaiting, stitching, and bark-insertion. Most of these disappeared when European commodities replaced local manufactures.[40] According to Denys, women wove "ornamental pieces the size of a foot ... on a frame, of which the warp is threads of leather from unborn Moose, a very delicate sort; the quills of Porcupine form the woof which they pass through these threads, just as one makes tapestry and it is very well made."[41] Collars, belts, and bracelets in quillwork also impressed European sojourners.

As in the Christian cultures of Europe, artistic expression often served spiritual purposes. Le Clercq was intrigued to discover that crosses were included among the iconography of the Gaspésians. Although he ruminated at length on this finding, it should hardly be surprising. The persistent efforts of Europeans to introduce Christian symbols might well have had some impact by the 1670s. Indeed, Jacques Cartier erected a ten-metre cross in the region in 1534, which must have left a lasting impression.

Before European contact, the Mi'kmaq depended on images and oral communication to pass knowledge to the next generation.[42] Shells woven into belts served to document treaties and other important events. According to Denys, people recited their genealogies at weddings and funerals "to keep alive the memory, and to preserve by tradition from father to son, the history of their ancestors, and the example of their fine actions and of their greatest qualities, something which would otherwise be lost to them, and would deprive them of a knowledge of their relationships, which they preserve by this means; and it serves to transmit their alliances to posterity." He also reported that the Mi'kmaq greatly valued the genealogical traditions that linked them to a line of "ancient chiefs" stretching back "more than twenty generations."[43]

As a people dependent upon oral tradition to pass on their cultural values, the Mi'kmaq were gifted storytellers. Denys explained:

There were some old men who composed them ... about Moose, the Foxes, and other animals, telling that they had seem some powerful enough to have taught others to work, like the Beavers, and had heard others who could speak ... When they told one of [these stories], it was always as heard from the grandfather. These made it appear that they had knowledge of the Deluge, and of matters of ancient Law. When they made their holiday feasts, after being well filled, there was always somebody who told them [a story] so long that it required all day and evening with intervals for laughing. They were great laughers ... During such times they never failed to smoke. They had a certain green tobacco, the leaf of which was not longer than the finger, nor any broader. They dried it, made it into a loaf, in the form of a cake, four inches thick. The smoke was not strong, the tobacco good and very mild.[44]

Tobacco was the drug of choice for the Mi'kmaq, and smoking figured prominently in their ceremonies and healing practices. Among the most unusual uses of tobacco was one reported by Sieur de Dièreville, a medical doctor, who explained how the Mi'kmaq saved drowned men who had capsized their canoe. After retrieving the victim, he claimed:

> They then fill with Tobacco smoke the bladder of some animal, or a long section of a large bowel, commonly used as receptacles for the preservation of their Fish & Seal oil, & having tied one end securely, they fasten a piece of Pipe or Calumet into the other, to serve as an injection Tube; this is introduced into the backside of the men who have drowned, & by compressing it with their hands they force into them the smoke contained in the bowel; they are afterwards tied by the feet to the nearest tree which can be found, & kept under observation; almost always follows the satisfaction of seeing that the smoke Douche forces them to disgorge all the water they had swallowed. Life is restored to their bodies.[45]

According to Denys, the Mi'kmaq used a local leaf, perhaps from the willow, to produce a mild tobacco, and they also smoked pukeweed (*lobelia inflata*) and tobacco obtained through trade with agricultural peoples to the southwest. Tobacco was so highly prized on both sides of the Atlantic that Europeans soon began to produce it and to include tobacco among the items exchanged for furs. Denys reported that pipes were made from wood, with the claw of a lobster for the bowl, and also of stone, which was hollowed out with bone, a process that took considerable time.

Time in Mi'kma'ki was calculated by the sun, moon, and seasons, and compared to most Europeans the Mi'kmaq had plenty of it. "Since they never expect that the fortunes of the children will be larger than those of their fathers," Le Clercq opined, "they are ... free from all those anxieties which we give ourselves in connection with the accumulation of property for the purpose of elevating children in society and in importance."[46] Celebrations – involving singing, dancing, feasting, smoking, and storytelling – could last for several days. Lescarbot noted that "the dances ... are performed without moving from one place; yet they are all in a round, or very nearly so, and they dance vehemently, striking the ground with their feet, and springing up in a half-leap ... And as for their hands, they keep them closed, and move their arms in the air, like a man who makes threatening gestures." Meanwhile, "there is but one who sings, be it man or woman: all the rest dance and say, *heh, heh*, like a man breathing hard. And at the end of every song, they all make a loud and long exclamation, saying *heeeee-e-e.*" He explained that "to be the more nimble, they commonly strip stark naked, because their dresses of skins hinder them; and if they have any heads or arms of their enemies, they carry them about their necks, dancing with this fair jewel, which they will sometimes bite, so great is their hatred even against the dead."[47]

As in most cultures, contests demonstrating skill and agility were popular among young men, who were eager to prove their prowess. Bones, sticks, and stones were used in various ways in games of chance. According to Lescarbot, the Mi'kmaq were addicted to gambling. He described one game, in which they "put in a platter a certain number of beans, coloured and painted upon one side, and having stretched out a skin on the ground, they play thereupon, striking with the dish upon the skin, and by that means the beans spring into the air, and do not all fall on the coloured side; and in that consists the hazard; and they have a certain number of quills made of rushes, which they distribute to the winners according to their luck in reckoning."[48]

The Spiritual Realm

Pre-contact peoples in the Americas shared a pantheistic worldview according to which humans were part of a cosmological order that encompassed all things, living and inanimate. According to the Mi'kmaq, the universe formed itself out of Power (*bouin* or *manitou*), which was manifested in people, animals, plants, and phenomena such as winds, weather, seasons, and directions.[49] Not only could one form of Power change into another – a person into a wolf, a stone into a person – but the character or state of mind of the Power force could also change – from good to evil, for instance, or strong to weak. This notion of Power made for an unpredictable universe, but it encouraged people to acquire and use Power responsibly through appropriate behaviour.

Dreams and trances helped an individual to acquire Power. By resorting to fasting, tests of endurance, and extended periods of isolation, altered states of consciousness could be achieved and one's particular source of Power identified. Spirit-beings could arrive out of the ocean fog, but they were usually encountered in the forest. Clothing, amulets, and objects such as animal hide, fur, ivory teeth, claws, bones, and feathers, which embodied Power, served as talismans to ward off evil. Based on their individual quest for Power, people would be accorded names such as Black Eagle or Loon Woman. Once acquired, Power could be lost by failure to respect the rules the belief system ordained.

For the Mi'kmaq, the sun and moon were the ancestors of "People," who lived on Earth, which was part of a spiritual universe made up of Six Worlds. Along with the Earth World, there was the World beneath the Water, the World beneath the Earth, the World above the Sky, and the World above the Earth. After death, the People went to the Ghost World, which a few managed to visit while still living. The Six Worlds were inhabited by good and evil forces embodied in horned serpents, giant man-eating birds, screaming monsters, roaring thunder, and spirits disguised as rocks or mountains. In this understanding of the cosmos, the dead could be reincarnated and even the part become the whole again. The bones of dead animals were therefore treated with respect and preserved so that the animal would wish to return to Earth and repeat the cycle. Conversely, an enemy must be entirely obliterated, and even then the ashes might return as mosquitoes and blackflies.

Spirits from the Ghost World were perceived to have the same needs as mortals. Thus, according to Le Clercq, the Mi'kmaq reserved a portion of their food for these "souls which are walking, say they, in the vicinity of their wigwams of their relatives and of their friends." Because everything was animated, "they went hunting the souls of beavers and of moose with the souls of their snowshoes, bows, and arrows." It is for that reason, Le Clercq concluded, "that "our Gaspésians have always observed inviolably the custom of burying with the deceased everything that was in their use during life."[50]

Funerals and burials were elaborate affairs. According to Le Clercq and Denys, bodies of the dead were sometimes embalmed by drying them through exposure on a brier, safe from hungry animals, or by smoking the skin in pieces and then reassembling it. The relatives and friends covered the body with moose skin or beaver pelts, which was then "bound with cords of leather or bark in such a manner that the chin touches the knees and the feet the back," Le Clercq reported. "Hence it comes about that their graves are quite round, of the form of a well, and four or five feet deep." Once everyone had assembled in the wigwam of the deceased, the body was carried to the burial ground and the body placed in the grave and "covered with bark and with the finest skins" and "with branches of fir and sprigs of cedar." The impact of European trade is clear from Le Clercq's list of grave goods that accompanied the body. "If it was a man, they add his bow, arrows, spear, club, gun, powder, lead, porringer, kettle, etc.; if it was a woman, her collar for use in dragging the sled or in carrying wood, her axe, knife, blanket, necklaces of wampum and of beads, and her tools used for ornamenting and painting the clothes, as well as the needles for sewing the canoes and lacing the snowshoes." Finally, the grave was "filled with earth, and upon it is placed a quantity of logs elevated three or four feet in the form of a mausoleum."[51]

The universe functioned harmoniously only when natural forces were in balance – a condition maintained by elaborate rituals. At the time of contact, people with special spiritual powers (*puoinaq*) played a major role in presiding over rituals and articulating appropriate ways of living in the world. Le Clercq reported that most spiritual leaders were men, but a few women also aspired to this status. In his words, they "usurped the quality and name of *religieuses*" and said "certain prayers in their own fashion." Unlike Le Clercq, who disapproved of women "usurping" men's roles, the Mi'kmaq embraced female spiritual leaders. "They look upon these women as extraordinary persons," he reported, "who they believe ... to hold communication with the sun, which they have all adored as their divinity."[52] People who today would be described as two-spirited, gay, lesbian, and transgendered were also perceived as possessing extraordinary spiritual powers. As in many societies, some people were believed to have precognition, able to see in advance coming events and be able to warn of dangers ahead. Signs of coming events were common in everyday life. The appearance of blood in a bowl, in a tobacco pipe, or on a Power-robe, for example, announced a coming death.[53]

Le Clercq managed to secure a bag belonging to a spiritual leader, which he described in minute detail. Constructed from the head of a moose with its ears cut off, it contained an *Oüahich*, which was a stone the size of a nut wrapped in a box which he called the house of his Devil"; "a bit of bark on which was a figure, hideous enough, made from black and white wampum ... in the shape of a little wolverine, which was adorned in black and white beadwork"; "a little bow a foot in length, together with a cord, two fathoms long, interlaced with porcupine quills"; "a very thin skin, on which were represented some little children, birds, bears, beavers, and moose"; "a stick a good foot in length, adorned with white and red porcupine quills," to which was attached dew-claws to make "a devilish noise"; and a "little wooden bird."[54] Given his extreme bias against Indigenous spiritual leaders, it might be wise to take with a grain of salt his interpretation of the roles of these items. The little bow with a cord, Le Clercq claimed, was used to deliver a blow to a mother's womb to induce an abortion, although women also had their own medicines to achieve that end. According to Le Clercq, the fragment of bark wrapped in a thin skin caused the death of the person depicted on the package, and the wooden bird brought success in the hunting of waterfowl.

Le Clercq reported explanations for how life began on earth: "They say that when the sun, which they always recognized and worshipped as their God, created all this great universe, he divided the earth immediately into several parts, wholly separated from one another by great lakes; that in each part he caused to be born one man and one woman, and they multiplied." After a great flood, in which all but a few people died, "God came then to console them ... after which he let them live upon the earth in a great and happy tranquillity, granting them ... all the skills and ingenuity necessary for capturing beavers and moose in as great number as were needed for their subsistence."[55]

Klu'skap seems to have been a much-revered culture hero for the Mi'kmaq and many Eastern Woodland peoples. Because the first documented reference to Klu'skap was reported only in the 1860s, after Christianity had been widely accepted, his role in the pre-contact period remains obscure. His character is variously represented as creator, teacher, or trickster, a person of greater Power than any ordinary human being. In many accounts, he has a grandmother, a younger brother or nephew, and a pair of dogs. After battling his evil twin brother, whom he turned to stone, and a frog monster, who on one occasion swallowed up Earth's water, Klu'skap set to work making Mi'kma'ki a "happy land for people." Many of the prominent geological features in Nova Scotia, such as Blomidon and Kelly's Mountain, provided a dwelling place for Klu'skap, who is described as roaming widely around the Atlantic region and beyond. Like the Christian deity, he created a gendered social order, commanding men to hunt animals in the forest and women to cook them.[56] Klu'skap "was the friend and teacher of the Indians," Stephen Hood explained to Baptist missionary and ethnographer Silas Rand in 1869, "all they knew of the arts he taught them ... He was always sober, grave, and good."[57] A highly ambiguous figure, Klu'skap clearly represents a time when he and his people reigned supreme in Mi'kma'ki.[58]

❧

With the arrival of Europeans, cultural practices among the Mi'kmaq began to change, slowly at first, but with tragic long-term consequences. One story collected by Rand describes Klu'skap's departure from the Maritimes. As related by Josiah Jeremy, the mighty Klu'skap, reputed to have come to Mi'kma'ki by sea from the east, was conveyed to "a distant land in the west" on the back of a large whale around the time of European contact. Jeremy explains that the Mi'kmaq "expect his return in due time, and look to an end of their oppression."[59] By the mid-nineteenth century, the Mi'kmaq in Nova Scotia had been marginalized, and European culture was ascendant everywhere. The transition was inevitably a painful one.

Chapter Three

Sixteenth-Century Encounters, 1497–1605

The global reach of European animals, microbes, people, plants, and systems of knowledge is one of the most significant developments of the past five hundred years.[1] Jutting into the North Atlantic, the Maritime region, along with Newfoundland and Labrador, occupied the front lines of European expansion. The newcomers initially experienced great difficulty transplanting their life-worlds in northern North America. After spending the winter of 1604–05 on Île Ste-Croix, during which thirty-five of the seventy-nine would-be colonists succumbed to malnutrition, the French explorer and cartographer Samuel de Champlain had grasped the essence of the region. "It is difficult to know this country without having wintered there," he conceded, "for on arriving in summer everything is very pleasant on account of the woods, the beautiful landscapes, and the fine fishing for the many kinds of fish we found there." Despite being located at the same latitude as France, the area that the French called Acadie had a much different climate: "There are six months of winter in that country," he warned.[2]

Surviving a Maritime winter was a challenge for European colonizers. Although contact with the Americas became continuous after the voyages of Christopher Columbus and John Cabot in the 1490s, it took more than a century for Europeans to establish a tenuous foothold on the northeastern coast of North America and even longer for settler societies to take root there. Living off the land proved difficult for people from European agricultural societies, with the result that colonization efforts collapsed unless they were supported by Indigenous peoples and received continuous assistance from overseas. In the sixteenth century, neither could be assured.

When assessing the early years of contact, it is important to keep two points in mind. First, the Europeans who sailed to North America after 1497 came from their own localized fields of knowledge, which varied greatly. Most of the early arrivals were men looking for *terra firma*, fresh water, and sex, along with fish, fur, and captives to take back home. Sojourners with great ambitions, they were often drunk and aggressive – not the types to make a good impression. When Europeans attempted to establish colonies in Mi'kma'ki, they were intent not only on making profits from their initiatives, but also on claiming territory for distant monarchs, converting the Indigenous population to Christianity, and enlisting them as allies in military conflicts. This behaviour inevitably created friction.[3]

Second, European settlement was initially possible only because the Mi'kmaq were prepared for their own reasons to accept the intrusion. Despite the great gulf separating the two cultures, there were many points of convergence that made accommodation possible. Both sub-scribed to gender norms that defined work and power relations, and both were governed by highly imaginative spiritual and ceremonial worlds that facilitated understanding, if not mutual respect. On both sides of the Atlantic, people were avid traders, eager to acquire new commodities for profit and pleasure. Warfare was endemic to both continents and barbarous practices prevailed everywhere. As Europe expanded overseas, its political and religious leaders at home unleashed a reign of religious terror that took the lives of tens of thousands of people. Slaughter on such a large scale was rare in North American. Disease gutted Indigenous societies after contact, but Europeans also suffered from pandemics, which, though less disastrous than those that swept the Americas after contact, took an enormous toll. In the mid-fourteenth century, the Black Death wiped out at least a third of the population of Europe, and plague periodically ravaged communities well into the nineteenth century. Crop failures and rampaging armies were usually followed by famine among hard-pressed European peasantry, for whom survival was always precarious, as it could be for the Mi'kmaq.

Europeans on the Move

Sagas had documented the far-flung explorations of the Nordic peoples, but it was only in 1960 that physical evidence of one of their settlements, established around the year 1000, was discovered at L'Anse aux Meadows in northern Newfoundland, setting off a flurry of speculation about the significance of the site. The current scholarly consensus is that it was a base camp for a region the Norse called Vineland, encompassing the Gulf of St Lawrence and perhaps beyond. Like the European explorers who came after them, the Norse were eager to identify wild grapes, a sure sign that the area had a climate that could sustain agriculture and produce the wine that was so valued for both dietary and religious purposes. The Norse abandoned L'Anse aux Meadows after a few years, not only because of the hostility of local inhabitants, but also due to the distance from their homeland. They continued to visit the northern reaches of North America until the Little Ice Age in the fourteenth century forced a final retreat.[4]

What is now the Maritimes almost certainly fell within the orbit of these early Nordic explorers, and the harbours of the Miramichi and the Margaree rivers have been suggested as locations where they might have tried to settle. Since their brief attempt at colonization seems to have had no long-term consequences, it is important primarily for the evidence it provides for both the long reach of the Norse in this period and the possibility of other contact episodes as yet undocumented. It is highly likely, for example, that fishermen from Europe, by chance or design, visited the shores of northern North America well before John Cabot's voyage in 1497, but these pioneers remain unnamed and unheralded. Claims that Henry Sinclair, Earl of Orkney, spent time in Nova Scotia in the 1390s have been received with scepticism.[5]

The Europeans who bumped against North America in the late fifteenth century had changed considerably in the five hundred years since the Norse initiative. Following the Black Death, Europe experienced a dynamic transformation of its feudal values and institutions.[6] By the end of the fifteenth century, a swirling cauldron of political ambition, commercial enterprise, religious turmoil, technological innovation, and artistic expression animated European societies. Other peoples in the world at the time – the Chinese, in particular – had the capacity to engage in overseas ventures, but it was the Europeans who took the lead. In the process, they created an Atlantic world in which the Americas, Africa, and Europe were increasingly interconnected by traffic in people, commodities, and ideas.[7]

A significant feature of the European transformation was a shift of gravity from the Mediterranean to the emerging nation-states on the western shores of the Atlantic Ocean. This reorientation was driven primarily by commercial priorities. When hostile Ottoman forces seized control of Constantinople in 1453, Europeans began searching for oceanic routes that would allow them to trade directly with Asia. New technologies made such options possible. With better maps, ships, and navigational devices, longer voyages became possible, and the lure of economic gain spurred sailors to push their seagoing technology to its limits. European expansion was further driven by rivalry among European monarchs, each determined to best the other in reaping the prestige and wealth that could accrue from overseas initiatives.

Enthusiasm for exploration was part of a dramatic cultural awakening in Europe fuelled by the Renaissance, a rebirth of interest in the achievements of ancient Greece and Rome. Under the influence of Renaissance thinkers, Europeans began to reflect on broad areas of knowledge, asking troubling questions about the nature of the physical world and religious beliefs. Johannes Gutenberg's invention of the mechanical printing press in the mid-fifteenth century made it easier to disseminate new ideas, and Europe quickly became a hotbed of intellectual ferment. In 1517 the German priest Martin Luther set in motion a protest against papal authority that fractured Christendom into warring Protestant and Roman Catholic factions. This disruptive context offered fertile ground for Europeans to take an interest in new peoples and places, and provided the justification to conquer anything in their path.

The Portuguese were the first to undertake the systematic exploration of the Atlantic. By 1488 their sailors had rounded the Cape of Good Hope at the southern tip of Africa, opening a sea route to India a decade later. The Italian Cristoforo Colombo (Christopher Columbus), sailing under the banner of Spain, reached the Caribbean in 1492. With the blessing of the pope, the Spanish and Portuguese divided the non-Christian world between them, an agreement sealed by the Treaty of Tordesillas in 1494. They lost little time in establishing themselves in Mexico, Central and South America, and Asia. By Iberian standards, England and France were trespassing when they tried to stake claims in North America. Since it was a poor consolation prize in the rush for spoils, Spain and Portugal made only intermittent protests.

King Henry VII of England was quick to probe the potential of the "new world." In 1496 he commissioned John Cabot (Zuan Chaboto), a citizen of Venice, "to sail to all parts, regions, and coasts of the eastern, western, and northern sea," and authorized him "to conquer, occupy, and possess whatever towns, castles, cities, and islands, he discovered." Cabot launched three expeditions from Bristol, which was England's second-largest port and the base for many overseas ventures financed by local and Italian capitalists.[8] Although his first voyage was aborted, Cabot reached the eastern shores of North America in June 1497, where he raised a cross and the banners of England and Venice. Before Newfoundland joined Canada in 1949, Nova Scotians took advantage of the ambiguity surrounding Cabot's landfall to suggest that he had reached Cape Breton, where the Cabot Trail was constructed in the 1930s as a tourist attraction. The official consensus for the purposes of quincentenary celebrations in 1997 was that Cabot initially landed at Cape Bonavista in Newfoundland.[9] Although Cabot might well have reached Cape Breton during his third voyage in 1498, it was assumed until recently that the expedition was lost at sea.[10] Cabot's 1497 voyage is important for the course of Atlantic Canadian and global history because he returned with the news that the waters of the region swarmed with fish "which can be taken not only with the net, but in baskets let down with a stone." Within a decade, European fishermen were making regular voyages to harbours along the coast of northeastern North America to exploit this abundant resource.

Cabot's findings not only stimulated the fisheries, but also launched a flurry of poorly documented exploration. Bristol merchant William Weston is believed to have led an expedition into the North Atlantic, probably in 1499,[11] and other voyages out of Bristol followed, including one by Cabot's son Sebastian in 1508–9.[12] Assuming that, like Brazil, some of this territory lay within his sphere, King Manuel of Portugal authorized several voyages by ocean-savvy sailors from the Azores. Under Portuguese auspices, both João Fernandes and Gaspar Corte-Real may have ventured as far as Greenland by the beginning of the sixteenth century. In 1501, Corte-Real, with three caravels, reached "Terre Verde," probably Newfoundland, where he captured at least fifty inhabitants. The captives arrived in Lisbon to much fanfare, but Corte-Real's vessel failed to return, and his brother Miguel was lost in a fruitless rescue expedition in 1502.[13]

After a brief hiatus, official interest in exploration was rekindled in the 1520s. João Alvarez Fagundes, who in 1521 registered his discoveries from an earlier overseas voyage, led a Portuguese expedition to establish a colony, probably on Cape Breton Island. Designed to be a self-supporting community, it included ten families from the Azores in the mix of settlers, and had the right to generate revenue through the manufacture of soap. A document written in 1570 suggests that Basque fishermen regularly visited the colony, and on one occasion brought back a request for the services of a priest. The failure of this initiative, about which little is known, has been attributed to the climate and the hostility of the local inhabitants.[14]

Not to be outdone, King Francis I of France gave his official sanction to Giovanni da Verrazzano, an Italian sponsored by French business interests, in his efforts to explore the Atlantic coast of North America in 1524. His purpose had been to find a passage to Asia, but instead he confirmed the existence of a continuous coastline from the Carolinas to Nova Scotia, part of which was now labelled "New France" on maps.[15] While most of the people Verrazzano met along the way seemed to have had little previous contact with Europeans, this was not the case for those living farther north. He reported that the inhabitants of what was perhaps the Penobscot area of Maine exchanged their wares by rope from ship to shore and had become cautious in their dealings with foreigners. They had good reason to be wary. In 1524–5 Estêvão Gomes retraced Verrazzano's voyage along the North American coast on behalf of Spain. Mindful that the Spanish king expected him to return with treasure that had proved elusive, he filled his ship with Indigenous people, likely from Nova Scotia, to serve as slaves in the court of Charles V. Fifty-eight captives were alive when they reached Spain, where they were subsequently set free, but to what future is unknown.[16]

Determined to emulate the success of Spain and Portugal in reaping wealth from their overseas ventures, King Francis I commissioned Jacques Cartier in 1533 "to discover certain islands and countries where it is said that a great abundance of gold and other precious things is to be found."[17] The following year, Cartier sailed through the Strait of Belle Isle and explored the perimeter of the Gulf of St Lawrence. After skirting the west coast of Newfoundland, he sailed north of the Îles de la Madeleine, and, on 30 June, caught sight of some local inhabitants in their canoes in what is now Cascumpeque Bay in Prince Edward Island. The next day, "a man came in sight who ran after our longboats along the coast, making frequent signs to us to return towards [North Cape]. And seeing these signs we began to row towards him, but when he saw that we were returning, he began to run away and flee before us." Cartier's next move suggests that he understood the diplomatic protocols that had developed in the previous three decades. "We landed opposite to him and placed a knife and a woolen girdle on a branch and then returned to our ship."[18] Eager to continue his explorations, Cartier moved on without meeting what almost certainly was a Mi'kmaw accustomed to seeing European vessels offshore.

During Cartier's next encounter with the local inhabitants, the balance of numbers was reversed. The expedition explored the east coast of New Brunswick, and then sailed into what Cartier called the Bay of Chaleur, where two "fleets" of canoes – Cartier estimated forty or fifty of them – came into view. "Upon one of the fleets reaching the shore, there sprang out and landed a large number of people, who set up a great clamour and made frequent signs to us to come on shore, holding up to us some skins on sticks," he reported. Since the French were exploring inshore waters in their vulnerable longboat, "we did not care to go," Cartier admitted, "so we rowed toward the other fleet which was on the water." Undeterred, those on shore "made ready two of their largest canoes in order to follow us," and they were joined by five more "that were coming in from the sea."[19] Cartier's crew was obliged to shoot cannon and launch fire lances to warn off their would-be trading partners.

On this voyage, Cartier also met St Lawrence Iroquoians fishing at Gaspé. Communication between the two groups proved difficult, but Cartier made a clear statement when he arrogantly erected a ten-metre cross, blazoned with three fleurs-de-lys and the words "Vive Le Roy De France." To add injury to insult, he then captured two sons of their chief, Donnacona, and took them back to France. Cartier returned to the St Lawrence region, spending two winters (1535–6 and 1541–2) near Donnacona's village of Stadacona (present-day Quebec City), but the rigours of the climate and the hostility of their hosts defeated these efforts to establish a permanent base in New France.

Cartier's voyages marked the end of the first phase of the European discovery of North America. Neither treasure nor a passage to Asia had been found, and all attempts to establish permanent settlements had failed. Preoccupied with other pressing matters, including bitter power struggles between Protestants and Roman Catholics throughout Europe, most monarchs temporarily lost interest in overseas empires. King Henry VIII of England earned the enmity of Catholics at home and abroad when he defied the pope by declaring himself the Supreme Head of the Church of England in 1534, while France erupted in a civil war between Catholics and Protestants (known as Huguenots), which raged intermittently from 1562 to 1598. Only private initiatives guaranteed a growing European presence in northern North America.

Fish and Furs

In value and the number of people employed, the cod fishery soon eclipsed all other economic activities in the Americas. Fish was an important source of protein in the European diet, especially for Catholics, who were obliged to observe more than 150 meatless days a year. As leaders in the industry, the French produced both a "wet" (or "green") cure, in which the fish were put in the ship's hold and heavily salted or packed in brine, and a "dry" cure, in which the fish were split, lightly salted, and then dried on shore. Although French palates preferred green fish, dry-cured fish kept better in the warmer climates of countries around the Mediterranean, which were major consumers of cod. The French Basques produced a dry cure as did the English, who ignored the domestic market to exchange their product for bullion, fruits, wine, and other Mediterranean goods.[20] French monarchs and policy makers also encouraged a sedentary fishery in the Atlantic region as a means of establishing claims to territory that was crucial to a successful fishery and to the creation of an overseas empire.[21]

By the end of the sixteenth century, the English had begun to control the harbours on the eastern coast of the Avalon Peninsula, and had given their name to English Harbour (now Louisbourg) in Cape Breton. Reflecting their dominance in the fisheries, the French – mostly Basques, Bretons, and Normans – ranged widely along the Atlantic coast. "Cap Breton" appeared on maps in the 1520s, but it is unclear whether the name derived from the ubiquitous fishermen from Brittany or from their Basque counterparts familiar with a place of the same name in southern France.[22] Harbours on the east coast of Cape Breton Island, including Ingonish, St Ann's, and Canso, initially served as shore bases for Basque and French fishermen.[23] Later in the century, they moved along the southern coast of the Nova Scotia peninsula and into the Bay of Fundy.

The Portuguese and Spanish also exploited the North Atlantic fishery, but their presence decreased with the centralization of power in Madrid in 1580 and the decline of Spain following the defeat of its armada by the English in 1588. As a result, the English and French fishing fleets expanded to meet the Iberian demand. Peter Pope has estimated that, by the end of the sixteenth century, some 10,000–12,000 French and 5,000–6,000 English fishermen, in as many as 500 boats, plied the waters of what is now Atlantic Canada.[24] They returned home with, on average, 200,000 tonnes of cod annually and more besides: halibut, mackerel, and salmon; oil from cod, seals, walruses, and whales; furs, hides, and tusks; and curiosities such as birchbark canoes, decorated leather bags, and Indigenous captives.

Over the course of the sixteenth century, trade in furs became an increasingly lucrative sideline of the fisheries. Algonkian peoples, skilled in the hunt, proved the most reliable partners in the fur trade. In Paris, hatters paid premium prices for beaver pelts with the outer guard hairs removed, producing a silky felt ideal for making hats. Pelts of fox, marten, otter, and lynx were also greatly prized as was leather from the cured hides of moose, deer, and seals. With immense profits to be made, French merchants began equipping vessels solely to trade in fur with people living along the coast from Labrador to Maine. The lure of finding more and better pelts eventually drew traders deeper into the continent, allowing them to tap regions farther north and west than was possible from bases along the Atlantic coast.

By the end of the sixteenth century, Tadoussac on the north shore of the St Lawrence River had emerged as a permanent base for French and Basque fur traders, who appeared each summer to barter for the winter catch.[25] Canso, on the mainland side of Chedabucto Bay, also served as a rendezvous for European fishers and traders. Laced with islands, Canso harbour offered shelter, trading opportunities, and a chance to exchange information after the long voyage across the North Atlantic. Marc Lescarbot mentioned stopping at Canso on his outward voyage to Acadie in 1606, learning from the Mi'kmaq there about developments at Port-Royal the previous year.[26]

With two commercial nodes to attract them and an endless coast-line for chance encounters, the Mi'kmaq embraced the opportunity to become intermediaries in the lucrative trade that quickly expanded through traditional North American networks. According to historian James Axtell, they were reported "sailing Basque shallops, wearing various items of European clothing, and speaking half-Basque, half-Indian trade jargon" as they exchanged furs and leather for European trade goods and then peddled their wares to their neighbours.[27] Lescarbot described the arrival in what is now Saco, Maine, in 1607 of two chiefs, one from the St John River and the other from La Have River, with "much merchandise which they come thither to sell – to wit, kettles, large, medium, and small, hatchets, knives, dresses, capes, red jackets, peas, beans, biscuits, and other such things."[28]

Details about how European traders operated in the sixteenth century can be found in surviving documents relating to a commercial expedition in 1583 led by Étienne Bélanger of Rouen, in Normandy.[29] Clearly familiar with overseas trade, Bélanger's vessel carried knives, mirrors, "and suche like small marchaundize" to exchange for what was on offer as he explored the coast from Cape Breton to the Gulf of Maine. He collected a valuable cargo that included hides and fine fur, castoreum ("a kynde of liquid muske or sivet taken out the Beaver stones"), dyes ("excellent Cullors, as scarlet, vermillion, redd, tawny, yellow, grey and watchett"), feathers ("the quils wherof are red as vermillion"), and "[a] kynde of mynerall matter," which was thought to contain silver and tin. In his account, Bélanger claimed to have reaped twenty times his investment from the sale of his North American treasures, which included enough beaver pelts to make six hundred hats. Like Cartier before him, Bélanger planted the coat of arms of his sponsor, the Cardinal de Bourbon, choosing the head of the Bay of Fundy to stake his claim, and gave names to many of the places he visited.

Bélanger's relations with Indigenous peoples varied. While he was returning home along the southern coast of Nova Scotia, the Mi'kmaq seized a pinnace used to explore inshore waters and at least two of its crew were killed. If Bélanger had any intentions of setting up a trading post in the area, which seems to have been the case, this encounter probably caused him to have second thoughts. According to Bélanger, international relations improved the farther they sailed from Cape Breton, where he found the inhabitants to be "more cruell and subtill of nurture than the rest." This finding might point to different characteristics among the Mi'kmaq, but it is more likely that, as familiarity increased, so too did contempt.

It is impossible to determine whether other Europeans managed to establish trading posts in what is now Nova Scotia in the sixteenth century. Nor do we know if they left behind sojourners to live with the Mi'kmaq and learn their language, as the Basques did on the St Lawrence in this period. Some of the sixteenth-century records for the ports of Rouen, Bordeaux, and La Rochelle are available, but those for St-Malo and the Basque ports of Bayonne, St-Jean-de-Luz, and Ciboure have been lost. Since the Basques seem to have had a significant impact on trade and even on the Mi'kmaw language, this loss has created a serious gap in our understanding of sixteenth-century Nova Scotia. It is also difficult to assess the effect on the Maritime region of the disruption of the fur trade in the Gulf of St Lawrence in the late 1580s. This was due to increased armed conflict between and among natives and newcomers for ascendancy in the area and to Russian furs flooding the European market through a new Dutch trading post established at Archangel in 1585. Oral evidence suggests that the Mi'kmaq participated in the wars that erupted in the Gulf of St Lawrence in this period, but we know few of the details.[30]

Ultimately, the European presence in Mi'kmaq'ki remained seasonal and dispersed in the sixteenth century. Although fishermen were usually sponsored by overseas merchants, each ship's master operated independently. It was first come, first served when it came to establishing a base on shore, but most captains returned each year to familiar harbours to erect shelters, fishing wharves, and facilities for salting and drying fish. Lescarbot mentioned meeting "a fine old sailor from St Jean de Luz, four leagues off Canso," who claimed to have made forty-two voyages to "these parts" by 1607. Captain Savalette employed sixteen men, and was harassed by the local inhabitants encamped in the region, who, Lescarbot reported, "too boldly and impudently went on board his ship and carried off what they listed," preferring whiting, bass, and halibut to the lowly cod. "And it would have been difficult to prevent this impertinence," Lescarbot concluded, "inasmuch as one would have been forced to remain constantly under arms, and work would have been at a standstill." Lescarbot added that his own countrymen sometimes "behaved worse than the savages, and conducted themselves towards [Savalette] as the gendarme does here [in France] to the peasants."[31] Such were the occupational hazards of the free-wheeling commercial frontier along the North American coast.

By the end of the sixteenth century, pirates also operated on the coasts of the Americas. They focused their efforts on the Caribbean, where Spanish ships carrying gold and silver could be intercepted, but they sometimes raided fishing vessels and shore bases in the North Atlantic to secure supplies and conscript crew members. Although a few of the "buccaneers" were commissioned by their monarchs to cripple enemy shipping – Queen Elizabeth's courtier Francis Drake is a good example – others were genuine outlaws, who benefited from there being "no peace over the line" drawn in the western Atlantic by the Treaty of Tordesillas.[32]

In the sixteenth century, new maps played a major role in helping Europeans come to terms with North America's geography (Figure 3.1).

Figure 3.1. This map of New France, published by Venetian cartographer Giacomo Gastaldi in 1556, offers a fascinating glimpse into the way Europeans initially imagined people and places in their "new world." Although areas frequented by fishermen are clearly marked – Newfoundland (Terra Nuova) looms large, and "Breton" appears on an island and two capes – the map would have been of little use to anyone trying to navigate the Atlantic region in the sixteenth century.
Giacomo Gastaldi, Nuova Francia, 1556. McGillLibrary-123671–2119 Identifier arc:/13960/t19k84h04 MARCXML https://archive.org/details/McGillLibrary-123671-2119.

The Venetian map maker, Giacomo Gastaldi, got some of it right in his 1556 map of New France, but the contours of the Gulf of St Lawrence and the Bay of Fundy were slow to take shape, and Newfoundland continued to be attached to the mainland in some maps until the end of the century. With the grasp of geography so tenuous, place names floated promiscuously around the region. "Norumbega," first applied by Verrazzano to part of the North American coast, gradually took root in northern New England and then disappeared entirely. He located "Arcadia," a name drawn from an idyllic landscape in Greece, near what is now Virginia, but it was subsequently represented farther north as "La Cadie" or "Larcadie," becoming the French colony of Acadie by the end of the century.[33] "Cap Breton" stayed put, as did "Labrador" after it drifted southward from Greenland, where it was first affixed by Fernandes. Derived from the Portuguese word for "land holder," Labrador was also applied to the saltwater lake on Cape Breton Island by the mid-sixteenth century. The Basque presence was represented in place names such as Baccaro (codfish) and Barachois (sand bar). In many instances, Europeans adopted versions of place names used by the Mi'kmaq, which in turn were anglicized in the eighteenth century as, for example, Chezzetcook, Joggins, Malagash, and Tusket – names reflecting a multilayered cultural evolution spanning centuries.[34]

The Mi'kmaq Discover Europeans

The response of the Mi'kmaq to the arrival of Europeans must be understood with the Indigenous worldview in mind.[35] Initially the invaders were the objects of great curiosity, perhaps even perceived as messengers bringing new spiritual practices from one of the other worlds that the Mi'kmaq believed made up their cosmos. The wine and ship's biscuit, basic supplies on French and Basque vessels, appeared at first to be birchbark and blood – strange sustenance indeed. No one could be sure what their arrival portended, but it was clear that the newcomers were aliens. Josiah Jeremy's account of a Mi'kmaw's first sighting of bearded European sailors and their tall-masted ships was recorded by Silas Rand.

> When there were no people in this country but Indians, and before any others became known, a young woman had a singular dream ... A small island came floating in towards the land, with tall trees on it, and living beings. [The shaman] pondered the girl's dream but could make nothing of it. The next day an event occurred that explained all. What should they see but a singular little island, as they supposed, which had drifted near to

the land and become stationary there. There were trees on it, and branches to the trees, on which a number of bears ... were crawling about ... What was their surprise to find that these supposed bears were men.[36]

Unable to understand each other's language, both peoples had great difficulty interpreting cultural codes and judging intentions. It was therefore prudent to tread carefully. While these visitors offered intriguing gifts, they also brought disease and wielded weapons of extraordinary power. The European "fire tubes" were less accurate in hitting their mark than the bow and arrow, but they impressed nonetheless. So, too, did other metal objects, particularly axes, fish hooks, kettles, knives, needles, and swords. Woven cloth and items of clothing – jackets, hats, scarves, and belts – were welcome supplements to leather and fur. Beads – perhaps first glimpsed in rosaries – bells, buttons, and coins had a special appeal as variants of the wampum so valued by the Mi'kmaq.

Over time, relationships evolved. Initially, both peoples probably stole what they wanted from each other when they could get away with it. Europeans quickly learned not to leave their vessels unprotected because they would either be confiscated or stripped of their metal fittings. Nails made sharp tips for arrows, while fish hooks had immediate practical use, as did copper and brass kettles, which were also refashioned into adornments with special spiritual powers. Since taking captives and killing enemies were practices understood by both sides, violent encounters were no doubt common. Diplomatic protocols gradually developed to reduce friction. Trust could be gained by leaving gifts in a conspicuous location, chiefs could be won over by special attention, participation in rituals encouraged bonhomie, and silent negotiation of equivalent value minimized haggling. For both sides, trade items were initially perceived as trinkets and trash – glass beads and used beaver skins, for example.[37] Trust could easily be broken, and violence always remained an option.

A century after first contact, Europeans still tried the patience of their hosts. Lescarbot, who had few illusions about the superior morals of his countrymen, reported that some men in his entourage desecrated a Mi'kmaw cemetery in search of furs and other valuable grave goods.[38] In 1610 Robert Gravé du Pont, who conducted trade on the St John River, precipitated a diplomatic row when he abducted an Indigenous woman.[39] The European persistence in taking captives played a major role in perpetuating the uneasy relationship with the Mi'kmaq. Displayed to curious onlookers in courts and town squares across Europe, most of them were destined to become slaves or to serve as interpreters if they were lucky enough to return to their homelands. Many captives succumbed to European diseases in foreign lands.

This story, told to Silas Rand by an unidentified informant in 1870, encapsulates the disgust that the Mi'kmaq felt about being objectified by their European captors.

> Shortly after the country was discovered by the French, an Indian named Silmoodawa' was taken to Planchean [France] as a curiosity. Among other curious adventures, he was prevailed upon to exhibit the Indian mode of killing and curing game. A fat ox or deer was brought out of a beautiful park and handed over to the Indian; he was provided with all the necessary implements, and placed within an enclosure of ropes, through which no person was allowed to pass, but around which multitudes were gathered to witness the butchering operations of the savage. He shot the animal with a bow, bled him, skinned and dressed him, sliced up the meat, and spread it on flakes to dry; he then cooked a portion and ate it, and in order to exhibit the whole process, and to take a mischievous revenge upon them for making an exhibition of him, he went into a corner of the yard and eased himself before them all.[40]

Despite their mutual sense of cultural superiority, both the Mi'kmaq and the Europeans were transformed by their discovery of each other. Europeans were sustained in their beliefs and practices when they returned home, but memories of egalitarian social conventions among the Mi'kmaq had a lingering impact. In Europe, resources were so depleted that hunting, fishing, and cutting timber were privileges available only to the nobility, but not so in Mi'kmaq'ki, where the abundance of natural resources inspired awe and greed.

After contact with the Americas, the pace of European trade and intellectual life quickened, and nation-states became more cohesive as rulers struggled to find ways of extending their powers beyond immediate territorial boundaries.[41] New foods – beans, corn, groundnuts, artichokes, potatoes, pumpkins, and tomatoes – appeared in the Old World diet, and tobacco soon became as popular in Europe as in the Americas.[42] Although slavery was integral to both European and Indigenous societies, the enslavement of large numbers of people from Africa and the Americas to sustain overseas plantations began to racialize labour practices. And with the annual return of European fishers and traders, these transformations in Europe doubled back on Mi'kma'ki in an increasingly interconnected Atlantic world.

The Mi'kmaq ultimately had the worst of the exchange, but initially only in one respect: the arrival of Europeans brought disease. It depleted their numbers and made it increasingly difficult for them to resist European settlement on a grand scale. At the same time, their mobile lifestyle enabled the Mi'kmaq to avoid being conquered in a territorial sense. There were no cities to possess, no fortifications to storm. If Europeans became too troublesome, the Mi'kmaq either eliminated the nuisance or moved on. They would not, could not, be enslaved. More subtle in its effect was the burden of desire embodied in European trade goods. For both practical and spiritual reasons, metal products, cloth, and new foods had wide appeal among Indigenous peoples. In the sixteenth century, these commodities served to enhance the lifeways of the Mi'kmaq, but, in hindsight, it can be seen that international trade had a transforming impact that was detrimental in its consequences.

After contact, the Mi'kmaq continued to fight and hunt with their traditional weapons. Muskets and, most crucially, ammunition became widely available only in the seventeenth century. The Mi'kmaq might have gained an early military advantage with iron-tipped arrows, which were more effective in taking down enemies than arrows tipped with bone. More fundamentally, the goal of hunting changed. By supplementing subsistence with overseas trade, men slaughtered more wildlife than they needed for the survival of their community, and women had more work to do preparing pelts and dressing hides. Since men were the principal traders, women's status might have been further diminished by contact, but Denys reported that women were also active traders, exchanging their handiwork for ship's biscuit and brandy.[43] According to Denys and other European commentators, the Mi'kmaq were skilled traders, developing ingenious strategies that would bring them the best prices for their wares.

Formal trading ceremonies, a regular spring ritual, included European food and alcohol. Early in the seventeenth century, Pierre Biard reported that "when our ships come, they never stop gorging themselves excessively during several weeks with various kinds of food" and "they get drunk, not only on wine but on brandy." Believing that providence provided the necessities of life, they enjoyed the present, with little thought of the future, Biard opined. "[n]evertheless, if they are by themselves and where they may safely listen to their wives (for women are better managers everywhere), they will sometimes make some storehouses for the Winter, where they will keep smoked meats, roots, shelled acorns, peas, beans, or prunes, bought from us."[44]

Writing in the 1670s, Denys described in graphic detail the violence that alcohol encouraged. Orgies, he noted, could last for two or three days, after which "heads, arms, and legs are badly bruised, and much hair is pulled out." Heavy drinking was primarily a man's game in both

Europe and North America, but women also became addicted to alcohol. Although a few women participated in the revelry, the "women and the older girls," Denys reported, "also drink much, but by stealth, and they go to hide themselves in the woods for that purpose. The sailors know well the rendez-vous. It is they who furnish the brandy, and they bring them into so favourable a condition that they can do with them everything they will."[45] The children resulting from such couplings were absorbed into Mi'kmaw communities.

The Mi'kmaq initially spurned Christianity, but their spiritual practices were transformed, subtly at first and then more dramatically. Reporting on four burial sites from the late sixteenth and early seventeenth centuries, Ruth Holmes Whitehead notes that they included kettles, knives, axes, and beads, although the quality of the European goods deteriorated over time as cheaper products were produced especially for the North American trade.[46] By the second half of the seventeenth century, Denys claimed, the Mi'kmaq no longer placed anything in their graves, and were "cured" of their "little superstitions," such as not giving animal bones to dogs.[47] Two centuries of contact had significantly altered the Mi'kmaw worldview, a process that greatly accelerated with European settlement and missionary endeavours.

Testing the Water's Edge

Neither the fisheries nor the fur trade required permanent settlement, and once they had experienced a North American winter, most would-be settlers had little enthusiasm for experiencing another. Yet European ambitions for overseas settlement remained alive. As the fur trade developed, monarchs, hoping to avoid the risks but reap the rewards of any successes, began offering trade monopolies to private companies in return for establishing settlements in the territories they claimed. Merchants had the most to gain if they could corral all the profits for themselves by securing a monopoly of the trade in fish and fur. Fuelled by the zeal of the Counter-Reformation, the Roman Catholic Church also supported "new world" initiatives, which afforded an opportunity to convert Indigenous peoples to its brand of Christianity. The nobility in European courts often envisioned recouping their failing fortunes or enhancing their reputations through a colonization project. For those roaming the streets and country roads; housed in orphanages, prisons, and poor houses; or enslaved and indentured to their masters, ambition had little to do with their involuntary participation in overseas expeditions.

Early colonizing efforts took place on the islands and shores of eastern North America because they were closest to the countries from which the colonizers came. Without a lifeline to the metropole, isolated colonies, which all of them initially were, proved vulnerable in the extreme – to Indigenous hostility, to enemy attacks and pirate raids, and, above all, to the lack of food and supplies. Even those sponsors most determined to sustain their colonizing enterprises often lost their supply vessels in storms, on dangerous reefs, or to enemy attacks, leaving their colonists stranded. And everything worked in slow motion by today's standards. It took at least three weeks, under ideal conditions, to sail from England to Newfoundland and almost as long again to reach the Bay of Fundy. The vessels carrying Sieur de Dièreville to Port-Royal in 1699 took fifty-five days to make the journey from La Rochelle, and that despite the effort to summon a favourable wind by flogging the cabin boy.[48] Given the dangers of oceanic travel, it is not surprising that early colonizers devoted major portions of their narratives to descriptions of the challenges they faced at sea. Prevailing westerlies, hurricanes, thunderstorms, icebergs, shoals, pirates, and inept or drunken captains all threatened life and limb, while contagious diseases and seasickness often made life on board ship a misery. On occasion no winds blew, prolonging the voyage until food and water ran perilously low. Little wonder that so much joy was expressed when a bird was sighted, signalling that land was nearby.

At the end of the sixteenth century, France again turned its attention to overseas colonization. Henri IV, the first Bourbon king of France (1589–1610), converted to Catholicism in 1593 and five years later brought a temporary end to the religious wars. As part of the peace settlement, the king issued the Edict of Nantes in 1598, which granted religious tolerance to Huguenots in an officially Roman Catholic state. In the same year, he signalled his long-standing interest in overseas colonization by appointing the Marquis de La Roche-Mesgouez as lieutenant-general of the territories named Canada, Newfoundland, Labrador, and Norumbega, with a monopoly of the fur trade. A supporter of the king, La Roche had been commissioned as viceroy of New France in 1578, but two expeditions, one in 1578 and another in 1584, failed to reach North America due to pirates and shipwreck. Caught up in the religious wars, which resulted in his imprisonment for nine years, he made a third attempt to establish a colony in 1598.

La Roche fixed his attention on Sable Island, which he renamed Île de Bourbon, in honour of the king. The location of the colony suggests that it was designed as an outpost for later, more ambitious settlement efforts on the North American mainland. In the meantime, the sandbar on the edge of the Scotian shelf served his commercial goals, having the advantage of being at the crossroads of the sea lanes between

Newfoundland and the Caribbean and relatively close to Europe. The colonists included ten soldiers and forty settlers, most of them vagabonds and beggars from Rouen. Once they were settled on the north shore of the island, La Roche set sail for the Newfoundland fisheries and then returned to France. He continued to send annual supplies of "wines, coats, and clothing," thanks to a subsidy from the king, but the settlers were obliged to live on fish and game, their vegetable gardens, and the cattle abandoned on the island by an earlier expedition. When no ship was sent in 1602, murder and mayhem ensued. Only eleven survivors made it back to France in 1603, where the king awarded them each 50 *écus*, much to the disgust of La Roche, who felt that the rascals should have been hanged for their lawlessness.[49]

La Roche continued to use Sable Island as a base for his commercial operations, but King Henri's favour passed to other entrepreneurs. In 1603 he appointed Pierre Dugua, Sieur de Mons, as viceroy of "la Cadie," "Canada," and "autres terres de la Nouvelle France," situated between the fortieth and forty-sixth parallels of latitude.[50] In return for a ten-year fur trade monopoly, de Mons agreed to sponsor sixty settlers annually, to support missionary efforts among the local population, and to explore the region with a view to finding precious metals. A native of the Huguenot stronghold of Saintonge, de Mons had distinguished himself in the religious wars, remained loyal to the king when he converted to Catholicism, and was rewarded with an annual pension and various public offices. Defying injunctions against the nobility participating in commercial activities, de Mons invested heavily in overseas trade. In 1600 he visited Tadoussac, where he quickly recognized that significant profits could be made in the fur trade if competition was eliminated.

Highly respected in business circles, de Mons found merchants, both Catholic and Protestant, in Rouen, St-Malo, La Rochelle, and St-Jean-de-Luz to invest his venture. He outfitted five ships, three of which were dispatched to the St Lawrence for trading and whaling, while the other two – the 150-ton *Don-de-Dieu* and the smaller *Bonne Renommée* – set course from Havre-de-Grâce for Acadie, which was earmarked, because of its warmer winters, for a settlement. François Gravé du Pont, commander of the *Bonne Renommée*, had made several trips to the St Lawrence, most recently in 1603. Although his interests were primarily commercial, his experience in North America proved valuable to the proposed colony.

The would-be colonists – all men – were drawn from a broad spectrum of French society.[51] A few noblemen, among them Jean Bienville de Poutrincourt et de Saint-Just, were keen to participate. Poutrincourt had fought with the Catholic League, but was prepared to put religious conflict behind him and dreamed of settling permanently in North America. Another dreamer, the explorer and cartographer Samuel de Champlain, also joined the expedition. Like de Mons, he hailed from Saintonge, had fought for the king in the final round of the religious wars, and gained royal favour, perhaps, it was rumoured, because he was one of Henri IV's many illegitimate children. Champlain's accomplishments alone would have recommended him to his betters. In addition to his sea-going skills, which he developed from an early age, he spoke several languages, and seemed driven by the desire to explore new frontiers. He had travelled to the Spanish colonies in 1599 and accompanied Gravé du Pont to the St Lawrence in 1603, in each case writing accounts of his explorations. Commissioned by the king to make a formal report on the expedition to Acadie, he would also leave an invaluable legacy in the form of the exquisite maps he made of the regions he visited.[52]

To get the infrastructure of a colony in place, de Mons recruited carpenters, masons, and labourers (*engagés*), typically on one-year contracts. Whether they volunteered or were commandeered for the venture is unknown. Swiss mercenaries accompanied the expedition to keep order among the colonists and to ward off enemies. A miner, a surgeon, an apothecary, numerous artisans, two Roman Catholic priests, and a Protestant cleric were among those destined for Acadie. Claims that Mathieu d'Acosta, a black man who knew "Acadian tongues," sailed with de Mons as an interpreter have been questioned, but there is little doubt that Africans served as crewmen in the multicultural labour force of the seaborne Atlantic world. In 1606 an unnamed black man died en route to Acadie, and, like some of his white counterparts, was dissected by the ship's surgeon to see what might have caused his demise.[53]

In what was now becoming a common practice, it was agreed that the two vessels bound for Acadie would meet at Canso. Champlain suggested that, while they were on the high seas, de Mons decided to make landfall farther along the southern coast of Acadie, but whatever its planned destination, the *Don-de-Dieu* overshot its mark and nearly came to grief on Sable Island. Turning northward, the explorers reached Acadie on 8 May at what they called Cap de la Hève, after the last point of land they had seen upon leaving home. They anchored on the shore of what is now Green Bay, where they met Mi'kmaq under the leadership of Messamouet. As the expedition continued along the South Shore, Captain Jean Rossignol, trading in what is now Liverpool harbour, was taken into custody and his ship confiscated for violation of de Mons's monopoly. Rossignol's name was subsequently given to the harbour he frequented, but it eventually moved inland to Nova

Scotia's largest lake. At Port Mouton – so called because a sheep fell overboard – the explorers delighted in a dinner of fresh mutton and set up camp. With Mi'kmaq as guides, de Mons dispatched a shallop to find the *Bonne Renommé*. Gravé du Pont, who seems to have had no difficulty finding Canso, had spent his time profitably by seizing four Basque vessels now deemed to be trading illegally.[54]

While waiting for Gravé du Pont, Champlain and eleven others explored the coast in a pinnace, describing geographical conditions and naming places as they went along. A dark rock resulted in the naming of Cap Nègre, while several islands, one of which was "completely covered with seals whereof we took as many as we wished," recommended another name. Since it was early June, some of the Seal Islands (*Îles aux loups marins*) also contained an "abundance of birds ... so great that no one would believe it possible unless he had seen it," Champlain declared. He then provided the earliest list of birds in North America offered by a European observer: "cormorants, ducks of three kinds, snow geese, murres, wild geese, puffins, snipe, fish-hawks, and other birds of prey, sea-gulls, plovers of two or three kinds, herons, herring-gulls, curlews, turnstones, divers, loons, eiders, ravens, cranes, and other kinds unknown to me."[55] Rounding a forked cape, which Champlain named Cap Forchu, the pinnace entered a bay he named St Mary's before returning to Port Mouton.

After transferring his cargo, Gravé du Pont moved on to the St Lawrence while de Mons began his search for a settlement site. What is now the Annapolis Basin was so impressive that Champlain, who reckoned that two thousand ships could ride anchor there, named it Port-Royal.[56] Seeking a place where he could bring his family, Pountrincourt expressed a desire to become the *seigneur* of Port-Royal, a wish that de Mons and ultimately the king granted. This initiative presaged a spectacular land rush that characterized all European colonizing endeavours.[57] Hoping to find a location closer to inland trading networks, the expedition explored the deeper reaches of the Bay of Fundy, which de Mons called Baie Française. The explorers kept watch for rumoured copper mines in the area, but although they detected veins of precious metals at Cape Chignecto and Cape d'Or, no operating mines were discovered. On 24 June, St-Jean-Baptiste Day, the expedition entered the mouth of a river that Champlain named in honour of this major religious holiday on the Catholic calendar. When the expedition sailed into Passamaquoddy Bay, de Mons found what he was looking for. A small island tucked inside the broad tidal estuary of what he named the Ste-Croix River seemed the perfect spot for a

European outpost. Once established, it would be a jumping-off point for a settlement farther down the coast.

The colonizers constructed their *habitation*, defended by cannon and a barricade, on Île Ste-Croix. Gardens were planted both on the island, where they were blasted by the sun, and on the adjacent mainland, where they flourished. Although the framework for the habitation had been brought from France, the colonists were obliged to cut down most of the trees on the island to finish their accommodations, which included storehouses, quarters for the soldiers, a bakehouse, and dwellings for de Mons and other gentlemen. No one could have imagined in the summer of 1604 that huge blocks of ice churned up by the winter tides of the Bay of Fundy could prevent the colonists from reaching the unlimited supply of firewood on the nearby shore. At the end of August, Poutrincourt sailed for France with the two larger vessels, while Champlain spent most of the month of September exploring the coast of Maine. Four days after his return to Ste-Croix on 2 October, snow fell.

The island site was chosen because it could easily be defended, but attacks by pirates and local inhabitants proved the least of their worries. Winter was their greatest enemy. Everything froze (except the Spanish wine), firewood ran out, and energies flagged. Without sufficient intake of vitamin C, scurvy began to take its toll. Champlain described the course of the hideous affliction:

> During the winter a certain malady attacked our people. It is called land-sickness, otherwise scurvy, according to what I have heard stated by learned men. There was engendered in the mouths of those who had it large pieces of superfluous fungus flesh (which caused great putrefaction); and this increased to such a degree in very liquid form. Their teeth barely held in their places, and could be drawn out with the fingers without causing pain. This superfluous flesh was often cut away, which caused them to lose much blood from the mouth. Afterwards, they were taken with great pains in the arms and legs, which became swollen and very hard and covered with spots like flee-bites; and they could not walk ... They had also pains in the loins, stomach, and bowels, together with a very bad cough and shortness of breath ... We opened several of them to determine the cause of the illness."[58]

The horror that unfolded on Ste-Croix mirrored earlier European settlement attempts in northern North America and might well have put an end to de Mons's new world ambitions. Only his dogged perseverance and that of Champlain and Poutrincourt, all veterans of the religious wars and no strangers to deadly horrors, ensured that they would make another effort to plant a colony in Acadie.

~~c~~2~

The European discovery of North America in the late fifteenth century opened a period of exploration and resource exploitation. Even if fishing and fur trading on the eastern shores of North America were only seasonal activities, the European presence was continuous and introduced a new trajectory of power on the continent. The Mi'kmaq adapted in differing ways to the new arrivals, developing relationships in which they had the upper hand at first. Inevitably both peoples meeting at the ocean's edge were changed by the encounter. As in the "middle ground" that Richard White describes emerging in the Great Lakes region in the second half of the seventeenth century, the Maritime region became a more violent, less predictable place after European contact. It developed into a borderland where two worlds overlapped and people of diverse backgrounds adjusted their differences through "creative, often expedient misunderstandings." In this fluid space, issues of power, sex, spirituality, trade, and violence were negotiated on a case-by-case basis, and new practices emerged to manage these important matters. This ccommodation occurred because there was, for a time, a mutual desire for what the other possessed and an inability on either side to impose its worldview on the other by force.[59] This equilibrium could not last forever.

Chapter Four

Colonial Initiatives, 1605–1670

Port-Royal, founded in 1605 by French colonizers in a region they called Acadie, is regarded as the first permanent European community in Canada. It had shaky beginnings. Unlike Quebec, which had a continuous history as an administrative and trading centre after its founding in 1608, Port-Royal never quite managed to live up to expectations. Quebec's location at the narrows guarding the St Lawrence River gave it a strategic and commercial value that no site in the Maritime region could emulate. With an ample coastline, impossible to administer in any effective way, Acadie emerged a contested space, vulnerable to the long reach of competing European economic, political, and religious interests. France established a commercial and administrative presence in the region in the seventeenth century, but its control remained tenuous.[1]

Port-Royal

As grim experience underscored, the French could not colonize Acadie until they had learned how to live there. It was not a skill that recommended itself to the faint-hearted. Not surprisingly, most of the forty-four men who survived the ordeal on Ste-Croix were eager to return to France on the supply ships that arrived in 1605. Champlain was prepared to chance another winter in North America, as were the pilot Pierre Angibault Champdoré and a young Breton nobleman, Fougeray de Vitré. One of the Roman Catholic priests and the Protestant minister (their names unknown) also persevered, determined to win the contest for Indigenous souls.

After exploring the coast as far as Cape Cod looking for a better base for their operations, de Mons finally chose Port-Royal, which Champlain described as "the most suitable and pleasant for a settlement that we had seen."[2] The commodious harbour, fertile soil, and temperate

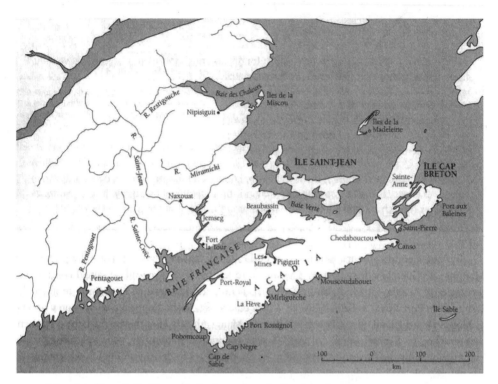

Map 4.1. French Settlements in Seventeenth-Century Acadie.
Adapted from John G. Reid, *Acadia, Maine, and New Scotland: Marginal Settlements in the Seventeenth Century* (Toronto: University of Toronto Press, 1981), 191–4, and Margaret R. Conrad and James K. Hiller, *Atlantic Canada: A History*, 3rd ed. (Don Mills, ON: Oxford University Press, 2015), 67.

climate were all good reasons for moving to Port-Royal, but it had another major advantage: the Mi'kmaq in the area welcomed the intruders. Having experienced a hostile reception from the people living farther along the coast during their explorations, the French colonizers were forcefully reminded that friendship with the local inhabitants was a necessary prerequisite in any attempt to establish a settlement.

Membertou, chief of the Mi'kmaq in the Kespukwitk region in which Port-Royal was situated, impressed the newcomers.[3] Exceptionally tall, Membertou sported a beard, an unusual feature among the normally smooth-faced Mi'kmaq. He claimed to be more than a hundred years old and to remember Jacques Cartier's visit to the region in the 1530s. Although it is impossible to determine if it was so, he might well have been the offspring of an early Mi'kmaw-European relationship. Membertou combined the roles of chief and spiritual leader, making him doubly powerful. According to Champlain, he had the reputation of being the "most treacherous" among his people, but the French declared him a *bon sauvage*, eager to have Europeans as allies in his efforts to triumph over his enemies.[4]

De Mons built his new "habitation" on the north shore of Port-Royal basin (Figure 4.1). More tightly constructed than the one at Ste-Croix, it included a cellar to protect food supplies from freezing during the winter. A palisade with four cannon pointing towards the harbour served as protection. Again the French planted gardens, and Champlain delighted in creating a little bower where he constructed a summer house, sowed seeds, and dug a reservoir for saltwater fish. The Mi'kmaq were keen observers of these activities and particularly fond of fresh bread, which the colonists made from corn flour ground in hand mills. With his monopoly under siege, de Mons returned to France early in September 1605, leaving his deputy François Gravé du Pont in charge of the colony. The hardy fur trader survived his first winter in North America, but at least a dozen of the forty-five Europeans at Port-Royal died before warmer weather returned. Among them were the squabbling clerics, thereby ending for the time being any pretence to formal missionary efforts.

In the spring of 1606, Poutrincourt, who was appointed governor of the colony, brought artisans and labourers to Port-Royal along with several relatives who would play important roles in the development of New France. These included his son, Charles de Biencourt; a cousin from Paris, apothecary and horticulturalist Louis Hébert; and another cousin from Champagne, Claude de Saint-Étienne de La Tour, who was accompanied by his fourteen-year-old son Charles. Gravé du Pont's son Robert was also included in the expedition, as was Marc Lescarbot, a lawyer and scholar from Paris, who described activities at Port-Royal in his *Histoire de la Nouvelle France*, published in 1609. Poutrincourt's charmed circle planned to have a French diet to sustain them during the long Maritime winter. According to Lescarbot, the missing cargo of one of their supply ships included: "six sheep, twenty-four hens, a pound of pepper, twenty pounds of rice, as many raisins and prunes, a thousand almonds, a pound of nutmeg, a quarter of a pound of cinnamon, half a pound of cloves, two pounds of lemon peel, two dozen lemons, as many oranges, a Westphalian ham, and six other hams, a cask of Gascon wine and another of Spanish, a hogshead of salt beef, four and a half pots of olive oil, a jar of olives, a barrel of vinegar and two sugar loaves."[5]

A Logemens des artifans.
B Plate forme où eftoit le ca-
    non.
C Le magafin.
D Logement du fieur de Pont-
    graué & Champlain.
E La forge.

F Paliffade de pieux.
G Le four.
H La cuifine.
O Petite maifonnette où' l'on
    retiroit les vtanfiles de nos
    barques ; que depuis le
    fieur de Poitrincourt fit

rebaftir, & y logea le fieur
Boulay quand le fieur du
Pont s'en reuint en France.
P (1) La porte de l'abitation.
Q (2) Le cemetiere.
R (3) La riuiere.

(1) Cette lettre manque dans le dessin ; mais la porte est bien reconnaissable tant par sa figure que par
l'avenue qui y aboutit. — (2) K, dans le dessin. — (3) L, dans le dessin.

p. 227

Figure 4.1. Champlain's Diagram of the Habitation at Port-Royal, 1605–6. The habitation at Port-Royal was similar to the ones built on Ste-Croix in 1604 and at Quebec in 1608. Surrounded by a palisade and armed with cannon, it was designed to protect French settlers and sojourners from attack by European and Indigenous enemies.
https://commons.wikimedia.org/wiki/File:Habitation-Port-Royal-1605.jpg

Learning from experience, the colonizers developed innovative responses to the challenges of living in Acadie. Poutrincourt built a grist-mill to relieve the effort of grinding grain by hand, an onerous task that the French schemed, without success, to secure Indigenous captives to do. Champlain established the Order of Good Cheer (*Ordre de Bon*

Temps), which obliged each gentleman to take turns providing game and fish for dinner. Elaborately staged events, they were attended by Membertou and at times other chiefs, who sat at the table while their families and followers observed from the sidelines. These nightly banquets, Champlain asserted, proved "more profitable than all sorts of medicines that we might have used" to ward off malnutrition. Still, seven people died during the winter of 1606–7.[6]

The leaders of the Port-Royal experiment were, above all else, Renaissance men, who shared a cultural sensibility centred on classical literature. Under Lescarbot's direction, the colonists performed a seaborne masque to welcome Poutrincourt, Champlain, and their crew when they returned in mid-November from two months of exploration along the Atlantic coast. As they anchored in the waters adjacent to the habitation, they were approached by Father Neptune, adorned with silvery locks and flowing beard, in a boat drawn by six Tritons and surrounded by Mi'kmaq in their canoes. The sea god, brandishing his trident, drew alongside Poutrincourt's longboat, addressing him in Alexandrine verse. After outlining what had been achieved through his command of the oceans – adventure, trade, exotic goods – Neptune reminded the explorers that

> If Man would taste the spice of fortune's savour
> He needs must seek the aid of Neptune's favour.
> For stay-at-homes who doze on kitchen settles
> Earn no more glory than their pots and kettles.[7]

Considered the first theatrical piece written by a European in North America, *Le Théâtre de Neptune* underscores the rich cultural life that the French brought with them to North America.

The French were doggedly determined to make the North American soil yield European crops. "Very often in the spring I was still at work in the moonlight," Lescarbot reported, deriving great pleasure from "digging and tilling my gardens, fencing them in against the gluttony of the swine, making terraces, preparing straight alleys, building storehouses, sowing wheat, rye, barley, oats, beans, peas, garden plants, and watering them."[8] Poutrincourt was so eager to prove the viability of agriculture at Port-Royal that he delayed his return to France in 1607 to wait for various grains to mature so that he would have samples to take with him. Not all ecological outcomes were intended. Seeds from European weeds, including the hardy dandelion, were among the early passengers on fishing vessels. So, too, were rats, which became a nuisance at Port-Royal. They quickly spread to the dwellings of the Mi'kmaq, attracted, Lescarbot surmised, by succulent fish oils.[9] By end of the seventeenth century, European cats, cattle, deer, pigs, rabbits, and sheep would be competing with bears, caribou, mice, and moose for the region's resources.[10]

The so-called Columbian exchange also worked in reverse. Although Acadie was not as rich in exotic commodities as were more southern regions of the Americas, it yielded objects of interest. De Mons included a live female moose, moose antlers, a hummingbird, horseshoe crabs, bows "taller than a man," and a birchbark canoe among the curiosities he transported to Paris in the autumn of 1605. The four-year-old dauphin, the future Louis XIII, was taken to see the moose, and marvelled at the speed of the canoe, propelled along the Seine by three sailors. On his return to France in 1607, Poutrincourt carried an eagle and Canada geese in his menagerie, but the eagle escaped and five of the geese died.[11] Seeds of red maples, the northeastern honeysuckle, and other local flora also crossed the Atlantic to be planted in the public and private gardens so popular in seventeenth-century France.

Despite Port-Royal's modest success in rooting Europeans in North America, it was ineffective as a base for controlling the fur trade. De Mons's monopoly was temporarily revoked in 1607. Facing financial ruin, he abandoned Acadie to concentrate his efforts on the St Lawrence. In the same year, the English established a colony at Jamestown, Virginia, and built Fort St George on the Kennebec River, the first moves in an effort to claim all the territory between the thirty-fourth and forty-fifth parallels. Acadie/Mi'kma'ki now sat uncomfortably as a borderland, not only between native and newcomer, but also between English Protestants and French Catholics as they competed for dominance in Europe and increasingly around the world.

Poutrincourt remained committed to his seigneury at Port-Royal. Leaving the habitation in Membertou's care, he returned to France in 1607 to mobilize the resources needed to sustain his estate. He, along with his son Charles, Louis Hébert, and the Le Tours, finally returned to Port-Royal in 1610. With them they brought a few colonists and a secular priest, Jessé Fléché, whose presence was designed to outflank the Jesuits, a powerful religious order determined to control missionary activities in Acadie. Fléché baptized Membertou and twenty members of his family, with Charles de Biencourt serving as interpreter. When they agreed to become Christians, the Mi'kmaq received new names: Membertou became Henri, in honour of the recently assassinated king; his wife was named Marie, after the queen; and his eldest son was given the name of the dauphin. Although he publicly renounced his earlier spiritual beliefs, Membertou probably saw his conversion as a gesture of alliance and friendship, rather than as the result of an understanding of Roman Catholic doctrine. He nevertheless replaced the shamanic bag that he wore around his neck with a cross, and reluctantly agreed, as he lay dying of dysentery in September 1611, to be buried in the French graveyard rather than with his ancestors.[12]

With a shipload of furs and proof of religious conversion in hand, Biencourt set sail for France in the summer of 1610 hoping to secure commercial backing and royal favour. The latter was now dispensed by Queen Marie, who served as regent for her young son. Biencourt was named vice-admiral of Acadie, but Poutrincourt was denied the fur trade monopoly he coveted. As a result, he was forced into an un-happy alliance in his efforts to find financial backing. The Marquise de Guercheville, a widowed lady-in-waiting to the queen, was prepared to support the colony, but she insisted that the Jesuits, who had become more influential at the French court following the death of Henri IV, would control missionary work in Acadie and become partners in the fur trade.

In May 1611 Biencourt returned to Port-Royal with thirty-six colonists and two Jesuit priests, Pierre Biard and Énemond Massé. The colony quickly dissolved into warring factions, with the Jesuits challenging Biencourt's authority. Determined to prevail, Guercheville obtained title to all the territories in Acadie outside of Poutrincourt's seigneury and moved the Jesuits from Port-Royal to St-Sauveur, a new colony established on Mount Desert Island in the Penobscot River of what is now Maine. Shortly after their arrival, the settlement was attacked by Samuel Argall, an English sea captain and adventurer. Some of the colonists at St-Sauveur were transported to Virginia; others were set adrift and managed, after a difficult voyage, to reach France. Eager to be rid of the French threat to the north, the governor of Virginia, Sir Thomas Dale, commissioned Argall to return to Acadie in the fall of 1613 to destroy all settlements there. Taking several of his French prisoners as guides, Argall sacked the surviving buildings at St-Sauveur and Ste-Croix, and destroyed everything but the gristmill and the barns at Port-Royal. Father Biard, one of the prisoners included in the expedition, said it all: "in an hour or two, the work of several worthy people had been reduced to ashes." Absent at time of the attack, the inhabitants of Port-Royal were left to the mercy of the elements. Biard wrote warmly of the "friendship and fidelity" of the Mi'kmaq, who offered them shelter during the fast-approaching winter.[13]

Returning to Port-Royal in 1614 to find complete ruin, Poutrincourt took most of the surviving colonists back to France. Biencourt and his cousin Charles de Saint-Étienne de La Tour, stayed on. Both teenagers when they arrived in Acadie, they were familiar with the customs of the country and had become fluent in native languages. Backed by merchants from La Rochelle and supported by the Mi'kmaq, Biencourt and his partners built a successful business in fish and fur, focusing their activities on the south shore of Acadie, where they could more easily intercept the interlopers who infested inshore waters. Robert Gravé du Pont, who traded furs on the St John River, plotted to overthrow the Poutrincourts, but was compelled to seek pardon for his treachery after Biencourt attacked his trading post in 1611.[14] To complicate matters further, the Dutch followed up Henry Hudson's exploration in 1609 of the river that now bears his name by issuing an exclusive patent in 1614 to the New Netherland Company for trade between the fortieth and forty-fifth parallels.

Following the death of Biencourt in 1623, the direction of Acadie was entrusted to Charles de La Tour, who had married a Mi'kmaw, likely a chief's daughter, from the Cap-Sable area. Their relationship, later blessed by a Récollet priest, produced three daughters, two of whom entered religious orders in France at a young age, suggesting that their mother had died. The eldest of the two, Antoinette, became renowned for her fine singing voice, which attracted the attention of Louis XIII's wife, Queen Anne of Austria. A third daughter, Jeanne, married a Basque fur trader, Martin d'Aprendestiguy, who in 1672 was granted a seigneury on the St John River. When he visited France in 1632, La Tour represented himself not only as "seigneur de la Tour" and lieutenant-general for the king in Acadie, but also as "Grand Sagamos des Souriquois, Etcherines, Pantegois et Quiniban." His entourage during this visit included two Mi'kmaq, Quichetect and Menougy, to whom he may have been related through marriage.[15]

Notwithstanding more than two decades of sustained effort by private interests sanctioned by the king, New France remained little more than a series of isolated trading posts: La Tour's bases at Cap-Sable and Port-Royal served as the major French presence in Acadie, while Quebec and Tadoussac anchored the St Lawrence colony known as Canada. None of these communities attracted many permanent settlers, and any military presence in the region consisted mostly of mercenaries employed by trading companies. If France was to outmanoeuvre its rivals in staking claims in North America, a new approach was necessary. In 1627 Louis XIII, following the recommendation of his chief advisor, Cardinal Richelieu, established the Compagnie des Cent-Associés (Company of One Hundred Associates), also called the Compagnie de la Nouvelle-France, to advance France's imperial interests in North America. A clause in the edict creating the company stated that only Roman Catholics were permitted to settle in New France. In

1628 the company dispatched four ships with supplies, soldiers, and four hundred settlers designed to transform Canada and Acadie into thriving colonies.

The Scottish Interlude

By this time, French claims to Acadie were being directly challenged by England and Scotland. In 1620 King James I of England (also James VI of Scotland) issued a royal charter for the Plymouth Council of New England, an organization created to establish colonies between the fortieth and forty-eighth parallels. The following year he granted rights within this broad territory of what are the present-day Maritime provinces and the Gaspé to his countryman Sir William Alexander. A proud Scotsman, poet, and scholar, Alexander was eager to see "New Scotland" added to the list of colonial enterprises that appeared on maps as New Spain, New France, New Netherland, and New England. In 1622 the Province of Maine, bounded by the Merrimack and Kennebec rivers, was awarded to Sir Fernando Gorges and John Mason. The English challenge to Acadie was borne out in 1626 when Claude de La Tour's trading post at Pentagouët on the Penobscot River was seized by a force from Plymouth Colony, established in 1620 by the first of several waves of Puritan settlers.[16]

Alexander's first attempts in 1622–3 to found a colony in Nova Scotia – the Latin term for New Scotland – failed, but he preserved, persuading the king in 1624 to create 150 knights-baronet who, in return for payment, would each receive a title and a land grant of 30,000 acres (12,150 hectares) in the colony.[17] Modelled on English colonization practices in Ireland, the scheme attracted little interest, but recommended itself to King James, who was eager to develop closer relations between Scotland and England. His son, Charles I, who ascended the throne in 1625, was equally interested in ruling over a "Greater Britain."

The outbreak of war between England and France in 1627, part of a series of European conflicts known as the Thirty Years' War (1618–48), stimulated further enthusiasm for contesting French claims to Acadie. With North American colonies now integral to European military strategy, Charles I commissioned David Kirke, the eldest son of a merchant with interests in London and Dieppe, and his four brothers to displace the French from "Canida."[18] In 1628 the Kirkes intercepted the inaugural expedition of the One Hundred Associates, and occupied Tadoussac. Among those taken prisoner was Claude de La Tour, who had prevailed upon the company to send support to his son at Cap-Sable. Quebec, blockaded by the English, surrendered in July 1629. William

Alexander's son, also named William, was on the scene as well in 1628 with another failed attempt to establish a colony. At the king's urging, the Kirkes and the Alexanders brought their common interests together in the Merchant Adventurers to Canada. This company planned two colonies in Acadie, one at Port-Royal under the command of William Alexander the younger, and another more strategically located in Cape Breton, commanded by Sir James Stewart, Lord Ochiltree, from Killeith in Scotland.[19]

Lord Ochiltree, supported by a £500 loan from the king, and William Alexander sailed to Nova Scotia in May 1629, arriving in Cape Breton early in July. They constructed a fortified base named Rosemar at Port-aux-Baleines, located near the northeastern cape from which the whole island took its name.[20] Alexander then moved on to Port-Royal while Ochiltree patrolled the fisheries, confiscating the vessels of those found fishing without a royal licence and levying a duty on all catches. According to Richard Guthry, who wrote an account of the expedition, the sixty settlers recruited for the Ochiltree colony included eight households of Church of England dissenters known as Brownists. After their arrival at Port-aux-Baleines, they announced that they had no intention of living among the main body of settlers. "Lord deliver all plantations from such people and root them out or convert them where they live," Guthry groused.[21]

Internal divisions had little to do with the demise of this Cape Breton colony. A ship under the command of Captain Charles Daniel, leader of an expedition dispatched by the One Hundred Associates to lift the siege of Quebec, lost its way in the fog off Newfoundland and fetched up at Grand Cibou on Cape Breton Island. Learning from the Mi'kmaq there that Quebec had surrendered to the Kirkes and that Ochiltree was asserting his authority on the island, Daniel captured and destroyed Fort Rosemar in September 1629, despite his knowing that a truce had been declared between England and France the previous April. The inhabitants of the fort were marched to Grand Cibou, forced to build Fort Ste-Anne for the French, and then shipped back to Europe in squalid conditions below deck. Using Ste-Anne as his base of operations, Daniel traded in the Gulf of St Lawrence as far as Miscou and Tadoussac on behalf of the One Hundred Associates until 1632, when he sold his interests in the company, which had failed to compensate him for his initiative on Cape Breton.[22]

Sir William Alexander's son had more success. After his capture by the Kirkes, Claude de La Tour agreed to accompany the Scottish colonizers to Port-Royal. There they constructed a fort, named in honour of King Charles, at the site of the present-day Fort Anne

National Historic Park. The colonists, seventy in all, planted gardens, delighted in the fertility of the soil, and revelled in the abundance of fish and wildlife. "We eat lobsters as bige as little children," Guthry marvelled.[23] Shortly after their arrival, the Scots entertained delegations from the Mi'kmaq and Wolastoqiyik, who appeared with presents, signalling their interest in trade and friendship. Their overtures received official recognition in the fall of 1629, when Chief Segipt, along with his wife and son, accompanied Claude de La Tour to England to be presented to the king. With an eye to his main chance, La Tour became one of Alexander's knights-baronet and married a lady-in-waiting to Queen Henrietta Maria, the youngest daughter of King Henri IV of France. On their return voyage in the spring of 1630, La Tour tried to convince his son at Cap-Sable to change sides with the offer of a knight-baronet, which he had secured on his behalf. This overture was vigorously rejected and the Scots, with Claude and his wife still in tow, continued to Charlesfort. Conditions there were grim. No more resilient in the face of a Maritime winter than their French counterparts, thirty of the colonists had died by the spring of 1630.[24]

Now having second thoughts about his earlier opportunistic decision, Claude de La Tour asked his son to be allowed to return to Cap-Sable, a request that was granted. Claude and his wife established an estate outside the walls of the fort and seemed to enjoy their lives as pioneer lairds in North America.[25] Charles de La Tour, meanwhile, benefited from the arrival of two vessels carrying artisans, labourers, supplies, and three Récollet priests sent by the One Hundred Associates. He was thus able to strengthen his base at Cap-Sable and make plans to construct a fortified trading post named Ste-Marie at the mouth of the St John River. In 1631 La Tour was appointed lieutenant-general of Acadie and a member of the One Hundred Associates.

European diplomacy, as would so often be the case in colonial matters, decided the fate of Scottish initiatives in Nova Scotia. In March 1632 the Treaty of St-Germain-en-Laye, which brought a formal end to the war, restored Acadie and Canada to France. King Charles threw the former French colonies into the balance to secure Queen Henrietta Marie's outstanding dowry, which would help restore the monarch's depleted coffers. In compensation for his dashed hopes for New Scotland, William Alexander was proclaimed the Earl of Stirling. Hostilities did not end there. When word of the peace treaty reached Port-Royal, its commander, Andrew Forrester, led an expedition across the Bay of Fundy to trash Fort Ste-Marie, taking special care to destroy the Roman Catholic cross and the king's coat of arms.

Civil War in Acadie

Following the Treaty of St-Germain-en-Laye, the French returned to the task of rebuilding their North American empire. Cardinal Richelieu commissioned his cousin, Isaac de Razilly, to take the surrender of Port-Royal, and appointed him the king's lieutenant-general for all of New France. A distinguished naval officer, Razilly had produced the report that convinced Richelieu to establish the Company of One Hundred Associates. Razilly was also an ardent Roman Catholic and had scars to show for it, having lost an eye in battle against the Huguenot stronghold of La Rochelle in 1625. Armed with impeccable military and religious credentials, Razilly brought energy and purpose to colonization matched only by his countryman in the colony of Canada, Samuel de Champlain.[26]

In September 1632, Razilly, with four ships carrying three hundred soldiers, artisans, and labourers and three Capuchin priests arrived at the mouth of the La Hève River, a location better suited to his commercial interests than Port-Royal. Most of his entourage probably came from the area around Auray in Brittany, the port of embarkation for three of Razilly's vessels. At the narrows of the river, Razilly constructed Fort Ste-Marie-de-Grâce, a chapel for the Capuchins, and several outbuildings. In December Razilly took possession of Port-Royal from the Scots, their seventeenth-century legacy to Nova Scotia including a name, a flag, and a coat of arms (Figure 4.2).[27] Since Charles de La Tour had also received royal approbation, some accommodation was necessary. Agreeing to share the profits from the fur trade, Razilly and La Tour dealt separately with the One Hundred Associates and managed to get along.

Thirty-six of the two hundred people who wintered at La Hève in 1632–3 died, due in part, it seems, to inadequate shelter. Undaunted, Razilly continued to lay the groundwork for a permanent French colony in eastern North America. One of his lieutenants, Nicolas Denys, began lumbering activities in the La Hève region and established a fishing base at Port-Rossignol. To protect his commercial interests more effectively, Razilly sent his officer Nicolas Le Creux to establish Fort St-François at Canso. Le Creux soon found himself defending his position against an attack by local Mi'kmaq allied with Jean Thomas, who was illegally trading furs in the area. A separate French company, which included Charles Daniel among its backers, was established in 1633 to exploit Cape Breton's resources of fish and fur from bases at Ste-Anne and St-Pierre.[28] In 1635 Razilly sent another of his lieutenants, Charles de Menou d'Aulnay, to take possession of Pentagouët, which by treaty had reverted to France but was still occupied by New Englanders.

Figure 4.2. Nova Scotia Coat of Arms. Granted in 1625, the Nova Scotia Coat of Arms, with its motto "One defends and the other conquers," was inspired by the Scottish Cross of St Andrew and the Royal Arms of Scotland. The unicorn was the imagined enemy of the lion, which was the symbol of the English monarchy. A Mi'kmaw, dressed in a feathered kilt and crown, was the only concession to "New Scotland." Largely ignored until the 1920s, the original coat of arms was restored by royal warrant in 1929, with mayflowers added to accompany the laurel and thistle. After Confederation, another coat of arms, with a salmon on a blue band between three thistles on a gold field, was designed, but never embraced by the people of the province.
https://www.canada.ca/en/canadian-heritage/services/provincial-territorial-symbols-canada/nova-scotia.html#a3

With these administrative details out of the way, Razilly turned to the challenge of recruiting settlers. Only a few families arrived in the first three years of the Razilly initiative, but a larger contingent followed in 1636. Seeking agricultural land, they established their farms in nearby Petite-Rivière. Good relations prevailed with the Mi'kmaq, and a number of immigrant men took country wives. Acadian families with names such as Boudrot, Comeau, Doucet, Gaudet, and Lejeune were among those who began their North American odyssey at La Hève.[29]

With Razilly's death of unknown causes in 1636, Acadie quickly lost its pre-eminence in New France. This was due in part to the character of d'Aulnay, deputized by Razilly's brother and heir to act on his behalf. Unlike his predecessor, d'Aulnay was unwilling to accommodate La Tour's territorial claims or to tolerate the commercial activities of other entrepreneurs. Lamenting "the envy of the French against each other,"[30] Denys retreated to La Rochelle for a decade before attempting another trading venture at Miscou, in what is now northeastern New Brunswick. D'Aulnay pursued him even there, seizing his trading post in 1647. En route, d'Aulnay captured the Compagnie du Cap-Breton's bases at Ste-Anne and St-Pierre.

La Tour was also living in exile by 1647, but he had refused to leave without a fight. When d'Aulnay decided to move most of the French settlers to Port-Royal from La Hève (families of mixed heritage stayed behind), he directly challenged La Tour's territorial and trading interests in the Bay of Fundy region. Bureaucrats in France made a bad situation worse by granting control of the area north of the Bay of Fundy to d'Aulnay and on the south side to La Tour. D'Aulnay's marriage in 1636 to Jeanne Motin, the twenty-year-old daughter of Razilly's lieutenant at Canso, seemed to confirm that he was in Acadie for the long haul and would leave progeny to inherit his North American domain.

Unwilling to concede defeat, La Tour contracted his own marriage, arranged through an intermediary, Guillaume Desjardins, Sieur du Val, a business partner based in La Rochelle. The legal document that La Tour sent to France was silent on the name of his intended wife, suggesting that Desjardins might have had carte blanche in fulfilling his mission. If so, he chose well. The marriage contract between thirty-seven-year-old Françoise-Marie Jacqueline and Charles de La Tour, signed on New Year's Eve 1639 in Paris, reveals the status of elite wives, especially those willing to brave the perils of colonization.[31] The bride brought no dowry to the marriage, but La Tour provided 2,000 livres for rings and other accoutrements, along with a 10,000 livre inheritance and a half-share in the wealth acquired during the marriage, as required by the laws that prevailed in Paris (*Coutume de Paris*). It was a generous offer, perhaps necessary to secure a willing recruit. In the spring of 1640, Françoise sailed to Cap-Sable, where she and Charles were married "in the presence of our Holy Mother Church." The couple then sailed to the St John River, where La Tour had constructed a new fort, commonly known as Fort La Tour.

By this time, the rivalry between d'Aulnay and La Tour had erupted into armed hostilities. Historians have difficulty confirming the details of the various confrontations, most of which were described by the highly biased combatants.[32] What is not in doubt is that the conflict caused both men to accumulate crippling debts. Defying the division of territory dictated by France, La Tour, with the help of his Indigenous allies, attacked d'Aulnay's operations on the north shore of the Bay of Fundy and then confronted him in the summer of 1640 in a brief but bloody engagement at Port-Royal. D'Aulnay emerged the victor, taking Charles and Françoise-Marie prisoner. His commission revoked because of his treachery, La Tour was forced to surrender his fort at Cap-Sable to d'Aulnay, who torched it along with the church and Récollet monastery. D'Aulnay was now triumphant, but La Tour still had his supporters, among them the aggrieved Récollets and some members of the Company of One Hundred Associates.

Refusing to return to France to explain the accusations against him, La Tour sought the assistance of Governor John Winthrop and the Council of the Massachusetts Bay Colony, founded in 1628. Its capital, Boston, was emerging as a substantial settlement, and the Council had the resources to provide ships and soldiers, if it were so inclined. Initially rebuffed, La Tour dispatched Françoise-Marie to intercede on their behalf in France. She managed to secure labourers, soldiers, and supplies, but was unable to deliver them due to a blockade of Fort La Tour by d'Aulnay's increasingly formidable naval resources. La Tour slipped away from the fort and proceeded to Boston, where the Council now proved open to his pleas for help. Leaving a mortgage on Fort La Tour as security, he advanced with four ships on d'Aulnay's vessels, chasing them back to Port-Royal. La Tour's force could not take the fort, but burned the gristmill, killed livestock, and confiscated furs and supplies in outlying storage buildings.

When word reached France that La Tour had enlisted the assistance of English Protestants to attack the governor of Acadie, he was again summonsed to Paris to account for himself, while his wife, who was back in France in the fall of 1643, was forbidden to return to Acadie. Probably with the collusion of members of the One Hundred Associates and Huguenots living on both sides of the Channel, Françoise-Marie managed to escape to England, where she hired a trading vessel to take her to Acadie. After a meandering voyage of more than six months, they were intercepted by d'Aulnay's imposing warship, the *Grand Cardinal*, and forced to proceed to Boston. There, the resourceful Françoise-Marie successfully sued the English captain for his failure to comply with the letter of his contract. While waiting for the outcome of the lengthy court proceedings, she took instruction in Church of England doctrine, suggesting that she might have had Huguenot leanings. In December 1644, she reached Fort La Tour, where supplies were running low.

Now outlaws in the eyes of the French, the La Tours weighed their options. Charles retuned to Boston for assistance in January 1645, leaving his wife in charge of the fort. In short order, she became embroiled in conflict with the Récollets, who, along with a few soldiers, decamped to Port-Royal. Learning the weakness of his enemy's position, d'Aulnay conducted a winter campaign that culminated in the storming of Fort La Tour in April. Françoise-Marie, who had valiantly led the defence, was forced to watch her surviving soldiers hanged, despite d'Aulnay's assurance that he would "give quarter to all" as a condition of surrender. She died three weeks later in unknown circumstances. With Acadie out of bounds, La Tour left Boston in a vessel belonging to David Kirke (now governor of Newfoundland), jettisoned his English crew at Cap-Sable, and sought refuge in Quebec. There he enjoyed the respect of the local community, participated in the wars against the Five Nations Confederacy of Iroquois (Haudenosaunee), and might have put Médard Chouart, Sieur de Groseilliers, in touch with businessmen in Boston who would later play a key role in the founding of the Hudson's Bay Company.[33]

Acadie had not seen the last of La Tour. After d'Aulnay died in a boating accident in 1650, La Tour managed to be reconfirmed, in February 1651, as governor of the colony. Two years later, he consolidated his territorial interests by marrying d'Aulnay's widow, becoming stepfather to her seven surviving children and producing five more offspring with his third wife. Nicolas Denys also returned to Acadie, operating, with the support of the One Hundred Associates, trading posts from Canso to the Gaspé, among them Chedabuctou (Guysborough), St-Pierre (St Peter's), Ste-Anne, and Nispisquid (Bathurst). Married to Marguerite Lafite in La Rochelle in 1642, Denys and his family lived primarily in St-Pierre until their property was destroyed by fire in the winter of 1669. They then relocated to Nispisquid, where Denys penned his remarkable two-volume description of Acadie in a futile effort to recoup his failing fortunes.[34] His son Richard, who participated in his father's commercial activities from an early age, married a Mi'kmaw, as did his brother Nicolas.[35]

Both La Tour and Denys were hounded by Emmanuel Le Borgne, an influential merchant from La Rochelle, who claimed jurisdiction over trade in Acadie as compensation for the extensive debts owed to him by d'Aulnay. In 1651 a force dispatched by Le Borgne occupied Port-Royal, and Denys's trading posts were subjected to repeated raids. The situation took another dramatic turn in 1654 when an English expedition led by Major Robert Sedgwick from Massachusetts captured Fort La Tour, Port-Royal, and Pentagouët. Although the settlers were allowed to stay, the Capuchins were expelled from Port-Royal, their new church and monastery torched, and the superior of their order executed. Taken captive by Sedgwick, La Tour was transported to England, where, in yet another twist on his ambiguous allegiances, he established his claim to Acadie on the basis of his status, secured earlier by his father, as one of William Alexander's knights-baronet.

The Sedgwick expedition was conducted in the context of civil war in England (1642–51), the beheading of Charles I in 1649, and the inauguration of a republic under Oliver Cromwell that lasted until the restoration of the monarchy in 1660. Cromwell's government, taking the view that Acadie had reverted to its former identity as Nova Scotia, recognized La Tour's territorial claims on the condition that he pay the costs of Sedgwick's expedition. To achieve this end and to satisfy the substantial demands of his Boston creditors, La Tour sold his rights in Acadie to Sir Thomas Temple and William Crowne, paid off his debts, and lived at Cap-Sable or Port-Royal, as his fancy dictated, until his death in the mid-1660s.[36]

Predictably the French government ignored English claims, appointing Le Borgne governor of Acadie in 1657. He and his son, Alexandre le Borgne de Belle-Isle, continued to attack English-occupied settlements until 1667, when, by the Treaty of Breda, Acadie was returned to France. Three years later, the English government forced Thomas Temple, who was reluctant to leave his new trading post at Jemseg, on the St John River, to let the French assume control. After the English withdrawal, Emmanuel Le Borgne and his sons enjoyed a monopoly over the fur trade in Acadie, and Alexandre Le Borgne, who married into the prolific La Tour family, became the seigneur of Port-Royal. Prone when in his cups to issuing conflicting land grants in his domain, he thoroughly muddled the already complicated inheritance rights in Acadie. He died in the early 1690s, pursued to the end by d'Aulnay's heirs, who continued to challenge the Le Borgne/ LaTour claims to Port-Royal. The issue was finally settled in Paris, with five La Tour and two Le Borgne heirs each receiving one-seventh of the property.[37]

What the few hundred settlers, most of them recruited from western France by successive governors, thought about their politically unstable new homeland is difficult to determine. Based primarily at La Hève and Port-Royal, they probably experienced their new world much as they had their old one, which was also periodically beset by warring factions. Acadie nevertheless had its advantages for settlers, including easier access to land, fish, and timber than was the case in France. If the settlers could avoid involvement in local conflicts and be free of pandemics, they might even prosper.

In the first half of the sixteenth century, Acadie was an open field for competing Capuchin, Franciscan, Jesuit, and Récollet religious orders, each determined to sustain Roman Catholicism in settler and Indigenous communities. The Capuchins were particularly active, dispatching as many as fifty-seven missionaries to Acadie between 1632 and 1658.[38] While they had some success in convincing the Mi'kmaq, Walostoqiyik, and Passamoquoddy to reconcile their beliefs with Christianity, they failed to establish a permanent base for Catholic missions in the region. Their churches and seminaries were trashed, and most clerical personnel returned to France after only a few years of service in the colony.

Acadie in the North Atlantic Context

The destructive squabbles among rival claimants to Acadie would be of little long-term import except that they reveal in the starkest way how the colony had become a pawn in European interests. With dreams of glory and profit ever before them, ambitious entrepreneurs built forts, raised armies, transported settlers, fought battles on land and sea, and had little to show for their pains other than the charred ruins of their "habitations" and indebtedness to European and, increasingly, Boston capitalists. There was good money to be made in fish, forest, and fur in Acadie, but only disaster for those who were determined to assert a monopoly over these resources. As a result of contests for ascendancy, French bases in Acadie were badly mauled, investments were wantonly squandered, and settlement languished. This was not the case in most nearby colonial jurisdictions. By 1660 the English colonies along the Atlantic seaboard had a European population approaching 70,000, New Netherland, which in 1655 absorbed a short-lived Swedish colony along the Delaware River, was home to a multicultural community of 5,000 immigrants, and even ice-bound Canada boasted more than 3,000 souls. Acadie, meanwhile, could count scarcely 500 year-round settlers, and shifting power relations in Europe called into question the very survival of Acadie as a French colony.

By the mid-seventeenth century, all European nations had been bested in their quest for overseas trade by the United Provinces of the Netherlands, which had achieved independence from Spain in 1579. While other jurisdictions were developing centralized monarchies, the Dutch had established a republican government characterized by elected officials, religious toleration, and support for capitalist enterprise. In the first half of the seventeenth century, the Dutch merchant marine grew dramatically, becoming larger than the combined shipping of England, France, and Spain. Other nations scrambled to catch up.

Beginning in the 1650s, England adopted a series of Navigation Acts designed to meet the Dutch challenge. Trade within its empire was restricted to English-built ships, crewed primarily by English subjects; colonial staples such as fish, furs, rice, sugar, and tobacco could be shipped only to England; and all European goods destined for the colonies had first to be sent through English ports, where they built up the nation's wealth by paying customs duties. These so-called mercantilist policies proved effective, more than doubling English shipping between 1640 and 1686.[39] The Navigation Acts provoked three Anglo-Dutch wars between 1652 and 1674, with long-term implications for Acadie. In 1664 an English expedition captured New Netherland, which was renamed New York. Its trading post at Fort Orange (renamed Albany) served as a major base for trade and military alliances with the Five Nations Confederacy, long-time enemies of the French and Algonkian peoples. The conditions were set for another round of fighting over control of northeastern North America.

Political troubles at home meant that France was slow off the mark in meeting the challenges posed by the Dutch and the English, but Louis XIV, who ascended the throne in 1643 at the age of five, would not long be eclipsed. In 1661 the young king assumed personal charge of state policy, a significant historical moment not only for France but also for Europe and the world. By creating administrative structures, legal regimes, military might, and symbolic gestures to sustain his monarchical powers against the claims of the nobility, the papacy, and other nations, the Sun King emerged as the most powerful force in European affairs. His efforts to extend France's reach during his long reign, which ended in 1715, sparked a series of wars that echoed around the world and determined the fate of Acadie.

The complicated geopolitical developments in this period left an indelible mark on the history of Nova Scotia. So, too, did the European settlers who set down roots in Mi'kma'ki before 1670.[40] Although their numbers were small, their staying power was impressive. The historian Gregory M.W. Kennedy has determined that the families brought by D'Aulnay from the Loudunais area of western France proved especially resourceful, becoming a major component of a closely knit Acadian community that reflected the cultural values, farming practices, and lifeways of their former homeland.[41] As another contestant for power in the struggle for ascendancy in the Maritime region, French settlers would continue to bear the brunt of Imperial and Indigenous rivalries but their commitment to Acadie remained a defining feature of their evolving identity.

Chapter Five

Louis XIV's Acadie, 1670–1713

During the reign of Louis XIV, France made a determined effort to expand its overseas empire. Acadie calculated in the king's ambitions primarily as a base for the migratory fisheries, a bulwark against New England, and a strategic location for shoring up Indigenous alliances. Unlike Canada, which guarded a major river leading to the interior of the continent, Acadie was initially neither a focus for settlement nor a site for military investment. Only 2,000 people of European origin made Acadie their home in 1713 when it passed from France to Britain by the Treaty of Utrecht, and the Mi'kmaq still dominated most areas of their traditional territory (Figure 5.1).[1]

Inventing Acadie

With overseas colonies at the centre of Louis XIV's power-building exercise, New France became the focus of intense attention. Jean-Baptiste Colbert was the administrator who orchestrated many of Louis XIV's early initiatives. Appointed controller-general of finances in 1665, he added the ministries of marine and commerce in 1669. Colbert introduced policies to reform national finances, promote economic self-sufficiency, and build a colonial empire defended by a massive navy. In theory at least, French colonies were endowed with a governor supported by a standing army; a legal regime based on the *Coutume de Paris*; a seigneurial system of land distribution that concentrated wealth in the hands of an aristocratic elite; a Roman Catholic church closely allied to the state; and a closed mercantile trading system designed to advance France's economic interests. Distance, administrative inefficiencies, and the king's preoccupation with European affairs meant that Acadie could circumvent many of the regulations imposed by officials based in Paris, but their decisions nevertheless reverberated across the Atlantic.

Figure 5.1. The success of Louis XIV in establishing his dictatorial regime was the envy of other monarchs who imitated his policies but never managed to outshine the "Sun King," who dominated European politics until his death in 1715.
https://commons.wikimedia.org/wiki/File:Louis_XIV_of_France.jpg

Louis XIV's first imperial initiative in North America involved establishing a colony at Plaisance, on Newfoundland's southeast coast, in 1662. Well positioned to serve as a base for the French fishing fleet, Plaisance was also designed to keep an eye on the English Shore of the Avalon Peninsula and to protect the approaches to the Gulf of St Lawrence. The colony of Canada attracted most of the king's attention, receiving an administrative apparatus, several thousand colonists, and a significant military presence between 1663 and 1673. Entangled in French-English relations until 1667, Acadie was finally declared a royal colony in 1670, with an administration subordinate to officials in Quebec.

The king appointed Hector d'Andigné de Grandfontaine, a captain in the Carignan-Salières regiment stationed in Canada, as Acadie's new governor. After arranging with his subordinates, Jean-Vincent d'Abbadie de Saint-Castin and Pierre de Joybert de Soulanges et de Marson, to take possession of the forts at Port-Royal, Cap-Sable, and Jemseg, Grandfontaine established his capital at Pentagouët, a better location, he decided, than Port-Royal to keep an eye on the aggressive New Englanders. It proved to be a disastrous decision. In 1674 a Dutch force under Jurriaen Aernoutsz razed Pentagouët and Jemseg, taking Joybert and the new governor of Acadie, Jacques de Chambly, captive to Boston.[2] Saint-Castin managed to escape to Quebec.

The Dutch were unable to follow up this victory, but the vulnerability of Pentagouët made it prudent to establish Acadie's administrative centre elsewhere. Unable to fix upon a strategic location, administrators experimented with Jemseg and Chignecto before finally returning to Port-Royal in 1683. The Company of Acadie (Compagnie de la pêche sédentaire de l'Acadie), commissioned by the king in 1682 to pursue a land-based fishery, chose to build their headquarters, Fort St-Louis, at Chedabuctou (now Guysborough). Lacking any geopolitical cohesion, Acadie continued to survive largely as a figment of European imaginations.

Most of the Europeans who stayed in the colony arrived between 1632 and 1654.[3] Both Razilly and d'Aulnay sponsored settlers, as did La Tour, but immigration was negligible during the English occupation from 1654 to 1670, and the state sponsored fewer than 130 settlers between 1670 and 1713. Although most newcomers came from France, individuals arrived from various points on the compass, including England, Scotland, Africa, and the West Indies. Initially the focus for settlement was Port-Royal, home to about five hundred people by the first decade of the eighteenth century. Beginning in the 1670s, young families in Port-Royal began on their own initiative to move up the Bay of Fundy to settle around the tidal estuaries of the Chignecto and Minas basins. These areas soon supported thriving communities based on agriculture, fishing, fur trading, lumbering, and smuggling with New England, which was a more reliable source of supplies than merchants in France.

Adapting quickly to their new environment, the settlers in Acadie managed to adjust to the longer winters, and thrived on the abundant resources that their new environment offered. The ambitious among them were encouraged by French authorities to dream large by the lifting of customary sanctions against nobles engaging in trade and artisans transgressing guild regulations. Even lawyers, blamed by the king for chicanery in judicial matters, were barred from the colonies. With fewer restrictions than they faced at home, some immigrants did exceedingly well. A young Jacques Bourgeois, for example, came to Port-Royal in 1642 to work as a surgeon in the community where his father served in the military. The following year, he married Jeanne, the daughter of Guillaume Trahan, an edge-tool maker who arrived in 1636, and together they raised a large family of three sons and seven daughters. Bourgeois became a prosperous farmer, shipbuilder, and trader, and along with several of his sons and sons-in-law, founded the settlement of Beaubassin, on the Isthmus of Chignecto in 1672. Located on the crossroads of transportation routes to the Gulf of St Lawrence and Quebec, the settlement offered opportunities beyond the watchful eyes of officials at Port-Royal. The Bourgeois family built mills to produce flour and lumber, and engaged in clandestine trade with Boston.[4]

Many newcomers to Acadie were artisans and labourers who stayed only long enough to fulfil their contractual obligations, but some of these sojourners left a lasting legacy. The ship carrying Guillaume Trahan to Acadie in 1636 brought seventy-eight passengers, among them five *saulniers* (salt marsh workers), at least three of whom returned to France after fulfilling their contracts to drain the marshes around Port-Royal for agriculture.[5] As a result of this initiative, dykeland farming became an enduring feature of the Acadian economy. Rather than clearing the forests, settlers worked together to accomplish the arduous task of reclaiming the rich alluvial soils flooded by the high tides of the Bay of Fundy. Using wooden clapper valves known as *aboiteaux* to control the flow of salt water, they transformed marshes into productive farmland suitable for growing wheat, barley, and fodder for livestock.[6]

By the beginning of the eighteenth century, Acadie was home to about 1,500 people of European heritage and the gender balance was nearly equal. Thereafter, with little immigration, the population doubled every twenty years.[7] This remarkable demographic feat was due in part to the thriving mixed economy that developed in the colony. Benefiting from easy access to fish and forest resources, Acadian farmers enjoyed a more diverse diet than their counterparts in France, and remained mostly free of the plagues that periodically ravaged European communities. The availability of land for those willing to cultivate it meant that women married young by European standards – around twenty-one on average – and few remained single. With a child born roughly every two years to married women of normal fertility, Acadian families were large, and children tended to stay in the region rather than seek opportunities elsewhere. Over time, most Acadians became related to one another, giving a society of varied origins the close-knit character of an extended family.[8]

Sieur de Dièreville, who visited Acadie in 1699–1700, commented in his memoir that large families were "the wealth of this country," and "the swarming of brats ... a delight to behold."[9] A poet, surgeon, and naturalist,[10] Dièreville described in verse the good fortune of "the Habitant," who escaped the burdensome taxes and tithes imposed on peasants in France:

Yet ever the Habitant content
With his abode; he only for
His living works, and no one speaks
To him of Taxes or of Tithes, nor are
There any payments to be made at all.[11]

It is widely held that Acadie was largely ignored by French officials, but the documentary trail linking the colony to Paris and Quebec suggests otherwise. Even the smallest administrative detail could produce a fat file of correspondence stretching over many years. When, for example, the king's lieutenant, Simon-Pierre Denys de Bonaventure, sired an illegitimate child with the twice-widowed Louise Guyon, Madame de Freneuse, word quickly reached the bishop of Quebec and officials in France. Bonaventure's wife and child were dispatched to Port-Royal to restore his reputation, and Madame de Freneuse was banished to Canada. Despite his popularity in Acadie – Bonaventure was a reliable source of supplies secured through trade with Boston – he was denied the position of governor in 1706 because of the scandalous affair. Madame de Freneuse, meanwhile, returned to Port-Royal shortly after its conquest by the British in 1710.[12]

Although state investment in the region remained minimal until the founding of Louisbourg, France was determined to establish European institutions in Acadie. Under the French regime, fifty-five seigneuries were granted in the colony in an effort to nurture a local aristocracy, which would be sustained through dues paid by tenants granted the right to cultivate portions of the seigneur's domain. The proprietorial system failed to create the robust class-based social organization that officials envisioned, but seigneurs asserted their authority when they could, and often served as community leaders. Tenants, meanwhile, resisted not only excessive seigneurial impositions, but also the demands of the state for supplies and military service.[13]

In their dealings with officials, seigneurs were even less submissive than commoners. In 1695 Commandant Joseph Robineau de Villebon complained to the minister of marine that the four Damours brothers, who had received seigneurial grants on the north side of the Bay of Fundy, were "so much given to libertinism and independent action during the ten or twelve years of their sojourn here that they cannot submit to authority."[14] This comment was prompted by their refusal to provide Villebon with copies of their concessions, which would almost certainly have confirmed their excessive land claims.

Philippe Mius d'Entremont was one of Acadie's most prominent seigneurs.[15] A childhood friend of Charles de La Tour, he moved to Acadie with his family in 1651, and was granted the barony of Poboncoup (Pubnico), stretching from Cap Nègre to Cap Forchu. Attracting a few young families from France and Port-Royal, he developed a community around his estate on Pubnico harbour. Two of his sons married daughters of Charles de La Tour and Jeanne Motin, while a third son married the daughter of Saint-Castin and his Abenaki wife, becoming the founder of families named Muis(e) in North America. One of his daughters, Marguerite, married Pierre Melanson, a founder of Grand-Pré, in the Minas area. With fourteen siblings, all of whom by French law inherited an equal share of the family estate, it is little wonder that Marguerite was prepared in the 1680s to move with her husband and growing family some distance upriver from her home near Port-Royal. Appointed king's attorney in 1670, Baron d'Entremont was typical of most seigneurs in New France whose income and status derived as much from trade, family connections, and government positions as from seigneurial dues.

The levelling influence of the North American frontier meant that seigneurs were often not much better off than the common folk, but most of them aspired to live in the manner appropriate to their class. When Parks Canada excavated the charred remains at the St-Pierre site of the perennially indebted Nicolas Denys, it yielded two rudimentary structures, one home to an opulent inventory of fine dinner services, upholstered furniture, and elegant fabrics.[16] Settlers with lower expectations remained content with pewter dishes, rough-hewn benches, home-spun wool and linen, leather moccasins, and wooden shoes. Although most homes were modest cottages with thatched roofs – Dièreville referred to them dismissively as "huts" (*cabanes*) – there were good reasons not to invest in substantial dwellings. Acadian communities were so often subject to destructive attacks that it must have seemed pointless to build with an eye to posterity.

It was certainly the case that the Acadians flouted the regulations forbidding trade with English colonies, but this practice was not unique to the colony, only more easily accomplished there.[17] After the transfer of power to the French in 1670, Boston merchants continued to maintain storehouses in Port-Royal, and, as Bonaventure's career documents, even French officials engaged in proscribed trade with "the enemy." The minister of marine hired the Company of Acadie to supply Port-Royal, but its ships and fort at Chedabuctou were vulnerable to attacks by pirates and by fishermen from Massachusetts, some of the latter operating with licences dispensed – for a price – by Acadie's governor, Michel Le Neuf de la Vallière de Beaubassin. He was recalled for this unsanctioned effort to supplement his salary, but the New Englanders remained ominously present. In the summer of 1688, they captured and trashed Fort St-Louis, crippling the Company of Acadie's commercial activities. As a result, Governor Louis-Alexandre des Friches de Meneval allowed two English vessels to deliver much-needed supplies to Port-Royal in 1689.

The Acadian economy was geared to simple exchange. Although furs were the main export, wheat, flour, hay, and feathers (the latter used for mattresses) found a ready market in New England, where alcohol, cloth, cooking utensils, corn, molasses, sugar, spices, tobacco, and tools were on offer. Acadian women were particularly fond of the red cloth, blue ribbons, and silk lace sold by Boston merchants. In 1690 several female litigants in Beaubassin launched a complaint against their parish priest when he withheld absolution because they defied sumptuary laws by wearing lace and ribbon.[18]

By the eighteenth century, most Acadians and Mi'kmaq were, in their own way, committed Roman Catholics. Protestants had been officially barred from Canada and Acadie since the 1620s, a policy that also prevailed in France following the Edict of Fontainebleau in 1685. Rather than convert to Catholicism, at least 200,000 Huguenots fled to Protestant countries, where they supported efforts to blunt France's imperial ambitions. Huguenot merchants had played a vital role in the founding of Acadie, and some of the settlers had Protestant leanings. In most cases, they abandoned their faith to avoid harsh penalties, but a few

sought refuge elsewhere. For example, Pierre Laverdure, the Huguenot founder of the Melanson clan, and his English wife Priscilla moved
to Boston after the restoration of French control in 1670, while their
sons, Charles and Pierre, remained in Acadie and converted to Catholicism. Another Huguenot, David Bassett, married Charles Melanson's
daughter Marie, moved to Boston, and participated in the attack on
Port-Royal in 1690.[19]

Claiming to be ruler by divine right, Louis XIV insisted on control
over the Roman Catholic Church both at home and in his colonies.
Religious conviction was difficult to police in Acadie, but clerics did
their best to root out heresy. In 1676 Louis Petit, a former captain in
the Carignan-Salières regiment who had entered the priesthood,
was appointed vicar-general of Acadie, under the jurisdiction of the
bishop of Quebec. Bishop Saint-Vallier appointed priests, established
parishes, urged the construction of churches, and in 1686 visited his
Acadian province. As elsewhere in New France, the Church in Acadie
was responsible for any schooling most young people received. Petit's
assistant taught boys in Port-Royal, and Petit himself taught catechism
to girls. From 1701 to 1710, a sister of the Congregation of the Holy
Cross conducted a school for girls at Port-Royal. Despite the best efforts
of diligent clerics, most Acadians remained illiterate.

In addition to ministering to the growing number of settlers, priests
were also charged with maintaining Indigenous missions. Their goal
was always twofold: to win souls for the Catholic Church and to sustain
military alliances for France. When the ship carrying Dièreville arrived
in Chibouctou (Chebucto) harbour (now Halifax harbour) in 1699, he
found the Mi'kmaq there mourning the loss of their priest, Louis-Pierre
Thury, who had been dispatched by the bishop of Quebec to Acadie in
1684. Initially located at Miramichi, where Richard Denys offered him
land for a mission, Thury was transferred to Pentagouët in 1687. There
he actively participated in Abenaki campaigns against the English
colonists at Pemaquid and York. Appointed vicar-general of Acadie in
1698, he planned to bring the Mi'kmaq together into one large community near Piziquid (now Windsor) on the Minas Basin, but he died
at Chibouctou in June 1699 before achieving this goal. Dièreville was
impressed by the stone monument that the Mi'kmaq had constructed
over Thury's grave and by the hymns they sung in Mi'kmaw, translated by their beloved priest.[20]

Legal records suggest that most Acadians followed Catholic injunctions relating to marriage and sexual conduct, but there was a limit
to how much clerical interference they would tolerate. In a highly
controversial case at Beaubassin in 1688, Abbé Claude Trouvé responded

to a paternity suit by insisting that not only the reputed father, Louis Morin, but also nineteen members of his family be expelled from the colony and their goods confiscated and given to the young woman's father. This draconian penalty outraged both the community and officials in Port-Royal. Mathieu de Goutin, the king's lieutenant of justice from 1688 to 1710, condemned the clerical edict, and neither the inhabitants of Beaubassin nor their neighbours in Minas would accept the hide-bound priest in their parish. In the end, Trouvé retreated to Port-Royal, Louis Morin was exiled to France, and the rest of his family moved to the Bay of Chaleur.[21]

The priest's rough justice seems outrageous by today's standards, but it was in keeping with the draconian punishments practised in the age of Louis XIV. Beheading, burning at the stake, breaking on the rack, and cutting out the tongue were common penalties for major misdemeanours such as blasphemy, counterfeiting, heresy, murder, rape, sorcery, and treason. Even theft could result in severe bodily mutilation. The French inquisitorial system of justice was based on the interrogation of the accused, with the final decision rendered by the judge, not, as in the British system, by a jury of peers. Depending upon the seriousness of the charges, the accused might even be subjected to judicial torture, *la question extraordinaire*, to extract a confession. Sentences tended to be more lenient in Acadie and Canada than in France, perhaps because of the close-knit nature of pioneer society and the paternal interest that Louis XIV took in his colonies. When Major Claude-Sébastien de Villieu punished two soldiers accused of stealing by applying burning wooden slivers to their hands and fingernails in 1703, the disabled soldiers were shipped to France, where they were examined in person by the king and granted a pension.[22]

The governor general and intendant based in Quebec had jurisdiction over Acadie, but the task of maintaining law and order on a day-to-day basis rested with an appointed council located at Port Royal. Headed by the governor, who was always a military man, the council enforced royal edicts with the assistance of a lieutenant, a notary, and a small garrison. Evidence suggests that officials had their hands full imposing laws made in Paris. When Jacques de Meulles, the Intendant of New France, conducted an extended tour of Acadie in 1685–6, he reiterated royal injunctions against the use of brandy in the fur trade and the practice of young men taking Indigenous wives and either living with them or bringing them into European communities. No one paid much heed. Liquor continued to flow freely on the fur trade frontier, while censuses recorded a few Mi'kmaq living in French settlements, both as families and as wives of Acadian men.[23]

In the opinion of most French officials, the Acadians were exceptionally independent, even republican in their behaviour. It could hardly
be otherwise. With an open frontier, close relations with Indigenous
peoples, and a governing apparatus that was largely ineffective beyond
Port-Royal, Acadians learned to be pragmatic in the face of political
conditions over which they had little control. Acutely understaffed,
governors were obliged to rely on priests and committees of prominent
residents in outlying communities to settle disputes. This practice gave
rise to vestry councils and parish committees that not only handled
local church matters, but also participated in negotiations with French
and, after 1710, British authorities.[24] It was not grassroots democracy,
but nor was it oppressive dictatorship.

Although the military played a major role in the thinking of imperial
authorities, it was a weak pillar in Acadie. Grandfontaine was accompanied by a few soldiers – twenty-five were reported in the census of
1671[25] – but it was not until 1685 that administrators were supported
by a permanent garrison. It consisted of soldiers from the Troupes
de la Marine, the army attached to the French navy. Numbers were
small, initially only seventy soldiers at Port-Royal and twenty at Fort
St-Louis. In 1702 the garrison at Port-Royal was increased to four companies, bringing the complement there to about two hundred. By that
time, the local militia, made up of able-bodied men between sixteen
and sixty capable of bearing arms, had been reorganized, and actually
turned out in 1707 to fend off an attack by the English. Most Acadian
men owned guns – also counted in some censuses – which were essential to hunting and security. In France it would have been unthink-
able to arm ordinary citizens, who were, in any event, denied hunting
privileges.

Despite its small size, the garrison was a significant institution in
Acadie and especially in Port-Royal. Not only did it offer protection
and economic stimulus to the community, it also supplemented the
small stable of prospective husbands and provided opportunities to
sons of Acadie's elite families. The historian Brenda Dunn notes that,
of the twenty-three officers stationed in Port-Royal between 1701 and
1710, nine married Acadian women and were absorbed into local society. Two Acadians, Louis Damours de Chaffours, who owned a seigneury on the St John River, and Charles de La Tour, a son of Jeanne Motin
named after his father, became ensigns in the Troupes de la Marine. In
some families, boys were earmarked at an early age for a military career.
Major de Villieu's son began carrying a musket in his father's company
at the age of five, and upon his father's retirement was appointed *garde
de marine* in France, the entry-level rank for young officers.[26]

Not all soldiers made a good impression. Some commandeered supplies from Acadians, were convicted of rape and murder, and deserted when the enemy appeared. So many soldiers seemed troubled by mental illness that one governor suggested in a letter to his superiors that he had more need of an insane asylum than a barracks.[27] Little wonder, then, that most governors supplemented their garrison with Indigenous allies and the Acadian militia. By the end of the seventeenth century, these auxiliary forces in outlying areas had become a law unto themselves, adept at terrorist practices common to *la petite guerre* – surprise attacks, taking captives and scalps, ritual executions, and torture – which inevitably was returned in kind by their enemies.[28]

Because Acadians were few in number and their presence provided valued opportunities to trade, they got on reasonably well with their Indigenous neighbours. Intermarriage decreased as settlement took root, but most communities served by unmarried French soldiers and traders included families of mixed heritage.[29] During the French regime, marriages between Indigenous women and French men played a significant role in cementing military alliances. Saint-Castin, for example, returned to Pentagouët after the Dutch attack in 1674 with a charge from the governor general of New France, Louis de Baude, Comte de Frontenac, to extend French influence among the Abenaki. Faced with the expansion of English settlers into their territory, they welcomed the support he offered during what is known as King Philip's War, which erupted in 1675–6 between settlers in New England and their Indigenous neighbours. Saint-Castin married Pidianske, daughter of the Penobscot chief Madockawando, succeeded him as chief, and helped bring the Abenaki, Penobscot, Passamaquoddy, Wolastoqiyik, and Mi'kmaq into a loose alliance – known as the Wabanaki ("Dawnland") Confederacy – to confront the aggressive New Englanders.[30] Although not a confederacy in the formal sense, it is a useful term to describe Indigenous peoples in the northeast of North America who were usually allied with the French as a means of forestalling the advancement of English settlement in the region.

The Impact of War, 1689–1713

Warfare dominated the final decades of Louis XIV's reign. Throughout the 1670s, he harassed the Dutch and asserted his right to occupy their territories. The Glorious Revolution (1688–9), which overthrew James II of England and put the Protestant ruler of the Netherlands, William of Orange, and his English wife Mary on the throne, spelled disaster for Louis XIV's ambitions to expand France's borders and champion the cause of Roman Catholicism. When William brought England into a defensive alliance in 1689, the War of the League of Augsburg (also known as King William's War or the Nine Years' War) quickly followed.

The Five Nations and the Wabanaki confederacies, representing Indigenous peoples threatened by European settlement, played a major role in how the conflict unfolded in North America. In August 1689, 1,500 Haudenosaunee (Iroquois) advanced on Montreal, while the Abenaki and their allies, led by Saint-Castin, attacked Pemaquid (now Bristol, Maine), capturing Fort Charles, killing settlers, and taking as prisoner nine-year-old John Gyles, who later published an account of his captivity.[31] In retaliation, Governor Frontenac launched winter raids along the New York and New England frontiers, and sent assistance to the Wabanaki in their attacks on Casco and Fort Loyal (Falmouth and Portland in Maine). With Boston now in jeopardy, New Englanders mobilized their resources to strike back.

In the spring of 1690, an expedition under the command of Sir William Phips, a colonial-born adventurer knighted for his success in recovering a sunken Spanish treasure-ship, attacked French posts on the Penobscot and Passamaquoddy, and then sailed to Port-Royal.[32] With his fortifications in shambles and lacking guns, Governor Meneval surrendered without a fight. Phips instructed his army to pillage the town and shipped Meneval, Vicar-General Petit, and most of the surviving French soldiers to Boston. Before leaving Port-Royal, Phips ordered Acadian men to assemble in the ruins of the church, where they were forced to swear allegiance to the English Crown, and then appointed a council of six residents to act as a local government. Fort St-Louis at Chedabuctou and La Hève were also easy marks, falling to a force led by Captain Cyprian Southack, a naval officer, cartographer, and entrepreneur based in Boston. Emboldened by these successes, Boston mobilized an expedition under Phips to take Quebec, but the sturdy defences of the walled town and advancing winter forced him to retreat. In 1691 Phips was appointed governor of Massachusetts, which now included "Accadia or Nova Scotia" as part of its territory in a new charter granted by King William.[33]

When a vessel owned by the Company of Acadie arrived at Port-Royal shortly after Phips's departure, the residents reaffirmed their allegiance to Louis XIV. Canadian-born Joseph Robineau de Villebon, the highest-ranking official in the colony, then decamped to the north side of the Bay of Fundy, thereby missing a second sacking of Port-Royal by the outraged New Englanders. Establishing his headquarters at Jemseg in the vain hope of avoiding a seaborne assault, Villebon later moved up the St John River to Nashwaak. The English appointed Colonel Edward

Tyng as commander-in-chief of Acadie, but he refused to stay in the colony because his Acadian advisors were unable to guarantee his safety. Indeed, Villebon captured Tyng in 1691 when he stopped to trade at the mouth of the St John River on his way back to Boston.

Villebon was well positioned at Jemseg to exert pressure on the Wabanaki Confederacy to attack settlers and forts on the New England frontier. Never an entirely unified force, the Abenaki, who were located on the front lines of English settlement in the district of Maine, welcomed French alliances but refused to be bound by them. Some elders counselled neutrality and even collaboration with the English to avoid the loss of human life that warfare entailed. In 1693 Governor Phips concluded an agreement with two Abenaki chiefs, Egermet and Madockawando, who probably did not have the authority to conduct negotiations on behalf of their people. Villebon managed to scuttle this diplomatic effort by calling upon the services of Taxous, a rival for authority, and Father Louis-Pierre Thury, who exploited divisions within Abenaki communities to undermine the peaceful diplomacy of the renegade chiefs.[34]

The European competition for Indigenous alliances, which promised military support and claims to territory, elevated the level of violence throughout northeastern North America. In his reports to the minister of marine, Villebon documented the Indigenous practice of taking scalps from their captives and wreaking vengeance on any of their own people found fighting alongside the English. He noted in one instance that an "English Indian" was given to "our Indians" to be burned "after he had been passed by one to another to expiate the death of a kinsman killed in war; no torment could have been added to those they had inflicted on him."[35] In contrast, John Gyles survived his six years of captivity among the Wolastoqiyik, who sold him in 1695 to Louis Damours. Gyles hunted with Damours and worked in his trading post at Jemseg until he was returned to Boston after the war ended.

Determined to maintain their control, French authorities established small garrisons at their bases north of the Bay of Fundy, and continued to send munitions and supplies, often through Baie Verte on the Northumberland Strait to avoid English vessels patrolling the Bay of Fundy. The audacity of French privateers who operated out of Port-Royal with the help of local recruits earned the town another drubbing by a force from Boston in 1693. By some accounts, Acadians outfitted French privateers reluctantly, having little recourse when importuned by aggressive buccaneers. The real story is more complicated. The France-born privateer, Pierre Maisonnat, *dit* Baptiste, for example, entered what were probably bigamous marriages – he reputedly had wives in both France and Holland – in 1693 and 1707 with women from Port-Royal, served as a militia captain, and died in Beaubassin in 1714.[36] Throughout the war, a few Acadians – including Abraham Boudrot and Charles de La Tour junior – played a duplicitous game, peddling wheat, lumber, and information to English merchants in Boston and to French authorities at Jemseg and Nashwaak. The worried populace, meanwhile, buried their valuables in the woods to protect them from being confiscated in a situation bordering on anarchy.

The summer of 1696 brought more military action. Canadian-born naval captain Pierre Le Moyne d'Iberville lifted the English blockade of the St John River, and, with the aid of a few Acadians and members of the Wabanaki Confederacy, captured Fort William Henry at Pemaquid (Figure 5.2). In retaliation, Benjamin Church led a force of New Englanders into the Bay of Fundy, where they pillaged Beaubassin and then conducted an unsuccessful siege of Fort Nashwaak in October. By that time, Iberville's Canadian, Acadian, and Wabenaki forces were in Newfoundland, where English settlers from Ferryland had overtaken Plaisance. Supported by French troops, Iberville's army captured and burned St John's and most of the English fishing bases on the Avalon Peninsula in a punishing autumn and winter campaign. Still not done, Iberville sailed to Hudson Bay, where he captured Fort York from the Hudson's Bay Company one week before peace was negotiated in Europe. The War of the League of Augsburg ended in September 1697 with the Treaty of Ryswick and without territorial losses to the French Empire in North America. The truce did not last long.

France used the breathing space to consolidate its position in North America. In an effort to extend his reach to Spanish territory on the Gulf of Mexico, Louis XIV dispatched Iberville to the mouth of the Mississippi River, where he constructed a fort near what is now Biloxi, Mississippi, in 1699. Another fort was constructed at Detroit to keep the Five Nations Confederacy under close surveillance. The English colonies along the Atlantic coast were now confined by French territorial claims running through the heart of the North American continent. To secure such a vast territory, France required the active support of the Indigenous peoples who lived there. Alliances were consolidated with fortified trading posts, which had less to do with the demand for furs than with the goals of military strategy. This approach seemed to work. In 1701 more than 1,300 representatives of nearly forty Indigenous nations from Acadie to the Mississippi, including the Five Nations Confederacy, assembled outside Montreal to negotiate peace among themselves and confirm alliances with France. The Great Peace of Montreal, signed by an Abenaki representative of the Wabanaki

Figure 5.2. Canadian Militiaman Going to War on Snowshoes. Locally recruited militia played a significant role in the intermittent warfare that prevailed in eastern North America during the French regime. This image is based on a member of Iberville's militia in his campaign in the Atlantic region in 1696–7. Library and Archives Canada, C-1854, "Canadiens en Raquette allant en guerre sur la neige," Claude-Charles Bacqueville de La Potherie, *Amérique septentrioale*, 1722. http://nlc-bnc.ca/008/001/008001-119.01-e.php? &document_id_nbr=106&ts_nbr=4&brws=1&&PHPSESSID=d5b6bcrge197fcrkasetghis06

Confederacy, was a diplomatic triumph for Louis XIV, who now seemed poised to achieve unrivalled European dominance.[37]

As people in North America were sorting out their relations, France became embroiled in another war. This time, Louis XIV planned to establish his grandson on the throne of Spain, thus uniting two of Europe's great empires. The War of the Spanish Succession began to rumble in the fall of 1701 with England and France ultimately ranged on opposing sides. In British North America, the conflict was known as Queen Anne's War, after the reigning British monarch from 1702 to1714. It was during Queen Anne's reign that the term "United Kingdom of Great Britain" came into common usage as a result of the terms of union, signed on 1 May 1707, between Scotland and England.

Before war was declared, French officials ordered Jacques-François de Monbeton de Brouillan to move Acadie's administrative centre back to Port-Royal from the mouth of the St John River, where it had been located at the end of the previous war. Governor Brouillan strengthened Port-Royal's fortifications, summoned Indigenous allies to supplement the reinforced garrison, and engaged a privateer to patrol the colony's coastline. With few resources at his disposal, he commandeered Acadians in the Bay of Fundy communities to work on fortifications and to submit to a levy on their wheat and cattle. When supplies of food and clothing ran short, Brouillan secured them from ever-obliging Boston merchants.

Brouillan and Governor General Vaudreuil were complicit in efforts to induce the Wabanaki Confederacy to wage brutal attacks on Wells, Saco, and Casco in the summer of 1703,[38] and on Deerfield, Massachusetts, in February 1704. In retaliation, Massachusetts dispatched an expedition led by Benjamin Church to the Bay of Fundy. Church had decades of experience in frontier warfare, and brought along as translator John Gyles, whose earlier captivity had afforded him the opportunity to learn native languages. The New Englanders sacked all major Acadian settlements except Port-Royal, which managed to hold out. Leaving a trail of broken dykes, burned homes, slaughtered cattle, and devastated crops, the New Englanders took fifty Acadian captives to Boston, targeting women and children to exchange for the equivalent English prisoners in Montreal and elsewhere. The Acadians were returned in 1706, among them at least two children born in captivity.[39]

The New Englanders were not yet finished. In June 1707, Colonel John March led an army of 1,100 British regulars, New England militia, and Indigenous warriors, supported by twenty-four vessels, against Port-Royal. Severely outnumbered, the new governor, Daniel d'Auger de Subercase, ordered buildings in the line of fire to be burned, and harboured more than 700 soldiers and civilians inside the fort. The siege was lifted with the help of Abenaki militia led by Saint-Castin's teenage son Bernard-Anselme, and sixty Canadians who had recently arrived as crew for the *Biche*, a frigate built at Port-Royal. Before they returned home, March's forces destroyed what was left of the town outside the fort, including, predictably, the Catholic church, and a ship still in stocks owned by Charles de La Tour. The day after March's departure, the privateer Pierre Morpain arrived with two New England vessels in tow. One brought much-needed supplies, including meat and flour; the other carried slaves, who were dispatched to the Caribbean island of Saint-Dominigue. Morpain was still in town when Colonel March returned later in the summer to face yet another defeat after a two-week siege consisting of deadly skirmishes outside the walls of the fort.

For the next two years, Subercase relied on Acadian farmers, shipments from Canada, and privateers to keep Port-Royal supplied. One of the privateer vessels, under the command of Bonaventure's brother Louis Denys de la Ronde, included Mi'kmaq and West Indians among the crew. They participated in the capture of St John's, Newfoundland, in 1708 and eventually fetched up in Canada. Morpain returned briefly in 1709, and in a ten-day period sank four British vessels and captured nine prizes. He took the occasion to marry the sixteen-year-old daughter of Seigneur Louis Damours.[40] In all, French privateers seized thirty-five vessels and took more than three hundred prisoners in 1709, fuelling the resolve of New Englanders to rid themselves of the French menace once and for all.

The Conquest

The siege of October 1710 resulted in what turned out to be the final capture of Port-Royal. Supported by a detachment of nearly 500 British infantry, marines, and grenadiers, General Francis Nicholson, a seasoned colonial officer and administrator, led a force 1,500 colonial militia and Indigenous allies to attack Port-Royal.

Conditions in the capital of the small colonial outpost were desperate. In a letter to his superiors written just before the siege, Subercase reported that morale was low. The English had blockaded Port-Royal, cutting off supplies, and he was obliged to remove canoes from the town so that the soldiers would not use them to escape. "I am as if in a prison from which nothing can be sent in or out," he complained. "I owe large sums of money that, through my industry, I have managed to borrow for the subsistence of the garrison during the last two years. I have paid what I can by selling all of my furniture and would give to my last shirt."[41] Few Mi'kmaq answered the governor's call for assistance.

Drawing on his knowledge of their seasonal rhythms, the historian William Wicken concludes that the Mi'kmaq would have had little time for warfare in early October, when the eel harvest was in progress.[42] Indeed, most Mi'kmaq might well have been oblivious to the attack.

After a week of bombardment, Subercase and his small demoralized garrison surrendered. The Articles of Capitulation, signed on 16 October 1710,[43] pertained only to the fort and a three-mile (4.8-kilometre) *banlieu* around it. Samuel Vetch, a Scotsman based in Boston who had championed a comprehensive campaign against New France, was appointed governor of Port-Royal, renamed Annapolis Royal in honour of the queen. While French administrators and soldiers, along with the Canadians and West Indians, returned to their respective homes, the 481 residents in the *banlieu* were given the option of moving to Plaisance or Canada within two years or taking the oath of allegiance to the British Crown. Most of them did neither, biding their time until help arrived from France or Canada and making life difficult for their conquerors by refusing to supply lumber, firewood, and food. When commissary Peter Capon was kidnapped and held for ransom during an attempt to purchase supplies from Acadians on the Annapolis River, Vetch sent a detachment of troops to seize the local church and take hostages, and dispatched their priest, Justinian Durand, to Boston.

Lacking a permanent garrison until the summer of 1712, Vetch held on with a mix of disgruntled New England militia, British regulars, and a company of unruly Mohawks led by his brother-in-law, John Livingston. Conditions worsened in the spring of 1711 with the arrival of a force of Abenaki and Wolastoqiyik led by Saint-Castin and accompanied by the missionary priest Antoine Gaulin. They threatened Acadians and Mi'kmaq with physical and ecclesiastical vengeance if they assisted the conquerors in any way, and sniped at the British when they tried to move beyond the narrow confines of their *banlieu*. In early June a detachment of seventy soldiers charged with securing lumber upriver from Annapolis Royal was decimated in a bloody ambush, prompting many of the Acadians living in the vicinity of the fort to withdraw for fear of reprisals. An outbreak of smallpox that ravaged the garrison in the spring of 1711, the presence of Mi'kmaq in area, and the failure later that summer of a massive British expedition led by Sir Hovenden Walker against Quebec further encouraged Acadian resistance to the impositions of their conquerors.

Not all Acadians shunned relations with the British. Some took the opportunity to make a little money by selling property in Annapolis Royal to the occupiers, and a few women found husbands among them. In 1711 Marie-Madeleine, daughter of the notorious privateer Pierre

Maisonnat and his wife Madeleine Bourg, married Lieutenant William Winniett; two years later Agathe de Saint-Étienne de La Tour married Lieutenant Edmund Bradstreet. Despite these individual accommodations, the situation for the conquerors remained tense. Vetch's position became even more difficult when Nicholson was named governor of Nova Scotia and Placentia in the autumn of 1712. As the two men vied for authority, the war gradually fizzled out.

The treaty ending the War of the Spanish Succession consisted of a complicated series of agreements signed at Utrecht in 1713 and 1714 involving Britain, France, Spain, the Netherlands, and other European governments. To secure the Bourbon dynasty on the Spanish throne, Louis XIV agreed in 1713 to abandon Hudson Bay, Newfoundland, and "la nouvelle Ecosse autrement dite Acadie" to the British and to recognize British suzerainty over the territory occupied by the Five Nations Confederacy. France retained fishing rights on the north coast of Newfoundland and kept islands protecting the entrance to the Gulf of St Lawrence, including Île du Cap-Breton and Île Saint-Jean. French settlers had the choice of swearing allegiance to a Protestant monarch or moving to French-controlled territory. The Mi'kmaq, Wolastoqiyik, and Passamaquoddy, who found their homelands awarded to their enemies without their knowledge or consent, had no place to retreat.

In retrospect, the Treaty of Utrecht marked the beginning of British ascendancy in northern North America, but this was not evident in 1713. Acadie had changed hands several times over the previous century, and another war might result in a return of French control. For many of the Acadians and Mi'kmaq who called the region home, this would have been the most desirable outcome. They were, after all, mostly French speaking and Roman Catholic. But it was a case of be careful of what you wish for. Its strategic location made the territory variously called Mi'kma'ki, Acadie, and Nova Scotia a potential battleground in any future European war, and its inhabitants would bear the brunt of the contest. As Elizabeth Mancke and John G. Reid argue, colonization and empire building were not the same process, and by the eighteenth century the latter had become the chief preoccupation of leaders in both Britain and France.[44]

Chapter Six

Contested Terrains, 1713–1749

The Treaty of Utrecht created more problems than it solved. Although Britain was theoretically in control of a place called Acadie, or Nova Scotia, the colony was, as Jeffers Lennox argues, largely a figment of European imaginations.[1] The challenge of governing the primarily French-speaking and Roman Catholic Acadians and Mi'kmaq initially defeated British authorities, whose interests lay elsewhere than in northeastern North America. In contrast, France, smarting from the loss of Acadie and Newfoundland, made a bold statement in Cape Breton with the founding of Louisbourg, and aggressively exploited the ambiguity of Nova Scotia's ill-defined boundaries, claiming that the area north of the Bay of Fundy and even parts of the peninsula were excluded from the term "la nouvelle Ecosse autrement dite Acadie" used in the treaty. British authorities inevitably took exception to the French position, while the Mi'kmaq and other members of the Wabanaki Confederacy insisted that European nations had no right to grant their homelands to each other in treaties. Caught in the middle, many Acadians tried to maintain a neutral stance, a position that ultimately proved untenable. Under these conditions, Mi'kma'ki drifted into chronic instability.

Benign Neglect

With colonies stretching from Newfoundland to South Carolina in 1713, Britain had no intention of making Nova Scotia a showcase for empire. The newly acquired colony served primarily as a buffer for New England against the French presence in the region, and few resources were initially committed to its administration. While the decision to revert to the name Nova Scotia, used off and on since 1621, made good political sense in context of the Act of Union of 1707, it attracted little enthusiasm from potential settlers in old Scotland or anywhere else in Britain and North America. Who would want to risk their lives in a contested borderland that threatened to erupt into violence under the slightest provocation?

Political uncertainty in Britain compounded the administrative neglect. In the immediate aftermath of the war, policy makers were preoccupied with the ascension of George I, the first monarch of the House of Hanover, whose rule was challenged by Jacobite uprisings designed to put Queen Anne's Catholic half-brother James Stuart on the throne. The struggle between supporters of constitutional monarchy, known as Whigs, and their conservative opponents, called Tories, played out across the Atlantic, sometimes paralysing administrative decisions. This situation, coupled with the hopelessly muddled machinery for colonial governance – the Lords of Trade and Plantations, the Secretary at War, the Secretary of State, the Paymaster's Office, the Board of Ordnance, and the Admiralty all had fingers in the administrative pie – meant that decisions were often buried in bureaucratic limbo.[2] When the uncompromising Whig Robert Walpole became the First Lord of the Treasury, Chancellor of the Exchequer, and leader in the House of Commons in 1721, positions he held until 1742, distant colonies remained low on the government's agenda.

In this context, none of the proposals to bring Protestant settlers to Nova Scotia got off the ground. The Wabanaki Confederacy's stout refusal to welcome European settlement in their homelands cast a pall over all colonizing efforts.[3] Even if this reality was ignored, as was often the case, the uncertain legality of the La Tour/Le Borgne seigneurial claims put title to new land grants in question. The British government finally decided to purchase the rights of the La Tour family from Charles de La Tour's granddaughter Agathe Campbell in 1734, but this dubious transaction had no immediate impact on colonization efforts.[4] With the British hold so tenuous, Acadians resisted taking any oath of allegiance that would require them to fight for a Protestant monarch against the French and their Wabanaki allies in the war that was sure to come.

As a fallback position, the British governed much as the French had before them. The administrative apparatus included an appointed governor and council supported by small garrisons based at Annapolis Royal and Canso. Little thought was given to introducing an elected assembly because only a handful of Protestant residents would be eligible to vote. During the few months that he spent in the colony in 1714, Governor Francis Nicholson succeeded in alienating nearly everyone, including the garrison upon which the success of his administration crucially depended. With his Whig connections, Samuel Vetch managed to replace Nicholson following the accession of George I, but Vetch stayed put in England. Lieutenant Governor Thomas Caulfield made a show of proclaiming the new monarch at Annapolis Royal, and tried to secure an oath of allegiance from the Acadians, but few were prepared to do more than sign a document recognizing George I as the legitimate sovereign.

Vetch was replaced in 1717 by Richard Philipps, an officer who had distinguished himself at the Battle of the Boyne on behalf of William of Orange in 1690. Equipped with a new regiment (the 40th), Philipps was charged with "laying the foundations of a Civill Government" similar to the one in Virginia, rather than the more democratic model that prevailed in the New England colonies. He finally arrived in Nova Scotia in 1720. After appointing a council of twelve men over which he presided, he tried to convince the Indigenous and Acadian residents in the colony to take an oath of allegiance. Only the Wolastoqiyik were prepared to promise peace and friendship. Philipps responded promptly to French and Mi'kmaw encroachments on Canso, moving to the area in 1721 to establish order, but he returned to England in the fall of 1722 convinced that British authority in Nova Scotia was little more than an elaborate fiction.

During his second tour of duty from 1729 to 1731, Philipps managed to extract a qualified oath of allegiance from Acadians living in Minas and Chignecto, but he accomplished little else before being recalled in 1731 to respond to complaints about his administration.[5] Although he officially remained governor until 1749, Philipps never again set foot in Nova Scotia. His subordinates John Doucett, Lawrence Armstrong, and Paul Mascarene did their best under difficult circumstances, but they lacked the resources to resolve the colony's inadequate defences or even to communicate effectively with Canso, which was on the front lines of a looming French presence in the region.

Île Royale

Cape Breton was rechristened Île Royale by the French in 1713 as a signal of its new strategic importance. To replace Plaisance, a fortified town was founded at Havre à l'Anglois, renamed Louisbourg in honour of the aging king (Figure 6.1).[6] It was designed to provide a base for the fisheries, to protect the Gulf of St Lawrence entrance to France's continental empire, and to serve as a linchpin in the burgeoning North Atlantic trade. The roughly two hundred Mi'kmaq who lived around Bras d'Or Lake on the island they called Unama'ki welcomed the trading opportunities and spiritual services that the French presence offered.

Figure 6.1. *Plan de Louisbourg 1731 en panorama couleur avec navires.*

This panorama of Louisbourg in 1731 was created by Claude-Étienne Verrier, son of the chief engineer at the fortress between 1724 and 1745. With the King's Hospital (left) and the King's Bastion (right) dominating the skyline, Louisbourg bore witness to the French talent for town planning in the eighteenth century and also to the design flaws that contributed to its relatively easy capture by British and New England forces in 1745.
https://commons.wikimedia.org/wiki/File:Plan_de_Louisbourg_1731_en_panorama_couleur_avec_navires.jpg

Well positioned to nurture friendly relations with the region's Indigenous peoples, Louisbourg became a hub for subsidized trade, annual
gift giving, and missionary influence among France's most loyal North
American allies.

In choosing Louisbourg as the site of their ambitious initiative, French
authorities were influenced by its proximity to good fishing grounds
more than by its strategic location. The primarily Newfoundland-born
settlers evacuated from Plaisance were the first to arrive, taking up
beach lots in and around Louisbourg in the fall of 1713. With financial
restraint foremost in their minds, French administrators experimented
with the more easily defended Port Dauphin (the former Ste-Anne) as
their official residence, but the royal government moved back to Louisbourg in 1720. By that time, more than eight hundred people were living in the community, which had also become a major base for seasonal
trade and the migratory fisheries. On 29 May 1720, Governor Joseph
de Monbeton de Brouillan, *dit* Saint-Ovide hosted a ceremony to commemorate the official founding of Louisbourg. New thinking in Paris
now determined that 4 million livres would be spent building elaborate
fortifications. Four times that amount would be required to maintain
the town over the next two decades.[7]

By 1734 the initial phase of construction had been largely completed.
Few could deny that Louisbourg, located on the western peninsula of
the harbour, was an impressive sight, especially when approached by
sea. The Kings Bastion and the King's Hospital dominated the skyline
of the walled town; a Royal Battery commanded the north shore; and
a lighthouse stood guard at the east side of the harbour entrance. By
the 1740s any enemy attacking Louisbourg confronted 215 embrasures,
150 mounted cannon, 7 mortars, and 64 swivel guns. Inside the walls,
chief engineer Jean-François du Vergery de Verville imposed a grid of
streets and public squares to serve as efficient thoroughfares for the
movement of troops and civilians. With the king's coat of arms, *fleur-de
lys*, plaques, and white flags ornamenting government-funded structures, visitors could be in little doubt that they had reached an important French stronghold.[8]

As was the case in Acadia until 1710, the governor and *commissaire-
ordonnateur* based at Louisbourg theoretically reported to officials in
Quebec, but in practice they communicated directly with France. The
fishing proprietors (*habitants-pêcheurs*) from Plaisance dominated the
island's economy, and were initially well represented on the Superior
Council. The Acadians, in contrast, were reluctant to leave their prosperous farms on the Bay of Fundy for the rocky soil of Île Royale. Even

Figure 6.2. Acadians, inset of painting by Samuel Scott of Annapolis Royal, 1751.
https://commons.wikimedia.org/wiki/File:Acadians%2c_Inset_of_painting_by_Samuel_
Scott_Annapolis_Royal%2c_1751.jpg

Figure 6.3. Acadians 2, inset of painting by Samuel Scott of Annapolis
Royal, 1751.
https://commons.wikimedia.org/wiki/File:Acadians_2,_inset_of_painting_by_Samuel_
Scott_of_Annapolis_Royal,_1751.jpg

the prospect of freehold land tenure – no seigneuries were granted on
Île Royale – failed to tempt them. Only sixty Acadian families, more
than 70 per cent of them from the area around Annapolis Royal, moved
to Île Royale between 1713 and 1734.[9] They settled primarily in areas
outside Louisbourg – Port Toulouse (St-Pierre), Île de Maurepas (Île
Madame), and Port d'Orléans (Niganiche) in particular – where they
could farm, fish, cut lumber, build vessels, and engage in coastal trade.
Continuity with previous French holdings was also ensured by rede-
ploying to Louisbourg the garrisons that had formerly served Plaisance
and Port-Royal.

Although a few German, Irish, Scottish, and Spanish sojourners
could be counted among Louisbourg's cosmopolitan population, most
of the residents came directly from France, especially from the Gulf of
St-Malo. French and Basque fishermen were prominent at Nérichac
(Arichat) and Petit-de-Grat on Île de Maurepas, which supported a
significant dry cod fishery.[10] Various religious orders – the Frères hos-
pitaliers, Récollets, and Soeurs de la Congrégation de Notre-Dame –
sustained by subsidies from France rather than a local tithe, provided
educational, medical, and spiritual services. In addition to Troupes de
la Marine, German and Swiss soldiers of the Karrer Regiment were stationed at Louisbourg from 1722 to 1745. Some of them were Protestants,

which seemed not to bother the minister of marine when it came to hiring mercenaries. A few soldiers were also based in Port Toulouse, located at the strategic portage between Bras d'Or Lake and the Atlantic.[11]

By the 1740s Île Royale had a civilian population of nearly four thousand, more than one-third of them living in Louisbourg, and a garrison approaching a thousand soldiers. Women accounted for only 12 per cent of the civilian population of Louisbourg in 1734. As a result, the average age of a female partner in marriage was under twenty. The gender balance in the outlying communities was also skewed towards men, most of whom made a living in the fisheries. While most men who had married on Île Royale by 1745 had come from France, more than 84 per cent of their partners had been born in New France.[12] About 11 per cent of the brides were pregnant when they married, a situation that elicited little official concern. What mattered most to both secular and spiritual authorities was that a man married the woman with whom he had sexual relations.

Control of sexuality among unmarried soldiers was another matter. As in most military towns, prostitution and venereal disease flourished, and cases of sexual assault were sometimes brought to court. Authorities occasionally deported prostitutes, and tried to punish sea captains and officers responsible for the presence of these *femmes de mauvais vie* in the colony, but with little effect.[13] Although seduction could bring a court order demanding marriage, elites were rarely penalized for such behaviour. Governor Saint-Ovide openly boasted of his youthful indiscretions, and when seventeen-year-old Sieur de Brise molested an eleven-year-old girl on board ship, he escaped censure after the surgeon determined that the girl had not experienced a "complete deflowering."[14]

Kenneth Donovan has determined that at least 216 slaves, two-thirds of them men, lived on Île Royale between 1713 and 1760.[15] More than 90 per cent were black, reflecting the close trading ties with the West Indies, where sugar, tobacco, indigo, and coffee plantations relied on enslaved labour from Africa. The remaining slaves were Indigenous people, called *Panis* or *sauvages*. Most *Panis* came from Canada, where they outnumbered slaves of African origin. In the French Empire, slavery was regulated, in theory at least, by the *Code Noir*, which was introduced in the West Indies in 1685. The Code obliged slave owners to house, feed, and clothe their slaves properly, to care for the aged and infirm, to encourage marriage, and to provide instruction in the Roman Catholic religion. Masters could whip their slaves, but not imprison or execute them without recourse to the courts; the law also forbade the sexual exploitation of slaves or the selling of a child separately from a

parent before reaching adolescence. Since the *Code Noir* was never registered in Île Royale, it is unlikely that its provisions were widely known
or observed. Slaves were often subjected to physical, psychological, or
sexual abuse, and had little hope of being released from bondage. Only
six slaves were freed during the French regime on the island, one of
whom was Marie-Louise, owned by the merchant Louis Jouet. During
her sixteen years of servitude, she gave birth to six children before being
released to marry a Breton fisherman who had moved to Louisbourg.[16]

A few people tried to escape the control imposed by the highly authoritarian government on Île Royale. When Louisbourg's lower court,
known as the *bailliage*, learned that two men were living in a cabin in
the nearby woods, surviving by hunting and fishing, they were ordered
to stop leading an idle life. Niganiche on the north shore posed a much
greater administrative challenge. The people there were closely tied to
Cap-de-Ré, a community on the south coast of Newfoundland, where
French and British settlers lived without any authority but their own. In
1724 officials in Louisbourg issued an order forbidding fishers to move
to Cap-de-Ré, and troops were sent to retrieve some of the migrants
living there. Nevertheless, relations across the Cabot Strait continued,
obliging *commissaire-ordonnateur* François Bigot to demand in the 1740s
that the local priest refuse to sanction marriage with residents from
Cap-de-Ré and to deny permission for two Niganiche women to join
their husbands living across the Strait.[17] This policy no doubt contributed to the growth of the rebellious community, where the population
had reached more than six hundred souls by 1737.

While administrators had their hands full maintaining control in the
outports, they also faced challenges in Louisbourg itself. The presence
of so many soldiers, the majority under the age of twenty-five (and a
surprising number under the legal limit of sixteen), meant that there
was plenty of youthful energy in the barracks. Although much of it
was harnessed to useful ends such as labour on the many construction
projects in the town, drunkenness, desertion, assault, and petty theft
were common among ordinary soldiers. Military justice was swift and
often fatal for major crimes, but most officers avoided imposing excessive physical punishment, such as running the gauntlet and confinement for long periods in a damp dungeon, because they wanted to keep
their soldiers healthy. With twenty-eight cabarets by 1734, Louisbourg
was awash with alcohol, and regular edicts to control its excessive
consumption among the civilian and military population alike failed
utterly. Soldiers earned a wage for their labour, but much of it ended
up in the hands of officers who sold them alcohol, equipment, food,
and other necessities at exorbitant prices in their privately operated

canteens. Since officers insisted that wages be routed through them, soldiers felt – and no doubt were – cheated in this early version of the "check-off."[18]

Like many eighteenth-century European societies, Louisbourg was riven by class and occupational hierarchies. Inside the walls, soldiers and civilians lived separate lives in their housing, justice, worship, and even cemetery burials. A wide gulf yawned between officers and the rank and file, and between administrative and mercantile leaders and ordinary civilians. As the reconstructed historical site at Louisbourg documents, the elite lived in impressive opulence, purchasing the best in clothing, furnishings, and tableware that eighteenth-century France had to offer. Those labouring on the docks and in the homes of the well heeled – whether enslaved, indentured, or earning a small pittance – experienced life differently. What they had in common was the cold, damp climate, which elicited comment from many sojourners. "There are, so to speak, only two seasons, winter and autumn," Thomas Pichon, secretary to Governor Jean-Louis Raymond, concluded in the early 1750s.[19]

Despite the challenges, Louisbourg quickly emerged as a major North Atlantic entrepôt. An average of 154 ships called at the port annually, a number exceeded in North America only by Boston, New York, and Philadelphia. Fish and fish oil made up more than 90 per cent of the locally generated exports, but the wharves in Louisbourg harbour were awash with much more: fishing gear, foodstuffs, and manufactured goods from France; molasses, sugar, and rum from the West Indies; foodstuffs and building supplies legally shipped from Canada or illegally imported from New England and Nova Scotia. There was a sixfold increase in French seaborne commerce in the years between 1710 and 1740, and Louisbourg was a major beneficiary of this growth. With the age of steam still a century away, the island's coal reserves were used primarily for heating purposes. Some effort was made to mine coal systematically at Port Morien, but it was widely available to anyone who took the trouble to dig it up.

France also tried to develop Île Saint-Jean, which was administered as a dependency of Île Royale. In 1719 the islands of Saint-Jean, Miscou, and Madeleine were granted to the French aristocrat the Comte de Saint-Pierre, with the stipulation that he sponsor settlement. The following year, his Compagnie de l'Île Saint-Jean sent out more than 250 colonists, who established themselves at Port-la-Joye (near Charlottetown), Havre St-Pierre (St Peter's), and other coastal locations. The company recruited a Sulpician priest, potential brides for their unmarried workers, and even a midwife. To encourage family life, indentured servants were promised release from their contracts if they married on Île Saint-Jean. Notwithstanding such careful family planning, the company failed, its efforts dogged by competition from interlopers (among them fishermen from Île Royale), crop failures, and ultimately bankruptcy.

To confirm French sovereignty, the governor of Louisbourg sent a detachment of thirty soldiers to occupy Port-la-Joye in 1726. It was a lonely outpost until Jean-Pierre Roma, an energetic Parisian merchant, established fishing operations on the island in the 1730s. He built roads to connect Trois-Rivières, his main base, with Havre St-Pierre and Port-la-Joye, and recruited settlers. According to a 1735 census, 432 colonists lived on Île Saint-Jean, about a third of them of Acadian origin. Among them were Michel Haché-Gallant, his wife Anne Cormier, and their twelve children, who had moved from Beaubassin to Port-la-Joye in 1720. The Gallants ultimately emerged as one of the most prominent families on the island.[20] During the summer, Mi'kmaq lived in the Malpeque area, where they grew corn, gathered the abundant shellfish, and travelled to meet with local religious and secular officials.

The Fisheries

As the foregoing suggests, the fisheries loomed large in French imperial policy. Profit from the cod fishery always exceeded that of the fur trade and its strategic value was represented in the experienced seamen it produced for the wartime navy. Should the North Atlantic cod fisheries be monopolized by another nation, the livelihood of thousands of families in the seaports of western France would have been threatened and France's military might compromised. When wars ended in 1713 and 1763, French negotiators were prepared to surrender territory in North America to the British, but they took special care to retain shore bases for their precious fisheries.

France dominated the North Atlantic cod fishery, its value twice that of the British fishery until the late eighteenth century. Contrary to often-repeated claims, cod was initially a luxury item, not a cheap source of protein, and the French pursued all aspects of the industry, not just the salt-intensive green fishery.[21] The Basques and Bretons predominated in the production of dried cod, while fishermen from Normandy pursued the green fishery on the Grand Banks, rarely setting foot in North America except for water and ship repairs. Cod dried on shore rather than packed in barrels on board ship required less salt and resulted in a higher-quality product, but it was a more labour-intensive enterprise and required shore bases for drying the fish.

Table 6.1. Value of the Île Royale Cod Fisheries,
1718–53 (in livres)

Year	Cod	Cod Oil
1718	3,130,000	313,000
1723	3,029,000	183,920
1733	3,307,300	181,830
1743	1,774,400	106,440
1753	1,969,000	98,450

Source: B.A. Balcom, *The Cod Fishery of Isle
Royale, 1713–58* (Ottawa: Parks Canada, 1984), 17.

Since the early days of contact, Newfoundland, Cape Breton, the Gaspé Peninsula, Île Saint-Jean, and the Îles de la Madeleine served as seasonal shore bases for the French migratory fishery and small, year-round settlements gradually took root. The resident fishery, over time, began to represent a larger portion of the dry cod industry. On Île Royale, shore-based fishermen copied New Englanders in making voyages of several days' duration to offshore banks in fast boats called schooners, where they wet-salted their catch onboard ship before drying it onshore. This resulted in an inferior product, but one that found a ready market in the Caribbean, where it was fed to the African slaves imported to work on plantations. The annual output of the resident fishery on Île Royale rose from about one-half to three-quarters of the total production of dried cod between 1718 and 1736, and in 1737 reached a high of 81 per cent.[22] When war threatened as it did by 1740, French fishing companies reduced their overseas investments in the knowledge that both their crews and their ships would soon be jeopardized (Table 6.1).

As on Île Royale, the output of the Nova Scotia fisheries increased following the Treaty of Utrecht, and colonial administrators in London, Boston, and Annapolis Royal kept a close watch on the industry. New Englanders dominated the Nova Scotia fishery, using Canso as their main base but drying their catch on any beach that suited their purposes. Each spring large transport vessels from Britain and New England arrived off Canso to take the processed cod to markets in southern Europe and the West Indies. Canso's summer sojourners supported a busy trade in barrels, construction materials, foodstuffs, fishing supplies, rum, salt, tobacco, and exotic commodities such as lemons and olive oil from the Mediterranean, much of it illegally shipped to Louisbourg. For a brief period in the 1730s, Canso was also the base of a whale fishery pursued primarily by residents of Nantucket. The production of

cod at Canso never reached the level reported by Louisbourg, the annual catch rarely exceeding 60,000 quintals, but the community was a
significant base for New Englanders, who viewed it as a component of
their growing commercial empire.[23]

The French and New Englanders operating in the Canso area managed to stay out of each other's way until 1718, when the governor of
Massachusetts dispatched Thomas Smart, a British naval officer tasked
with keeping North American waters safe from pirates and expelling
the French from Canso, either by diplomacy or by force. When his discussions with Governor Saint-Ovide failed to bring the desired resolution, Smart confiscated French vessels in the Canso area and escorted
them to Boston. This incident led to prolonged diplomatic wrangling
over the ownership of Canso Island, and inspired Governor Philipps to
help the New Englanders build a fort there to protect their interests in
the region. In addition to installing a small garrison at Canso, Philipps
and his subordinates made efforts to establish a local militia, appoint
justices of the peace, and grant shore and garden lots. This might have
been more attention than the community had bargained for, given the
threat these institutions posed to the clandestine Louisbourg trade, but
it underscored the importance of Canso in the larger imperial agenda.[24]

The Wabanaki Confederacy

Members of the Wabanaki Confederacy had not been represented at
Utrecht, but they soon learned what had transpired there. In the summer of 1713, Governor William Dudley and other colonial officials from
Massachusetts met with Wabanaki delegates at Portsmouth and Casco
to outline the treaty's main provisions with the hope of negotiating a
lasting peace. Some 40 Wolastoqiyik and 20 Mi'kmaq were among the
358 Indigenous delegates assembled at Casco, but only the Abenaki
were signatories to a treaty that permitted limited British settlement
but not new forts on their territory.[25] None of the other members of the
Wabanaki Confederacy was prepared to accept that they had forfeited
control of their territory to the British or that it was ever France's prerogative to give it away.

The Mi'kmaq were especially insistent on this point. With a population of roughly 3,500 in 1713, the Mi'kmaq were more numerous than
either the Acadians (2,000) or the British (400, including the garrison).[26]
This balance would change dramatically over the next half-century,
but for the time being the Mi'kmaq were the dominant force in Nova
Scotia both numerically and militarily. Inevitably, the growing presence of New England fishermen and merchants in the region following

the conquest made the Mi'kmaq anxious. Governor Dudley had argued in vain for government-regulated trade in what were known as "truck-houses" because, he claimed, "a Trade managed by private Persons will be liable to be corrupted by extorted Prices and selling them Drink."[27] Sharp practices by New England traders sometimes ended in violence and confirmed the Mi'kmaq in their preference for trade with the French based on Île Royale, who were subsidized to trump their British competitors. In 1719 Governor Saint-Ovide began meeting annually with the Mi'kmaq to shore up trade and military alliances.

The Mi'kmaq needed no encouragement from France in their resistance to the British. Determined to assert control over their territory, the Mi'kmaq regularly challenged New England fishermen when they tried to dry their fish on Nova Scotia's coastline. The Boston-based merchant Cyprian Southack, who had been involved in several campaigns against Acadia, established fishing operations at Port Roseway (now Shelburne) in 1715, but was warned away by two local inhabitants, who informed him that a hundred warriors were coming to expel him. Southack wisely fled before the Mi'kmaq torched his facilities.[28] Others in the region that year were not so fortunate. When Mi'kmaw mariners seized Massachusetts fishing vessels off Cape Sable, they were reported to have declared that "the Lands are theirs and they can make War and peace when they please."[29]

French fishermen stayed away from Canso after the British began constructing a fort there, but the Mi'kmaq were not so easily intimidated. In the summer of 1720, they attacked the community, touching off a conflict that included a two-hour naval battle between New England fishermen and Mi'kmaq manning captured sailing ships. The fishermen eventually prevailed, but they knew it would not be their last encounter with a determined enemy. As a warning to survivors, New Englanders decapitated the corpses of Mi'kmaq that washed ashore and set their severed heads on pikes near Canso's makeshift defences.[30]

The standoff with the Mi'kmaq in Nova Scotia blended into the Abenaki's concern over the encroachment of British settlement in the Kennebec area of Maine in violation of the agreement reached in 1713. The result was a full-fledged "Indian War" – known as Dummer's War, after the lieutenant governor of Massachusetts, or Father Rale's War, after a Jesuit priest who had established a mission on the Kennebec – which ranged along the New England-Nova Scotia frontier. Mi'kmaq and Wolastoqiyik captured eighteen New England vessels trading in the Bay of Fundy in 1722 and attacked fishermen at Canso and along the eastern shore of Nova Scotia. Philipps outfitted two sloops to protect the Canso fishery, but Annapolis Royal lay dangerously exposed and was short of provisions because the Mi'kmaq had intercepted ships bringing supplies. When approached by local authorities, most Acadians refused to sell their produce to them, for fear, they claimed, of reprisals by the Mi'kmaq.

The approximately fifty Mi'kmaq living in the vicinity of Annapolis Royal bore the brunt of administrative anxiety. Lieutenant Governor Doucett took twenty-two captive, most of them women and children, as hostages against an attack. The strategy failed. In early July 1724, fifty-six Mi'kmaq and Wolastoqiyik descended on Annapolis Royal, burning part of the town, killing a British soldier, and taking several captives before retreating. In response Doucett executed a hostage on the spot where the soldier had been killed, burned three Acadian homes in retaliation for the destruction of property, and expelled two priests believed to have abetted the outrage. Prudent Robichaud, a prominent Acadian living in Annapolis Royal, was imprisoned for trading with the enemy "to terrify the other Inhabitants from Clandestine Practices of betraying English subjects into the Indian hands."[31]

In December 1725 a peace agreement was reached in Boston between delegates from New England and Nova Scotia – council member Paul Mascarene, a Huguenot officer in the 40th Regiment, represented Nova Scotia – and negotiators from the Wabanaki Confederacy, with the stipulation that each Indigenous nation would be required to ratify the treaty. Sixty-four delegates representing Mi'kmaq, Wolastoqiyik, and Passamaquoddy attended a ratification ceremony held at Annapolis Royal in June 1726. The articles were read in English and French and then translated into Mi'kmaw and perhaps other languages by Prudent Robichaud and Abraham Bourg. At the close of the ceremony, Doucett entertained the delegates, offered presents, and released the remaining hostages. When a delegation of Wolastoqiyik from Meductic, on the St John River, arrived the following year, the process was repeated.[32]

The Treaty of 1725–6 would have significant long-term implications for Nova Scotia. Consisting of two documents, the first part outlined practices that the Wabanaki Confederacy would be obliged to follow in their relations with the British colonies of Massachusetts, New Hampshire, and Nova Scotia. The signatories recognized British sovereignty, promised not to molest any of "His Majesty's Subjects" or harbour deserting soldiers, and were obliged to follow "His Majesty's Laws" in seeking redress for any "Misunderstanding, Quarrel or Injury" between themselves and the British. The second part of the treaty outlined Britain's obligations, including the promise that Indigenous peoples would not "be molested in their Persons, Hunting [,] Fishing and Shooting & planting ... nor in any other [of] their Lawfull occasions."[33]

Since formal treaties were a British innovation and each side in the negotiations took away oral memory of what had been decided, only time would tell whether the agreement was worth the paper on which it was written. The Indigenous signatories undoubtedly interpreted the negotiations in the spirit of peace and friendship, implying that trade and gift giving would follow and that the land and its resources would be shared but not bargained away.[34] The British, in contrast, thought in terms of land ownership in the context of European institutions of governance and law. It was unclear how these divergent perspectives would be reconciled. What is clear is that the Treaty of 1725–6, like most written documents, took on a life of its own. It was subsequently violated by both sides and renegotiated in 1760–1, but Canadian courts have confirmed that it was never superseded. By the Constitution Act, 1982 and subsequent court cases, including the Marshall decision of 1999, the Treaty of 1725–6, along with the agreements signed in 1760–1, became the legal foundation on which Indigenous rights in the Maritimes stand.[35]

Pirates on the Horizon

From the early seventeenth century, the waters in the Atlantic region swarmed not only with privateers officially sanctioned to capture enemy shipping, but also with pirates – outlaws who terrorized merchant vessels and plundered seaports for their own benefit. The number of pirates mushroomed after the War of the Spanish Succession in part because wages for seamen plummeted when sailors were discharged from the British Navy. Although the Caribbean, West Africa, and the Indian Ocean attracted the most attention from pirates, the Atlantic region was a regular stop on the seasonal round for many of the "enemies of all mankind." The vessels involved in the North Atlantic fisheries and carrying trade offered worthy prizes, including fish, wine, bread, boats, and bullion, and provided a particularly rich recruiting ground for both forced and voluntary sailors.[36]

One of the most successful pirates in this period was Bartholomew Roberts, known by the posthumous nickname "Black Bart." Ambitious and ruthless, he dressed lavishly, flew an array of menacing flags, and employed musicians to play for his pleasure and to add dramatic emphasis during attacks. He began his career in 1719, focusing on West Africa and the Caribbean, but when the governors of Barbados and Martinique hired armed ships to hunt him down, Roberts sailed north. In 1720 he appeared off Canso, where he harassed New England fishing vessels, and then moved on to Trepassey, a harbour south of St John's.

He met no resistance from the twenty-two terrified ship captains in the port, who readily yielded men and supplies under the threat of losing their ships. After bombarding the community, Roberts moved to the waters off Île Royale, where he amassed a small fleet of vessels and a crew of more than two hundred men. This achievement enabled him to inflect a reign of terror in the busy shipping lanes between North America and Britain before heading back to the Caribbean. Although highly successful – Roberts captured some four hundred ships, fifty-five of them in the Atlantic region – his career was short, ending in a battle with HMS *Swallow* off the coast of Africa in February 1722.

Other pirates soon followed. In June 1722, Ned Low, notorious for his viciousness, attacked New England fishermen at Port Roseway, looting the thirteen vessels in the harbour, commandeering a new schooner for his own use, and taking on unwilling crew for further escapades off Newfoundland and Canso. One of his surviving captives, Phillip Ashton, described his experience on Low's vessel as a "floating hell," where "prodigious Drinking, monstrous Cursing and Swearing, hideous Blasphemies, and the open defiance of Heaven and the contempt of Hell was the constant employment." In addition to torturing and killing many of his captives, Low made a point of slitting the nose of any New England captain caught in his grip. He returned to the Canso area in April 1723, capturing eleven vessels. Low met a grisly end in 1724, when his ship was overtaken by his unhappy captives. They threw his body overboard, pickled his head in salt, and mounted it on the masthead before setting off for Boston. With their seaborne commerce under threat, Britain and France quickly put more energy into suppressing piracy, but its legacy continues in Nova Scotia through rumours of pirate treasure buried in such places as Oak Island and Ile Haute.

British Nova Scotia

Until 1749 the British presence in Nova Scotia remained confined primarily to Annapolis Royal. The gap between British administrators and Acadians widened after the conquest, as many of the latter withdrew from the capital and the former felt too vulnerable to carve out estates in the countryside. Closely tied to Boston – only a week away by sea – and London – a much longer run – the residents of Annapolis Royal introduced a variety of British institutions to sustain them in their anxious isolation. The origins of some of Nova Scotia's most cherished cultural practices date from this transitional period in the province's history.

By the 1740s Annapolis Royal was home to about eighty families, almost equally divided between Acadian and British. British administrators, merchants, and officers of the 40th Regiment and the Royal Artillery formed a tight little clique, bound together over time by marriage.[37] With up to two hundred men in the garrison, Annapolis Royal, like Louisbourg, was dominated by the military. Only five people were licensed to sell liquor in the community before 1744, all of them garrison wives who probably operated out of their homes. It was highly unlikely that their monopoly would be seriously challenged. When it was revealed in the summer of 1733 that tailor William Haw was selling liquor illegally to soldiers, he was paraded through the town, while being whipped a hundred times by the cat-o'-nine-tails.[38]

When they were not on extended leave – Annapolis Royal was deemed an undesirable clerical posting – Church of England clergy ministered to soldiers and civilians. In 1728 the Reverend Isaac Watt, acting garrison chaplain, was employed by the Society for the Propagation of the Gospel to operate a school, which initially enrolled fifty students. The leading English families were preoccupied with the well-being of their children as represented by their success in securing government positions, military commissions, and worthy marriage partners. To help advance the prospects of their offspring, well-placed Annapolis Royal families often sent them to Massachusetts or overseas to be educated. Paul Mascarene, who maintained his family in Boston, sometimes offered room and board to children of his Nova Scotian colleagues.

Boston and London offered better opportunities to experience high society, but the residents of Annapolis Royal replicated as much of metropolitan culture as they could manage. They enjoyed sleigh rides in winter, played bowls and grew gardens in the summer, hosted dinner parties and balls throughout the year, and celebrated special occasions on the royal calendar with salutes and toasts. King Gould, who served as the London-based agent for the garrison, sent British newspapers, magazines, and sheet music – "Purcell's music for fiddle" was dispatched in 1738 – to his clients in Nova Scotia. In Boston, newspapers carried reports on activities in Nova Scotia, among them a play performed for "Officers and Ladies" in the winter of 1744, the first, it seems, since the early years of Port-Royal. No information is provided as to what play provided amusement, but Mascarene's papers included an English translation of Molière's *La Misanthrope*, which might have appealed to an audience eager to see human foibles satirized.[39] In 1738 officers of the garrison established a Masonic Lodge, following from the founding of the First Grand Lodge in London in 1717 and a branch in Boston in 1733.

Although most of the labour in Annapolis Royal was performed by soldiers and indentured servants, a few families were sufficiently affluent to purchase slaves. Isaac Provender, a ten-year-old "Bound Servant" to the family of Edward Amhurst and Mary Winniett, came to public attention in 1737 when he burned down his master's house and barn. Since no one in the town had legal training, the council sought advice from Boston. Unlike Marie-Joseph Angélique, who protested her enslavement in a similar way in Quebec in 1734, Provender escaped the death penalty. He was sent to Boston, where he accompanied the Louisbourg expedition in 1745 and was court-marshalled the following year for trying to escape.[40]

Only three families were reported living permanently in Canso in 1729, but numbers there were much larger from May to November, when New England fishermen and merchants operated in the area.[41] By 1736 seasonal and permanent residents alike benefited from the services of a Church of England chaplain, a chapel, and a school. Canso's most prominent citizen was Edward How, an Irish-born merchant who served as justice of the peace, sheriff, and militia captain. Like most merchants, he lived in the style appropriate to his class. Excavations of his property by the staff of Parks Canada unearthed Chinese porcelain, fine furniture, and other material possessions easily available through illegal trade with Louisbourg. How's daughter Deborah received an excellent education, perhaps taught at home by her mother Deborah Crawley, a member of a merchant family from Marblehead, Massachusetts, or by the Society for the Propagation of the Gospel teacher resident in Canso from 1736 to 1743.[42]

In New England, where democratic institutions such as elected legislative assemblies, town meetings, and self-governed Congregational churches flourished, Nova Scotia was perceived as a tyrannical dictatorship. The council included as many military as civilian appointees, while justices of the peace, also appointed, were sometimes intimidated by officers. Since the council also sat as a court of judicature beginning in 1721, executive and judicial powers were conflated. That justice was, overall, meted out with an even hand is a tribute, Thomas Barnes argues, to the men who possessed no legal training but understood that justice must be seen to be done.[43] Although a few Acadians seeking redress appeared before the council, they kept largely to themselves, served as they had been before the conquest by priests – permitted by the Treaty of Utrecht to minister to both Indigenous and Acadian residents of Nova Scotia – and prominent members of the community, who selected delegates for negotiations with authorities in Annapolis Royal.

By far the largest bone of contention between the Acadians and British administrators was the oath of allegiance. Culture and tradition predisposed most Acadians to support the French, but their experience suggested that they should try to remain neutral in the struggle between France and Britain. After two decades of futile efforts to extract an unqualified oath, British authorities lived with the accommodation made by Philipps, which included a verbal promise that Acadians would not be forced to fight against France. Maurice Basque has underscored the obvious point that Acadians were not a monolithic group – that some Acadians formed close ties with the British, others with the French, and still others with neither – but the British were convinced that at least some of the "neutral French" would operate as a dangerous subversive element in wartime.[44] Meanwhile, Acadian farmers in Minas and Beaubassin were as defiant of authority as they had always been, cheekily driving their cattle overland through Tatamagouche to the Strait of Canso for transshipment to Louisbourg.

The Acadian strategy of playing both sides had its limits. French officials viewed the Acadian and Indigenous inhabitants of Nova Scotia as their main bulwark against the British, and refused to accept neutrality as a permanent posture. Using Roman Catholic priests as political agents, French authorities kept a watchful eye on these potential sources of military support. Antoine Gaulin, appointed vicar-general in 1702, continued his ministry after the conquest until 1732, establishing missions at Mirliguèche, Antigonish, Shubenacadie, La Have, and Cape Sable. In 1727 he conducted a census of Acadians, an exercise designed to account not only for souls but also for potential soldiers. Pierre-Antoine-Simon Maillard ministered to Roman Catholics in the region from 1735 until his death in 1762. Adept at learning Indigenous languages, he established a mission at Île de la Ste-Famille (Chapel Island) on Île Royale, which served as the site for an annual celebration combining worship, gift giving, and trade. Beginning in 1738 Jean-Louis Le Loutre ministered to mainland Mi'kmaq from his base at Shubenacadie and at French posts brazenly located at Beaubassin and Tatamagouche. According to a 1735 census undertaken by priests in the region, as many as 550 warriors could be assembled among Mi'kmaq living from Gaspé to Cape Sable.[45]

Naomi Griffiths has described the years between 1713 and 1744 as a "golden age" for Acadians, largely because it was a rare period of peace.[46] Unlike the Mi'kmaq and British populations, which remained static, the numbers of Acadians exploded, reaching more than 10,000 on mainland Nova Scotia and 4,000 on Île Saint-Jean and Île Royale by 1754.[47] Family life flourished and agriculture benefited from the expansion of markets in the region. Literate English men, on whose comments we must rely for much of what we know about Acadians in this period, were particularly interested in the women they encountered.

According to one male commentator, Acadian women were slovenly in their dress – their stockings settled around their ankles – and swarthy in complexion, typical attributes of women who worked outdoors as well as in the home.[48]

King George's War, 1744–8

The three decades following the Treaty of Utrecht were not always peaceful in Nova Scotia, but the level of violence increased after the War of the Austrian Succession erupted in Europe in 1740. While Britain and the Dutch Republic supported the right of Archduchess Maria Theresa to rule Austria, France and Prussia opposed it on the grounds that power should devolve to a male heir in the Hapsburg line. The conflict merged with the War of Jenkins' Ear between Britain and Spain, which was fought primarily in the Caribbean beginning in 1739, resulting in a formal declaration of war between Britain and France in March 1744. It was dubbed King George's War in English North America, after the second Hanoverian king of Britain. It marked the beginning of what historian Jerry Bannister describes as the Forty Years' War in Nova Scotia, which paved the way for settler sovereignty in the region.[49]

During the war, George II's rule was challenged by what turned out to be the last Jacobite attempt to restore the Stuart dynasty to the throne. "Bonnie" Prince Charlie's primarily Scottish army, supported and supplied by France, invaded England in November 1745, but was routed at Culloden the following spring. Until then, Britain had few resources to commit to North America. New Englanders, their numbers having grown impressively, proved more than willing and able to pick up the slack, signalling the arrival of a new node of power in the North Atlantic, one that would soon make its mark on a global scale.

News that war had been declared reached Louisbourg several weeks before it arrived in Annapolis Royal and Boston. Taking advantage of this intelligence, Louisbourg's governor, Jean-Baptiste-Louis Le Prévost Duquesnel, authorized privateers to attack New England shipping, and dispatched a small military expedition under Captain François Du Pont Duvivier, a native of Port-Royal, against Canso. The eighty-seven soldiers stationed there were caught off guard and surrendered almost immediately in May 1744, perhaps because Duvivier's force had been augmented by at least sixteen Mi'kmaq, who for good reasons struck fear in the hearts of Canso's inhabitants. After pillaging the site, the victors carried the garrison and civilians to Louisbourg. One of the officers captured in the attack was John (baptized Jean-Baptiste) Bradstreet, the second son of Edmund Bradstreet and Agathe de Saint-Étienne de la

Tour. Bilingual and deeply involved in clandestine trade with Louisbourg while stationed in Canso, he played a major role in arranging the prisoner exchange and subsequently provided valuable information on conditions in Louisbourg to Governor William Shirley of Massachusetts.[50]

Early in July, a force of 230 Mi'kmaq, accompanied by a French officer and Abbé Le Loutre, attacked Annapolis Royal, but withdrew two days later when a company of Massachusetts volunteers arrived from Boston. Duquesnel had promised support for the campaign, but it failed to materialize. Determined to prevent Annapolis Royal from falling to the French, Governor Shirley sent more troops, including a small detachment of Pigwackets – Abenaki who had allied themselves with the British. Later in the summer, Duvivier, with about 55 soldiers from Louisbourg and Port-la-Joye, 130 Mi'kmaq, and 70 Wolastoqiyik, accompanied by Abbé Maillard, began a month-long siege against Annapolis Royal. Paul Mascarene, who had been appointed lieutenant governor, might well have been forced to surrender, but once again assistance from Louisbourg failed to appear, while a much-feared company of New England Rangers, most of them Pigwackets under Captain John Gorham, managed to reach Annapolis Royal. By the time Captain Denys de Bonaventure arrived with naval support, fifty-four soldiers, and at least sixty Mi'kmaq, Duvivier's force had withdrawn.[51] The collaboration of Acadians in the region, whether under duress or not, troubled Shirley and undermined Mascarene's policy of conciliating the "neutral French."[52]

Moving quickly to gain the initiative, the New Englanders declared war against the Mi'kmaq and Wolastoqiyik, offering bounties of up to £100 for their scalps and up to £105 for live captives.[53] Gorham's Rangers patrolled the Bay of Fundy seeking scalps, and only Mascarene's intervention managed to deflect three vessels sent by Shirley to punish the Acadians. By May 1745 Annapolis Royal was again under attack, this time by a Canadian expedition consisting of more than six hundred Troupes de la Marine led by Lieutenant Paul Marin de la Malgue. Like Duvivier, Marin commandeered supplies and labour from Acadians. Before the siege could be resolved, Marin was ordered to Louisbourg, which was experiencing its first test as a military stronghold.

In the spring of 1745, a volunteer militia of 4,300 men, led by the New England-born merchant and politician William Pepperrell, supported by a naval squadron of more than a hundred British and New England vessels under the command of Commodore Peter Warren, laid siege to Louisbourg. Dragging their cannon over difficult terrain from their landing site at Gabarus Bay, the New Englanders pounded their objective for nearly seven weeks. In the ultimate indignity, the attackers captured the Royal Battery, which had been abandoned, and trained its guns on the town. The failure of the French to fortify the area around the lighthouse also gave the New Englanders another vantage point for their offensive.[54]

Governor Louis Du Pont Duchambon faced a dismal prospect. The previous December, the troops stationed at Louisbourg had mutinied almost to a man over their poor food and living conditions and briefly took over the town. François Bigot managed to restore order by promising to address grievances, but the soldiers continued to maintain the upper hand over the winter. Declaring themselves "slaves" to the mutinous throng, royal officials were obliged to tread warily, and refused to deploy soldiers outside the town walls for fear they might desert. Indeed, it was only after authorities promised not to punish the leaders of the mutiny that the soldiers agreed to fight. The lack of supplies, the problem that sparked the mutiny, became acute once the attackers blockaded the harbour and began their bombardment.

With his town in ruins, its inhabitants facing starvation, and his Mikmaw allies engaging the enemy in outlying areas running out of ammunition,[55] Duchambon surrendered on 17 June. The New Englanders destroyed outlying communities on Île Royale and Île Saint-Jean, including Roma's base at Trois-Rivières. Almost all the conquered people, including the garrison, were shipped to France to await the outcome of the war, while the New England soldiers dug in, hoping to consolidate their victory. Living conditions in the dilapidated town were atrocious, resulting in an uncommonly high death rate among the unhappy soldiers charged with protecting Louisbourg from recapture.

Declaring that promises of amnesty had been made under duress, French authorities put the Louisbourg mutineers on trial. Four soldiers in the Karrer Regiment and eight of the Troupes de la Marine were found guilty of inciting mutiny.[56] While François Bigot thought this outcome would serve as an example to other potential mutineers, he, too, should have taken a lesson from the fracas. Supplying the regiment was his responsibility, one that enabled him to bilk the colony by commandeering resources and selling them illegally. Promoted to intendant of New France in 1749, Bigot continued his corrupt practices in Quebec, where he and a ring of conspirators stretching from Canada to Bordeaux made huge fortunes. This time Bigot paid for his excessive greed. After New France was conquered, he was thrown into the Bastille for nearly a year, stripped of his property, and spent the rest of his life in exile.[57]

In 1746 the French tried to regain the initiative in the Atlantic region. They mobilized sixty-four ships and 11,000 soldiers and crew under the Duke d'Anville, to proceed to Canada if it were under attack, and if not, to capture Louisbourg, Annapolis Royal, Placentia, and perhaps even Boston.[58] D'Anville planned to meet a detachment of seven hundred Troupes de la Marine under Captain de Ramezay arriving from Canada and the Wabanaki force under Marin that had been involved in the attack on Annapolis Royal the previous year. From the beginning things went terribly wrong. Adverse winds and storms slowed the transatlantic crossing, in which typhoid, typhus, and scurvy took their toll. When the expedition finally took refuge in Chibouctou harbour in September, three months after leaving France, only forty-four vessels remained. Forty per cent of the men who decamped at Chibouctou soon died or became seriously ill. Six days after his arrival, d'Anville succumbed to a stroke and his successor resigned after trying to commit suicide. The Marquis de Jonquière, who was en route to his posting as governor general of New France, assumed control and proceeded with a plan to attack Annapolis Royal in conjunction with three hundred of de Ramezay's soldiers. Employing the expertise of fifty Acadian pilots, 1,500 soldiers and their officers were loaded on vessels to advance on Annapolis Royal, but the expedition encountered more difficulties rounding the South Shore and was aborted. By the end of October, the tattered remnants of the d'Anville expedition had limped back to France without firing a shot at the enemy. Its major legacy was typhus, which the Acadians and Mi'kmaq who had interacted with their visitors carried back to their communities.[59]

Its navy devastated, France could no longer support military campaigns in North America, but de Ramezay and his Indigenous allies, who had retreated to Beaubassin, were not deterred. Learning that Governor Shirley had sent five hundred colonial militia to keep the Acadians in the Minas area under surveillance, de Ramezay dispatched Captain Louis Coulon de Villiers and Louis de la Corne with three hundred troops to confront them. Using sleds and snowshoes to travel in winter conditions, they conducted a twenty-one-day march that took them through Baie Verte and Tatamagouche to Grand-Pré, where the New Englanders were quartered in Acadian homes. Using information provided by sympathetic Acadians, the French surrounded the houses where the New Englanders were sleeping, killed seventy, including their commander Colonel Arthur Noble, and forced the rest to surrender. What the English described as the "Massacre of Grand Pré," proved disastrous for the Acadian strategy of neutrality. British administrators now had convincing evidence that Acadians could be pressed into supplying the French and their allies with billets, intelligence, and provisions. Whether their compliance was voluntary or extracted under duress was immaterial.

⁓❧⁓

The Treaty of Aix-la-Chapelle in 1748 temporarily averted reprisals. In what was essentially a draw, Britain and France agreed to return what each had captured from the other, outraging the New Englanders who had spent blood and treasure on the capture of Louisbourg. The Mi'kmaq and their Wabanaki allies made no agreement to end hostilities and, like the European nations which signed the treaty, understood that it represented a truce rather than a final settlement. In Mi'kma'ki the peace of 1748 would not last long.

Chapter Seven

Reinventing Nova Scotia, 1749–1775

Between 1749 and 1775, Britain's ascendancy in Nova Scotia was confirmed and the colony's cultural landscape transformed. This was achieved at great cost to the Indigenous and Acadian inhabitants, who were caught in the vortex created by the contest between Britain and France for world dominance. A flashpoint for imperial ambitions, Mi'kma'ki temporarily assumed an international significance, bringing the military might of Europe to its shores. Modern Nova Scotia was forged in the bloody wars that punctuated the mid-eighteenth century, setting the trajectory for the province's evolution that still plays out today.[1]

1749: A Pivotal Year

In the spring of 1749, two European fleets set sail for northeastern North America. One came from France to reoccupy Louisbourg; the other marked Britain's first serious attempt to colonize the territories acquired by the Treaty of Utrecht. With some exceptions – among them the mutinous Karrer Regiment – the roughly 3,000 settlers and soldiers in the French expedition had made Île Royale their home before 1745. In contrast, few of the 2,576 would-be settlers who sailed from the River Thames to Nova Scotia in 1749 – most of them artisans, labourers, servants, and discharged soldiers – had ever crossed the Atlantic.[2] Enticed by offers of free transport, land, work, and provisions for a year, they were expected to become the founders of a military stronghold named after George Montagu Dunk, 2nd Earl of Halifax, who presided over the Board of Trade and Plantations from 1748 to 1761. Dunk brought a new sense of purpose to the Board and focused his attention on Nova Scotia, which he believed had the potential to serve as a model for a reformed strategy of colonial governance.[3]

Louisbourg in 1749 still bore evidence of the bombardment four years earlier, but the French moved quickly to restore fortifications, repair old buildings, and construct new ones to accommodate a larger population. Fearing the ravages of another attack, many of the former settlers from outlying districts now sought refuge in the walled town. The garrison also expanded impressively, from 1,050 in 1749 to 2,100 in 1755. Although the troublesome community of Niganiche on the north shore was not re-established, Port Toulouse grew in size and new areas of the island were settled as more Acadians arrived from Nova Scotia to escape the chaos unfolding there.[4] France also dispatched troops from Quebec to the lower St John River and Chignecto areas of what is now New Brunswick. Their commanders, Charles Deschamps de Boishébert and Louis de la Corne, were charged with building fortifications, mobilizing Indigenous allies, and organizing militias among the Acadians, who would be "persuaded" to move to the disputed territory north of the Bay of Fundy.[5]

Halifax, meanwhile, rose from the shores of Chibouctou harbour to take on the French challenge (Figure 7.1). In what must have seemed like a minor miracle, most of the passengers on the thirteen crowded vessels bound for Halifax survived their ocean voyage. This was a result in part of the decision to install ventilators to improve air circulation below decks, an innovation recently developed by clergyman and scientist Stephen Hale for use on slave and prison ships.[6] Colonel Edward Cornwallis, a thirty-six-year-old veteran of the recent Scottish campaign, had been chosen to oversee the construction of the fortified town and to serve as governor of Nova Scotia.[7] A disciplined and purposeful administrator, Cornwallis convened a meeting of his council within three weeks of his arrival late in June. John Gorham, Edward How, and Paul Mascarene, who had served at Annapolis Royal, were included among his advisors, and the 40th Regiment was relocated to the new capital.

Cornwallis ignored his instructions to establish an elected assembly until British settlement had taken root. In the early months of the town's development, this objective seemed doubtful, as more than a third of the immigrants from England disappeared on vessels returning to Boston, which served as the major source of supply for Halifax in the early years of settlement.[8] The emigrants were replaced by merchants, artisans, and labourers eager to profit from government contracts and to escape their creditors. In an effort to encourage immigration, British authorities decreed that residents of Nova Scotia could not be sued for debts incurred outside the colony, a law that remained on the books until 1762. Authorities also ignored imperial proscriptions against Jews

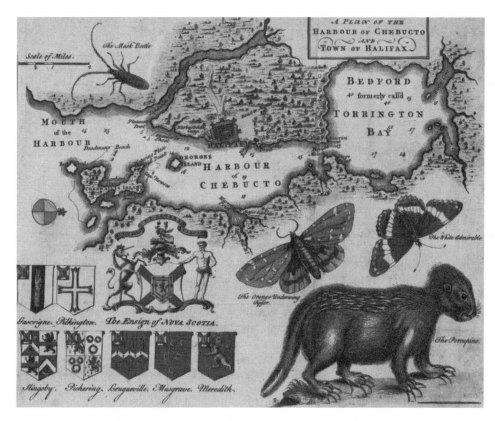

Figure 7.1. *A Plan of the Harbour of Chebucto and Town of Halifax*, Moses Harris, 1750. A naturalist as well as a surveyor, Moses Harris focused on the flora and fauna of Nova Scotia rather than the town of Halifax in this illustration. While the butterflies are accurately rendered, the porcupine is a less impressive likeness.
McGill Library-rbsc-maps_G3422_H3_1750_H3–17130, catalogue record MARCXML; published in *Gentleman's Magazine* 20 (July 1750): 295.

receiving royal favour. In the initial allotment of land in August 1749, John Franks, Samuel Jacobs, and Isaac Solomon were awarded town lots, and more Jews found their way to Halifax from Boston, Newport, and New York.[9]

Merchant Joshua Mauger, born on the Channel Island of Jersey, emerged as the most powerful figure in the colonial capital. In 1747 he arrived in Louisbourg, where he became a supplier to the Royal Navy's North American squadron, established during the campaign of

1745, and he followed it to Halifax in 1749. Mauger engaged in clandestine trade with Louisbourg while it remained under French control and extended his mercantile interests to include the West Indies trade, selling slaves, speculating in land, supplying the military, and manufacturing rum, over which he and his sometimes partner John Fillis enjoyed a virtual monopoly. During the 1750s, he was largest shipper in Halifax, owning wholly or in part twenty-seven vessels, some purchased in New England, others acquired through privateering or purchased at public auction.[10]

Cornwallis had his hands full convincing the shiftless settlers to build shelter and defences for the imperial outpost. With the arrival of British troops evacuated from Louisbourg in late July, the governor had more military muscle at his disposal, but he was obliged to secure labour from Acadian communities and increase wages to get the job done. After a year of hard work, Halifax was protected on the landward side by a palisade and five forts, while three batteries secured the water approaches. Inside Halifax's defences, rigidly rectangular streets were laid out on the steep slope leading from the waterfront towards Citadel Hill. A Grand Parade in the centre of the town served as the focus of military exercises and community life, while the harbour sheltered the North Atlantic squadron. In outlying areas, Fort Sackville, built on the shores of Bedford Basin by Gorham's Rangers, guarded the entrance to a road to the Minas Basin settlements, and the town plat of Dartmouth, across the harbour from Halifax, was surveyed by Charles Morris in 1750.[11]

Sustained by parliamentary grants, Halifax gradually acquired civilian institutions. By the summer of 1750, the Church of England was served by St Paul's, an elegant building constructed adjacent to the Grand Parade with timber shipped from Boston. It served both its own congregation and worshippers of other Protestant denominations until Mather's Meeting House, which initially catered mostly to New England and Scottish Congregationalists, opened its doors in 1754. In year-round communication with the North Atlantic world, Haligonians were kept informed about the latest developments by their local newspaper, the *Halifax Gazette*, first published on 23 March 1752 by New Englander John Bushell.[12] Amid "Foreign Advices," "Plantation News," and shipping schedules, readers of the *Gazette* were alerted to local opportunities, among them Hannah Hutchinson's offer, on 18 April 1752, to teach young ladies "Needle-Work and Embroidery either with Cruels, Gold, or Silver," along with French and Country Dances in her home on Carpenter's Row. During the early years of settlement, smallpox and typhus took the lives of many immigrants, ensuring plenty of occupants for the burying ground outside the palisade. A government-funded hospital began receiving patients in the spring of 1750, and an orphanage was opened two years later. Once government provisions were discontinued, poverty and petty crime stalked the streets of Halifax, prompting the construction of a "House of Correction" in 1754. The only school in the town that served the poor was sponsored by the Society for the Propagation of the Gospel, which operated sporadically beginning in 1751.[13]

Unimpressed with the mostly urban and military settlers who had accompanied him in 1749, Cornwallis urged the Board of Trade to send him immigrants with farming experience from continental Europe. Nearly 2,500 people from various German states, Switzerland, and the Netherlands arrived in Nova Scotia between 1750 and 1753.[14] Recruited by Rotterdam merchant John Dick, the "Foreign Protestants," many of them Lutherans, initially remained in makeshift accommodation in Halifax because it was too dangerous to settle them in outlying areas. Some were put to work on construction projects to pay off their passage, and nearly all had difficulty surviving in their enforced limbo. As discontent mounted and dozens deserted to Île Royale and other French strongholds, authorities in Halifax were compelled to take action.[15]

In June 1753, Lieutenant-Colonel Charles Lawrence, accompanied by a contingent of troops and 1,453 of the impatient immigrants, founded the town of Lunenburg, on Mirliguèche harbour, across the river from La Have.[16] Over the objections of the colonists, who were eager to get settled on their land, Lunenburg was designed as a compact community that could be defended in the event of attack. Such caution was warranted. The area formerly had been home to a population of Acadians and Mi'kmaq, who bequeathed several hundred acres of cleared land to the new settlers.[17] Although the chief in the La Have region, Claude Gisiquash, appeared before the council in April 1753 to offer peace and friendship, many Mi'kmaq perceived the British occupation of Halifax and Mirligueche as acts of aggression (Map 7.1).

Trouble in Mi'kma'ki

One of Cornwallis's first objectives was to reach an accommodation with the Indigenous peoples living in greater Nova Scotia. In August 1749, four delegates representing the Mi'kmaq, Passamaquoddy, and Wolastoqiyik, gathered from areas north of the Bay of Fundy by Edward How, met with the council in Halifax. Working through Acadian and Indigenous interpreters, they reaffirmed the peace of 1726. This agreement made it easier for the British to challenge French claims to disputed territory in northern sections of the colony, but it was signed by only one Mi'kmaw, Jean Pedousaghtigh from the Chignecto region.[18]

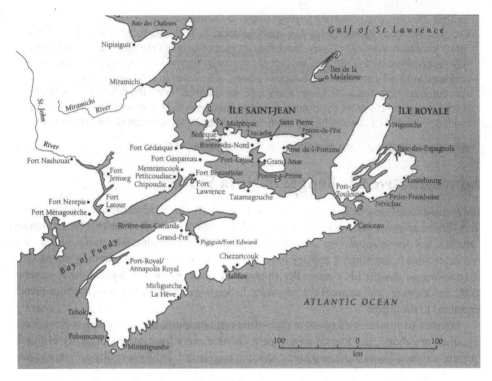

Map 7.1. Settler Communities in the Maritime Region, 1755.
Adapted from Jean Daigle, ed., *Acadia and the Maritimes* (Moncton: Université de Moncton, Chaire d'études acadiennes, 1995), 33, R. Cole Harris, ed., *Historical Atlas of Canada, I: From the Beginning to 1800* (Toronto: University of Toronto Press, 1987), plate 30, and Margaret R. Conrad and James K. Hiller, *Atlantic Canada: A History*, 3rd ed. (Don Mills, ON: Oxford University Press, 2015), 67.

Most Mi'kmaq were in no mood to sign treaties. Some of them attacked British ships and settlers at Beaubassin and Canso, and met with French authorities at Port Toulouse in September to determine how to deal with the British invasion. Abbé Maillard was on hand to help craft, in both Mi'kmaw and French, a message to Cornwallis. It read in part: "The place where you are, where you are building dwellings, where you are now building a fort ... this land of which you wish to make yourself now absolute master, this land belongs to me. I have come from it as certainly as the grass, it is the very place of my birth and of my dwelling, this land belongs to me ... I swear, it is God who has given it to me to be my country for ever ... Show me where I, the Indian, will lodge? You drive me out; where do you want me to take refuge?"[19]

The guerrilla war that followed is sometimes called Le Loutre's War because of the French priest's dogged persistence in challenging the British occupation. In July 1749 Le Loutre had reported to his superiors: "As we cannot openly oppose the English ventures, I think we cannot do better than to incite the savages to continue warring on the English." Le Loutre's plan was to persuade them "to send word that they will not permit new settlements to be made in Acadia ... I shall do my best to make it look to the English as if this plan comes from the savages and that I have no part in it." Ordered by the ministry of marine to move his mission from Shubenacadie to Beauséjour Ridge, on the Isthmus of Chignecto, Le Loutre continued to create problems for the British from his new base of operations. Cornwallis understandably perceived Le Loutre as "a good for nothing scoundrel as ever lived."[20]

Well-schooled in methods of "pacifying" dissidents in Scotland after the Battle of Culloden, Cornwallis took a much tougher approach towards the Mi'kmaq and their political priests than that of his predecessors. He responded not by declaring war on the Mi'kmaq – to do that, he reasoned, "would be ... to own them a free and Independent people" – but by ordering British subjects to "take or destroy the savages commonly called Micmacks wherever they are found." He offered bounties "to be paid upon producing such savage taken or his scalp (as is the custom of America)," and put a price of £50 on Le Loutre's head.[21] Not surprisingly, the attacks by Mi'kmaw and Acadian militants continued, fuelled by French authorities at Louisbourg and Quebec, who also paid for captives and scalps. The Dartmouth side of Halifax harbour was especially vulnerable to attack, prompting Cornwallis to have a fort constructed there in 1750. It did little good. For nearly a decade, Dartmouth and Halifax remained subject to raids in which scores of settlers and soldiers were killed or taken captive.

As tensions mounted, the Acadians were pressed by both the British and the French to take sides. Shortly after his arrival, Cornwallis summoned Acadian deputies to Halifax, demanding that the people they represented take an unqualified oath of allegiance. They refused, fearing reprisals by the Mi'kmaq and French forces in the region. Their caution was justified. Everywhere in greater Nova Scotia, militias made up of Acadian and Indigenous militants threatened the lives and property of anyone found to be collaborating with the British.

In the fall of 1749, Cornwallis ordered the construction of Fort Vieux Logis in Grand-Pré to intimidate the populous Minas settlements. Indigenous and Acadian militia attacked the fort in November and carried the commander and eighteen soldiers to Chignecto. The following spring, Cornwallis sent Gorham's Rangers to secure the road to the

Minas Basin in preparation for the construction of Fort Edward at Piziquid. En route, they became engaged in a three-day encounter with a contingent of Mi'kmaq, who were finally routed by reinforcements from Fort Sackville. Meanwhile, Colonel Lawrence, dispatched to the Isthmus of Chignecto to construct fortifications there, received a blistering welcome and was forced to retreat. As a pre-emptive move, Le Loutre and Le Corne had the village of Beaubassin torched, forcing the community's inhabitants to move across the Missaguash River to Beauséjour Ridge. Lawrence returned to the region in September with enough troops to achieve his objective. During one standoff, Edward How, who had lost an arm in the Battle of Grand-Pré, was killed by a sniper while operating under a flag of truce, adding more fuel to the conflict.[22] Lawrence managed to build a fort, which bore his name, but the French, installed at Fort Beauséjour on the other side of the Tantramar marshes, continued to have the upper hand. To protect their position, they built Fort Gaspereau at Baie Verte and Fort Menagouàche at the mouth of the St John River.

Under pressure by militias and priests, Acadians began moving in significant numbers to the Chignecto region, Île Saint-Jean, and Île Royale. Le Loutre oversaw a massive dyke construction project north of the Missaguash in an effort to get agricultural production back on track for export to Louisbourg, but just supplying themselves proved a major challenge for the displaced Acadians. Instead of producers, they became consumers of provisions, creating a significant drain on French supplies. The Mi'kmaq, now almost constantly engaged in guerrilla warfare, also became dependent on the French for food. Despite these difficulties, the French still managed to move freely in the Bay of Fundy and Northumberland Strait. The Marquis de Chabert even managed to chart the Atlantic coast of Nova Scotia for France in 1750–1, with little fear of being challenged.[23] His survey was designed to support French efforts to establish their claims against Britain in a commission that met in Paris between 1750 and 1753 to settle the boundaries of Acadia/ Nova Scotia. With neither side willing to give way in the claims and counterclaims over cartography and historical documentation, discussions ended in deadlock.[24]

Unable to obtain from London the military and naval resources he needed to secure the colony from its enemies on land and sea and claiming ill-health, Cornwallis returned to England in 1752. His successor, Peregrine Thompson Hopson, concluded a peace treaty with Jean-Baptiste Cope, Chief of the Mi'kmaq, at Shubenacadie in September 1752, and several chiefs on the South Shore were prepared to sign the document, but it was not clear who they represented other than themselves. Raids, skirmishes, and reprisals continued. In 1753 Le Loutre reported that the extraordinary sum of 1,800 livres was paid for eighteen British scalps from the region. By this time, these grisly trophies and enemy captives had become a major source of wealth for guerrilla fighters on the frontiers of New France throughout eastern North America, and the demand for scalping knives from overseas increased dramatically.

Le Grand Dérangement

The Seven Years' War raged from 1756 to 1763 on the European continent, but formal battles between Britain and France began earlier in North America. Following clashes with the French and their Indigenous allies on the Ohio frontier in 1754, the British and aggrieved settlers in their American colonies organized a four-pronged attack against the outer defences of New France: Fort Duquesne in the Ohio Valley, Fort Niagara in the Great Lakes region, Fort Frédéric on Lake Champlain, and Fort Beauséjour in Nova Scotia. In the winter of 1755, Vice-Admiral Edward Boscawen received secret instructions to intercept the flotilla from France bringing soldiers and supplies to Louisbourg and Quebec. Most of the enemy vessels eluded him, but his squadron, reinforced by more ships of the line under Rear Admiral Francis Holburne, blockaded Louisbourg, capturing twenty-four French fishing and merchant ships between June and September.[25]

The British offensive of 1755 proved a failure on all fronts except one. A colonial militia of 2,500 men commanded by Colonel Robert Monckton captured Fort Beauséjour after a two-week siege. With only 160 regular soldiers and a militia of 300 men, the French commander, Louis Du Pont Duchambon de Vergor, capitulated on 16 June. The British were assisted in their objective by Thomas Pichon, who had been transferred to Beauséjour from his clerical post in Louisbourg. In return for payment, Pichon kept the enemy informed about conditions inside the fort, encouraged the Acadians to demand an early capitulation, and even offered advice on how the assault might be successfully conducted. Le Loutre managed to elude capture and make his way to Quebec, but he was still a marked man. In September, the ship carrying him to France was intercepted by the British, who held him prisoner until 1763. Le Loutre's able assistant, Abbé Jean Manach, who had arrived from France in 1750, remained committed to his Indigenous and Acadian flock until 1761, when he was arrested by authorities and taken to Halifax.[26]

The discovery that Acadians made up the majority of the people defending Fort Beauséjour marked a turning point in their history.[27]

They protested that they had been forced to fight against their will – and the Articles of Capitulation had granted them pardon – but the authorities in Halifax were no longer willing to believe them. With rumours circulating that the French were preparing to launch a counterattack, Colonel Lawrence, acting governor in Hopson's absence, decided to force all Acadians to bend to his will. As a preliminary step, Acadians were obliged to surrender their firearms, which most of them agreed to do. Delegates from the Acadian communities were then summoned to Halifax and ordered to take an unqualified oath of allegiance. Despite the changed circumstances, they refused to do so. The thirty men from Annapolis Royal reported that the people they represented had charged them "strictly to contract no new oath."[28] Told that deportation would be the result of their refusal, they stuck to their position.

Unfortunately for the Acadians, the strategies they had pursued in the past would no longer work. Plans had been made to expel the Acadians in the Chignecto region who persisted in their refusal to take an unqualified oath of allegiance, but now the fate of all Acadians hung in the balance. On 28 July, after the latest delegation of Acadian deputies had proved obdurate, Lawrence and his council confirmed the order for a wholesale deportation. Chief Justice Jonathan Belcher, a New England-born lawyer and scholar who had been appointed to his position the previous year, offered legal justification for the decision to impose such a harsh penalty on people who were arguably British subjects. Although it clearly lacked humanity, deportation would solve the problem of the "neutral French" once and for all, and had long been the "final solution" recommended by Governor William Shirley of Massachusetts.

Lawrence moved quickly. Orders were sent to the military commanders at Chignecto, Piziquid, and Annapolis Royal instructing them to seize the men and boys, along with all boats, so that women and children would not try to escape. At the same time, soldiers were dispatched to Tatamagouche to cut trade with Louisbourg. Abijah Willard, who participated in the raid, noted in his diary: "I went with a Small party of men over a Large River Tatmagoush wher[e] I Burnt 12 Buildings one of which was a Storehouse with Rum and molasas and Iron ware and another of Rum[,] sugar and molasas & wine and a masshouse[.] I ordered the men to Draw as much Rum as they had bottles to Cary which they Did and sot fire to the Rest."[29] In August, Boscawen sent a warship to destroy French communities between St George's Bay and Port-aux-Basques on the south coast of Newfoundland. Sixty-seven of their residents were dumped on Île Royale, where they faced a second deportation in 1758. Beginning in September, the Acadians captured in the summer of 1755 were herded onto transports from Boston and distributed to British colonies along the Atlantic seaboard.

The expulsion of the Acadians is one of the most horrifying events in Nova Scotia's history. With farming activities absorbing their attention, the Acadians in the Minas area were caught by surprise when the British soldiers arrived. Men were imprisoned at Fort Edward in Piziquid and in the church at Grand-Pré while awaiting their deportation. At Annapolis Royal, where four decades of living in close proximity muddled the strategy, many Acadians had prior warning, enabling many to escape before the authorities issued their fatal order. A small group of refugees from the town led by Pierre Belliveau spent a difficult winter on an island off present-day Belliveau's Cove in St Mary's Bay, where many of them died. Even Acadians who had taken an unqualified oath of allegiance were not spared. In 1754 Antoine Henri, who had moved his family to Île Royale, willingly took the oath before the council in Halifax as a condition to being allowed to return to his former home in Cobequid, but he received no special consideration. Acadians in the Minas area who now accepted their grim reality begged to take an unqualified oath of allegiance to stay on their land, but it was too late to make amends.[30] Like the campaign against the rebellious Scots after the Battle of Culloden, the expulsion of the Acadians and the seizure of their land cleared the decks for anglicizing a territory that British authorities were determined to control.

At Chignecto, where men were imprisoned in Fort Cumberland (formerly Fort Beauséjour) and Fort Lawrence, the British met spirited resistance. Boishébert blew up the fort at the mouth of the St John River before Monckton could capture it, and, with the help of an Acadian and Indigenous militia, forced British soldiers to retreat from Petitcodiac on 3 September.[31] In October, eighty-six captives at Fort Lawrence escaped by digging a tunnel under the walls and fleeing with their families to the nearby woods. Some of the Acadians who remained at large made their way to Canada, Île Royale, and Île Saint-Jean; others lived in refugee camps at Shediac, Miramichi, and Restigouche, where they, along with the Mi'kmaq and Wolastoqiyik, continued their opposition to British forces pursuing them.

Whether free or captive, loyal or not, few Acadians escaped the tragedy that engulfed their communities. British and New England soldiers put their homes, barns, and churches to the torch and sent the deportees on their way, taking only the goods they could carry with them. Their land and livestock became the property of the Crown and helped to cover the costs of their transports supplied by Boston merchants Charles Apthorp and Thomas Handcock. The departure brought more heartbreak as extended families were separated and the land they loved so much was left behind. When the transports finally arrived, Colonel John Winslow, stationed at Grand-Pré, noted on 8 October that "the Inhabitants ... went off very Solentarily and unwillingly, the women in Great Distress Carrying off their Children in their Arms, Others Carrying their Decrepit Parents in Carts and all their Goods moving in Great Confusion and appeared a scene of Woe and Distress."[32] Not surprisingly, Winslow declared that this "troublesome affair" was "more grievous to me than any service I was ever employed in," a sentiment echoed by Major Handfield in Annapolis Royal.

The horrors of the deportation did not end with the embarkation. Since authorities in the receiving colonies had not been informed in advance, they offered little assistance, and some even refused to accept their quotas of deportees. One boatload of passengers managed to overwhelm their captors and run the ship into the mouth of the St John River, but most Acadians had little hope of escaping their dismal fate. Although the deportation had not been authorized by Lawrence's superiors in London, they had little difficulty in sanctioning it, and promoted him to governor of Nova Scotia in 1756. The bloody resistance everywhere in the region by Indigenous and Acadian militias only stiffened Lawrence's resolve to rid the colony of the terrorist menace. Expulsions in Pubnico and other areas in southwestern Nova Scotia began early in 1756.

Despite the odds against them, Indigenous peoples in the region refused to submit to the British. In May Lawrence instructed both soldiers and civilians to "annoy, distress, take, and destroy the Indians inhabiting different Parts of this Province," and increased the price paid for scalps and captives. Two officers stationed in Halifax raised troops of rangers to take advantage of this lucrative opportunity. Lawrence's policy was prompted, in part, by attacks on Lunenburg. In one audacious raid in May 1756, Wolastoqiyik dispatched by Boishébert descended on the home of Louis Payzant in Mahone Bay, killing him, his son, a servant, and her child. A pregnant Marie-Anne Payzant, her four remaining children, and her husband's scalp were carried to Aukpaque, a Wolastoq'kew community near the French community at Pointe Ste-Anne (now Fredericton). While the children remained with their captors, Marie-Anne, a French-speaking Huguenot, was taken to Quebec. In 1757 the Payzant children were ransomed through the intervention of a Jesuit missionary, Charles (Carolus) Germain, and also taken to Quebec, where the family remained until 1760.[33] By that time, the attacks on Lunenburg, which had cost the lives of at least thirty-two settlers, were coming to an end.

Brutal as it was, the expulsion of the Acadians and the genocidal campaign against Indigenous peoples in the region had the military impact Lawrence intended. The lack of food and other supplies reached crisis proportions in Louisbourg, where the authorities were besieged by destitute refugees.[34] Neither in Louisbourg nor in Versailles was there much concern about the fate of the deported Acadians or of their erstwhile military allies. After all, the French had also been involved in expulsions and exterminations in their imperial crusades, and viewed these human tragedies as nothing more or less than the inevitable consequences of military strategy.[35]

The Seven Years' War, 1756–63

Warfare in North America merged into the Seven Years' War in 1756. This time, France, Austria, and eventually Spain squared off against Britain and Prussia. Fought in Europe and its colonies around the world, the war permanently altered the balance of power in North America and put Nova Scotia on the front lines of the global conflict.[36]

The gridlock in Parliament that hampered the British war effort was lifted in the summer of 1757, when William Pitt, the popular Whig leader in a new coalition government, launched a more comprehensive strategy that included a major thrust in North America. By this time, three enormous French squadrons, loaded with war matériel, provisions, and troops for Louisbourg, had eluded the British blockade on both sides of the Atlantic. The presence of the French fleet, under the command of seventy-four-year-old naval veteran Comte Du Bois de la Motte, put an end to British plans to attack Louisbourg in 1757. Although Lord Loudon, commander of the British Army in North America, and Admiral Francis Holburne had about 13,000 troops between them, roughly matching the strength of their opponents, they decided to abort the mission. British warships cruised off Louisbourg beginning in August, but both fleets were badly mauled by a September hurricane. With his ships battered and his forces laid low by typhus, Du Bois de la Motte retreated to France, taking the pestilence to French ports. Discouraged by delays and disease, a Wabanaki force assembled for the defence of Louisbourg also dispersed. Pitt, meanwhile, ordered eight ships of the line to winter in Halifax to prepare for an early start on a blockade of Louisbourg in the spring.[37] The decision to build a North American base in Nova Scotia was finally beginning to pay off.

With their naval forces better organized, the British managed to delay or thwart the departure of two of the three French squadrons earmarked for the defence of Louisbourg in 1758. Even the ship carrying the intended commander, Charles de Blénac-Courbon, failed to reach Louisbourg in time for the siege. The British also experienced delays, leaving troops cooling their heels in Halifax. Brigadier-General James Wolfe took the opportunity to host a lavish dinner for forty-six of his friends at Great Pontack House on 24 May. British soldiers were obliged to drink a daily ration of spruce beer to ward off scurvy, but Wolfe's guests were medicated with stronger elixirs: seventy bottles of Madeira, fifty bottles of claret, and twenty-five bottles of brandy.[38] Three days later, Boscawen's fleet departed for Louisbourg without Major General Jeffery Amherst, commander of the army, whose ship caught up with the expedition as it rounded Cape Sambro.

By 3 June, Governor Augustin de Drucour, with a civilian population of about 4,000 and 8,500 soldiers, sailors, and militia, faced one of the largest military forces ever to campaign in North America: 27,000 British and colonial soldiers and sailors conveyed by 157 vessels. On board were several hundred women who, as wives, mistresses, cooks, cleaners, and caregivers, were an integral part of almost all military operations.[39] Governor Drucour held out as long as he could, but once the British troops landed on 8 June, a stiff bombardment soon had the town in ruins. Boishébert arrived in Port Toulouse early in July with a small force of Troupes de la Marine, Acadians, and Indigenous allies, but his exhausted, disease-ridden contingent had little impact on the siege. With supplies of food and ammunition running short, Drucour agreed to terms of surrender on 26 July. The historian John Johnston has calculated that 371 British soldiers died in the battle for Louisbourg, while on the French side only 93 were killed. If civilian and Indigenous casualties are added, the number of fatalities might have been closely matched (Figure 7.2).[40]

The Mi'kmaq in the region fled with Abbé Maillard to the refugee camp at the mouth of the Miramachi, but there was no place to hide. In consolidating his victory, Amherst sent troops to Île Saint-Jean, Gaspésie, Miramichi, and the St John River to bring Indigenous enemies to their knees and round up Acadians for deportation. Even Amherst, no stranger to military brutality, was shocked when he learned of the bloody campaign against the Acadians living along the St John River by New England Rangers under Moses Hazen. "I gave a Commission of Captain to Lieutenant Hazen as I thought he deserved it," he wrote. "I am sorry to say what I have since heard of that affair has sullied his merit with me, as I shall always disapprove of killing women and helpless children."[41] A similarly aggressive policy was carried out in Gaspésie by James Wolfe, who had played a conspicuous role in the siege of Louisbourg and was put in charge of the British attack on Quebec in 1759.[42] The last battle in the Maritime region occurred in July 1760

Figure 7.2. *Britain's Glory, or the Reduction of Cape Breton by the Gallant Boscawen & General Amherst*, 1758. There was much rejoicing in Britain and its North American colonies when Louisbourg was captured for a second time in 1758.
New Brunswick Museum John Clarence Webster Canadiana Collection W907, available online from the McCord Museum at http://collections.musee-mccord.qc.ca/en/collection/artifacts/W907

in the Baie des Chaleurs, where Commodore John Byron intercepted a small French expedition bringing supplies to Montreal. The French retreated into the Restigouche River, where, aided by local Acadians and Mi'kmaq, they mounted a fierce resistance but were ultimately defeated.

The fall of Louisbourg led to the removal of settlers from Île Royale and Île Saint-Jean, with most of the captives being sent to Britain and France. When a French expedition occupied St John's, Newfoundland, in the summer of 1762, nervous authorities in Halifax rounded up six hundred Acadians imprisoned in various forts around the colony and shipped them to Boston. Having had enough of supporting refugees,

Boston sent them back. This was the last of the formal deportations. Between 1755 and 1762, nearly 11,000 Acadians out of a total of more than 14,000 had been sent into exile.[43] How many survived the ordeal is difficult to calculate. Some of the ships carrying the deportees capsized, while disease among a weakened and heartsick population took many lives. The deadliest removal was from Île Saint-Jean. Of the more than 3,000 Acadians shipped from the island in 1758, 679 drowned at sea and another 970 died from various causes before reaching their destinations.[44] For many of those who survived, the deportation marked the beginning of a lifetime of wandering. It took many of them to Louisiana, where their descendants, known as *Cajuns*, still live; to Canada, the Îles de la Madeleine, St-Pierre, the West Indies, French Guiana, Britain, France, and, most improbably, the Falkland Islands. While France offered homes to displaced Acadians after the war ended, many of those who took up the offer felt like strangers and sought opportunities to return to North America.

The resistance fighter Joseph Broussard, known later in life as Beausoleil, has emerged as one of the heroes of the Acadian tragedy. Born in Port-Royal in 1702, Broussard was a rebel from an early age, embroiled in land disputes with his neighbours and, though married, named by the midwife in a contentious paternity suit. Fluent in Mi'kmaw, he participated in attacks on Annapolis Royal in 1724, on Grand-Pré in 1747, and on British settlements in Nova Scotia after the founding of Halifax. He led a militia unit outside the walls of Fort Beauséjour in the siege of 1755. Captured and imprisoned in Fort Lawrence, he managed to escape. Along with his brother Alexandre, who made his way back from imprisonment in South Carolina, and their seven sons, Broussard helped Boishébert organize militia units to inflict misery on British and colonial troops. Following his surrender in November 1760, Brossard was kept under close guard in prison, ending up on Georges Island in Halifax Harbour. After the war, the Broussards gathered six hundred Acadians and hired ships to take them to the French island of Saint-Domingue. From there they moved to Louisiana. Shortly after his arrival there in 1765, Beausoleil died of yellow fever at the age of sixty-three. He was buried in the present-day town of Broussard, named in his honour.[45]

The historian John Mack Faragher argues that the Acadian expulsion fits the United Nations definition of "ethnic cleansing," a term coined in the early 1990s to describe violent conflict in the Balkans.[46] While this conclusion has generated some debate, there is little disagreement about the impact on the Acadians. They had developed a sense of themselves as a separate people in North America by 1713, but the painful experience of the *le grand dérangement* added new substance and cohesion to their identity. As the defining moment in their collective memory, it would long shape the cultural perceptions and political actions of their descendants, especially those living in the Maritimes and Louisiana, where Acadian culture continued to evolve. The expulsion became a blot on Nova Scotia's historical record to the point where, in 2003, the Crown issued a Royal Proclamation acknowledging the "trials and suffering experienced by the Acadian people during the Great Upheaval," and designated "A Day of Commemoration" commencing on 28 July 2005, the 250th anniversary of the decision by Lawrence and his council to deport the Acadians from the colony.[47]

As French power collapsed, the Mi'kmaq, Passamaquoddy, and Wolastoqiyik made their accommodations with the British. They were encouraged to do so by Maillard, Germain, Manach, and other missionary priests who knew the extreme deprivation facing France's Indigenous allies. Without ammunition and other supplies, they could neither hunt nor fight effectively and faced complete annihilation. Beginning in 1760, most bands sent delegates to Halifax to sign formal treaties, which acknowledged "the jurisdiction and Dominion of His Majesty George the Second over the Territories of Nova Scotia or Accadia," and affirmed that signatories to the treaty would respect existing British settlements and those "lawfully to be made."[48] These treaties promised what Indigenous peoples needed most urgently – government-operated trading posts – but they made no mention of homelands protected from rapacious settlers. Nor, significantly, did the treaties explicitly state that Indigenous peoples had surrendered their land to the British, an omission that would become the basis for comprehensive territorial claims in the second half of the twentieth century. At the time of their signing, the treaties were perceived by the British as instruments of submission to the Crown, while Indigenous signatories would have viewed them as a confirmation of peace and friendship. The differing understandings still resonate today.

In June 1761, Chief Justice Belcher, who assumed control of the colony following the sudden death of Lawrence due to complications from a cold, hosted a ceremonial burying of the hatchet at his farm on Spring Garden Road in Halifax. Abbé Maillard served as interpreter for Belcher's eloquent speech to several chiefs, in which he declared a "covenant of peace" from which a bright future would flow. "In this Field," Belcher promised, "you will reap Support for yourselves and your Children, all brotherly affection and Kindness as fellow Subjects, and the fruits of your Industry free from baneful weeds of Fraud and Subtlety."[49] The future was less glowing than Belcher envisioned. Instructed by the British government to draw up a proclamation forbidding encroachment on Indigenous lands, Belcher obeyed his orders but refused to publicize the resulting document because, as he told his superiors, "If the proclamation had been issued at large, the Indians might have been incited ... to have extravagant and unwarranted demands, to the disquiet and perplexity of the New Settlements in the province."[50] In 1762 Belcher set aside a broad swath of land from Musquodobit River to the Baie des Chaleurs for the Mi'kmaq, but this plan was rejected by the Board of Trade.[51]

By 1760 British victories at Quebec and Montreal had sealed the fate of New France, releasing military resources for the Caribbean front, where several French and Spanish islands were captured. The last battle in the Seven Years' War in North America occurred in Newfoundland. For three months in the summer of 1762, a French expedition occupied St John's and several major outports. A British force assembled in New York and Nova Scotia defeated them at the Battle of Signal Hill in September.

The Treaty of Paris formally ended the war early in 1763. Eager to repossess some of its conquered Caribbean colonies, France agreed to give up its North American empire. French negotiators fought hard to keep Île Royale for the migratory fishery, but settled for the right to fish on the Treaty Shore in Newfoundland and possession of the islands of St-Pierre and Miquelon. To prevent France from trying to recapture Louisbourg, William Pitt ordered it destroyed. The razing of the town's defences began in 1760, and the final contingent of British soldiers sailed away in 1768. Now the only major British naval base in the region, Halifax became a more elegant place when much of the cut stone used in the construction of Louisbourg was repurposed in the capital. In a final irony, the bell that summoned *Louisbourgeois* to mass was installed in the "little Dutch church" on Brunswick Street that served German-speaking adherents of the Church of England.

A Royal Proclamation, issued on 7 October 1763, outlined in broad strokes, how Britain intended to manage its territories in the Atlantic region. Île Royale (renamed Cape Breton) and Île Saint-Jean (anglicized to the Island of St John) were annexed to Nova Scotia, while Anticosti Island, the Îles de la Madeleine, and "the Coast of Labrador" were placed under the governor of Newfoundland. As before the war, the boundary between Nova Scotia and the Province of Maine, which was administered by Massachusetts, remained undefined, but much of the territory known variously as Mi'kma'ki, Acadie, and Nova Scotia was brought together under one colonial administration.

The proclamation also set out the Crown's policy regarding Indigenous peoples. European settlement was banned west of the Alleghany Mountains, where an uprising inspired by the Ottawa chief Pontiac was creating havoc at the former French posts occupied by the British. Elsewhere, all lands in the colonies not ceded or purchased by the British government were to be reserved for Indigenous peoples, and no private individual was authorized to buy land from them. Conceived with the western frontier in mind, these policies were studiously ignored by administrators in Nova Scotia, which now became the principal focus in North America of Britain's post-war colonization and land speculation schemes. John Reid has argued convincingly that the Indigenous peoples in the Maritime region remained a military threat to settler society until 1775, but the odds that Nova Scotia's original inhabitants could buck the trends working against them were hardly promising.[52]

During the war, Britain had begun an extensive exercise exploring and mapping its expanding empire. Three men whose scientific skills had contributed to the success of the Louisbourg and Quebec campaigns – James Cook, Samuel Holland, and Joseph Frederick Wallett DesBarres – were appointed to conduct surveys in the Atlantic region. While Cook turned his attention to Newfoundland, Holland carried out surveys of the Gulf of St Lawrence, including St John's Island, the Îles de la Madeleine, and Cape Breton.[53] Between 1764 and 1773, DesBarres painstakingly charted the waters of the Maritime region. His findings and those of Holland, along with exquisite drawings by DesBarres, were published in several volumes as *The Atlantic Neptune* (1774–84), a major achievement in cartographic history (Figure 7.3). To accommodate new settlers, the Boston-born surveyor Charles Morris, who had survived

Figure 7.3. *Wreckers' Den near the Pond on the Island of Sable*. J.F.W. DesBarres included this representation of Sable Island, with a view of a Wreckers' Den and wild horses in the distance, in his *Atlantic Neptune* (1777). So many ships came to grief on the shores of Sable Island that it became known as "the graveyard of the Atlantic," and provided a rich treasure trove for seaborne scavengers.
J.F.W. DesBarres, 1777. Killam Library, Dalhousie University, Halifax.

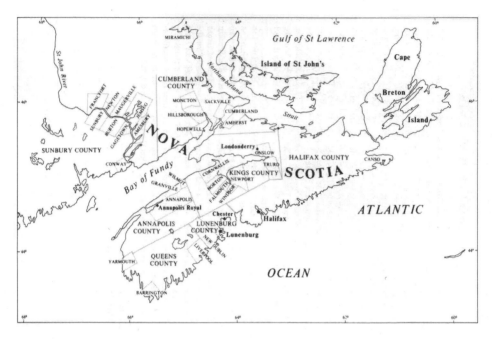

Map 7.2. Planter Nova Scotia, 1767.
Adapted from Margaret Conrad, ed., *They Planted Well: New England Planters in Maritime Canada* (Fredericton: Acadiensis Press, 1988), 8.

the 1747 attack at Grand-Pré, helped to lay out Halifax and Lunenburg and supervised the drawing up of Nova Scotia's county and townships boundaries. Meanwhile, Lieutenant Joseph Peach and Lieutenant John Marr made the first comprehensive British survey of the St John River and its main portage to the St Lawrence.[54]

In the process of charting, surveying, and mapping, the British assigned new names to the Maritime landscape, which they imagined as largely empty space and which they claimed as their own by virtue of military might. Some names stuck, others did not. Few of the country and parish names that Holland applied to Cape Breton were adopted, and even on the mainland Indigenous and Acadian nomenclature persisted (Map 7.2).

Planter Nova Scotia

The expulsion of the Acadians, the razing of their communities, and the reduction of Louisbourg to rubble struck major blows to Nova Scotia's economy. While such wonton destruction was nothing new in the region, the colony would have evolved much differently had the port town of Louisbourg survived, Acadians been allowed to remain on their productive farms, and the Mi'kmaq offered guarantees to a significant portion of their homeland.[55] Since none of these policies prevailed, Nova Scotia started over again, its population dominated by new settlers. The process began with the founding of Halifax and Lunenburg, but continued in earnest once Louisbourg had been captured, most of the Acadians deported, and the surviving Mi'kmaq pacified.

Wartime conditions made it difficult to recruit settlers from overseas, but New Englanders, who had long set their sights on the northeastern frontier, were near at hand. With their numbers growing impressively – reaching 350,000 by 1750 – and their expansion westward temporarily blocked by the continuing war in the interior, Nova Scotia offered the best alternative for those seeking new areas for settlement. Accustomed to considerable social and political autonomy, New Englanders were reluctant to move to a colony where their "rights as Englishmen" were in question. To overcome this obstacle, the Board of Trade instructed a reluctant Governor Lawrence to call Nova Scotia's first elected assembly in 1758 – a reform long demanded by the Halifax merchant community – and to issue a proclamation, widely circulated though New England newspapers, inviting immigrants to Nova Scotia. A second proclamation followed early in 1759, specifying the rights that settlers would enjoy: two elected assembly representatives for each settled township, a judicial system similar to the one in "Massachusetts, Connecticut, and the other Northern Colonies," and freedom of worship for Protestant dissenters. Calvinists, Lutherans, and Quakers were specifically mentioned as having "liberty of conscience" and the right to be "excluded from any Rates or Taxes to be made and levied for the Support of the Established Church of England." Because aggrieved Acadians and Indigenous peoples still constituted a threat, the proclamation assured would-be settlers that "Forts are established in the Neighbourhoods of the Lands proposed to be settled."[56]

What really got the attention of New Englanders was the offer of free land exempt from taxes for ten years: 100 acres (about 40 hectares) for each head of household, with an additional 50 for each family member and servant. The language of the proclamation suggests that authorities felt it necessary to be clear on issues of gender and race: 100 acres of "wild Wood-Lands" was allowed "to every Person, being Master or Mistress of a Family," and 50 acres "for every White or Black Man, Woman or Child" in each family. In other words, families headed by widows and slave owners were welcome. To avoid abuse by land speculators who had no intention of settling in the colony, each grantee was obliged to "Plant, Cultivate, improve, or inclose" a third of their land within ten years and no grantee was allowed more than 1,000 acres (just over 400 hectares). In the initial rush for spoils, speculators such as Benjamin Franklin could be found on the list of potential grantees, but they risked escheat of their land if they failed to settle on it.

With their political and religious concerns addressed and the carrot of free land dangling before them, nearly 8,000 people from Massachusetts, Connecticut, Rhode Island, and New Hampshire moved to Nova Scotia between 1759 and 1775. Known as "Planters," the old English term for colonist, they established communities along the South Shore (Yarmouth, Barrington, Liverpool, and Chester), in the Annapolis Valley (Annapolis, Granville, Wilmot, Cornwallis, Horton, Falmouth, and Newport), and in Cobequid (Onslow, Truro, and Londonderry), Chignecto (Sackville, Cumberland, and Amherst), and Petiticodiac (Moncton, Hillsborough, and Hopewell). In 1762 James Simonds, James White, and William Hazen – New England merchants associated with Joshua Mauger – established trading operations near the mouth of the St John River. When families from Essex County, Massachusetts, squatted on land occupied by Acadians and Wolastoqiyik, Mauger intervened to ensure that the newcomers prevailed. The grateful settlers named their community Maugerville in what became Sunbury County. The tide of New England migration receded in 1768 when the Treaty of Fort Stanwix opened western lands for settlement, but by that time the "Yankee" tone of Nova Scotia society had been firmly set.

The authorities in Halifax expected the new colonists to settle on their town lots as the founders of Lunenburg had been obliged to do, but the plucky New Englanders in agricultural townships quickly traded their holdings into one large farm. Luckily for them, the end of the war reduced the incidence, if not the threat, of Indigenous attacks. Some of the immigrants received assistance from Halifax to transport them to their new homes, but most made their way by forming voluntary associations to manage the process or by striking out on their own.[57] According to family tradition, Elizabeth and Edmund Doane dismantled their two-storey house in the Cape Cod community of Eastham and loaded it, together with their seven children, livestock, and provisions, on a boat for bound for Barrington. Bad weather and shipwreck dogged their journey northward in the fall of 1761, but they finally reached Barrington the following spring with little more than the clothes on their backs. Elizabeth Doane served as doctor and midwife for her neighbours, and received land in her own name to support her services. When she became too old to make house calls by foot, two men carried her in a basket suspended by a pole across their shoulders. She died in 1798 at the age of eighty-two.[58]

Most of the New Englanders could read when they arrived in Nova Scotia. Although many could also write, the two skills were often taught sequentially in this period. Learning to read was important for New Englanders whose dissenting religious beliefs were rooted in a personal knowledge of the Bible.[59] In the early years of Planter settlement, children were taught at home by one or both parents or an older sibling, a local minister, or itinerant teacher. Most teachers were men, but literate women, often a widow or a spinster, sometimes taught local children in their homes. Teachers sponsored by the Society for the Propagation of the Gospel also served in the colony, but most New Englanders looked upon them with suspicion because they were charged with teaching the Church of England catechism.

As a result of their relatively high level of literacy, Planters left a legacy of account books, diaries, and letters to help historians understand their settlement experience. The most remarkable example is a personal diary kept between 1766 and 1812 by Simeon Perkins. One of sixteen children born to a family from Norwich, Connecticut, Perkins moved to Liverpool in 1762, where he became a prosperous merchant and shipbuilder and held a variety of government positions, including justice of the peace, judge, militia captain, and member of the assembly.[60] His diary provides information on his public and private life in one of Nova Scotia's most prosperous Planter communities. While less detailed, the diaries of the Reverend John Seccombe, a Congregational minister from Harvard, Massachusetts, and of his daughter Mercy offer delightful insights into everyday activities. The good parson was especially attentive to the meals he ate in his Chester parish, providing one of the best records we have of culinary tastes and dietary standards in Planter Nova Scotia. Dining with a parishioner in October 1761, Seccombe recorded that he was served boiled bacon, pork, carrots, turnips, squash, cheese, and cake, all washed down with "Good Wines & Spruce Beer."[61] Clearly the fall harvest had yielded a groaning table. Mercy's attention, meanwhile, was focused on the weather, which determined the daily rhythms of her domestic life.

For the most part, the New Englanders who chose to settle in Nova Scotia came from more humble origins than did Perkins and Seccombe.[62] Many belonged to families with a large number of children, who had little hope of inheriting or purchasing enough land to support themselves in their long-settled New England communities. Attracted by the possibility of receiving 500 acres (202 hectares) – the size of most grants – to begin anew, they were investing in the well-being of their descendants for up to three generations. The availability of cleared land in areas where the Acadians had once lived was an added bonus, but New Englanders lacked the skills to manage the dykes, which had been breached during a violent storm in September 1759. Halifax came to the rescue, employing Acadian prisoners to bring the dykelands back into production.[63]

Unlike immigrants from across the Atlantic, the New Englanders were close to their former homeland and drew easily on its resources. They recruited ministers for their Congregational churches in New England, traded their fish and farm produce in Boston and other New England ports, and returned periodically to visit family and friends. Although most Planters came with little capital and some of them needed government provisions to help them through the first difficult years, many reached a modest level of comfort in one generation. The widespread ownership of land meant that the majority of men were "proprietors," able to vote and participate in local government. The New Englanders, along with other "planters" who arrived before 1775, laid the foundation for a study yeomanry in colonial Nova Scotia, but, as Graeme Wynn has noted, the potential for a thriving agrarian economy was limited from the outset by the colony's endowment of climate and soil.[64]

A Multicultural Mosaic

New Englanders were not the only "planters" in Britain's new Nova Scotia. After the Seven Years' War, Acadians who took the oath of allegiance were again permitted to settle in the Maritime region. This policy followed a plea in 1764 from Jersey-born merchant Jacques Robin, who was eager to hire French-speaking workers for his fishing operations in Cape Breton and the Bay of Chaleur. To accommodate the Acadians, the Nova Scotia government exempted them from legislation passed in 1758 declaring that "no papist hereafter shall have any lands or grants of land from the Crown." Laws against the presence in the colony of any "popish person, exercising ecclesiastic jurisdiction" or attempting to establish Roman Catholic schools remained in place until 1767, when Charles-François Bailly de Messein was appointed by the bishop of Quebec to minister to the Acadians and Indigenous peoples in the Maritime region.[65]

Offered smaller grants of land than their New Englander counterparts – commonly eighty acres (32 hectares) for each head of family and forty acres (16 hectares) for each family member – Acadian settlers were deliberately dispersed throughout the colony. They sunk deep roots in Argyle in the Cape Sable area and Clare in southwestern Nova Scotia;

Chezzetcook, near Halifax; Havre-Boucher, Pomquet, and Tracadie on St George's Bay; Île Madame and Cheticamp in Cape Breton; the western end of St John's Island; the head of the Bay of Fundy (Minudie, Nappan, and Maccan) and Memramcook areas; and the northeastern shore of what would later become New Brunswick. While settled by Acadians, the Îles de la Madeleine were administered by Quebec after 1774. Many of the Acadians who had found homes in St-Pierre and Miquelon moved to Cape Breton in 1792 when they were again obliged to swear an oath of allegiance, this time to the revolutionary government in France. Scratching a hardscrabble existence from the inferior soil typical of most of the land grants they received, Acadian settlers soon turned to the forests and sea for survival. Acadians were less likely than their anglophone neighbours to be served by formal institutions designed to promote their culture, but it survived anyway, nurtured by close-knit French-speaking communities that kept to themselves.

Individuals who fetched up in Nova Scotia from various backgrounds also sought and sometimes received free land. Among them was Marie-Anne Payzant, who returned from Quebec after it fell to the British and was granted 500 acres (202 hectares) in Falmouth Township in 1761. The following year, she married an Irish immigrant, Malachi Caigin. Prone to violent outbursts, Caigin was murdered by Peter Manning, another Falmouth grantee, also originally from Ireland, who was hanged for his crime in 1776. Marie-Anne died in 1796 at the age of eighty-five and was buried in a corner of her property, which was then being farmed by her son Lewis and his growing family. Another son John married Mary Alline, the daughter of a neighbouring Planter family from Rhode Island, and was caught up in a religious awakening inspired by Mary's brother Henry. Marie Anne's eldest son, Philip, received a grant of 300 acres (about 120 hectares) in Chester Township when he reached the age of seventeen, sold it along with a Lunenburg town lot still owned by the Payzants, and moved to Boston in 1772, where he later joined the American revolutionary army. By the 1770s his sister Mary was living in South Carolina with her husband, John James Juhan, a Swiss teacher, who had boarded with the family in Falmouth. Marie-Anne's youngest child Lisette, born in Quebec, married Joseph Jess, the son of a New England Planter who originally had been a linen weaver in Belfast, Ireland. While perhaps more mobile than most families, the Payzants offer a fascinating glimpse of the complicated identities and geographical range of the uprooted migrants floating around the North Atlantic world in the mid-eighteenth century.

The program sponsored by the state to attract families to Nova Scotia was supplemented by an older method of encouraging settlement. In an attempt to populate the region on the cheap and at the same time to promote a land-based aristocracy, British authorities made large land grants to "proprietors" on condition that they recruit Protestant settlers, improve their properties, and pay quitrents to sustain the colonial administration. In one seventeen-day period in October 1765, more than 1 million hectares of mainland Nova Scotia, much of it along the St John River, was handed over to speculators. Two years later, in an even more spectacular display of largesse, sixty-four of the sixty-seven lots surveyed on St John's Island by Samuel Holland were granted to favourites of the king and court, including the ubiquitous Joshua Mauger. Cape Breton was spared this indignity. With its timber and coal resources reserved exclusively for the military, land grants were suspended temporarily on an island inhabited primarily by Acadians, Mi'kmaq, and seasonal fishermen from New England.

Although most of the proprietors failed to meet the conditions of their grants, a few tried to do so. Alexander McNutt, an Irish-born soldier stationed at Fort Cumberland in 1760, planned to settle thousands of Protestants from Ulster on grants amounting to 2,300,000 acres (about 9,300 square kilometres), but authorities in London opposed having Ireland depopulated for the benefit of Nova Scotia. In the end, McNutt managed to bring several hundred Protestants from Ireland and New Hampshire to the Cobequid townships of Truro, Onslow, and Londonderry and to New Dublin in Lunenburg County. Fearing that the Ulster immigrants would manufacture linen on a commercial basis, the British government passed legislation to keep manufacturing jobs at home.[66] McNutt persisted in his immigration schemes, and ultimately settled on an island at the entrance to Port Roseway, where he also received a township grant, but he was unable to attract many settlers.

Another would-be aristocrat, the surveyor J.F.W. DesBarres, acquired by grant or purchase 80,000 acres (about 32,000 hectares) while stationed in Nova Scotia between 1762 and 1774. He used managers, tenant farmers, and enslaved labour to develop his properties in Tatamagouche, Falmouth, Minudie, Maccan, Nappan, and Petitcodiac. By 1768, he had established his headquarters at Castle Frederick in Falmouth Township, where he worked on his surveys during the winter. When he returned to England in 1774, he left his mistress Mary Cannon, whom he had met in 1764 when she was in her early teens, in charge of his estates. Mary continued to live at Castle Frederick, which Desbarres finally deeded to their four surviving children in 1819.[67]

Authorities in Halifax also participated in the land grab. Some 60,000 acres (about 24,000 hectares) of land was granted to councillors and other friends of the government in the Windsor area.[68] Located on the shores of the Minas Basin, Windsor was fast becoming not only the country seat of the Halifax elite but also a commercial centre of some importance. In 1767 it hosted the colony's first agricultural fair, a testimony to the industry of the new immigrants who had settled in the fertile farmlands around the Minas Basin.

Other groups were also attracted to what Nova Scotia seemed to offer. In 1765 a handful of pacifist German Protestant families from Pennsylvania settled on the Petitcodiac River, where they became the founders of Hopewell, Hillsborough, and Moncton. The Philadelphia plantation, granted in 1765 to fourteen proprietors in what became Pictou County, attracted a few Scottish settlers from Pennsylvania under the supervision of physician John Harris, but the majority of its early inhabitants, 190 Presbyterians from Loch Broom, arrived directly from Scotland in September 1773 on board the *Hector*. Since the challenge that confronted them on the tree-lined shore was greater than they had anticipated, nearly two-thirds of the passengers moved to other areas of Nova Scotia before the onset of winter.[69] Always alert to trading opportunities, Scottish merchants were drawn to Halifax, but their influence was felt throughout the colony. In 1765 William Davidson and John Cort received a grant of 100,000 acres (nearly 40,500 hectares) on the Miramichi River, where they developed a salmon fishery and diversified into timber and shipbuilding. Settlers also came from England. About a hundred immigrants from the West Country, an area long associated with the North Atlantic fisheries, settled at Blandford (just west of Halifax), where they mingled with migrants from Lunenburg.

Between 1772 and 1776, nearly a thousand people arrived from Yorkshire, many of them followers of John Wesley, the leader of a Methodist reform movement in the Church of England. Most of them settled in the Chignecto area. Pushed out of England by high rents, land enclosure, and their own ambitions, they arrived with commercial and farming skills of a high order. Some of them had sufficient capital to purchase their farms outright, while others rented their farms until they could afford to buy their own.[70] Their move to Nova Scotia had been encouraged by Lieutenant Governor Michael Francklin, himself a land speculator, who had failed to attract New England settlers to his holdings. Despite opposition from British authorities, Francklin employed agents to promote Nova Scotia in Yorkshire communities. Among the immigrants was the draper William Black, whose son became a popular itinerant Methodist preacher in Nova Scotia.

In this period Lunenburg's "Foreign Protestants" were gradually spreading to locations along the South Shore. Some of them supplemented their farming activities by fishing, and were widely regarded as a hard-working, if stubborn lot. In Lunenburg the Reverend Jean-Baptiste Moreau, a former Roman Catholic priest, had established the Church of England parish of St John in 1753, where he ministered to all Protestant denominations. Moreau died in 1770, by which time sixty German Reformed families had left the St John congregation to form a separate church. After failing to find a minister, they chose Bruin Romkes Comingo, a local fisherman respected for his piety and integrity, but lacking theological training. The Presbyterian and Congregational churches in Nova Scotia shared a common confession with the German Reformed Church, and they declared themselves an ad hoc presbytery for the purpose of carrying out Comingo's ordination at Mather's (later St Matthew's) Church in Halifax in 1770.[71]

Most of the unsettled grants in Nova Scotia eventually reverted to the Crown, but this was not the case on St John's Island. By having the island proclaimed a separate colony in 1769 and controlling its administration, the proprietors succeeded in frustrating all attempts to settle "the land question" in favour of freehold tenure. The new colony (named after Prince Edward in 1798) thus became saddled with a proprietorial land system that was increasingly out of step with land-granting policies in the rest of the Maritime region.[72]

Halifax in War and Peace

While the rural areas of mainland Nova Scotia were filling up with settlers, Halifax adjusted to the slower pace of peacetime conditions. During the Seven Years' War, the town was a lively place, its commodious harbour crammed with ships and its streets filled with soldiers and sailors, sometimes in the tens of thousands. Taverns, brothels, and gambling dens on Water Street and elsewhere kept the rank and file amused and both military and civilian courts busy. Following the frenzy associated with the Louisbourg and Quebec campaigns, one well-placed observer commented that "the business of one-half of the town is to sell rum and the other half to drink it."[73] With labour always in short supply, indentured servants, many of them Irish, fetched up on the waterfront, and camp followers sometimes remained behind when armies and navies departed. Francklin, Mauger, and other Halifax worthies outfitted privateers, reaping enormous profits in the auctions of their plunder. In 1762–3 the British fleet involved in the capture of Havana overwintered in Halifax with an estimated £400,000 sterling to spend. Church officials complained about the dissipation that ensued, but they, too, reaped rewards. Among the loot auctioned in Halifax was a pump organ from Cuba that found a home in St Paul's.

As the war wound down, Halifax faced a crisis. The population declined sharply and many of those who remained were casualties of the war – alcohol addicted, crippled, mentally unstable, and lacking the support of kin. To compound the misery, London stopped funding amenities such as hospitals, midwives, surgeons, orphanages, and workhouses, and cut back on the annual parliamentary grant. The colonial government, struggling to cope with mounting debt, was unwilling to fill the gap. Labourers congregated in what became known as Irishtown, at the south end of Halifax, and children whose parents were unable to care for them were bound out as child labour. At the other end of the social spectrum, the smart set, consisting mostly of the families of military officers and government officials, continued to enjoy fine dining, fancy-dress balls, and Sunday strolls along Pleasant Street (now part of Barrington Street). Horse racing on the North Common became a popular pastime after the war, and Michael Francklin developed a stud farm on his property in Windsor to advance the sport. As was typical of seaports throughout the North Atlantic world, Halifax was a multicultural community, where people of various identities mixed and intermarried. A Scottish Guild of Merchants and a North British Society documented the sense of identity and networking skills of a small group of ambitious immigrants. With its military establishment and elite families, Halifax was home to half of the 101 "Negroes" reported to be living in Nova Scotia in 1767. Most of them were enslaved or indentured labour with little hope of ever exercising civil rights.

Although much of the bustle vanished after the war, Halifax was still Britain's North American base for the Royal Navy. This status was enhanced with the construction of a naval yard north of the town walls, beginning in 1758. As well as careering facilities, where vessels could be cleaned, caulked, and repaired, the yard included storage sheds, wharves, housing, a mast pond, and all of the ancillary activities – blacksmithing, sail making, and woodworking – required to keep great sailing ships afloat. Britain invested more than £515 in the naval yard by 1783, a sum which yielded sixteen buildings, including a hospital, all surrounded by a mile and a half of brick walls. Julian Gwyn argues that the naval yard, which usually employed between one hundred and two hundred men, was the largest industrial complex in British North America before 1820, bringing welcome capital and skilled labour to a region that lacked both.[74]

Following the Seven Years' War, Halifax was expected to play a leading role in Britain's efforts to tighten control over imperial trade. The Navigation Acts had long been widely flouted in British North

America, where merchants took the opportunity to trade directly with European countries and their Caribbean colonies when it suited their purposes. In 1763 Parliament approved legislation to permit the Royal Navy to police smuggling – a role more commonly performed by the thirty-eight customs offices in North America – and Halifax became the site of a Vice-Admiralty Court, which handled cases involving vessels suspected of violating mercantile regulations. To encourage enthusiasm for their mission, the proceeds of any seizures, after being verified and assessed by the court, were shared between the Crown and the captain and crew. Since Nova Scotia was far removed from the main lanes of commercial activity and generated little trade itself, this role initially had little impact on the fortunes of most Nova Scotians.[75]

Halifax was, above all else, the seat of government in the rapidly evolving colony. Following Lawrence's death, governors came and went with alarming regularity. Successive administrators, including Jonathan Belcher (1760–3), Montague Wilmot (1763–6), William Campbell (1766–73), and Francis Legge (1773–6), tried to constrain the powerful mercantile clique in Halifax – especially by regulating the taxes imposed on the importation, sale, and manufacture of rum – but they soon found themselves removed from office, and the offending legislation was rescinded by British authorities sympathetic to the appeals of the mercantile community.

The growth of settlement increased the number of assembly seats, which reached thirty-seven in the 1770 election. Since most people in rural areas were too busy to travel at their own expense to Halifax, there was considerable absenteeism during sittings of the assembly, and the town's merchant clique remained in control. They made it their goal to frustrate any effort to impose taxes on unsettled land to help defray the colony's mounting debt and to escape penalties when they abused their positions to enrich themselves.[76] During his two stints in the assembly (1765–9 and 1774–5), John Day, who had married into the powerful Cottnam family based in Newport Township, offered a principled critique of the "Junto of cunning and wicked Men, in Halifax who added to the Distresses of the Community in order to promote a slavish Dependence on themselves." His career as a politician was cut short when he drowned at sea in 1775.[77]

In this period Michael Francklin, the English-born man-for-all-seasons, was the steady administrative constant. After arriving in Halifax in 1752 at the age of nineteen, he fell in with Mauger, a former associate of Francklin's relatives, who sponsored his young protégé as owner of a tavern. From there Francklin branched into other mercantile interests, which flourished during the wartime boom. He was elected to the assembly in 1759 and appointed to the council in 1762. Largely because of Mauger's influence, Francklin was awarded the position of lieutenant governor in 1766. He possessed important qualifications for his position, including the ability to speak Mi'kmaw and French, but he often overstepped his authority. He was a poor manager of Mauger's business interests in Nova Scotia, eliciting a string of rebukes from his patron for carelessness, greed, and indolence. As tensions between Governor Legge and Halifax merchants escalated, Francklin retired to his estate at Mount Martock, outside Windsor; he was replaced as lieutenant governor in 1776.[78]

Like the French before them, the British conducted censuses in Nova Scotia to measure their success in colony building. The 1767 census recorded 13,494 settlers living in greater Nova Scotia, but if Indigenous and Acadian inhabitants had been enumerated more accurately, the population might well have approached what it was before 1755.[79] The census probably also overestimated the proportion of people who were Protestant, calculating it at 85 per cent. Because many of the immigrants came as families, and unattached men tended to drift away, the gender balance was nearly equal. More than 45 per cent was under age sixteen, promising rapid population growth in the future. The colony was home to about 2,100 Irish and 1,900 Germans, but more than half of the population was designated as "American-born," not counting the 1,100 Acadian and twenty-eight Indigenous inhabitants separately enumerated. In Halifax and most areas of the countryside, the "American-born" were overwhelmingly New Englanders, a feature of the colony's demography that would have troubling implications when war again loomed on the horizon.

In the period from 1749 to 1775, Nova Scotia entered a second round of colonization. Almost all of the settlers in rural areas were in the pioneering stages, content to produce enough for subsistence with a little surplus to barter for rum, sugar, tea, and cloth from Halifax or Boston. When John Robinson and Thomas Rispin, two travellers from Yorkshire, visited the colony in 1774, they found poverty aplenty and evidence that the population was draining away as opportunities on the western frontier of North America beckoned. They also found potential in a colony that, they believed, was "as well situated as any place in the world."[80] They criticized the farmers, especially those from New

England, as exceedingly lazy, addicted to rum, and exploited by local and Boston-based merchants. What Nova Scotia needed, these visitors concluded, were more agricultural surpluses generated by improved farming methods and better business practices to keep more of their money at home. Time would tell whether settler society in Nova Scotia could rise to these expectations.

Chapter Eight

The Great Divide, 1775–1792

In the mid-eighteenth century, Nova Scotia was brutally reconstructed in the crucible of global warfare. The American Revolution (1775–83) brought more difficult adjustments. As a result of the rupture between Britain and thirteen of its North American colonies, Nova Scotia's population more than doubled with the influx of 35,000 American Loyalists and disbanded soldiers. In 1784, to accommodate the horde of demanding immigrants, British authorities carved two new colonies out of Nova Scotia: New Brunswick and Cape Breton, with capitals at Fredericton and Sydney, respectively. The arrival of the Loyalists confirmed that an Anglo-British society would prevail in the Maritimes, but historians continue to puzzle over why the region failed to succumb to the revolutionary fervour that engulfed its southern neighbours.[1] The reasons are complicated and remain open to new interpretations (Figure 8.1).

The Road to Revolution

Following the Seven Years' War, Britain's efforts to impose greater control over its expanding North American empire and to reduce its enormous wartime debt made many colonists uncomfortable. The Royal Proclamation of 1763 restricting settlement and trade in Indigenous territories west of the Appalachians became an early cause for grievance. This ruling was followed by several contentious pieces of parliamentary legislation, among them the Sugar Act (1764), imposing tariffs on a wide range of luxury goods such as sugar, coffee, and wine imported into the American colonies; the Stamp Act (1765), placing a tax on printed materials, including commercial transactions, legal documents, licences, and newspapers; and the Quartering Act (1765), requiring colonial legislatures to house and feed British troops sent to North America. The soldiers were charged with providing protection against

Figure 8.1. *New Settlement on the Island of Cape Breton in Nova Scotia in the Year 1785 by Lieutenant William Booth*. This image of Sydney was drawn by British military engineer William Booth, who was stationed in Nova Scotia from 1785 to 1789. His legacy included drawings, paintings, military records, and personal journals that offer valuable insights into the early years of Loyalist society. McCord Museum-M20079.

Indigenous aggression on the frontier, but conveniently positioned in seaport towns to keep a watchful eye on mercantile law breakers.

Settlers in the older colonies quickly mobilized resistance against what they viewed as a conspiracy to subvert their rights as British subjects. In October 1765 delegates to an Intercolonial Stamp Act Congress in New York passed a series of resolutions condemning the British policy of taxing citizens without their consent. Meanwhile, paramilitary groups calling themselves the Sons of Liberty began intimidating colonial officials charged with implementing the odious regulations. The Stamp Act was withdrawn in March 1766, but Parliament continued to assert its right to impose unwelcome legislation. The Townshend Acts, introduced in 1767, included a duty on imported glass, lead, paint, paper, and tea, stirring up more unrest in colonial ports. In March 1770 tensions reached a fever pitch when British troops fired into a Boston mob, killing five people. Another protest in Boston precipitated the final round of conflict leading to war. On 16 December 1773, self-styled "Patriots" disguised as Mohawks boarded three East India Company ships and dumped their cargo of tea into the harbour.[2]

The British government responded to the Boston Tea Party in the spring of 1774 with a series of measures collectively known as the Coercive Acts, dubbed the "Intolerable Acts" by the aggrieved colonists. In addition to closing the port of Boston, the legislation suspended the Massachusetts legislature, restricted town meetings, and placed the colony under

Crown rule. The Quebec Act, passed by Parliament at the same time, further inflamed colonial ire by annexing the Ohio country to Quebec and granting political privileges to Roman Catholics. When General Thomas Gage arrived in Boston in May 1774 to replace civilian governor Thomas Hutchinson, he met stiff resistance from Committees of Safety, which had evolved from the Sons of Liberty to serve as alternative forms of local government and as vehicles for extracting loyalty oaths from newly elected Patriot assemblies. In September delegates from twelve British colonies in North America – all but Georgia, Newfoundland, St John's Island, Nova Scotia, and Quebec – met in Philadelphia to coordinate a response to Britain's heavy-handed policies.

The First Continental Congress demanded the repeal of the Coercive Acts. When London refused to back down, the colonial militia was placed on alert. British troops dispatched in April 1775 to capture a weapons depot at Concord confronted the Patriot militia there and at nearby Lexington. Another military engagement occurred at Bunker Hill in June. As Massachusetts erupted in violence, a Second Continental Congress voted to raise an army under George Washington to defend "American liberty." In addition to driving the British out of Boston, the Patriots planned to capture Quebec. The invasion of Quebec, launched in the fall of 1775, failed miserably, but Washington's army succeeded in forcing Gage to withdraw to Halifax in March 1776. On 4 July 1776, thirteen rebellious colonies declared independence and resolved to fight a war to make good their intentions.

Nova Scotia at a Crossroads

Nova Scotians suffered many of the indignities associated with parliamentary legislation, but they remained peripheral to the Patriot movement. Like Georgia, established as a Crown colony in 1732 to serve as a buffer against the Spanish in Florida, Nova Scotia was a borderland colony and still highly dependent on parliamentary grants. Moreover, many settlers had received land from the Crown on exceptionally favourable terms, and were reluctant to become rebels for fear, as seemed likely at the outset of the war, that British forces would prevail. Georgia was eventually swept into the Patriot embrace, but Nova Scotia and the other North American colonies ceded in 1713 and 1763 by France continued to spin in the British orbit.[3]

This outcome was not a foregone conclusion. By almost any measure, Nova Scotia should have become the fourteenth North American colony to secede from the British Empire. Its population was dominated by New Englanders and its economic and social ties were as much North American as they were British. Nor were American-born settlers the only ones to respond positively to the Patriot rhetoric casting King George III and his aristocratic ministers as agents of tyranny. Many of Nova Scotia's Scots and Irish immigrants, along with most Acadians, Mi'kmaq, and Wolastoqiyik, harboured deep resentment against British authorities. For the settlers who subscribed to Congregational, Methodist, and Presbyterian beliefs, practical concerns such as access to glebe lands in the townships and the right to perform marriages predisposed them to cast a jaded eye on colonial officials who upheld the prerogatives of the Crown and the Church of England. And under no circumstances would the general population willingly submit to new taxes, whether imposed by Halifax or London.

Neither the Royal Proclamation nor the Quartering Act had much impact on Nova Scotia, but the Stamp Act was another matter. The rush of land grants in 1765 was precipitated by taxes on government documents that came into effect on 1 November, and newspaper editors, now obliged to print on stamped paper, were outraged by the legislation. In Halifax, Anthony Henry, the Montbéliard-born printer of the *Halifax Gazette*, and his assistant Isaiah Thomas, recently arrived from Boston, kept their readers informed about resistance to the Stamp Act and championed its repeal. Both men soon found themselves unemployed. While Thomas returned to Massachusetts to continue his agitation there, Henry established the *Nova Scotia Chronicle and Weekly Advertiser*, which became so popular with its coverage of political developments animating the North Atlantic world that it absorbed the less popular *Gazette* in 1770.[4]

Interest in the issues creating tensions between Britain and its North American colonies was not confined to Halifax. When word was received in the South Shore community of Liverpool in early June 1766 that the Stamp Act had been repealed, Simeon Perkins reported in his diary that the town erupted in a "day of rejoicing" during which the cannon at Fort Lawrence was fired, colours were flown on all ships, and the militia "marched to the home of Major Doggett and were entertained." Once in the festive mood, Perkins revealed, the good citizens of Liverpool "made a bonfire out of the old house of Capt. Meyhew, a settler here, and continued all night, and part of the next, carousing."[5] Liverpudlians might have been prone to partying, but it is clear that the Stamp Act was highly unpopular in the community. So, too, were the customs duties imposed under the Townshend Acts, which created tensions in many colonial ports. Merchants in Halifax debated whether they should accept tea shipped by the East India Company that was subject to the hated tax, but the promise of profits ultimately trumped principles.

As the issue of political rights became the focus of attention on both sides of the Atlantic, Nova Scotians began to reflect on their own colonial condition. In February 1768 Anthony Henry published Governor Lawrence's proclamations, reminding his readers that town meetings, in which residents chose their community officials, had been eclipsed by Halifax-appointed justices of the peace meeting in quarter sessions to determine candidates for local government. Unauthorized gatherings were held in various areas of the colony, prompting the council in 1770 to threaten prosecution of anyone calling meetings "for Debating and resolving on Several Questions Relating to the Laws and Government of this Province."[6] Since Governor Francis Legge was obliged to issue a similar warning in 1774, it was apparent that settlers paid little attention to dictates from Halifax.

Nova Scotia's loyalty to Britain, proclaimed by the assembly, the council, and the governor in the summer of 1775, masked mounting tensions. As battles raged in Massachusetts, merchants in Halifax hinted darkly in communications with London that Nova Scotia might also resort to rebellion if Legge persisted in his rigorous efforts to root out corruption and put the colony on a sounder financial footing. His attempted reforms had little impact in the townships, but efforts to mobilize the colony for its own defence generated widespread discontent. In October 1775 the Halifax-dominated assembly passed a militia bill and imposed a tax on landholdings to support it. Where would the country folk get the currency to pay the tax, and how would they protect their families from Patriot attacks if they were called away to Halifax?

In short order, Committees of Safety were established in Sunbury and Cumberland counties and in the Cobequid townships to mobilize opposition to the militia policy and to correspond with Patriot leaders in Massachusetts. Legge dispatched Captain John Stanton to the Annapolis Valley to gauge the mood of the people there, but the officer's summary of his findings, submitted early in December 1775, brought little comfort to the dispirited governor:

Their Principles are Republican –
Their Views, to subvert the English Constitution in the Province –
Their Sentiments, taken generally, are, that there is too much power vested
    in the Governor ... –
Their Wishes are, that the Rebels of New Hampshire and New England
    may invade this Province in the ensuing Spring –
Their Hopes are, to profit by the confusion which they imagine will be the
    necessary consequence of the Invasion –
Their Fears are, least by mistake they should join the weaker Party & suffer
    with them accordingly.[7]

Despite this unwelcome intelligence, Legge felt compelled to put the colony on a wartime footing. The Patriot invasion of Quebec spread panic in Halifax, where the garrison had been depleted to support Gage's campaign in Boston. On 5 December 1775, the governor declared martial law and tried to mobilize rural militias for the defence of the capital. Few men in the townships responded to the call of duty, in part because their own communities were now being threatened. In the autumn of 1775, the Continental Congress began licensing ship captains to plunder, burn, or sell at auction vessels bringing munitions and supplies to British forces in Boston.[8] Even worse, most ports in Nova Scotia were now visited by American privateers, who ranged as far as Labrador in their search for plunder. Freebooters out of Machias cruised the Bay of Fundy in the summer of 1775, inspiring fear in coastal communities and trashing Fort Frederick at the mouth of the St John River. Halifax was well enough protected to avoid attack, but Charlottetown was looted in November and the colony's governor, Phillips Callbeck, taken prisoner.

Admiral Samuel Graves, commander of the Royal Navy in North America, ordered his warships to sink the "pirates" and to "lay Waste" to any community that harboured them. Since Nova Scotians traded with the Patriots, they, too, were subject to these penalties. What this could mean was manifested in October 1775, when an expedition led by Lieutenant Henry Mowat levelled much of the town of Falmouth, Maine, in retaliation for the Patriot capture of an armed sloop sent to Machias to protect efforts by the Boston merchant Ichabod Jones to secure firewood and lumber for Gage's forces.[9]

The war at sea quickly commanded the attention of almost every Nova Scotian. In a memorial dated 8 December 1775, the proprietors of Yarmouth tried to explain the difficulties they faced in what for them had become a civil war:

> We do all profess to be true Friends & Loyal Subjects to George our King. We were most all of us born in New England, we have Fathers, Brothers & Sisters in that Country, divided betwixt natural affection to our nearest relations, and good Faith and Friendship to our King and Country, we want to know, if we can at this time remain in a peaceable State, as we look on that to be the only situation in which we with our Wives and Children, can be in any tolerable degree safe.[10]

During the previous week, Yarmouth's militia officers had been carried off on two armed vessels whose Patriot captains threatened worse should the inhabitants take up arms against them. If they were not allowed to remain "neuter," the memorialists argued, "we have nothing to do, but retire from our habitations either to Halifax or New England." Similar petitions begging for relief from militia duty outside their own communities and from the militia tax came from Cumberland, Onslow, and Truro. "It would be utterly Impossible for a number of us to raise money if it were to save our lives," the petitioners from Truro declared. In Kings County, country squire Henry Denny Denson reported that the "Implacable Rancour of the People ... against His Majesty's Government &c is prodigious."[11]

Nowhere was the militia bill more contentious than on the Isthmus of Chignecto in Cumberland County, the key to any military strategy to invade the Nova Scotia peninsula by land. During the early winter of 1776, John Allan, a Scottish-born assembly member, and other Patriot sympathizers in the region made plans to seize provisions destined for Halifax and to attack Fort Cumberland. Assembly representative Samuel Rogers and former assembly member Jonathan Eddy, along with Isaiah Boudreau, departed for Boston early in February with a petition appealing George Washington for support of their proposed military campaign. By that time, Washington had met with delegates from the Wolastoqiyik and Passamaquoddy, who were willing to play both sides in their efforts to secure much-needed ammunition, clothing, and supplies.[12] Legge and the council capitulated late in February, rescinding the militia call-up and deferring the land tax. In May the governor sailed to London to answer charges levelled against him by his enemies.[13]

Legge's timely departure removed the focus of grievance, and in his absence the acting administrator, Commodore Mariot Arbuthnot, encouraged harmony by fraternizing with members of the assembly, visiting outlying communities, and refusing to take harsh measures even when they might have been warranted.[14] In the early summer of 1776, the Royal Fencible American Regiment, raised by John Gorham's brother Joseph to serve as a home guard, was installed at Fort Cumberland to keep an eye on developments in the rebellious region.[15] Two Yorkshire settlers, William Black Sr and Christopher Harper, agreed to serve as justices of the peace and enthusiastically exercised their power to root out dissidents, perpetuating what the historian Ernest Clarke describes as the "the balance of petty viciousness" that characterized the Chignecto area.[16] With a price on their heads, Eddy and Allan fled to Machias. In Sunbury County, where settlers were importuned by Wolastoq'kew insurgents, American privateers, and their Congregational minister Seth Noble, a meeting held in Maugerville in May resulted in a declaration of support for the Patriot cause signed by 125 men in the district.

Notwithstanding these rebellious tendencies, the groundwork for Nova Scotia's Loyalist stance had been laid. The colonial economy, in the doldrums for a decade, began to recover as wartime demand brought renewed prosperity. For both merchants and producers, profiting from the war was preferable to taking up arms. Had Halifax succumbed to the revolutionary spirit, the colony might well have been lost, but the mercantile community there thrived on government contracts and never gave serious consideration to confronting the military establishment, even when it was represented by no more than a hundred soldiers. A few dissidents in the town sabotaged military stores and engaged in espionage, but they failed to become the nucleus of a Patriot movement. As an imperial creation, Halifax remained firmly fixed in the British Atlantic, which the historian Stephen Hornsby argues was oceanic, commercial, and naval in its orientation.[17]

Nova Scotia's loyalism was reinforced by British legislation passed in March 1775 excluding the rebellious colonies from the bank fisheries. As a result, a few New England fishermen and merchants moved to ports from Passamaquoddy to Canso, becoming, in effect, the first Loyalist migrants to Nova Scotia from the disaffected colonies. More Loyalists arrived in Halifax in the spring of 1776 aboard the fleet that evacuated Gage's army of 9,000 soldiers and 2,000 civilians from Boston. Although New York became the headquarters for the British military later in the summer, Halifax continued to play a supporting role in the transshipment of soldiers, prisoners, provisions, and war matériel. The town also became the temporary home for families of British soldiers fighting elsewhere. If the volume of complaints about price gouging is any indication, Haligonians made the most of their wartime opportunities.

Revolution Forestalled

The presence of a British fleet in the North Atlantic discouraged Washington from any serious thought of invading Nova Scotia in the early stages of the war, but the threat of rebellion in outlying districts remained high. Within a week of the Declaration of Independence in July 1776, the Massachusetts council met with a delegation of ten Mi'kmaq and Wolastoqiyik in Watertown, on the outskirts of Boston, where they signed a treaty of "Alliance and Friendship."[18] Washington hoped to raise a regiment of Indigenous allies to do his fighting in the northeast, but the delegates lacked the authorization to sign an agreement binding their peoples. Unwilling to commit themselves to either side, the Passamaquoddy and Mi'kmaq rejected the treaty, while the Wolastoqiyik were divided on the matter.

This response greatly disappointed Allan and Eddy, who continued with their plans for an attack on Fort Cumberland. At the beginning of August 1776, Eddy was back in Boston with a request for military assistance and a letter of support from Patriot sympathizers in Onslow Township. Since the General Court was not in session, he was dispatched to the Congress in Philadelphia, where all eyes were focused on the British occupation of New York, which became a magnet for refugee "royalists." Eddy was sent on his way with only military supplies, provisions, and general encouragement to pursue his good intensions.

In the face of Indigenous neutrality and Patriot preoccupations, Allan decided that the attack on Fort Cumberland should be postponed, but Eddy persevered. Gathering up what support he could muster in Machias, Passamaquoddy, and Maugerville, Eddy and his "army" – some seventy-two men, including sixteen Wolastoqiyik under their leader Ambroise St-Aubin – proceeded in canoes and small boats along the north shore of the Bay of Fundy to Shepody. The outpost there was easily captured on the evening of 29 October. Efforts to recruit locally brought Eddy more disappointment, netting twenty-one Acadians, four Mi'kmaq, and about a hundred settlers from Chignecto, Cobequid, and Pictou. In the end, Gorham's Royal Fencibles, which had suffered deaths and desertions over the summer, roughly matched Eddy's contingent.[19] After a month-long siege, in which local inhabitants showing British sympathies were badly mauled by Eddy's poorly disciplined recruits, the attackers were put on the run with the belated arrival of a company of Royal Marines from Halifax, via Windsor, on 27 November.

The victors torched the properties of families that had supported Eddy, making the Isthmus of Chignecto once more a burned-over district. Among the victims were John Allan's wife Mary and her five children (including seven-month-old George Washington Allan), who finally found refuge from the ravages of the late autumn weather inside Fort Cumberland. Although a few diehard Patriot supporters such as William How, the son of Edward How, were rumoured to be allied with "Indians and French Acadians ... to burn all the houses belonging to Yorkshire Familys and other Government friends at Fort Lawrence,"[20] Gorham managed to reduce the cycle of vengeance by issuing a conditional pardon to all but the ringleaders of the rebellion. Only two of the forty rebels captured following the siege – Dr Peter Clarke and Thomas Faulkner – were convicted of high treason. Before they could be executed, they unaccountably escaped from their Halifax jail and, along with about three hundred other Patriot sympathizers, fled to the United States.[21] While live-and-let-live seemed to be the operating principle in Halifax, the tensions between rebels and royalists had a lasting impact on the Chignecto region, where arson, looting, and civil litigation continued for more than a decade. As late as 1788, the house of Christopher Harper, who as a magistrate "had made himself obnoxious to most of the principal settlers," was burned to the ground.[22]

Following the attack on Fort Cumberland, authorities in Halifax implemented policies to suppress dissent. Nova Scotians in rebellious areas were obliged to swear their loyalty to the Crown, and most of them did so. When a majority of the proprietors in Onslow and Truro townships refused to take the oath in 1777, their elected representatives were denied permission to take their seats in the assembly. In addition, a few prominent men perceived to be contravening wartime regulations and counselling sedition were hauled into court. Among them was Chester Township's founding father Timothy Houghton, who was convicted of "high misdemeanor" for stating that oaths of allegiance were non-binding because King George had broken his own coronation oath by accommodating Roman Catholicism under the Quebec Act. In the winter of 1777, Malachy Salter, a merchant and office holder in Halifax, was tried for sedition, and continued to be legally harassed for trading and communicating with the enemy until his death in 1781. A native of Boston, Salter was an active member of Mather's Congregational Meeting House, which put him in the company of other New Englanders who believed that the insurgents had every right to stand up to British tyranny. Even the Reverend John Seccombe faced charges of preaching a seditious sermon.[23]

As the war progressed, most Nova Scotians, eager to avoid prosecution and the devastation resulting from armies marching through their communities, became loyal British subjects by default. Others were prepared to profess their loyalty. At the time that Stanton reported almost universal republican sympathies in the Annapolis Valley, seven hundred inhabitants of Halifax, Kings, and Annapolis counties entered into an association "acknowledging their duty and fidelity to His Majesty." Legge's unpopularity made it difficult for him to fill the ranks of his Loyal Nova Scotia Volunteers, but the response was more positive for enlistment in Gorham's Royal Fencibles and in the 2nd battalion of the Royal Highland Emigrant (the 84th) Regiment, both of which recruited locally. By 1777 militias in most communities willingly fought alongside regular soldiers in their efforts to stave off privateer attacks. A few intrepid Nova Scotians, most of them based in Halifax and Liverpool, became involved in their own privateering ventures against the rebellious Americans.[24]

The failure of Eddy's campaign sustained Nova Scotia's loyalist stance, but the threat of insurgency remained. In May 1777 John Allan, appointed a colonel in the Continental Army with responsibility for "Eastern Indians," led about a hundred men from Machias to the St John River, making his headquarters at the Wolastoq'kew community of Aukpaque. This was meant to be the initial move in an invasion of 3,000 soldiers authorized by Congress, but a contingent of Royal Fencibles under Gilfred Studholme forced Allan's militia and his Wolastoq'kew allies to retreat to Machias. Thereafter, enthusiasm evaporated for the larger campaign. A fleet from Halifax led by Commodore Sir George Collier attacked Machias in August, but withdrew in the face of a spirited defence in which Patriot stalwart Jonathan Eddy played a conspicuous role.[25]

Earlier in the year, an expedition under Colonel Arthur Goold had arrived on the St John River to root out Patriot sympathizers. Mary Coy remembered being "greatly frightened" as a six-year-old child when a swarm of soldiers entered her home, but she was won over by the toys that the well-prepared diplomats had brought with them.[26] Under military pressure, most of the 125 residents of the Maugerville area who had earlier declared their support for the Patriots agreed to take an oath of allegiance in return for a pardon. Israel Perley, the clerk of the treasonous town meeting, was arrested, while parson Noble joined Allan, Eddy, and other Patriot leaders, in Machias.[27]

In November 1777, after Portland Point received another drubbing by American privateers, Studholme returned to the St John River, charged with constructing adequate defences. Fort Howe, named after William Howe, commander of the British forces in North America, protected the area from seaborne attack, but the Indigenous threat continued to haunt authorities. To address this concern, Michael Francklin was brought out of retirement to serve as Superintendent of Indian Affairs, charged with securing the allegiance of the Mi'kmaq and Wolastoqiyik. He tried to court dissidents north of the Bay of Fundy by offering presents, agreeing to issue land grants, and importing an Acadia-born missionary priest, Joseph-Mathurin Bourg, who had taken up his calling in France after being expelled from Grand-Pré in 1755, but these efforts brought mixed results.[28] Following the American victory at Saratoga in the fall of 1777, France and Spain joined the war on the side of the United States, renewing Indigenous memories of happier alliances. A threat to Fort Howe by the Wolastoqiyik in 1778 and sporadic attacks by Mi'kmaq on settlers in the Miramichi area underscored the fragility of British control in the region. Peace and friendship agreements were signed in 1778–9, but neither side put much faith in them.

Recognizing that a major show of force was required, Francklin hosted what must be one of the most ambitious diplomatic initiatives ever mounted in the Maritime region. According to his own report, he assembled "three hundred fighting men besides six hundred women and children" at the mouth of the St John River early in the summer of 1780 to meet with delegates from "the Ottawas, Hurons, Algonkins, Abenakis and other nations from Canada." The visitors, staunch allies of the British, promised to wage war against any Mi'kmaq or Wolastoqiyik aligned with the Americans.[29] Although this extraordinary effort at intimidation seemed to work, Patriots and French operatives remained active in the Machias area. If the United States and France decided to launch an attack on Nova Scotia, it was unclear where Indigenous – or indeed many settler – sympathies would lie. Most people just wanted the fighting to stop, and supported whichever side seemed to have the upper hand.

Fortunately for those responsible for keeping Nova Scotia in the imperial fold, a full-scale invasion failed to materialize, and continuing attacks by sea extinguished most lingering Patriot support. Liverpool, Lunenburg, and Annapolis Royal were trashed during the course of the war, and British coal-mining operations in Cape Breton remained under constant threat. In September 1777 the American naval commander John Paul Jones menaced the collieries at Spanish Harbour (now Sydney) and raided the fisheries at Île Madame and Canso, where he impressed local recruits to fill vacancies in his crew. Captains of British naval vessels also tried to press Nova Scotians into service, a practice that became legal in 1775 when Parliament lifted the colonial exemption from impressment that had been in place since 1709.[30] After riots over impressment erupted in Halifax in 1779, authorities insisted that press gangs be forbidden to operate on shore, but the ruling was sometimes disregarded, and seagoing Nova Scotians remained vulnerable to impressment throughout the war.

To address the ongoing challenge of American privateers, Halifax arranged convoys to protect coastal shipping, dispatched vessels to patrol inshore waters, and installed small garrisons in outlying communities to support local militias. In June 1779 Nova Scotia's western flank became more secure when a British force under Brigadier General Francis McLean occupied Penobscot Bay. By that time, most of the fighting had moved to the central and southern states, and any plans to invade the northern British colonies brought the threat of a renewed French presence in North America, an outcome that no Patriot would welcome. French vessels nevertheless remained a menace to shipping in the North Atlantic. In July 1781 two French frigates engaged a British convoy of eighteen vessels in a bruising encounter off Spanish Harbour.[31]

It was in this worrisome context that an evangelical religious revival, led by the charismatic itinerant preacher Henry Alline from Falmouth, gained momentum in Nova Scotia. Beginning in the 1730s, New Englanders had experienced a "Great Awakening" that split many of their Congregational Churches into "Old Light" Calvinist and "New Light" evangelical branches. New Lights were responding to a North Atlantic pietistic movement that emphasized individual spiritual rebirth, emotional engagement, and a disciplined personal life. In newly settled areas such as Nova Scotia, fiery exhortation by "born-again" preachers invariably had a much wider appeal than the scholarly sermons read from the pulpit by Old Light, academically trained ministers. Alline's message that good Christians should pursue spiritual rather than military battles especially resonated among the New England Planters, who were also comforted by Alline's assertion that they had been called by God from the dark clouds hanging over their former homeland to pursue God's plan in a peaceful corner of North America.

Alline's ministry was short – he began preaching in 1776 and died in 1784, while preaching in New Hampshire – but he laid the foundations of an evangelical tradition that is still strong in many areas of the Maritimes.[32] This tradition was reinforced by the ministry of William Black Jr, who began his long career as a Methodist preacher in 1781. Like Alline, Black was born again, untrained in theology, and emphasized a disciplined life. His message was initially well received in communities settled by his fellow immigrants from Yorkshire, but he soon gained a wider following.[33] With the American Revolution as their backdrop, Alline and Black helped many Nova Scotians to assert their own notions of empowerment to sustain them in apocalyptic times. Largely safe from the ravages of wartime armies, they were, as Alline claimed, "a people highly favoured by God."

As the American Revolutionary War wound down, Irish Catholics living in Halifax made a concerted effort to repeal the legislation of 1758–9 proscribing the practice of Roman Catholicism in Nova Scotia and denying Catholics the right to own property. A petition for this reform was presented in the legislature in 1781. After much bureaucratic foot dragging, repeal legislation was approved by King George III in December 1783, to take effect the following year. Catholics were still barred from public office, but the institutional development of the Roman Catholic Church in British Nova Scotia dates from July 1784, when a chapel was erected in the south end of Halifax on the property where St Mary's Basilica stands today.[34]

The Spirit of 1783

After the victory of French and American forces at Yorktown, Virginia, in October 1781, the British abandoned their continental campaign to concentrate on challenges from France and Spain in the Caribbean, Europe, and India. Guerrilla warfare continued on the North American frontier and in deeply divided communities everywhere as diplomats based in Paris tried to sort out the implications of the Patriot triumph. Determined to prevent France from muddying the terms of peace, British negotiators tended towards leniency, an approach that had significant implications for Nova Scotia.

British thinking on colonial policy was also influenced by the spirit of austerity. The most damning indictment of Nova Scotia's drain on the national treasury was uttered in the House of Commons by the Irish politician Edmund Burke in February 1780: "The province of Nova Scotia was the youngest and the favourite child of the Board [of Trade]. Good God! What sums the nursing of that ill-thriven, hard-visaged, and ill-favoured brat has cost to this wittol nation! Sir, this colony has stood us in a sum of not less than £700,000. To this day it has made no repayment – it does not even support those offices of expense which are miscalled its government; the whole of that job still lies upon the patient, callous shoulders of the people of England."[35] Burke, who considered the expulsion of the Acadians a travesty and was appalled by British efforts to suppress the rebellious American colonies by force, went on to argue that the "*neutral French*" had done a much better job of colonization than the British had managed to do since taking possession of Nova Scotia. No doubt this view was widely shared among parliamentarians.

In the Treaty of Paris (1783), Britain recognized the independence of the United States of America, leaving Newfoundland, Nova Scotia, St John's Island, Quebec, and the Hudson's Bay Company territory to form what was left of "British" North America. The treaty also created an ill-defined boundary separating Nova Scotia from New England along the St Croix River, thus relinquishing much of the territory in Maine that had been occupied by British forces since 1779. In another significant concession, Americans were allowed to fish in the Gulf of St Lawrence, on the offshore banks, and along the Newfoundland coast outside the French Treaty Shore, and were given the "liberty" to dry fish on the unsettled coasts of Nova Scotia, the Îles de la Madeleine, and Labrador. British negotiators gave some thought to extending free trade with the new United States – free trade generally had been promoted by Scottish intellectual Adam Smith in *The Wealth of Nations*, published in 1776 – but that idea was ultimately rejected.[36]

Policy relating to the people in the Thirteen Colonies who had remained loyal to the British proved a major sticking point in Paris. For the American negotiator Benjamin Franklin, the issue was profoundly personal. His acknowledged illegitimate son William, a former governor of New Jersey, actively supported the British cause and had become estranged from his father, who was disinclined to accommodate the hated "Tories." So outraged was the elder Franklin by his son's loyalism that he cut him out of his will except for the books and papers that William already possessed and the property that his father still claimed in Nova Scotia.[37] The Franklins were not untypical. Many families were ripped apart, both emotionally and physically, by the conflict.

After prolonged discussion, the Americans agreed only to a weak clause in the treaty (Article V) promising that Congress would "earnestly recommend" to state legislatures that they "provide for the restitution of all estates, rights, and properties, which have been confiscated belonging to real British subjects." Most Loyalists who tried to recoup their lost fortunes under this provision were met with derision, harassment, and even death. With the experience of mass violence perpetrated by Patriot enthusiasts etched on their memories, many Loyalists, like the Acadians a generation earlier, were set adrift to find a new homeland.

The Maritimes became the destination for more than 40 per cent of the 75,000 civilian refugees and disbanded soldiers who were forced or who chose to leave the United States when the war ended. Sir Guy Carleton, the British officer in charge of the evacuation of the Loyalists, argued convincingly that they should be offered free land in the remaining British colonies, thereby not only rewarding them for their sacrifices, but also establishing firm foundations for a revitalized empire in North America. Although Loyalists began moving to Nova Scotia before hostilities ended, most arrived between 1782 and 1784 on fleets departing from New York, Charlestown, and Savannah, where refugees had gathered under British protection during the war. Still others found their way to Nova Scotia from Britain, Florida, the Bahamas, Jamaica, and other sites of refuge in their restless quest for a safe haven.[38]

The tidal wave of Loyalist immigrants swamped the old colony of Nova Scotia and posed enormous administrative challenges.[39] Arriving to take up his new post in the fall of 1782, Governor John Parr moved quickly to escheat unoccupied land and carve out townships for the Loyalists, but surveying took time and the migrants were impatient. Charles Morris Jr, who had succeeded his father as surveyor general in 1781, was especially hard pressed, referring to his experience getting the Loyalists settled on their land as "next to Egyptian Slavery."[40] Given the numbers of people to accommodate, bottlenecks inevitably occurred in arranging food, shelter, and land grants, thus generating much grumbling, genuine hardship, and sometimes bitter conflict. The situation would have been much worse had the British not acquired valuable experience in managing and provisioning large armies in North America during the recent war.

Despite the difficulties, Loyalists were eventually located in communities scattered across the Maritime region. Some 14,000 of them arrived at Portland Point, founding the city of Saint John and establishing farms along the lower St John River. Acadians in this region, once again dispossessed, were offered grants farther upriver in Madawaska, where they were finally left alone. Even more Loyalists and disbanded soldiers – approximately 19,000 – went to peninsular Nova Scotia, many of them initially fetching up in Shelburne (the former Port Roseway), which for a time became the largest city in British North America, with a population of more than 12,000.[41] When it failed to develop into the prosperous commercial metropolis its founders had expected, most of the immigrants moved on. Many of them returned to the United States when they judged it safe to do so; others found homes in another British colony or moved to one of the smaller Nova Scotia communities, including Antigonish, Aylesford, Clements, Digby, Guysborough, Parrsboro, Ramsheg, Rawden, Sheet Harbour, Ship Harbour, Weymouth, and Wilmot, where land was available. Fewer than five hundred Loyalists made their way to Cape Breton, and a similar number settled on St John's Island, the latter unpopular because of its proprietary landholding system.

Although the Loyalists shared the common experience of being "great sufferers," they came to their fate in a myriad ways.[42] Many Church of England clergy, having sworn an oath of allegiance to the king as symbolic head of their church, had refused to forsake the British monarchy and the values of hierarchy, stability, and tradition it represented.[43] The Reverend Jacob Bailey, a Harvard-trained Church of England minister in Pownalborough, Maine, paid a heavy price for sticking to his principles. Harassed by Patriots as early as 1774, his position became untenable after he refused to read the Declaration of Independence from his pulpit. Reduced to extreme poverty and threats of violence, Bailey and his family sailed on a small boat to Halifax in June 1779. The good parson was dispatched by the Society for the Propagation of the Gospel to Cornwallis Township, where he found "Whigs, independents, Anabaptists, new lights, and beltgurded Connecticut saints," the number of "King Killers" there "in proportion ten times greater than in the dominions of Congress."[44] Never fully reconciled to the values of a revolutionary age, Bailey finally made his home in Annapolis Royal, where he ministered to his Church of England flock and became one of Nova Scotia's earliest literary figures, writing satirical verse, essays, novels, and plays, most of which circulated in manuscript form.

Many Loyalists were people who simply had backed the wrong horse during the war and suffered the consequences. In the early 1770s Edward Winslow was a young man with great prospects. As a Harvard graduate, the only son of a prominent New England family with valuable estates in the Plymouth area, and a minor office holder, he stood up to the Sons of Liberty, fought with the British forces at Lexington, and was evacuated to Halifax in spring 1776. During the war, he served as muster master general of the colonial troops in New York, where his parents and two sisters also found refuge. The Patriot seizure of the Winslow estates meant that these *Mayflower* descendants lacked the resources required to establish themselves in England, a land they had never seen. In 1783 Edward, his mistress Mary Symonds, their three children, and several servants and slaves moved to Nova Scotia. The rest of the family followed him there. While Winslow worked in Halifax as the agent for colonial regiments settling in the colony, Mary and the children were installed at Granville, near Annapolis Royal, where rents were cheaper than in the overcrowded colonial capital. Winslow urged the British government to create a separate colony for the Loyalists north of the Bay of Fundy, which he hoped to make the "envy of the American states." Ultimately he settled on the outskirts of Fredericton, where he farmed and secured enough government positions to maintain his family in shabby dignity, but he died a pauper in 1815. The following year, the New Brunswick assembly granted £100 to each of Winslow's two unmarried daughters in recognition of his "numerous services" to the province.[45]

A handful of highly placed colonial officials and Harvard-trained professionals were in the Loyalist mix, but most were artisans, farmers, labourers, and merchants. Only 110 of those granted land in Nova Scotia were considered of sufficiently high status to receive 1,000 acres (405 hectares) of land, rather than the usual grant of half that much.[46] To men such as Winslow, the lower orders were unsuited to the challenges facing them in establishing Loyalist colonies. The New Brunswick assembly, he quipped, was another Lilliput composed of "fellows here who three years agoe did not know the Magna Charta was not a Great pudding." Class prejudices, not surprisingly, bedevilled efforts to establish new communities under stressful circumstances. When fifty-five prominent Loyalists petitioned while still in New York for estates of 5,000 acres (over 2,000 hectares), the majority of the refugees vigorously protested and the request was denied.

Concluding that the new city of Saint John was both too crass and too close to the American border, Governor Thomas Carleton, brother of Sir Guy, chose Fredericton (formerly St Anne's Point) as the capital of New Brunswick, which he hoped would become a stable agricultural society led by a landed gentry. His dreams of social harmony were quickly shattered. During the first general election in the colony in the fall of 1785, some of the inhabitants of Saint John violently protested the condescension and corruption of the government based in Fredericton.[47] Clearly, many Loyalists were as "levelling" in their political views as the Patriots who hounded them.

More than half the Loyalists were women and children, whose fortunes were dictated by family decisions to support the British cause.[48] In a few cases, widows of Loyalists received land grants in their own name. Whether married or widowed, women faced the challenges associated with a pioneering life, and often brought with them troubling memories of harassment by Patriot relatives and neighbours while their fathers, husbands, and brothers fought the Patriots or languished in unhealthy prisons. The "settling in" process inevitably caused enormous stress as mothers tried to care for their children while living in the holds of vessels and in tents and crude huts that barely sheltered them from the elements. Jacob Bailey described the conditions in Annapolis Royal, which received its first shipload of refugees in December 1782: "In affecting circumstances, fatigued with a long and stormy passage, sickly and destitute of shelter from the advances of winter ... Several hundred are stowed in our Church, and the larger numbers are still unprovided for ... Nearly four hundred of these miserable exiles have perished in a violent storm, and I am persuaded that disease, disappointment, poverty and chagrin will finish the course of many before the return of another spring."[49]

In these conditions, family life was often strained as husbands failed to offer the domestic security their wives craved and wives fell short of the obedience husbands – and the law – felt was due them. At Shelburne a tomb stone bore this sad inscription documenting the experience of one self-sacrificing woman: "The wife of John MacLean who died the 18th March, 1791, aged 32 years. She left her native country, Scotland and numerous friends and companions, to follow the fortunes of her husband during the war with America in 1780. And when New York became no longer an asylum to loyalty, she joined him again on the rugged shore of Nova Scotia."[50]

Elizabeth Lichtenstein Johnston, the daughter of a prominent Georgia Loyalist, was arguably one of the most mobile of the Loyalist refugees.

The Great Divide, 1775–1792   171

In 1779, at the age of fifteen, she had married William Johnston, a captain in the New York Volunteers. Elizabeth followed her husband to New York, Savannah, and Charleston, and then joined the Loyalists evacuated to the British colony of East Florida in 1782. When Florida was ceded to Spain the following year, the Johnstons were forced to relocate. They moved to Scotland, where William pursued his medical studies, and then to Jamaica, where he established his practice. Elizabeth and her growing brood – she gave birth to ten children – often travelled to Britain to escape the unhealthy Caribbean climate, which took the lives of several of her offspring. After William died in 1806, Elizabeth moved to Annapolis Royal, where her father and one of her daughters had settled. By the time she wrote her memoirs in 1836, she had become the matriarch of a prominent Nova Scotia family. One of her sons, James William Johnston, served as Conservative premier of Nova Scotia, and another son, John, was a member of the assembly.[51]

A significant proportion of the migrants were soldiers, with their own demons to bear. During the war, about 19,000 men from the colonies fought in what were known as "Provincial" regiments. They became eligible for land grants in Nova Scotia,[52] as did many of the regular British, Irish, and Hessian soldiers discharged from the military when the war ended. As was the case with the founding of Halifax, disbanded soldiers, especially the young and unmarried, were inclined to sell their grants and drift away. Deputy Surveyor Benjamin Marston, a Loyalist merchant evacuated from Boston to Halifax in 1776, was singularly unimpressed with the eighty-four officers and men of the Nova Scotia Volunteers who received 22,000 acres (8,900 hectares) of land in Antigonish. "Such another set of riotous vagabonds never were," he sniffed.[53]

For older soldiers, whether family men or not, the prospect of settling in Nova Scotia must have been daunting. This was surely the case for Allan MacDonald, who had married Flora MacDonald in Scotland in 1750. Famous for her involvement in smuggling Bonnie Prince Charlie out of Scotland after the Battle of Culloden, she and other Jacobite collaborators were granted amnesty in 1747. In 1774 the MacDonalds migrated to North Carolina, just in time to be caught up in the American Revolutionary War. Allan MacDonald joined the Loyalist militia, which was defeated by Patriot forces at Moore's Creek Bridge in February 1776. Held prisoner until September 1777, he was freed under a prisoner exchange and found security behind British lines in New York. In 1778 he was appointed commander of the Royal Highland Emigrant Regiment stationed at Fort Edward, Nova Scotia. Flora, suffering the wrath of the Patriots for her Loyalist stance, joined him there during the winter of 1779, but decided to return to Scotland later that year. When the war ended, Allan, now in his sixties, received a grant of 3,000 acres (about 1,200 hectares) on the Kennetcook River, but gave up his new world dreams to join his wife in 1785.[54]

Cultural background and race as well as class divided the Loyalists. Although most of the migrants were colonial born, more than 20 per cent of those who settled in mainland Nova Scotia were recent immigrants from Britain, Ireland, and elsewhere.[55] Scots, including those serving in the military, could be found in every community, but many of those who stayed in Nova Scotia quickly gravitated to northeastern areas of the peninsula, including what are now the counties of Cumberland, Colchester, Pictou, Antigonish, and Guysborough, where their fellow countrymen were putting down roots. People of Dutch and Huguenot ancestry, many of them from New York, swelled the Loyalist ranks. So, too, did those who by religious conviction were pacifists. Quakers fell into this category, and a few of them found their way to the Maritime region, among them entrepreneurs from Nantucket who established a whaling operation in Dartmouth. As early anti-slavery advocates, Quakers tried to ban slave owners from settling in their communities.[56] This policy did not sit well with slave-owning Loyalists, who brought at least 1,500 – the number, Harvey Amani Whitfield contends, was likely much higher – of their unhappy chattels with them.[57]

The Black Loyalists

About 3,500 free African Americans, known as Black Loyalists, chose to settle in Nova Scotia. During the war, the British had encouraged slaves to leave their Patriot masters by promising them their freedom if they joined the British cause. At least 20,000 did so. They worked behind British lines, and some men fought in segregated units, including the Ethiopian Regiment, Black Pioneers, and Black Brigade. Like the Loyalists generally, the Black Loyalists generated diplomatic tensions at the negotiating table. Article VII of the Treaty of Paris stipulated that the British "would not carry away any Negroes, or other Property." In an effort to prevent Black Loyalists from being re-enslaved, Carleton established a board made up of four British and three American commissioners in New York to determine the legitimacy of their claims. The names and demographic details of those appearing before the board were recorded in "The Book of Negroes," a unique document in Nova Scotia's colonial history.[58] Those who managed to establish their status in New York were issued a certificate of freedom, most of them signed by Brigadier General Samuel Birch. Two Nova Scotia communities were named Birchtown, one in Shelburne County and another in Guysborough County, by their grateful founders.[59]

Shelburne was the initial destination of nearly half of the Black Loyalists who came to the Maritime region. Driven to the opposite side of the harbour, they struggled to farm in the rocky soil, which was all that Birchtown offered. Stephen Blucke, a Barbadian who had fought in the Black Pioneers, played a significant role in the founding of the community, but the Black Loyalists put greater stock in their religious leaders. Many of the Birchtown settlers subscribed to Methodist beliefs and were under the pastoral care of Moses Wilkinson, a former slave who was blind from birth. A persuasive preacher, he inspired his fellow Loyalists Boston King and John Ball to take up the ministry. One-quarter of the Methodists in Nova Scotia were African Americans after the arrival of the Loyalists, a situation that impressed the movement's founder, John Wesley. In a letter to the white Methodist Loyalist James Barry in July 1784, Wesley noted: "The work of God among the blacks in your neighbourhood is a wonderful instance of the power of God; and the little town they have built is, I suppose, the only town of negroes that has been built in America – nay perhaps in any part of the world, except only in Africa." Wesley vowed to keep his black followers supplied with religious literature and encouraged white Methodists to "give them all the assistance you can in every possible way."[60]

Not all of Birchtown's residents were Methodists. The Reverend John Murrant attracted about forty families to the evangelical Church of England sect known as the Huntingdonians, named after Countess Huntingdon, who funded their missions. David George, the most controversial and successful of the Black Loyalist preachers, was a Baptist. His meetings were attended by both black and white settlers, but even Birchtown residents found his message too radical. In addition to their emphasis on salvation through faith rather than good works, Baptists insisted on adult baptism and baptism by immersion instead of sprinkling. Such "free will" practices defied the teachings of established churches, and were widely perceived as encouraging republican tendencies. As George's following grew throughout the Maritime region, he incurred hostility from people who liked neither his message nor the colour of his skin. Violence against George escalated into a nasty race riot in Shelburne in the summer of 1784 when disbanded soldiers attacked black labourers in the vicious competition for wage-paying work.

Prejudice dogged Black Loyalists wherever they went. Usually forced to live in segregated areas, they were often denied provisions and received much smaller grants of land than white settlers did – if they received any land at all.[61] Many black settlers received only a licence of occupation for a plot of 10 acres (4 hectares), which could easily be revoked if their white neighbours coveted the land. Even communities where blacks formed the majority, among them Brindley Town (near Digby), Preston (near Halifax), and Little Tracadie (near Guysborough), were defined, like Birchtown, by poverty and wretchedness. Dr Bray's Associates, the missionary arm of the Church of England, established separate schools for blacks, taught primarily by black teachers, but literacy remained secondary to survival in their hierarchy of needs.[62] When wheat blight struck Nova Scotia in 1791, blacks and whites alike faced starvation, but the poorest suffered most. Methodist preacher Boston King reported that some of his followers were forced to sell their clothes and eat their cats and dogs "to support life." Even with that, "several of them fell down dead in the streets, thro' hunger."[63]

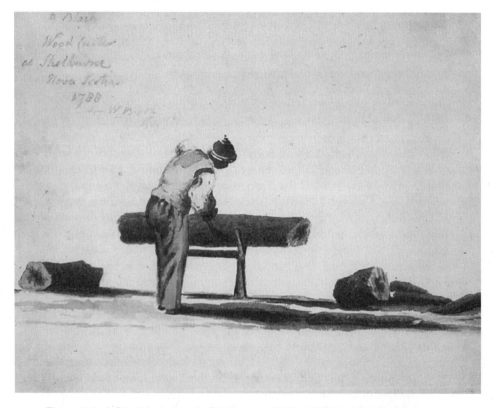

Figure 8.2. A Black Labourer in Shelburne, 1788, by William Booth. Most African Americans in the Loyalist migration to Nova Scotia, such as the woodcutter represented here, survived by working as labourers. LAC-040162. W.H. Coverdale Collection of Canadiana.

Figure 8.3. Rose Fortune was a well-known entrepreneur in Annapolis Royal by the time this portrait of her was painted by an unknown artist around 1830. Nova Scotia Museum, Halifax.

Although most of the Black Loyalists who arrived in Annapolis Royal moved to Lequille, on the outskirts of the town, the enterprising Fortune family from Pennsylvania was an exception. Their daughter Rose, ten years old in 1784, proved especially ambitious. In her adult life, she made a living by carting baggage from ships arriving at Annapolis Royal to nearby inns, and she later kept a public house. Her efforts to maintain order among the roughs on the waterfront later earned her unofficial recognition as Canada's first policewoman. Such was her local fame that renowned author Thomas Chandler Haliburton mentioned her in one of his short stories, and an unknown artist painted a watercolour portrait of her wearing an overcoat over a dress and apron and a straw hat on top of a lace cap tied under her chin.[64]

Other than poverty and violent attacks, the major threat to Black Loyalists was re-enslavement.[65] Evidence shows that unscrupulous men sometimes kidnapped free blacks, dumped them on a vessel bound for the southern United States or the West Indies, and pocketed the profit from their sale. In some cases, blacks in dire economic circumstances were tricked into signing long-term indentures that essentially amounted to enslavement. Lydia Jackson, who settled in Manchester (now Guysborough), signed such a contract after the death of her husband and was immediately sold to Dr John David Bolman, a Hessian regimental surgeon living in Lunenburg. He treated her brutally even when she was pregnant. After three years, Lydia escaped to Halifax, where she re-established her freedom.[66]

Mary Postell's well-documented story offers evidence of the processes used to exploit free blacks in Loyalist Nova Scotia. After having her certificate of protection stolen in Charlestown, she was caught up in the lives of two Loyalist brothers, Samuel and Jesse Gray, who moved to East Florida. In 1785 Jesse Gray found his way to Argyle, Nova Scotia, taking Mary and her two daughters, Flora and Nellie, with him. When he tried to sell Flora in 1786, Postell took Gray to court to establish her free status, but he prevailed on the undocumented claim that he had purchased Mary from his brother. Gray then sold Mary to his neighbour for 100 pounds of potatoes and later sold Flora, who ended up enslaved in North Carolina. Mary went to court again in 1791 to protect Nellie, but Gray was once more acquitted; a black witness, Scipio Wearing, had his house torched for testifying on Mary's behalf.[67]

The dream of a "promised land" where they could escape prejudice, own property, and live independently had inspired Black Loyalists to move to Nova Scotia. When their dream turned into a nightmare, they found a spokesman in Thomas Peters, who had served as a sergeant in the Black Pioneers. Peters and two hundred of his fellow soldiers initially settled in Brindley Town, near Digby, but they were denied the three years of provisions accorded to white Loyalists, offered smaller grants of land, and forced to work on construction projects rather than on their own farms. Peters petitioned the governor of New Brunswick, Thomas Carleton, for land, but this request was denied. In 1790 Peters travelled to London to continue his crusade for fair treatment. While there, he met abolitionists Granville Sharp and Thomas Clarkson, who were planning to resettle emancipated slaves in the new colony of Sierra Leone. The British government provided funding for this venture, which seemed to offer the opportunity that free African Americans were looking for. Early in 1792 nearly 1,200 Black Loyalists, including Peters, almost all religious leaders, and the long-suffering Lydia Jackson, moved from Nova Scotia and New Brunswick to Sierra Leone. This loss of leadership inflicted a devastating blow on the embattled black minority in Nova Scotia. Despite continuing challenges, the Black Loyalists left a legacy of literacy, religious conviction, and self-help in both of their adopted homelands, where the story of their particular war for independence remains an essential component of their collective historical memory.

Cape Breton

While the population of Nova Scotia and New Brunswick grew dramatically with the arrival of the Loyalists, Cape Breton languished. It had been declared a separate colony largely on the strength of a scheme by New York Loyalist Abraham Cuyler to attract 3,000 Loyalists from Quebec, but he managed to bring only 140 to Louisbourg and St Peter's in the fall of 1784. The rest had second thoughts about moving to Cape Breton when western sections of Quebec, which in 1791 became the colony of Upper Canada, were opened to settlement. A few hundred Loyalists from a variety of locations eventually found their way to Cape Breton, most of them settling in Baddeck, Port Hood, Sydney, and the Gut of Canso, but it never became the Loyalist haven that Cuyler originally envisioned. Because Cape Breton was still a colony in embryo, it was to remain subordinate to Halifax until such time as an assembly could be called.

Cuyler's disappointment was compounded when the position of lieutenant governor went not to himself but to the famous cartographer J.F.W. DesBarres.[68] In some respects DesBarres was an inspired choice for the position. He had participated in the siege of Louisbourg and had surveyed Cape Breton's shores and harbours. This knowledge could serve him well in developing the territory deserted by the British in the 1760s. Early in the winter of 1785, DesBarres arrived at Spanish Harbour to establish the new capital there, named, like the capital of Australia, after Lord Sydney, President of the Board of Trade and Plantations. DesBarres recruited 120 settlers from England, who vied with the Loyalists for access to provisions and offices. Although Cuyler was appointed to the executive council, he, along with his Loyalist friend David Matthews, soon locked horns with DesBarres, as did the garrison commander Lieutenant-Colonel John Yorke. DesBarres was recalled in

1787, but his successor William Macarmick also alienated Cuyler, who moved to Montreal in 1791.

The small population of Cape Breton, many of them Roman Catholic Acadians and Mi'kmaq, provided an excuse for authorities to delay calling an assembly. This left the appointed officials in Sydney, including the Connecticut-born Church of England minister Ranna Cossit, to squabble among themselves.[69] The colony's coal, fish, and timber resources remained largely untapped, and the most British authorities asked was that Cape Breton not require any major financial outlays. In this context, Sydney had difficulty living up to the ambitious town plan laid out by DesBarres, who imagined a grid of streets and tree-lined avenues. Only the governor's house and the garrison church, the latter constructed from stone salvaged from Louisbourg, documented the enthusiasm for Georgian architecture that brought elegance to many colonial capitals in this period. A soldier arriving in 1789 reflected that, having "passed a great part of my life in America and been in many unpleasant and disagreeable situations ... I so declare without exaggeration that I think Sydney is by far the worst." Not surprisingly, most immigrants drifted away from the shabby British outpost, which counted fewer than two hundred people in 1795.[70]

The Loyalist Order

Having experienced persecution, defeat, and exile, the Loyalists had an obsessive need to restore order, security, and status,[71] but few felt they could reach their potential in what they sneeringly called "Nova Scarcity." Many of the migrants were former city dwellers and soldiers, ill-equipped to carve out homes in what seemed a howling wilderness. The challenge proved too much for some, who retreated into alcoholism, mental illness, and suicide. For others, getting back to their homeland became a major goal. Esther Clark Wright has estimated that as many as 25 per cent of the Loyalists who settled in New Brunswick returned to the United States; the proportion was probably even greater in Nova Scotia and Cape Breton.[72] Shelburne is the poster child for Loyalist outmigration, but Carole Troxler has documented a similar rapid decline in population in communities such as Rawdon and Ship's Harbour, settled by Loyalists from South Carolina and Georgia.[73]

Notwithstanding high levels of outmigration, Indigenous peoples, who had remained a force to be reckoned with before the war, now found themselves overwhelmed.[74] Leaders of the Mi'kmaq, Wolastoqiyik, and Passamaquoddy petitioned for land, which was sometimes granted, but it was often blatantly stolen by squatters who knew they would not be prosecuted for breaking the law. The Passamaquoddy were dispossessed when a community of Loyalists who had settled in the Penobscot region while it was under British occupation moved to St Andrews following the Treaty of Paris. In Cape Breton the Mi'kmaq managed to hold on to Chapel Island, which was granted to them by the government in 1792, but by that time resource depletion was beginning to have an impact even on this sparsely settled colony. The council minutes for 1789 report that nearly 9,000 moose had been killed by visiting hunters "merely for the sake of their skins."[75] For people who depended on the hunt for a significant portion of their diet, this wonton destruction could spell disaster. Even more telling is the growing preponderance of poor settlers participating in the fur trade, which hitherto had been almost exclusively under the control of the Mi'kmaq.[76]

The experience of the Alexey family is exceptional only in that it is so well documented. In 1786 Charles Alexey, a spokesman for the Mi'kmaq in the Cape Sable region, travelled to Halifax to secure government support to help them maintain control of their land. The recent grant of much of the area to Loyalists had not only ejected the Mi'kmaq in the region from their garden plots, but also privatized areas where they had customarily fished and hunted. After Alexey made another complaint to authorities, the superintendent of Indian Affairs, George Henry Monk, reported in 1794 that "the French people and some English have taken away the land that he had cleared and made a Garden of." The Alexey family complained of its difficulty accessing the fishery in 1800 and again in 1803, and John Bartlett Alexey was among the twenty families still petitioning for land in 1823, after having "settled on three grants of Land and have also been removed." In October 1807 the Court of General Sessions in Yarmouth and Argyle convicted Miner Vander-Horn for assault "against the body" of Jane Alexis (Alexey), suggesting that violence played a role in keeping the Alexeys on the move.[77]

Tensions also ran high between the old and new settlers. While the former chafed at the superior attitude of the "damned Refugees," the latter resented being exploited by Nova Scotians who had profited from the war and continued to benefit from the peace. When the smug Halifax elite refused to embrace the newcomers by offering appointments to the council and other high offices, the better-placed Loyalists became leading voices of the opposition in the assembly. They mocked Parr, calling him "Cock Robin" because of his quick, jerky walk, or the "Bashaw of Siberia" and the "Pontiff," in reference to his imperious manner in political and religious matters.[78] In return Parr accused them of promoting republican principles, a common put-down for anyone challenging appointed officials.

Figure 8.4. Micmaw Encampment by Hibbert Newton Binney, c. 1791. This idealized image is a far cry from the reality faced by most Mi'kmaq at the end of the eighteenth century.
Nova Scotia Museum.

To Parr's dismay, his title was downgraded to lieutenant governor when the British North American colonies were reorganized in 1786 and placed under the supervision of a governor-in-chief located in Quebec. By that time, Parr had expanded the size of the assembly to accommodate the increase in Nova Scotia's population, and Harvard-educated Loyalist Samuel Blowers had been appointed attorney general, a position coveted by the Irish-born member from Sackville Township, Solicitor General Richard John Uniacke. Loyalist efforts to have incompetent judges dismissed led to extreme bitterness, which was played out during a by-election in Halifax in 1788. During the three days of violence that accompanied the contest between Charles Morris, son of the colony's first surveyor general, and Loyalist candidate Jonathan Sterns, skulls were cracked and one man was killed.[79] Morris won by a wide margin, but the "judges' affair" smouldered until a new chief justice, Thomas Andrew Strange, who possessed impeccable qualifications for his position, arrived from England in 1790.

The Loyalists finally triumphed in Nova Scotia when John Wentworth, the former governor of New Hampshire, replaced Parr in 1792. Having aristocratic tastes and pretentions, John and his wife Frances had long angled for a better position than that of surveyor general of the King's Woods, which he had been awarded at the end of the war. Frances Wentworth's intimate relationship with Prince William Henry, who visited Halifax with the North Atlantic squadron in the 1780s, is widely believed to have sealed her husband's advancement.[80] While the Loyalist elite revelled in the court-like atmosphere surrounding the Wentworths, the pioneer experience had a levelling effect, especially outside Halifax, where Loyalist roots counted for little in a colony where nearly everyone now claimed to have supported the British cause.

Opposition to Wentworth's charmed circle centred around Nova Scotia-born William Cottnam Tonge, elected to the assembly for Newport Township in 1792. While motivated by personal ambition as much as by ideology, Tonge and his supporters shared a concern for the rights of elected representatives, and championed the rural constituencies over the narrow interests of the capital. The debate around political principles, which coalesced during the American Revolution, was further heightened in 1789 when a popular revolution broke out in France, resulting in the creation of a republican government. In 1791 the Nova Scotia assembly secured complete control of revenue bills, a concession to popular sentiment, but one guaranteed to bring elected officials into conflict with lieutenant governors and their appointed councillors.

Loyalist elites were unable to curtail the democratic tendencies taking root in the era of the American and French revolutions, but they managed to add political weight to the conservative side of the political spectrum. In 1787 Charles Inglis, the former rector of Trinity Church in New York, was consecrated as the first bishop of Nova Scotia, with jurisdiction over all the British North American colonies, including Newfoundland and Bermuda. The Society for the Propagation of the Gospel, the Church of England's missionary arm, helped to defray the salaries of clergy and the cost of building churches. In an effort to sustain the hierarchical class structure so admired by conservatives, Inglis supported the founding of an academy in Windsor in 1788 (which evolved into King's College in 1802) as an exclusive institution for the sons of the Church of England elite, and a Grammar School in Halifax in 1789. Inglis and his clergy strenuously opposed evangelical enthusiasm and the democratic tendencies it seemed to encourage, but without much success.[81]

The arrival of the Loyalists brought unprecedented investment in the Maritime region. Not only did Britain spend prodigiously to transport,

feed, and shelter the refugees, it also offered bounties for the construction of sawmills and ships, invested in roads and bridges, and came to
the rescue when crop failures and drought threatened survival during
the early years of settlement. More capital arrived in the form of half-
pay for retired military officers and compensation for losses that a few
Loyalists received when the United States failed to conform to the provisions of Article V. Given the colony's economic underdevelopment,
much of the money quickly drained away on imports from Britain
or smuggled from American ports. Even in rural areas, people were
increasingly caught up in the expanding market economy, exchanging their output from farming, fishery, forest, and quarries (notably
building stone, coal, grindstones, gypsum, and salt) for manufactured
goods, including luxury items such as cotton, mirrors, snuff boxes, and
wine glasses.[82]

Despite hopes to the contrary, Nova Scotia initially proved unable
to challenge New England's commanding role in the North Atlantic
fisheries and the West Indies trade. The Maritime region could scarcely
meet its own agricultural needs, let alone supply external markets, and
few Loyalists turned their energies to a commercial fishery on a scale
that matched the output of metropolitan merchants. Since owners of
colonial vessels, even if locally built, were legally unable to secure cargoes in New England or operate outside the Navigation Acts, trade languished. Consequently, communities such as Boston, Portsmouth, and
Salem, with a vast hinterland to supply them, easily bested Sydney,
Halifax, Liverpool, Shelburne, and Yarmouth in the rapidly expanding
global carrying trade and in such profitable ventures as the Pacific coast
sea otter trade, in which many New England entrepreneurs made extensive profits in the late eighteenth century.

Culture and Community

Loyalists and other Nova Scotians negotiated their new identities in the
context of a vibrant intellectual environment that was gradually transforming the Atlantic world. In cultural terms, they were children of the
Enlightenment, a movement originating in Europe that emphasized progress in human affairs and promoted new ideas about economics, philosophy, politics, religion, science, and society. Both the American and
French revolutions were borne on the tide of Enlightenment ideas, which
challenged not only political and religious traditions, but also conventional beliefs about class, race, and gender. The adjustment to "modern"
ways of thinking was often painful, but it culminated in the formation of
institutions and values that remain deeply rooted in Nova Scotia.[83]

The Enlightenment thrived on literacy, which was increasingly perceived as a source of personal empowerment, pleasure, and even salvation. By contemporary standards, the Loyalists were a literate lot, among them parsons, printers, teachers, and writers who reinforced the interest in intellectual pursuits apparent in Nova Scotia before the American Revolution. Like their counterparts throughout the Anglo-Atlantic world, literate Loyalists produced poems, essays, pamphlets, and sermons, wrote letters and kept diaries, and discussed British political tracts, fiction, and advice books in drawing rooms, coffeehouses, and the pages of their newspapers.[84] John Howe, a Loyalist printer from Massachusetts, and William Cochran, a Church of England clergyman and classical scholar, attempted to provide a forum for colonial writers through their *Nova-Scotia Magazine and Comprehensive Review of Literature, Politics, and News*, published in Halifax from 1789 to 1792.[85] At its peak it had no more than three hundred subscribers and received few submissions from local writers, but it ranks as the first literary journal in the British North American colonies. One pseudonymous contributor no doubt reflected the thinking of many Nova Scotians with the comment: "Were I to name the most striking peculiarity of our neighbours in the United States, I would say that they are set apart from the rest of mankind by a certain *littleness*."[86] By implication, being Britons meant participating in a larger and more important undertaking.

Schooling remained largely a family matter in late eighteenth-century Nova Scotia, but with the arrival of the Loyalists, more families had the opportunity to send their children to private schools. Although grammar schools excluded girls, they nevertheless had access to private schooling of a high order. Among the teachers in the Loyalist diaspora was Deborah How Cottnam, who had been raised near Canso.[87] Deborah's daughter Martha was married to Winckworth Tonge, an Irish army officer who resided in Windsor, served as the colony's naval officer, and held an assembly seat for much of the period between 1759 and 1792. Before the American Revolution, Deborah and her unmarried daughter Grizelda Elizabeth taught girls in the Cottnam home in Salem, Massachusetts, but they were forced by Patriot hostility to move back to Nova Scotia in 1775. Two years later they were operating a boarding and day school for the colonial elite in Halifax, its numbers expanded by the first wave of Loyalists. In a letter to her aunts in Boston in November 1777, fifteen-year-old Loyalist Rebecca Byles reported that she and her sisters attended Cottnam's "Female Academy," her younger sisters to learn "plain sewing & Reading," she to "Writing, learning French (parley vous Francais Mademoiselle) and Dancing."[88]

It is from the pen of Rebecca Byles that we receive an oft-quoted comment on the gendered nature of education in this period. Boys, she opined, were poorly educated because they were "all intended for the Army or Navy, or some Post under Government, where neither Knowledge [n]or Honesty are required." In contrast, she maintained, "Girls ... have the best Education the place affords, and the accomplishment of their Minds is attended to as well as the adorning of their Persons; in a few years I expect to see Women fill the most important Offices in Church and State."[89] It was not only the daughters of the Loyalist elite who took up new ideas about the status of women. A harbinger of the "New Dispensationalism" that would call into question conventional Christian morality was recorded in 1791 by New Light preacher John Payzant, who reported that Lydia Randall from Cornwallis had publicly announced the libertarian notion that "marriage was from the Devil" and "that she had sooner see [young women] have children by any Man [than] to marry."[90]

A few Loyalists included libraries among their household effects, and added to them by purchasing books directly from publishers in Britain or from booksellers such as Alexander Morrison who set up shop in Halifax in 1786. Even peddlers sometimes included a book or two, most often a Bible, almanac, spelling book, or even a music primer, in their backpacks.[91] Many people believed that literature should be devoted to moral improvement, but the jury was still out on the value of novels, which became popular after the publication of *Pamela, or Virtue Rewarded* by Samuel Richardson in 1740. For some Nova Scotians, the novel was added to drinking, dancing, and frivolous fashion on the list of evils to be avoided by right-thinking people. When Rebecca Bailey, the nineteen-year-old daughter of the Anglican rector of Annapolis Royal, absconded to Boston in 1801, he blamed her behaviour on having become a "reader of novels and romances" and being seized by the "religious prensy or disorder" sweeping the community. The flight to Boston was all part of a piece for an inconsolable Loyalist father who disapproved of novels, of evangelical enthusiasm, and of the United States.[92]

Moralists were particularly disgusted with Halifax, where the presence of sojourning soldiers and sailors ensured that grog shops and prostitution flourished. To add to the ethical challenge, the military sponsored live theatre, which often involved ribald humour and thinly veiled political criticism. Dramatic performances by local and visiting thespians had been held in venues such as the Great Pontack Inn since the 1750s, but conditions for theatre-goers improved when the Garrison Officers' Theatrical Society launched the New Grand Theatre on Argyle Street on 28 February 1789. Capable of holding up to five hundred patrons, the New Grand opened with productions of Shakespeare's *The Merchant of Venice* and Arthur Murphy's farce *The Citizen* to a large and enthusiastic audience.[93] Two weeks later the garrison presented *The Beaux Stratagem*, a late Restoration comedy by Irish-born playwright George Farquhar. The announcement for this production in the *Nova Scotia Gazette and Weekly Chronicle* made a plea for "the ladies" to "dress their heads as low as possible, as otherwise the persons sitting behind cannot have the sight of the stage," a reference to the cumbersome headdresses fashionable for women in this period.

New enthusiasms percolating in the North Atlantic world in the late eighteenth century were propelled by voluntary organizations, both religious and secular. They were hallmarks of an engaged citizenry, who increasingly exerted their influence on society and pursued their interests through cooperative endeavours outside the family and the formal political arena. By participating in organized sociability, they were laying the foundations of a strong civil society in a world where death, migration, and war put kinship ties to the test.[94] Dissenting churches were the most obvious example of voluntarism, and their "extracurricular" activities, which included prayer meetings, revivals, and Sunday school, brought people together on a denominational basis for intellectual stimulation and social interaction.[95] Singing schools, usually taught in the winter months by an itinerant or local singing master, were also promoted by many churches, although not the more radical wing of Presbyterianism, where even Isaac Watt's hymns were forbidden. A prolific poet, Henry Alline wrote hymns that became a popular feature of public worship, and can still be found in evangelical Christian hymnbooks.[96]

Non-denominational service organizations, meanwhile, promoted charity and self-help, none more successfully than the Freemasons, who sustained fourteen separate lodges in Halifax by the end of the eighteenth century, most of them associated with military regiments based in the town. Halifax also boasted several coffee houses, which sold a wider array of beverages than the name implies. Like taverns, coffee houses were popular venues for meetings, and served as places to pick up mail and to read newspapers from home and abroad.[97] Nova Scotians might have been on the periphery of the Atlantic world, but they were no less engaged in the latest cultural trends because of that.

~~~

The American Revolution marks an important watershed in Nova Scotia's modern history. At a local level, the arrival of the Loyalists completed Britain's ascendancy in Acadie/Mi'kma'ki.[98] Henceforth, Nova Scotia evolved in the context of an expanding British Empire, which hardly skipped a beat with the loss of the Thirteen Colonies. This did not mean that political culture and relationships among the colony's heterogeneous peoples remained static. As Maya Jasanoff has noted, the "spirit of 1776" launched the United States on the road to democratic republicanism, but the "spirit of 1783" inspired another experiment in North America, one characterized by constitutional monarchy, centralized government, and humanitarian ideals.[99] Both were ultimately based on liberal principles and rule of law. What separated Nova Scotia (and British North America generally) from the United States, historian Jerry Bannister argues, was loyalism, not liberalism, an ideology that continues to be debated and to evolve throughout the North Atlantic world.[100]

Chapter Nine

Entering the Nineteenth Century, 1792–1820

In 1792 the name "Nova Scotia" applied only to a stubby peninsula jutting into the Atlantic Ocean. Much of this area's best arable land was now claimed by immigrants, the majority of whom had arrived from other British colonies in North America after 1749. Although its frontier character was gradually receding, Nova Scotia remained underdeveloped and outmigration had become a worrying trend. Economic conditions improved dramatically during Britain's wars with France and the United States between 1793 and 1815, but post-war retrenchment forced painful adjustments. Among them was the restoration of Cape Breton to Nova Scotia's jurisdiction in 1820, where it has since, and sometimes resentfully, remained. By the dawn of the new century, immigration from Ireland and Scotland was resetting the balance of European and American-born settler populations and pushing the Mi'kmaq further to the margins, but everyone faced the challenge of a new world order focused on making progress in human affairs.

The French Revolutionary and Napoleonic Wars

Following the outbreak of the French Revolution in 1789, Britain became embroiled in another war with France. The final round of the Anglo–French rivalry began early in 1793, when Britain joined the coalition of European countries resolved to stop revolutionary France from trying to impose its republican principles on everyone else. In 1799 Napoleon Bonaparte engineered a coup against the dysfunctional French republic, and then concentrated power in his own hands. After little more than a year of peace following the Treaty of Amiens, signed in March 1802, Napoleon's ambitions to expand his empire across Europe prolonged the conflict until 1815. As British authorities struggled to contain their nemesis, they ruffled feathers in the United States, which

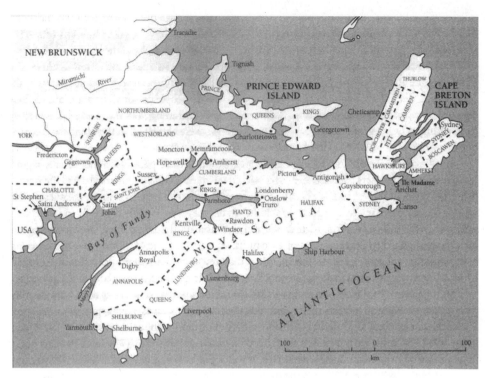

Map 9.1. Nova Scotia and Cape Breton at the End of the Eighteenth Century.
Adapted from R. Cole Harris, ed., *Historical Atlas of Canada, I: From the Beginning to 1800* (Toronto: University of Toronto Press, 1987), plate 32, and Margaret R. Conrad and James K. Hiller, *Atlantic Canada: A History*, 3rd ed. (Don Mills, ON: Oxford University Press, 2015), 108.

declared a second war of independence against its former mother country. The War of 1812 in North America brought the global conflict closer to home – but not too close – and provided Nova Scotians with unprecedented opportunities to line their pockets.

During the first phase of the war with France, American shippers proved more adept than their Nova Scotian counterparts in supplying the expanding overseas demand for fish, foodstuffs, and timber. This situation was abetted by the Treaty of Amity and Commerce – commonly called Jay's Treaty, after the American chief justice who helped negotiate the agreement – signed in 1794, which addressed contentious issues between Britain and the United States arising from the American Revolutionary War. In addition to abandoning its fur-trading posts south of the Great Lakes, Britain gave American shippers access to their West Indies trade, which perpetuated Nova Scotia's disadvantage against its closest competitors.

Prospects for the colony's merchants and producers gradually improved after 1803 as Napoleon extended his reach across continental Europe and relations between Britain and the United States deteriorated. With the Navigation Acts working in their favour and alternative sources of supply cut off, Nova Scotians found ready markets in Britain for their exports, and began competing successfully in the carrying trade to the West Indies. Halifax became a busy entrepôt for cargoes shipped under convoy to Britain and the Caribbean, while outlying ports benefited from opportunities for trade and privateering. Making a good situation even better, the expanded British military and naval presence in the colony generated investment in defence infrastructure and increased the supply of hard currency. Julian Gwyn estimates that British spending in the colony between 1793 and 1815 amounted to £5 million.[1] While much of the capital drained away to distant suppliers, enough remained to support the claim that this period marked a new phase of economic development. The founding of the Halifax Committee of Trade in 1804 (and resuscitated in 1822 as the Halifax Chamber of Commerce) signalled the growing sense of collective purpose among a mercantile elite that had a major impact on Nova Scotia's destiny.[2]

Timber was the most important commodity for a pre-industrial empire based on sea power.[3] Beginning in the mid-eighteenth century, Britain had reserved large stands of forests in North America for the Royal Navy, but most of its supplies still came from the Baltic region. After Napoleon gained control of sea routes to northern Europe, Britain introduced tariff policies to develop a secure supply of ship timber from North America. New Brunswick emerged as the quintessential "timber colony," but Nova Scotia also benefited from the almost unlimited demand for forest products to keep the Royal Navy afloat. Shipbuilding, which had been gaining ground since the 1780s, flourished in Halifax and in outports such as Liverpool, Shelburne, Yarmouth, Annapolis Royal, and Pictou. Although most vessels were built primarily to handle the growing coastal trade and for privateering, a few were employed in overseas trade and sometimes sold in Britain and the West Indies. Investment in shipbuilding in this period was larger than in any other sector of the Nova Scotia economy, with the possible exception of agriculture, which also expanded under the stimulus of wartime demand for grains, hay, livestock, and potatoes.[4]

William Forsyth emerged as one of the most successful of a new generation of ambitious Scottish entrepreneurs who figured prominently in mercantile activities throughout British North America. Having gained business experience on the River Clyde, Forsyth moved to Halifax in 1784, and quickly established commercial contacts in New Brunswick, Lower Canada, and Newfoundland. He exchanged goods dispatched by his Scottish partners and various British manufacturers for fish and timber, which were shipped to markets in the North Atlantic region. In 1788 Forsyth's company won a seven-year contract to provide the Royal Navy with masts, yards, and spars, demand for which skyrocketed after 1793. Forsyth was appointed to the council in 1801 and participated in a number of unsuccessful development schemes, including plans to build a canal from Halifax to the Bay of Fundy, to establish a chartered bank, and to secure a twenty-one-year monopoly on coal mining in the colony. Forsyth moved back to Scotland in 1809, leaving his partner John Black, also from Scotland, to supervise the company's Halifax operations, which finally wound down when the wars ended.[5]

As Britain's primary naval base in North America, Halifax thrived under the impact of war. The naval yard expanded in size, the military complement grew, and the demand for labour escalated. With rising wages as an incentive, migrants from outlying communities and from Ireland moved to Halifax, which boasted a population approaching 8,500 by the turn of the century. The Vice-Admiralty Court was kept busy throughout the war assessing enemy shipping and contraband-carrying neutral vessels captured on the high seas by the Royal Navy and privateers. And, as in previous wars, the brothels and taverns of lower town were periodically flooded with soldiers and sailors eager to let off steam before shipping out to their next assignment.

Halifax also hosted more exotic sojourners whose temporary presence kept colonial tongues wagging. From 1794 to 1800, King George III's son, Prince Edward Augustus, and his French mistress, Julie de St-Laurent, made their home in Nova Scotia. As commander of the British military forces in the region, Prince Edward (who in 1799 became the Duke of Kent and Strathearn) attempted to improve defences and to impose strict military discipline, which included drilling the garrison on the Grand Parade every morning at 5 a.m. Unimpressed by the dilapidated state of the town's public buildings, he inspired the construction of three exquisite round structures – St George's Church of England, the Old Town Clock, and the Prince's Lodge Rotunda – which still bear testimony to the elegance of Georgian architecture. In November 1798 the British government approved a proposal to rename St John's Island after the popular young prince, who forsook his mistress in 1818 to produce a legitimate heir to the throne. The future Queen Victoria was born on 24 May the following year.[6]

In 1796 nearly 550 Maroons, freedom fighters recently defeated in a war with Jamaican authorities, were exiled to Nova Scotia. The men were put to work on public and private projects in Halifax, and organized into a militia unit to defend the town from a potential French invasion. Spurred by a grant from the Jamaican government, Lieutenant Governor John Wentworth tried to make the exiles comfortable in their new homes located in Preston, Boydville (Sackville), and other areas outside the capital. Not surprisingly, the Maroons had difficulty adjusting to their new environment. After their first difficult winter and efforts by Wentworth to exploit them as labourers on his property in Preston, they petitioned the British government to find them a more congenial place to live. Authorities on both sides of the Atlantic were slow to accede to their wishes, but most of them were finally shipped to Sierra Leone in 1800. Accustomed to hunting down runaway slaves in Jamaica, they assisted the governor of Sierra Leone in crushing an uprising initiated by a group of Black Loyalists demanding a "settler constitution." Among the Maroons who stayed behind in Nova Scotia was Wentworth's mistress, Sarah Colley, whose son George Wentworth Colley inherited his father's summer house in Preston.[7]

Nova Scotia also served as a temporary home for prisoners of war. As soon as hostilities were declared, an expedition launched from Halifax captured the French islands of St-Pierre and Miquelon, returning with more than six hundred prisoners. Engagements at sea soon brought a steady stream of French and a few Spanish captives. While some of them were housed in military barracks or on prison ships anchored in the harbour, others were allowed to wander freely in the town until their release was negotiated. The presence of potentially dangerous sojourners created tensions between civilian and military authorities in Halifax, leading to a decision in 1803 to build prison facilities on Melville Island (actually a peninsula) on the North West Arm. Some 1,535 French prisoners were housed there between 1803 and 1815. During the War of 1812, the arrival of more than 8,000 Americans captured on privateers and in battles in Upper and Lower Canada led to the expansion of the Melville Island facilities.[8] Prisoners who died during their incarceration were buried in graves on adjacent Deadman's Island.

The Mi'kmaq posed little immediate threat, but authorities worried that they might complicate security in the region. After war was declared, George Henry Monk, who had been superintendent of Indian Affairs in the early 1780s, offered his services, which were called upon when Mi'kmaq began gathering near Windsor in the autumn of 1793. Wentworth authorized gifts of food and clothing so that "the peace of our scattered Inhabitants may not be disturbed by them, and also that they will join in case of an invasion." Both Monk and Wentworth understood that extreme poverty among the Mi'kmaq was a major cause of their discontent, and British authorities were initially sympathetic to providing annual relief, but plans to survey reserves of land and to support farming initiatives failed to materialize. When the Mi'kmaq applied for land grants, bureaucrats offered only licences of occupation, perhaps fearing the hostility of settlers who coveted "unoccupied" land for themselves and their offspring.[9]

The War of 1812

Relations between Britain and the United States, which were reasonably amicable in the aftermath of the Treaty of Paris, deteriorated during the lengthy war with France. As a neutral country, the United States insisted on its right to trade with both sides, offering plenty of opportunity to offend one or other of the belligerents.[10] Both Britain and France insisted on searching neutral merchant vessels for contraband, and imposed harsh penalties for violations – typically the confiscation of the ship and its cargo. In the early years of the war, France was as aggressive as Britain in the matter of neutral shipping, but the balance of naval power shifted after Nelson's victory at Trafalgar in 1805. Napoleon tried to regain the initiative in 1806 by issuing a decree forbidding all French, allied, and neutral trade with Britain. In response, British authorities issued orders-in-council blockading French and allied ports and requiring neutral vessels to be inspected at British ports before sailing to Europe. France retaliated by declaring that it would seize any neutral ship that obeyed these regulations.

Caught in the crossfire, President Thomas Jefferson imposed a temporary embargo on American trade to all belligerents in December 1807. This initiative crippled American exporters and also wreaked havoc with the British war effort, which depended on supplies from, or shipped through the United States. In an effort to circumvent the embargo, British authorities granted "free port" status to Halifax, Saint John, Shelburne, and St Andrews. New England shippers, angered by Jefferson's trade restrictions, took advantage of this strategy. As a result, Britain continued to receive American imports, and the designated free ports became busy commercial centres in the expanding regional economy.

The growth of the American merchant marine to meet the wartime demand added another source of friction by challenging the Royal Navy's efforts to maintain its wartime complement of more than 100,000 sailors. During the course of the war, thousands of actual and potential

British naval recruits attempted to avoid the Royal Navy's harsh discipline and low pay for more lucrative positions on American merchant ships. Britain's attempt to retrieve deserters and draft-dodgers from American vessels created enormous resentment in the fledgling republic. In 1807 American outrage reached new heights when the British warship *Leopard* opened fire on the USS *Chesapeake* off the coast of Virginia, killing or wounding twenty-one men and taking four alleged deserters for trial in Halifax. All four of the prisoners had served in the Royal Navy and were technically deserters, but only one, Jankin Ratford, was British-born. He was hanged from the yardarm before the assembled fleet, while the other three captives, two of them African Americans, remained in prison, no doubt relieved when their death-defying sentences of 500 lashes were commuted.[11]

Tensions over "free trade and sailors' rights," coupled with Indigenous policy on the western frontier, finally goaded the United States into declaring war on Britain in June 1812 and launching an attack against Upper Canada. Buffered by the New England states, whose leaders refused to participate in the war, Nova Scotia was spared a military invasion, but it was well positioned to benefit from what was essentially a naval war between two unequal belligerents. Trade with the United States was now illegal, but it was sanctioned by Lieutenant Governor Sir John Coape Sherbrooke, who was determined to keep supply lines open. Nowhere was clandestine trade more successfully pursued than "along the lines" in the Bay of Fundy, where colonial products such as coal, fish, grindstones, gypsum, and timber, together with British manufactures, were exchanged for American and Caribbean products. According to the historian Joshua Smith, the region surrounding the Bay of Fundy emerged as one of the great smuggling centres of the North Atlantic world in this period, ranking with St Mary's on the Georgia–Spanish Florida border and Heligoland in the North Sea.[12] Even legitimate trade flourished, with the documented revenues collected at the port in Halifax tripling between 1812 and 1814.[13]

As was the case during the American Revolutionary War, the United States commissioned privateer vessels to attack British shipping. They inflicted considerable damage during the first year of hostilities and caused panic in coastal communities, but by the summer of 1813 the Royal Navy had imposed an effective blockade of the entire American coast. In Halifax, the Vice-Admiralty Court processed 714 "prizes" seized from the enemy during the war, more than double the number brought to judgment between 1793 and 1811.[14] Naval ships made two-thirds of the captures, but several of the forty-two local privateers that preyed on enemy shipping were highly successful.[15] The *Liverpool*

Packet, a former slave ship purchased in 1811 at prize court by Enos Collins, is reputed to have captured fifty vessels worth in total $1.5 million.

A native of the Planter community of Liverpool, Enos Collins emerged as one of Nova Scotia's most successful entrepreneurs. He moved to Halifax before the War of 1812 to be better positioned to pursue his mercantile interests, which included supplying British armies involved in the European campaign against Napoleon. Along with other merchants, naval officers, and government officials in the capital, Collins enhanced his fortune by buying captured vessels at prize auctions and selling their contents elsewhere at immense profit. Success in this enterprise was ensured through corrupt practices whereby captured ships and their contents were undervalued by court officials so that bidders with inside information could enhance their profits.[16] Alexander Croke, who presided over the Vice-Admiralty Court from 1801 to 1814, was admired for his legal expertise, but thoroughly despised by many people in Halifax for his bad temper, inflexible judicial style, and the high fees he charged for his services.[17]

On Sunday, 6 June 1813, Haligonians thrilled to the spectacle of HMS *Shannon* arriving in port with the infamous USS *Chesapeake* in tow after a brief but bloody engagement off Boston (Figure 9.1). The town's citizens, among them a young Thomas Chandler Haliburton, flocked to the harbour to witness the scene, and would long remember this "most brilliant achievement," which at the time and subsequently was much memorialized in image and song. At the helm of *Shannon* was twenty-two-year-old Provo Wallis, who assumed command after Captain Philip Broke was seriously wounded and his second lieutenant killed. The son of a Halifax shipwright, Wallis was registered on the books of several naval vessels from the age of four, and went to sea when he was fourteen years old. After a long and distinguished career in the Royal Navy, he was named admiral of the fleet in 1877. By that time he had abandoned his native soil for England, where he died in 1892 at the age of 100.[18]

The majority of Nova Scotians employed by the Royal Navy in this period had little choice in the matter. With volunteer recruits always in short supply, the coast guard hovered outside Halifax harbour to impress crews serving on merchant and fishing vessels entering the port, while residents from outlying communities ran for cover when a Royal Navy ship appeared on the horizon. Authorities tried to restrict the operation of press gangs on shore, but relented if the lack of sailors threatened to render naval vessels inoperable. Since Nova Scotian ports were popular places for mariners to desert their posts, press gangs were also often on the lookout for their missing comrades. Most warrants for "the

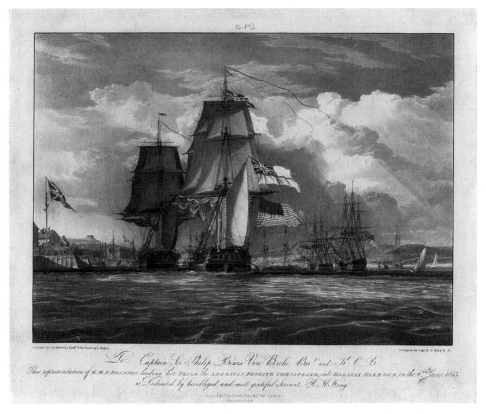

Figure 9.1. *HMS Shannon leading her prize, the American Frigate Chesapeake into Halifax Harbour, on the 6th June 1813*, by John C. Schetky. The arrival of HMS *Shannon* in Halifax Harbour with the USS *Chesapeake* in tow on 6 June 1813 was celebrated throughout the British Empire, and was later commemorated with this painting by Scottish marine artist John C. Schetky. Nova Scotia Archives, Documentary Art Collection, accession no. 1979–147 142.4/ negative N-2301 CN-1139.

press" on land eventually included quotas and time restrictions, along with exemptions for freeholders, merchant crews, and militiamen, but desperate naval captains sometimes ignored the letter of the law. In 1805 anti-press gang riots in Halifax, which left one man dead and others injured, brought more restrictions to impressment in Nova Scotia ports, among them exemptions for fishermen. This and other concessions eased tensions but failed to stop unauthorized conscription until peace was declared in 1815.[19]

With its outstanding seafaring tradition in the fisheries and the West Indies trade, Liverpool was especially hard hit by impressment. Historian Keith Mercer has calculated that some two hundred Liverpool men were pressed into service between 1759 and 1815. Half of the unwilling sailors were plucked from Liverpool's privateer vessels, which ranged as far as the Caribbean in pursuit of enemy shipping.[20] The stress that the Royal Navy's impressment polices inflicted on the small community can readily be gleaned from entries in the diary of Simeon Perkins, himself an investor in Liverpool's privateering ventures. In June 1805, Perkins reported that the arrival of HM Schooner *Whiting* created "Some rumpus" in the town and resulted in three black men barring themselves in his house after being "chased by the men of wars people."[21] As this comment suggests, disadvantaged minorities often bore the brunt of the press in Nova Scotia, as did recent male immigrants from Britain and the United States, most of whom were fair game.

The tide of war turned decisively in the summer of 1814. With Napoleon exiled to Elba, Britain focused its attention on North America. British troops and freed slaves led by Rear Admiral George Cockburn attacked Washington in August, burning the presidential residence and other public buildings before being forced to withdraw. Later in the same month, a British army of more than 2,500 men under the command of Lieutenant Governor Sherbrooke set sail from Halifax to occupy part of the coast of Maine, which was achieved with little resistance from the local inhabitants. The Federalist governments of the New England states were so opposed to the war that they sent delegates to a secret meeting in Hartford, Connecticut, in November to discuss a separate peace with the British. Even the possibility of secession from the United States was mooted. Although Britain's long-term goal was to establish a colony named New Ireland in the occupied territory, it initially served primarily as a conduit for a lucrative trade, much of it in prize goods seized from American vessels condemned in Halifax's Vice-Admiralty Court.[22]

These dramatic developments encouraged diplomatic efforts to bring the war to a speedy conclusion. By the Treaty of Ghent, signed on 24 December 1814, both parties agreed to peace and the return of captured territory. No mention was made of "free trade and sailors' rights," and these issues never again became a source of contention between the two nations. While Nova Scotia's militia was at the ready throughout the war, it saw little action. Only one of its members, William Harding of the 22nd Battalion, claimed compensation for his wounds, the result of the accidental discharge of his musket.[23]

At the Battle of Waterloo in June 1815, a coalition army led by the Duke of Wellington ended the military exploits associated with Napoleon Bonaparte, who had escaped from Elba earlier in the year. Nova Scotians no doubt breathed a collective sigh of relief when they learned that he had finally surrendered to the British squadron at Rochefort in July. On 4 September, eighteen-year-old Louisa Collins, living near Cole Harbour outside of Halifax, noted in her diary (with decidedly uncertain spelling) that "there is nuse of Bonnyparts being taken – I hope it is true, there is no punnishment two grate fer sich a rech--homenny lives has bin sacrefised for his ambition."[24]

Although the War of 1812 brought no territorial gains, the Anglo-American Convention of 1818, which tied up loose ends resulting from the war, redefined fishing rights. American vessels were no longer permitted to fish within three nautical miles of the Nova Scotia shoreline, but they were granted the right to enter bays and harbours in the Maritime region to take shelter, for repairs, and to secure wood and water – a convenient loophole for smuggling, which had become a way of life in most outport communities. The United States was also granted access to the inshore fisheries of Labrador and along large portions of Newfoundland's coast. In an earlier agreement, St-Pierre, Miquelon, and fishing rights in northwestern Newfoundland were restored to France. By making these concessions, the British ensured that the United States and France remained major competitors in European and Caribbean markets for cod.

The Convention also addressed American claims for the return of, or compensation for, the slaves in the Chesapeake region who had sought freedom behind British lines during the 1814 campaign. By the time the agreement was signed, more than 2,000 freed African Americans, known as "Black Refugees," had moved to the Maritimes, the vast majority of them to Nova Scotia. Those who survived the post-war smallpox epidemic and unhealthy living conditions in temporary locations such as the Halifax Poor House and Melville Island Prison were settled in Halifax, Preston, Hammonds Plains, Beechville, and along the roads to Truro and Windsor. Like the Black Loyalists, they received small land grants, waited many years for them to be processed, and were shamefully treated by their white neighbours.[25] The assembly even went so far in 1815 as to urge the prohibition of further Black immigration because "the proportion of Africans already in the country is productive of many inconveniences; and that the introduction of more must tend to the discouragement of white labourers and servants, as well as to the establishment of a separate and marked class of people, unfitted by nature to this climate, or to an association with the rest of His Majesty's

Colonists."[26] Despite such hateful attitudes, the Black Refugees valued their freedom and the anti-slavery sentiment that had prompted Parliament to abolish the African slave trade in 1807.

Slavery was still practised in many British colonies, but its days were numbered in Nova Scotia. Growing anti-slavery sentiment, the lack of statutory legal protection, and the agency of those suffering enslavement put slave holders at a distinct disadvantage. In 1803 James Delancey, a prominent Loyalist in Annapolis Royal, tried unsuccessfully in court to regain his slave, known only as Jack, who had escaped to Halifax to work as a free man. With their unhappy chattel increasingly following Jack's example, twenty-seven residents from the counties of Annapolis and Digby petitioned the legislature in 1807 for the "right of holding property in Negroes upon the same ground that they possessed the right of holding any other species of property," or to be granted compensation. As in previous efforts to secure formal legalization of slavery in Nova Scotia, their pleas fell on deaf ears.[27]

New Scotland Confirmed

"Happy state of Nova Scotia!" one anonymous author wrote in a letter to the *Acadian Recorder* in May 1814. "[A]mongst all this tumult we have lived in peace and security; invaded only by a numerous host of American doubloons and dollars, which have swept away the contents of our stores and shops like a torrent."[28] Nova Scotians were so flush with cash in 1814 that the legislature voted a grant of £2,500 for "the distressed Inhabitants of Upper Canada," who had suffered greatly as contending armies criss-crossed their territory.[29] A year later, economic conditions warranted less generosity. Markets and military investment shrivelled at war's end and in 1819 the Halifax naval yard closed completely in favour of Hamilton, Bermuda.[30] With American producers again shipping directly to Britain and the West Indies, Halifax no longer played the role of linchpin in the expanding North Atlantic trade.

In this context, hard currency, including the much-valued British sterling and Spanish dollars (on which "Halifax Currency" was based) quickly vanished. "A man at the present time may travel from Cape Sable to Pictou and not find a dollar in his way," Isaiah Shaw, assembly member for Granville Township, lamented in 1818.[31] Not everyone was pessimistic about what Nova Scotia had to offer. Immigration from Britain, which had continued throughout the wars, escalated in peacetime, while a new generation of Nova Scotians built on the successes of their immigrant forbears to create a moderate level of comfort and, for some,

Table 9.1. Estimated Population of Nova Scotia and Cape Breton, 1791–1817

Year	Nova Scotia	Cape Breton	Total
1791	45,000	1,500	47,000
1801	63,000	3,000	66,000
1811	71,000	5,000	76,000
1817	81,700	8,000	89,000

Source: Julian Gwyn, *Excessive Expectations: Maritime Commerce and the Economic Development of Nova Scotia, 1740–1870* (Montreal: McGill-Queen's University Press, 1998), 23.

great opulence. The colony's population nearly doubled between 1793 and 1820, a likely sign that economic growth would follow (Table 9.1).

In this period, Nova Scotia finally began receiving a large number of settlers reflecting its seventeenth-century name.[32] Scots arrived both from the more prosperous Lowlands, where the new industrial order was beginning to take root, and from the Hebrides and the Highlands, where tenant farmers were being pushed out by a variety of factors, including the disintegration of the clan system in the wake of the Battle of Culloden, escalating rents imposed by profit-seeking landlords, and a population boom precipitated by the lowly potato, which improved the general health of the population. By the 1790s, the enclosure movement, which substituted sheep for tenant farmers, added impetus to the exodus. The collapse of the kelp industry (important in making soap and glass) in the second decade of the nineteenth century and the recession that followed the Napoleonic Wars further increased the movement of Scots to overseas locations.[33] In 1803 British authorities tried to staunch the flow of emigrants with the Passenger Vessels Act, which imposed regulations to mitigate the cramped conditions on ocean-going vessels, but it had little impact. After the war British authorities sanctioned the "shovelling out of paupers" to the colonies as long as they could finance their own way.

Nova Scotia and Cape Breton were popular destinations for hard-pressed Scots looking to improve their prospects. Living in what was primarily a barter economy, tenant farmers in Scotland had difficulty mobilizing the capital required to move to more distant frontiers in the United States and Upper Canada, which arguably offered better land and more opportunities than the Maritime region. Industrial jobs were expanding in Britain, but they were shunned by many tenants who dreamed of becoming lairds in their own right and of replicating a way of life that was now under intense pressure. In eastern Nova Scotia and Cape Breton, land was still easy to come by, and with its rolling

hills and ocean access, the area was reminiscent of their beloved homeland. Many immigrants simply squatted on unoccupied land and applied for ownership later, which was almost always granted. This was
especially the case in Cape Breton, where the processes for surveying
and granting land were uneven at best. Inevitably, those who arrived
first occupied the best locations, and those who came later were rele-
gated to interior districts with poor soil and little access to rudimentary
transportation routes, creating what historian Rusty Bittermann has described as a "hierarchy of the soil" that defined social relationships in
most rural areas.[34]

The overseas rush of Scots was facilitated by the expanding timber
trade, which continued after the war and offered convenient transatlantic passage on vessels bound for Charlottetown, Halifax, Pictou, Sydney, and other seaport towns in the Maritimes. Since most of the land
in Prince Edward Island was owned by proprietors, immigrants who
arrived there often moved across the Northumberland Strait to access
freehold tenure. The majority of Scots emigrated in kin and community
groups, and in some cases were mobilized by self-appointed agents
such as "Major" Simon Fraser. The son of a military officer who had
settled in Pictou after the American Revolution, Fraser had business
interests in Fort William, Scotland, and began shipping migrants to Pictou in 1791. He soon earned the nickname "Nova Scotia" for his zealous recruiting practices. Once the migrations started, a steady stream of
family and friends followed. Because immigration records are incom-
plete and many ship captains dumped their human ballast wherever it
was convenient, it is impossible to determine exactly how many Scots
settled in Nova Scotia and Cape Breton between 1773 and 1851. The
scholarly consensus puts the number conservatively at 50,000, making
the Scots the largest ethnic group to settle in these two colonies.[35] With
their arrival, the Scots, who were no different from other settlers in their
attitudes, usurped the last refuge of the Mi'kmaq, who now had few
areas of their homeland to call their own.

Scottish immigrants were more diverse than their stereotype as
a clannish, penny-pinching people suggests. Although a significant
proportion were Presbyterians, the church had fractured in the 1730s
and 1740s, and the schisms followed them across the Atlantic. Roman
Catholic Scots often stuck to themselves, and were accused by some
observers of being less ambitious than their Presbyterian neighbours.
Since many of the Catholic immigrants were Gaelic speakers, integration into an overwhelmingly Protestant anglophone society inevitably
took a little more time. In the end, the Pictou area, where most of the
best land was taken up by the first decade of the nineteenth century,

emerged as a predominantly Protestant community, while Antigonish attracted Catholic settlers, but neither county was homogeneous. Cape Breton attracted Protestants and Catholics in roughly equal numbers, many arriving from the islands of Barra, Harris, Lewis, and the Uists, in the Outer Hebrides.

With them the Highland Scots brought their rich musical and oral culture. Emigrating bards chronicled their leaving of Scotland and how they felt about their new homeland. John Maclean (1787–1848), born in Tiree, moved to Pictou County in 1819. He ultimately regretted his decision, as one of his Gaelic compositions, *The Deception*, suggests:

I soon discovered that far-away fields
are not so green as reported.
Imagine what a trying experience it is
to lose one's ears in the cold spring.

Allan MacDonald (1794–1868), who settled in Mabou, was happier in his new home, composing a song that outlined the advantages of New Scotland:

Now that you have come across the sea
to this fair land,
you will want for nothing the rest of your life;
everything prospers for us.
You'll get honey from flowers,
Sugar and tea;
Better than the land you left
With the rabble in charge of the forests.[36]

While most Scottish immigrants struggled to put down roots, a few had the resources to take advantage of the opportunities Nova Scotia had to offer. One of the most successful was Edward Mortimer, who, in the late 1780s, settled in Pictou, where he became a prosperous merchant. In addition to his interest in fish, timber, and shipping, he outbid his competitors in 1818 for a twenty-one-year lease to operate coal mines in the Pictou area. As the pre-eminent merchant in the county, he held a variety of local offices and sat in the assembly for two decades. Many immigrants in eastern Nova Scotia were perpetually indebted to him, prompting his friends in Halifax to dub him the "King of Pictou" and "our Oat Meal Emperor from the East." Mortimer's death in 1819 cut short his reign over Pictou, but his massive stone residence (later named Norway House) stood until 2013. It was built by carpenters and masons Mortimer brought from Scotland in 1810 especially to build a home worthy of his status.[37]

Ireland, like Scotland, was experiencing major social and economic upheavals. In the wake of the Irish Rebellion of 1798, the British Parliament passed the Acts of Union, which incorporated Ireland into the United Kingdom on 1 January 1801. Repressive measures against Roman Catholics under British rule, along with periodic famines among a poor tenant population overly dependent on the potato, contributed significantly to the stream of emigrants to North America. Newfoundland was the initial destination of Irish labourers involved in the cod fishery, and from there they often shipped to other North American ports. Poor Irish Catholics settled in remoter and often less fertile areas of Nova Scotia, worked in the colony's forest and seafaring industries, and were hired as outdoor labourers and domestic servants. As the most likely place in the colony to find wage-paying work, Halifax had been a magnet for Irish immigrants since its founding. By the 1830s more than a third of the town's population claimed Irish ancestry. Irish men were often accused of being addicted to alcohol and prone to violence, but research conducted in Halifax court records suggests that these traits were shared equally with most other residents in the hard-drinking town.[38]

In January 1786, the Charitable Irish Society was founded in Halifax to raise money for "the relief of such of their poor and indigent Countrymen and their Descendants as hereafter may be found worthy of their countenance and protection." The Society's articles of incorporation were signed by 136 members, an indication that Halifax had a substantial number of relatively well-heeled sons of Erin who were willing to assist "any of the Irish Nation who shall be reduced by sickness, Old age, shipwreck or other misfortune," without making a distinction with respect to religious affiliation.[39] The Society's roster included prominent politicians and businessmen, but none was more ambitious or more successful than its first president, Richard John Uniacke.

Born in 1753, Uniacke left Ireland as a young man and made his way to Philadelphia, where in 1774 he met Moses Delesdernier, who was recruiting settlers for Hopewell Township. After arriving in Nova Scotia, Uniacke married Delesdernier's twelve-year-old daughter, with whom he had a dozen children. Uniacke was briefly imprisoned for his suspected involvement in the Eddy Rebellion, but he was promptly released, enabling him to return to Ireland to study law. When he arrived back in Halifax in 1781, he used his Irish connections to rise quickly to prominence. His fellow countryman Governor John Parr appointed him solicitor general in 1781 and advocate general of the Vice-Admiralty

Court in 1784. The latter position was awarded as a consolation prize when Loyalist Samuel Salter Blowers was named attorney general. By 1815 Unaicke had amassed a considerable fortune from the fees that accrued from this lucrative office.

Loathed by many Loyalists for, among other things, his alleged Patriot leanings during the American Revolution, Uniacke managed to overcome all obstacles by the sheer force of his personality. Utterly fearless, he was twice challenged to a duel in the 1790s by Blowers, the second time in 1797 after Uniacke had given Jonathan Sterns, the Loyalist assembly member for Halifax, such a vicious public beating that it likely contributed to his death the following year.[40] The fracas revolved around Uniacke's success in bringing pressure to bear from the Colonial Office to insist that he be appointed attorney general over Sterns, who was Wentworth's candidate for the position. Uniacke's biographer Brian Cuthbertson notes that "Later generations remembered as grand and remarkable the sight of Uniacke and his six sons, all of whom were over six feet tall, walking through the streets of Halifax." His country home, Mount Uniacke, built during the War of 1812 on an 11,000-acre (4,450-hectare) estate northwest of Halifax, documents his rise from relative obscurity to the pinnacle of colonial society.[41]

Few people in Nova Scotia lived as well as the Uniackes. For post-war immigrants who often ended up in remoter areas of the colony, life could be grim. This was especially so in 1815, when a plague of field mice swept through the colony devouring crops – in some places so plentiful that they formed a "ridge like seaweed along the edge of the sea."[42] As if this tragedy were not enough, 1816 brought "the year without a summer," the result of the volcanic eruption of Mount Tambora in Indonesia the previous year.[43] The climate crisis, which brought frosts during the summer months, coincided with the government's decision to build a road from Halifax to Annapolis to accommodate soldiers whose regiments were disbanded after the war. With communities planned at Sherbrooke, Dalhousie, and Wellington, the road was designed to open the interior of the colony to settlement. About 270 members of the Royal Newfoundland Fencibles and the Nova Scotia Fencibles opted in 1816 to take up land offered on the proposed road; over the next few years, others followed their example. As was usually the case, soldiers, especially those without a family to help them get established on the land, made poor farmers. Despite considerable public expenditure on rations, implements, and wages, most of the settlers drifted away. Dalhousie and New Ross (the former Sherbrooke) survived, but as smaller communities than originally envisioned, and the road remained unfinished.[44]

Similar results followed the arrival in Halifax of one hundred Welsh immigrants aboard the ship *Fanny* in 1818, bringing smallpox with them. Fearing a pandemic, worried authorities urged vaccinations for residents living as far away as Hammonds Plains, and the council quickly approved a grant of £200 to help the survivors settle in Shelburne. Neither the four hundred white settlers nor the Mi'kmaq in the area welcomed the newcomers. After tense negotiations, seventeen adults and twenty-nine children settled on the western shores of the Roseway River, calling their community New Cambria. Welsh immigrants continued to arrive in the Maritimes in the post-war period, but most settled in New Brunswick. In 1819 the Nova Scotia assembly granted £90 towards building a road from Shelburne to Annapolis Royal as a means of introducing cash into the struggling community, but the majority of the Welsh settlers moved on.[45]

Unlike their predecessors, most nineteenth-century immigrants received no offers of provisions and implements to get them started on the land, and periodic efforts to provide assistance proved inadequate to the need. In 1818 one Halifax commentator noted that newcomers were allowed to wander neglected "through our streets – the outcasts of the old world, and intruders on the new." Many immigrants, their numbers impossible to determine precisely, shipped off to the United States or the Canadas soon after their arrival in Nova Scotia. Road-building projects provided temporary work, and 90,000 acres (36,400 hectares) of unoccupied Loyalist grants were escheated between 1819 and 1821, but these gestures were not enough to make the colony a haven for immigrants who had the wherewithal to settle elsewhere.[46]

Writing to a contact in England in 1812, William Hersey Otis Haliburton, the privileged offspring of New England Planters living in the Windsor area, summed up the traits of the multicultural society that had taken root in the colony since 1749:

The Irish are strong and ... often the best Labourers, but, in general, are not inventive or quick of apprehension, and are much addicted to strong Liquors. The English are the Best, and natural Farmers and Mechanics, but they are the least likely to come abroad. The Germans are the most industrious and persevering in every thing they undertake ... [but] they *will* drink, and are mulish if you interfere with them in their manner of doing their work [and] are not willing[ly] taught; the German women are the best Settlers America ever knew, laborious, persevering and as prolific as Rabbits. The New Englander would be the best Settlers were they steady'r. There are no ... people, in any degree so inventive, which quality to a new settler is invaluable ... but, in general, they are liable to shift about from one place or occupation to another, and ... [are], in general, inveterate Republicans. Black people are good House servants, and make very good common hands on board vessels; they make indifferent Country Labourers – and never become Masters of others ... [They are] sober, honest, industrious ... love their own Society and are very talkative.[47]

Haliburton ignored the Acadian, Mi'kmaq, and Scots in his commentary, but he underscored the ethnic stereotypes that were common among local elites and that would inform the writings of his son, Thomas Chandler, who became one of Nova Scotia's most celebrated authors.

Town and Country

Two decades of war lifted the financial gloom that had previously paralysed Nova Scotia's political life. By 1796 the colony's long-standing debt was discharged, and thereafter political tensions increasingly revolved around the division of the spoils. Elected assembly members were for the most part drawn from the same class of merchants, lawyers, and office holders that made up the governor's appointed council, so they were disinclined to demand political reform of the kind that sparked upheavals in the United States and France. Instead they debated how much money should be collected from customs and excise duties (the main source of public funds other than imperial grants), and where the income should be spent. The differences of opinion often fell along the fault line between town and country.

For much of this period, town-country tensions were manifested in the personalities of Sir John Wentworth and William Cottnam Tonge. The latter won a by-election in Newport Township in 1792, the year Wentworth became lieutenant governor.[48] The son of an Irish-born army officer, assembly member, and major landowner, Tonge's roots in the colony ran deep. His great-grandfather was Edward How, who had moved to Canso from Massachusetts in the early 1720s. While Wentworth championed the interests of Halifax merchants eager to reduce duties on imports, Tonge and his supporters were determined to spend windfall revenues on roads and other public improvements beyond the confines of Halifax. When the assembly tried to win the contest by withholding approval of revenue bills, the council blocked appropriations supported by the assembly. Deadlock and recriminations ensued.

Tonge's career signalled the rise of country towns whose merchants were prepared to challenge the dominance of the capital. In 1799 Tonge and two other prominent country representatives, James Fulton from Londonderry and Edward Mortimer from Pictou, ran for seats in Halifax County (which at the time encompassed much of central Nova Scotia), all four of which had previously been held by Wentworth's supporters. The three men topped the polls with the help of votes from outlying areas of the constituency, but Tonge was later disqualified as a representative for Halifax County because he lacked sufficient property qualifications there. As the member for Hants County, he remained a thorn in the side of the lieutenant governor. Tonge, who traded in gypsum, timber, and farm produce, brought popular pressure to bear on authorities to make Windsor a customs port, a policy that not only threatened the ascendancy of mercantile interests in Halifax, but also raised the spectre of democratic excesses among the masses.

Wentworth ultimately resolved to rid himself of the troublesome country squire. Using tactics that brought howls of protest from those who championed the rights of elected representatives, Wentworth refused to recognize Tonge's election as speaker of the assembly in 1806. The following year he ordered the sheriff in Hants County to suppress public meetings "professing reform," and dismissed Tonge as Naval Officer, a position that had been passed down from his father in 1792. The uproar that followed and the prospect of war with the United States prompted British authorities to replace Wentworth in 1808 with Sir George Prevost, whose military experience recommended him to the position.[49] Prevost made a point of courting Wentworth's goodwill and later in the year appointed him deputy commissary general for his military expedition to the West Indies. Following Prevost's successful campaign in Martinique, Tonge found positions in the West Indies and never returned to Nova Scotia.[50]

Prevost initially managed relations with the assembly better than his predecessor and even secured approval in 1809 for an excise duty on distilled liquors to defray the costs of arms and uniforms for the militia. When Prevost and the council agreed in 1810 to appropriate half of the Arms Fund to assist the churches, schools, and colleges of the Church of England, the assembly, whose membership was dominated by adherents of dissenting churches, cried foul.[51] The council also refused to accept the assembly's bill relating to the travelling expenses of its members. Since the cost of attending meetings in Halifax posed a considerable burden, country representatives were understandably aggrieved. Before these issues could be resolved, Prevost was appointed governor general of British North America and dispatched to Quebec. The War of 1812 diverted everyone's attention during the lieutenant governorship of Sir John Sherbrooke, who, like his predecessor, brought military experience to his position and followed Prevost to Quebec in 1816.[52]

Sherbrooke was replaced by George Ramsay, the 9th Earl of Dalhousie. A veteran of the recent wars, Dalhousie was an ambitious and conscientious Scot, determined to make his mark in colonial governance. To better achieve this goal, he toured the countryside, all the while keeping a journal and accompanied by his official draftsman, John Elliott Woolford. Both men bequeathed invaluable written and artistic records of life in colonial Nova Scotia. Dalhousie's aristocratic values made him uncomfortable with the levelling influences he encountered in the colony, and he was quick to detect the lack of ambition among ordinary folk. At the same time, he was critical of the exclusiveness of King's College, and spearheaded plans for an institution of higher learning open to men of all religious backgrounds. This initiative was launched in 1818 with £7,000 from the customs duties levied at Castine during the War of 1812. In 1820 Dalhousie laid the cornerstone on the Grand Parade for a college named in his honour, but lack of funds and political bickering postponed its opening.

One of the most contentious issues during Dalhousie's term in office was the lack of hard currency and the difficulty of assessing the value of the various coins and notes circulating in the colony. In 1818 the assembly debated a plan to create paper currency, but it was rejected because a majority of the members feared it would drive away any remaining coin. Farmers wanted government loans to tide them over until economic conditions improved, while merchants favoured creating a bank to manage currency, an idea that had been mooted as early as 1801, but deferred on the insistence of the "interior parts of the Country." Because of the standoff between the assembly and the council, neither a bank nor a province-wide system of loan offices – only Annapolis and Kings counties were briefly beneficiaries of this program – were approved, and the currency crisis rumbled on.[53]

By the time Dalhousie followed his predecessors on the well-worn path to Quebec in 1820, he and his council were at odds with the assembly on a number of other issues, including the rights of dissenting churches and road appropriations. When the assembly used a ruse to withhold funding for the militia in 1819, Dalhousie declared to be "disappointed & vexed that a very few cunning Yankees ... should have outwitted, & defeated me."He was so incensed with the speaker of the assembly, Simon Bradstreet Robie – that "ill tempered crab, deeply tinctured in Yankee principles" – that he was prepared to block his election for another term in office and, in a fit of pique, rejected the assembly's gift of 1,000 guineas upon his departure from Nova Scotia.[54] As Dalhousie's comments suggest, the tensions between town and country and the differences of class, culture, and values these designations seemed to imply had become a defining feature of colonial politics.

The Country in Bloom

Both town and country had been drawn closer to Britain during the French and Napoleonic Wars, but rural areas were less influenced by metropolitan standards than the capital. While British merchants, officers, and officials circulated through Halifax and the established churches of England and Scotland had pride of place there, outlying communities produced their own leaders and adopted their own religious perspectives. Authorities in Halifax tried to control their hinterland through the appointment of local officials over which they had almost total control, but the seacoasts were too porous and state powers too anemic to have an overwhelming impact. As a result, the two decades of war opened a space for the consolidation of a community life in the countryside that was neither British nor American but distinctly Nova Scotian.

Religion played a central role in how most Nova Scotians defined themselves at the turn of the nineteenth century. Whether they traced their origins to the Thirteen Colonies, Britain, or continental Europe, most settlers were heirs to a factional Christianity that was transatlantic in scope and that continued to evolve wherever it was planted. Dissenting beliefs – New Light Congregational, Methodist, Baptist, German Reformed, and Secession Church Presbyterian, among others – arrived with various waves of immigrants after 1749, and then struggled to find ways of remaining relevant in a new and pluralistic environment. Henry Alline drew on New Light Congregational practices during the American Revolution to give birth to what the historian David Bell describes as a "distinctive, self-confident religious culture," especially in the townships dominated by New England Planters.[55] To this powerful movement was added dissenters from the Church of England, who founded a separate Methodist church after the death of their leader John Wesley in 1791. Baptists were the radicals of their time, demanding a personal and public discipline of a uniquely high order, especially around issues of salvation (experiential awakening), baptism (adult immersion), and communion (closed to all but those baptized as an adult). By the time Presbyterianism began to take root in eastern Nova Scotia and Cape Breton, it had twice fractured over the relationship between church and state, first when Ebenezer Erskine led a secession from the established Church of Scotland in 1733 over the rights of the congregation to appoint ministers, and then when the Session Church divided over church governance into Burgher (civil oath-taking) and Associate Synod (non-juring Anti-Burgher) branches in 1747. Many of the "Foreign Protestants" from the German and Swiss states were Lutherans, the denomination whose namesake had launched the Reformation, and by the 1770s they, too, spawned a German Reformed wing in Nova Scotia.

The triumph of the Baptist church over its Congregational and Methodist rivals is one of the most significant and surprising developments in this period. As late as 1797, there were at most four Baptist churches in Nova Scotia, three of them in the communities of Halifax, Preston, and Shelburne, which had significant black populations.[56] The other was located in Horton (now Wolfville). Three years later, the Nova Scotia Baptist Association was founded, an achievement attributed to Horton pastor Thomas Handley Chipman, a close associate of Alline and his associate Edward Manning who had moved from Ireland as a young child with his family to Falmouth Township. Within a few years of its founding, the Baptist Association had absorbed most Congregational and Allinite churches according to a "mixed church" plan whereby both close and open communion congregations were accepted. John Burton, who ministered to his mostly black congregation in Halifax beginning in 1795 according to close communion principles, remained outside the Baptist Association until 1811. The Congregationalists in Liverpool also resisted the Baptist tide. Their pastor was Allen's brother-in-law John Payzant, who had been trained by Jesuits in Quebec, and might have harboured strong feelings about the murder of his step-father by Edward Manning's father in 1776.[57] Bishop Charles Inglis, who spent much of his time ensconced on his rural estate near Aylesford in the Annapolis Valley, was appalled by "the rage for dipping," which he claimed was "frequently performed in a very indelicate manner before vast collections of people."[58] Such condemnations notwithstanding, the Baptists went from strength to strength.

The abrupt shift of allegiance to the Baptist church resulted in part from an outbreak in the 1790s of religious enthusiasm, known as the "New Dispensationalism," which denied the necessity of formal church rules and stressed a direct relationship with God. While this position was in keeping with Alline's teachings, the scandalous personal behaviour – much of it relating to sexual licence, alcohol consumption, and questionable religious rituals – of the new dispensationalists brought widespread censure, and was certainly not reflective of Alline's disciplined example. Seeking respectability and conformity in church practices, a group of charismatic young preachers gravitated towards Baptist beliefs as a means of distancing themselves and their followers from past indiscretions. They were sustained in this direction by Samuel Stillman, a leading Baptist minister in Boston who was in direct communication with Chipman. The support of the Boston Baptists contrasted sharply with the lack of interest in their Nova Scotia brethren by Congregational and Methodist leaders in the United States.[59]

While the fine points of theology might have generated vigorous debate among dissenting church leaders, the people who filled their pews wanted above all else to experience a personal awakening or the revival of an earlier ecstasy that would quicken their religious commitment. This longing was satisfied in the first decade of the nineteenth century when the Second Great Awakening swept through northeastern North America. Moved by emotional sermons delivered by visiting preachers from New England and local preachers such as Harris Harding, Joseph Dimmock, and James and Edward Manning, people abandoned their daily routines to celebrate what they saw as the work of God in their midst. The day after a revival meeting in Liverpool in early March 1807, John Payzant reported that "the streets were filled with people of all descriptions ... going from house to house. There was no business done that week and but little vituals dressed. The people were so many for there was young and old, rich and poor, male and female, Black and White, all met together and appeared to be as one."[60] Thousands of Nova Scotians were "awakened" at the height of the revival in 1806–8. While the spiritual excitement gradually abated, requiring another revival to rekindle it, the new sense of community, empowerment, and moral uplift generated by the Second Great Awakening left a lasting legacy of evangelical enthusiasm, and echoed the secular search for liberty, equality, and citizenship that now animated much of the Atlantic world.

By 1809 Baptist leaders felt powerful enough to force close communion on member churches. The rigid conformity demanded by the Association flew in the face of the inclusive approach adopted by Alline, and divided many congregations. As a result of the differing opinions, two Baptist traditions emerged, one Calvinist in its emphasis on election and close communion, the other more inclusive and ultimately designated by the America term "free will." In Nova Scotia the Calvinist Baptists became the more influential of the two, gradually gaining a larger following. In the 1820s even leading families in Halifax succumbed to the "rage for dipping," which would have a significant impact on the colony's political life.

Another dissenting religious orientation prevailed among the Presbyterian Scots who settled in eastern Nova Scotia and Cape Breton. By the late eighteenth century, many Presbyterians were heirs of the

Scottish Enlightenment, which produced such intellectual giants as Adam Smith and David Hume. Presbyterian Scots demanded not only an educated clergy but also a laity that could understand philosophical and doctrinal issues. Typically trained at universities in Aberdeen, Edinburgh, Glasgow, or St Andrews, Presbyterian pastors were deeply immersed in the debates that had created divisions in their church, counselled reason over superstition in religious practices, and supported publicly funded parish schools such as those that encouraged widespread literacy in Scotland.

As soon as they arrived in their new settlements, Scottish immigrants appealed to their homeland to send out pastors. By the early 1770s, Daniel Cock and David Smith, dispatched by the Burgher Synod in Scotland, were ministering to the Scots-Irish population living in the townships of Truro and Londonderry. Pictou applied for a minister in 1784, and two years later received James MacGregor, a highly educated Gaelic speaker trained in the Anti-Burgher tradition. When he was asked to join the Presbytery of Truro being formed among four Burgher ministers, MacGregor refused on principle to do so. A passionate anti-slavery activist, MacGregor then took to task his slave-owning countryman Daniel Cock in a stinging rebuke published in Halifax in 1788. The standoff continued when two more Anti-Burgher pastors, John Brown and Duncan Ross, arrived in 1795 and joined with MacGregor to form the Associate Presbytery of Pictou. MacGregor gradually relaxed his rigid doctrinal position, but it was not until 1817 that the presbyteries of Pictou and Truro united as the (Secessionist) Presbyterian Church of Nova Scotia, with MacGregor as the first moderator.[61]

The Presbyterian congregation in Halifax stood aside from the Secessionist Church. With roots in both New England Congregationalism and Scottish Presbyterianism, the Protestant Dissenting Church (formerly Mather's and later St Matthew's) became firmly fixed in the orbit of the established Church of Scotland, when the growing rift between the two groups over the timing of communion, the singing of hymns, and the origins of ministers was settled through the intervention of Scottish rector Andrew Brown, a brilliant young cleric who ministered in Halifax from 1787 to 1795. The "auld Kirk" was reinforced in 1817 by the arrival of the Gaelic-speaking Donald Allan Fraser, who organized the first Church of Scotland congregation outside Halifax at McLellans Mountain in Pictou County. He became the moving figure behind the founding of the Church of Scotland Presbytery of Pictou in 1823, and served as the first moderator of the Synod of Nova Scotia, established ten years later.[62]

The bureaucratization of the Baptist and Presbyterian churches in Nova Scotia was motivated by the need for structures to ensure the training and ordination of home-grown pastors. Since King's College remained unwilling to grant degrees to dissenters, MacGregor determined to establish a separate institution of higher learning in Nova Scotia that would follow the example of Scottish universities in being accessible to male students of all denominations. In this goal he was joined by the Anti-Burgher pastor Thomas McCulloch, who had initially been assigned by the Associate Synod to Prince Edward Island. When the ship on which McCulloch was travelling to his new mission landed in Pictou in November 1803, the townsfolk urged him to stay, his library and globes providing clear evidence that this was a scholar who could improve educational opportunities in their community.[63]

In 1806 McCulloch opened a school, and following the Napoleonic Wars he spearheaded efforts to establish an academy in Pictou that would be open to all religious denominations. The incorporation bill passed without division in the assembly, but the council added the caveat that the trustees and teachers of the proposed institution must adhere to the established churches of England or Scotland. It was also denied a a permanent subsidy and the right to grant degrees, privileges available only to King's College. Despite their disappointment, the Presbyterians accepted these restrictions, and Pictou Academy was launched in 1818, with McCulloch as principal. In his address at the opening of the academy building, he argued that a higher education must include both classical studies and the sciences, an advanced perspective at the time. "A liberal education is valuable," McCulloch argued, "not so much on account of the information which a young man picks up in college as for the habits of abstraction and generalization which he imperceptibly contracts in the course of his studies."[64]

Roman Catholics had less latitude than dissenters when it came to doctrine, but they had their own axes to grind. Although they were allowed to establish churches, receive grants of Crown lands, and had been able to vote if they possessed the requisite property qualifications since 1789, Catholics could not stand as candidates for assembly seats nor officially hold high public office. Viewed by most Protestants as the anti-Christ, Catholics were subject to much derision and discrimination. Efforts to overcome their second-class status were hampered by the cultural and linguistic differences separating the various peoples – Mi'kmaq, Acadian, Irish, and Scots – attached to Catholicism and by their subordination to the bishop of Quebec. Bishop Joseph-Octave Plessis made pastoral visits to the Maritimes in 1811, 1812, and 1815, but the vast scope of his diocese meant that he had only sporadic interest in his eastern flock, many of whom had no regular access to a priest.

Like other denominations in the colony, Roman Catholics had difficulty securing clergy. Lower Canada, Ireland, and Scotland rarely had missionaries to spare, and few local boys had the wherewithal to study abroad. The bilingual Abbé Bourg, based at Tracadièche (Carleton), on the Gaspé Peninsula, made annual visits to southwestern Nova Scotia from 1780 to 1783, and in 1784 was asked to move to Halifax, where a growing population of Catholic Loyalists and Irish demanded a priest. Bourg returned to Lower Canada when Father James Jones arrived from Ireland in 1786. Appointed superior of the missions in Nova Scotia, Cape Breton, the Îles de la Madeleine, St John's (Prince Edward) Island, and part of New Brunswick, Jones had little hope of fulfilling his extensive responsibilities without a stable of clergy willing to minister in remote and often poor regions of the Maritimes.

In 1786 Father William Phelan arrived from Ireland to minister to Catholics in Arichat, on Île Madame, but he proved more trouble than he was worth. Phelan found his primarily Acadian and Mi'kmaw parishioners "extremely rude and ignorant" in "everything regarding church discipline or civil society," and "totally unacquainted with any sort of restraint or subordination." His popularity quickly plummeted when he tried to claim land already occupied, opened a store to enhance his income, and charged fees for his services.[65] In addition, he began to discredit James Jones, perhaps hoping to replace him as superior of the Roman Catholic Church in the region.

In the 1790s help came from France, where priests who refused to accept the revolutionary government's Civil Constitution of the Clergy were seeking work in more welcoming environments. Several émigré priests settled in Nova Scotia, among them François Lejamtel, from Miquelon, who succeeded Phelan in Arichat in 1793, and served the community until 1819. In 1799 Jean-Mandé Sigogne, a highly educated priest from the Loire region of France, made his way to Nova Scotia, where he ministered to the Acadians in southwestern Nova Scotia from his headquarters at Baie Ste-Marie. He remained there until his death in 1844. Admired by authorities for his learning and urbanity, he antagonized his parishioners with his authoritarian administrative style. He, in turn, was appalled by the lax religious practices and spirit of independence that he encountered among his parishioners. As the most educated man in the area, Sigogne served as justice of the peace for many years, and played a towering role as a community leader.[66] He even managed to add Mi'kmaw to the several other languages in which he was proficient to accommodate Catholics from the Bear River reserve who arrived in Ste-Marie each year on 26 July to celebrate the feast of St Anne.

In 1801 Edmund Burke, an Irish-born priest educated at the Université de Paris, was dispatched to Halifax to serve as vicar general of Nova Scotia. His efforts to establish a seminary failed due to the lack of qualified teachers and to the general hostility from both established and dissenting churches to any expansion of Catholic influence. Burke stood up to his detractors, most notably Inglis and McCulloch, and after lobbying the pope, he was appointed vicariate apostolic in 1817, a position placed under the jurisdiction of Rome, rather than Quebec. While he was unable to mobilize the resources to build a seminary, Burke opened Catholic schools for boys and girls in Halifax and laid the cornerstone of St Mary's Cathedral on 24 May 1820, just a few months before his death.[67]

The prevalence of dissenting churches in the countryside blunted efforts by successive Church of England bishops to uphold the prerogatives of the established church in Nova Scotia. Denied the advantages of a colonial tithe and therefore reliant on funds generated locally or from overseas, the Church of England had exclusive rights to perform marriages by licence and to the revenues derived from the sale of land set aside for churches and schools in each township, but these privileges were deeply resented. In 1819 the legislature approved a bill extending to ministers of all denominations the right to marry by government licence, but Dalhousie reserved the bill for imperial approval, which was not forthcoming. While prepared to extend the privilege to the Church of Scotland, he was unwilling to grant concessions to dissenting preachers whom he despised. Not surprisingly, this approach did not go over well with many Nova Scotians.

Cape Breton Redux

The growing number of settlers in Cape Breton also resented the high-handedness of their political masters. With a population of only a few thousand until the second decade of the nineteenth century, administrators ruled without an assembly and liked it that way, but they would not be able to resist the democratic tide for long. The French Revolution not only kept the dream of more liberal political practices alive, it also brought a measure of prosperity to Cape Breton, which had coal, fish, and timber on offer. Sydney thrived under the impact of war and so, too, did the largely Acadian community on Île Madame. During his second visit to Arichat in 1815, Bishop Plessis noted that, "Even within the last three years there is a notable difference and a considerable betterment. The houses are more attractively constructed, and the people dress better. They eat more food, such as bread (which the Acadians know so well how to do without); not that their fields produce more grain, for they do not cultivate them but because they have enough money to buy flour."[68]

By the turn of the century, immigrants began arriving in significant numbers.[69] As early as 1775 a group of Scots from St John's Island had settled in Judique, on the Gulf shore, and others followed them from the Island and also from mainland Nova Scotia. The first boatload of immigrants directly from Scotland arrived in Sydney harbour in 1802 with more than four hundred passengers. Eager to prevent the newcomers from "farther Emigration to A Foreign Country," the council offered every man, woman, and child a subsidy to stay. Most of them settled near Sydney and along the Mira River, where the land originally had been granted to Loyalists. The migrations continued, escalating after 1817 when the British government relaxed its restrictions on freehold grants in Cape Breton. Thereafter, until the generous conditions were withdrawn ten years later, a married man could acquire 200 acres (81 hectares) by paying a fee of £3 to £5 to cover the cost of surveying and registering the grant and by fulfilling settlement requirements, which included erecting a house, clearing 3 of every 50 acres received, and acquiring three cattle within three years. The Margaree Valley and the Bras d'Or Lakes were the first to attract settlers, but less accessible areas were soon claimed by people eager to own land and as much of it as they could get.[70] By 1820 Cape Breton was home to about 10,000 people, the majority of them immigrants from Scotland.

During its short life as a separate colony, Cape Breton had only three lieutenant governors. The second, following DesBarres, was William Macarmick, who arrived in Sydney in 1787. Nothing seemed to go right for Macarmick. In 1789 the British government suspended free land grants in the Maritimes, hoping to raise money from the sale of land, and the garrison in Sydney was withdrawn to Halifax, a decision prompted by the outbreak of the French Revolution. His efforts to form a colonial militia brought stiff resistance, but he managed to secure the help of Jerseymen and Loyalists to keep a close watch on the Acadians, who, it was feared, might support any French invasion of the colony. When his perquisites from the sale of coal from mines leased to private operators were withdrawn in 1794, Macarmick was outraged. He left Cape Breton in a huff the following year, but held his position *in absentia* until his death in 1815.

Few of the administrators in charge of the colony in Macarmick's absence had much of an impact. The exception was Major General John Despard, who experienced a decidedly shaky start to his term in office. Appointed by the Duke of Kent as military commander and civil administrator of Cape Breton in the summer of 1799, Despard was unable to wrest his position from the incumbent, Brigadier General John Murray, and his militant supporters until September of the following year. Once in control of the council, Despard initiated policies designed to make Cape Breton a functional colony. He escheated land granted to absent Loyalists, approved the construction of a new market-house in Sydney, supported the building of gristmills in outlying regions, and called upon Halifax merchant John Corbett Ritchie to help put the poorly managed coal mines into more efficient production for markets in St John's and Halifax.[71]

Lacking the funds to support his policies, Despard convinced his council and authorities in London to impose a duty on rum. This measure opened the way for those demanding an assembly to advance their cause. Since the revenue bill had not been approved by elective representatives, it smacked of "taxation without representation," a policy put to rest by British authorities during the American Revolution. Richard Gibbons, son of the colony's former chief justice, emerged as the spokesman for the growing opposition to Cape Breton's authoritarian regime. By 1807 Despard decided that he had better things to do with his time than manage a dysfunctional colony, and returned to England. Cape Breton never recovered its administrative momentum. In 1816 the taxation issue was pursued in court, with Gibbons acting for the aggrieved taxpayers and the colony's attorney general, Richard John Uniacke Jr, for the Crown. The jury found the tax illegal, and the colonial treasury faced bankruptcy.

By this time, Lieutenant Governor George Ainslie had assumed office, but he was no better equipped to deal with Cape Breton than were his predecessors. He had little respect for the local inhabitants, whom he described as "the refuse of three kingdoms" (England, Ireland, and Scotland), too poor, and illiterate, he felt, to support an assembly. When Gibbons drew up a petition claiming that all rulings of the council were illegal because an assembly had never been called to approve them, Colonial Secretary Lord Bathurst determined that Gibbons had a point. The reform strategy backfired disastrously. Tired of the troublesome colony and eager to reduce administrative expenditures, British authorities decided to make Cape Breton once again part of Nova Scotia.

On 16 October 1820, Sir James Kempt, who had succeeded Dalhousie as lieutenant governor, officially proclaimed the demise of Cape Breton as a separate colony. The island became one constituency in Nova Scotia, with three judicial units administered from Arichat, Port Hood, and Sydney. Seven townships were established (Sydney, St Andrew, St Patrick, Canseau, Port Hood, Ainslie, and Margaree), but they were only empowered to hold annual meetings for the support of the poor.

As elsewhere in Nova Scotia, appointments to most local offices were controlled by authorities in Halifax. All government officials in Cape Breton were dismissed except for the surveyor general, Thomas H. Crawley, and for the time being the island had no representative on the council. Shocked by the dashing of their dream of a separate colony, reformers in Cape Breton tried for a generation to reverse the decision.[72]

As a county of Nova Scotia, Cape Breton had two seats in the forty-one-member assembly. The election in November 1820 returned Richard John Uniacke Jr and Lawrence Kavanagh. The son of one of the first anglophone families to settle in Cape Breton, Kavanagh, like many assembly members, was a well-placed merchant. When only fourteen years old, he and his older brother James had inherited a prosperous business from their father, who had been a supplier to the British army after the capture of Louisbourg in 1758. While James moved to Halifax, young Lawrence took charge of their interests in Cape Breton, amassed a large fortune, and built an impressive estate at St Peter's. Only one obstacle stood in the way of Kavanagh's assuming his seat in the assembly: he was a practising Roman Catholic. Although he agreed to take an oath of loyalty to the Crown, he was not prepared to take an oath denying transubstantiation, the belief that at Mass the bread and wine are transformed into the body and blood of Christ.

Kempt sensed that Nova Scotians were now more willing to confer full civil rights on Catholics, and the Colonial Office offered no objections to Kavanagh's taking his seat without swearing the problematic oath. When he appeared early in the 1822 session, he was denied admission, but the council presented a formal address to the Crown asking for the removal of the oath, which was granted. A last-ditch effort to exclude him, launched by members from the overwhelmingly Protestant areas of Lunenburg, Cumberland, and the Annapolis Valley, failed to pass. In April 1823 Kavanagh took his seat in the assembly. Outside Quebec, where Catholics were accorded the right to sit in the assembly in 1791, this was a major breakthrough in the movement for Catholic emancipation that was now gaining momentum in Britain.

The Spirit of Improvement

The prolonged post-war slump dulled the optimism that had prevailed in 1814, but many Nova Scotians remained undaunted. With steam power transforming production processes, a new age of material well-being seemed within reach. Indeed, the idea of unending progress in human affairs championed by enlightened thinkers was confirmed by recent developments in Nova Scotia itself. Despite setbacks, many

people looked forward to a brighter future. Even the poor and op-
pressed, it was thought, might be liberated from their unhappy condition if they only developed new skills and adopted new ways of
thinking that were rooted in a faith in free markets, private property,
and self-interest, concepts that became the hallmarks of the modern age
in the Western world.

No one represented the enthusiasm for improvement better than
Walter Bromley.[73] Stationed in Halifax from 1808 to 1810, Bromley re-
tired from the army in 1811 and used his half-pay pension to launch a
career in social activism. Under the auspices of the British and Foreign
School Society, sponsored by the Duke of Kent, Bromley returned to
Halifax, where he opened the Royal Acadian School in the fall of 1813.
Unlike grammar schools, which were offered a subsidy under legislation passed in 1811 and catered primarily to boys of elite families,
Bromley's institution offered low-cost education for the middle class
and free education for the poor, and taught boys and girls of all denominations. It used the monitorial system of teaching, whereby advanced
students taught younger ones to keep costs low. Concerned about the
problems of poverty and unemployment, Bromley also established a
workshop to teach practical skills. Progressive for its time, Bromley's
school drew support from liberal-minded men in Halifax and beyond,
who served on the school's advisory board. The success of Bromley's
initiative shamed the Church of England clergy in Halifax into sponsoring the National School in 1816 to cater to the poor. With winter unemployment a growing problem in Halifax, Bromley became a leading
figure in the Poor Man's Friend Society, founded in 1820 to promote
"the adoption of such measures, as would more effectually relieve the
wants of the numerous poor, and destroy the system of public begging."

Bromley also focused his energies on Indigenous peoples, eliciting
support from the New England Company for efforts to teach farming
skills to the Mi'kmaq and Wolastoqiyik. This initiative prompted Abbé
Sigogne in 1814 to prepare a petition for the lieutenant governor from
Paussamigh Pemmeenauweet (Louis-Benjamin Peminuit Paul) and
his three brothers, Jean-Lucien, Pierre, and François, on behalf of 120
Mi'kmaq for land in Shubenacadie, "not in the back woods," but fit for
agriculture. By August 1818 some twenty-two families were settled on
the grant and 50 acres (20 hectares) cleared. Another settlement took
root in Gold River, but Bromley ran into financial difficulties, and no further initiatives among the Mi'kmaq materialized.[74] Bromley returned to
England in 1825, but the rage for reform would be carried on by others.

At the same time that Bromley was championing progressive education, his contemporary, John Young, sparked a movement to improve

agricultural practices.[75] Young arrived in Halifax from Scotland in 1814, just in time to participate in trading activities, both legal and otherwise, circulating around Castine. He used the profits from these ventures to develop his mercantile business, but he had higher ambitions. Appalled by the state of Nova Scotia's farms and inspired by the liberal thinking of Adam Smith, he wrote sixty-four letters to the *Acadian Recorder* between 1818 and 1821 under the pen-name "Agricola," outlining what needed to be done to increase agricultural output. The enthusiastic response testified not only to the reform impulse that characterized the post-war period, but also to the growing influence of newspapers. By December 1818 agricultural societies had been formed in four counties, and a Central Board of Agriculture was being organized with the support of Lieutenant Governor Dalhousie. Another nineteen societies were established over the next two years. As president of the Central Board, Young proved unable to devote the time required to be efficient in the delivery of seeds, the transportation of breeding stock, and responding to the many letters of enquiry he received. His own business interests and political ambitions took precedence, with the result that in 1826 the assembly cancelled the annual grant to the Central Board, and local agricultural societies languished. Nevertheless, like Bromley, Young generated interest in reform beyond the institutions he helped to create. Unlike Bromley, Young remained in the colony, where he served in the assembly from 1824 until his death in 1837.

No Nova Scotian was more successful in experimenting with crops and farming methods than Charles Ramage Prescott. The son of an early immigrant to Halifax, Prescott retired in 1812 from the successful business partnership of Prescott, Lawson and Company to live at Acacia Grove, his country estate in Cornwallis Township, where he tested strains of wheat, Swedish turnips, and fruit trees imported from England, the United States, and Lower Canada. In his extensive orchards, he grew more than a hundred varieties of apples, including the popular Gravenstein, which grew well in the region. Generous in sharing his successful varieties with farmers throughout the area, he laid the groundwork for what became a major export crop in the Annapolis Valley.[76]

Despite such achievements, it is difficult to determine how far the spirit of industry and improvement penetrated the fabric of Nova Scotian society. For most people, these concepts were represented in the efforts they took to keep food on the table. Other than local merchants who were able to accumulate wealth through trade and keeping customers permanently "on the ledger," most landed families were adept at what today would be called multitasking. They cobbled together a subsistence by planting crops, raising animals, fishing, hunting, cutting firewood, and taking wage labour when it was available. Women wove cloth, fashioned clothing, made butter and cheese, and preserved food for the use of their families or to barter at the general store for iron pots, spices, tea, tools, and other "luxuries." When they could, women tried to sell their skills as teachers, housekeepers, and care givers. In 1799, Margaret Doucett, who lived in the Acadia community of Clare, advertised in the Halifax *Weekly Chronicle* her "Great Cures" for cancer "in all its various Stages, with the most trifling pain to the Person afflicted."[77] Children, meanwhile, were assigned chores at an early age, and were sometimes hired out to learn practical skills and to keep down the number of mouths to feed.

Poverty stalked every community, and could be found not only among the landless, the alcohol addicted, the mentally ill, and those lacking kin to serve as a social safety net.[78] The death of a spouse, ill-health, a disastrous fire, failing crops, sick animals, or the lack of winter employment sometimes threatened the very survival of families, whose individual members were then forced to rely on the compassion of neighbours and the parsimony of the poor law. For many families, survival depended on a credit system in which merchants advanced supplies and paid for local products in goods rather than in cash. This practice encouraged dependence and sometimes resulted in creditors' foreclosing on properties, but it enabled producers to participate, at least minimally, in the market economy. Because disaster could strike at any time, ethnic groups stuck together for the greater likelihood of finding mutual aid, church pews were filled with parishioners eager to solicit God's blessing, and men such as Edward Mortimer and Lawrence Kavanagh, who sometimes displayed mercy rather than mendacity towards those down on their luck, earned the devotion of the people they exploited. In this, Nova Scotians were little different than most other people living in the North Atlantic world, where survival was often precarious.

Its uneven opportunities notwithstanding, Nova Scotia had been transformed in the years between 1793 and 1820. The consumer revolution, which had been gaining ground since the mid-eighteenth century in the Atlantic world, sunk deep roots in the colony during the war, fuelling notions of the good life that extended beyond basic subsistence and spiritual salvation. While rural communities still seemed rough-hewn by European standards, the countryside now boasted estates worthy of an English gentleman. Joseph Brown Comingo, the grandson

Figure 9.2. Government House, Halifax, 1819, by John Elliott Woolford. As this watercolour by John Elliott Woolford suggests, Government House, opened in 1811, impressed visitors with its symmetrical windows and hipped rooflines, typical of Georgian architecture that was common in early nineteenth-century Halifax.
https://en.wikipedia.org/wiki/Government_House_(Nova_Scotia)#/media/File:Government_House_NS.jpg (or LAC C-3559).

of Lunenburg's first German Reformed minister, managed to make a modest living between 1808 and 1820 by painting watercolour portraits, family groups, and landscapes for an expanding middle class.[79] Governor Wentworth added to the stock of Georgian structures in Halifax with a new gubernatorial residence whose cornerstone was laid in September 1800. Perceived by the assembly as built "on a scale far beyond the wants and circumstances of the Province," it was constructed with local stone, much of it procured at Wallace, in Pictou County (figure 9.2).[80] Stone was also used in the construction of a new building to house the legislature, a project launched in 1811 and completed in 1819. Both Government House and Province House were built to last, and are still in use for their original purposes.

Chapter Ten

Bluenoses and Britons, 1820–1854

Shaped by more than two centuries of intermittent warfare, Nova Scotia's settler society coalesced during the four decades of peace following the War of 1812. The population increased, primary industries expanded, and the carrying trade flourished. By the 1850s settlement had reached its territorial limits, and further economic growth rested on embracing the opportunities associated with the Industrial Revolution. Everyone in the colony got caught up in the great transformation that roiled societies in the industrial age,[1] but not everyone benefited to the same degree.

A Maturing Colonial Society

In the first half of the nineteenth century, many Nova Scotians became ambitious participants in a rapidly evolving North Atlantic economy. Halifax emerged as a banking, shipping, and wholesaling centre in the Maritime region, and boasted a powerful clutch of merchant-shippers – two hundred strong by mid-century – whose outlook was international in scope. Outlying communities also reaped the rewards of an expanding global economy and, along with Halifax, sprouted churches, colleges, literary societies, mechanics' institutes, newspapers, schools, and reform organizations to sustain a vibrant intellectual and social life. As they adjusted to the challenges facing them, Nova Scotians became more British in orientation, but paradoxically they also became more aware of their own separate identity.

According to the 1851 census, 276,854 people were making Nova Scotia their home, more than double the 123,630 enumerated in 1827. Large families, averaging six or seven children, were the bedrock of a youthful society where more than half of the population was under the age of twenty. Three-quarters of Nova Scotians were classified as

Figure 10.1. Lochaber Lake, County Sydney, Nova Scotia, 1830. Engraved by J. Clark. Stumps of trees felled by pioneer settlers litter the landscape in this engraving of Lochaber Lake in rural Cape Breton.
From *Letters from Nova Scotia; Comprising Sketches of a Young Country* by Captain W. Moorsom (London, 1830), p. 178. Nova Scotia Archives Library: AK F100 M78.

Protestant, with the Presbyterian (73,000) and Baptist (42,600) churches reporting the most adherents. While nearly 70,000 Roman Catholics lived in Nova Scotia, Antigonish and Richmond were the only counties in which they formed a substantial majority. Fewer than 5,000 people were designated as "Coloured," and about 1,000 as "Indians," both figures almost certainly underestimations. Cape Breton Island, still a rugged settlement frontier, reported a population of 55,000 (figure 10.1). The 1851 census made no mention of people's origins, but records from a decade later reveal that 90 per cent was native-born, a clear indication that immigrants no longer dominated the social landscape.[2]

Then as now, census takers focused on economic output, which operated on a much smaller scale than is the case today. They paid close attention to the household economy, recording not only crops and livestock, but also the production of butter, cheese, maple sugar, and cloth. Only coal and gypsum were reported under the category of "Minerals," while grindstones, bricks, soap, and candles made up what were described as "Various Manufactures." In a table devoted to "Shipping and Fisheries," the census counted 30,154 nets and seines, along with 812 "fishing vessels" employing 3,681 men; another 6,713 men operated 5,161 smaller boats. Shipbuilding was flourishing, with 486 vessels and 2,654 boats under construction.[3] By volume, dried cod, fish oil, herring, and mackerel were the major products of the sea, caught in nearby waters with small boats and larger vessels that ranged as far as Labrador for their catch. Nova Scotia's rivers were awash with more than 2,000 mills and factories producing beer, cloth, flour, iron, leather, and timber, most of them small operations employing one or two people. Only ten were powered by steam. Drawing on these and other records, Julian Gwyn has concluded that the economy barely kept pace with population growth in this period, a situation that called into question the colony's capacity to adjust to the enormous economic transformation sweeping the Atlantic world.[4]

These limitations were not obvious to many Nova Scotians, who were beginning to develop a sense of themselves that transcended narrow identities of class and culture. "Bluenose," a term applied by the Loyalists to the New England settlers they encountered upon their arrival, was becoming a popular moniker for all Nova Scotians, but its origins remain obscure. A word used since the seventeenth century to imply puritanical morals, "bluenose" might have been a reference to the evangelical values embraced by many Nova Scotians. Another explanation is that it was a derogatory term referring to the bracing Maritime climate and perhaps also to the blue dye transferred by thick woollen mittens when Nova Scotians wiped their noses. Others, including the author Thomas Chandler Haliburton, speculated that the bluenose potato, an early variety peddled in the holds of sailing ships, was the source of the nickname.

Whatever its origins, the journalist, poet, politician, and publisher Joseph Howe entitled one of his poems "The Blue Nose." In it he crowed:

> Let the Frenchman delight in his vine-covered vales,
> Let the Greek toast his old classic ground;
> Here's the land where the bracing Northwester prevails
> And where jolly Blue Noses abound.[5]

Clearly steeped in the cultural traditions of the Western world, Howe was also a proud Nova Scotian. His poem "Acadia," which remained unpublished during his lifetime, was a heartfelt celebration of his native land in images that evoke a widely understood sense of place. Devoting whole stanzas to fragrant mayflowers, autumn colours, and lofty pines, Howe was also sensitive to dark shadows in the colony's story, noting the depredations of "white men" who "thoughtlessly remove the stones" that Mi'kmaw "hands had gather'd o'er his parents' bones," and "saw them fell the trees which they had spared / And war, eternal war, his soul declared."[6]

Like Joseph Howe, many Nova Scotians took pride in their identity as Bluenoses, a people with a colourful history and a growing list of accomplishments to their credit. In 1829 Howe published Haliburton's *Historical and Statistical Account of Nova-Scotia*, which outlined major developments in the colony's dramatic past. Best known as the author of *The Clockmaker* (1836) and *The Old Judge* (1849), Haliburton imagined a prosperous future for Nova Scotians, whom his fictional character, Yankee clock peddler Sam Slick, compared unfavourably with the "go ahead" denizens of the United States. Slick commented that "these Bluenoses have no motion in 'em, no enterprise, no spirit, and if any critter shows any symptoms of activity, they say he is a man of no judgment, he speculative, he's a schemer."[7] Through the use of satire, Haliburton, whose knowledge of Nova Scotia was enriched by his travels as a circuit court judge, hoped to spur his countrymen to rise to their potential.

Haliburton and Howe were Nova Scotia-born but looked to Britain as the centre of their cultural universe. While Haliburton ended his political career as a Conservative member of the British Parliament from 1859 to 1865, Howe's path led in 1869 to a position in John A. Macdonald's Liberal-Conservative coalition cabinet in the Dominion of Canada. These destinies reflect the transatlantic citizenship that membership in the Empire offered Bluenoses, and document the rapidly evolving geopolitical scene that Britons everywhere experienced in the mid-nineteenth century.[8]

As Howe's literary work suggests, pride in Nova Scotia's development was increasingly expressed in the vocabulary of nationalism, which inspired militant movements throughout the Atlantic world in the nineteenth century, bringing diverse peoples together in new nation-states. Unlike Germany and Italy, which emerged as unified nations in this period, conquered peoples in the British Empire, including the Irish, French Canadians, and Acadians, pondered how best to nourish a separate identity in a context where anglophone culture and power were dominant. For anglophone Nova Scotians, the trick was to disentangle British and colonial variants of their identity, without severing ties with the Empire as the United States had done.

Beamish Murdoch, a contemporary of Haliburton and Howe, wrestled with how best to imagine a worthy destiny for his homeland. Called to the bar in 1822, Murdoch embraced the spirit of improvement and philanthropy at an early age, and while barely in his twenties expressed the wish that Nova Scotia be "classed among those countries that have reared and produced the benefactors of the human race."[9] In 1828 he founded the *Acadian Magazine* with the express goal of overcoming the impression, "far too prevalent abroad, and particularly in the Mother Country, that we are comparatively ignorant and barbarous." The magazine survived for less than two years, but most of its submissions came from Maritimers, suggesting that the region now sprouted a respectable number of aspiring writers. Successful in capturing a Halifax seat in the 1826 election, Murdoch was unable to repeat this achievement in 1830, and turned his energies to producing a four-volume *Epitome of the Laws of Nova Scotia*, published by Howe in 1832 and 1833. In it he declared that the values of liberty and equality, which were fundamental to the British legal system, found their clearest reflection in the progressive North American context of his native province.

Dreams and Schemes

Progress was certainly on the minds of ambitious entrepreneurs who were determined to see Nova Scotia live up to its economic potential. The post-war recession finally lifted in the mid-1820s, due in part to changes in the mercantile system that worked in Nova Scotia's favour, but sustained prosperity proved elusive.[10] Writing in 1834 after another downturn in the economy, John Homer, a prominent shipper and assembly member for the South Shore constituency of Barrington, lamented that Nova Scotians were unable to produce enough wheat to "bread" themselves, relying instead on "superfine" flour imported from the United States.[11] This practice meant that locally grown wheat and coarser grains such as oats, barley, and rye, which arguably were better suited to the Nova Scotia climate, sold at a discount. To address this problem, Homer suggested that the legislature take a number of measures to boost agricultural output, among them the introduction of "Corn Laws" similar to those operating in Britain. This was not a new idea. In 1820 Halifax merchants had petitioned the assembly for bounties to encourage the production of wheat at home and duties against the importation of flour from the United States.

Restrictions imposed in 1818 by the United States on trade with British North America meant that Nova Scotia shippers could no longer profitably secure cargoes of flour, beef, pork, and lumber in American ports for sale in the West Indies. Rather than develop local sources of supply, Homer and other merchants in the colony simply registered their vessels in Boston. The British government declared Halifax a free port in 1826 to address this absurdity, and permitted trade with non-British islands in the West Indies, but it was easier to smuggle American products directly into outport communities than to route them through the capital. "In the twenty years of peace," Homer reckoned, "we have paid mostly to the middle and slave holding states of America, nearly two million of pounds sterling for bread and other articles which ought to have been produced here by our own country."[12] Raised on agrarian and mercantile notions of economic well-being, Homer dismissed Nova Scotia's abundant coal resources as a means of generating wealth, and painted a decidedly unflattering picture of the working conditions and fractious class structure associated with extensive mining operations.

Others were more enthusiastic about the opportunities associated with the industrial age. Using Sam Slick as his mouth piece, Haliburton argued that railways would "enlarge the sphere and the means of trade, open new sources of traffic and supply, develop resources, and what is of more value perhaps than all, beget motion." In particular, a railway linking Halifax to the Bay of Fundy would enhance the trading potential of the capital, which in this period was surpassed by Saint John in population and industrial development. If Nova Scotians failed to keep up with the times, Slick warned, "our folks will buy them out, and they must recede before a more intelligent and active people."[13]

Contrary to Slick's opinion, Nova Scotians had some motion in them, but their efforts sometimes fell short. In 1826 Charles Rufus Fairbanks, an entrepreneur and assembly member for Halifax, established a company to build a canal along the Grand Lake-Shubenacadie River system to improve communication with the Bay of Fundy. Supported by a grant of £15,000 from the Nova Scotia legislature and both state and private capital from Britain, this "great public road," as Fairbanks dubbed it, became mired in debt, engineering problems, and disgruntled workers. After sinking £80,000 in the venture, construction was halted in the early 1830s. One of Fairbanks's sons supervised the canal's completion by 1861, but by then it was no longer competitive with a railway being built along the same route.[14]

While Fairbanks was pursuing his dream, another initiative was underway in areas with extensive reserves of coal, which was fast replacing wood as a source of heat and power. The Crown claimed subsurface mineral rights, and in the late eighteenth century began leasing coal resources in Nova Scotia and Cape Breton to local entrepreneurs who paid rents and royalties for the privilege. In 1788 George III assigned rights to other mineral resources in Nova Scotia to his profligate son, the Duke of York, who in turn transferred them, with coal added, to one of his creditors, Rundell, Bridge, Bigge, and Rundell, in 1824. They moved quickly to establish a monopoly, extinguishing all existing local leases and adding Cape Breton, which had been a separate colony at the time of the duke's initial windfall, to their holdings. The General Mining Association (GMA), the company formed to operate the mines, signed an agreement with the Crown in 1828. In return for a sixty-year lease covering all the coal reserves in Nova Scotia, the GMA agreed to pay a rent of £3,000 per annum and a royalty of 2 shillings on each cauldron of coal mined in excess of 20,000. Sydney and Pictou were declared free ports to facilitate the export of coal to the United States. Compared with previous leases awarded to local entrepreneurs, it was an exceptionally good deal.[15]

By the time the agreement was signed, two industrial towns were already under construction, one at Albion Mines (now Stellarton), in Pictou County, and the other at Sydney Mines, in Cape Breton County. The GMA hired Richard Smith, son of a Staffordshire coal mine operator, to supervise the company's activities. In the spring of 1827, local residents watched in amazement as Smith, two hundred miners, and tons of machinery were installed at Albion Mines. In short order, brickworks, coal yards, coke ovens, a foundry, a sawmill, wharves, and workers' housing were built; track was laid for a horse-drawn railway; and a seventy-five-foot smokestack dominated the skyline. The GMA's first coal was produced from a 212-foot pit in September 1827, and three months later a twenty-horsepower steam engine began to pump water and hoist coal at the mine. Mount Rundell, Smith's imposing brick mansion located on a landscaped estate overlooking the new community, also inspired awe. Meanwhile, Richard Brown, a young British mining engineer, had arrived at Sydney Mines to oversee, under Smith's supervision, a similar miracle of modern industry. By the early 1830s, the GMA employed more than nine hundred men, most of them miners from lowland Scotland and northern England, and produced 50,000 tons of coal annually.[16] The age of industrial capitalism had arrived in Nova Scotia.

In 1839 the GMA hosted celebrations to mark the inauguration of the colony's first modern railway line, powered by steam engines named *Samson, Hercules,* and *John Buddle* (the latter named after a prominent English mining engineer), to carry coal the six miles from Albion Mines to the harbour at New Glasgow (Figure 10.2). As the Reverend George Patterson reported in his *History of the County of Pictou, Nova Scotia,* published in 1877, the opening of the line was "an occasion of general rejoicing."

Figure 10.2. The *Samson*, shown above in the early 1880s, was one of three locomotives shipped in pieces from Newcastle-on-Tyne and the first to be assembled for a test run before the official opening of the Albion Mines Railway in September 1839.
History Collection, Nova Scotia Museum, Halifax, NSM27.38 copy neg. N-3563.

The two steamers, Pocahontas and Albion, with lighters attached, each carried from Pictou about 1,000 persons to New Glasgow, whence they were taken by train to the mines. Crowds of people on horseback and on foot were there assembled from all parts of the country. Here a procession was formed of the various trades, the Masonic lodges, the Pictou Volunteer Artillery Company ... A train of waggons, fitted up to receive passengers, had been attached to each engine, and, being filled with the crowd, now made the first trip to New Glasgow and back again, giving a new sensation to multitudes.

According to Patterson, "On their return, a feast was given to the employees of the Company, for which 1,100 lb of beef and mutton, with corresponding quantities of other articles, were provided; a dinner was given to invited guests, and the night was spent in general festivity."[17]

The owners of the GMA had deeper pockets than most local entre-preneurs, but home-grown businessmen also made their mark. Among them was Samuel Cunard, the second son of Abraham Cunard, a Quaker Loyalist from Pennsylvania.[18] In addition to working as a master carpenter for the British Army, Abraham Cunard pursued private business interests, buying up land, trading in timber with Britain and the West Indies, and participating in other lucrative opportunities available in wartime Halifax. A. Samuel and Son, founded in 1812, survived the post-war slump by securing government contracts to transport immigrants to outlying districts and to carry mail to Boston, St John's, and Bermuda. The son in the firm's name was Samuel, who, upon his father's death in 1824, assumed full control of the company.

Like other ambitious entrepreneurs, Samuel Cunard was constantly on the lookout for investment opportunities. He registered at least seventy-six vessels in Halifax during his career, and his shipping interests flourished as the pace of North Atlantic trade quickened. In the 1820s he became a partner in the Halifax Banking Company, served as vice-president of the Shubenacadie Canal project, and invested in whaling ventures in waters off Brazil. A man unwilling to take no for an answer, he convinced the East India Company to award him its lucrative North American tea agency rather than to merchants in Quebec, which, he argued, was a less efficient port than Halifax because it was ice-bound half of the year. Quarterly tea auctions began at Cunard's stone warehouse on the waterfront in June 1826, and from there much of the precious commodity was re-exported to other British North American colonies and to the West Indies. He also expanded his trade with Britain in manufactured goods, helping to make Halifax the leading wholesaling centre in the Maritime region.[19] In 1830 Cunard's status was confirmed by his appointment to the legislative council.

Recognizing that Nova Scotia was well positioned geographically to meet the escalating demand for coal, Cunard offered to lease the Cape Breton reserves on better terms than those offered by the GMA, but the British capitalists prevailed – at least for a time. In 1827 Cunard secured a contract to provide wharf space in Halifax for the GMA, and in 1834 he succeeded Richard Smith as the company's local business agent. Cunard's investments extended into New Brunswick, where, with his brother Joseph, he developed extensive timber and shipping operations centred on the Miramichi River. In 1838 the brothers became involved in a land company to purchase estates on Prince Edward Island. Samuel emerged as one of the Island's largest landowners, and proved no less eager than other proprietors to discredit the Escheat Movement that was gaining ground in the colony.[20]

Cunard easily survived the decline of the West Indies trade following the abolition of slavery in 1833, shrewdly betting on steamships as the way of the future. In 1830 he became a founding director of the Halifax Steamboat Company, which built a steamship, the *Sir Charles Ogle* (named after the commander-in-chief of the Royal Navy's North American Station), to provide more reliable transportation between Halifax and Dartmouth. Cunard was also one of more than two hundred shareholders of the Quebec and Halifax Steam Navigation Company, incorporated in 1831 to inaugurate steamship service between Halifax and Quebec. The *Royal William*, launched from Quebec shipyards, sailed to Halifax in August, calling at Miramichi and Pictou along the way. Losing money on the venture, the owners decided to sell the vessel, which used steam engines for most of its twenty-five-day transatlantic voyage from Pictou to Gravesend, England, in June 1833, the first ship to do so. Cunard also commissioned a coastal steamship for mail service to Prince Edward Island and elsewhere in the region.

With this experience behind him, Cunard was ready when the British Admiralty advertised in 1838 for tenders to carry transatlantic mail by steamship. Believing "that steamers properly built and manned might start and arrive at their destination with the punctuality of railway trains on land," Cunard travelled to England to submit his successful bid for an "ocean railway."[21] In July 1840 his company's first purpose-built steamer, *Britannia*, sailed from Liverpool to Halifax in thirteen days and then on to Boston. Charles Dickens, who travelled to Halifax en route to the United States in January 1842, complained of the cramped conditions on board the *Britannia* – which he described as "not unlike a giant hearse with windows on the side." Words, the celebrated author declared, could not convey the agony of the rough winter passage that resulted in breaking glass, tumbling waiters, and seasickness all around.[22] Cunard's steamships gradually offered improved accommodations and, with a reputation for speed and safety, dominated ocean-going passenger service. In the 1840s Cunard increasingly left his Nova Scotia operations in the hands of his sons to spend more time in London, while his vessels bypassed Halifax to dock in Boston and New York.

Cunard was not the only Nova Scotia–based entrepreneur to seize opportunities as they arose. Following the War of 1812, Enos Collins went from strength to strength, engaging in banking, lumbering, shipping, and whaling. He invested heavily in the United States, and it was rumoured that he was persuaded not to move there only by the offer of a seat on the legislative council in 1822. After several unsuccessful attempts to secure a banking charter from the legislature, Collins and seven of his associates founded a private bank in 1825. Collins was the dominant partner in the Halifax Banking Company, which operated in his Water Street premises.[23] As a member of the council, Collins tried to intervene in matters relating to his own interests, which tarnished his reputation and added fuel to the fire for political reform that was spreading throughout British North America. After being replaced on the legislative council in 1840, Collins lived in semi-retirement on his Gorsebrook estate, where he and his wife Margaret Halliburton, the eldest daughter of a prominent judge, entertained lieutenant governors and other well-placed Haligonians. His wealth, estimated to be more than $6 million in the 1860s, made Collins one of the richest men in British North America.[24]

Edward Kenny was not far behind Collins in wealth and prestige by the second half of the nineteenth century. In 1824 Edward and his older brother Thomas arrived in Halifax from Ireland as clerks and then partners in the mercantile establishment of James Lyons, who remained in Cork during the winter months. The brothers soon branched out on their own, developing a thriving wholesaling business and diversifying into banking, manufacturing, real estate, and utilities. More socially engaged than his bachelor brother, Edward married Ann Forrestell in 1832, and together they raised ten children. Eager to challenge the Protestant establishment, both in Nova Scotia and Ireland, Kenny became involved in Howe's reform movement, actively supported the incorporation of Halifax as a city in 1841, and was elected mayor the following year. Courted as a prominent leader of the city's increasingly powerful Roman Catholic community, he was appointed to the legislative council in 1843. He also became actively involved in a range of community organizations, among them the militia and the Charitable Irish Society, which he twice served as president, and he was a founding member of the exclusive Halifax Club in 1862.[25]

With its population approaching 20,000 by mid-century and a significant military presence that infused money into the economy, Halifax offered an expanding local market for commodities such as beer, which slaked the thirst of soldier and civilian alike. In 1817 Scottish-born Alexander Keith, a brewer trained in England, moved to Halifax, and three years later bought out his employer. Alexander Keith Brewery prospered, and by the 1830s its owner had become a powerful figure in Halifax, serving as president of the North British Society, Provincial Grand Master of the Freemasons, and a director of the Bank of Nova Scotia. He was also prominent in the founding of various fire, life, and marine insurance companies, sat on the board of directors of the Halifax Gas, Light, and Water Company, founded in 1840, and was elected to the first council formed after Halifax was incorporated. In 1843 he was elected mayor and appointed to the legislative council.[26]

In 1821 William Murdoch, also from Scotland, arrived in Halifax, where he established a dry goods business and became a successful wholesaler. Like many other merchant capitalists, he branched into shipping and banking, and supported such initiatives as the Inland Navigation Company, established to reboot the dormant Shubenacadie Canal project. A bachelor, he used his wealth to support civic and philanthropic initiatives, among them the Protestant Orphans' Society and Young Men's Christian Association, both founded in 1853. Murdoch eventually moved to London, where in 1862 he helped to establish the Imperial Bank to finance commercial ventures in British colonies. Upon his death in 1866, several Halifax institutions were beneficiaries of his will, among them St Matthew's Church, a public hospital, and a residential school for the hearing impaired. He also left a legacy to establish a home for the blind.[27]

Despite facing ups and downs in the volatile colonial economy, William Machlin Stairs remained in Halifax, where he had been born in 1789. He was raised in the puritanical Sandemanian tradition, but joined the Presbyterian Church when he married in 1814. By the 1830s he had established a thriving hardware business, and from there he branched into chandlery, shipbuilding, shipping, and manufacturing. A supporter of the Reform Party, he served as a member of the assembly from 1841 to 1843 and as mayor of Halifax from 1847 to 1848. In 1850 he was appointed to the legislative council, a fitting reward for his role in keeping the Reform Party and its most articulate spokesman, Joseph Howe, solvent. William's son and namesake became a partner in the business, and in 1854, with his son-in-law Robert Morrow, they founded William Stairs, Son and Morrow, one of the few mercantile operations in Halifax to make a successful transition to industrial capitalism. Stairs senior withdrew from involvement in the company to become a founder and president in 1856 of the Union Bank, the fourth such institution in the city, which had become a major financial hub for the Atlantic region.[28]

The Halifax area was arguably the best location in Nova Scotia from which to exercise entrepreneurial initiative, but rural areas could also be harnessed for capitalistic ventures. In the Bay of Fundy community of Minudie, Amos Peck Seaman, a son of New England Planters of Welsh extraction, emerged as the "Grindstone King" of North America. By 1810, with his brother Job as a business partner, Seaman was trading with New England and the West Indies in vessels built in his own shipyards. He became a tenant on the DesBarres estate in 1823, and collected rents for the proprietors. Between 1826 and 1834, Seaman and his partner William Fowler leased the stone quarries on the property and developed a thriving trade with the United States in grindstones used in milling operations. In 1834 Seaman purchased the DesBarres estate, including the fertile marshlands called the Elysian Fields, which had been dyked by Acadians before the expulsion and worked by Acadians and other tenants while the DesBarres family owned the property. Through the purchase of more land, and reclaiming 1,500 acres (600 hectares) from the sea, Seaman accumulated one of the largest landholdings in Nova Scotia.

Seaman was determined to monopolize the output of the quarries on his estate, which had long been a source of supplementary income for tenant farmers and other members of the community. Treating the resource as common property, they had regulated its exploitation more or less cooperatively among themselves. After years of legal wrangling and the eviction of one-third of his tenants, Seaman prevailed over the "transient" quarry workers in 1838, but only through the intervention of Colonial Secretary Lord Glenelg, who was prepared to replace the idea of a people's commons with capitalistic notions of property rights. Seaman's request that Minudie be made a free port was denied, although ports such as Windsor, Parrsboro, Shelburne, and Lunenburg were granted that status in 1839.

Together with his major competitor Joseph Read, who operated primarily on the New Brunswick side of the Bay of Fundy, Seaman dominated the burgeoning grindstone trade along the eastern seaboard of North America. Nearly two hundred men were employed in Seaman's operations, which also included mills and shipyards. Like many entrepreneurs in small-town Nova Scotia, Seaman ruled his empire paternalistically, serving as a local magistrate, building schools and churches, and establishing a Freemasons Lodge. He also constructed Nova Scotia's first steam-powered gristmill, consolidated the weir fishery along the shores of Cumberland County, and took an interest in cattle breeding. In 1850 he called for the early completion of a railway to the St Lawrence to make accessible the market "now shut to us by circuitous navigation."[29] Following his death in 1864, lawsuits relating to inheritance sent Seaman's empire into a downward spiral, a common outcome for many family-owned businesses.

Poverty was endemic in many families trying to make a living in Cape Breton, but even there, merchants who controlled markets and credit could do well. By the 1830s William McKeen, who began his mercantile career in Truro, had established himself as a gentleman farmer and prosperous merchant in Mabou, on Cape Breton's west coast. He dominated the market for local produce – mostly butter, cattle, pork, potatoes, salt fish, and woollen cloth – which he sold in Canso, Halifax, Sydney, and St John's. Since the trade was based largely on barter, producers often became indebted to him and were sometimes dispossessed of their property when the exchange became uneven.[30] Early in the 1850s, McKeen was attacked in his home by a gang of local men, an indication that he was not universally admired in Mabou. In nearby Port Hood, Peter Smyth, another well-heeled merchant, was damned by a delightfully graphic curse: "May he fall off a bridge and may the lobsters devour his private parts."[31]

Comers and Goers

In this period, immigrants continued to arrive, the majority of them from Ireland and Scotland. Artisans and others pushed aside by the new industrial order in Britain now joined crofters and the victims of periodic famines in the exodus. Halifax, Pictou, and Sydney were the main points of entry, but ship captains sometimes tried to avoid quarantine regulations by unloading their sickly passengers on remote shores. Few areas of the sea-girt colony were spared this burden. In 1831 local residents were confronted with sixty disease-ridden passengers dumped on the shores of Digby Gut by a vessel from Galway bound for Saint John.[32] Even with good health and sympathetic treatment, immigrants often had difficulty surviving in their new environment. Cases of extreme distress brought temporary relief from authorities, but such help could not ensure long-term well-being for those who struggled to eke out a living by squatting in backcountry areas or by taking poorly paid employment.

Cape Breton, where half the settlers in the 1830s were squatters, remained the most challenging location in which to put down roots. John Stewart, a Presbyterian missionary from Scotland, was shocked by the misery he encountered on the island in 1834. "I have," he reported, "baptized the child of a parent lying on a pallet of straw, with five children in the state of nudity," and tried "to afford the consolations of religion at a dying bed, in a habitation where no food existed, but what was supplied by neighbours who could ill spare it.[33] Stewart had been sent to Cape Breton by the Glasgow Colonial Society with funds raised by its auxiliary, the Edinburgh Ladies' Association. Under the leadership of the indefatigable Isabella Gordon Mackay, the Association dispatched ministers and teachers to Cape Breton in the 1830s and 1840s, and helped to organize a parish system, which kept its distance from the Presbyterian Church of Nova Scotia until 1860.[34]

Stewart, meanwhile, moved to New Glasgow with his Scottish bride in 1838, no doubt feeling more at home in this prosperous Pictou County community than in backcountry Cape Breton.

In 1827 the Nova Scotia legislature introduced a passenger act designed to put an end to the "coffin-ships" that discharged destitute immigrants and to forestall British plans to assist pauper emigration to the colony. Surveyor General Thomas Crawley huffed that "the lazy inmates" from English poor houses would surely "sink into despair at the sight of stubborn forests and terrific winters" in Cape Breton and only become a charge on the public purse.[35] Although the Passenger Act was later withdrawn, the government was determined to put an end to the arrival of paupers, whose need for food, shelter, and medical care continued to present unwanted challenges to colonial authorities. Their concerns were well founded. In 1827 an outbreak of typhus fever took 800 lives in Halifax out of a total population of about 11,000.[36]

The threat of cholera in 1832, which created havoc in Saint John, Quebec, and Montreal that year, prompted the legislature to impose a head tax of 5 shillings on each immigrant arriving in Nova Scotia and to establish Boards of Health in Halifax and outlying communities to manage epidemics brought by newcomers. Cholera bypassed the colony in 1832, but the tax remained, increasing the hardship facing immigrants. Richard John Uniacke Jr, the assembly member for Cape Breton County, declared in 1834 that he had seen "poor children begging in the streets of Sydney for the means of paying that exaction to which they had become liable, by venturing from one part of the Empire to another."[37] Cholera finally arrived in Halifax in 1834, further galvanizing anti-immigrant sentiment. Overwhelmed by the crisis, in which 284 people died, the government billed the Colonial Office for the cost incurred in sending back to England twenty-nine widows and orphans of pensioners from Chelsea who had died of cholera, along with forty-seven recent arrivals requiring assistance.[38] British immigrants continued to appear each year – including 8,300 Scots between 1839 and 1851 – but they were unwelcome unless they had enough capital to get established.[39] A famine in Ireland, caused by a potato blight, brought a rush of immigrants to North America between 1846 and 1851, but few of them stayed long in Nova Scotia.

By mid-century authorities were faced with a new problem: the exodus of Bluenoses to greener pastures. The potato blight that disrupted Ireland also swept through Scotland and eastern North America, prompting thoughts of emigration among families dependent on subsistence farming.[40] In Cape Breton, where the population relied on the potato more than in other regions of Nova Scotia, many families pulled through only with government support. This often came in the form of "Indian" meal (corn meal), which was widely distributed throughout the island. According to an oral account by a woman identified only as "Katy Mary," settlers from Loch Lomond walked thirty miles to the nearest distribution point. "The poor women were barefooted and each woman took her knitting along with her and knitted as they walked," she reported. "Each man and woman was supplied with half a barrel of Indian meal, then they cried for something to eat." When the barrel was rolled out, they "poured the water from the brook into the barrel and made raw cakes and passed [them] around to each person. All ate heartily, then each man and woman took their half-barrel on their backs and sang 'Ben Dorian' as they left for their homes."[41] Despite the severe hardship, government assistance meant that fewer people in Cape Breton starved to death than in Ireland, but crop failures certainly soured many settlers on their adopted homeland. Emigration gripped Cape Breton between 1847 and 1851, dispersing desperate settlers in the thousands near and far.

The potato blight proved to be the last straw for the Scots living in St Ann's, Cape Breton. In 1820 a settlement had been established there by the dissident preacher Norman McLeod and his followers. They had left Pictou County to establish a separate community in the Ohio Territory, but took shelter from a storm in St Ann's and liked it so much that they decided to stay. Their community thrived under the disciplined leadership of their autocratic pastor, whose clerical status was confirmed in 1827 by the Presbytery of Geneva, in New York State. When the potato crop failed in the late 1840s, McLeod decided "in this evening of his days" – he was approaching his seventieth year – to move to Australia, where his eldest son was living. In 1851 McLeod and his family left "this now desperate & dreary place" in a boat built in the community, for "a kind of comparative Paradise" halfway around the world. By the end of the decade, some eight hundred of his followers had joined him, not in their initial destination of Melbourne, where a gold rush had created a society too godless for McLeod's liking, but in Waipu, New Zealand, which still bears the stamp of these zealous Normanites.[42]

McLeod was not the only Presbyterian parson to abandon Nova Scotia. In 1843 the established Church of Scotland experienced yet another crisis over congregational governance, and more than a third of its members, led by Thomas Chalmers, left the General Assembly to form the Free Church of Scotland. This "Disruption" was preceded by an evangelical movement that had been gaining momentum for several decades, especially among Gaelic-speaking Highlanders, who resented their well-educated Presbyterian ministers, many of whom increasingly identified more with landlords than with their hard-pressed parishioners.[43] Within months of its founding, Free Churches began forming in Nova Scotia, led by John Stewart's congregation in New Glasgow. With Stewart's encouragement, the Nova Scotia Synod repudiated the established Church of Scotland in 1844, and a Free Church College, later named Pine Hill Divinity Hall, opened in Halifax in 1848. All but two ministers of the established church in Nova Scotia and Prince Edward Island returned to their homeland to fill pulpits left vacant by the schism, leaving the Free Church dominant in the Maritimes.[44]

Many Nova Scotians looked to the United States for opportunities. After the War of 1812, the Americans swept aside Indigenous peoples south of the Great Lakes and opened the Ohio Territory to settlement. The annexation of Texas in 1846 and a nasty war with Mexico extended American jurisdiction to the Pacific coast. When gold was discovered in California in 1848, a rush of fortune seekers overwhelmed the local population. Nova Scotians were quick to follow the money, to Ohio, to California, and especially to nearby Massachusetts, the cradle of industrialization in United States. In *The Old Judge*, published in 1849, Haliburton commented that Nova Scotia had become a land of "comers and goers." Among the latter, he reported, were "mature females, who are about to seek their fortunes in the great republic, where they are to cease being servants, and become factory ladies.[45] In this way, "factory ladies" and other peripatetic Nova Scotians were planting their culture across the continent and around the world.

A Great Awakening

In 1933 archivist and historian Daniel Cobb Harvey argued that, between 1815 and 1835, the descendants of diverse peoples "actually began to think as Nova Scotians." Thereafter, he maintained, they "united to produce an intellectual awakening, with its culminating achievement in responsible government."[46] Literacy, which many Nova Scotians prized, served as the foundation for staying intellectually awake. Not only was the ability to read and write valuable for religious and professional purposes; these skills were also essential to the new economic order that demanded disciplined and enlightened citizens capable of making their way in the industrial age.[47]

In this period most children were still taught at home, but the demand for access to public elementary schooling was steadily gaining ground. The assembly appointed a commission in 1824 to survey the state of education in the colony and to advise on policy. Its report estimated that "barely the fourth part of the children in a rapidly increasing population are taught at all," and complained that male teachers were hard to find because they were paid a "pittance" by local school trustees. Eager to put Nova Scotia in the vanguard of education reform, the commissioners recommended a system of "free," universal, and compulsory schooling, such as prevailed in Massachusetts and in many Scottish parishes, and that a general tax be levied to pay for this ambitious undertaking. Such a radical suggestion encountered widespread opposition. Why should people without school-aged children be assessed to pay the cost of educating other people's offspring? Where would poor families, some of them unable to clothe their children adequately to attend school, get the money to pay the tax? And why should children waste time in the classroom when they ought to be contributing to the family economy? Even more contentious was the question of how racial relations and religious instruction would be handled in schools open to children of all cultural backgrounds. These were important questions, and the reactions to them reflected a less cohesive society than Harvey imagined.[48]

When the motion for a general assessment to finance public schools failed in the assembly by a vote of 24–12, the government fell back on piecemeal policies to encourage local initiatives. Periodic reports on schooling underscored the inadequacy of this approach. Acadians had little access to education in their own language other than in areas such as Clare and Île Madame, where francophone priests and lay teachers offered basic training. In communities settled by Highland Scots, Gaelic-speaking teachers from their homeland were eagerly sought, but the German-speaking population of Lunenburg County had little access to schooling in their own language and shunned the English-language teachers available to them. Blacks and Mi'kmaq, unwelcome in most classrooms, were the objects of philanthropic efforts – the Associates of the Late Dr Bray and the Society for the Propagation of the Gospel still operated schools for black children in a few communities – but such initiatives fell far short of the publicly funded and uniform system of education reformers demanded.

In 1828 John Alexander Barry, the representative for Shelburne Township – a man who never minced words and even served prison time for refusing to retract accusations of smuggling against a fellow member of the assembly – explained why formal schooling was necessary. He lamented the declining influence of the Royal Acadian School after Bromley's departure, arguing that, when it was "in full operation, and encouragement given to its teacher, [the streets] were not thronged as they are now were with idle and uneducated children." According to Barry, it was now impossible "to pass from one corner to another, without the ear being assailed by oaths, by curses, and by language such as ought not to proceed from the mouths of any individual, much less from the lips of a child," while "on Sunday ... the playing of marbles and the tossing of coppers was a common amusement." For Baptist educator Edmund Crawley, writing in 1840, the argument for a reformed education policy was clear and unassailable: "Places of education are like roads, bridges, and inns: they facilitate our progress."[49]

In 1841 the legislature established a Central Board of Education and made schools where instruction was conducted in French, Gaelic, and German eligible for grants. The number of schools increased in the 1840s, but remained absent in poorer areas, especially on the Eastern Shore. At the same time, new items appeared on the educational agenda: a Normal School to train teachers and the appointment of a superintendent of education to oversee the general advancement of learning.[50] These were worthy goals, but the immediate need for basic schooling remained a daunting challenge: the 1851 census recorded only 1,096 schools attended by 31,354 students, scarcely one-third of the 88,452 children under the age of ten.

While Nova Scotians dragged their feet on the matter of general assessment, either locally or province-wide, church-operated schools filled some of the gaps. In 1850 Halifax established a Board of School Commissioners, which promptly offered a subsidy to a school for Roman Catholic girls founded the previous year by the Sisters of Charity of New York. Its enrolment soared to four hundred, half of the students exempt from fees.[51] By this time, Arichat was developing as a hub of learning under the steady guidance of the Reverend Colin Francis MacKinnon. Born in Antigonish County in 1810, MacKinnon showed so much intellectual promise that he was sent to Rome in 1829 for higher education. Upon his return to Cape Breton eight years later, he ministered in the Sydney area, where he founded the St Andrews grammar school. He was appointed bishop of Arichat in 1851, a diocese established in 1844 to accommodate the growing Roman Catholic population in eastern Nova Scotia and Cape Breton. MacKinnon founded St Francis Xavier College in Arichat in 1853, and three years later welcomed the sisters of the Congregation of Notre-Dame to undertake the education of girls. The college was moved to Antigonish in 1855, and MacKinnon soon followed, testimony to the growing influence of Scottish clerics in power struggles among Roman Catholics of various cultural backgrounds.[52]

Higher education in Nova Scotia relied primarily on private initiative after Lord Dalhousie's idea of a religiously inclusive, Halifax-based college foundered on denominational rivalries. In 1824 a crisis erupted in St Paul's when Bishop John Inglis, son of Nova Scotia's first Church of England bishop, blocked efforts to appoint an evangelically oriented rector. Disaffected members, including up-and-coming young men such as Edmund Crawley, son of the surveyor general, and James William Johnston, the Jamaican-born offspring of a prominent Loyalist family, founded Granville Street Baptist Church in 1827, and appointed a Boston cleric to their pulpit. The Granville Street converts brought new energy to what hitherto had been a primarily rural church. They helped to establish Horton Academy in Wolfville in 1828, and provided recruits for the ministry, including Crawley, who, after studying at Andover Seminary and Brown University, was appointed pastor of the Granville Street Church in 1831. In 1837 the Baptists founded a denominational newspaper, *The Christian Messenger*. When Crawley was passed over for a position at Dalhousie in 1838, his aggrieved co-religionists promptly secured a charter for what became known as Acadia College, which opened its doors to students in 1839. Crawley justified this initiative as a means of preventing young men from "leaving us, to seek, in other countries, a more advanced education, perhaps never to return."[53]

Other denominations were not far behind the Baptists. Once Catholic emancipation was formally declared throughout the British Empire in 1829, the Roman Catholic hierarchy renewed efforts to educate its adherents. This goal was complicated in Nova Scotia by tensions between Scottish and Irish Catholics when Edmund Burk's successor, the Scottish-born, Gaelic-speaking priest William Fraser, remained in Antigonish following his consecration in 1827. As a result, two Roman Catholic educational institutions emerged, one in Halifax (Saint Mary's, 1841) and another in Arichat/Antigonish (St Francis Xavier, 1853). Even the Congregationalists were inspired by the boom in higher education, establishing Gorham College in Liverpool in 1848 with an endowment from the estate of local businessman James Gorham. The college opened in 1851 under the direction of the Reverend Frederick Tompkins, who had studied at University College, London, but a disastrous fire in 1854 put an end to the initiative. The Methodists, meanwhile, had founded Mount Allison College in 1843 in nearby Sackville, New Brunswick.

Still denied degree-granting status and a permanent grant, Pictou Academy remained the major Presbyterian educational institution in Nova Scotia until Dalhousie College, theoretically non-denominational, was launched in 1838 with Thomas McCulloch as its first principal. Hounded by supporters of the established Church of Scotland and undermined by conservatives in the Church of England and the Roman Catholic Church, McCulloch was saddled with two professors of the "auld Kirk" persuasion, which made it seem to most onlookers that Dalhousie College had been captured by the Presbyterians. Had Crawley been appointed to the Dalhousie faculty as originally planned, this perception might well have been blunted, but bigotry triumphed. Some reformers, including Joseph Howe, urged that the separate colleges be brought together under one non-denominational umbrella in Halifax to increase efficiency, but the decentred college system prevailed, and the new institutions were granted charters. By the time McCulloch died in 1843, Dalhousie College was struggling, and its doors closed two years later, the victim of the highly charged political and religious rivalries of the mid-nineteenth-century. In this context, King's, which abandoned its confessional regulations in 1829, insisted on maintaining its exclusive access to government grants, while the newer colleges, including Mount Allison, which drew many of its students from Nova Scotia, were determined to have their fair share.[54]

The presence of local institutions of higher education by no means discouraged ambitious young men from pursuing degrees elsewhere. Among them was J. William Dawson, who received his early education at Pictou Academy. There he developed an interest in geology, no doubt inspired by McCulloch's natural history museum, which impressed John James Audubon when he visited Pictou in 1833.[55] In the 1840s Dawson studied sciences in Edinburgh, where he was encouraged by the eminent geologist Charles Lyell to conduct fieldwork in Nova Scotia. The results of Dawson's research were published in the *Quarterly Journal* of London's Geological Society, which elected him a fellow in 1854.[56] Dawson taught at Pictou Academy and Dalhousie, served as Nova Scotia's first superintendent of education from 1850 to 1853, and was hired by various colonial governments and entrepreneurs to search for commercial mineral deposits. In 1855, the year his much-praised *Acadian Geology* was published in London and Edinburgh, Dawson was lured to Montreal to serve as principal of McGill University.

Literacy made it possible for people to enjoy the books, magazines, and newspapers flying off English-language presses – if one could gain access to them. To that end, Truro sustained a subscription library between 1812 and 1820, Haligonians sought memberships in the garrison library established by Lord Dalhousie in 1818, and Yarmouth formed a Book Society in 1822. Mechanics' Institutes, founded in Scotland to disseminate scientific education among the artisan class, took root in Nova Scotia, beginning in Halifax in 1831. In addition to offering lectures on a broad range of topics and hosting various artistic activities, the institute sponsored a library designed to supply "useful knowledge at a cheap rate for all who desire it." The first order of sixty-two books included thirty-five works of fiction. Mechanics' Institutes were also established in Yarmouth (1835) and Sydney (1837).[57] In smaller communities, literary and scientific societies were formed to keep members abreast of the times – one was convened by young men in Mabou in the winter of 1843–4[58] – while travelling lecturers and bookselling peddlers slaked the thirst for knowledge in many outlying areas.

In the nineteenth century, newspapers served as the major vehicle for engaging the wider world and for promoting new notions of what was possible at home.[59] Nova Scotia had the most newspapers of any British North American colony in 1820, with twenty-nine founded between 1801 and 1820.[60] Usually larger than their eighteenth-century counterparts and appearing on a weekly or by-weekly basis, they included more local news, and published novels in serial form. One of the first works of fiction produced in British North America came from the pen of Thomas McCulloch, whose *Stepsure Letters* initially appeared in the *Acadian Recorder* between 1821 and 1823. Using gentle humour and satire to encourage disciplined behaviour and more progressive attitudes, McCulloch's fiction was sufficiently popular to prompt him to submit a manuscript to Blackwell's in Edinburgh. "Auld Eppie's Tales," was a wordy effort, but that, it seems, was not the reason for its rejection. Instead it was judged too coarse in the ribald tradition of Jonathan Swift and Walter Scott for an increasingly refined reading public.[61]

Joseph Howe's *Novascotian* had a broad readership, in part because its editor travelled throughout Nova Scotia to sell subscriptions, and also because Howe made a special effort to generate local content. In addition to publishing accounts of debates in the assembly and of his eastern and western "rambles" in the colony between 1828 and 1831, Howe reported the creative output of a small group of men, their names undisclosed, who gathered from time to time in Halifax for "good conversation, good port, and the taste of a fine Havana." Some fifty-two satires, songs, dialogues, and dramas were produced by "the Club" between 1828 and 1831, laying the groundwork for the Mechanics' Institute. Haliburton's *Clockmaker*, which first appeared in the *Novascotian* in 1835–6, was almost certainly inspired by earlier club deliberations.[62]

Although Howe became Nova Scotia's most prominent newspaper editor, the competition for readers was fierce. Along with denominational publications such as the *Christian Messenger*, *Presbyterian Witness*, and Antigonish *Casket* – the latter a small bilingual (English and Gaelic) Catholic weekly[63] – newspapers focusing on commerce, farming, and social reform were founded. Several newspapers were closely allied with emerging political divisions based on conservative and liberal values. In 1813 Anthony Henry Holland launched the *Acadian*

Recorder, which was associated with moderately liberal views, while the Halifax-born publisher Edward Ward founded the *Free Press* in 1816 to champion conservative perspectives.[64] The *Patriot*, a Pictou-based newspaper established in 1827, introduced more radical notions into the mix. Its editor, lawyer Jotham Blanchard, engaged Howe in newspaper debates that elevated the level of political discussion and led Richard John Uniacke Jr to demand that Blanchard be reprimanded in the assembly for supporting republican principles.[65]

As Dawson's career testifies, interest in new scientific thinking and its practical applications were central to the intellectual awakening animating colonial society. The growing enthusiasm for "natural history" inspired artist Maria Morris, a descendant of prominent Nova Scotia surveyors, to publish an illustrated volume entitled *Wildflowers of Scotia* in 1839.[66] Funded by subscriptions, it was the first of four books in a series that together comprised 99 prints representing 146 species of British North American flora. Titus Smith, a talented botanist who had been commissioned by Governor Wentworth to survey the interior of the colony in 1801, provided text to accompany Morris's watercolours. Described by Howe in 1828 as "the Rural Philosopher of Dutch Village Road," Smith was a regular contributor to various newspapers on matters relating to farming and natural sciences. In 1833 he received a grant of £15 from the legislature to collect specimens of geology, botany, and mineralogy for the Mechanic Institute's museum, the precursor to the Nova Scotia Museum, founded in 1868. He also served as secretary to the Central Board of Agriculture, re-established in 1841, a position he held until his death in 1850.[67] By then Haligonians could escape the "dust and din" of the city in a public gardens, established in 1841 on the edge of the Halifax Commons at the behest of the Nova Scotia Horticultural Society, founded in 1836.[68]

Abraham Gesner, born in Cornwallis Township in 1797, pursued a resolutely practical approach to scientific discoveries. After twice being shipwrecked in his efforts to export horses to the West Indies, Gesner studied medicine in London, where he developed a keen interest in earth sciences. He practised medicine in Parrsboro because of its exceptional geological features, which figured prominently in his first book, *Remarks on the Geology and Mineralogy of Nova Scotia*, published in Halifax in 1836. As a result of this achievement, Gesner was hired to conduct geological surveys of New Brunswick and Prince Edward Island. While in New Brunswick, he became acquainted with a natural bitumen deposit known as albertite (named for Albert County), and distilled from it a new substance to provide lighting, which he called "kerosene." Gesner moved to New York in 1853 to commercialize his invention, but an earlier British patent for a similar product undercut his profits. By the end of the decade, petroleum produced in Pennsylvania and Canada West put Gesner out of business.[69]

Patent issues also prevented Charles Fenerty from capitalizing on his discovery of how to make paper from wood pulp. Given the rapid expansion of newspapers and publishing generally, printing shops were fast running out of rags, the material from which newspaper was usually made. German weaver Friedrich Gottlob Keller is credited with inventing the groundwood process for making paper in 1840, but Fenerty claimed to have devised a similar method at least a year earlier. Still a teenager at the time of his breakthrough, he made his findings public only in 1844, when he published a letter in the *Acadian Recorder* about his pulpwood paper, which, he claimed, "is as firm in its texture, as white, and to all appearances as durable as the common wrapping paper, made from hemp, cotton, or the ordinary materials of manufacture."[70]

Men were at the forefront of new literary and scientific initiatives in the first half of the nineteenth century, but the ability to read and write also offered women a path to self-expression and public acclaim. Born in the Annapolis Valley in 1807, Eliza Chipman was encouraged by her Baptist pastor Edward Manning to keep a record of her spiritual journey, a practice she began at the age of sixteen. Despite being mother to twelve children, step-mother to eight more, and performing the public duties demanded of a minister's wife from the age of nineteen, she continued to write in her diary, the existence of which was revealed on her deathbed in 1853. Moved by her spiritual commitment, William Chipman published his wife's journal to serve as an inspiration to other women.[71] Like Eliza Chipman, many literate Nova Scotians kept private records of their spiritual and worldly journeys, and in the process shaped an individual sense of who they were in a rapidly changing society.

Few women ventured into the newspaper business, but two Halifax-based sisters, raised in the Wesleyan Methodist tradition, both briefly entered the field. In 1844 Sarah Herbert took on the editorship of the *Olive Branch*, a periodical devoted to social reform and in which she published poetry and serialized novels produced by herself and other writers from home and abroad. Her career was cut short when she died at the age of twenty-four in 1846. Like her sister, Mary Eliza Herbert was a prolific writer, and her founding of the *Mayflower or Ladies' Acadian Newspaper* in 1851 provided an outlet for her work. Devoted to those who wished "to roam awhile in the flowery field of romance – to hold communion with the Muses," the *Mayflower* survived for only three issues, and most of the contributions came from Herbert herself. Early in 1852, another Halifax writer, Mary Jane Katzmann, founded the *Provincial, or Halifax Monthly Magazine*. It was ambitious in its scope, publishing travel accounts, history, essays, plays, and fiction. When her financial backing evaporated in December 1853, Katzmann opened a bookstore and continued to publish the output of her busy pen. Under her married name of Lawson, she produced an award-winning history of the townships of Dartmouth, Preston, and Lawrencetown in 1887, the achievement for which she is most remembered.[72]

No author in Nova Scotia emulated Haliburton's success in attracting international attention, but a few tried. While still in his teens, William Charles McKinnon, the grandson of a Loyalist who had settled in Sydney, began producing poetry and founding newspapers. His intellectual interests were supported there by a Literary and Scientific Society, a Mechanics' Institute, and John Bourinot's well-stocked bookstore. Inspired by Walter Scott, McKinnon published "The Battle of the Nile," in 1844, a romantic epic on Nelson's defeat of Napoleon in 1798. His early novels, published serially in his newspaper, the *Commercial Herald*, in the winter of 1850, fictionalized Cape Breton history. The first, *St Castine: A Legend of Cape Breton*, was set in Louisbourg during the 1758 siege, and involved a British spy disguised as a larger-than-life Mi'kmaq, "armed merely with a scalping knife." McKinnon's editorials and fictional pieces drew attention in Pictou and Halifax, but he longed for a wider readership. In 1850 he moved to Boston, where several of his novels appeared in the *Waverly Magazine*. Ill-health apparently forced him to return to Nova Scotia, but did not prevent him from running unsuccessfully as a Reform candidate in Victoria County in 1851. Facing rejection in politics and a poor reception for his literary work – Mary Jane Katzmann declared his "windings and contradictions" in *St George, or the Canadian League*, a novel constructed around the Lower and Upper Canadian rebellions, as subjects for only "the most peculiar mind" – he turned to the ministry and was ordained a Methodist minister in 1857.[73]

No writer had more influence on making Nova Scotia's name known to the wider world in this period than New England poet Henry Wadsworth Longfellow. Although he never set foot in the Maritimes, Longfellow immortalized the deportation of the Acadians at Grand-Pré with his epic poem *Evangeline, A Tale of Acadie*, published in 1847. It became an instant success at a time when romantic poetry was in vogue. Translated into French in the 1860s, it was embraced by many Acadians, and helped to consolidate a sense of identity among a people scattered across the Atlantic world. The historical accuracy of Longfellow's portrayal of the star-crossed lovers Evangeline and Gabriel has been called into question by critics, but the emotional authenticity of the story was never in doubt. No other literary character has had a larger impact on Nova Scotia than Evangeline. By the end of the nineteenth century, promoters were touting the "Land of Evangeline" to encourage tourists to visit the Annapolis Valley, and when movies began to shape popular culture, Evangeline became the subject of Canada's first feature-length film, produced by the Halifax-based Canadian Bioscope Company in 1913. The movie found enthusiastic audiences in both Canada and the United States, where portions of Longfellow's most popular poem had appeared in successive generations of school textbooks. Indeed, American producers had released film versions of the Evangeline story in 1908 and 1911.[74]

Longfellow's poem also launched a frenzy of soul-searching among anglophones. Could Britain's brutal treatment of the Acadians in the 1750s not be justified in some way, they wondered? For those aware of the new evidence-based research methods gaining attention in Europe and the United States, the truth of the situation seemed to lie in a close examination of historical records. Thomas Beamish Akins, who as a young man had been trained in the law offices of his cousin Beamish Murdoch and had assisted Haliburton with his historical research, lobbied for a Depository of Colonial Records as early as 1841. His proposal for a Public Records Commission "to cause the ancient records and documents illustrative of the history and progress of society in this province to be examined, preserved, and arranged," was approved unanimously by the assembly in 1857. Akins hoped "to explain the reasons for the expulsion of the Acadians, and in large measure exculpate the Imperial and provincial administrators of the day," but he cast a wide net in his diligent efforts to amass public documents, and laid a firm foundation for the first public archives in British North America.[75] Beamish Murdoch drew upon these archival resources to produce a three-volume *History of Nova Scotia, or Acadie* (1864–7), written to provide "a useful record of the varying events that ... have made Nova Scotia a happy, free and intelligent province, progressive and prosperous." Murdoch failed to provide the final word on the Acadian deportation, and the debate over the morality of the tragedy continues to preoccupy historians.[76]

Longfellow was not the only American writer to influence literate Nova Scotians. While still an adolescent, Theodore Harding Rand travelled from his home in Canard, Kings County, to Boston, where he found employment in a drugstore. He eagerly embraced the new ideas put forward by abolitionists, liberal theologians, and transcendentalists in Massachusetts, and was inspired by the philosophy of Ralph Waldo

Emerson. After enrolling at Horton Academy in 1854, he was caught up in one of the revivals that periodically swept through Baptist institutions, helping him to escape what he described as "the frigid zone of rationalism." A romantic at heart, he wrote poetry and planned to pursue a literary career after graduating from Acadia College in 1860, but instead assumed the chair of English and Classics at his alma mater. In 1864, at the age of twenty-nine, he was appointed superintendent of education. He presided over the inauguration of a public school system in Nova Scotia in 1864–5, and then accomplished the same goal in New Brunswick in 1871.[77]

Sporting activities flourished in Nova Scotia's maturing colonial society.[78] Organized play was still in its infancy, but Halifax was large enough to sustain cricket, curling, horse racing, rowing, and yachting clubs. The military participated in many sporting initiatives, including the first rowing regatta in 1826 and the founding of the Halifax Yacht Club in 1837. In 1824 Scottish residents inspired the founding of a curling club in Halifax, and by mid-century Dartmouth, Truro, Pictou, New Glasgow, Albion Mines, and Sydney each spawned a club and would soon be hosting bonspiels.[79] Hockey, also called "hurley," "shinny," or "ricket," was played in the early 1800s by the students at King's College in Windsor, and the game became popular whenever ice conditions made it possible to play. "Most of the soldier boys were quite at home on skates," one diarist in Halifax commented in 1847. "They could cut the figure eight and other fancy figures, but shinney was their first delight."[80] In the 1860s John Forbes and Thomas Bateman, two employees in John Starr's steam-powered factory in Dartmouth, developed a spring mechanism that revolutionized ice skating. Starr's Acme skates ultimately sold more than 11 million pairs around the world in a variety of styles until they were superseded by the boot skate early in the twentieth century.[81]

Not everyone was pleased by the growing enthusiasm for sports. Evangelical reformers complained about games being held on Sunday, women joining the rowdy spectators, and the gambling, profanity, and violence that sometimes accompanied sporting events. Their concern might have been justified. Horse racing on the Halifax Common, a popular pastime since the 1760s, often included sales of alcohol, card games, dancing, and fisticuffs, all frowned upon by zealous reformers. In 1841 a brawl broke out during the races, after which, the *Acadian Recorder* reported, "the combatants could be seem washing the gore from themselves."[82] These public displays of increasingly frowned-upon behaviour invited efforts to impose regulations that reflected a more refined society.

Progress Deferred

While settler society was buoyed by the promise of progress, the Mi'kmaq struggled for survival. How could a minority population divided among four colonies and numbering little more than 3,000 souls ever develop the capacity to sustain its culture and participate as equals in the new economic order? The challenges they faced were formidable. Settlers continued to steal the land on which the Mi'kmaq lived, even when they had a licence of occupation. At the same time, the newcomers aggressively defended their own property rights, which meant that mobile fishing, hunting, and gathering strategies no longer sustained a healthy lifestyle. Poverty, disease, and demoralization were the inevitable result.

In this period, responsibility for policy relating to the Mi'kmaq gradually devolved from the Crown to local authorities. Lieutenant governors such as Lord Dalhousie and Sir James Kempt were well-meaning in their efforts to establish fixed reserves on which the Mi'kmaq could become farmers, but without adequate resources they were no better equipped than poor immigrants to make a living on the marginal lands carved out for them. When the British government conducted an enquiry into the state of Indigenous peoples throughout the Empire in 1834, Lieutenant Governor Sir Colin Campbell ignored the request for information until ordered to respond by the colonial secretary. The British government, meanwhile, reduced treaty rights to the annual distribution of blankets and sporadic relief in times of crisis. One colonial official went so far as to argue in 1841 that, although the Mi'kmaq possessed "an undeniable Claim to the Protection of the Government as British Subjects," they had no "military title" to systematic relief, as did the Indigenous peoples of the province of Canada who had fought with the British against both the French and the Americans.[83] The distinction between the deserving and undeserving poor was finely honed in colonial Nova Scotia, and proved to be a useful tool for bureaucratic bean counters trying to protect the provincial treasury.

It was not that the Mi'kmaq refused to adjust to the commercial economy of the now dominant culture in Nova Scotia. By the nineteenth century, most bands had taken up subsistence farming and wage-earning labour when they could do so, and sold their crafts and wild berries door-to-door and in community markets. The quality of their handiwork was widely recognized and sought by collectors around the world, but downswings in the economy undermined a stable income from artistic production. When the Mi'kmaq attempted to establish farms, they were harassed by hostile neighbours, and, like them, suffered greatly when crops failed. The Mi'kmaq were willing to work for wages, but needy settlers were invariably the first to be hired.[84]

As was the case from the beginning of contact with Europeans, Mi'kmaq protested their treatment. In 1821 Chief Andrew Meuse appeared before the assembly in a successful effort to prevent the passage of a bill to end the porpoise hunt in the Annapolis Basin on which his community depended. The following year, he began to lobby for a grant of land at Bear River, travelling with Walter Bromley to London in 1825 to plead his case. Meuse failed to secure a freehold grant, but the requested land was surveyed and divided into 30-acre (12-hectare) lots in 1827. In the same year, reserves were confirmed for the Mi'kmaq living at Grand Lake, Indian Brook, Middle River, Malagawatch, Pennall's, New Ross, and Wycocomagh, and other grants followed.[85]

Meuse also collaborated with Grand Chief Paussamigh Pemmeenauweet to organize a petition calling for banning the sale of alcohol to the Mi'kmaq. The legislature acceded to this request in 1829, and attached a provision to the prohibition bill requiring any school receiving public funding to instruct Mi'kmaw children free of charge. Like reserve policies, this legislation was inadequately enforced. Meuse paid a second visit to London in 1831–2, where he consulted with philanthropist Elizabeth Fry and was presented with a medallion by King William IV. Although the Bear River reserve experienced difficulties and Meuse himself succumbed alcohol abuse, he remained a powerful figure in his community until he died in 1850.[86]

On 25 January 1841 the Colonial Office received an eloquent petition addressed to Queen Victoria from the aging Grand Chief Paussamigh Pemmeenauweet, who outlined in his own words the ongoing plight of his people.

I cannot cross the great Lake to talk to you for my Canoe is too small, and I am old and weak. I cannot look upon you for my eyes not see so far. You cannot hear my voice across the Great Waters. I therefore send this Wampum and Paper talk to tell the Queen I am in trouble. My people are in trouble ... No Hunting Grounds – No Beaver – no Otter – no nothing. Indians poor – poor forever. No store – no Chest – no Clothes. All these Woods once ours. Our Father possessed them all. Now we cannot cut a Tree to warm our Wigwam in Winter unless the White Man please. The Micmacs now receive no presents, but one small blanket for a whole family. The Governor is a good man but he cannot help us now. We look to you the Queen. The White Wampum tell that we hope in you. Pity your poor Indians in Nova Scotia. White Man has taken all that was ours.[87]

Within days of receiving this heart-breaking missive, the Colonial Office ordered Lieutenant Governor Lord Falkland to respond. New to his gubernatorial office, Falkland called upon Joseph Howe for his thoughts on the matter. Howe offered no new strategies, but he underscored the need to appoint an official to work with chiefs in getting their people settled on reserves, to act against squatters, and to arrange for Mi'kmaq to attend local schools. The following year, legislation embodying this advice was adopted, and Howe was appointed to the unpaid position of Indian commissioner. After less than two years, he quit in frustration. Howe's home was besieged by supplicants, and it served in the absence of other physical facilities as a place to store clothing and supplies.

The position of Indian commissioner remained vacant until 1847, when Abraham Gesner took on the challenge. He struggled to make a difference in the lives of the Mi'kmaq, but the story remained the same, and even worsened in the late 1840s when the potato blight and Hessian fly devastated crops of potatoes and wheat. "We have never been in a worse condition than now. We suffer for clothes and for vituals," several chiefs reported in 1849. "We cannot sell our baskets and other work, the times are so hard. Our old people and young children cannot live. The potatoes and wheat do not grow, and good people have nothing to give us. Where shall we go, what shall we do? Our nation is like a withering leaf in a summer's day."[88]

No longer considered a threat to European dominance, the Mi'kmaq became marginal, though ever-present, in colonial society. Each summer they emerged from their winter retreats to sell their wares, and they were invited to add colour on ceremonial occasions, including the celebrations in Halifax in June 1838 to mark Queen Victoria's coronation (Figure 10.3). A central feature of Nova Scotia's contribution to the Great Exhibition in London in 1851 consisted of "a canoe, paddles, a dress, cradle, chairs, mats, cigars, fans, purses, hoods, moccasins, and baskets" of Mi'kmaw manufacture.[89] These blurred lines of Nova Scotia's cultural identity reflected ambiguities in relations between the Mi'kmaq and their colonizers that remain unresolved.

In the 1850s Mi'kmaq throughout the Maritime region became the objects of the proselytizing efforts of Silas Tertius Rand, a Baptist minister endowed with exceptional language skills. Rand was drawn to foreign missionary work, but family obligations stood in his way. Acquainted with the Mi'kmaq since his childhood in Cornwallis Township, he undertook the study of their language, and enlisted the support of evangelical philanthropists in Halifax to establish a Micmac Missionary Society in 1850. Rand had genuine sympathy for the Mi'kmaq, but his mission was based on the misguided belief that their failure to join the

Figure 10.3. *Celebration on Halifax Common of the Coronation of Queen Victoria, 28th June 1838*, by William Eager. In this painting, Irish-born artist and art teacher William Eager portrayed Haligonians, including three Mi'kmaq on the far right, celebrating Queen Victoria's coronation in 1838. In the same year, Eager organized an ambitious exhibition that featured 125 works by his students.
Royal Ontario Museum, 955.218.1.

age of progress could be attributed to "the darkness, superstition and bigotry of Romanism."[90] Although Rand's missionary efforts had little lasting impact on religious beliefs among the Mi'kmaq, who remained resolutely Catholic, he played a major role in preserving their culture by collecting their oral history and compiling a dictionary.

African Nova Scotians

The Baptist Church was more successful in attracting adherents among African Nova Scotians. Like the Acadians and Mi'kmaq, the black population in Nova Scotia was scattered in separate communities around the colony. Major settlements such as Birchtown, Brindley Town, and Tracadie traced their origins to the Black Loyalist migration, while

Preston, which had seen most Black Loyalists and Maroons come and go, finally developed a stable population with the arrival of the Black Refugees. What these and other black communities in Nova Scotia held in common with one another and with the larger white community was a strong disposition towards evangelical beliefs, which many black immigrants had brought with them from the United States and then nurtured in their new homeland.

After most of their leaders, including the popular Baptist preacher David George, departed for Sierra Leone in 1792, African Nova Scotians in and around Halifax were served by John Burton, a white immigrant from England who settled into his colonial ministry in 1795. Burton began his career as a Methodist missionary, but converted to the Baptist faith in the United States, and it was from there that he secured funds to build a small chapel at the corner of Birmingham and Barrington streets in 1802. Its membership soared from thirty-three in 1811 to more than three hundred in 1819, making it the largest Baptist church in the colony.[91] Although a few whites were included in this number, most were Black Refugees, who valued Burton's help in getting settled in the Halifax area.

In 1816 a recently emancipated slave, described as more than six feet tall and "light skinned," arrived in the colony from Virginia in search of his mother. He found her in Preston, and took the name of her community. A gifted orator, Richard Preston was encouraged by Burton to become an itinerant preacher, and he quickly gained a following among the black population throughout the colony. Burton's church in Halifax was disrupted in 1825 by the arrival of would-be Baptists from St Paul's who tried to expel blacks from the congregation. With the help of enlightened deacons, money was collected to send Preston to England to study for ordination and to purchase land for a separate black church. He was well received in London, where activists such as William Wilberforce and Thomas Buxton were leading a powerful movement for the abolition of slavery.[92] Preston was ordained by the West London Baptist Association in 1832, and returned to Halifax with more than £600 to help construct a chapel on Cornwallis Street, which he served as pastor. Completed in 1833, the year the British Parliament passed a bill to abolish slavery throughout the Empire, Cornwallis Street Baptist church became a beacon for black Baptists living in Nova Scotia.

The spectacular growth of Baptist churches under Preston's leadership culminated in the creation of the African United Baptist Association, an alliance of twelve churches, in 1854. The Association became a lynchpin in the struggle for social justice in a society consumed with racial prejudice. One of the twelve, Campbell Road Baptist church, founded in 1849, was located in the north end of Halifax. The church documented the migration of African Nova Scotians to the city, which offered better employment opportunities than could be found in most black communities. As the numbers living on Campbell Road increased, the community took on the name of Africville.[93]

Blacks living in Nova Scotia were under no illusion that the formal abolition of slavery would overcome racist attitudes. In 1834 the assembly had passed legislation to "Prevent the Clandestine Landing of Liberated Slaves" from the West Indies, a measure struck down later in the decade by the British government. Britain's support for the abolition of the slave trade and ultimately slavery throughout the Empire warmed the hearts of blacks living in Nova Scotia. When members of the African Friendly Society, founded in Halifax 1831, marched in the parade to commemorate Queen Victoria's coronation, they carried a banner emblazoned with the words "Victoria and Freedom." One of the reforms most desired by many blacks living in the Halifax area was to have their provisional land grants converted to freehold tenure so that, as landholders, they could vote. During the 1840 election, blacks from outside Halifax marched on the polling station at the Court House demanding that they be allowed to exercise their political rights.[94]

Poverty and racism made it difficult for blacks to mobilize resources to establish schools. In 1815 the legislature provided funding for a one-room school and a small house for the school master in both Hammonds Plains and Preston, where white teachers were subsidized by the Society for the Propagation of the Gospel. The growing number of black people living in Halifax, approaching five hundred by the 1830s, prompted the founding of the African School in 1836. Supported by funds raised locally and in England, it was open to both sexes and taught day school, night school, and Sunday school. Inspired by a visit to the Halifax African School, a small group of black settlers founded a school in Port La Tour, near Barrington. Blacks living in Salmon River, outside Yarmouth, petitioned for school funding in 1839, but other priorities came first for subsidies. As with religious observance, schooling for the black population in communities where numbers warranted evolved into a primarily segregated experience.

Even the movement to abolish slavery throughout the world spawned separate organizations in Nova Scotia. Under Preston's leadership, a Negro Abolitionist Society was founded 1846. It played a modest role in advancing the anti-slavery cause in the United States, but it kept up a steady round of activities in Halifax, hosting abolitionist speakers, presenting musical entertainment, organizing annual summer picnics, and raising support for slaves fleeing from the outrages of the Fugitive Slave

Law passed in the United States in 1850. Despite a general sense among most Nova Scotians that slavery was a blot on American society, the Society was unable to enlist much support from Halifax's white community in establishing an interracial front against slavery, not even when Harriet Beecher Stowe, author of the wildly popular anti-slavery novel *Uncle Tom's Cabin*, stopped in the city en route from Boston to Britain in 1854.[95]

Reform, Refinement, and Respectability

As the foregoing attests, the rage for reform animated people of all classes and cultures in Nova Scotia. It could scarcely have been otherwise. Located at the crossroads of popular movements in both Britain and the United States, the colony was awash with new ideas about how to achieve good governance, elevate the poor and marginalized, and reduce the cruelty and violence that punctuated all aspects of community life. The new middle class of reformers was willing to strengthen the powers of the authorities with laws, police, and prisons to achieve these ends, but hoped to encourage self-discipline through church attendance and public schooling, so that the values of peaceful relations and civic virtue would be internalized, making force unnecessary to maintain social control. The result of their efforts ushered in what became known as the Victorian Age, after the popular queen who championed moral rectitude during her long reign from 1837 to 1901.[96]

Without question, there was much that needed reforming in Nova Scotia, especially in Halifax, which, like most seaport towns, was renowned for violent and illegal activities. By mid-century the city's waterfront was home to a thick underworld of boarding-house keepers, crimps (traffickers in crewmen), and prostitutes, who took advantage of soldiers and sailors sojourning in the city.[97] In August 1838 a two-day riot broke out when a discharged soldier claimed to have been robbed by prostitutes, bringing his friends and soldiers into the streets to redress the transgression. Violence between townsfolk and visiting sailors could erupt at any time, as Mayor Alexander Keith discovered early in March 1853, when the *Winchester*, an American-registered vessel travelling from Liverpool to New York, limped into the harbour after being battered by a storm off the Grand Banks. Within a few hours of its arrival, the captain charged eleven of the crew with mutiny. The alleged mutineers were subsequently attacked by a mob, outraged by a report that three female passengers from Ireland had been sexually harassed by the mutinous male crew and an Irish-born physician. The mayor read the Riot Act and summoned 150 soldiers from the Citadel to prevent a lynching. Although the three sailors charged with assault were acquitted in a hastily convened trial in which the women's testimony was flatly contradicted by the male witnesses, it was clear, as the historian David Sutherland argues, that new values around class, ethnicity, and gender were complicating contentious issues in Victorian Halifax.[98] The political significance of the trial was signalled by the status of the lawyers involved: Premier James B. Uniacke for the persecution and opposition leader J.W. Johnston for the defence.

Violence played a significant role in most elections. This was inevitable, given that voting was conducted orally, voters were liberally treated with alcohol, and intimidation served as a practical strategy for carrying the poll. In 1832 the contest for the new riding of Cape Breton County was particularly violent as GMA manager Richard Smith took on William Young, the son of the agricultural reformer John Young. Smith spent lavishly to attract support, and employed a gang of miners to guard the hustings in Sydney, where he won handily (394–7). Meanwhile, Young, a resident of Halifax, was greeted with cries of "Down with Nova Scotians," a reference to lingering resentment against the union of 1820. The contest turned in Young's favour in Arichat and Cheticamp, where Catholic Scots supported his candidacy. In Cheticamp, 150 Highlanders seized the poll to prevent Smith's supporters from voting. The otherwise progressive town of Pictou was especially prone to violence on polling day. During a by-election in 1843, tension between the adherents of the established Church of Scotland and the Secessionists was so acute that Pictou's sheriff constructed a ten-foot barrier across the street to the hustings to keep the warring factions apart.[99] Given the violence that surrounded elections, women were warned to stay away from the polls. An exception was made during the bitterly fought election of 1840, when a few single women and widows in Annapolis County who met the property qualifications for the franchise were "carried up to the hustings" in an effort to win the poll.[100]

Pictou County bore out John Homer's concerns about contentious class relations associated with the mining industry. The workers at Albion Mines were not easily intimidated, temporarily walking off the job or moving elsewhere – often to Pennsylvania, where both the climate and wages for coal miners were better – if they felt they were treated unfairly. In the early years of mine operations, as in most industrial enterprises, relations between managers and workers were conducted along paternalistic lines. Richard Smith even felt obliged to descend regularly into the mines, which were plagued by gaseous emissions, to satisfy his men that working conditions were safe. Their caution was well founded. In December 1833 the miners held a parade to commemorate the first anniversary of a disastrous fire, attributed to incendiaries, which killed fourteen horses and shut down the mines for six months.

GMA officials got a stronger taste of collective action in 1840, when the miners struck for and won better wages. With markets for Nova Scotia coal collapsing due to increased production in the United States, the company tried to roll back wages in the late autumn of 1841. A three-months' strike of almost all mine employees ensued. The company timed its announcement of a wage reduction to coincide with the winter slowdown, which made its decision to cut off coal supplies to miners and access to the company-controlled store a genuine hardship. Samuel Cunard arrived on the scene to manage the crisis, and both sides agreed after two weeks of negotiations to split the difference, but not before more than a hundred angry wives and children descended on Mount Rundell to give mine manager Henry Poole a fright. In the spring Pictou County's parsimonious magistrates petitioned the assembly to make Albion Mines a separate poor district so that they would never again have so many miners on their relief rolls.[101]

Interpersonal relations in Nova Scotia also included a level of violence that reformers hoped to avoid. Under British common law, which prevailed in the colony, wife beating was rarely prosecuted, and the foundation of discipline at home and at school was based on the old adage "spare the rod and spoil the child." Men were especially inclined to settle their differences through violence, with the more gentlemanly among them resorting to formal duels, despite a growing opposition to such confrontations since 1819, when Richard John Uniacke Jr killed his opponent, resulting in a sensational trial.[102] Even cruelty to animals was everywhere in evidence. Cock fights and bear baiting were popular pastimes, wild beasts were slaughtered in large numbers for sport, and domesticated animals often bore the brunt of their owners' angry frustrations. For marginalized peoples, institutional violence in the form of courts, prisons, and reformatories produced systemic outcomes in which they did not fare well.

Spearheaded by churches, the reform of personal behaviour became a widespread movement. Family life especially required attention, starting with the abandonment of extramarital relations such as those publicly displayed by the Wentworths and the Duke of Kent. In the prescriptive literature of the period, companionate marriages were encouraged. Women were told that their place was in the private sphere of the home, while men were the designated providers and possessed with personal, political, and professional rights in the public sphere that were withheld from women. One of the most best articulations of this doctrine was presented to the Young Men's Christian Association in Halifax in November 1856 by Robert Sedgewick, a Presbyterian minister who had emigrated from Scotland in the late 1840s. "Woman is the complement of man," he argued, and "the sphere of woman is home and whatever is co-relative with home in the social economy." In her role as daughter, sister, wife, mother, teacher, friend, member of the church, and messenger of mercy, Sedgewick asserted, a woman found her "true" vocation.[103] His lecture served as a counterpoint to liberal feminist perspectives, which were boldly outlined in the Declaration of Sentiments produced at a much publicized women's rights convention in Seneca Falls, New York, in 1848.

As Nova Scotia women began their long struggle for equal rights, they became enthusiastic supporters of a movement to improve men's behaviour. The most obvious route to this end was to encourage temperance in the consumption of alcohol, which fuelled so many of the violent outbursts in public and private life. In the early nineteenth century, imported and locally produced alcohol, most notably rum, was consumed at an alarming rate in Nova Scotia – reputedly 10 gallons (more than 45 litres) per capita every year.[104] Alcohol was the elixir of choice in colonial society for social occasions and for anyone suffering from mental or physical distress. It also figured prominently in most barter exchanges, and was regularly doled out to workers on waterfronts, in lumber camps, and during militia exercises. Some communities became notorious for drunken behaviour. In 1824 Catholic priest James Grant was dispatched to Manchester (Guysborough) charged not only with carrying out his clerical duties, but also paid by the government to establish order at nearby Fox Island and Crow Harbour, where alcohol-induced brawling was creating havoc.[105] The two communities were locked in competition for ascendancy in the mackerel fishery, which had expanded with the introduction of jigging technology developed in Massachusetts and the growing demand for a plentiful fish commonly used as bait.[106]

While efforts to limit the consumption of alcohol were common enough at various times in the Western world, the modern temperance movement began in the early 1800s in the United States. Beaver River in Yarmouth County and West River in Pictou County established British North America's first temperance societies in 1828. According to local tradition, the Beaver River organization was formed after a shipwreck washed ashore multiple copies of a wildly popular sermon by Lyman Beecher, a Presbyterian minister who had co-founded the American Temperance Society in 1826. The presence of the printed sermon on board the blighted vessel testifies to the enthusiasm for a movement whose time had come. The benefits of temperance were immediately apparent to its promoters. On 17 September 1828, Pictou's *Colonial Patriot* reported:

On Friday last the frame of a large house, the property of Mr. Geo. Mc-Donald, of West River, was erected WITHOUT THE USE OF RUM! In lieu of it ale and beer were used, so that the work was completed in a superior manner, while neither abusive language, nor profane swearing was heard, no black eyes nor drunken men seen; but peace and friendship pervading the concourse. That this change of custom, in this part of the country will be followed in future (at least to a great degree) may be reasonably expected, since it tends not only to promote the harmony, health and respectability of those who assemble on such occasions, but the interest of the builder.[107]

In the early days of the movement, most temperance societies were aligned with churches, which encouraged their adherents to take the pledge. Nova Scotians did so in the thousands, despite being obliged to follow strict regulations that resulted in expulsion for backsliders and even for personally temperate merchants who trafficked in the demon rum. In 1834 a temperance convention was held in Halifax, and by 1837 Nova Scotia boasted more than eighty temperance societies. While churches continued to play a central role in the temperance movement, it took on a more non-denominational tone with the founding of the Sons of Temperance in New York in 1842. Five years later, a Sons of Temperance local was founded in Yarmouth, and within a year thirteen organizations convened a Grand Division in Nova Scotia.

What began as a movement for personal discipline focusing on the consumption of hard liquor gradually turned into a demand for state intervention to stop the manufacture, sale, and consumption of all alcoholic beverages. Total prohibition was by any measure a radical idea. It threatened not only deeply rooted social and commercial practices in colonial society; it also would cut seriously into the wealth of the colonial treasury, which relied for as much as half of its revenue on import duties and licence fees applied to alcohol. As the movement spread, the Church of England and the Roman Catholic Church took up the cause, but replacing wine with non-fermented grape juice at communion, a practice favoured by evangelicals, was deemed as going a little too far. Inevitably, Irish and Scottish Catholics took separate approaches, with Bishop Fraser controlling the Church's Total Abstinence Society and Irish Catholics sustaining the less rigorous Temperance Society. Acadians, separated by language and culture, and Catholic Scots in Cape Breton were the least likely to embrace temperance in an organized way, but no one was immune from the view that respectable folks no longer drank alcohol to excess.[108]

The temperance movement failed to stop but it certainly reduced the consumption of alcohol.[109] It also prompted a number of important side effects, among them a more prominent role for women in the public sphere. Although women in colonial Nova Scotia occasionally petitioned the government individually for land or relief, they usually did not sign petitions or petition collectively. This reticence receded as male temperance advocates sought allies in their cause. In 1835 the *Yarmouth Herald* published a list of ways women could participate in the movement, including attending meetings of temperance societies, "patronizing temperate taverns and groceries," and "refraining from forming any connexions with one who habitually drinks distilled or fermented liquors."[110] Empowered by the temperance crusade, women soon began pushing the boundaries of their participation, signing petitions and forming separate female temperance organizations. Women's involvement in temperance activities extended to fund-raising initiatives to support Sunday schools, colleges, and foreign missions. In the 1830s Baptist women in the Maritimes helped to raise money – again, much knitting was involved – to establish Acadia College, and formed Female Mite Societies to support missionary endeavours.

Nova Scotia's Protestant churches were at the forefront of the overseas Christian missionary movement. In 1845 Maritime Baptists collaborated to send Richard Burpee to Burma under the auspices of the American Baptist Foreign Mission Board. Secessionist Presbyterians were not far behind, sponsoring John Geddie, who had migrated to Pictou as a toddler in 1817, to establish a mission to the New Hebrides in 1846. Closer to home, the Baptists donated money to the Grande Ligne Mission in Montreal, designed to wean French-speaking Catholics from the error of their ways. Obed Chute, pastor of the Wallace Bay Baptist Church, visited the Grand Ligne Mission for five months in 1852 before beginning his work among the Acadians in southwestern Nova Scotia. Like the Mi'kmaq, they proved impervious to the proselytizing of overzealous Baptist missionaries.

⟳⟲

By the mid-nineteenth century, leading Nova Scotians could look back with some pride on how well their generation had adjusted to major challenges, among them a prolonged post-war slump, mass immigration, economic uncertainty, and new values associated with the Industrial Revolution. Their sense of collective identity, though still fragile, was represented in movements for improving themselves and their communities and, as we shall see in the next chapter, for reforming a system of colonial governance that seemed increasingly out of step with the liberal ideologies sweeping across the North Atlantic world.

Chapter Eleven

Making Progress, 1820–1864

In 1848 Nova Scotia became the first colony in the British Empire to be granted what was cautiously labelled "responsible government," a system whereby political power devolved from officials appointed by the Crown to elected local elites. This milestone coincided with a period of unprecedented economic transformation inspired by advances in communications technologies that collapsed time and space at a dizzying pace. Taking advantage of its dominance in international commerce and a calamitous famine in Ireland, Britain embraced free trade and abandoned the lingering restrictions of the Navigation Acts between 1846 and 1849. This momentous shock demanded new strategies for colonies nurtured in the cocoon of the mercantile system. Ultimately, the transition proved less disastrous than many had feared. Nova Scotia's producers and shippers welcomed better access to global markets, many of which were already open to them as participants in Britain's expanding commercial empire. A major exception was the United States, but markets there became less restricted in 1854, when Britain negotiated reciprocal free trade in primary products for its North American colonies. In place until 1866, the Reciprocity Treaty, along with the demand generated by the Crimean War (1854–6) and the American Civil War (1861–5), boosted production and trade. It was a good time for making progress.

The Solution of 1848

The peaceful transition to self-government is one of Nova Scotia's greatest political achievements. Under representative government instituted in 1758, power had been weighted towards appointed institutions: the lieutenant governor, legislative council, and judicial apparatus. The legislative council, the so-called Council of Twelve, also served as the executive council, advising the lieutenant governor on policy matters. With few exceptions, political appointments were biased towards Halifax, the Church of England, and mercantile success, awarded to men who seemed increasingly out of step with liberalizing tendencies in the Western world. In 1828, Thomas Chandler Haliburton, by no means a radical critic, described the Council of Twelve as "pensioned old ladies," most of whom "think all the world is contained within the narrow precincts of Halifax."[1] Over time the elected assembly served as a forum for critics – among them Loyalists, rural members, and an emerging middle class of artisans, entrepreneurs, evangelicals, and professional men – to protest an oligarchic government, but it had little power to implement significant policy changes.[2]

Responsible government turned the old representative system upside down. Instead of power emanating from the top of the political hierarchy, it derived from the majority in the assembly, ideally embodied in a cohesive political party, which alone chose members of the executive council and to which it was collectively responsible. Under responsible government, the lieutenant governor relinquished his authority and accepted the recommendations of his democratically elected advisors. The same political revolution was taking place in Britain itself, where the Reform Act of 1832 rooted out some of the worst abuses of the electoral system, but on both sides of the Atlantic there was much muddling through and sometimes violent confrontations before the mechanics of parliamentary democracy and constitutional monarchy were fully sorted out.[3]

Under representative government in Nova Scotia, the Council of Twelve, which met in secret, could block measures passed by the assembly, with one important exception: money bills. Tensions between appointed and elected members of the legislature over such issues as bank charters, funding for roads and bridges, grants to denominational colleges, import duties, and quit-rents on property came to a head in 1830 in the so-called Brandy Election. In 1826 the assembly had imposed a duty of 1s 4d on imported brandy to raise revenue, but a technicality enabled customs officials to collect a smaller amount. When Enos Collins and other shippers discovered this discrepancy, they refused to pay any part of the levy, and used their position on the council to block the assembly's revised legislation.

The election of 1830, fought around the issue of the brandy tax, was hotly contested and resulted in the death of one man in Pictou, where Kirk supporters rioted against Secessionists, crying "Fear God and hate the Anti-Burghers." The new assembly reimposed the duty on brandy, and the council accepted it but came off looking badly. This was also the case two years later when the council, which included five directors of the Halifax Banking Company, tried to restrict the powers of the new Bank of Nova Scotia. In the ensuing rumpus, the duelling banks created a financial crisis that compounded a general economic recession and generated more disgust with the ruling oligarchy.

The Brandy Election was a defining moment for Joseph Howe, who ultimately made a name for himself as a champion of political reform (Figure 11.1). It was not a position he came to naturally. As a young man he had embraced the conservative values of his parents, who were adherents of the Sandemanian sect in Boston, members of which were branded as Loyalists for their pacifism. Howe's father was a printer, and in the early 1800s was appointed king's printer and postmaster general, positions he transferred to his eldest son. As a younger off-spring in a large family, Joseph was obliged to make his own way in the world. He was well equipped to do so, being home schooled, and set to work as an apprentice in his father's print shop from the age of thirteen.

After assuming the editorship of the *Novascotian* in 1827, Howe observed at close range the Council of Twelve's self-serving practices and the outright corruption of the men appointed to their positions for life by their friends in high places. Members of Howe's family had been beneficiaries of official favour, but they were equipped with strict ethical values and a sense of duty that some government appointees clearly lacked. Integrity and merit mattered to Howe, and the governing structures demonstrated neither when men such as Halifax County's negligent treasurer William Cleaveland remained in office because the grand jury that presided over municipal affairs refused to accede to his dismissal.[4] Even more damning were the practices of W.H. Roach, the acting commissioner of the Bridewell, who used the prison's facilities, employees, and inmates to enrich himself. Richard Tremaine, a commissioner on the board overseeing the Poor Asylum, behaved no better, bilking the institution by supplying inferior provisions at exorbitant prices.

With a flourishing newspaper at his disposal, Howe was in a position to call into question Nova Scotia's political institutions. On 1 January 1835 the *Novascotian* published a letter, signed by "The People" – written by Howe's friend George Thompson – alleging that, in "the last thirty years, the Magistracy and Police [in Halifax] have, by one stratagem or other, taken from the pockets of the people, in over exactions, fines, etc., etc., a sum that would exceed in the gross amount £30,000."[5] This statement was actionable under British law, which held that it was libellous to publish anything that degraded a person or disturbed the public peace, and that the truth of the charge could not be used as a

Figure 11.1. Portrait of Joseph Howe, from a painting by T. Debaussy, London, 1851. This portrait of Joseph Howe captures the young "conservative reformer" who hoped to make Nova Scotia the "normal school" for colonial development in the British Empire.
From *The Speeches and Public Letters of Joseph Howe*, vol 1, 1804–48 (Halifax: Chronicle Publishing, 1909), frontispiece.

defence. In 1820 William Wilke, a descendant of one of the founders of Halifax, had been sentenced to two years in prison for publishing a pamphlet criticizing money-grubbing magistrates.[6]

Howe pleaded his own case in a six-hour oration, a clever strategy because he could present arguments that would be off-limits to trained lawyers. His long litany of corruption by political appointees reportedly brought some men in the crowed courthouse to tears, and the jury took only ten minutes to return a verdict of "not guilty." With public opinion on his side, Howe emerged as the darling of liberals everywhere. Haligonians erupted in two days of celebration, and Howe appeared in the Exchange Coffee House on 30 March to receive a silver pitcher sent by his admirers in New York in recognition of his contribution to freedom of the press.[7] Although journalistic freedom would continue to be violated in Nova Scotia and libel law remained unreformed in the British Empire until 1843, the significance of Howe's case was widely acknowledged.

In the 1836 election, Howe won a seat for Halifax County. He quickly emerged as the spokesman in the assembly for the Reform Party (called the Liberal Party by the mid-1850s). Its supporters included the colony's first Acadian members, Simon d'Entremont from Argyle and Frederick Robicheau from Clare, documenting a resurgent sense of purpose among a hitherto politically dispersed Roman Catholic minority. At the same time, Laurence O'Connor Doyle, a lawyer trained in Richard John Uniacke's office, brought energy to the Reform cause and represented an increasingly cohesive Irish Catholic bloc, first as a member for Arichat Township (1832–40) and then for Halifax County (1843–7) and Halifax Township (1847–1855).

In 1837 Doyle sponsored the Quadrennial Act, which limited assembly terms to four years rather than seven, while Howe introduced twelve resolutions calling for, among other things, an elected legislative council, executive responsibility "to the Commons," and the exclusion of judges and churchmen from the council.[8] The Colonial Office rejected the elective principle, but bowed in the direction of reform by dissolving the Council of Twelve and creating separate executive and legislative councils, a structure already in place in the Canadas since 1791 with no obvious advantage to liberal principles. Lieutenant Governor Sir Colin Campbell initially tried to swamp the councils with church officials, and even appointed James W. Johnston, a leading spokesman for the embryonic Conservative (or Tory) Party, to both of the new bodies, but Howe remained outside Campbell's charmed circle.[9]

Howe's involvement in political reform coincided with mounting tensions leading to rebellions against oligarchic rule in both Lower and Upper Canada in 1837–8. Eager to avoid further violent outbursts, the British government appointed John George Lambton, Lord Durham, a man known for his liberal views, to make recommendations for reforms in colonial governance. Drawing on advice from Robert and William Baldwin in Upper Canada, Durham recommended a system of "responsible government," which required colonial governors to choose their advisors from those who had the support of the majority in the assembly. Neither the colonial secretary, Lord John Russell, nor Tories on either side of the Atlantic were prepared to go that far, but Howe was a convert to this position, arguing as early as 1836 that Bluenoses should enjoy the same political rights as "our brethren across the water." In a letter to Lord Russell in September 1839, Howe elaborated on this point: "Every poor boy in Nova Scotia ... knows that he has the same right to honours and emoluments of office as he would have if he lived in Britain or the United States; and he feels that while the great honours of the empire are almost beyond his reach, he ought to have a chance of dispensing the patronage and guiding the administration of his native country without any sacrifice of principle or diminution of self-respect."[10]

Howe's comments were written in response to Russell's ten resolutions, which withheld responsible government but authorized governors to replace their executive councillors from time to time to reflect the complexion of the assembly. Much depended on how far governors would go in this matter. When Campbell refused to bend, the Reformers carried a motion of non-confidence in his executive council and demanded the governor's recall. Tensions between Conservatives and Reformers ran so high that Howe was forced to fight a duel with John Halliburton, son of the chief justice. No lives were lost – Halliburton missed and Howe fired his pistol into the air – but authorities were alarmed, and Governor General Charles Poulett Thompson was dispatched to Halifax in the summer of 1840 to encourage harmony between the opposing sides. Two avowed Reformers, Howe and James McNab, joined a coalition executive of nine members convened by the new lieutenant governor, Lord Falkland, in October 1840, but it was a poor reflection of the recently elected assembly. Some Reformers were critical of Howe, accusing him of putting ambition ahead of principle. Herbert Huntington, representing Yarmouth in the assembly, was the most consistent proponent of party solidarity, but Howe, obsequiously loyal to Britain and greedy for public office, was prepared to give the new system a try.[11]

In the context of a Reform-dominated assembly and councils decidedly Conservative in their sympathies, political harmony proved elusive. Enmity between the two parties intensified in 1843 when Howe supported a motion to withdraw government grants to sectarian colleges and devote them to the creation of one non-denominational university in Halifax. This move put Acadia College in jeopardy and stiffened Johnston's resolve to restrict the power of the Reformers. During the same session, Howe announced his intention to push ahead with full responsible government, including "the formation of a cabinet composed of heads of departments." Johnston interpreted this statement as a demand for rule by "political factions," and predicted that it would "lead to the oppressive and corrupting use of patronage."[12] He was right, of course, but party rule and control of patronage – some nine hundred appointments were at stake – were exactly what the Reformers demanded.

With his executive council in disarray, Falkland dissolved the assembly and called an election in the autumn of 1843. During the campaign, he tried to shore up his position by appointing Johnston's brother-in-law, Mather Byles Almon, to both the executive and legislative councils. This was too much for Howe, McNab, and James Boyle Uniacke, who resigned from the executive council in protest. A late convert to the Reform movement, Uniacke saw which way the political winds were blowing and acted accordingly. Johnston won the support of a slim majority in the assembly due to the loss of eight Reform seats in primarily Baptist constituencies, but the Conservatives now controlled the government, and would have to relinquish their power if they lost a general election.

Over the next four years, the Reformers laid the groundwork for victory. Howe assumed editorial control of the *Novascotian* and the *Morning Chronicle*, both owned by his political ally William Annand, where he kept the Tories on their toes. Never one to hold his tongue, Howe blunted his chances of becoming the first premier under responsible government by poking fun at Falkland in newspaper coverage that was deemed less than refined by the standards of the day – in particular a bit of doggerel that began "The Lord of the Bed-chamber sat in his shirt" – setting opposition tongues wagging. Howe compounded his offence by arguing in the assembly that had the author said that "the Lord of the Bedchamber had no shirt, or that it stuck through the pantaloons, there might have been good grounds for complaint."[13]

Despite Howe's coarse language, the Reformers managed to woo more Catholic voters in Halifax, thanks to Johnston's bigoted sentiments, and three Lunenburg seats were ripe for turning. The Reformers triumphed on 5 August 1847 after a bitter campaign in which simultaneous voting was introduced into the electoral process. This measure eliminated some of the corruption associated with the previous system, but it did little to prevent race and religion from being exploited for partisan advantage. Johnston alleged that the Reform Party's Irish supporters were plotting to establish "Catholic ascendancy" in Nova Scotia, and gangs of black Conservatives and Irish Reformers, often rivals for any low-paying jobs on offer, clashed violently in Halifax, raising concerns that the city might descend into chaos.[14] Although the Reform Party won a clear majority of seats in 1847, Johnston remained in office in the hope of reconstructing the coalition, but such a solution to the "colonial question" was no longer possible. When the assembly met early in 1848, it voted non-confidence in the executive council, and Johnston resigned. Both Lieutenant Governor Sir John Harvey, who had served in the three other Atlantic colonies before arriving in Nova Scotia in 1846, and the third Earl Grey, colonial secretary in Lord John Russell's Whig administration, bowed to the inevitable.[15]

On 2 February 1848 the Reformers, under the leadership of James Boyle Uniacke, formed the first "responsible government" in British North America. The province of Canada followed the same path a few weeks later. This achievement was only one step – admittedly an important one – on the road to full autonomy. The Colonial Office remained a powerful influence in policies relating to defence, external affairs, legal matters, and constitutional amendment, and governors still exercised important discretionary powers. Nor was responsible government the democratic triumph it is sometimes made out to be. Voting rights were restricted to men over twenty-one years of age who owned property, and only a narrow pool of candidates was eligible for public office. And party rule brought its own demons, including playing to interest groups and currying favour in ways that brought political institutions into disrepute. Nevertheless the solution of 1848 was significant, setting in motion democratic processes that gradually yielded broader citizen engagement.

Responsible Government in Action

Before introducing long-delayed reforms, the new administration was obliged to adapt provincial institutions to make responsible government work. Colonial Secretary Earl Grey had agreed to the principle of party rule in Nova Scotia, but he had to be persuaded by Lieutenant Governor Harvey of the need for cabinet responsibility on the British model. This innovation meant dismissing appointees to the executive council and sorting out their pensions, which many people judged to be unnecessarily generous. More shaking of heads followed the transfer of Crown revenues to the province, which was now required to pay administrative salaries, including that of the lieutenant governor. Determined to end lifetime appointments, the Liberals introduced bills to have Supreme Court judges, the provincial treasurer, and the surveyor general serve at the pleasure of the government.[16]

Many of the issues the Reformers hoped to address had long been the subject of debate. Public schooling and college grants were high on the agenda, as were ways of improving conditions for private investors. In their first session, the Reformers introduced bills to provide limit liability for co-partners in business enterprises and to place Dalhousie College under the scrutiny of a government-appointed board of governors. Opposition both within and outside the government prevented Dalhousie from getting established as a non-denominational provincial college and stalled the creation of a public school system. Undaunted, the Reformers laid the groundwork for progress by appointing J. William Dawson as Nova Scotia's first superintendent of education in 1850, and by establishing a provincial Normal School, which opened its doors in Truro in 1855.

Genuinely alarmed by the revolution transforming political processes, Conservatives in the assembly and the legislative council made as much trouble as they could for the Reform government. Harvey described them as "a violent, fractious opposition,"[17] an assessment no doubt fuelled by their demand that his salary be reduced. In the legislative council, Conservatives tried to water down the judges' bill, and Bishop John Inglis, who hitherto had paid little attention to his privileges in the upper chamber, voted on every issue to protect the prerogatives of the Crown and the permanent grant to King's College. Through appointments and persuasion, the Reformers managed to carry their modest 1848 program in the legislative council, but when Harvey acceded in 1849 to the dismissal of more than a hundred justices of the peace, tensions reached the breaking point. Despite a swarm of angry petitions to the Colonial Office demanding the measure be rescinded, Grey, with some coaching from Howe, held firm.

The Conservatives were outraged by their diminished influence, but they proved more restrained in their response than their counterparts in Lower and Upper Canada, which in 1840 had been cobbled together by the British government into one colony. Following the achievement of responsible government in the united province of Canada, the new Reform government under the leadership of Robert Baldwin and Louis-Hippolyte LaFontaine passed legislation awarding compensation to rebels whose property had been damaged by British forces during the 1837–8 uprisings. In response, a Tory mob torched the legislative building in Montreal and pelted Governor General Lord Elgin with refuse. Meanwhile, many of the city's merchants, smarting from Britian's abandonment of the Navigation Acts, protested their loss of protected markets by signing a petition calling for annexation to the United States. The province of Canada seemed poised to dissolve into the kind of political chaos sweeping many European capitals in this period and inspiring radical ideas such as those advocated by German philosophers Karl Marx and Friedrich Engels in the *Communist Manifesto*, published in 1848.

An intercolonial conference, with LaFontaine serving as chair and Howe as secretary, was convened in Halifax in September 1849 to consider less disruptive ways of dealing with common economic challenges. The delegates agreed to ask the British government to negotiate free trade in natural products with the United States and to seek approval from their legislatures for removing tariff barriers to intercolonial trade. The latter policy was slow to materialize because of the potential loss to provincial treasuries of money from low-revenue-generating tariffs imposed by each self-governing colony after Britain had adopted free trade. In British North America, as elsewhere in the modernizing world, governments faced a common problem: how to generate sufficient revenue to pursue their ambitious programs.

Uniacke was officially the leader of Nova Scotia's Reform government, but Howe, appointed provincial secretary, did most of the heavy lifting. No issue animated Howe more than the new communications technologies. After its successful testing by American inventor Samuel Morse in 1844, telegraphic communication became an immediate necessity. Howe moved quickly to establish a board of commissioners to oversee the construction of a telegraph line to the New Brunswick border. This was part of a larger project orchestrated by Frederic Newton Gisborne, an English-born engineer from Canada East, who was appointed superintendent of Nova Scotia's telegraph lines in 1849.[18] One exciting chapter in this communications story was the operation of a pony express, financed by the Associated Press, to carry mail the 146 miles (235 kilometres) from Halifax to Digby Gut, from where it was shipped to Saint John and relayed to cities along the Atlantic seaboard. Once the telegraph line was completed to Halifax in November 1849, the pony express went out of business, but during its ten months of operation it generated a great deal of excitement in communities where the mad dash, which took as little as eight hours to complete, could be witnessed. After several failed attempts, a cable was finally laid across the Atlantic Ocean in 1866, making communication between the two continents almost instantaneous.

At Howe's insistence, the telegraph line to New Brunswick was constructed as a government project to keep it out of the hands of "speculators," and he hoped to build railways the same way. Three projects competed for attention: a railway running from Halifax through Amherst and Saint John to Portland, Maine; an intercolonial line linking Halifax to Quebec City; and shorter routes from Halifax to Windsor, Truro, and Pictou. With the Colonial Office refusing to support any of them, Howe travelled to Britain in the fall of 1850 to secure an £800,000 loan from private investors. He was, he declared, responding to a cry from Nova Scotia for "further industrial development; active employment for the people; new and improved facilities for business and social intercourse."[19] It would not be the last time Nova Scotia's political leaders would make just such a pitch to outside investors.

Howe's five-month sojourn in Britain focused on making "my little country, God bless her snow clad hills," better known and more respected.[20] To that end, he peppered Colonial Secretary Grey with memoranda and delivered a well-received speech in Southampton urging Britons to pay more attention to the potential of their developing overseas colonies. Howe's imperial dream coalesced around visions of a railway across British North America, mass immigration from Britain, and representation of the self-governing colonies in the British Parliament. In March the cabinet approved a loan guarantee for railways in the Maritimes, but it was later rescinded for the Portland line and then abandoned altogether. Still fixated on transportation, Howe pursued plans for the provincial government to build local railways, while Johnston demanded that private enterprise take the risks of such costly undertakings.

During Howe's absence in England, his colleagues agreed to privatize the province's telegraph line in return for its expansion to Yarmouth and Sydney. They also withdrew the permanent grant to King's, thus putting it on an equal footing with other colleges, but this move was rejected by the Colonial Office. Neither outcome pleased Howe. Nor did he welcome Johnston's crusade in support of electing legislative councillors and municipal officers. To most observers, this approach smacked of American republicanism, but it was better, Johnston argued, than giving the government of the day exclusive control over appointments. His proposals failed to gain much traction, leaving politicians on both sides of the assembly puzzling over how best to define citizenship and patronage in an increasingly democratic age.

To fulfil their 1847 promise of an expanded franchise, the Reformers sponsored a bill in 1851, introduced by Laurence O'Connor Doyle, to allow voting privileges to adult men who paid county and poor rates. This reform was meant to address the inadequacy of voting regulations in place requiring a voter to have property worth or generating an annual income of 40 shillings. The new franchise regulations dropped property qualifications and increased the number of men eligible to vote, but the payment of county taxes proved to be an even less satisfactory measure of wealth and further expanded partisanship in the election process. Disgusted by the corrupt electoral practices that resulted from tampering with the thoroughly inadequate assessment rolls, Johnston recommended that universal manhood suffrage be instituted instead. The Reformers reluctantly agreed, and this policy was adopted in 1854. Women were excluded from the franchise in 1851 whether they were ratepayers or not, while Indigenous people and paupers who received public assistance from the provincial government or county magistrates were denied the vote in 1854. The expanded franchise led to at least a 56 per cent increase in the electorate between 1847 and 1855, benefiting primarily young men and male labourers, renters, and tenant farmers.[21]

In 1855 Johnston convinced the assembly to adopt legislation permitting municipal incorporation, a measure designed to enable communities to sponsor policies their residents deemed important to their well-being. Only Yarmouth took advantage of the opportunity, and quickly reversed itself when the cost of local government escalated under the new system. Johnston also promoted the union of the self-governing British North American colonies, an idea advanced as early as the 1780s, raised by Lord Durham, and even promoted by Howe when he was in full rhetorical flight. For the moment, this goal seemed premature both to authorities in London and to most members of the assembly, feasible only when a railway was constructed to hold such a dispersed political entity together.

With the Conservatives fighting a rearguard action, the Reformers easily won the 1851 election. They proceeded on a number of initiatives, including the repeal of a law passed in 1816 that made labour unions illegal. They also stuck down the 1758 statute declaring the Church of England the established church in Nova Scotia, and finally revoked the permanent grant to King's College. In 1854 the Reformers managed, after Johnston's efforts to enlist private investors failed, to establish a Railway Board to supervise the building of provincial lines, beginning with the one from Halifax to Windsor. Howe himself assumed the position of chief commissioner to ensure that the project proceeded quickly and efficiently. Disgusted by this violation of laissez-faire economic principles, William Stairs resigned from the legislative council, but this gesture did little to diminish support for the government. William Young succeeded Uniacke as premier in 1854 and led the Reform Party to victory the following year.

An important item on the government's agenda was reform of the legal system to make it more accessible and consistent with modern thinking. In 1850 Howe had introduced a Free Trade in Law Bill, which allowed any litigant to be represented by a lay person, and a statute set court costs at £1 a day. Other legal reforms took longer to achieve, among them the abolition of imprisonment for debt, the repeal of usury laws, a new bankruptcy code, and granting married women the right to own property and conduct business in their own names. In 1855 legislative councillor Jonathan McCully introduced bills to address some of these matters, but they failed to carry in the assembly, where many rural members insisted on maintaining the status quo. The Court of Chancery, which handled cases relating to the interpretation of foreclosures, property settlements, and wills, had little hope of surviving reform sentiment. It had long been a source of criticism for its cumbersome processes on matters that potentially had an impact on every family. In 1855 Chancery functions were reassigned to the Supreme Court. It was not until 1866 that a Court for Divorce and Matrimonial Causes was created to deal with failed marriages, although Nova Scotia had been an outlier in the British Empire since 1766 in granting divorces on the grounds of cruelty, the result of following New England precedents.[22]

In the 1855 election, Howe was defeated in his Cumberland riding by the energetic Tory candidate Charles Tupper. The son of a prominent Baptist pastor, Tupper had attended Horton Academy and earned a degree from the Royal College of Surgeons in Edinburgh in 1843 before returning to his hometown of Amherst to practise medicine.[23] Tupper's success at the polls was due in part to Howe's absence during much of the campaign in a clandestine effort to enlist volunteers in the United States for Britain's war against Russia in Crimea. Not only was his mission on foreign soil ill-advised and arguably illegal, it was also conducted in such a way that his "volunteers," many of them unemployed Irish Americans, were recruited under the false pretence that they were signing up for construction work on Nova Scotia's railway. William Condon, president of Halifax's Charitable Irish Society, alerted his countrymen in the United States to this deception, forcing Howe to make a hasty retreat from New York when an angry mob gathered outside his hotel. Irish Catholics were particularly vocal in their opposition to Britain's imperial campaigns in Crimea and elsewhere, a political stance inflamed by the brutal suppression of the 1848 Irish rebellion for national independence.

Once it became public, Howe's mission provoked a diplomatic row, resulting in the expulsion of the British ambassador to Washington for his part in the subterfuge. It also had disastrous consequences for Howe and the Liberal Party. In reaction to being taunted by Protestants, Irish railway workers in the Windsor area turned on their harassers at Gourley's Shanty in May 1856. The militia was called out to quell the violence and capture its perpetrators. Tried in court, they were defended by Johnston and no jury would convict them. Howe became involved in the ruckus, and could not resist making bigoted remarks about Irish Catholics who threatened his beloved Empire. Obliged to resign from the Railway Board for his indiscretion, Howe won a by-election in Windsor Township by acclamation, and was complicit in the dismissal of Condon from his minor government position.

This petty reprisal galvanized Catholics of all ethnic backgrounds. Encouraged by Tupper, eight Catholic assembly members and two Protestants who represented ridings with significant Catholic populations – Antigonish and Digby – deserted the Liberals. So, too, did prominent merchant Edward Kenny, who resigned his seat in the legislative council over the issue. A Protestant Alliance, spearheaded primarily by Free Church clergy, championed the Liberal cause, but it had little immediate effect. Backed by an unlikely coalition of Baptists and Catholics, the Tories voted out the the Liberals, installed a Johnston government without an election, and restored Kenny to the council.[24]

Religious antagonism was nothing new in Nova Scotia, but it took on a more venomous tone during Johnson's short-lived administration. With Howe and Tupper going head-to-head in debates over the impact of Rome and the Protestant Alliance on matters large and small, the assembly accomplished little. Tupper led a Nova Scotia delegation to London in 1858 to participate in talks on British North American union and the construction of an intercolonial railway, projects actively pursued by Canadian finance minister Alexander Galt, but the discussions generated little sustained enthusiasm. An exception to the dismal litany of failure was finalizing an arrangement, initiated by the Liberals in 1856, to end the General Mining Association's monopoly over Nova Scotia's mineral resources. The higher prices for coal the company charged its local consumers compared with buyers in the United States had long been a source of complaint, and neither the Liberals nor the Conservatives were prepared to defend the GMA's exclusive privileges. The policy adopted in 1858, while perpetuating some of the company's leases, finally opened the province's mineral assets to new investment.[25]

In May 1859 Nova Scotians faced another election, with Protestants deserting the Conservatives in such large numbers that Johnston won his largely Baptist riding in Annapolis County by only seventeen votes. The Liberals squeaked through with a slim majority, but their position was precarious because several "loose fish" voted on policy rather than on party lines. Eager to escape the fractious political scene, Young assumed the position of chief justice in 1860, and Howe became premier. He tried to push ahead with the construction of an intercolonial line to Quebec, the route most likely to attract British investment, but without success. The Canadian government, mired in debt and political deadlock, withdrew from negotiations, unable to commit to any railway policy without risking collapse.

Determined to secure imperial favour and disappointed by the failure of his government to achieve its ambitious goals, Howe accepted the position of imperial fisheries commissioner in December 1862, gradually relinquishing responsibility for party leadership to Truro native Adams Archibald. William Annand, dubbed "Boots" for his unswerving loyalty to Howe, continued to keep a firm editorial hand on the *Morning Chronicle* and the *Novascotian*.[26] Never reconciled to mass democracy and bested by the Tories when it came to buying votes, the Liberals introduced legislation in 1863 to replace universal manhood suffrage with an assessment franchise and to make the executive rather than the assembly the source of money bills, the latter move encouraged by the need for tighter financial control as the state became involved in major projects such as railways.[27] The legislative council, where the Liberals held a majority of only one seat, amended the franchise bill so that it would take effect after the forthcoming election. With Tupper's organizational skills at the ready and soon-to be-disenfranchised voters flocking to the polls, the Liberals were crushed, winning only fourteen of the fifty-five assembly seats. Nine of them went to the Conservatives by acclamation, and even Howe, who ran in Lunenburg, was defeated by nearly five hundred votes.[28]

Golden Opportunities

Although the state might have fallen short of its potential in the era of responsible government, Nova Scotia's economy entered what came to be seen as a "golden age." Consumption increased, markets expanded, and fleets of locally built vessels sailed the oceans of the world seeking cargoes that their merchant-capitalist owners could "buy cheap and sell dear." Scholars have argued that the age was more bronze than golden, and that the accumulated wealth was concentrated among the top 5 per cent of the population, but few deny the significance of the period from 1848 to 1866, when the prospects for economic growth seemed unlimited.[29]

What was not entirely clear at the time was the extent to which railways could undercut as much as enhance Nova Scotia's geographical advantages in the global economy. Although the province offered ice-free ports on the Atlantic crucial to year-round trade and military security in British North America, it was distant from the inland frontier of settlement, which, once accessible by rail, made Montreal, Toronto, and New York booming metropolises with control over growth-fuelling hinterlands. Even if Halifax managed to overcome the tyranny of distance, its future as a genuine metropolis was compromised by competition from Saint John and other ports in the region with similar advantages. This truth was confirmed in 1853, when Portland, Maine, was connected by rail to Montreal. By the end of the decade, Canadian merchants were linked to the interior of the continent by the Grand Trunk Railway, which stretched from Quebec City to the American border at Sarnia. The Maritimes had literally missed the train.

The continental drift, which ultimately defined Nova Scotia's marginal position in the North Atlantic world, was signalled by the 1854 Reciprocity Treaty between Britain and the United States.[30] As requested by the self-governing colonies, and pressed most consistently by the Canadians, who depended heavily on American markets, the British government had begun discussions with the United States on free trade in 1852. Premier Young assumed he would join Governor General Lord Elgin and representatives from Canada and New Brunswick in Washington to participate in the final negotiations, but he received no formal invitation. This omission, inadvertent or not, explained Young's absence at the bargaining table, where access to the inshore fisheries was a deal-breaker for the United States.

Under the Convention of 1818, Americans had been excluded from a three-mile coastal zone in most British North American waters. Repeated violations of the ruling prompted the Nova Scotia assembly to adopt in 1836 what was known as the Hovering Act, making it an offence punishable by confiscation for foreign vessels to hover within three miles of the coast or to navigate the Strait of Canso without paying lighthouse dues. To ensure compliance, the assembly granted £500 to police the legislation.[31] British naval vessels arrived on the scene to demonstrate imperial support for the policy, but "hovering" continued, in part because so many Nova Scotians benefited from illegal trading and the roughly 4,000 seasonal jobs offered by the Yankee fishing fleet each year. As treaty discussions loomed, a more concerted effort was made to force the United States to comply, creating a significant bargaining chip for British negotiators. Young was no doubt relieved that he had not been officially consulted on Article I of the Reciprocity Treaty, in which inshore fisheries were sacrificed to the larger goal of free trade.

When details of the agreement were released, angry denunciations poured forth from both political parties in the Nova Scotia assembly, but the grumbling soon died down. Most producers welcomed Article III, which provided legal access to one of the most lucrative markets in the world for the products of farms, forests, fisheries, and mines, and which specifically mentioned several of Nova Scotia's valued exports, among them building stone, firewood, grindstones, gypsum, and rags. To provide security for those willing to test the value of the agreement, it was slated to last for at least ten years and thereafter to remain in effect for twelve months after one side gave notice of termination. Studies of the impact of the Reciprocity Treaty on the Nova Scotia economy suggest that it helped to sustain the province's pre-treaty level of American trade, which stood around 30 per cent of the total, and expanded markets for coal, dairy products, mackerel, and potatoes. It also reduced the prices of imported cod, tobacco, and wheat, which was a boon to shippers seeking cargoes for export.[32] The decision by the Nova Scotia government in 1860 to follow the province of Canada in adopting decimal currency is testimony to the growing influence of the United States in monetary matters.

Assessing the impact of the Reciprocity Treaty is complicated by the American Civil War, which pitted the industrializing northern states against the agricultural southern states over the issues of slavery and national unity. The conflict raged between Confederate and Union forces from 1861 to 1865, threatening to engulf Britain and its colonies in the chaos. Without the war, it is unlikely that economic growth in this period would have reached the levels it did, nor would the cancellation of Reciprocity in 1866 by the triumphant North bent on a protectionist policy have proved so disastrous. In addition to the expansion of trade, Nova Scotians also benefited from the decline of the American merchant fleet, crippled by the war. Shippers based in Nova Scotia were well positioned to pick up the slack, and ports such as Yarmouth and Halifax bustled with American vessels transferred by their owners to the protection of the British flag in an effort to elude Confederate raiders.[33]

Even before the stimulus provided by reciprocity and war, shipping and shipbuilding in Nova Scotia had become major enterprises. They had been nurtured by mercantilist policies that favoured colonial ships and products, but they continued to thrive in the free trade environment of the mid-nineteenth century. With timber near at hand, many Nova Scotia ports built a wide range of vessels for diverse purposes: schooners, small dories, and brigs for fishing and the coastal trade; larger brigs, barques, and ships to carry bulky cargoes to distant markets; and floating transports of all kinds to sell to buyers, a significant portion of them located in Liverpool, the main port in England's industrial heartland. Nova Scotia's larger ocean-going vessels, most of them built with spruce and pine, had improved in quality by mid-century and were in high demand for the expanding commodity trade. They required no special protection to compete successfully with carriers from Britain, Norway, and the United States, the three great ocean-going nations of the world. Registered shipping tonnage increased dramatically in the middle of the nineteenth century. By the 1870s the Dominion of Canada stood fourth in registered shipping tonnage (1.3 million tons and 7,500 vessels), more than 70 per cent of it based in the Maritimes.[34]

In Nova Scotia, shipping companies were concentrated in Halifax, where half the province's tonnage was registered. Vessels built in Bay of Fundy ports were often registered in Saint John, which boasted the largest shipping fleet in the Maritime region. Wealthy Halifax-based merchant-shippers such as Samuel Cunard and Enos Collins had their counterparts throughout the province, among them Thomas Killam in Yarmouth, Ezra Churchill in Hantsport, William D. Lawrence in Maitland, James William Carmichael in New Glasgow, and Thomas Dickson Archibald in Sydney.[35] Although owners and captains were usually Maritime-born, they increasingly relied on foreign crews to do the hard and dangerous work associated with the carrying trade. Shipping to distant ports for about $20 a month was a rite of passage for many young Nova Scotian men, but most of those who survived the experience returned to land-based occupations once their wanderlust had been satisfied. The few women who worked in the sea-going trades were rarely welcome, with the exception of captains' wives, who occasionally shared the excitement and risk associated with globetrotting. It took courage to embark on vessels that could be away for a year or more before returning to home port and might never return at all. One-third of the ships in service in any given year were stranded, wrecked, or lost at sea. For this reason, shipbuilders usually amassed capital by selling shares and spreading their investments over a number of vessels to avoid losing everything in one disaster at sea. The age of sail ultimately seemed more glamourous in retrospect, but it put Nova Scotia on the map, making the province better known internationally in the mid-nineteenth century than is the case today.[36]

Land-based industries thrived on the prosperity generated by the carrying trade, which required not only cargoes of fish, farm produce, forest products, and minerals to sell abroad, but also chandlery services for vessels and provisions for crews, which averaged twenty-three men for a 1,200-ton three-masted ship. In ports where ocean-going craft were being built, there was plenty of work for blacksmiths, caulkers, coopers, sailmakers, and shipwrights. The chandlery operations of William Stairs, Son and Morrow thrived on the expansion of shipping out of Halifax, as did William Moir's bread-baking business, which also catered to the military. Capitalizing on the growing demand for his products, Moir built a new factory on Argyle Street in 1862, equipping it with the latest steam technology imported from Britain and the United States. Moir's machines mixed dough for crackers and hard bread, important staples of the carrying trade, along with soft bread, popular in the local market. In 1865 Moir built a flour mill to supply his bakery, relying on wheat imported from the United States and the province of Canada.[37]

The success of Nova Scotia's shipping industry was a source of local pride, but it might have blunted the emergence of a more robust manufacturing base in the province. While Toronto, Montreal, and Saint John sprouted factories producing an impressive array of consumer goods, Nova Scotians tended to rely on imports, rather than introduce protective tariffs to nurture home-grown industries. Nor did many entrepreneurs initially capitalize on the province's coal and iron resources to produce the machinery, rails, and iron ships that defined the industrial age. Halifax merchants and their counterparts in outport communities used their influence in the assembly to maintain low tariffs – the key, they believed, to their success in international trade. The situation was different in New Brunswick, where "the industrious classes" organized a Provincial Association in 1844 and pressed the government to introduce a 15 per cent protective tariff on a wide range of consumer goods, including agricultural implements, cigars, hats, iron castings, pianos, sleighs, and wagons, helping to make Saint John the most advanced industrial city in the Maritime region by the 1860s.[38]

Despite the odds against succeeding, a few entrepreneurs eagerly embraced the opportunities the industrial age seemed to offer. Ten years after he arrived with his parents from Ireland in 1838, a young Alexander Robb opened a small shop in Amherst to mend iron stoves. He branched into selling stoves imported from Boston, and then began manufacturing his own stoves in 1856, producing 2,500 stoves annually in a modern steam-powered factory with twenty employees. Robb was not the only resident of Amherst eager to reap the rewards of new production processes. In 1867, fifteen merchants, farmers, craftsmen, and politicians, among the latter Robert B. Dickey and Charles Tupper, invested in the Amherst Boot and Shoe Factory. Both companies went from strength to strength when a railway connected "Busy Amherst" to markets near and far in the 1870s.[39]

Not surprisingly, the smart money both at home and abroad focused on the province's extensive mineral resources. Twenty-seven new collieries opened between 1863 and 1867, expanding coal-mining activities not only around Pictou and Sydney, but also in Inverness, Victoria, and Cumberland counties. In 1866 coal accounted for 15 per cent of provincial exports and provided employment for 3,074 men and boys.[40] The primary market for the increased output of the mines was the United States, where the Civil War had compromised access to Pennsylvania's coal fields. Excess capacity would dog the industry once the war and reciprocity ended, despite efforts by entrepreneurs to use local coal in the production of pig iron from iron deposits in Londonderry and Clementsport.[41]

Coal and iron were the workhorses of the industrial age, but gold attracted widespread attention after "rushes" erupted in California (1849), Australia (1851), and British Columbia (1858). By 1861 Nova Scotia was experiencing its own gold rush, prompted by recent finds along the Eastern Shore at Mooseland-Tangier and Sherbrooke, and at the Ovens in Lunenburg County. More discoveries followed. Eager to avoid the lawlessness that characterized other gold rush areas and to develop another revenue stream for the government, Howe's administration established sixty-four mining districts and required miners to bring their ore to Halifax to be weighed and taxed. Since many gold seekers no doubt ignored this ruling, the amount of gold extracted in Nova Scotia is difficult to estimate. Recorded yields from 1862 to 1871 indicate that 192,772 troy ounces of the precious metal was produced by an average of seven hundred miners each year.[42] As with other Eldorados, Nova Scotia's first gold rush gradually petered out, and sojourners hoping to strike it rich moved on.[43]

For all the excitement generated by mining and shipping, the fisheries remained central to the economy of Nova Scotia, which was by far the largest fish producer in British North America outside of Newfoundland. The mainstay of the industry was still dried cod, which was caught and processed in much the same way as it had been for more than three centuries. The markets for cod, too, remained much the same – southern Europe and the Caribbean – although the demand declined in the British West Indies after slavery was abolished there in 1833. Fresh fish was also exported, mostly to nearby markets in the United States, where it could arrive in fairly good condition when packed in ice.[44] At mid-century, fishermen from France began using bottom set trawls (long lines of baited hooks) and lightweight dories to catch cod, a practice gradually adopted in the Atlantic region, helping to boost ocean harvests. Although the export trade was gradually centralized in Halifax, outports continued to ship their fish directly to international markets, increasingly to the Spanish West Indies and Brazil, where slavery survived for another generation after it was abolished in British jurisdictions. The fishing industry was so important to Nova Scotia's economy that politicians ignored it at their peril.[45]

According to the 1861 census, the 14,322 men involved in the fishery produced nearly 400,000 quintals (40 million kilograms) of dried cod annually, along with large quantities of bait fish such as herring and mackerel, and fish oil, much of the latter used in the tanning industry. Fishing remained primarily a seasonal occupation, integrated into the yearly round of farming and forestry work. While men plied the inshore, Bank, Gulf, and Labrador fisheries in the spring and summer, women and children maintained the family farm and pitched in when the catch needed salting, pickling, and packing onshore. Every county in the province supported a fishery but ports along the South and Eastern Shores and in Cape Breton produced the largest volumes of "merchantable" cod and mackerel, for which the government paid bounties to encourage output. Profits from the fisheries were accumulated by merchants and shippers, not by ordinary families in coastal communities. In good years the abundance of fish drove down prices; in bad years yields were insufficient to cover previous cost overruns to merchants for provisions and fishing gear. The so-called truck system left many fishing families cash poor and perpetually in debt.

Lunenburg emerged as one of the most successful fishing ports in this period, and was also gaining a reputation for producing high-quality vessels, most of them destined for the fishery. With forty-six schooners among the fifty ships on building blocks in Lunenburg in 1859, a Halifax journalist reported that "These Dutchmen have done more for to foster the art of shipbuilding in Nova Scotia than any other class of people within our borders." Claiming that Lunenburg vessels were "marvels of neatness," the journalist declared that their builders "lavish a greater amount of money in ornamenting their craft – in carving and gilding – than they would be willing to disburse in decorating their frows [fraus] and daughters."[46] The point might also have been made that similar decorative skills were applied to the wooden houses constructed for prosperous Lunenburgers, leaving a nineteenth-century legacy that helped to make the town worthy of a UNESCO heritage designation in 1995.[47]

Given the expansion of construction and shipping, old-growth forests in Nova Scotia all but disappeared in this period. Pine, hemlock, spruce, and other species were turned not only into boards and deals, but also into barrels, boxes, firewood, pit props, shingles, and staves. Unlike New Brunswick, where the Crown retained control of a significant proportion of the woodlands, Nova Scotia's forests were mostly privately owned, encompassed in the land grants offered by the government since the 1750s. Landowners liked it that way because it gave them a source of supplementary income, but it made conservation measures, in the rare instances they were considered, difficult to implement. By the 1860s the operations of the approximately 1,400 sawmills in the province choked rivers with dams and sawdust, impeding the annual migration of salmon. In 1865 eighty-five-year-old Peter Paul reflected on the abundance he had experienced growing up in Pictou County, where his family preserved salmon as they had done for centuries for consumption during the winter. The timber industry, he reported, now "make country cold, make rivers small," and "sawmills, sawdust, and milldam send all the fish away."[48] Clearly progress had its downside.

As in earlier decades, most Nova Scotians engaged in at least part-time farming, either on their own land or that of others. The standard of living varied widely between the prosperous commercial farms in the Annapolis Valley and the hardscrabble homesteads typical of the rocky interior, but, on average, rural folk consumed ever-larger quantities of imported goods, primarily chinaware, cloth, coffee, flour, molasses, rum, sugar, tea, and tools.[49] To secure these items, they sold or bartered their labour, cloth, coarse grains such as oats, consumed by both horses and people, butter, hay, livestock, and root vegetables. Farmers nearly doubled their yield of potatoes after the blight subsided in the 1850s. According to the 1861 census, the province produced 3,824,814 barrels and boxes of potatoes, with Kings Country accounting for nearly a quarter of the total.[50] The staple food on most colonial tables, in lumber camps, and on sea-going vessels, the hardy tuber survived reasonably well in the holds of ships and found markets in the Maritimes and abroad.

Despite aspirations to the contrary, Nova Scotia would never become an agricultural paradise. Canada West, Ohio, California, and many other areas of North America were better served by climate and soil to produce commercial crops.[51] Settlers living on soil-deprived farms could easily be lured to opportunities elsewhere, and by the 1860s abandoned homesteads were beginning to dot the rural landscape. For those who could afford it, new machinery such as iron ploughs, seed drills, and threshing machines were beginning to alleviate some of the back-breaking work typical of agriculture pursuits, but nothing could induce Nova Scotia's rocky soil, the legacy of ancient geological forces, to yield a wealth-generating abundance for the majority of farm families.

This reality was far from the minds of provincial politicians when they planned their exhibits for the International Exhibition held adjacent to the gardens of London's Royal Horticultural Society in 1862. Eager to showcase the progress made in Nova Scotia over the previous decade, the Liberal government convened a high-powered committee under the secretaryship of Robert Grant Haliburton, son of the famous author, to assemble the best the province had to offer. The submissions included a huge vein of coal up to thirty-six feet wide from the Albion Mines, a sample of pig iron from the Acadia Iron Works in Londonderry, fish preserved in alcohol, and a variety of fruit and vegetables. Nova Scotia apples arranged in flat trays with partitions and packed in bran won prizes, and prompted the London *Times* to remark that "the beauty of the apples beat anything we have ever seen."[52] The following year Haliburton and other Annapolis Valley farmers re-established the Nova Scotia Horticultural Society to promote fruit growing, an industry that would come into its own once regular steamship service and refrigeration made large-scale export to British markets possible.[53]

Nearly every community in Nova Scotia experienced the quickening pace that characterized the age of sail, but Halifax often failed to impress visitors. During her brief sojourn there in 1854, a young Isabella Lucy Bird remarked on the filth that defined the city's streets, which in the summer were strewn with "oyster-shells, fish heads and bones, potato-skins, and cabbage-stalks," and in December "ankle-deep in mud." She was also struck by the shabby wooden structures that dominated the streetscape.[54] With the examples of urban improvements appearing on both sides of the Atlantic, city councillors began to rectify these unflattering conditions by installing sewers and sidewalks. After four fires ripped through Hollis and Granville streets between 1857 and 1861, the council purchased steam-powered fire engines, expropriated the privately run water services, and imposed regulations requiring brick and stone buildings in the downtown core.[55] Meanwhile the Commons, which was shared with the military and roaming cattle, began to shrink with the leasing of building lots on Spring Garden Road.

Despite these advances, a few well-travelled observers concluded that, while Halifax might compare favourably with seaport towns in England, it lacked the bustle of major cities in the United States or even of Saint John.[56] Halifax was a financial, military, and shipping hub, but it had a sluggish manufacturing base and even left most of the ship-building activity to the flourishing outports. Although Haligonians did their best to impress Prince Albert when he visited the city in 1860, the foreign journalists who accompanied him were as dismissive as Isabella Bird. *Harper's Weekly* reported that Halifax had an "old and decrepit look, as if blight had fallen upon its energies somewhere about the close of the last American war." Even more scathing, the correspondent for the *London Times* concluded that Halifax was a "quaint, rickety little village ... stagnant and lethargic without being quiet – noisy without being busy."[57]

Working in Changing Times

While politicians were chasing progress and shippers extended their reach, ordinary Nova Scotians were coming to grips with the rapid pace of change. The triumph of industrial capitalism in the mid-nineteenth century underscored Benjamin Franklin's earlier insight that time is money, and introduced a new ethic of materialism that challenged traditional spiritual values. It also encouraged the growth of cities at the expense of the countryside, created a new class structure based on relationship to production rather than heredity, drove a wedge between the public world of work and the private realm of the family, and altered the relationship of human beings to their natural environment. It was not by chance that Haliburton chose clock pedlar Sam Slick to make his point that notions of time were being transformed. With factories, railways, and steamships running to strict schedules, the rhythms of the sun, seasons, and family life came under intense pressure. The advantage rested with those who paid attention.

The opportunities available to attentive Nova Scotians at mid-century are documented by the experiences of Margaret Dickie. Born in 1827 on a farm near Halfway River (renamed Hantsport), she was educated locally, and taught children in her home after she married mariner Simeon Michener in 1849. Eager for her husband to escape the dangers of seafaring, she eagerly embraced the idea of joining others in their community who were planning to move to Ohio once it became open to settlers. Simeon died of fever in 1850 while scouting the potential of the American settlement frontier, leaving Margaret bereft but still determined to pursue new horizons. She furthered her education at Miss Kidson's Academy in nearby Wolfville, and in 1856 married Robert McCulloch, an Irish immigrant who worked as a caulker in Hantsport's shipyards. They raised two daughters and Margaret served as the town's telegraph operator. When the American Civil War ended, the McCullochs moved to Delaware to try peach farming, but the carpetbagging venture did not go well, and they returned to Hantsport, where the shipbuilding industry still offered employment.[58]

Margaret had been trained by her father to bind leather shoes, but she had never worked as a cobbler's assistant, and this skill soon became obsolete. Over the course of the nineteenth century, machines and managers increasingly controlled the output previously produced by artisans. Each craft industrialized on its own schedule, which was determined largely by the timing of the introduction of new machinery, scale of production, and level of skill retained by those who did the work.[59] In this context the guild system, in which master craftsmen trained apprentices and journeymen according to strict contracts laying out the duties and obligations of both sides in the agreement, gradually broke down. Employers in the new industrial order paid the lowest wages possible, often hiring women and children, who were routinely paid less than men, and employees learned on the job, often in life-threatening conditions.

Unless there was a labour shortage, unskilled workers never had much bargaining power with their employers because they could easily be replaced and the law was never on their side. In 1856 George Chute, a fish packer on the Halifax waterfront, took his "Master" to court for assaulting him when he insisted on "a whole day's wages for three-quarters of a day," the shorter hours due to inclement weather. The court found no merit in Chute's case, as his employer had every right to throw out of his shop any employee who challenged his authority, using force if necessary.[60]

Skilled labourers were beginning to form cooperatives, fraternal associations, and unions to improve their prospects, but the chances of success in bargaining with employers were limited.[61] Although it was no longer illegal after 1851 to engage in organized efforts to press for better working conditions, there was no law preventing employers from firing someone who tried. The state could also be depended upon to supress labour unrest. When the workers at Sydney Mines went on strike for better wages in 1864, GMA managers demanded that the provincial government intervene. One of Johnston's last acts as premier was to introduce a bill, based on a British statute of 1825, making it illegal for an employee to use coercion or force against any other employee or against an employer on pain of a mandatory jail sentence of twelve months. Such was the consensus on this matter that all three readings of the bill passed in a morning's sitting, by which time the government had authorized a hundred soldiers to be shipped from Halifax to the disaffected area.[62]

The new labour legislation designed to keep the mines running smoothly had little impact on organizing efforts by workers in Halifax. In 1864 shipwrights and caulkers on the waterfront unionized; truckmen forced the city to increase their pay; and 150 journeymen carpenters walked off the job in a largely unsuccessful bid to secure better wages. By this time, the movement for a "half-holiday" on Saturday was gaining support among the male clerks who staffed the city's banks, businesses, and shops six long days a week. Whether this burst of labour activity had any direct link with the efforts associated with the founding of the International Workingmen's Association in London in September 1864 is unknown. What is clear is that labourers in Nova Scotia were eager to find ways to maintain their status and improve their working conditions in the rapidly changing economic climate and under a political system in which voting privileges were restricted to men who owned at least $300 in real and personal property.

For minorities shunted aside by the majority culture, possessing a skill offered the best chance of improving one's income. Shippers in Halifax had difficulty keeping up with the demand for barrels, providing an opportunity for African Nova Scotians in Hammonds Plains and other communities around the city to earn money from their small land holdings.[63] The production of barrels was slow to mechanize, but the skill required to make them was widespread, and the competition for sales kept prices low. Mi'kmaq also produced barrels, and their baskets, boxes, brooms, and canoes sold well in the mid-nineteenth century, arguably the apex of craft production in Nova Scotia, both in quantity and quality, before factories undermined the profitability of such efforts.

When gifted artisans took their craft to a higher level, it fetched a better return and was sometimes sought by collectors. Julius Cornelius, a Prussian-born jeweller who arrived in Halifax from Boston in the mid-1850s, won first prize and a Diploma of Honour at the International Exhibition in 1862 for his exquisite pieces crafted from Nova Scotia gold.[64] Even more outstanding was Mi'kmaw artisan Mary Christianne Paul Morris, who won international recognition for her needlework, quillwork, and splint baskets. By mid-century one of her magnificently decorated costumes could sell for as much as $150. In 1855 she moved from Dartmouth to the Northwest Arm, where she built a house from her own earnings. Such was her reputation that her portrait, painted by London-based artist William Gush, who spent time in Halifax in 1858, was presented to eighteen-year-old Albert, Prince of Wales, when he visited Halifax in 1860, a reminder perhaps of her quillwork cradle that was gifted to the prince at the time of his birth (Figure 11.2).[65]

Few women managed to emulate Morris's achievements. Welcomed only as assistants in artisan shops, they were formally excluded from craft guilds. If they acquired skills, it was often as a member of a family of artisans and producers. John and Susannah Oland, who emigrated from England with their children in the early 1860s, rose to prominence on the strength of Susannah's "Brown October Ale" recipe, which she initially brewed in a shed behind their home in Dartmouth. When the Turtle Cove Brewing Company was incorporated in 1867, it was registered in the name of Susannah's husband, but she continued

Figure 11.2. Quillwork cradle by Mi'kmaw artist Mary Christianne Paul Morris. Morris developed an international reputation for her needlework, quillwork, and splint basketry.
Mary Christianne Paul Morris, Sweetgrass Arts Centre Public Education Program, online at https://sweetgrassartscentre.wordpress.com/sweetgrass-arts-centre-public-education-program/.
DesBrisay Museum collection, Bridgewater, N.S. acc. 184

to preside over the running of the business. In 1877 she used an inheritance to buy out a partner and changed the name of the company to S. Oland and Sons.[66]

Other enterprising women living in urban areas translated their household skills into dress-making shops and bakeries, became boarding-house keepers, and worked as caregivers, domestic servants, and tutors, typically female occupations that expanded with the rise of an affluent middle class in the mid-nineteenth century. Young women living in the countryside continued to work in the homes of extended family members and neighbours before they set up their own households, but as the population expanded many young women gravitated to towns and cities, where wages were usually higher. By the 1860s women outnumbered men in Halifax, which offered single women and widows better prospects than most rural areas for making a living.[67]

Ambitious young white women increasingly found work in the expanding field of primary education, but they faced obstacles to advancement. Paid less than men for their labour, female teachers were eagerly sought by penny-pinching school trustees trying to minimize expenses. Most women taught with a permissive licence, thus reducing the charge on local school boards. After it opened in 1855, the Normal School admitted female students but other institutions of higher learning catered to an exclusively male clientele. Tired of being excluded, six young Nova Scotia women travelled to Massachusetts between 1856 and 1858 to attend Mount Holyoke Female Seminary, a liberal arts college widely recognized for its excellence under the direction of its founder, Mary Lyon. Among these pioneers was Alice Shaw, who established Grand Pré Seminary in Wolfville in 1861.[68]

Women at the lower end of the social scale were especially vulnerable in the mean streets of Halifax, where unscrupulous boarding-house keepers, tavern owners, and pimps made a good living by exploiting people down on their luck. For women convicted of selling sex, having an illegal abortion, or disposing of their unwanted babies in back alleys, on church doorsteps, or in the harbour, the law imposed jail sentences. The experience of eighteen-year-old domestic servant Olivia Gibson is perhaps typical. After discharging her baby in an outdoor privy in 1865, her employer discovered and reported her crime. She confessed in a deposition that the father of her child was a bombardier in the Artillery. Although the outcome of Olivia's brush with the law is unclear, she apparently died shortly after this incident. Domestic servants predominated among those convicted of infanticide, a testimony to the lack of wage-paying options for women and the double standard that prevailed around sex outside of marriage.[69]

The underclass living near the waterfront and on Barrack Street (now part of Barrington Street) below Citadel Hill expanded dramatically in this period. Although an 1862 pamphlet, *Halifax: "Its Sins and Its Sorrows,"* no doubt exaggerated the worst features of what was considered immoral behaviour in the city – Sabbath desecration, drunkenness, and prostitution topping the list – it is difficult to overstate the misery experienced by anyone caught in a cycle of poverty, exploitation, and institutionalization in the seaport city. Deemed by a journalist in 1869 as "The Wickedest Woman in Halifax," Margaret Howard had a long and colourful career on the streets. A native of St John's, Newfoundland, she first appeared in Halifax police court on a charge of drunkenness in 1863 at the age of twenty. She opted for thirty days in prison, no doubt unable to pay the optional two-dollar fine. Historian Judith Fingard has determined that, over the next sixteen years, Howard served more than fifty prison terms and attempted suicide at least six times. Although she was probably safer in prison than on the streets, she resisted incarceration, and at least once managed to escape her confinement. Female prisoners made up nearly half of the repeat offenders, in part because the police kept a close eye on women who failed to conform to ladylike behaviour. Not surprisingly, black women, the poorest people in Halifax, were overrepresented among the prison population.[70]

The good citizens of Halifax established a dazzling array of institutions to address the conditions they saw as a threat to social stability. In addition to constructing a new prison in the north end of the city in 1860 and a new poorhouse nine years later, they founded a City Mission (1852), Ragged School (1852), House of Refuge for Fallen Women (1854), Visiting [Medical] Dispensary (1855), Mount Hope Asylum (1859), Sailors Home (1862), and Temporary Home for Young Women Seeking Employment as Domestic Servants (1869). Other than Rockhead Prison and the Poors' House, these institutions depended largely on fluctuating charitable funding, much of which was raised by the city's twenty-five churches.[71]

As in earlier periods, Nova Scotia men found work in the ranks of the British Army or Royal Navy. One who made a name for himself was William Hall. A descendant of a Black Refugee family that had settled in Horton Bluff, he shipped out of Hantsport in his teens and served briefly on American vessels before joining the Royal Navy as an able seaman in 1852, while still in his early twenties. During the Crimean War, he saw action with a gun crew in the siege of Sevastopol, and was awarded the Victoria Cross for his bravery in helping to put down an Indian mutiny against the British at Lucknow in 1857. Hall was the first black man and the first Nova Scotian to receive this prestigious medal. In 1876 he retired to live with his two unmarried sisters on their ancestral farm, his income supplemented by a military pension of £50.[72]

Even more opportunities for military service were available upon the outbreak of the American Civil War. Estimates of the number of British North Americans who fought in the war vary widely, ranging up to 55,000. The official numbers, based on birth records, lean towards this higher figure, but many of the recruits born in "the provinces" had lived in the United States for decades, had voted there, and never expected to return to the land of their birth.[73] Whatever their sense of identity, most Nova Scotia–born combatants fought on the Union side, reflecting their location in and adjacent to the northern states and a common pre-dilection to support the issues for which the Union armies fought. Jo-seph Howe was a Union supporter on principle, and his son Frederick volunteered to fight, a decision that caused his father so much anxiety that he travelled to the battlefields of Virginia to satisfy himself that his offspring was still alive.[74]

African Nova Scotians might have had the most incentive to become involved in the war, especially after President Abraham Lincoln's government issued the Emancipation Proclamation in 1863 and later offered bounties to men who enlisted. In 1864 twenty-nine-year-old Benjamin Jackson from what is now Lockhartville, a community near Hantsport, became one of the seventy-three African Nova Scotians to serve in the Union Navy during the war. Jackson was an experienced sailor and no doubt welcomed the bounty that came with his enlist-ment. He also received payment for taking the place of a drafted Amer-ican, Lewis Saunders, whose name Jackson used when he signed up. Employed as a gunner on the USS *Richmond*, he was wounded during an attempt to remove a mine from the Mississippi River. Returning a hero, Jackson received a monthly pension of $4 under his assumed name. He continued his career as a sailor for a time, then peddled fish and vegetables in his community. Not surprisingly, his application for a disability pension in 1878 encountered bureaucratic resistance until the confusion over his identity was resolved by the American consul in Halifax nine years later.[75]

Many Nova Scotians who fought in the Union Army were enticed by the hard cash offered by recruiters or payment to serve as substitutes for well-heeled drafted men. William Charles Archibald, a farm boy from the Musquodoboit Valley, was working as a teamster in the Maine lumber woods when he was approached by a recruiting agent who of-fered him a generous bounty for signing up. Archibald survived the war, returned home, and became one of the few soldiers to write about his experiences.[76] Recruiting agents also operated illegally in Nova Scotia, flushed with greenbacks for any man willing to serve. British soldiers in Halifax were attracted by the higher pay American recruit-ers offered. Others were forced into service. When an enlisting agent drugged a young man from Bridgetown and slapped him in a schooner bound for Boston, daring lads from Digby, armed with a warrant from the local justice of the peace, took to the water and chased down the culprits. Although the number of Mi'kmaq attracted to military service is unknown, Ben Christmas reputedly became a bounty broker among Indigenous people in Maine and the Maritimes.[77]

Despite the general bias towards the North, Confederate sympathizers could be found throughout Nova Scotia, especially in Halifax, where prominent families such as the Almon-Johntson clan favoured the conservative values the South seemed to represent. Halifax physician William Johnston Almon was reputedly personally thanked by Confederate president Jefferson Davis for his "efficient and disinterested support of the cause," while his wife Elizabeth Lichtenstein Ritchie Almon served on the Halifax Committee of the Southern Prisoners Relief Fund. Their son, William Bruce Almon, ran the Northern blockade at the age of twenty-three to serve as a physician to Confederate soldiers in Virginia. A nephew and namesake of Alexander Keith even worked as a secret agent for the Confederacy.[78] After its founding in 1862, the elite Halifax Club hosted Confederate dignitaries and officers from blockade runners, and both Church of England and Roman Catholic clergy publicly supported the South.[79]

Warring Neighbours

From the Confederate attack on Fort Sumter in April 1861 to Abraham Lincoln's assassination by John Wilkes Booth four years later, Nova Scotians followed the battles in the American Civil War in their newspapers and worried that the war might escalate into another global conflict. Their fears were justified. Despite support in Britain for ending slavery, powerful industrial interests were at stake. Entrepreneurs whose factories depended on raw cotton grown by enslaved labour in the South were prepared to help the Confederacy evade the Northern blockade, and British shipbuilders willingly sold iron-clad vessels, among them the formidable *Alabama*, *Florida*, and *Shenandoah*, which contributed to the Confederacy's successes at sea during the war. These economic interests help to explain the British decision to remain neutral during the conflict, rather than endorsing the Union cause as the North had hoped. In such circumstances, diplomacy could easily give way to war, putting all of British North America in the bull's eye.

This galvanizing prospect was highlighted on 8 November 1861, when Captain Charles Wilkes of the USS *Jacinto* intercepted the *Trent*, a British mail packet travelling from Havana to London, and removed two Confederate diplomats charged with negotiating assistance from overseas. This violation of British neutrality prompted a stiff ultimatum: release the envoys from prison in Boston or face a declaration of war. The Union government finally backed down on 26 December, but tensions remained high, and Britain dispatched 15,000 troops to supplement the 5,000 already stationed in British North America. Arriving in mid-winter, most of them were obliged, as were soldiers during the War of 1812, to travel overland in winter to reach the province of Canada, emphasizing the military necessity of an all-British rail line to an ice-free port in the Maritimes. The Nova Scotia assembly passed legislation in 1862 to increase the size and efficiency of the militia, whose numbers reached a reported 46,000 by 1864, and the British government embarked on an extensive overhaul of Halifax's defences.[80] The *Trent* affair dampened sympathies for the North in the British Empire, giving permission, if any were needed, to side with the underdog against the Union bullies.

Throughout the war Nova Scotians found themselves uncomfortably close to the action as Confederate and Union vessels chased each other in the waters off their shores and entered their harbours to escape capture, purchase provisions, and make repairs. At least 230 Union and 25 Confederate vessels visited Maritime ports during the war. As an epicentre of ocean communication in British North America, Halifax served as a base for blockade runners, and hosted both Union and Confederate visitors. If they could get that far, American deserters and draft dodgers sought refuge in the Maritimes, where they were likely to be safe from authorities trying to track them down. The townsfolk in Mulgrave on the Strait of Canso claimed in 1865 that they had been inundated during the war with people they described as "the scum of all nations, with a good sprinkling of skedaddlers," arriving from the United States on Yankee fishing boats.[81]

Given the multiple sources of friction, it was only a matter of time before Maritimers themselves precipitated a diplomatic crisis. The most dramatic incident of this kind occurred in December 1863, when Confederate sympathizers disguised as passengers seized the SS *Chesapeake* off Cape Cod en route from New York to Portland, and steered the propeller-driven steamer towards the Bay of Fundy. This act of piracy, which included the murder of the second engineer, was led by a pair of schemers, John Clibbon Brain, a London-born resident of Ohio, and Vernon Locke, a native of Shelburne, Nova Scotia, who had been living in North Carolina for two decades. Among the crew were eleven New Brunswickers recruited in Saint John, where aspects of the plot had been hatched.[82] Chased by Union vessels, the *Chesapeake* picked up Locke and another crew member off Grand Manan, discharged their captives in Saint John, and then headed for Nova Scotia to secure coal and supplies. It visited the ports of Yarmouth, Shelburne, La Have, and Petite Riviere before being intercepted at Sambro by two Union warships and escorted into Halifax harbour. International law required that the lawful possession of the *Chesapeake* be determined by the Vice-Admiralty

Court, which ruled that the captured vessel be returned to its original owners, not to either belligerent.

This was only the official narrative in what became an elaborate farce. While the Vice-Admiralty Court deliberated, high-placed Confederate sympathizers in Halifax helped the "pirates" escape, adding to the outrage of the Union government. The vehemently anti-British New York *Herald* was scathing in its condemnation of the ship's capture "by a party of men of the kind known as Blue Noses – men with the cold blood and feeble circulation of reptiles."[83] At the insistence of Lieutenant Governor Sir Arthur Hastings Doyle, who was determined to be seen as upholding British neutrality, warrants were issued for the arrest of William Almon, Alexander Keith's nephew, and Dr Peleg Smith for physically attacking a police officer during an altercation on the Queen's Wharf when the Americans finally released three British subjects shackled in irons. With so much sympathy for the South in the city and friends in the judicial system, the accused were eventually acquitted due to "insufficient evidence" by the Supreme Court. Warrants for Brain and three others were issued in New Brunswick, where the courts were no less sympathetic to the alleged criminals, and Brain moved on to more adventures on Lake Erie.[84]

The following August, Halifax was again the site of a diplomatic row when the British-built Confederate raider *Tallahassee* refuelled there after a destructive rampage along the northeast coast in which twenty-six vessels were destroyed and seven captured. Neutrality laws limited its stay in Halifax to twenty-four hours, but Captain John Taylor Wood was given an extension to fix his rigging, and a mainmast obligingly supplied by Dr Almon. The Union's secretary of state, William Seward, informed the British envoy in Washington, Lord Richard Lyons, that he was "a good deal disturbed" by the warm reception the *Tallahassee* received in Halifax, and claimed that Alexander Keith's order in New York for a ship's compass and 3,000 barrels of pork was destined for the Confederate vessel. Believing incorrectly that Nova Scotians were among the *Tallahassee*'s crew, the *New York Times* took the opportunity to complain that the province's "large seafaring population, needy, greedy, courageous, and unscrupulous" could outfit fifty such vessels.[85] Haligonians were certainly guilty of what the *Times* described as "codling and feasting" the crew of the *Tallahassee*, who were entertained by a volunteer band playing secessionist tunes such as "Bonnie Blue Flag" and "Dixie." Fearing capture by Union warships, Wood hired skilled pilot "Jock" Flemming to guide his ship out of the harbour through the narrow eastern passage under the cloak of darkness, but with twenty-five desertions while in port, he sailed with a skeleton crew.

Meanwhile Maritime waters swarmed with Union vessels on the hunt for the *Tallahassee*. Concluding that discretion was the better part of valour, Halifax authorities tightened their regulations relating to visiting warships until the conflict ended in April 1865.[86]

~~~⚬~⚬~~~

Important for the opportunities it offered ambitious Nova Scotians and the excitement it generated in many communities, the American Civil War was also a defining moment in the geopolitical history of North America. Had the Confederacy made good its bid for independence, at least four rather than three nation-states would have spanned the continent, bending the arc of history along a different trajectory. But the North prevailed, and the aggressive expansionism of the revitalized United States served as the backdrop against which British North American politicians worked out their path to industrial development and material well-being.[87]

Chapter Twelve

Confederation and Its Discontents, 1864–1873

"It was the best of times, it was the worst of times." This opening sentence of *The Tale of Two Cities*, published in 1859 by popular British novelist Charles Dickens, must have resonated with his devoted readers in Nova Scotia. The novel's plot centres on the chaos unleashed by the French Revolution in the 1790s, but the mid-nineteenth century offered an equally paradoxical environment. Despite what seemed like progress in human affairs, disruptive new ideas and technologies imposed painful adjustments, while wars, rumours of wars, and terrorist attacks made everyone nervous. Among the strategies that triumphed in these troubling times was union of the British North American colonies, launched in 1867 with New Brunswick and Nova Scotia joining Quebec and Ontario. Two years later, Rupert's Land and the North-West Territory, the domain of the Hudson's Bay Company, was annexed to the Dominion of Canada, which was soon extended to British Columbia (1871) and Prince Edward Island (1873). This drive across northern North America must be judged in retrospect as an impressive feat of empire building, mimicking the expansion of the United States in the 1840s.

Tupper's Dream

One of the major architects of this achievement was Charles Tupper, who became a dominant force in the Conservative Party after he was elected to the Nova Scotia assembly in 1855. During the 1863 campaign, Tupper and long-time party leader James W. Johnston had pitched an expanded railway network and a publicly funded education system to the electorate. The Liberal administration led by Joseph Howe from 1860 to 1863 had been equally eager to pursue these goals, but had been hamstrung by dissention in its own ranks over which railway line should be tackled first; how, if at all, Roman Catholic schools

Figure 12.1 Charles Tupper, 1870.
Library and Archives Canada MIKAN 3221859

would be accommodated in a provincial school system; and where to find the capital to finance such costly ventures. At various times, Howe, Johnston, and Tupper had participated in negotiations to finance a railway connecting the Maritimes with the province of Canada and had endorsed British North American union as a means of enhancing the power of the state to effect economic and social progress, but no concrete action had been forthcoming.

These matters would be resolved under Tupper's watch, first as provincial secretary in Johnson's administration and then as premier when Johnston retired to the bench in May 1864. Emboldened by the Conservative Party's comfortable majority in the assembly, Tupper hired Sandford Fleming, a Scottish-born engineer living in Canada West, to oversee the extension of the Nova Scotia Railway from Truro to Pictou. It was completed as a government project ahead of schedule and on budget in May 1867, notwithstanding strong objections from within the Conservative Party. The same determination ensured that the line from Windsor to Annapolis Royal began operation two years later. Inevitably, provincial deficits soared, but nothing could deter the "ram of Cumberland" once his mind was set.

In the field of education, Tupper introduced a Free School Act in 1864, establishing a state-supported system under the supervision of a Council of Public Instruction composed of the members of the executive council and the superintendent of education. When more than half the province's school districts balked at imposing compulsory assessments to help fund the initiative, Tupper introduced a second education bill in 1865 to force compliance. This unpopular measure drew stiff resistance throughout the province, but the premier refused to budge. Nor did he give in to protests from Catholics over the appointment of Theodore Harding Rand, a "born-again" Baptist, as the first superintendent of education under the new system. Refusing to allow a narrow evangelical vision to prevail in Nova Scotia's schools, Tupper negotiated a compromise with Roman Catholic Archbishop Thomas Connolly whereby confessional schools would receive public funding provided that teachers followed the provincially prescribed curriculum and offered religious instruction only after school hours. Since the executive council now regularly included Catholics, their interests, Tupper argued, would be protected. It was a leap of faith on Connolly's part to accept what was only a "gentleman's agreement." Isaac LeVesconte, the Jersey-born Conservative member from Richmond County, introduced a motion in 1865 calling for the formal endorsement of separate schools, but Tupper's will prevailed.[1]

Tupper's hard-headed drive also figured in the relaunch of Dalhousie College. In what must have seemed like a minor miracle, the squabbling Presbyterian synods began to take a more accommodating approach to their differences, first in the union of the Presbyterian Church of Nova Scotia and the Free Church in 1860 (as the Presbyterian Church of the Lower Provinces), and then in the good sense of two Pictou County clerics of the "auld kirk," George Munro Grant and Allan Pollok, to improve provincial educational facilities for their clergy. In 1862 Tupper agreed to join an interdenominational board of governors for Dalhousie College and the Liberals introduced a new bill of incorporation, which became law in April 1863. Faced in the winter session of 1864 with a flood of petitions against the legislation, including one from Acadia College, Tupper overrode opposition in his own party, a third of whom supported a motion for repeal introduced by the Conservative member for Annapolis County, Avard Longley. After quashing Longley's motion with the support of fifteen Liberals, Tupper travelled to Wolfville in June to beard the Baptist lions in their own den.[2] It was an impressive performance, and one that served as a warning to anyone trying to override the premier.

Securing funding for an intercolonial railway proved to be more complicated. By the early 1860s, banking institutions in London, the world's financial centre, had become leery of investing in British North American transportation projects. The Grand Trunk Railway, completed in 1859 from Quebec City to Sarnia amid a haze of debt and corruption, failed to yield the profits expected of it, and brought prominent London financiers such as Thomas Baring and George Carr Glyn close to bankruptcy. The Grand Trunk extension to Rivière-du-Loup in 1860 only added to the company's financial woes. As a result, bankers had little interest in responding favourably to pleas for investment in what would almost certainly be another money-losing railway.

The British government, whether dominated by Conservatives or Liberals, was equally reluctant to pour good money after bad in British North America. Indeed, principled laissez-faire liberals, including William Ewart Gladstone, chancellor of the exchequer in Lord Palmerston's administration from 1859 to 1866, were dubbed "Little Englanders" for their view that colonies were only a playground for the aristocracy to waste taxpayers' money. In particular, they disapproved of the expensive military bases scattered throughout Britain's far-flung Empire. The most extreme Little Englanders, among them Goldwin Smith, professor of modern history at Oxford, argued that the North American colonies should be set adrift to pursue their own destinies so that Britain would not be drawn into costly wars to protect them. While few British politicians were prepared to go that far, they were obliged to tread carefully when it came to providing loan guarantees for any risky railroad project in the colonies.

The financial crisis generated by the poor performance of the Grand Trunk galvanized bankers, imperial enthusiasts, politicians, and railway promoters into action. Early in the winter of 1861, British MP Joseph Nelson and Canadian cabinet minister John Ross, who was president of the Grand Trunk Railway, contacted Howe about reviving

Nova Scotia's involvement in talks on colonial union and what was now believed to be its essential partner, the "Intercolonial Railway." Howe was slow to respond to their solicitations, but a personal visit that summer from Nelson and British MP Edward Watkin, who had assumed the presidency of a reorganized Grand Trunk Railway Company, convinced him to attend meetings in Quebec and London to discuss financing for the Intercolonial. The outbreak of the American Civil War in April 1861 added a sense of urgency to the discussions, while the *Trent* incident, which erupted in November, offered incontrovertible evidence of the military value of an all-British rail line connecting military bases in Halifax and Quebec. In this context, Palmerston and the Duke of Newcastle, colonial secretary from 1859 to 1864, warmed to the idea of support for the Intercolonial.[3]

The presence in London of colonial emissaries seeking railway funding served as a catalyst for the founding in January 1862 of the British North American Association (BNAA), an organization designed to lobby on behalf of the colonies.[4] It counted among its members not only men with banking, land, and railway interests, but also seventeen British MPs, including Nova Scotia expatriate Thomas Chandler Haliburton. While plans for colonial union were slow to coalesce, efforts on behalf of the Intercolonial went ahead under the direction of the BNAA's purposeful secretary, Joseph Nelson. In April 1862 Palmerston's cabinet voted by a narrow margin to support the long-sought loan guarantee. All that remained was to work out the financial details for cost sharing the project.

Some of the members of the BNAA dreamed large, envisioning a railway and a political union under British suzerainty extending to the colonies of British Columbia and Vancouver Island on the Pacific coast. To that end, Watkin became the moving spirit behind the creation of the International Financial Society, which purchased the Hudson's Bay Company in 1863. If their dreams were realized, investors in the company would reap lucrative returns from the development of a huge swath of North American real estate. The fact that Indigenous peoples lived in the region was conveniently ignored.

Just when plans seemed to be progressing as the lobbyists had hoped, Canada's Bleu-Conservative government headed by George-Étienne Cartier and John A. Macdonald was defeated in May 1862 on a militia bill designed to improve the province's defences. The new Liberal ministry, headed by John Sandfield Macdonald and Louis-Victor Sicotte, was understandably cautious when it came to contentious defence and transportation initiatives, focusing instead on slaying the deficit and, most crucially, holding their wobbly coalition together. In September

1863, after a year of foot-dragging, the Canadians officially withdrew from discussions on financing the Intercolonial. This outcome created consternation in the Maritimes, and convinced Colonial Office officials and London financiers that political consolidation was a necessary prelude for any progress on the Intercolonial. Negotiations with one colonial government was bad enough, but orchestrating several unpredictable provinces was akin to herding cats.

Promoters of British North American union were forced to tread water until the province of Canada achieved a greater level of political stability.[5] In the meantime, the Colonial Office focused on Maritime union as a preliminary step to the larger goal. This idea had been in the air for decades and was popular in Nova Scotia, rectifying, as the *Acadian Recorder* put it on 2 April 1864, "a mistake under which these colonies have been suffering for eighty years or more." With encouragement from the Colonial Office, lieutenant governors in the region, most of them eager to raise the tone of what they perceived as petty colonial politics and to broaden the scope for their own ambitions, became instrumental in advancing the cause of Maritime union.

No one was more enthusiastic about uniting the Maritimes provinces – or more disdainful of colonial politicians – than Arthur Hamilton Gordon, New Brunswick's lieutenant governor from 1861 to 1866.[6] The son of former British prime minster Lord Aberdeen, Gordon exuded a breath-taking arrogance that ruffled the feathers of New Brunswick's Liberal premier, Leonard Tilley, who led his party to victory in June 1861. Tilley was as eager as Howe and Tupper to see the Intercolonial completed. Most of the "missing link" between Rivière-du-Loup and Truro would run through New Brunswick, bringing much-needed investment and opening new areas of the province to settlement. It would also complement the grandiosely named and money-hungry European and North American Railway running from Saint John to Shediac, a project completed in 1860.

In the summer of 1863, Gordon began laying plans for a meeting of premiers and lieutenant governors to discuss Maritime union. Tupper was in agreement on the ends of the proposal but not the means, insisting that Gordon's small executive committee be expanded to include a bipartisan legislative delegation from each province. Not much pleased to have his plans amended by a lowly colonial, Gordon denounced Tupper in a letter to Newcastle as a man possessed of but "very moderate abilities, considerable obstinacy, and a large share of vanity,"[7] traits that might well have been applied to Gordon himself. Tupper's approach was well calculated, designed not only to deflect interparty wrangling, but also to reduce the influence of meddlesome lieutenant governors.

Even the Duke of Newcastle understood that any initiative for constitutional change in self-governing colonies must now come from elected provincial politicians, not from aristocratic men responsible to the Colonial Office.[8]

On 28 March 1864, Tupper introduced a motion in the assembly to convene a conference on Maritime union. His dream was to make Nova Scotia an industrial powerhouse in a modern nation-state extending to the Pacific, but this goal, he argued, was impractical for the time being, and "no wiser step could take place than the union of the Maritime Provinces in the first instance."[9] Given a general consensus that political union would yield economic benefits and perhaps a sense that, like other similar constitutional initiatives, little would result from this one, Tupper's motion passed in the assembly without dissent, and it was largely ignored by the press. Enabling resolutions were also passed in New Brunswick and Prince Edward Island, but no action was taken until June, when Viscount Monck, governor general of British North America, contacted Nova Scotia's newly appointed lieutenant governor, Sir Richard Graves MacDonnell, enquiring if a Canadian delegation could attend the proposed conference on Maritime union.

By this time, a seismic political shift had occurred in the province of Canada, where the government had collapsed in the autumn of 1863. After a prolonged period of instability, a "grand coalition" was forged the following June under the titular leadership of elder statesman Étienne Taché. It included three of the most powerful political leaders in the province: George Brown, George-Étienne Cartier, and John A. Macdonald. The moving force behind the coalition was Brown, leader of the Reform Party in Canada West and editor of the *Globe*, Toronto's most influential newspaper. He was determined to secure Canada West's ability to chart its own destiny free from what he saw as the conservative French Catholic forces of Canada East that hobbled the united province. To that end, Brown had spearheaded a bipartisan constitutional committee, which, after much discussion behind closed doors in the spring of 1864, agreed that the dysfunctional union of Upper and Lower Canada be dissolved and replaced by either a union of the self-governing British North American colonies or, failing that, a federation of Canada East and Canada West. Aware that constitutional talks were being planned in the Maritimes, the Canadians decided to insert themselves into the discussions.

MacDonnell, who had been dispatched to Nova Scotia with instructions to advance Maritime union, was not altogether pleased by the Canadian request, but he dutifully put plans in motion for a meeting in Charlottetown on 1 September. This location would not only help to overcome Prince Edward Island's reluctance to participate in the discussions; it was also the most convenient point of arrival for the visitors from Canada, many of whom sailed from Quebec City on the government-owned steamboat *Queen Victoria*. Other Canadian delegates took a more circuitous route, travelling along the Grand Trunk line from Montreal to Portland, then by sea to Saint John, where they caught the European and North American Railway to Shediac, and there boarded another vessel to take them to Charlottetown.

This was not the first Canadian delegation to visit the Maritimes in the summer of 1864. Well before the coalition government had been cobbled together, nearly one hundred Canadians, among them politicians and journalists, had responded to an invitation from the Saint John Chamber of Commerce and the City of Halifax to tour Nova Scotia and New Brunswick in August. This initiative was the brain-child of Thomas D'Arcy McGee and Sandford Fleming, two of the few Canadians ever to visit the "Lower Provinces." Amid alcohol-fuelled dinners, balls, and bonhomie in Saint John, Fredericton, and Halifax, the Canadians had their first chance to lobby on behalf of their plans for British North American union. Apparently they made a good impression. Even Joseph Howe, who was taking a break in Halifax from his duties as fisheries commissioner, rose to the occasion, announcing in an after-dinner speech that "the day was rapidly approaching when the Provinces would be united, with one flag above their heads, one thought in all their bosoms, with one sovereign and one constitution."[10]

The conviviality that marked the Canadian visit in August also served as a backdrop to subsequent conferences at Charlottetown and Quebec leading to what would soon be described by the ambiguous term "confederation." Without developing informal relationships in this way, negotiations on political union would never have proceeded as smoothly as they did. Canadians and Maritimers in the early 1860s were surprisingly distant cousins. While they shared common allegiances, ambitions, and political structures, they were often in closer contact with people in Britain, the United States, and the wider world than they were with each other. Less than 6 per cent of Maritime trade was with the province of Canada and, as Archibald McLelan, a merchant-shipper and assembly member for Colchester, observed, Nova Scotia probably had "more ships in the Port of Calcutta, in any day of the year, than ... in all the ports of Canada."[11] Time would tell whether closer personal relations with the "Upper Canadians" would encourage respect or only breed contempt among suspicious Maritimers, who were still smarting from what they perceived as Canadian duplicity in recent railway negotiations.

Nova Scotia's Fathers of Confederation

At the end of August, twenty-three delegates from Canada and the Maritimes converged on Charlottetown. Tupper's efforts to keep constitutional discussions under the control of provincial legislatures had been successful. Although lieutenant governors were invited to the conference, MacDonnell decided not to attend. It was left to the five delegates from Nova Scotia – Adams George Archibald, Robert Barry Dickey, William Alexander Henry, Jonathan McCully, and Charles Tupper – to determine their province's position in the discussions on colonial union.

Nova Scotia's Fathers of Confederation had much in common. All five men had been born in the province, and four of them traced their surnames to Protestant immigrants from Ireland. As a descendant of New England Planters, Tupper had the deepest roots in North America, his ancestor having arrived in Massachusetts in 1635. Dickey, McCully, and Tupper called Cumberland County home; Archibald hailed from Truro, in Colchester County; and Henry, born in Halifax, grew up in Antigonish County. Except for Tupper, who was a medical doctor, they had all trained as lawyers, and each had become involved in public life early in their professional careers. They were family men, having married between 1841 (Henry) and 1846 (Tupper). Only Henry, whose first wife died in childbirth, married a second time. Among them they had twenty-two children, with Henry father to eight. Born between 1809 (McCully) and 1821 (Tupper), they were middle-aged men by 1864, with impressive records of political achievement to bring to any constitutional talks.

While Nova Scotia's delegates all lived in middle-class comfort, Jonathan McCully (1809–77) had worked hardest to get there.[12] The income from his family's 60-hectare farm in Cumberland County was insufficient to provide more than a local education for Jonathan and his eight siblings, but he managed to accumulate enough money by teaching school – Tupper was one of his pupils – to pay for his apprenticeship as a lawyer. After he was admitted to the bar in 1837, he became involved in the fractious political scene in Halifax as a supporter of Joseph Howe's reform movement. McCully contributed articles to the *Acadian Recorder* under the pseudonym of "Clim o' the Cleugh," and was rewarded for his services with a seat in the legislative council in 1848. He was also appointed a judge of probate in 1853 and a railway commissioner in 1854. As the leading editorial writer for the Halifax *Morning Chronicle* in the 1850s, McCully played a pivotal role in bringing down Johnson's government in 1859. He was appointed solicitor general in Howe's cabinet, and served as the province's commissioner for railways from 1860 to 1863. Leader of the Liberals in the legislative council, McCully was an obvious choice for the bipartisan Charlottetown delegation, but he had been initially passed over, perhaps because Tupper was unimpressed by his penny-pinching management of the Railway Board. McCully's date with destiny was not to be denied. When John Locke, a Liberal merchant from Shelburne County, withdrew from the delegation, McCully, at Archibald's suggestion, was chosen to replace him.

Adams George Archibald (1814–92) was the scion of a prominent Colchester County family that had emigrated from Londonderry, Ireland, in the early 1760s.[13] Tutored by a relative before attending Pictou Academy, he apprenticed with William Sutherland, a leading barrister in Halifax. In 1836 Archibald established a legal practice in Truro, where he benefited from his extensive family connections, gathering up appointments as justice of the peace, registrar, school commissioner, and judge of probate before following in the footsteps of six previous family members by winning a seat in the assembly in the 1851 election. As attorney general in Howe's administration, Archibald, along with McCully, had been involved in railway negotiations in Quebec and London in 1861, and three years earlier had accepted Johnston's invitation to accompany him to London in a bipartisan effort to put an end to the General Mining Association's monopoly. After Howe assumed his imperial duties, Archibald led the Liberals in the assembly, and in this capacity became a Father of Confederation. Neither Archibald nor McCully, who represented the Liberal Party in Nova Scotia's delegation to Charlottetown, had ever expressed much interest in political unions, large or small, but they had actively supported progressive policies – public schools and state-operated railways among them – designed to meet the challenges of the industrial age.

William Alexander Henry (1816–88) was the son of an Irish immigrant who moved his business interests from Halifax to Antigonish in the second decade of the nineteenth century.[14] Tutored by Secessionist Presbyterian pastor Thomas Trotter, Henry studied law with Alexander MacDougall, whom he defeated in the 1840 election. Henry lost his seat in 1843, but regained it in 1847 and served in William Young's cabinet as solicitor general. In 1857, shortly after being appointed attorney general, Henry switched party allegiance when the government dismissed William Condon, president of Halifax's Charitable Irish Society, for his role in exposing Howe's covert army recruitment practices in United States. This potentially career-limiting move enabled Henry to retain his seat in his largely Roman Catholic constituency.

Appointed solicitor general in Johnston's cabinet shortly before the government collapsed, he was serving as attorney general under Tupper when he joined the delegation heading for Charlottetown in the summer of 1864. Henry's commitment to the Intercolonial Railway and to economic development generally ensured that he was in step with the premier on the issues that had prompted constitutional discussions, but his aristocratic ways – he reportedly effected the style of a country gentleman by carrying white riding gloves and riding crop with an Irish setter at lead – might have raised eyebrows among many voters in Antigonish County.[15]

Robert B. Dickey (1811–1903) was born in Amherst, the son of Robert McGowan Dickey, a Conservative member of the assembly from 1836 to 1851.[16] Educated at Truro Grammar School and Windsor Academy, Dickey began the study of law at age fifteen with Alexander Stewart, representative for Cumberland County in the Nova Scotia assembly. Dickey practised law in Amherst, and was appointed to the legislative council in 1858. He also served as a consular agent for the United States, and sat on the Nova Scotia Electric Telegraph Company's board of directors. Fully aware of the value of the Intercolonial Railway, if only to make the journey over the Cobequid Hills to Truro less onerous, he had participated in negotiations on railway financing in London in 1858, and he could see the potential benefits of Maritime union for his province and especially for his strategically placed constituency.

Charles Tupper (1821–1915) might well have been guilty of obstinacy and vanity, as Gordon asserted, but the lieutenant governor was wrong to accuse him of limited abilities. A whirling dervish of energy and purpose, Tupper was schooled at an early age to hard work and self-discipline by his father, a prominent Baptist minister and scholar.[17] Like McCully, Tupper taught school for a time, but he was obliged to borrow money to finance his costly education in Edinburgh. There he earned the best medical degree then available anywhere in the world, and abandoned the restrictions on his personal behaviour demanded by his rigorous Baptist upbringing. As one of the province's most highly trained physicians, he helped to establish the Medical Society of Nova Scotia in 1854, and was elected its president in 1863. If nothing else, Tupper was adept at multitasking. At the same time that he was knee-deep in controversy over his government's education and railway policies, and preoccupied by Confederate raiders infesting Nova Scotia's coastal waters, he plunged into efforts to unite the British North American colonies. Like Dickey, he saw advantages for his hometown and for himself – Tupper had extensive investments in Cumberland County's coal mines – but he also had a broader vision of what British

North America might become. In a speech on "The Political Condition of British North America" delivered to the Mechanics' Institute in Saint John in 1860, he championed union of the colonies "stretching from the Atlantic to the Pacific." This "British America," Tupper declared, which was "untrammeled either by slavery or the ascendancy of any dominant Church, presenting almost the only country where the great principles of civil and religious equality really exist," would "in a few years exhibit to the world a great and powerful organization, with British institutions, British sympathies, and British feelings, bound indissolubly to the Throne of England."[18] The following year, Tupper seconded a motion put forward by Howe's administration to investigate the processes by which any discussion of colonial union might be conducted.[19] Tupper's vision and political skills were exceptional among the men representing Nova Scotia at meetings in Charlottetown and Quebec in 1864. Although his political acumen would be put to the test in the years that followed, his confidence in the potential of British North American union never wavered.

Notwithstanding their achievements, Nova Scotia's Fathers of Confederation were hardly representative of the geographical scope of the province, let alone its demographic makeup. There was no representation from Cape Breton, southwestern Nova Scotia, or the Annapolis Valley, no farmers, fishermen, or even mercantile interests to speak of, and no Acadians or Roman Catholics in the delegation. African Nova Scotian, Mi'kmaw, and female representatives were beyond imagining.[20] What united the five men dispatched to Charlottetown "for the purpose of arranging a preliminary plan for the union of the three provinces under one government and legislature" was their commitment to political efficiency and economic progress as represented by the building of railways, and specifically the Intercolonial, which would serve communities where four of the five delegates lived. And Tupper's dream of a powerful and prosperous transcontinental nation-state that could defy the United States while maintaining the British connection would soon inspire them all.

The challenge facing Maritime politicians at the constitutional bargaining table was their region's small size relative to the province of Canada, which had gone from strength to strength in the early nineteenth century. It had the largest population (more than 2.5 million compared with less than 664,000 in 1861; see Table 12.1) and the most railway mileage (85–90 per cent), along with the lion's share of capital investment (84 per cent), government revenue (78 per cent), and industrial output (nearly 87 per cent). Canada also generated the bulk of the overall public debt (84 per cent), much of it resulting from grants to the Grand Trunk and other railway lines.[21]

Table 12.1. Population of British North America, 1851–71

	1851	1861	1871
Canada West/Ontario	952,004	1,396,091	1,620,851
Canada East/Quebec	890,261	1,111,566	1,191,516
Nova Scotia	276,854	330,857	387,800
New Brunswick	193,800	252,047	285,594
Prince Edward Island	62,678[a]	80,857	94,021
Newfoundland[b]	–	122,638	158,958
British Columbia/Vancouver Island	55,000	51,524	36,247[c]
Manitoba	–	–	25,228
Northwest Territories	–	–	48,000

[a] Figure is from 1848.
[b] Figures are from 1857 and 1874.
[c] This figure understates the Indigenous population of the province by about 15,000.
Sources: "Series A2–14. Population of Canada by province, census dates, 1851 to 1976," in *Historical Statistics of Canada,* 2nd ed., ed. F.H. Leacy (Ottawa: Minister of Supply and Services, 1983); and James Hiller, "Confederation Defeated: The Newfoundland Election of 1869," in *Newfoundland in the Nineteenth and Twentieth Centuries: Essays in Interpretation,* ed. James Hiller and Peter Neary (Toronto: University of Toronto Press, 1980).

Conferences in Charlottetown and Quebec

The fifteen Maritime delegates in Charlottetown on Thursday, 1 September 1864, convened in Prince Edward Island's elegant neoclassical Province House, built in the late 1840s. After selecting the Island's Conservative premier John Hamilton Gray as their chair and Tilley and Tupper as joint secretaries, the delegates agreed they would listen to what the Canadians had to say before addressing the question of Maritime union. This made perfect sense, as they had little on which to focus their discussions. As far as we know, not one of the Maritime delegates had so much as scratched a plan for union on the back of a used envelope.

The Canadians, in contrast, came prepared, having spent the previous two months producing detailed proposals for British North American union. Eager to convince their listeners of the wisdom of their efforts, they took three days to outline their vision. Macdonald and Cartier offered assurances that the united provinces would remain as firmly tied to Britain as they had been in their status as separate, responsibly governed colonies, and explained that any union, while ideally highly centralized, must be a federal one to preserve provincial identities. By dividing Canada into two provinces as was planned, French Canadians in Canada East would have a local government in which they were a majority – the bottom line for Cartier. Canada's finance minister, Alexander Galt, outlined funding arrangements for the proposed federation, assigning to the national government control over tariffs and commercial policy generally, while also absorbing provincial debts. George Brown presented the legislative apparatus: an appointed upper house, where regional representation would prevail, and a lower house elected on the basis of population. Although none of the Fathers of Confederation was a democrat in any radical sense, "rep by pop" was a rallying cry for Brown's Reformers, and would be a deal-breaker for the delegates from Canada West, which was poised by sheer numbers to dominate any strictly democratically structured federation.

After spending a fourth day probing the Canadian proposals, the Maritime delegates returned to the question of regional union on Wednesday, 7 September. Their discussions were now focused by Tupper's sweeping motion: "Whereas in the opinion of this conference a Union of Nova Scotia, New Brunswick, and Prince Edward Island under one government and legislature would elevate the status, enhance the credit, enlarge the influence, improve the social, commercial, and political condition, increase the development, and promote the interests generally of all these provinces, resolved that the time has arrived when such Union should be effected." The motion never had a chance. Unlike Nova Scotia, whose assembly had authorized its delegates to arrange "a preliminary plan" for Maritime union, the New Brunswick and Prince Edward Island representatives were charged by their legislatures only to "consider" or "discuss the expediency" of such an initiative. As Premier Gray quipped earlier in the year: "If the provinces of Nova Scotia and New Brunswick were to be annexed to Prince Edward Island, great benefits might result, but if this colony were to be annexed to these provinces, the opposite might be the effect."[22] The restoration of "Greater Nova Scotia" was swiftly sidelined, while talks on British North American union were slated to continue the following month in Quebec.

In the meantime, constitutional talks continued in Nova Scotia and New Brunswick. Most of the delegates sailed out of Charlottetown early on the morning of 9 September on the *Queen Victoria* to Pictou, where those who had sufficiently recovered from a grand ball hosted by Lieutenant Governor George Dundas at Province House disembarked to tour the coal mines at New Glasgow. They then took horse-drawn coaches to Truro and the train from there to Halifax, arriving within hours of the *Queen Victoria*, which had sailed through the Strait of Canso. Discussions among the delegates continued amid more elaborate socializing in Halifax on Saturday and Monday – Sunday was set aside as a day of rest – and continued in Saint John and Fredericton. In New Brunswick, Cartier, Galt, and Brown were guests of Lieutenant Governor Gordon, who was not much pleased to learn that plans for Maritime union had been abandoned.

By 10 October 1864, Nova Scotia's Fathers of Confederation were immersed in another round of discussions in Quebec City. The obliging Canadians had sent the *Queen Victoria* to pick up delegates from Gulf of St Lawrence ports, starting in Pictou. Unlike New Brunswick and Prince Edward Island, which had each increased their delegations by two members, Tupper stuck with his four original colleagues, but this time he brought along his wife Frances and teenage daughter Emma. Archibald's wife and daughter and Dickey's daughter were also included in Nova Scotia's entourage, as were Lieutenant Governor MacDonnell and his wife, perhaps because they were eager to visit Canada and had relatives there, not because the lieutenant governor had any role to play in the discussions. When the meetings ended in Quebec, the delegates planned to promote their resolutions in major Canadian cities, including Ottawa, where new provincial parliament buildings were under construction. For those who were interested, a visit to Niagara Falls, one of the world's great tourist attractions, was on the agenda.

In Quebec, the delegates from Canada and the Maritimes were joined by two "observers" from Newfoundland, which had not been represented at Charlottetown. The meeting also drew journalists from as far away as New York and London, along with a few Grand Trunk Railway officials, but they were denied access to formal discussions, which were held in private and only partially documented in the official minutes. What was leaked, to whom, and with what purpose during informal occasions will never be known. Nor is it possible to determine the degree of dissention within each provincial caucus. Only the final vote was recorded for posterity.

More than two weeks of intense negotiations in the reading room of the legislative council chamber in Quebec yielded seventy-two resolutions. Although the delegates from the Atlantic region had plenty to say, the discussions were dominated by the Canadians, who had put the most energy into the union plans and were determined to protect them from unwelcome amendments. Brown had initially tried to have the Maritimes vote as a single unit, a position from which he retreated when firmly challenged by the region's representatives. On other matters, the Canadians were less willing to give way. The motion presented by Prince Edward Islander Edward Palmer and seconded by

Robert Dickey that each province have one vote was rejected; Canada was awarded two votes to reflect its founding colonies, which would ultimately be named Ontario and Quebec. Significantly, the Maritime provinces still had the majority of votes, but without a coherent plan for what they wanted out of the negotiations, they were divided and less effective than they might have been in securing any regional advantage.

The rigidity with which the delegates approached union discussions was demonstrated in the treatment of Prince Edward Island, whose representatives were eager for assistance to settle the proprietary land question that was generating social unrest in their province. In earlier talks with Gordon and Tilley, Tupper had argued that this issue needed to be addressed to ensure the Island's involvement in any union, but the delegates would have no part of it; nor would they increase the number of seats in the lower house from five to six to provide balanced representation for the Island's three counties. Ultimately, neither Newfoundland nor Prince Edward Island would accept the "scheme" devised in Quebec, and withdrew from further negotiations. New Brunswick and Nova Scotia had more at stake, most notably the Intercolonial Railway, and their delegates soon bore the brunt of the criticism unleashed against their handiwork.

The Quebec resolutions put in official language what had been outlined by the Canadians in Charlottetown.[23] Since legislative union was unacceptable to Canada East and the Maritimes, a federal system with two levels of jurisdiction, national and provincial, would define the governance structure. Members of what, following British precedent, would be called the "House of Commons" were to be elected on the basis of population, giving the two sections of Canada, with their far greater numbers, overwhelming control: 143 out of 194 seats, which for the purposes of the meeting in Quebec included the eight seats projected for Newfoundland. The upper chamber, still described as the "Legislative Council," was designed to provide a regional counterbalance, but it was rendered ineffective by a widely held belief that the power of the individual states had been a significant cause of the American Civil War. As a result, a majority of the Maritime delegates were reluctant to insist on equal provincial representation in what became known by the American term the "Senate."

The debate over representation in the upper house was prolonged and acrimonious. In the Canadian plan, twenty-four seats were allotted to each of Canada West, Canada East, and the Maritimes. Eager to achieve a better outcome, Tilley and Dickey proposed that the Maritimes have thirty-two seats, but their motion was defeated. The first day of discussion on this matter ended without a resolution. Frustration over the deadlock perhaps accounts in part for the mayhem that erupted at the grand ball and dinner hosted for eight hundred guests that evening by the Government of Canada. The governor general's sister-in-law Frances Monck recorded rumours that the festivities ended at four in the morning amid "drunkenness, pushing, kicking and tearing ... the supper room floor was covered in meat, drink, and broken bottles."[24] In a letter to his wife Anne, Brown informed her that he had left at midnight with a headache, missing most of the uproar, as no doubt had Tilley, one of the few teetotallers among the Fathers of Confederation.

Although the Maritimers pushed the debate into a third day, most of them rejected a motion by Prince Edward Island delegate Alexander Macdonald to have equal provincial representation in the upper house. They settled instead for a poor compromise proposed by Tupper whereby four additional seats would be allocated to Newfoundland if it decided to join the union. To compound the Islanders' distress, the delegates agreed to award ten seats each to Nova Scotia and New Brunswick, leaving Prince Edward Island only four. To be doubly sure that the upper chamber remained ineffective, the Canadians insisted that its members be appointed for life by the federal government, not elected as was the case for the legislative councils of both Canada and Prince Edward Island in 1864. Such a concession to democracy and decentralization was too progressive – and likely too American – for most of the Charlottetown delegates to swallow in the 1860s.[25]

The debate over representation in the upper house was a harbinger of what was to come after Confederation. In any situation where regional issues were at stake, the less powerful provinces, either singly or united, would be obliged to give way. Accommodating the Canadians soon became part of the DNA of most Maritime politicians. Putting a fine point on it, George Brown assessed the critics of his plans for the upper house in a letter to Anne on 17 October 1864: "The conference proceedings go well considering we have a great deal of talkee-talkee and not very much practical administrative talent among our Maritime friends."[26]

As the Canadians ordained and the Maritimers conceded, power in the proposed union would be highly centralized, and lay squarely in the elected House of Commons. The federal government was given legislative control over matters relating to "the peace, welfare and good government of the Federated Provinces," and to this end had responsibility for criminal law, currency and banking, defence, foreign policy, Indian affairs, interprovincial trade, transportation, and, most important, customs and excise duties, the major source of state revenues in this period. Residual powers – "all matters of a general nature not specifically and exclusively reserved for Local Governments and Legislatures" – were assigned to the federal government, further extending the authority of the House of Commons.

Provinces would fund their responsibilities from an annual federal grant of 80 cents per capita and, if their elected leaders had the courage to legislate them, by direct taxes on land and other natural resources over which they had control. As enumerated in the resolutions, provincial responsibilities were onerous enough, and they would expand dramatically over time: commerce within their borders, natural resources, civil law, municipal government, education, and social services. Three areas of responsibility – agriculture, fisheries, and immigration – were to be jointly administered. In recognition of the huge debt – up to $62 million – that the Canadians brought to the federal table compared with that of the Maritimes, a clause in the agreement provided 5 per cent interest on the amount by which the debts of Nova Scotia and New Brunswick fell below $8 million and $7 million, respectively. Tilley also negotiated a special grant for his province – $63,000 a year for ten years – in recognition of its immediate financial needs relating to the European and North American Railway. Awarding provincial control over duties on the export of timber, logs, masts, spars, deals, sawn lumber, coal, and other minerals was designed in part to appeal to the Maritimes, as was resolution 68, which stated: "The General Government shall secure, without delay, the completion of the Intercolonial Railway from Rivière-du-Loup, through New Brunswick, to Truro in Nova Scotia."

The delegates might have resisted a political apparatus that smacked too much of American republicanism, but they showed no similar distaste for following the United States in its romp across the continent. Resolution 10 specifically stated that "The North-West Territory, British Columbia and Vancouver [Island] shall be admitted into the Union on such terms and conditions as the Parliament of the Federated Provinces shall deem equitable, and as shall receive the assent of Her Majesty; and in the case of the Province of British Columbia or Vancouver, as shall be agreed to by the Legislature of such Province." Resolution 69 authorized executive action on westward expansion, though in less specific terms than the clause relating to the Intercolonial: "The communications with the North-Western Territory, and the improvements required for the development of the Trade of the Great West with the Seaboard, are regarded by this Conference as subjects of the highest importance to the Federated Provinces, and shall be prosecuted at the earliest possible period that the state of the Finances will permit." The vision of a united transcontinental British North America was now officially on the drawing board.

Confederation in Question

Since the provinces represented at the Charlottetown and Quebec conferences operated under the rules of responsible government, their leaders were obliged either to call elections or to have their legislatures endorse the Quebec resolutions. They passed easily enough in Canada, but were greeted less enthusiastically in New Brunswick and Nova Scotia. Shortly after the details of the agreement were reported in the press, critics began raising objections. Tilley was immediately taken to task by commercial interests in Saint John, began losing support even in his own cabinet, and decided to call a winter election to clear the air. Tupper was confident that his majority in the assembly would make short work of the gathering storm of opposition to the Quebec resolutions in Nova Scotia, but he had seriously misjudged the situation.

By December it was clear that Tupper would have a major battle on his hands. Lieutenant Governor MacDonnell, like his New Brunswick counterpart, was uncomfortable with the direction that constitutional talks had taken, while Dickey, who had disagreed with his fellow caucus members on a number of issues, broke ranks, publicly announcing his reservations about the financial arrangements in the union agreement. Archibald valiantly defended the work of the Quebec delegates, but most members of the Liberal Party deserted him. Early in January 1865, William Annand's son Charles, owner of the *Morning Chronicle*, dismissed McCully, who soldiered on, founding a newspaper he christened the *Unionist and Halifax Journal*. His efforts seem to have had little impact. Every newspaper outside Halifax except Pictou's *Colonial Standard*, edited by Conservative stalwart Simon Holmes, condemned the Quebec resolutions. When the assembly convened in February, members were confronted with a flood of anti-union petitions containing thousands of signatures.

Under Annand's control, the *Morning Chronicle* became the mouthpiece for a coalition of anti-Confederates, which included supporters of both political parties. Their position was thoroughly aired in a series of "Botheration Letters," published anonymously – but the style was obviously that of Joseph Howe – from 11 January to 2 March 1865. Claiming that the union proposal was "neither fish, flesh, nor good red herring," Howe summarized his opposition to the Quebec resolutions in a letter to British prime minister John Russell on 19 January 1865:

1 That by adopting the principle of Representation by population, the Maritime Provinces will be forever swamped by the Canadians.

2 That, if the Canadas, always in trouble of some sort, and two or three times in open rebellion, should repeat such eccentricities, we should be compromised, and our connexion with the Mother Country endangered.

3 [That] because the plan of double Legislatures, tried in Scotland and Ireland and swept away, is cumbersome and expensive, and cannot be carried out without raising our ad valorum duty, which is now only 10 per cent to 20.

4 That, when we raise our duties to this point, for the benefit of 3,000,000 Canadians, we burthen our trade with the Mother country and with our British brethren in fifty other Colonies scattered all over the world.

5 That when the tariff is thus raised, but £250,000 currency will be left for defence, a sum utterly inadequate for any such purpose while nothing is gained by weakening the unity of command and control now promised by Her Majesty's Government.[5]

Having made his reputation as the champion of responsible government, Howe was determined that his beloved Nova Scotia not bargain away its hard-won powers. Opposition to the Quebec resolutions ultimately became the last major battle of his long political career.

Powerful mercantile interests, both in and outside the assembly, quickly weighed in on the union proposals. The threat of higher tariffs imposed by a federal government dominated by the province of Canada spooked businessmen such as Thomas Killam, John Locke, William Stairs, and his son William James Stairs into public opposition to Confederation. Ninety-year-old Enos Collins, who still kept a close eye on political affairs, was so incensed by the Confederation agreement that he resigned from the Conservative Party. According to Joseph Howe, Collins declared that, "if he was twenty years younger, he would take a rifle and resist it."[27] A few members of the mercantile community supported the union initiative, but worried about the details of the Quebec agreement. If shippers were forced to pay higher prices for their cargoes because of tariffs on imported tea, cotton, sugar, and other foreign commodities imposed by the federal government, the cost would cut into their profits, and even if they managed to survive the shock, the monies accumulated would go to Ottawa, not to the province, which was tied to the 80 cent per capita grant. Although vastly oversimplified, McCully captured the essence of differing attitudes in the business community towards Confederation in Nova Scotia when he quipped that opponents were those who had "money made," while supporters hoped to be "money making."[28]

Facing an ever-higher wall of opposition, Tupper wisely chose not to submit the Quebec resolutions to the assembly for fear they would be rejected. This uncharacteristic caution probably saved him from the fate that befell Tilley, whose government was crushed – Tilley lost his own seat – early in March by an anti-Confederation coalition led by a former Liberal cabinet minister Albert Smith. Tupper and MacDonnell crafted a Maritime union proposal that made no reference to Confederation, which passed in the Nova Scotia assembly on 21 April 1865, but the new colonial secretary, Edward Cardwell, was opposed to anything that might divert attention from the main goal. Following instructions from Cardwell, MacDonnell withdrew from active support for Maritime union and travelled to Fredericton to convince Gordon not to try to revive his pet project.

International forces intervened to keep Confederation from being scuttled. During the Quebec Conference, supporters of the Confederate States based in Canada East had raided the town of St Albans, Vermont, looting banks and destroying property before retreating across the border, where thirteen of the culprits were apprehended. Designed as a desperate attempt to open a northern front in the Civil War, the St Albans Raid failed miserably in its objective but resulted in collateral damage. When a sympathetic Montreal magistrate released the raiders on a technicality, the Union government retaliated by serving notice in December that it would withdraw from the Reciprocity Treaty. This decision was anticipated in any event because the North, now the likely victor in the conflict, was eager to protect its industrializing economy from foreign competition, but coming as it did in the midst of controversy over Confederation, the announcement dramatically changed the optics.

So, too, did debates in Palmerston's cabinet in 1864–5 over imperial defence policy in which the desirability of greatly reducing Britain's military presence in North America was discussed.[29] Although this troubling idea remained on the back burner for the time being, the prospect of inadequate defence created anxiety. Unfinished business left over from the Civil War was generating ongoing tensions that underscored colonial vulnerability to American aggression. Britain's willingness to trade with the Confederacy and supply it with commerce raiders was a particular sore point in Washington, bringing demands for compensation, including the possibility of territorial concessions. As the war drew to a close, Secretary of State William Seward resurrected the view that it was the "manifest destiny" of the United States to control the whole North American continent. This was more than an idle threat. In July 1866 the House of Representatives introduced a bill calling for the annexation of British North America and incorporating its provinces and territories into the union. Although the bill was buried in committee, the Americans purchased Alaska from Russia in 1867 and actively opposed the ill-fated effort by Napoleon III of France to establish a monarchical regime in Mexico, ominous signs that the United States had resumed its course of continental domination.

Relations between Britain and the United States were further complicated by the Fenian Brotherhood, an Irish nationalist organization determined to repeal the Acts of Union of 1800. One branch of the Fenians concocted a plan to invade British North America from American soil in the hope of touching off a larger war and capturing territory that could be exchanged for Irish independence. With so many recently discharged American soldiers of Irish descent facing unemployment when the Civil War ended, the Brotherhood had little difficulty finding recruits for their cause. Fenian raids in New Brunswick and Canada West in the spring of 1866 were easily deflected, but they put the defence issue squarely in the spotlight at a key moment in the Confederation debate.

By the winter of 1866, Albert Smith's government had dissolved into factions, giving Gordon the excuse he was seeking to force another election in New Brunswick. This time the Liberal Party promised major revision of the Quebec resolutions. The formal end of Reciprocity in March 1866, a Fenian raid on Campobello Island in April, support from Roman Catholic bishops and timber merchants, and money from the Canadians and their Grand Trunk railway allies all helped to secure a decisive Liberal election victory early in May. Although Tilley regained his seat and remained the province's primary spokesman for Confederation, he was no longer premier. That position was held by Miramichi lawyer and lumber baron Peter Mitchell, who had led the party from his seat in the legislative council after the 1865 debacle.

As in New Brunswick, the lieutenant governor's office was used to advance Confederation in Nova Scotia. MacDonnell, who was a lukewarm ally in the Confederation cause, was replaced in November 1865 by Sir William Fenwick Williams, a native of Annapolis Royal and a hero of the Battle of Kars in the Crimean War. Highly popular in Nova Scotia, he helped Tupper to convert enough anti-Confederates to pass a resolution in the assembly authorizing continued discussion of British North American union. Three of the anti-Confederates courted by Williams later received senate appointments – Caleb Bill (Kings County), John Bourinout (Cape Breton County), and William Miller (Richmond County) – but considerations other than gubernatorial influence also might have been at play, among them a growing conviction in Cape

Breton of the importance of the Canadian market for coal once the Reciprocity Treaty ended.[30] Fearing that Tupper was trying to destroy the Liberal Party by bribing its members, Archibald, who had survived an attempt by Annand to depose him as party leader, agreed to support a watered-down union motion, but on one condition: that he and McCully receive the lieutenant governor's assurances that he would oblige Tupper to keep his promise to share with the Liberals any patronage appointments resulting from Confederation.

Tupper's motion in the assembly on 10 April 1866 made no reference to the Quebec resolutions, which had been thoroughly discredited. Instead he attempted to appeal to those who had reluctantly come to his own position: that union was inevitable and the best hope for Nova Scotia was to seek changes to the agreement. By the autumn of 1865, Annand also had accepted this reasoning, as had William Miller, a Liberal member from Richmond County, who upstaged both Tupper and Annand by proposing, on 3 April 1866, that a conference be convened in London to discuss a better plan for Confederation. A week later, Tupper introduced a motion in favour of union in principle, which passed by a vote of 31–19:

> Whereas in the opinion of the House it is desirable that a Confederation of the British North American provinces should take place:
>
> Resolved – That the Lieutenant Governor be authorized to appoint delegates to arrange with the Imperial Government a scheme of Union which will effectively assure just provisions for the rights and interest of the Province; each Province to have an equal delegation, Upper and Lower Canada being for this purpose considered as separate provinces.

Disgusted by Tupper's sleight of hand, diehard anti-Confederates demanded a referendum on British North American union, but their motion was rejected 31–18.

This turn of events prompted Howe to return from New York, where he had planned to become editor of a newspaper following the loss of his fisheries appointment at the end of Reciprocity. After meeting with Thomas Killam and other anti-Confederates in Halifax, he helped them to write an address to Queen Victoria, signed by eighteen members of the assembly and five members of the legislative council, protesting the undemocratic way in which political union was being forced on Nova Scotia. To reach a broader audience, the anti-Confederates established the League of the Maritime Provinces – also known as the Anti-Union League – and Howe embarked on a tour of the western counties, where much of the opposition to Confederation was focused. Unionists tried to discredit the League by accusing its members of disloyalty and even treason, but these smear tactics had little effect. With men such as W.J. Stairs serving as first vice-president and its major financial backer, the League quickly gained a credibility that was difficult to undermine.[31]

The Colonial Office kept up the pressure to bring Nova Scotia into line. The end of the Reciprocity Treaty not only struck fear in the hearts of primary producers in the provinces and put Howe out of work; it also reintroduced the long-standing issue of American access to the inshore fisheries. Since the fisheries ranked high among Nova Scotia's industries, Tupper's government was eager to police inshore waters when the treaty ended. The Canadians, with less at stake and without consulting with the Maritime provinces, introduced a licensing system to accommodate the Americans. This was their prerogative, of course, but when Tupper appealed for assistance from Britain to protect Nova Scotia's inshore waters from foreign interlopers, he was informed that Canada's policy was good enough for all of the provinces. Even more galling, Tupper was told that he would not be included in negotiations relating to the end of Reciprocity because Governor General Monck and his Canadian advisors were adequate to the task.[32] The message could not have been clearer: Confederation and Canada's leadership in that initiative served the best interests of the British Empire, whose leaders were eager to reduce financial commitments in North America. If the Maritimes hoped to have any influence on British policy, the route to that end was through representation in a federal government dominated by the province of Canada. In other words, Nova Scotia's interests were insignificant in the larger scheme of things.[33]

Clinching the Deal

With only a year left in his term of office, Tupper hoped to have the British Parliament pass union legislation before Nova Scotians went to the polls in 1867. He proceeded to London in July with Archibald, Henry, and McCully in tow, along with two members of his cabinet, both lawyers, who held seats in the legislative council: Solicitor General John W. Ritchie, the son of a prominent family from Annapolis Royal, and Alexander McFarlane, son-in-law of Amos Seaman in Cumberland County. Tilley and his team were also there, but the Canadians delayed their arrival until November, leaving their Maritime colleagues to cool their heels overseas for more than four months.

During the interval, Howe and Annand appeared on the scene in an effort to arouse British public opinion against Confederation, or at least to delay negotiations until Tupper was forced to call an election. Howe wrote pamphlets and letters to newspapers emphasizing the devious processes used to bring Nova Scotia into the union and arguing that the British Empire would be better served by an imperial federation centralized in London than by colonial union in North America. With the assistance of the Earl of Carnarvon, colonial secretary in Lord Derby's Conservative government, Tupper took on the opposition, and seems to have carried the argument, despite the arrival of anti-Confederate reinforcements to bulk up the cause: William Garvie, secretary of the Anti-Union League, now in London to study law at Lincoln's Inn, and Hugh McDonald, a member of the assembly from Antigonish.[34]

The final negotiations on Confederation took place in London from 4 to 23 December 1866. Although the Canadians refused to make any substantive changes to the Quebec resolutions – and refused Tupper's request that they pass enabling legislation similar to that adopted by the Nova Scotia assembly – several amendments were agreed upon. Significantly, the clause relating to the Intercolonial was strengthened to avoid any confusion or delay, providing for the railway's "immediate" construction "by the Government of Canada." As a result of the unwavering determination of the Maritime delegates, Canada's founding constitution is unusual in having the construction of a railway by the state among its provisions.

Other amendments to the Quebec resolutions also had significant implications for Nova Scotia's future development. In accordance with British and Canadian wishes, the federal government assumed exclusive rather than joint control of the fisheries, which had become an irritant with the end of Reciprocity. Tupper concluded that Nova Scotia's delegates had little hope of changing powerful minds on this matter. And it was Tupper who requested that coal be removed from the list of commodities on which provinces could impose excise duties. As he explained to the assembly, he expected "the possession of coal mines, together with other natural advantages" to make Nova Scotia "the great emporium of manufactures in British America," and "in taking out the power of any Legislature to double the amount of royalty, we were giving a guarantee to capitalists who might come in and invest their money in coal mines."[35] In a move that would later create problems in establishing provincial rights to offshore fish and petroleum resources, Tupper had Sable Island tacked on a list that included beacons, buoys, and lighthouses as a federal responsibility.

Despite a strong lobby by Archbishop Connelly, who travelled to London to press his case, the delegates refused to provide legal support for separate schools in the Maritimes as was confirmed for Ontario and Quebec. A concession was made to religious minorities in the Maritimes by a clause authorizing the federal government to pass remedial legislation to protect "Separate or Dissident Schools" where they had been established by provincial legislation both before and after Confederation. Another concession of sorts was allowing Nova Scotia and New Brunswick to divide the twenty-four Maritime senate seats between the two provinces now that Prince Edward Island was out of the picture. Since Nova Scotia was likely to enter Confederation with a much higher debt than had been predicted, due largely to the costs incurred by railway construction and public schools, Tupper tried to secure changes to the provincial grant but without success. Phillip Buckner concludes that Tupper seems to have been convinced that the advantages of union would offset the immediate financial difficulties that the Quebec resolutions imposed on the province, but it was a huge gamble.[36] As a shipping and wholesaling hub, Nova Scotia had the highest per capita income of all the British North American colonies from revenue-generating tariffs, and their loss would be sorely felt.

As the resolutions adopted in December were being prepared for legislation, a few changes were made to the wording. In Section 91, which outlined federal responsibilities, the word "welfare" was replaced by "order," so that "peace, order, and good government" became the national watchword. The concept of "welfare" disappeared entirely, with the provinces accorded powers prosaically described as being of "merely local or private nature." Although there was easy agreement that the new federation be called Canada, there was some question about how it should be categorized. Tilley is credited with suggesting that Canada be described as a "dominion" of the British Empire. A term used as early as the seventeenth century in relation to Virginia and New England, it had also been applied to England, Ireland, Scotland, and Wales, the constituent "dominions" of the United Kingdom. Tilley might have been dimly aware of this backstory, but his inspiration almost certainly came from a recent reading of Psalm 72, which includes the phrase: "He shall have dominion from sea to sea, and from the river unto the ends of the earth." Given the ambitions of the Fathers of Confederation, it was an appropriate choice, one calculated to avoid the word "kingdom," which seemed pretentious in a North American setting and might well have offended American republican sensibilities. In anticipation of the continental scope of the new dominion, the British government had Vancouver Island annexed to British Columbia in August 1866, making one less cat to herd. Since neither of the west coast colonies enjoyed responsible government, Vancouver Island's misgivings could readily be dismissed.

The British North America Act (now the Constitution Act, 1867), passed by the British Parliament after brief and ill-informed debates in both the Lords and House of Commons, received Royal Assent on 29 March 1867. It was accompanied by legislation to provide financing for the Intercolonial Railway. The instability of the British government after the introduction of the Second Reform Act in 1866 helps to explain imperial inattention to the birth of Canada, but the general consensus around British North American union had long been established. Most politicians were just determined to get this colonial file off the agenda. At the last minute, Edward Hamilton, MP for Salisbury, delayed approval of Canada's constitution when he asked whether women were qualified to vote in the District of Algoma, where every householder was enfranchised. His sensitivity on this matter had been generated by recent debates over voting privileges in Britain, where John Stuart Mill, an influential advocate of women's rights, had made such a question relevant. The rattled authorities quickly inserted "male" in the offending sentence of Section 41, thus requiring the bill to be returned to the House of Lords for their approval, which was given without discussion on 12 March.[37]

When the Dominion of Canada came into being on 1 July 1867, it was essentially the old province of Canada writ large. Its name, capital, civil service, currency, laws, militia policy, tariff schedule, and taxes on newspapers and bank notes were imposed on Nova Scotia and New Brunswick. As expected, Sir John A. Macdonald, who had received a knighthood for his role in bringing Confederation to fruition, was chosen by Governor General Monck to lead the first federal administration, an extension of the province of Canada's coalition of Conservatives and Liberals. Based on the evidence, it is hard to disagree with Philip Girard, who concludes that New Brunswick and Nova Scotia were "annexed to Canada" in 1867 (Map 12.1).[38]

Tupper's final days in office before handing over the premiership to Hiram Blanchard, a Liberal who supported Confederation, were taken up with administrative details. Preparation for the new constitution included reducing the size of the assembly from fifty-five to thirty-eight seats and the legislative council from twenty-one to eighteen; passing legislation to prevent dual representation in the provincial and federal parliaments; and selecting Nova Scotia's twelve senators, in which Tupper kept his word to share appointments with the Liberals. What Tupper had not anticipated was his exclusion from Macdonald's first cabinet.

As 1 July loomed, the soon-to-be Canadian prime minister ran into difficulty forming a government. Obliged to accommodate both

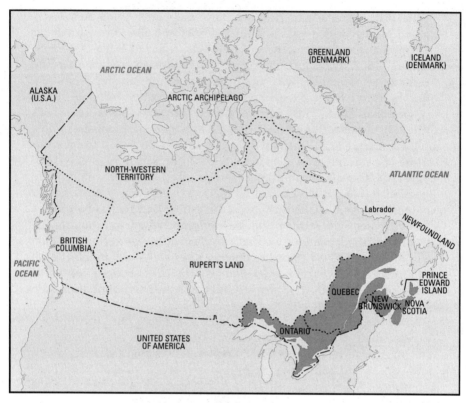

Map 12.1. The Dominion of Canada, 1867. In 1867, the Dominion of Canada consisted of only four provinces clustered on the eastern seaboard, the St Lawrence River, and the Great Lakes.
Map courtesy of Donald Fyson. Base map courtesy of Natural Resources Canada.

political parties and powerful ethnic, linguistic, regional, and religious sensibilities, Macdonald was reluctant to expand the number of cabinet positions for fear of throwing the whole balance out of whack. Ontario insisted on having one more cabinet position than Quebec, while English Protestants in Canada East demanded a seat at the table, and Cartier held firm on having at least three French Canadians. This left out Irish Catholics. When Macdonald threatened to resign, raising the possibility that Monck might call upon the dreaded George Brown, who had withdrawn from the coalition government in 1865, to lead the national government, Tupper proposed that he and D'Arcy McGee, the spokesman for the Irish Catholics of Canada East, stand aside.

It was typical of Tupper to break the logjam in this self-sacrificing way, but the compromise might have further damaged the Confederate cause in his home province. In the end, Nova Scotia was represented in Canada's first federal cabinet by Senator Edward Kenny, an Irish Roman Catholic, who was appointed receiver general, and Adams Archibald, who served as secretary of state for the provinces.[39] The idea that Nova Scotia might receive a third cabinet position to make way for one of the major architects of Confederation seemed too much to concede. Macdonald offered Tupper the chair of the Intercolonial Railway Commission, but Tupper declined, arguing that it "would weaken my influence in rendering the Union of the Provinces acceptable to the people of Nova Scotia."[40]

Newspaper comment in Nova Scotia on Confederation Day reflected mixed feelings.[41] Refusing to bow to on-going anti-Confederate sentiment, the *Pictou Standard* predicted on 2 July: "As loyal subjects [and] lovers of our country, we will celebrate [July 1st in future years], with feelings of fervent gratitude and joy, as the birth-day of what [is] destined to become one of the great nations of the earth." The *Morning Chronicle*, in contrast, grieved the death of the self-governing province, and mocked efforts by union supporters to attract a crowd to the events planned for the public holiday in Halifax, which saw many businesses remain open. In some areas black flags were flown to signal disapproval of the new constitutional arrangement. On 3 July the *Eastern Chronicle and Pictou County Advocate* printed birth, marriage, and death notices for "John Bluenose," and issued a warning:

> Nova Scotians, you are now said to be Canadians, by Act of Parliament, against your wishes. Do you accept the will of the despots who have forced this measure upon you, or do you reject the imputation as an insult upon your intelligence, and a trampling upon your right to be heard in deciding your own destiny? The coming Election will decide whether Nova Scotia is to be ruled according to the well-understood wishes of the people of this Province, or according to the commands – the impudent demands – of the rebels and corruptionists of Canada.

Pictou County resident James Barry, who subscribed to the *Halifax Citizen* as well as the *Eastern Chronicle*, found culprits closer to home. On 30 June 1867, he reported that "Tomorrow we will be swallowed up in the Dominion of Canada. Nova Scotia will become a province of Canada and Canadians will rule and suck the life blood out of it. Damn TORYISM say I."[42]

Enfranchised Nova Scotians finally had their say when provincial and federal elections were held on 18 September. At both levels, old party allegiances gave way in most ridings to Confederate and anti-Confederate candidates, who engaged in a contest that was even more corrupt and vicious than usual. The outcome was unambiguous.[43] At the federal level, Tupper was the only Confederate to win a seat, beating William Annand by a thin margin of 1,368 to 1,271 votes. Even Archibald went down to defeat, nearly bankrupting himself in the process. Many of the eighteen successful anti-Confederates won by acclamation when no one could be persuaded to run as a unionist in the counties of Cape Breton, Guysborough, Shelburne, Victoria, and Yarmouth. Archbishop Connolly's last-minute appeal to his co-religionists to support union candidates did little to stop anti-Confederates from topping the polls in largely Catholic ridings. Confederate candidates in Halifax were endorsed by Connolly and managed to carry the city districts, but anti-unionists Patrick Power and Alfred Gilpin Jones were elected with the votes from outlying regions of the constituency.

At the provincial level, the outcome was equally decisive. Only two Confederates held on: Hiram Blanchard in Inverness and Henry Gesner Pineo in Cumberland. No one could be found to run on a union ticket in the counties of Shelburne and Cape Breton, and four seats were automatically forfeited when the Confederates, in a futile effort to achieve at least limited success, ran only one candidate in the double-seat ridings of Antigonish, Inverness, Richmond, and Yarmouth. In Digby County, the anti-Confederates were so divided that they ran two candidates, and even then, one of them – William Vail, a former Conservative – managed to win. The extent to which anti-Confederate feelings shattered old party allegiances is revealed by the final tally, showing that sixteen anti-Confederate members in the new assembly had previously identified as Conservatives and fifteen as Liberals.[44] Although the party system in Nova Scotia had been shaky before Confederation became a policy issue, and Tupper had poached Liberals to achieve other goals, the Confederation issue blew traditional alliances to smithereens. It would take another decade to reconstruct a functioning two-party system in the province.

The Repeal Movement

Now successful beyond their wildest expectations, the anti-Confederates were confronted with what to do. Macdonald believed that Joseph Howe was the key to pacifying Nova Scotia, but the prime minister overestimated the old tribune's power to put the anti-union genie back in the bottle. A caucus meeting of elected federal and provincial anti-Confederate members held in Halifax on 6 October authorized the provincial legislature to petition the Crown for repeal of the union. While Howe bided his time until a reply was received from London, Tupper refused to take Archibald's position in Macdonald's cabinet because this move might further compromise his dwindling influence in the province.[45]

With so many people of various political stripes having jumped on the anti-Confederation bandwagon, forming a provincial government proved difficult. After Richard McHeffey, the senior Liberal member in the legislative council, tried without success to put together a ministry, Annand was appointed to the council and assumed the role of premier on 7 November. Martin I. Wilkins, an eccentric Tory lawyer from Pictou and former solicitor general in Johnson's administration, led the anti-Confederates in the assembly. Although Annand and Howe were long-time allies, their relationship became strained under the pressure of coordinating strategies and managing patronage in the two levels of government. Relations between the federal and provincial wings of the party worsened when Annand's caucus passed a resolution protesting against MPs who had taken their seats in Ottawa, as Howe had done – an act Wilkins described as unconstitutional.[46] James William Carmichael of Pictou and Thomas Killam from Yarmouth publicly agreed with the provincial ministry, and refused to return to Ottawa for the winter session.

Conditions quickly deteriorated after the autumn session of Parliament extended the Canadian tariff rate to the Maritimes, a policy introduced by Leonard Tilley, who served a minister of customs in the federal cabinet. The high tariffs on sugar to protect Montreal refineries and on imported grains to support Ontario farmers were anathema to shippers in the Maritimes, who now could say "I told you so." Even worse, no protection was offered to Nova Scotia coal, no doubt because Ontario and Quebec had soon resumed their pre–Civil War practice of securing most of their supply from the United States. The uproar in Nova Scotia was loud and prolonged, but Macdonald refused to listen, telling McCully on 2 January, "You must remember that we have a distinct policy in view as to our dealing with the United States and that policy must not be interfered with from any accidental poverty in one section."[47]

At this point Howe lost any ability he might have had to restrain the more radical elements in the anti-Confederation movement. Twenty-seven public meetings were held between the last week in December and mid-February, many of which passed resolutions demanding immediate repeal of the union, some even advocating violence – customs houses being a suitable target – to achieve that end.

In a few areas, southwestern Nova Scotia in particular, annexation to the United States was beginning to gain traction, and a short-lived newspaper, dubbed *Bluenose*, was founded to champion this destiny for the province. A Repeal Association headed by W.J. Stairs emerged from the chaos, and Nova Scotian discontent rumbled on. Although Howe's concern for loyalty to the Crown and public order might have been shared by a majority of Nova Scotians, feelings ran high nearly everywhere. In Pictou County several militia companies, protesting the imposition of Canadian regulations, refused to muster, and the constables who unwisely tried to collect fines for non-compliance were attacked by a force of two hundred men.[48]

The assembly conducted no regular business in the winter session of 1868, focusing instead on fifteen resolutions presented by Wilkins demanding Nova Scotia's release from the British North America Act. Since the legislative council was still dominated by Conservative appointees, the petition was forwarded directly from the assembly to London, and a delegation, which included Howe and Annand, was authorized to lobby there on the province's behalf. The Repealers attracted more attention than had been the case in 1866, but the result was the same. Although the issue of repeal was debated in Parliament with some seriousness, it was rejected, as was the request for a committee of enquiry into the province's grievances, the latter losing by a vote of 181–87. The colonial secretary, a position now held by the Duke of Buckingham and Chandos, had no intention of granting repeal, but he encouraged Macdonald to do more to address Nova Scotia's concerns. It was now Ottawa's job to herd British North American cats.

In an attempt to get in front of what was emerging as a serious secession crisis for the new dominion, Macdonald dispatched Tupper to London with promises of better terms. His meetings with Howe ended badly, despite Macdonald's advice that his emissary adopt a more conciliatory tone. Determined to humiliate Howe both privately and publicly, Tupper leaked information that undermined Howe's authority both with his anti-Confederate colleagues and with the new lieutenant governor, Sir Charles Hastings Doyle. While Tupper's mean-spirited approach might be explained in part by the distress he felt in seeing his dream turn into a nightmare, it was clear that he no longer was the right man for a policy of quiet diplomacy.

The political ground began to shift ever so slightly in April, when Tilley introduced legislation reducing tariffs on imported corn, corn meal, flour, and sugar, and postponing the extension of Canadian currency into Nova Scotia and New Brunswick, to give the region more time to adjust. Although this was a good start, more needed to be done to soften the blow of a number of policies that rubbed Nova Scotians the wrong way. The Canadian legal system applied the death penalty for more crimes than was the case in Nova Scotia, and the Canadian civil service, which initially included only two Nova Scotians, knew little about the Maritime region. Even worse, civil servants from the province of Canada whose jobs had been abolished because of adjustments relating to Confederation received pensions from the dominion government, but their Maritime counterparts did not. Where was the fairness in that?

In June 1868 an official dispatch to Governor General Monck formally denied Nova Scotia's right to repeal. The Colonial Office no longer communicated directly with its former self-governing colony, a stark reminder of Nova Scotia's diminished status. Fearing social unrest and growing annexation sentiment, Howe leaned towards negotiating with Ottawa for better terms, but this position remained so unpopular that Annand, anticipating a revolt among his assembly supporters, dared not be seen as one of the "compromisers." Even anti-Confederates who welcomed a negotiated peace refused to back down, seeing a united front as the best way to squeeze concessions out of Ottawa. Others were determined to find an alternative to Confederation. In July 1868 meetings were held in Yarmouth that included talk of annexation to the United States. This was preferable, some reasoned, than being attached to Canada, which was so hostile to the province's interests. With the collapse of the fisheries in 1867–8 and the economic slump that followed the end of both the American Civil War and Reciprocity, annexation seemed a perfectly logic step to restore prosperity in the aggrieved province.[49]

The escalating secessionist movement finally jolted Macdonald into action. With Tilley acting as go-between, the prime minister accepted an invitation from Howe to visit Halifax in August 1868 to apply his legendary charm to prevent the union from unravelling. Ensconced with the lieutenant governor, Macdonald focused his attention on Howe, refusing even to entertain a meeting with Annand, who was twice turned away from Government House when he attempted to join the discussions. This exclusionary tactic underscored the prime minister's view that negotiations should be carried out by federal members from Nova Scotia, not in consultation with the recalcitrant provincial government. Appealing to Howe's ego, Macdonald agreed to work with him on better terms, and promised that, if Howe agreed to enter the cabinet, all federal political appointments designated for Nova Scotia would be channelled through him.

This approach proved counterproductive, offending long-suffering union supporters, undercutting Tupper's influence, and further alienating the provincial government. Determined to wreak their revenge for being rebuffed, the assembly expelled Blanchard on the grounds that he had been appointed legal adviser for the federal government in Nova Scotia. Howe, meanwhile, was slow to respond to Macdonald's request to determine what might constitute better terms for fear that he would be unable carry anti-Confederates on his coattails no matter how generous the federal offer. Clutching at one last straw, Annand decided to test the waters of repeal with Gladstone's Liberal government in London, which assumed office early in December.

Finally, on 15 January 1869, Joseph Howe and Archibald McLelan, the federal MP for Colchester County, travelled to Portland, Maine, to meet Minister of Finance Sir John Rose to discuss better terms for Nova Scotia. The result was a higher debt allowance ($9,040,439 rather than $8,000,000) and a special annual grant of $82,698 for ten years similar to the one Tilley had secured for New Brunswick in 1864. A federal order-in-council approved these measures on 25 January, five days before the arrival of a dispatch from the British government rejecting Nova Scotia's most recent plea for repeal. On the same day, Macdonald released the agreement for better terms, and announced that Howe would enter the cabinet as president of the Privy Council. The Nova Scotia assembly had not been asked to approve the agreement nor had it been informed in advance of the details.

The outraged anti-Confederates were now determined to punish the compromisers. When Howe agreed to join Macdonald's cabinet, he resigned his seat in Hants County to run as a Confederate candidate. A Repeal League was formed in Halifax on 25 January to organize a campaign against Howe and to encourage unity among the diverse anti-Confederate factions. Two other federal seats, Yarmouth and Richmond, had also become vacant due to the recent deaths of their incumbents, Thomas Killam and William Croke. After erratic manoeuvring on the part of the Confederates, Lieutenant Governor Doyle and the ever-unpredictable Wilkins, the date of 20 April was set for all three by-elections so that a loss in Yarmouth, which was a foregone conclusion, would not influence the vote in the other two ridings.

The anti-Confederates conducted a ruthless campaign, especially in Hants County, where Howe fell dangerously ill trying to keep up a frenetic campaign agenda. As criticism against Howe mounted, even McCully's former newspaper, the Halifax *Unionist*, included an anonymous outburst, attributed to William Henry, against the better-terms agreement. Willing to swallow his negative feelings towards Howe, Tupper brought what energy he could to bear on Hants County voters,

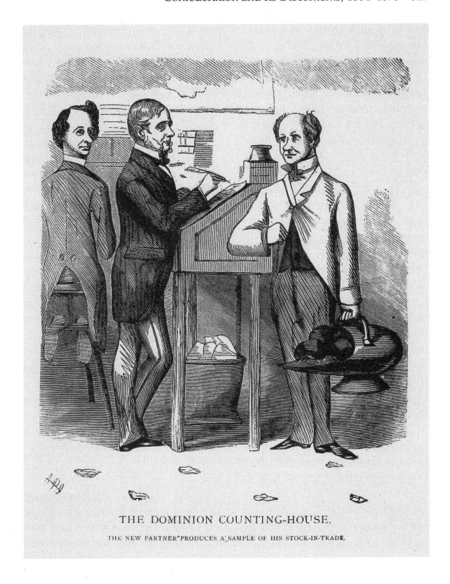

THE DOMINION COUNTING-HOUSE.

THE NEW PARTNER PRODUCES A SAMPLE OF HIS STOCK-IN-TRADE.

Figure 12.2. *The Dominion Counting-House: The New "Partner" Produces a Sample of His Stock-in-Trade*, J.W. Bengough 1869. In this cartoon, J.W. Bengough portrays Joseph Howe accepting his seat in the federal cabinet bearing a coal scuttle, while Minister of Finance John Rose and Prime Minister John A. Macdonald look on with approval.
McCord Museum M994X.5.273.35.

and even offered his own seat if it were needed. Archbishop Connolly also got into the act, bringing to heel two recalcitrant priests who had not forgotten Howe's earlier anti-Catholic diatribes. Money poured in for both sides. As much as $30,000 was spent in support of Howe – his friends in Ottawa being particularly generous – while his opponent, merchant and former Confederate Monson Goudge, had about $20,000 at his disposal, most of it raised in Halifax. The Halifax *Citizen* joked that the Repeal League had purchased pigs and cattle "at fabulous prices to such an extent" that it "will shortly open an Agricultural show," and that the price offered for shingles "gave the Goudge committee a monopoly of the market."[50]

In the end Howe carried most districts in his riding, and won by a comfortable margin of 383 votes, but had they not been guilty of the same offence, his opponents might well have launched a suit against him for bribery. It was certainly not Howe's finest hour. Nor did his victory give much comfort to the Confederates, who witnessed twenty-four-year-old Frank Killam carry every district in his father's former constituency, notwithstanding Macdonald's promise to extend the rail line from Annapolis to Yarmouth if the Confederate candidate was successful. Isaac LeVesconte, who had refused to run in 1867, won in Richmond against his opponent William Henry, who detested Howe. Although LeVesconte shared this antipathy, he was less of a danger to the compromisers than Henry would have been. The hostility expressed by Ontario's Liberal MPs towards the better-terms arrangement when it was debated in the House of Commons ensured that Nova Scotia's MPs would gravitate towards Macdonald, who at least had patronage to dispense. When McLelan stepped down to take the position of railway commissioner, Archibald easily won back his former seat in a by-election held in the summer of 1869.

In desperation, anti-Confederates became more radical, focusing on annexation to the United States as their only hope for escape from a hostile Canada and an unfeeling "mother country." A convention held in Halifax in June, produced a manifesto that proclaimed: "Our only hope of commercial prosperity, material development and permanent peace lies in closer relations with the United States. Therefore, be it resolved that every legitimate means should be used by members of this convention to sever our connection with Canada and to bring about a union on fair and equitable terms with the American Republic."[51] At meetings held over the summer, the League promoted annexation, drawing most of its support from the fishing and shipping counties of southwestern Nova Scotia, the coal-mining districts of Pictou County and Cape Breton, and Halifax and Saint John, where some members of the mercantile community continued to stew over the indignities imposed by Confederation. In May Dr George Murray from Pictou County presented a petition from his constituents asking that conditions for entry into the United States be explored, and when Archibald was appointed lieutenant governor of Manitoba in 1870, Robert Chambers ran unsuccessfully on an annexationist platform in the Colchester riding.[52] John Cudlip, an anti-Confederate from Saint John, introduced a motion supporting annexation to the United States in the New Brunswick legislature in 1869, but the assembly in the Loyalist province refused to entertain it.[53] Rather than representing the beginning of renewed purpose, annexation proved to be the last gasp of the secessionist movement – at least for the time being. Improved economic conditions and an expanding American market that even high tariffs could not completely undermine helped to refocus attention on making accommodation with Ottawa.

By the early 1870s, more regionally sensitive national policies gradually wore down some of the rough edges of Confederation. New Brunswick's Peter Mitchell build a Department of Fisheries that played to Maritime interests, and the Treaty of Washington, which addressed issues bedevilling relations between Britain and the United States, opened the American market to Canadian fish in return for access to Canadian inshore waters. Macdonald, the only Canadian represented at the bargaining table, almost fumbled even this limited concession, but merchants on both sides of the border were determined to avoid further controversy over the fisheries. There was criticism in Nova Scotia and elsewhere in the dominion over Britain's sacrifice of Canada's interests in the negotiations, but only two Nova Scotia MPs voted against the treaty. When work finally began on the Intercolonial Railway under the supervision of Sandford Fleming, it brought jobs and business to the communities along its circuitous route from Truro to Amherst, which was opened in November 1872. At the provincial level, Annand managed to work within the constitutional framework in which his government was largely ignored by Ottawa, but it would take more time to bring stability to the party system. Annand led his newly christened Nova Scotia Party to victory in the 1871 election on a platform of provincial rights, a rallying cry that other provinces would enthusiastically embrace.

Prince Edward Islanders met the same fate as their Maritime cousins in 1873, but they received a better deal by negotiating one-on-one with the Dominion of Canada when an orgy of railway building gutted their provincial treasury. Not only did the Island's Confederation agreement concede what had been demanded in Quebec – a sixth Member of Parliament and a grant to assist in phasing out the proprietorial land system – it also provided funds to cover railway debts, and offered a guarantee of "Efficient Steam Service for the conveyance of mails and passengers ... between the Island and the mainland of the Dominion, Winter and Summer, thus placing the Island in continuous communication with the Intercolonial Railway and the railway system of the Dominion."[54] An extra seat in the House of Commons for the Islanders could scarcely be denied after the province of Manitoba, created in 1870, had been granted four MPs, rather than the one that its population warranted.

When British Columbia joined Confederation in 1871, a railway to the Pacific was written into the union agreement. It was now better terms all around. The leading proponent of Confederation on the west coast was the controversial politician Amor de Cosmos. Born in Windsor, Nova Scotia, de Cosmos was christened William Smith and honed his liberal political values in his home province before making his way via the California gold fields to Victoria in the 1850s.[55]

As Howe's health declined, Tupper succeeded him as president of the Privy Council in June 1870, finally achieving the cabinet position he deserved. Howe, appointed secretary of state for the provinces in the fall of 1869, became lieutenant governor of Nova Scotia in May 1873, a position he held for only a few weeks before dying. In the 1872 federal election, five of the sitting anti-Confederate MPs were defeated, while Conservatives and compromisers carried fifteen of the twenty-one seats and received 51 per cent of the votes cast, compared with 41 per cent in 1867. Macdonald, whose administration just managed to squeak through, was grateful for the support that Nova Scotia's MPs offered in the House of Commons, and more crumbs from the federal patronage table were forthcoming.[56]

After the Macdonald government was forced to resign over the Pacific railway scandal in November 1873, most of the remaining anti-Confederates were brought into the Liberal government led by Alexander Mackenzie. In the winter election of 1874, only two Conservatives, Tupper and Cape Breton County candidate William McDonald, survived the wrath of the Nova Scotia electors, and even McDonald soon moved into the Liberal camp. Tupper played a key role in rebuilding the Conservative Party before the 1878 election, enjoyed life as high commissioner to London beginning in the early 1880s, and served briefly as prime minister in 1896. The last living Father of Confederation died in 1915 at the home of his daughter Emma in Bexleyheath, England, where Sir Charles and Lady Tupper had retired after his defeat in the 1900 election.

Confederation in 1867 was not inevitable. A fortuitous sequence of events, timely coincidences, and purposeful politicians and business leaders on both sides of the Atlantic made it happen. Although the jury is still out on whether it was the best option for Nova Scotia, the Dominion of Canada gradually assumed the status its supporters predicted. It is now a powerful nation-state, boasting one of the highest standards of living in the world. Nova Scotians played a major role in, and are beneficiaries of, this outstanding achievement. Those who warned that Nova Scotia would not fare well in the race for economic success under the Confederation agreement have also been vindicated. Between 1880 and 1930, one in three Maritimers voted with their feet by moving elsewhere, most of them to the United States.[57] Tupper's dream that Nova Scotia would become a major industrial node in North America failed to materialize, the geographies of industrial capitalism having been established well before 1867.

The tide of outmigration after 1867 included Margaret and Robert Dickie and their two daughters. In the early 1880s, they pulled up stakes in Hantsport, where the shipping and shipbuilding industry was in decline, to move to Bay City, Michigan. Robert found work in the shipyards there, while Margaret was hired as a school inspector. She was also active in the Baptist Church, which was taking root in the community. After retiring from her public duties to care for her ailing husband, Margaret continued to add to the family income. She knitted mittens for the local woollen factory, all the while, her daughter reported, churning butter "with the old-fashioned dasher" and reading "a paper pinned to the wall ... the paper was generally 'The Christian Messenger' or 'The Presbyterian Witness,' which was father's paper."[58] Like many Nova Scotians, the Dickies were hard-working citizens of the Anglo-transatlantic world, whose culture they shared and helped to shape throughout North America.

Afterword

It is a common misconception that historians deal only with the past. Nothing could be further from the truth. The role of historians is to remind us of the presence of the past in our daily lives. Indeed it is impossible for historians to do anything else. While we strive for distance and objectivity when analysing historical evidence, we are shaped by our own histories that determine what we select to bring into the present from the vast reservoir of past events.[1] History is, above all, a creative exercise. Each day offers developments requiring us to reflect anew on the various ways in which the past contextualizes the present and on how this knowledge might help us in addressing current challenges.

Anyone living in Nova Scotia in the twenty-first century needs no reminder that history is always with us. While writing this narrative, I was obliged to take into account contentious debates over the statue of Edward Cornwallis in Halifax; how legal regimes, political institutions, religious organizations, and universities should address their racist and sexist pasts; where Indigenous demands for truth and reconciliation will take us as a society; and to what extent the mindless pursuit of economic growth will result in environmental disaster. Most of these issues are rooted in unequal accommodations made in the eighteenth century among the peoples jostling for power over what are now the Maritime provinces of Canada. None of the outcomes of current policy debates is preordained by history, but we risk monumental failure if we are not informed by an understanding of how we arrived at the present state of affairs.

This volume is, among other things, an attempt to situate "greater" Nova Scotia – also known as Mi'kma'ki, Acadie, and the Maritimes – in an early and dramatic chapter in the expansion of Europe. As we are now acutely aware, this imperial thrust at the ocean's edge had a devastating impact on the land, sea, and original peoples, an experience that ultimately became common to the planet. Nova Scotians often boast of the "firsts" in their history, but being at the forefront of settler colonialism and environmental degradation is hardly a cause for celebration. Instead, insights from the outcomes of European expansion encourage us to think more critically about the values that motivated so many of the settlers and their descendants who have made their home in Nova Scotia since 1500.

As I have pitched it in this narrative, Nova Scotians entered Confederation with their capitalist practices, Christian idealism, public institutions, and historical consciousness already well established. The dreams of economic growth, individual achievement, and social harmony that inspired the Fathers of Confederation still inform public policy, in some cases couched in the very same words used to support nineteenth-century efforts to bring Nova Scotia into the industrial age. It is not that Nova Scotians have resisted making adjustments to national and global trends since 1867, but rather that continuity as much as change has defined the results of the adjustment process. After all these years, the economic dependence, demographic challenges, and sense of backwardness that troubled policy makers at the time of Confederation still dominate the provincial agenda and define the stereotypical view that people in the Maritimes are never quite able to get their act together.[2] What happened to shatter the dreams of Joseph Howe, Beamish Murdoch, Charles Tupper, and other nineteenth-century idealists who imagined Nova Scotia leading the world in humane and progressive achievements?

Looking Backwards

The post-Confederation history of Nova Scotia can best be understood by looking at the wider regional framework.[3] After 1867 Nova Scotia shared an economic destiny with New Brunswick and Prince Edward Island, and all three Maritime provinces became obsessed with finding solutions to their failure to sustain a level of prosperity equal to most other regions of southern Canada. The usual culprits identified as thwarting this objective include corporate exploitation, debilitating conservatism, and a flawed political structure set in motion in 1867 that hobbled the region's ability to achieve desired goals. When Newfoundland – officially Newfoundland and Labrador since 2001 – joined Canada in 1949, it, too, felt the sting of second-class provincial status in a nation-state beginning to make its mark on the world stage. In the twenty-first century, the "Atlantic region" remains the "sick man" of Canada, caught, it seems, in a time warp from which there is no escape.

Following the Second World War, historians began accumulating evidence of how unfairly the Atlantic region had been treated by Ottawa.[4] This narrative, which I have had a small part in crafting, often presumes that national policies inevitably disadvantaged the region and were implemented against strong objections by Maritimers themselves. Neither was consistently the case. After the introduction of the National Policy tariff in 1879, it became a source of endless debate, but it was not a central Canadian plot designed to disadvantage the Maritimes. This initiative was introduced by Minister of Finance Leonard Tilley from New Brunswick, who, like Charles Tupper and many other MPs from the Maritime region, supported an aggressive industrial strategy modelled on the highly successful protectionist policies pursued by the United States after the Civil War ended in 1865.

In the early 1880s manufacturing in the Maritimes, especially in Saint John and in communities along the route of the Intercolonial Railway, expanded impressively. Locally owned factories producing consumer goods such as bread, confectionery, cotton, glass, rope, spices, and textiles found national markets, and Nova Scotia's coal industry flourished, but not for long. In the late 1880s powerful interests in Boston, Montreal, and Toronto began gobbling up Maritime companies.[5] The region's financial institutions, among them the Bank of Nova Scotia and the Royal Bank, met a similar fate at the turn of the century, by which time the Maritimes were well on their way to becoming a branch-plant economy. None of this could have occurred without the collusion of Maritimers themselves. Prominent among them was New Brunswick's Max Aitken, who honed his savvy business practices working for financier John F. Stairs in Halifax. Aitken then moved to Montreal, where he presided over the most aggressive corporate consolidation movement yet experienced in the Canadian economy. By 1911 he was living in London, where, as Lord Beaverbrook, he kept a close eye on his Canadian interests and stirred up controversy in his role as a powerful newspaper baron.[6]

In 1886 Nova Scotians briefly flirted with another repeal movement, this time led by Liberal premier William S. Fielding, who hankered for a renewal of reciprocity with the United States to improve markets for primary producers in his province. Withdrawal from Confederation was predicated on New Brunswick and Prince Edward Island joining the initiative, but they showed little enthusiasm for partnering with empire Nova Scotia.[7] Prime Minister John A. Macdonald dismissed the region's discontent as partisan nonsense, and his Conservative Party was endorsed by the majority of Nova Scotia voters in the federal election of 1887, taking fourteen of the province's twenty-one seats. No thought was given to holding a referendum to determine what the general population thought about negotiating new constitutional arrangements. Like their better-off counterparts, ordinary folks simply moved to areas where economic growth outpaced that of their homeland. The exodus of Maritimers was as much a cause for, as a result of, the ongoing weakness of the region's economy, which failed to develop metropolises strong enough to absorb the drift of people from rural to urban occupations in the industrial age.[8]

This phenomenon underscores an ongoing reality: Nova Scotians might have had nostalgia for the salt sea air and breath-taking ocean views, but opportunities elsewhere trumped long-term commitment to the province. Migrants left traces of their homeland in the areas they settled – Waipu in New Zealand, for example, or a community named Scotia on the northern coast of California – but most globetrotters quickly blended into the evolving transatlantic culture. I stumbled across Scotia while driving along the west coast of the United States in 1982. According to *Wikipedia*, the name of the mill town was chosen in the 1880s because so many of its people came from the Maritimes, and a coin toss determined whether it was to be called Scotia or Brunswick.[9] In 1905, American sociologist Albert J. Kennedy reported that "Provincial" women from Canada, most of them from the Maritimes, made up an estimated 70 percent of the nurses working in Massachusetts, testimony to the attractiveness of the "Boston States" to young women eager to seek economic independence.[10]

While other areas of North America attracted immigrants in large numbers at the turn of the twentieth century, most newcomers either bypassed the Maritimes or left soon after they arrived for better opportunities elsewhere. Fielding, meanwhile, found a larger stage for his free trade objectives, becoming minister of finance in Wilfrid Laurier's Liberal administration in 1896. By 1911, when a federal election was fought largely around the adoption of a draft trade agreement with the United States, the power of a new generation of capitalists concentrated in Ontario and Quebec was clear for all to see. The Conservative Party, led by Halifax lawyer Robert Borden, won the contest – although only nine out of eighteen seats in Nova Scotia – and his government spurned the American overture.

With outmigration dominating demographic trends, the region's representation in the House of Commons began to shrink. In the first decade of the twentieth century, Prince Edward Island and New Brunswick challenged the policy that tied representation to population all the way to the Judicial Committee of the Privy Council in London, but lost their case.[11] Population also determined the Maritime region's provincial grants, which were renegotiated at the 1906 Dominion-Provincial Conference, but other regions fared better, especially the new provinces of Alberta and Saskatchewan, which received higher per capita grants than existing provinces. Arguably, Prince Edward Island's needs also merited attention, as evidenced by its introduction in 1894 of Canada's first provincial income tax. In 1912 great swaths of the remaining Northwest Territories were handed to Manitoba, Ontario, and Quebec, which doubled in size without any compensation to provinces lacking resource-rich hinterlands. Small gestures were made to accommodate Maritime protests, including the 1915 amendment to the British North America Act whereby no province in Canada was to have fewer elected MPs than senators, guaranteeing Prince Edward Island four seats and New Brunswick and Nova Scotia ten each as long as the Senate survived.[12]

Following the First World War, the industrial base of the Maritimes collapsed well before the Great Depression of the 1930s threatened economies everywhere. The region's coal and steel industries, which became a national success story in the first decade of the twentieth century, were "streamlined" in a haze of labour unrest, and most remaining branch plants were shuttered. Between 1920 and 1926, 45 per cent of the manufacturing jobs in the Maritime region disappeared. The "rationalization" of freight rates after the Intercolonial was integrated into the government-operated Canadian National Railway, incorporated in 1919, exacerbated the crisis.[13] When American capital drifted across the tariff-protected border in the 1920s to produce the automobiles, clothing, and household appliances fuelling mass consumer society, it gravitated to the St Lawrence–Great Lakes heartland, where most of the population was concentrated.

Post-war discontent in Nova Scotia – and perhaps the influence of female voters who had won the franchise during the war – was reflected at the polls in the 1920 provincial election. The upstart United Farmers and Labour parties captured seven and four seats, respectively, prolonging a Liberal regime that had already been in power for thirty-eight years. In 1921 the Liberals captured every one of the of the province's fourteen federal ridings, a clear rejection of the wartime regime. With so few seats, Nova Scotia had little clout in William Lyon Mackenzie King's minority Liberal government, which depended for survival on the support of the sixty-five representatives of the newly formed Progressive Party and its affiliated United Farmers MPs. Although the rural population throughout Canada shared a sense of grievance over their declining power in a rapidly urbanizing society, the Progressive Party had little interest in issues facing the Maritimes, where it claimed only one seat. Narrow regionalism thwarted any attempt by the Prairie and the Maritime provinces to collaborate in readjusting the imbalance of Confederation.[14]

Struggling to address the challenges facing them and outraged by a sense of injustice, Maritimers came together in the 1920s to wrestle concessions from Ottawa. A genuinely regional phenomenon, the Maritime Rights Movement was dominated by professionals and businessmen – the Conservative Party and the Maritime Provinces Board of Trade both played conspicuous roles – but it received widespread support from people of all classes and cultures. The Nova Scotia Conservatives, led by Amherst-born politician and industrialist Edgar N. Rhodes, fought the 1925 provincial election under the banner of Maritime Rights, winning forty out of forty-three seats (figure 13.1). The Conservative premiers of New Brunswick and Prince Edward Island were quick to jump on the protest bandwagon. The extent of regional unrest prompted King's government to appoint a Royal Commission on Maritime Claims chaired by the British industrialist Sir Andrew Rae Duncan. Although the commission's report, submitted in 1926, recognized the fiscal problems facing poorer provinces, the notion of special "rights" for the Maritimes was too much for the rest of Canada to swallow. The region was pacified by programs to improve transportation policies and provide assistance to flagging industries such as fisheries and coal mining.

Once other areas of Canada shared the Maritime experience of economic crisis in the 1930s, Ottawa began to grasp the problem of fiscal imbalance, which made it difficult for poorer provinces to meet their constitutional obligations or even to participate in national cost-shared programs, such as old age pensions and mothers' allowances, to improve social conditions. King was slow to see the full implications of the Depression, which contributed to the success of the Conservative Party, led by Richard Bedford Bennett, in the 1930 election. The fourth Conservative prime minister with Maritime roots – the others were John Thompson, 1892–4; Charles Tupper, 1896; and Robert Borden, 1911–20 – Bennett was eager to eliminate the poverty that gripped the country, and supported welfare measures, but his party was divided over what to do. On the eve of the 1935 election, Bennett embraced a progressive platform reflecting aspects of Franklin D. Roosevelt's New Deal in the United States, but it was too late to save himself or his party.[15]

Early in 1935 Bennett's minister of trade and commerce, Harry H. Stevens, had resigned his position to become leader of the Reconstruction Party, which championed the rights of the "little man" against the

Figure 13.1. "Let's Keep it at the Masthead," *Halifax Herald*, 2 May 1925. This image, created by Cape Breton–born cartoonist Donald McRitchie, captures the spirit of the Maritime Rights Movement that helped to define issues in the provincial and federal elections of 1925 and 1926.

big interests whose outrageous greed was exposed in the 1934 Royal Commission on Price Spreads. King and the Liberals easily defeated their divided Conservative rivals and other new parties on the scene – the Co-operative Commonwealth Federation (CCF) and Social Credit Party – in the October 1935 election. The whiff of the Depression so crippled the Conservative Party nationally that it had little chance of success at the polls. In a herculean effort to appeal to voters, the party's king makers invited John Bracken, the Progressive premier of Manitoba, to serve as leader, and gave birth to the Progressive Conservative Party in 1942.[16] Two years earlier, the constituency of Cape Breton South had elected coal miner and United Mine Workers activist Clarence Gillis as the first CCF MP east of Montreal.

Many Nova Scotia voters, especially in Cape Breton and eastern areas of the mainland, had voted for the breakaway Reconstruction Party in 1935. This was also the heartland of the Antigonish Movement, launched in the 1930s by St Francis Xavier University's Extension Department under the direction of Roman Catholic priests Jimmy Tompkins and Moses Coady. Promoting adult education, self-help, and cooperative enterprises in banking, marketing, and retail, the Antigonish Movement quickly gained support throughout the Maritimes, especially among Roman Catholics, who were encouraged by their clerical leaders to seek a "middle way" between the political extremes of both right and left that attracted support in the conditions wrought by the two-decades-long depression in the region.[17]

In 1933 the Liberals returned to power in Nova Scotia under the leadership of Angus L. Macdonald, a Cape Bretoner who practised and taught law in Halifax. One of his early initiatives was to establish a three-man commission of enquiry into the effects of national policies on Nova Scotia's economy. It was chaired by J. Harry Jones, a professor from Leeds University in England, and included University of Toronto political economist Harold Innis and the former deputy minister of fisheries Alexander Johnston, a native of Richmond County. While the commission's 1934 report recognized that federal subsidies were "seriously inadequate" for smaller jurisdictions, and offered creative solutions to provincial inequalities, it was significant primarily in serving as an impetus for a national Royal Commission on Dominion-Provincial Relations, established by the King government in 1937.[18]

Among the studies conducted for the commission was the first systematic analysis of economic conditions in the Maritime region, produced by New Brunswick-born Stanley Alexander Saunders, who had studied under Harold Innis at the University of Toronto. Saunders concluded that either the federal government must assume the costs of new social services and development projects or grant the provinces greater taxation powers and larger federal subsidies.[19] The commission's report finally appeared in 1940, by which time Canada was involved in another world war. Notwithstanding the delay in addressing fiscal challenges, Ottawa's superior spending capacity in the 1930s might have spared poorer provinces the bankruptcy that forced Newfoundland to surrender its self-governing institutions in 1934 and be administered by a British-appointed commission until it was again self-supporting.[20]

During the Second World War, the Maritime region's industrial infrastructure and political clout were so weak that none of the twenty-eight Crown corporations created by the federal government to run an efficient war effort was located in the region. Military bases were another matter – the Maritimes were located on the front lines of the Battle of the Atlantic after all. Halifax and Sydney attracted significant defence dollars, while powerful politicians such as Finance Minister James L. Ilsley made sure that his riding of Digby-Annapolis-Kings received investment in the form of military bases in Greenwood and Cornwallis.[21] Defence spending during the Cold War kept many wartime bases afloat and justified the creation of more, but this was not enough to ensure a thriving regional economy.[22] In 1955 the per capita income of the Maritimes stood at 33 per cent below the Canadian average.

Newfoundland, whose per capita income was little more than half that of Canada, joined Confederation in 1949, after two referenda offered its citizens three options: commission government, Confederation, or responsible government. Annexation to the United States, which had established a significant military presence in the colony during the war, was also in the air, spurring political leaders in both the United Kingdom and Canada to urge a speedy, and to their minds logical, conclusion to the colony's destiny. Newfoundlanders were divided on what direction to take, but under the leadership of popular radio personality Joseph Smallwood, the Confederation option won by a margin of 4.6 per cent over responsible government in a second referendum. Term 29 of the union agreement stipulated that a Royal Commission would be established within eight years to determine what level of assistance was required to maintain adequate public services while keeping taxes comparable to those of the Maritime provinces, not those of Canada as a whole.[23] The regional fix was in for what now would become known as the "Atlantic provinces."

In the 1950s business and political leaders came together after some prodding by the Maritime Board of Trade to address the region's position as an economic laggard. They generated a series of recommendations that intersected with a brief period of enthusiasm for regional development and social welfare to improve the quality of life for all Canadians. As a result of what historian W. Stewart MacNutt called the "Atlantic Revolution," new national policies were adopted – equalization payments (1956), unemployment insurance for fishermen (1956), Atlantic Provinces Adjustment Grants (1958), and a flurry of federal, regional, and provincial development agencies – which halted the region's decline relative to the rest of the nation.[24] Policies that would now be seen as extraordinarily interventionist – including the consolidation of Newfoundland outports, Prince Edward Island's comprehensive development plan, Louis Robichaud's Programme of Equal Opportunity in New Brunswick, and ambitious efforts by Robert Stanfield's Progressive Conservative government to attract industry to Nova Scotia – transformed the lives of many Atlantic Canadians, and provided opportunities at home for young people that their parents could scarcely have imagined. Although some scholars have argued that these policies generated a culture of state dependency, they worked in terms of employment and population growth – at least for a time.[25]

The politics of regionalism offers significant insights into the way federal political parties positioned themselves after the Second World War. When John Diefenbaker led the Progressive Conservative Party to victory in 1957, he purposefully created a cabinet that for the first time had a majority of ministers from the Western and Atlantic provinces.[26] Regional tensions made governing difficult and ultimately played a significant role in undermining Diefenbaker's administration. The Liberal Party, which has never chosen a leader from outside Ontario and Quebec, returned to office under Lester Pearson (1963–8) and Pierre Elliott Trudeau (1968–79; 1980–4), both of whom focused their attention on the threat of Quebec separatism. While much is made of Trudeaumania, it is worth noting that neither the Maritimes nor the Prairie provinces gave the Liberal Party a majority of their seats in the elections of 1968 and 1972, setting the margins against the middle for a significant showdown when the oil crisis and "stagflation" engulfed Canada in 1973.

Given the popularity of equalization programs in the poorer provinces, it is not surprising that efforts were made to integrate the concept of fiscal equality into the Constitution Act, 1982. The Atlantic provinces collaborated with Manitoba and Saskatchewan to produce Article 36, which obliged the federal government to make equalization payments "to ensure that provincial governments have sufficient revenues to provide reasonably comparable levels of public services at reasonably comparative levels of taxation."[27] To date this clause has not been tested in the courts, and it might well be entirely worthless given the vague reference, not once but twice, to "reasonably." Is it reasonable that people in Alberta pay only a 5 percent goods and servives tax, while the Atlantic provinces are subjected to a 15 percent harmonized sales tax (the highest in Canada) to maintain services that just barely meet the notion of "reasonably comparable"? Most federal leaders would be leery, if they valued their jobs, of seriously engaging such a question.

There was little collaboration among the Atlantic provinces to ward off the neoliberal template that descended on Canada in the 1980s. Embraced nationally by the Progressive Conservative government led by Brian Mulroney following the report of the Royal Commission on the Economic Union and Development Prospects for Canada (1985), the new orthodoxy promoted balanced budgets, deregulation, free trade, and lower taxes to ensure global competitiveness. The Liberals became committed to the same polices once the party achieved power under Jean Chrétien in 1993. A torrent of criticism directed against equalization payments, universal social welfare state programs, and unionized labour became commonplace among "think tanks" established to promote the new world order. Scholars such as David Alexander and Ernest Forbes warned that Canadian unity would be endangered if transfer payments to people and regions were undermined,[28] but it was Quebec, not the Atlantic provinces, which drew on the argument that the draconian austerity program initiated by Chrétien's finance minister Paul Martin was yet another good reason to hold a second referendum on independence in 1995.

By the 1990s provincial governments in Atlantic Canada began toppling at an alarming rate as premiers wrestled with declining revenues and an ideology that discounted the value of state intervention in economic affairs. Even the New Democratic Party government in Nova Scotia from 2009 to 2013 conformed to the new reality, promising balanced budgets, rather than radical measures to help people falling through the cracks of neoliberal policies. A less intrusive state and a larger role for corporations proved to be a bad bargain for everyone except for those on top of the social ladder, and wreaked havoc with people treading water to survive. In the Atlantic region, gross domestic product levels stagnated, unemployment escalated, and outmigration again dominated demographic trends. The overall population in the Atlantic region has remained almost static (around 2,400,000 in 2020), while that in every other province of Canada and most other areas of the world has grown. By the second decade of the twenty-first century, the Atlantic provinces made up less than 7 per cent of the Canadian population, down from more than 20 per cent for the Maritimes in 1871.

Newfoundland and Labrador Making Waves

It is tempting to argue that the region's political leaders could have been shrewder in their negotiations with Ottawa, but they had little leverage in the perennial search for "better terms." When they demanded reforms to improve their region's prospects, the pushback was formidable and often couched in victim-blaming language. In the 1920s *Maclean's* magazine compared the Maritime provinces to a housewife who, having married for money, which failed to materialize, "neglected her housework, went down to the seashore ... watched the ships go by and pouted."[29] Ralph Klein, premier of Alberta from 1992 to 2006, was particularly dismissive of transfer payments, often described as "shit" or "crap," that sustained the "creeps and bums" from "the east,"[30] but political leaders outside of Atlantic region usually curbed their criticisms when their own jurisdictions were in need of federal assistance.

Unlike people in the Maritimes, who tend to settle for accommodation with Ottawa, Newfoundlanders took a more aggressive approach. Joseph Smallwood, premier from 1949 to 1972, was never shy about taking Ottawa to task, and Clyde Wells, the Liberal premier from 1989 to 1996, stands out as one of the most thoughtful politicians on matters relating to constitutional reform designed to improve conditions for smaller provinces. During the discussions around the Meech Lake and Charlottetown Accords, which Brian Mulroney's government initiated as a means of bringing Quebec into the Constitution, Wells swam against the tide, arguing for a stronger federal government to ensure economic equality across the country and an elected Senate in which all provinces had an equal voice. Wells was even prepared to reverse his province's acceptance of the Meech Lake Accord, but credit for its defeat ultimately went to Manitoba, where Elijah Harper, distressed by the lack of consultation on Indigenous rights, cast a negative vote that made it impossible for Gary Filmon's Progressive Conservative government to extend the deadline for accepting the Accord.[31] In tight corners, even small provinces and one vote can sometimes make a difference.

Newfoundland and Labrador's confrontation with Ottawa over royalties from Atlantic Canada's offshore resources is instructive on how "have-not" provinces in Confederation are sustained in their secondary status.[32] By the early 1980s, the United Nations Law of the Sea Convention had enabled Canada to expand exclusive jurisdiction over fisheries and mineral resources from twelve to two hundred miles of the coastline. This policy offered a unique opportunity for the Atlantic provinces to transcend their "have-not" status, but the Trudeau government fought to maintain federal control over coastal areas, and the Supreme Court of Canada sided against Newfoundland when it challenged Ottawa's claims to exclusive jurisdiction. Eager to deescalate the tensions, Mulroney's administration signed an Atlantic Accord with Newfoundland and Nova Scotia in 1985 to give the two provinces a share of income from offshore oil and gas development. When the royalties began to flow in the late 1990s, it became clear that they would offset transfer payments. The inability to make progress in slaying the accumulated provincial debt and setting his province on a stable economic path after the cod moratorium of 1992 threw 30,000 people out of work prompted Newfoundland and Labrador's Liberal premier Roger Grimes to establish a Royal Commission on to explore how best "to renew and strengthen" the place of his province in Canada.

The commission's report, tabled in 2003, was largely ignored following Grimes's defeat at the polls that year, but his Progressive Conservative successor, Danny Williams, would brook no opposition in his crusade to make good on the promise of Confederation. Backed by Nova Scotia's Progressive Conservative premier John Hamm, Williams fought a battle for 100 per cent of offshore petroleum royalties until his province had achieved a standard of living and burden of taxation approaching the Canadian average. This time Ottawa got the message. Through political manoeuvring during the 2004 election campaign and dramatic posturing, which included walking out of meetings and removing the Canadian flag from provincial government buildings, Williams forced Paul Martin's minority Liberal government to negotiate a better agreement on offshore resource royalties with his province and Nova Scotia in 2004–5.

The standoff leading to the compromise was a shabby affair and left bitter feelings. During negotiations with Ottawa, offers to concede full royalties initially came with strings attached that revealed the centrist bias of Ottawa bureaucracies: the new royalty regime would be capped so that Newfoundland and Labrador's per capita fiscal capacity would not exceed that of Ontario; the province would be required to run a balanced budget; and the agreement would have an eight-year time limit. Comments about Williams in the *Globe and Mail* were disparaging, with Margaret Wente comparing the premier to a "deadbeat brother-in-law who's hit you up for money a few times too often," and describing Newfoundland and Labrador as the world's most "scenic welfare ghetto."[33] Inevitably, people in the province, where the population had dropped from 580,000 in 1984 to 509,000 in 2007, and many of those remaining forced to endure a long commute to jobs in Alberta, were outraged. Other provinces, meanwhile, were hot on the trail of increased transfer payments, among them Ontario, which in 2005 quietly received $5.75 billion to address its claim that it paid more than its fair share into the federation.

When Stephen Harper assumed office in 2006, he tried to "rationalize" equalization payments, prompting Williams to wage a highly successful ABC (Anything But Conservative) campaign in his province during the 2008 federal election. In the same year, his government expropriated the assets of AbitibiBowater after it closed its paper mill in Grand Falls-Windsor in 2008, throwing eight hundred people out of work. The company filed for compensation under Chapter 11 of the North

American Free Trade Agreement, but Williams refused to pay, leaving the federal government to pick up the $130 million tab on the grounds that it was responsible for negotiating this corporate-friendly policy.[34]

More troubling for Williams was the deeply flawed contract signed in 1969 by BRINCO (British Newfoundland Corporation) with Hydro-Québec for the rights to transmit power at a ridiculously low fixed price from Churchill Falls in Labrador to markets in Canada and the United States. Quebec played hardball throughout the negotiations to the point of demanding a renegotiation of the 1927 Labrador boundary. Despite having constitutional control of interprovincial trade, the federal government refused to intervene against a province threatening to secede and that gave the Liberals enough votes to keep them in office. Since the mid-1970s, Quebec has collected windfall profits, so far averaging more than $1 billion a year. Backed by Supreme Court decisions, Quebec refuses to budge, and no federal government has been prepared to remedy the injustice.[35]

There is little likelihood that the general trends will change in the immediate future. By the twenty-first century, the centre of gravity in Canada had shifted decisively westward, and the Ontario–Western provinces axis, with nearly 70 per cent of Canada's population, will almost certainly hold.[36] Quebec has abandoned earlier expectations of having parity in national institutions, and the Atlantic region might be forced to concede any representation at all if the commission established in 2016 to investigate murdered and missing Indigenous women and girls is any indication. This, notwithstanding that the Liberal Party had won all of the thirty-two seats in the Atlantic provinces in the 2015 election. Given the region's lack of power in Confederation, bloc voting has proved to be a largely useless strategy, and Atlantic Canadians know it. Scholars exploring Canadian political culture in the 1970s discovered that people living in the region expressed "a low sense of efficacy" or, as Stephen Harper dubbed it in 2002, "a culture of defeat."[37] With the region's political institutions so compromised by democratic processes, it might be more accurate to call it a culture of realistic expectations.

Going Forward

If we accept that living in a poorer region of a prosperous country produces debilitating cultural side-effects, the question arises whether there was a smarter alternative to hitching the region's wagon to the Canadian star. Since 1867 critics of Confederation have suggested other political destinies for a part or all of the Atlantic region of Canada. They fall into several broad categories, including integration into the British

Empire, annexation to the United States, Maritime union, and provincial autonomy. Because they can never be proven one way or another, counterfactual analyses have their limits, but they stimulate the mind wonderfully, encouraging new ways of assessing where to go from here.

The most vocal advocate for colonial representation in the British Parliament was Joseph Howe, who tried desperately to convince the Colonial Office that this option, along with appointing worthy colonials such as himself to positions in the imperial bureaucracy, was the best route to advancing not only Nova Scotia but all of the Empire.[38] In the 1880s a broad imperial federation movement, in which Maritimers such as George M. Grant and George Parkin played prominent roles, gained support in English Canada, but it failed to develop institutional legs and the idea gradually dissolved into the looser Commonwealth arrangement when national independence became the global ideal following the First World War.[39] Northern Ireland and Scotland offer a comparative perspective for imperial integration as a means to a more prosperous end. It is doubtful that Maritimers would ever have had the influence in London that they felt was warranted, and the tyranny of distance would have taken its toll. In retrospect, we can be grateful that this option slipped off the agenda, sparing us the direct agonies of Brexit.

Since the 1860s Maritimers have been prominent among Canadians who have supported annexation to the United States. Radical repealers in Nova Scotia and New Brunswick at the time of Confederation cast their eyes longingly south of the border, eager to restore the lucrative trade that the Reciprocity Treaty and the American Civil War had generated.[40] Although annexation sentiment continued to be expressed in the Maritimes and in Canada generally well into the twentieth century, it never advanced much beyond an interest in access to American markets. A free trade agreement was signed with the United States in 1988 and extended to Mexico in 1992. Since then, annexation has attracted little support for reasons that have little to do with trade. Most observers agree that Empire America is experiencing a near-death experience, and it is fortunate that Atlantic Canadians are at one remove from the political shenanigans plaguing our nearest neighbour.

Between 1604 and 1758, "Acadie" was a distinct, if ill-defined, region of New France, and for a brief period after 1758 Nova Scotia included what became the colonies of Prince Edward Island in 1769 and New Brunswick in 1784. Union of the three provinces is not a far-fetched political goal, and in the age of sail there was much to recommend it. Before railways reoriented transportation networks, the Atlantic Ocean, the Bay of Fundy, and the Straits of Canso and Northumberland bound the Maritimes together,[41] while the notion that small regions off large continents could achieve global greatness had been proven by Britain itself. Charles Tupper, whose political base in Amherst was located at the junction of the three provinces, warmed to the idea of Maritime union, and it was his motion in the Nova Scotia assembly in 1864 that set the ball rolling for the Charlottetown Conference. Most historians conclude that the meeting on Maritime union very likely would never have taken place at all had the Canadians not asked to join the discussions. The alacrity with which Maritime delegates dropped the less ambitious project for the larger one speaks to the relief the representatives of all three provinces felt in salvaging at least a remnant of the limited provincial autonomy achieved in the mid-nineteenth century.[42]

Since the 1880s, calls for Maritime union have periodically attracted political support. Fielding's overtures to New Brunswick and Prince Edward Island in 1886 failed to gain traction, and the Royal Commission on Maritime Claims steered away from the union idea. It caught on in 1965, to the extent that the legislatures of both New Brunswick and Nova Scotia passed motions calling for a high-level study of the matter. Funded in part by the federal government and chaired by the principal of Queen's University, John J. Deutsch, the Commission on Maritime Union (1968–70) examined the potential impact of a single political unit on such issues as fiscal policy, social services, and the fate of the French language in the region. Maritime union has been a preferred option for the federal government at any time – fewer poor provinces to placate – and the Deutsch Commission report fell into line with that goal. So, too, it seems, did people in the region. A poll was conducted in 1969 with more than 3,000 Maritimers on the question, "Would you vote for complete union into a single province?"Two-thirds of the respondents were in favour – the "yes" vote was 68 per cent in New Brunswick, 64 per cent in Nova Scotia, and 58 per cent in Prince Edward Island. Despite an apparent alignment of the stars, provincial autonomy prevailed, but formal collaboration was embodied in such institutions as the Council of Maritime Premiers (Atlantic Premiers after 2000) and the Maritime Provinces Higher Education Commission.[43]

Conservative senators from the Maritimes reactivated the union idea in 2012, but by then popular opinion proved less enthusiastic. A poll conducted with 1,500 Atlantic Canadians revealed that in Nova Scotia 28 per cent of respondents completely or mostly supported a union of the four provinces; in New Brunswick the figure was 34 per cent; and in Prince Edward Island 26 per cent. Newfoundland and Labrador proved most resistant, with just 16 per cent supporting the idea.[44] In the intervening years, provincialism had gained strength in Canada, and regional collaboration orchestrated by the Council of Atlantic Premiers had squeezed most of the "efficiencies" out of administrative operations. For those longing to reduce the role of the state, regional union is still attractive,[45] although it is difficult to imagine exactly how a single Maritime or Atlantic province would do more than create a larger – still poor – political unit in which old provincial loyalties jostled for prominence. In much the same way that Norway spun off the union with Sweden in 1905, or the short-lived Federation of the West Indies fell apart in 1962, one or more of the provinces would almost certainly demand, sooner or later, that their independence be restored if policies failed to work to their advantage. The turmoil afflicting the European Union offers an object lesson in this respect, with Mediterranean countries particularly aggrieved about the impact of centralized monetary policies on their economic well-being.

This leaves the Nordic model: independence for smaller political jurisdictions in a globalizing world. Cuba, Iceland, New Zealand, and a great many other of the planet's small nations also come to mind in this category, suggesting outcomes that range from failed states to highly successful ones. Many anti-Confederates after 1867 believed that restoring provincial autonomy would enhance their ability to secure a separate trade agreement with the United States. Although there is little evidence to suggest that Americans in the 1860s were interested in anything other than annexation – and even that would have been strongly resisted by the recently defeated southern states – Newfoundland managed to negotiate a draft free trade treaty with the United States in 1890. This prospect was so alarming that Canadian politicians insisted that the British government squelch this initiative because it would only reinforce ongoing separatist tendencies in Nova Scotia.[46]

Newfoundland's bankruptcy in the 1930s served as a cautionary tale for Maritimers thinking of cutting ties with Canada, but it is a mistake to assume that any or all of the Maritime provinces would have suffered a similar fate had they remained outside Confederation. In his analysis of economic growth in the Atlantic region between 1880 and 1940, political economist David Alexander underscored the diversity of resources in the Maritimes, which served as a cushion in hard times. He also concluded that the economy of the Maritime provinces shrank relative to both Newfoundland and Canada in this period. Although it is impossible to determine whether conditions would have been better for the Maritimes outside Confederation, Alexander's findings confirm that Canadian federalism failed to generate the prosperity that its political leaders sought.[47]

What must be acknowledged is that no provincial government in the Maritimes was ever prepared to embrace radical alternatives to structures that sucked money, people, and power to growth centres elsewhere.[48] Saskatchewan, whose economy contracted to a level similar to that of the Maritime provinces in the 1930s, pursued a social democratic solution to its troubles under the premiership of Tommy Douglas, who led the CCF to victory in 1944. The Scandinavian countries, which experienced problems of poverty and outmigration similar to those afflicting the Atlantic region, also opted for social democracy after the Second World War. As independent states, the Atlantic provinces could have evolved into the Scandinavia, rather than the Mediterranean, of North America, but they lacked a cultural distinctiveness to boost social cohesion and their economies, whether in or outside Confederation, were too closely aligned with North American capital markets and liberal values to embrace dramatic departures from the old familiar ruts.[49] That point conceded, politicians in the region, many of them steeped in the values of the Protestant social gospel, Reformist Catholicism, human rights, and democratic socialism have played a significant role in promoting a "progressive" slant in both the Conservative and Liberal parties beginning in the 1930s.

The depth of liberal political values in Canada and in the Atlantic region can be gauged by comparing their responses to the financial crisis of 2008 with that of tiny Iceland (population 331,778 in 2016, up from 267,454 in 1995), which succumbed to neoliberal strategies at the turn of the twenty-first century. Devastated by the economic shock, Iceland's post-crisis government let banks pay for their lack of diligence, enhanced the tourist potential of Icelandair, and built the spectacular Harpa concert hall and conference centre to prime the economic pump.[50] Small states can often get away with policies that larger jurisdictions cannot.

Given that economic and social trends have long been global in scope, an argument can be made that Atlantic Canada would be no better off in the second decade of the twenty-first century had its leaders successfully pursued any of the other political options potentially available to them. It can also be argued that joining Confederation was the best road to take in the long run for those seeking security, economic well-being, and global status. While much academic energy has been spent exploring the negative impact of Confederation on the region, less effort has been made to analyse the benefits that have accrued, among them investment in railways, highways, and information technology well beyond what small jurisdictions might have managed. The fisheries have had good years and bad, but they often received purposeful attention under federal ministers, and Ottawa was generous in helping the region to address the fisheries crisis of the 1990s. By the second decade of the twenty-first century, Nova Scotia led the country in the value of its fisheries, but for how long is uncertain given the rapid depletion of the ocean's wild species. For capitalists in the Atlantic region, among them Craig Dobbin, Roy Jodrey, Harris and Wallace McCain, Kenneth C. Irving, John Risley, Harry Steel, and Frank Sobey, federal policies provided the support they needed to build their business empires. And the status that Nova Scotians achieve from being attached to Canada is nothing to sneeze at: it has developed into one of the world's wealthiest nation-states, with all the opportunities and responsibilities associated with this privileged economic position.

Quebec's experience documents that, even within Confederation, there are few impediments to thinking creatively about "provincial" powers. For the moment, the options are endless, but they essentially boil down to two broad directions. The Atlantic provinces can continue with high unemployment that is typical of underdeveloped states, content in the safety valve of outmigration to more prosperous regions and confident that transfer payments will always, at least minimally, maintain a basic standard of living. Alternatively, Atlantic Canadians can imagine better ways to address the challenges that characterize the age of anxiety. While it is still unfashionable to suggest that economic growth is not the be-all-and-end-all of public policy, continuing down this road is no longer a realistic option. Ways of living in what is by global standards one of the world's most favoured regions might offer strategies for surviving the deep challenges that climate change and corporate values are pressing upon us. And nowhere is it written that the four provinces will sing from the same page of the hymn book in making adjustments to current demographic and environmental realities. Geography and history give the region a similar angle of vision on Confederation, but each province has a history long and deep enough to sustain separate political destinies in a world where the choices are to sink or swim together.[51]

The Atlantic region serves as an uncomfortable reminder to the rest of Canada that unfettered market forces often fall short. Even the economic meltdown of 2008, when states propped up a system riddled by greed and irresponsibility, failed to stop ideologues from preaching that less government is the best government. Since the gap between rich and poor is not only manifested geographically across regions, but is also encompassed in class, ethnic, gender, and race relations, it is important to invest in an activist state that encourages a fairer distribution of nature's bounty and that works to achieve sustainable living standards for everyone. The region's good fortune is that it is part of a country as rich and as politically creative as Canada. The larger geopolitical framework offers security in hard times, provides opportunities outside Atlantic regional boundaries and sometimes within, and – in theory at least – subscribes to the values of equal opportunity and social welfare. In addition to guaranteeing equalization payments, Article 36 of the Constitution declares that the Government of Canada and the provincial governments are committed to "a) promoting equal opportunities for the well-being of Canadians; b) furthering economic development to reduce disparity in opportunities; and c) providing essential public services of reasonable quality to all Canadians." The interests of smaller jurisdictions in Canada invariably take a back seat to more powerful ones, but nothing prevents the Atlantic provinces, individually or together, from working to ensure that Canada live up to the high-minded principles enshrined in the Constitution.

After Confederation Nova Scotians continued to pursue an evolutionary, rather than a revolutionary, approach to effecting change, a practice championed by Joseph Howe but common to many provincial efforts to achieve political and social change. Progressive policies were nudged along by courageous individuals such as Edith Archibald, James B. McLachlan, Moses Coady, Viola Desmond, Donald Marshall and Léger Comeau, who were backed by civil society organizations such as the Woman's Christian Temperance Union; United Mine Workers of America; the Extension Department of St Francis Xavier University; the Nova Scotia Association for the Advancement of Coloured People; the Union of Nova Scotia Indians; and the Fédération acadienne de la Nouvelle-Écosse. Some lived long enough to see their goals embraced by major political parties. It is not the time to abandon this valuable, if imperfect, democratic process.

By focusing on the regional question for so long, Nova Scotians might well have been missing the main point of where we are as a species in the twenty-first century. The unresolved issues resulting from the expansion of Europe beginning five centuries ago – the legitimacy of imperial expansion, environmental exploitation, and social inequality – demand urgent attention and invite innovative solutions. With the digital communications revolution transforming our most basic institutions – community, family, politics, and work among them – and sinister forces positioned to shape "the Internet of Things" in destructive ways, Nova Scotians are obliged, as they were at the dawn of the industrial age, to bend the arc of history in positive directions, gathering our individual and collective energies to make a difference.

Notes

Introduction

1 John G. Reid and Thomas Peace, "Colonies of Settlement and Settler Colonialism in Northeastern North America, 1450–1850," in *The Routledge Handbook of the History of Settler Colonialism*, ed. Edward Cavanaugh and Lorenzo Veracini (London: Routledge, 2017), chap. 6. See also Lorenzo Veracini, *Settler Colonialism: A Theoretical Overview* (New York: Palgrave Macmillian, 2010).

2 Two periodicals, *Acadiensis* and the *Journal of the Nova Scotia Historical Society*, and two websites *Borealia* (https://earlycanadianhistory.ca) and *ActiveHistory* (http://activehistory.ca) have contributed enormously to advancing the fields of early Canadian history and Atlantic Canada Studies.

3 Jerry Bannister, "Atlantic Canada in an Atlantic World? Northeastern North America in the Long 18th Century," *Acadiensis* 43, no. 2 (2014): 2. On historical consciousness, see Margaret Conrad, Kadriye Ercikan, Gerald Friesen, Jocelyn Létourneau, Delphin Muise, David Northrup, and Peter Seixas, *Canadians and Their Pasts* (Toronto: University of Toronto Press, 2013).

4 John G. Reid, *Nova Scotia: A Pocket History* (Halifax: Fernwood, 2009), 10. This question is explored more fully in Reid's "The Nova Scotia Historian: A Creature of Paradox?" *Journal of the Nova Scotia Historical Society* 5 (2002): 106–21.

5 Ian McKay, "The Liberal Order Framework: A Prospectus for a Reconnaissance of Canadian History," *Canadian Historical Review* 81, no. 4 (2000): 617–45. For illuminating commentaries on this argument, see the essays in Jean-François Constant and Michel Ducharme, eds., *Liberalism and Hegemony: Debating the Canadian Liberal Revolution* (Toronto: University of Toronto Press, 2009).

6 Interview, 23 September 1987, in Douglas Keay, *Women's Own Magazine*, 31 October 1987, 8–10.

1. Ancient History

1 George F. MacDonald, "Debert: A Paleo-Indian Site in Central Nova Scotia," *Anthropology Papers* (Ottawa: National Museum of Man, 1968). For a brief outline of more recent archaeological developments in and around Debert, see Robyn Crook and Matthew Munro, "The Many Layers of Debert: Exploring Nova Scotia's Oldest Archaeological Site," in *Underground Nova Scotia: Stories of Archaeology*, ed. Paul Erikson and Jonathan Fowler (Halifax: Nimbus, 2010), 1–10. See also Robson Bonnichsen, David Keenlyside, and Karen Turnmire, "Paleoindian Patterns in Maine and the Maritimes," in *Prehistoric Archaeology in the Maritime Provinces: Past and Present Research*, ed. Michael Deal and Susan Blair (Fredericton: New Brunswick Archaeological Services, 1991), 1–36.
2 "Kluskap," in Ruth Holmes Whitehead, *Stories from the Six Worlds: Micmac Legends* (Halifax: Nimbus, 1988), 165–7.
3 Joggins Fossil Cliffs UNESCO World Heritage Site, available online at http://jogginsfossilcliffs.net/.
4 Peter R. Eakins and Jean Sinnamon Eakins, "Sir John William Dawson" and Loris S. Russell, "Abraham Gesner," in *Dictionary of Canadian Biography Online*.
5 Atlantic Geoscience Society, *The Last Billion Years: A Geological History of the Maritime Provinces* (Halifax: Nimbus, 2001).
6 For a detailed description of nature's endowment of land forms, climate, vegetation, and soils, see Andrew Hill Clark, *Acadia: The Geography of Early Nova Scotia* (Madison: University of Wisconsin Press, 1968), chap. 2.
7 R. Cole Harris and Geoffrey Matthews, eds., "Plate 1: The Last Ice Sheets, 18,000–10,000 BC," *Historical Atlas of Canada* (Toronto: University of Toronto Press, 1987).
8 Brian Fagen, *The Little Ice Age: How Climate Made History, 1300–1850* (New York: Basic Books, 2000).
9 Atlantic Geoscience Society, *Last Billion Years*, 188.
10 For a summary of human development in the period before European contact, see Stephen A. Davis, "Early Societies: Sequences of Change," in *The Atlantic Region to Confederation: A History*, ed. Phillip A. Buckner and John G. Reid (Toronto; Fredericton: University of Toronto Press and Acadiensis Press, 1994), 3–21, and David Sanger, "Pre-European Dawnland: Archaeology of the Maritime Peninsula," in *New England and the Maritime Provinces: Connections and Comparisons*, ed. John Reid and Stephen

Hornsby (Montreal: McGill-Queen's University Press, 2005), 15–31. The larger context is covered in Arthur J. Ray, *I Have Lived Here since the World Began: An Illustrated History of Canada's Native Peoples*, rev. ed. (Montreal: McGill-Queen's University Press, 2011); Olive Patricia Dickason, *Canada's First Nations: A History of Founding Peoples from Earliest Times*, 4th ed., with David T. McNab (Don Mills, ON: Oxford University Press, 2008); Bruce Trigger and Wilcomb Washburn, eds., *Cambridge History of the Native Peoples of the Americas*, 3 v. (Cambridge: Cambridge University Press, 1996); and James V. Wright, *A History of the Native People of Canada*, 3 v. (Ottawa: Canadian Museum of Civilization, 1995–2004).

11   Sanger, "Pre-European Dawnland," 16–17.

12   For the theories relating to Northeast Asian migration to North America, see E. James Dixon, "When and How Did First Peoples Come to North America?" *Athena Review* 3, no. 2 (2002). See also E. James Dixon, *Bones, Boats, and Bison: Archaeology and the First Colonization of Western North America* (Albuquerque: University of New Mexico Press, 1999); Gary Haynes, *The Early Settlement of North America: The Clovis Era* (Cambridge: Cambridge University Press, 2002); David B. Madsen, ed., *Entering America: Northeast Asia and Beringia Before the Last Glacial Maximum* (Salt Lake City: University of Utah Press, 2004); David J. Meltzer, *First Peoples in a New World: Colonizing Ice Age America* (Berkeley: University of California Press, 2009); and Dennis J. Stanford and Bruce Bradley, *Across Atlantic Ice: The Origins of America's Clovis Culture* (Berkeley: University of California Press, 2012).

13   Sanger, "Pre-European Dawnland," 22.

14   Susan Blair, ed., *Wolastoqiyik Ajemseg: The People of Beautiful River at Jemseg*, vol. 2, *Archaeological Results* (Fredericton: New Brunswick Archaeological Services, Heritage Branch, Culture and Sports Secretariat, 2004).

15   James A. Tuck, "The Archaic Period in the Maritime Provinces," in *Prehistoric Archaeology in the Maritime Provinces: Past and Present Research*, ed. Michael Deal and Susan Blair (Fredericton: New Brunswick Archaeological Services, 1991), 29–65. See also, James A. Tuck, *Maritime Prehistory* (Ottawa: National Museum of Man, 1984).

16   Sanger, "Pre-European Dawnland," 18–19.

17   Bruce J. Bourque, *Diversity and Complexity in Prehistoric Maritime Societies* (New York: Plenum Press, 1995).

18   Ken Donovan, "Precontact and Settlement: Ingonish and Northern Cape Breton from Paleo-Indians to the 18th Century," *Nashwaak Review* 22/23, no. 1 (2009): 331–6.

19   David Sanger, *Cow Point: An Archaic Cemetery in New Brunswick*, Archaeological Survey of Canada, Mercury Series 135 (Ottawa: National Museum of Man, 1987), and Davis, "Sequences of Change," 9–10.

20   A comparison of languages supports the hypothesis that people moved from the Great Lakes into the St Lawrence Valley between 3,000 and 2,000 years ago. See Sanger, "Pre-European Dawnland," 26.

21   Stephen A. Davis, *Micmac* (Tantallon, NS: Four East Publications, 1991), 18.

22   Wright, *History of the Native Peoples of Canada*, vol. 2, 803.

23   Jason Hall," Maliseet Cultivation and Climatic Resilience on the Wəlastəkw/St John River During the Little Ice Age," *Acadiensis* 64, no. 2 (2015): 3–25.

24   Robert McGhee," Canada Y1K: The First Millennium," *Beaver* (December 1999–January 2000): 9–17.

25   Dickason, *Canada's First Nations*, 12.

2. Mi'kma'ki

1   General studies of the Mi'kmaq include Stephen A, Davis, *Micmac* (Tantallon, NS: Four East Publications, 1991); Daniel N. Paul, *We Were Not the Savages*, 3rd ed. (Halifax: Fernwood, 2006); Harald E.L. Prins, *The Mi'kmaq: Resistance, Accommodation and Cultural Survival* (Fort Worth, TX: Harcourt Brace College, 1996); and Ruth Holmes Whitehead, *Elitekey: Micmac Material Culture from 1600 AD to the Present* (Halifax: Nova Scotia Museum, 1980). On the Wolastoqiyik and Passamaquoddy, see Susan Blair, ed., *Wolastoqiyik Ajemseg: The People of Beautiful River at Jemseg*, vol. 2, *Archaeological Results* (Fredericton: New Brunswick Archaeological Services, Heritage Branch, Culture and Sports Secretariat, 2004); Robert Ferguson, "Wolastoq: Commemorating a People," in *Underground New Brunswick: Stories of Archaeology*, ed. Paul Erickson and Jonathan Fowler (Halifax: Nimbus, 2013), 55–64; and Vincent O. Erickson, "Maliseet-Passamaquoddy," in *Northeast*, vol. 15, *Handbook of North American Indians*, ed. William C. Sturtevant (Washington, DC: Smithsonian Institution, 1978), 123–36. Bruce J. Bourque has argued that the Wolastoqiyik, Passamaquoddy, and Abenaki are not direct descendants of the Etchemin, but rather a consolidation of various peoples resulting from European contact; see Bruce J. Bourque, "Ethnicity on the Maritime Peninsula, 1600–1759," *Ethnohistory* 36, no. 3 (1989): 257.

2   Ralph Pastore, "The Sixteenth Century: Aboriginal Peoples and European Contact," in *The Atlantic Region to Confederation: A History*, ed. Phillip A. Buckner and John G. Reid, 22–39 (Toronto; Fredericton: University of Toronto Press and Acadiensis Press, 1994).

3   I am grateful to John G. Reid for checking the English translations against the French to ensure their accuracy.

4   James F. Pandergast, "The Confusing Identities Attributed to Stadacona and Hochelaga," *Journal of Canadian Studies* 32, no. 4 (1998): 149–67.

5 For various perspectives on the numbers of Mi'kmaq at the time of contact, see Virginia P. Miller, "Aboriginal Micmac Population: A Review of the Evidence," *Ethnohistory* 23, no. 2 (1976): 117–27, and "The Decline of the Nova Scotia Micmac Population, AD 1600–1850," *Culture* 2, no. 3 (1982): 107–20. See also John D. Daniels, "The Indian Population of North America in 1492," *William and Mary Quarterly*, 3rd series, 49, no. 2 (1992): 298–320, and Paul, *We Were Not the Savages*, 2nd ed. (2000), 45–6.

6 Cole Harris, *The Reluctant Land: Space and Environment in Canada before Confederation* (Vancouver: University of British Columbia Press, 2008), 46–7.

7 Pierre Biard, *Relation of New France* (Lyons: Louys Muguet, 1616), reprinted in *Jesuit Relations and Allied Documents*, vol. 3, *Acadia, 1611–1616*, ed. R.G. Thwaites (Cleveland: Burrows Brothers, 1896), 105.

8 Ibid., 73.

9 Prins, *Mi'kmaq*, 25

10 Nicolas Denys, *The Description and Natural History of the Coasts of America*, ed. William F. Ganong (Toronto: Champlain Society, 1908), 447–8, 413.

11 Biard, *Relation of New France*, 86–7.

12 Ibid., 89.

13 Prins, *Mi'kmaq*, 39–41.

14 Marc Lescarbot, *The History of New France*, 3rd ed. (Paris: Adrian Perier, 1618), in *The History of New France*, vol. 2, trans. W.L. Grant (Toronto: Champlain Society, 1911), 357.

15 Chrestien Le Clercq, *New Relation of Gaspesia, with the Customs and Religion of the Gaspesien Indians* (Paris 1691), ed. William F. Ganong (Toronto: Champlain Society, 1910), 136.

16 Biard, *Relation of New France*, 90.

17 Le Clercq, *New Relation of Gaspesia*, 237; see also 265–73.

18 Lescarbot, *History of New France*, vol. 3, 216.

19 Le Clercq, *New Relation of Gaspesia*, 107.

20 Ibid., 105–6.

21 Biard, *Relation of New France*, 77–81.

22 Laurie Lacey, *Mi'kmaq Medicines*, 2nd ed. (Halifax: Nimbus, 2012).

23 Whitehead, *Elitekey*, 8.

24 Le Clercq, *New Relation of Gaspesia*, 118–19

25 Lescarbot, *History of New France*, vol. 2, 309.

26 Denys, *Description and Natural History of the Coasts of America*, 430.

27 Le Clercq, *New Relation of Gaspesia*, 265.

28 Biard, *Relation of New France*, 99.

29 Ibid., 75.

30 Le Clercq, *New Relation of Gaspesia*, 109.

31 Ibid., 260–1.

32 Ibid., 239.
33 Ibid., 228.
34 Biard, *Relation of New France*, 99.
35 Le Clercq, *New Relation of Gaspesia*, 89–90.
36 Cited in Ruth Holmes Whitehead, *The Old Man Told Us: Excerpts from Micmac History*, 1500–1950 (Halifax: Nimbus, 1991), 11–12; translated by Margaret Anne Hamelin from "Lettre à Madame de Drucourt," n.d. [c. 1750], in *Les Soirées Canadiennes* (Quebec: Brousseau Frères, 1863), 300–1.
37 Le Clercq, *New Relation of Gaspesia*, 296.
38 Ibid., 253.
39 On this subject, see Ruth Holmes Whitehead, "I Have Lived Here since the World Began: Atlantic Coast Artistic Traditions," in *The Spirit Sings: The Artistic Traditions of Canada's First Peoples* (Toronto: McClelland & Stewart and Glenbow Museum, 1987) and *Micmac Quillwork: Micmac Indian Techniques of Porcupine Quill Decoration, 1600–1950* (Halifax: Nova Scotia Museum, 1982).
40 Whitehead, *Micmac Quillwork*, 15.
41 Cited in ibid., 6.
42 Pierre Déléage, "L'écriture attaché des Mi'kmaq, 1677–1912," *Acadiensis* 42, no. 1 (2013): 3–36.
43 Denys, *Description and Natural History of the Coasts of America*, 410.
44 Ibid., 418–19.
45 Sieur de Dièreville, *Relation of the Voyage to Port Royal in Acadia or New France*, trans. Mrs. [Alice Lusk] Webster, ed. John Clarence Webster (1708; Toronto: Champlain Society, 1933), 180.
46 Le Clercq, *New Relation of Gaspesia*, 107.
47 Lescarbot, *History of New France*, vol. 3, 183–4.
48 Ibid., 197–8.
49 Ruth Holmes Whitehead, *Stories from the Six Worlds: Micmac Legends* (Halifax: Nimbus, 1988), 1–21. For a more detailed discussion, see Anne-Christine Hornborg, *Mi'kmaq Landscapes* (Aldershot, UK: Ashgate, 2008).
50 Le Clercq, *New Relation of Gaspesia*, 214.
51 Ibid., 300–1.
52 Ibid., 229.
53 Whitehead, *Stories from the Six Worlds*, 9
54 Le Clercq, *New Relation of Gaspesia*, 221–2.
55 Ibid., 84–5.
56 Whitehead, *Stories from the Six Worlds*, 165–7.
57 Cited in Prins, *Mi'kmaq*, 21.
58 Hornborg, *Mi'kmaq Landscapes*, 100–17.
59 Silas Tertius Rand, *Legends of the Micmacs*, ed. Helen Livermore Webster (New York: Longmans, Green, 1894), 31–2.

3. Sixteenth-Century Encounters, 1497–1605

1 Alfred J. Crosby, *Ecological Imperialism: The Biological Expansion of Europe, 900–1900* (Cambridge: Cambridge University Press, 1986); Jared Diamond, *Guns, Germs, and Steel: The Fates of Human Societies* (New York: Norton, 1998); and John E. Richards, *The Unending Frontier: An Environmental History of the Early Modern World* (Berkeley: University of California Press, 2005).

2 *The Works of Samuel de Champlain*, vol. 1, *1599–1607*, ed. H.P. Biggar (Toronto: Champlain Society, 1922), 307.

3 Alfred G. Bailey, *The Conflict of European and Eastern Algonkian Cultures, 1504–1700* (Toronto: University of Toronto Press, 1969).

4 Birgitta Wallace, "The Norse in Newfoundland: L'Anse aux Meadows and Vinland," *Newfoundland Studies* 19, no. 1 (2003): 5–43, and "Nova Scotia's Place in Vineland: On the Trail of the Elusive Norse" in *Underground Nova Scotia: Stories of Archaeology*, ed. Paul Erikson and Jonathan Fowler (Halifax: Nimbus, 2010), 139–153.

5 Mark Finnan, *The Sinclair Saga* (Halifax: Formac Press, 1999) and Brian Smith, "Earl Henry Sinclair's Fictitious Trip to America," *New Orkney Antiquarian Journal* 2 (2002). An amended version is available online at http://www.alastairhamilton.com/sinclair.htm.

6 George Huppert, *After the Black Death: A Social History of Early Modern Europe* (Bloomington: Indiana University Press, 1998).

7 David Armitage, "Three Concepts of Atlantic History," in *The British Atlantic World, 1500–1800*, ed. David Armitage and Michael J. Braddick (Basingstoke, UK: Palgrave Macmillan, 2002). For an Atlantic Canada perspective, see Luca Codignola, "How Wide is the Atlantic Ocean? Larger and Larger," and John G. Reid, "How Wide is the Atlantic Ocean? Not Wide Enough," *Acadiensis* 34, no. 2 (2005): 74–80, 81–7. See also Elizabeth Mancke and Carol Shammas, eds., *The Creation of the British Atlantic World* (Baltimore: Johns Hopkins University Press, 2005) and Gilbert Held et al., eds., *Britain's Oceanic Empire Atlantic and Indian Ocean Worlds. c. 1550–1850* (Cambridge: Cambridge University Press, 2012).

8 Francesco Guidi-Bruscoli, "John Cabot and His Italian Financiers," *Historical Research* (2012), available online at https://onlinelibrary.wiley.com/doi/abs/10.1111/j.1468-2281.2012.00597.x.

9 Peter E. Pope, *The Many Landfalls of John Cabot* (Toronto: University of Toronto Press, 1997) and Brian Cuthbertson, "John Cabot and his Historians: Five Hundred Years of Controversy," *Royal Nova Scotia Historical Society Journal* 1 (1998): 16–35.

10 Research conducted by British scholar Alwyn Ruddock and those following her lead suggests that at least part of the expedition returned in 1500

after exploring the coast from Newfoundland to the Caribbean. See Evan
T. Jones, "Alwyn Ruddock, John Cabot and the Discovery of America,"
Historical Research 81 (2008): 224–54, and "Henry VII and the Bristol Expeditions to North America: the Condon Documents," *Historical Research*
83 (2010): 444–54. Following Ruddock's death in 2005, research on her
claims were centred at the University of Bristol, where Evan Jones and
Margaret Condon coordinate the Cabot Project: http://www.bristol.
ac.uk/history/research/cabot.html.

11   Evan T. Jones and M.M. Condon, "William Weston" and David Loades,
"Sebastian Cabot," *Oxford Dictionary of National Biography*.

12   R.A. Skelton, "Sebastian Cabot," *Dictionary of Canadian Biography Online*.

13   L.-A. Vigneras, "Gaspar Corte-Real" and "Miguel Corte-Real," and A.
Davis, "João Fernandes," *Dictionary of Canadian Biography Online*. General studies of the early period of European exploration include Robert
McGhee, *Canada Rediscovered* (Ottawa: Canadian Museum of Civilization, 1991); David B. Quinn, with Alison M. Quinn and Susan Hillier,
eds., *New American World: A Documentary History of North America to
1612*, 5 v. (New York: Arno Press, 1979); and Tryggvi J. Oleson, *Early
Voyages and Northern Approaches, 1000–1632* (Toronto: McClelland &
Stewart, 1963).

14   Emily Burton, "Portuguese Settlement in Northeastern North America:
The 1520s Fagundes Expedition," *Nashwaak Review* 22/23 (Spring/Sum-
mer 2009): 413–46.

15   Luca Codignola, "Another Look at Verrazono's Voyage, 1524," *Acadiensis*
29, no. 1 (1999): 29–42, and William F.E. Morley, "Giovanni Da Verrazzano," *Dictionary of Canadian Biography Online*.

16   L.-A. Vigneras, "Estevão Gomes," *Dictionary of Canadian Biography
Online*.

17   *The Voyages of Jacques Cartier*, Introduction by Ramsay Cook (Toronto:
University of Toronto Press, 1992), 117.

18   Ibid., 17.

19   Ibid., 20–1.

20   In addition to Harold Innis's classic study, *The Cod Fisheries: The History
of an International Economy* (New Haven, CT: Yale University Press, 1940),
see David J. Starkey, Jon Thor, and Ingo Heidbrink, eds., *A History of
the North Atlantic Fisheries*, vol. 1, *From Early Times to the Mid-Nineteenth
Century* (Bremerhaven: German Maritime Museum, 2008) and D.J.
Starkey and J.E. Candow, *The North Atlantic Fisheries: Supply, Marketing
and Consumption, 1560–1900* (Hull, UK: Studia Atlantica, 2006). For an
excellent brief summary of the literature on the fisheries, see Peter Pope,
"Comparisons: Atlantic Canada," in *A Companion to Colonial America*, ed.
Daniel Vickers (Oxford: Blackwell, 2003), 492–6.

21 Mario Mimeault, "La pêche à la morue des Français d'Amérique du Nord de 1500 à 1763: un atout dans la géopolitique française," *Acadiensis* 47, no. 2 (2018): 26–49. See also Mimeault, *La pêche à la morue en Nouvelle France* (Quebec City: Septentrion, 2017).

22 Peter Pope, "Transformation of the Maritime Cultural Landscape of Atlantic Canada by Migratory European Fishers, 1500–1800," in *Beyond the Catch: Fisheries of the North Atlantic, the North Sea and the Baltic, 900–1850*, ed. Louis Sicking and Darlene Abreu-Ferreira (The Hague: Brill, 2009), 127.

23 Oral history suggests that the Portuguese also might have used Ingonish as a base for their fisheries. See Ken Donovan, "Precontact and Settlement: Ingonish and Northern Cape Breton from the Paleo-Indians to the 18th Century," *Nashwaak Review* 22/23, no. 1 (2009): 336–40.

24 Pope, "Transformation of the Maritime Cultural Landscape," 139.

25 Laurier Turgeon, "French Fishers, Fur Traders, and Amerindians during the Sixteenth Century: History and Archaeology," *William and Mary Quarterly*, 3rd series, 55 (1998): 585–610.

26 Marc Lescarbot, *The History of New France,* 3rd ed. (Paris: Adrian Perier, 1618), in *The History of New France*, vol. 2, trans. W.L. Grant (Toronto: Champlain Society, 1911), 309.

27 James Axtell, *After Columbus: Essays in the Ethnohistory of Colonial North America* (New York: Oxford University Press, 1988), 177. On the matter of linguistic development, see Peter Bakker "'The Language of the Coastal Tribes is Half-Basque': A Basque-American Indian Pidgin in use between Europeans and Native Americans in North America ca. 1540–ca. 1640," *Anthropological Linguistics* 31, nos. 3–4 (1989): 117–47.

28 Lescarbot, *History of New France,* vol. 2, 323.

29 D.B. Quinn, "The Voyage of Etienne Bellenger to the Maritimes in 1583: A New Document," *Canadian Historical Review* 43, no. 4 (1962): 328–43.

30 Turgeon, "French Fishers, Fur Traders, and Amerindians during the Sixteenth Century," 587, 599.

31 Lescarbot, *History of New France,* vol. 2, 362–3.

32 Dan Conlin, *Pirates of the Atlantic: Robbery, Murder and Mayhem off the Canadian East Coast* (Halifax: Formac, 2009), 7–15.

33 Alan Rayburn, "Acadia: The Origin of the Name and Its Geographic and Historical Utilization," *Canadian Geographer* 10, no. 1 (1973): 26–43.

34 Joan Dawson, *The Mapmaker's Eye: Nova Scotia through Early Maps* (Halifax: Nimbus and Nova Scotia Museum, 1988); William Francis Ganong, *Crucial Maps in the Early Cartography of Atlantic Canada* (Toronto: University of Toronto Press, 1964); and William B. Hamilton, *Place Names of Atlantic Canada* (Toronto: University of Toronto Press, 1996).

35 Cornelius J. Jaenen, "Amerindian Views of French Culture in the Seventeenth Century," *Canadian Historical Review* 55, no. 3 (1974): 261–91, and

George R. Hamell, "Strawberries, Floating Islands, and Rabbit Captains: Mythical Realities and European Contact in the Northeast during the Sixteenth and Seventeenth Centuries," *Journal of Canadian Studies* 21, no. 4 (1986–7): 72–94.

36 Josiah Jeremy to Silas Rand, 26 September 1869, cited in Ruth Holmes Whitehead, *The Old Man Told Us: Excerpts from Micmac History* (Halifax: Nimbus, 1991), 8.

37 Axtell, *After Columbus*, 144–81.

38 Lescarbot, *History of New France*, vol. 2, 352.

39 George MacBeath, "Robert Gravé du Pont," *Dictionary of Canadian Biography Online*.

40 Silas Tertius Rand, *Legends* (New York: Longmans, Green, 1894), 91.

41 I am indebted to Elizabeth Mancke for this insight.

42 Victoria Dickenson, "Cartier, Champlain, and the Fruits of the New World: Botanical Exchange in the 16th and 17th Centuries," *Scientia Canadiensis* 31, nos. 1–2 (2008): 27–47.

43 Denys, *Description and Natural History of the Coasts of America*, 446–9.

44 Pierre Biard, *Relation of New France* (Lyons: Louys Muguet, 1616), in *Jesuit Relations and Allied Documents*, vol. 3, *Acadia, 1611–1616*, ed. R.G. Thwaites (Cleveland: Burrows Brothers, 1896), 105.

45 Denys, *Description and Natural History of the Coasts of America*, 449.

46 Ruth Holmes Whitehead, *Nova Scotia: The Protohistoric Period, 1500–1630* (Halifax: Nova Scotia Museum, 1993), 78.

47 Denys, *Description and Natural History of the Coasts of America*, 442.

48 Sieur de Dièreville, *Relation of the Voyage to Port Royal in Acadia or New France*, trans. Mrs. [Alice Lusk] Webster, ed. John Clarence Webster (1708; Toronto: Champlain Society, 1933), 57, 80.

49 Gustav Lanctot, "Troilus de a Roche de Mesgouez," *Dictionary of Canadian Biography Online*.

50 David Hackett Fischer, *Champlain's Dream* (New York: Alfred A. Knopf, 2008), 38–41, and George MacBeath, "Pierre du Gua de Monts," *Dictionary of Canadian Biography Online*.

51 Lescarbot, who recognized that women were necessary to the success of French colonization, noted that in the past women had gone to sea but that it was no longer customary. Lescarbot, *History of New France*, vol. 1, 45–6.

52 Fischer, *Champlain's Dream*, 42–7.

53 John Johnston, "Mathieu Da Costa along the Coasts of Nova Scotia: Some Possibilities," *Journal of the Nova Scotia Historical Society* 4 (2001): 152–64.

54 *Works of Samuel de Champlain*, vol. 1, 238.

55 Ibid., 248.

56   Ibid., 259.
57   John C. Weaver, *The Great Land Rush and the Making of the Modern World, 1650–1900* (Montreal: McGill-Queen's University Press, 2003).
58   *Works of Samuel de Champlain*, vol. 1, 303–5.
59   Richard Wright, *The Middle Ground: Indians, Empires, and Republics in the Great Lakes Region, 1650–1815* (Cambridge: Cambridge University Press, 1991), chap. 2.

4. Colonial Initiatives, 1605–1670

1   For specific details on the extraordinary characters who populate the narrative of French early colonizing activities in Acadia, I have drawn on Elizabeth Jones, *Gentlemen and Jesuits: Quests for Glory and Adventure in the Early Days of New France* (Toronto: University of Toronto Press, 1986); M.A. MacDonald, *Fortune and La Tour: The Civil War in Acadia* (Halifax: Nimbus, 2000); and Brenda Dunn, *A History of Port-Royal/Annapolis Royal, 1605–1800* (Halifax: Nimbus, 2004). On the larger context in which Acadia's history unfolded, see John G. Reid, *Acadia, Maine, and New Scotland: Marginal Colonies in the Seventeenth Century* (Toronto: University of Toronto Press, 1981); N.E.S. Griffiths, *From Migrant to Acadian: A North American Border People, 1604–1755* (Montreal: McGill-Queen's University Press, 2005); Gregory M.W. Kennedy, *Something of a Peasant Paradise? Comparing Rural Societies in Acadie and the Loudunais, 1604–1755* (Montreal: McGill-Queen's University Press, 2014); and Jean Daigle, "Acadia from 1604 to 1763: An Historical Synthesis," in *Acadia of the Maritimes*, ed. Jean Daigle (Moncton: Université de Moncton, Chaire d'études acadiennes, 1995), 1–43. The British context of this struggle is explored in Nicholas Canny, ed., *The Origins of Empire: British Overseas Enterprise to the Close of the Seventeenth Century* (Oxford: Oxford University Press, 2001); Bruce Lenman, *England's Colonial Wars, 1550–1688* (London: Longmans, 2000); and David Loades, *England's Maritime Empire: Seapower, Commerce and Policy, 1490–1690* (London: Longmans, 2000). See also John G. Reid and Elizabeth Mancke, "From Global Processes to Continental Strategies: The Emergence of British North America to 1783," in *Canada and the British Empire*, ed. Phillip Buckner (Oxford: Oxford University Press, 2008), chap. 2, and Elizabeth Mancke, "Spaces of Power in the Northeast," in *New England and the Maritime Provinces: Connections and Comparisons*, ed. Stephen J. Hornsby and John G. Reid (Montreal: McGill-Queen's University Press, 2005), chap. 3.
2   *The Works of Samuel de Champlain*, vol. 1, *1599–1607*, ed. H.P. Biggar (Toronto: Champlain Society, 1922), 259.

3   W.P. Kerr, *Port-Royal Habitation: The Story of the French and Mi'kmaq at Port-Royal, 1604–1613* (Halifax: Nimbus, 2005), 35, and Lucien Campeau, "Henri Membertou," *Dictionary of Canadian Biography Online.*

4   *Works of Samuel de Champlain,* vol. 1, 384.

5   Marc Lescarbot, *The History of New France,* 3rd ed. (Paris: Adrian Perier, 1618), in *The History of New France,* vol. 2, trans. W.L. Grant (Toronto: Champlain Society, 1911), 353.

6   *Works of Samuel de Champlain,* vol. 1, 447–9.

7   Cited in Jones, *Gentlemen and Jesuits,* 93. See also Jerry Wasserman, *Spectacle of Empire: Marc Lescarbot's Theatre of Neptune in New France* (Vancouver: Talonbooks, 2006).

8   Lescarbot, *History of New France,* vol. 2, 266.

9   Marc Lescarbot, *The History of New France,* vol. 3, trans. W.L. Grant (Toronto: Champlain Society, 1914), 227.

10 Ramsay Cook, "1492 and All That: Making a Garden out of a Wilderness," in *Consuming Canada: Readings in Environmental History,* ed. Chad and Pam Gaffield (Toronto: Copp Clark, 1995), 62–80.

11 Jones, *Gentlemen and Jesuits,* 63–3, 116–19.

12 Lucien Campeau, "Henri Membertou," *Dictionary of Canadian Biography Online.*

13 Biard, *Relation of New France,* 73.

14 George MacBeath, "Robert Gravé du Pont," *Dictionary of Canadian Biography Online.*

15 MacDonald, *Fortune and LaTour,* 44–5.

16 George MacBeath, "Claude de Saint-Étienne de la Tour," *Dictionary of Canadian Biography Online.*

17 On the colonization efforts of the Alexanders, father and son, see N.E.S. Griffiths and John G. Reid, "New Evidence on New Scotland, 1629," *William and Mary Quarterly,* 3rd Series, 49, no. 3 (1992): 492–508; John G. Reid, *Sir William Alexander and North American Colonization: A Reappraisal* (Edinburgh: University of Edinburgh, Centre of Canadian Studies, 1990); and D.C Harvey, "William Alexander, Earl of Stirling," and "Sir William Alexander," and John S. Moir, "Sir David Kirke," in *Dictionary of Canadian Biography Online.*

18 The complicated background of the Kirke family is summarized in Andrew D. Nicholls, *A Fleeting Empire: Early Stuart Britain and the Merchant Adventurers to Canada* (Montreal: McGill-Queen's University Press, 2010), 78–80. See also Peter E. Pope, *Fish into Wine: The Newfoundland Plantation in the Seventeenth Century* (Chapel Hill, NC: Omohundro Institute and University of North Carolina Press, 2004).

19 Andrew D. Nicholls, "'The purpois is honorabill, and may conduce to the good of our service': Lord Ochiltree and the Cape Breton Colony, 1629–1631," *Acadiensis* 34, no. 2 (2005): 109–23.

20   A.J.B. Johnston, *Storied Shores: St. Peter's, Isle Madame, and Chapel Island in the 17th and 18th Centuries* (Sydney: University College of Cape Breton Press, 2004), 25.

21   Richard Guthry, "A Relation of the Voyage and Plantation of the Scots Colony in New Scotland under the conduct of William Alexander Younger, 1629," 503, transcribed in Griffiths and Reid, "New Evidence on New Scotland, 1629," 500–8.

22   René Baudry "Charles Daniel," *Dictionary of Canadian Biography Online.*

23   Guthry, "Relation of the Voyage and Plantation of the Scots Colony," 504.

24   Dunn, *History of Port-Royal/Annapolis Royal*, 9–14.

25   MacBeath, "Claude de Saint-Étienne de la Tour."

26   George MacBeath, "Isaac de Razilly," *Dictionary of Canadian Biography Online.*

27   Mora Dianne O'Neill, *Royal Connections: The Royal Province of Nova Scotia and the Crown*, Exhibition, John and Norma Oyler Gallery, Art Gallery of Nova Scotia, 14 September 2013–30 March 2014.

28   Robert Le Blant, "Les companies du Cap-Breton, 1629–1647," *Revue d'histoire de l'Amérique française* 16, no. 1 (1962): 81–94.

29   Joan Dawson, "Colonists or Birds of Passage? A Glimpse of the Inhabitants of LaHave, 1632–1636," *Nova Scotia Historical Review* 9, no. 1 (1989): 42–61.

30   MacDonald, *Fortune and LaTour*, 67.

31   Ibid., appendix A. See also George MacBeath, "Francoise-Marie Jacqueline," *Dictionary of Canadian Biography Online.*

32   Where accounts diverge, I have relied on Dunn, *History of Port-Royal/Annapolis Royal*, chap. 1.

33   MacDonald, *Fortune and LaTour*, 177.

34   George MacBeath, "Nicolas Denys," *Dictionary of Canadian Biography Online.*

35   Alfred G. Bailey, "Richard Denys de Fronsac," *Dictionary of Canadian Biography Online.*

36   Dunn, *History of Port-Royal/Annapolis Royal*, 27.

37   Ibid., 28, 65. See also MacBeath, "Charles de Saint-Étienne de la Tour," Mason Wade, "Emmanuel LeBorgne," and Clément Cormier, "Alexandre Le Borgne de Belle-Isle," *Dictionary of Canadian Biography Online.*

38   Luca Codignola, "Competing Networks: The Roman Catholic Ecclesiastics in French North America, 1610–58," *Canadian Historical Review* 80, no. 4 (1999): 539–84.

39   For a brief summary of these developments, see Alan Taylor, *Colonial America: A Very Short Introduction* (New York: Oxford University Press, 2013), chap. 7.

40   For the larger context of French imperialism in this period, see James Pritchard, *In Search of Empire: The French in the Americas, 1670–1730*

(Cambridge: Cambridge University Press, 2004); John G. Reid et al., *The "Conquest" of Acadia, 1710: Imperial, Colonial, and Aboriginal Constructions* (Toronto: University of Toronto Press, 2004); and Jeffers Lennox, *Homelands and Empires: Indigenous Spaces, Imperial Fictions, and Competition for Territory* in *Northeastern North America, 1690–1763* (Toronto: University of Toronto Press, 2017).

41   Kennedy, *Something of a Peasant Paradise?* 10–11, 138.

5. Louis XIV's Acadie, 1670–1713

1   For the larger context of French imperialism in this period, see James Pritchard, *In Search of Empire: The French in the Americas, 1670–1730* (Cambridge: Cambridge University Press, 2004); John G. Reid et al., *The "Conquest" of Acadia, 1710: Imperial, Colonial, and Aboriginal Constructions*, (Toronto: University of Toronto Press, 2004); and two books by N.E.S. Griffiths: *From Migrant to Acadian: A North American Border People, 1604–1755* (Montreal: McGill-Queen's University Press, 2005) and *The Contexts of Acadian History, 1686–1784* (Montreal: McGill-Queen's University Press, 1992).

2   William I. Roberts, "Jurriaen Aernoutsz," *Dictionary of Canadian Biography Online*.

3   Muriel K. Roy, "Peuplement et croissance démographique en Acadie," in *Les Acadiens des Maritimes*, ed. Jean Daigle (Moncton: Centre d'Études Acadiennes, 1980), 135–207. On the origins of the immigrants to Acadia, see Ronnie-Gilles LeBlanc, "Les origins français du peuple acadien avant 1714," in *Le fait acadien en France: histoire et temps présent*, ed. André Magord (La Crèche, France: Geste éditions, 2010), 25–48, and Stephen A. White, *Dictionnaire Généologique des familles acadienne* (Moncton: Chair d'études acadiennes, 1999).

4   Sally Ross and Alphonse Deveau, *The Acadians of Nova Scotia Past and Present* (Halifax: Nimbus, 1992), 29. See also Clément Cormier, "Jacques Bourgeois," *Dictionary of Canadian Biography Online* and "Family of Jacques Bourgeois & Jeanne Trahan," available online at http://homepage.ntlworld.com/pitretrail/myline/paternal/JBourgeois.htm.

5   Brenda Dunn, *A History of Port-Royal/Annapolis Royal, 1605–1800* (Halifax: Nimbus, 2004), 17–18.

6   Now a classic, Andrew Hill Clark's *Acadia: The Geography of Early Nova Scotia to 1760* (Madison: University of Wisconsin Press, 1968) offers a detailed examination of the region's environment.

7   Gisa I. Hynes, "Some Aspects of the Demography of Port Royal, 1650–1755," *Acadiensis* 3, no. 1 (1973): 3–17.

8   Maurice Basque, "Family and Political Culture in Pre-Conquest Acadia," in Reid et al., *"Conquest" of Acadia*, 48–63.

9 Sieur de Dièreville, *Relation of the Voyage to Port Royal in Acadia or New France*, trans. Mrs. [Alice Lusk] Webster, ed. John Clarence Webster (1708; Toronto: Champlain Society, 1933), 93–4.

10 Jacques Rousseau, "Dièreville," *Dictionary of Canadian Biography Online.*

11 Dièreville, *Relation of the Voyage to Port Royal in Acadia or New France*, 90. The English translation by Alice Lusk Webster is not a literal transition but better, John Reid contends, than a literal rendering; John Reid to Margaret Conrad, 5 August 2018.

12 Dunn, *History of Port-Royal/Annapolis Royal*, 60–1, 95.

13 Gregory M.W. Kennedy, *Something of a Peasant Paradise? Comparing Rural Societies in Acadie and the Loudunais, 1604–1755* (Montreal: McGill-Queen's University Press, 2014), chap. 4.

14 M de Villebon to Count Pontchartain, 1 October 1695, in John C. Webster, ed., *Acadia at the End of the Seventeenth Century: Letters, Journals and Memoirs of Joseph Robineau de Villebon, Commandant in Acadia, 1690–1700, and Other Contemporary Documents* (Saint John: New Brunswick Museum, 1934), 86.

15 Clément Cormier, "Philippe Mius d'Entremont, *Dictionary of Canadian Biography Online.*

16 Birgitta Wallace, "An Archaeologist Discovers Early Acadia," in *Looking into Acadie: Three Illustrated Lectures* (Halifax: Nova Scotia Museum, 1997), 21–5.

17 Jean Daigle, "Nos amis les enemies: relations commerciales de l'Acadie avec le Massachusetts, 1670–1711" (PhD diss., University of Maine at Orono, 1975).

18 Brenda Dunn, "Lives of Women in Ancienne Acadie," in *Looking into Acadie*, 39–40, and Dunn, *History of Port-Royal/Annapolis Royal*, 34–5.

19 Basque, "Family and Political Culture in Pre-Conquest Acadia," 52.

20 René Baudry, "Louis-Pierre Thury," *Dictionary of Canadian Biography Online.*

21 Dunn, "Lives of Women in Ancienne Acadie," 44.

22 Dunn, *History of Port-Royal/Annapolis Royal*, 63.

23 Ibid., 34, 66.

24 Kennedy, *Something of a Peasant Paradise?* chap. 5.

25 "Census of 1671, Acadie," in *Censuses of Canada, 1665–1871*, vol. 4 (Ottawa: Statistics Canada, 1876), 10.

26 Dunn, *History of Port-Royal/Annapolis Royal*, 49–51.

27 Ibid., 77.

28 Geoffrey Plank, "New England and the Conquest," in Reid et al., *"Conquest" of Acadia*, 70.

29 Recent research documents only eight marriages between an Acadian and an Indigenous person and five with a Métis. See LeBlanc, "Origins

français du peuple acadien avant 1714," 35. See also William Wicken, "Re-examining Mi'kmaq-Acadian Relations, 1635–1755," in *Vingt ans après, Habitants et marchands: lectures de l'histoire des XVIIe et XVIIIe siècles canadiens*, ed. Sylvie Dépatie, Catherine Desbarats, Danielle Gauvreau, Mario Lanlancette et Thomas Wien (Montreal: McGill-Queen's University Press, 1998), 93–114.

30 Georges Cerbelaud Salagnac, "Jean-Vincent d'Abbadie de Saint-Castin, Baron de Saint-Castin," *Dictionary of Canadian Biography Online*.

31 W.S. MacNutt, "John Gyles," *Dictionary of Canadian Biography Online*.

32 Emerson W. Baker and John G. Reid, *The New England Knight: Sir William Phips, 1651–1695* (Toronto: University of Toronto Press, 1998).

33 The Charter of Massachusetts Bay, 1691, available online at http:// avalon.law.yale.edu/17th_century/mass07.asp.

34 Jeffers Lennox, *Homelands and Empires: Indigenous Spaces, Imperial Fictions, and Competition for Territory* in *Northeastern North America, 1690-1763* (Toronto: University of Toronto Press, 2017), chap. 1, and René Baudry, "Louis-Pierre Thury," *Dictionary of Canadian Biography Online*.

35 M de Villebon to Count Pontchartain, 13 October 1691 to 25 October 1692, in *Acadia at the End of the Seventeenth Century*, 42.

36 W. Austin Squires, "Pierre Maisonnat, dit Baptiste," *Dictionary of Canadian Biography Online*.

37 Giles Harvard, *The Great Peace of Montreal of 1701: French-Native Diplomacy in the Seventeenth Century* (Montreal: McGill-Queen's University Press, 1991), 122.

38 John G. Reid, "Unorthodox Warfare in the Northeast, 1703," *Canadian Historical Review* 73, no. 2 (1992): 211–20.

39 Dunn, "Lives of Women in Ancienne Acadie," 43.

40 Bernard Pothier, "Pierre Morpain," *Dictionary of Canadian Biography Online*.

41 Dunn, *History of Port-Royal/Annapolis Royal*, 82.

42 William Wicken, "Mi'kmaq Decisions: Antoine Tecouenemac, the Conquest, and the Treaty of Utrecht," in Reid et al., *"Conquest" of Acadia, 1710,* 86–100.

43 Dates in Britian conformed to the Julian calendar until 1752, when it was replaced by the Gregorian calendar, used in France since the sixteenth century. Eleven days separated the two calendars, thus creating confusion both then and now. For convenience, the Gregorian date is used throughout this book.

44 Elizabeth Mancke and John G. Reid, "Elites, States, and the Imperial Contest for Acadia," in Reid et al., *"Conquest" of Acadia, 1710*, 47.

6. Contested Terrains, 1713–1749

1   Jeffers Lennox, *Homelands and Empires: Indigenous Spaces, Imperial Fictions, and Competition for Territory in Northeastern North America, 1690–1763* (Toronto: University of Toronto Press, 2017). See also Geoffrey Plank, *An Unsettled Conquest: The British Campaign against the Peoples of Acadia* (Philadelphia: University of Pennsylvania Press, 2001); John G. Reid, "The Conquest of 'Nova Scotia': Cartographic Imperialism and the Echoes of a Scottish Past," in *Essays on North Eastern North America, Seventeenth and Eighteenth Centuries* (Toronto: University of Toronto Press, 2008), 87–102; and John G. Reid and Elizabeth Mancke, "From Global Processes to Continental Strategies: The Emergence of British North America to 1783," in *Canada and the British Empire*, ed. Philip Buckner (Oxford: Oxford University Press, 2008), 22–42.

2   Barry Moody, "Making a British Nova Scotia," in *The "Conquest" of Acadia: Imperial, Colonial, and Aboriginal Constructions*, ed. John G. Reid et al. (Toronto: University of Toronto Press, 2004), 137.

3   John Reid, "Imperialisms, Diplomacies, and the Conquest," in Reid et al., *"Conquest" of Acadia*, 101–23.

4   Ibid.

5   Maxwell Sutherland, "Richard Philipps," *Dictionary of Canadian Biography Online*.

6   Louisbourg is the subject of three fine books by A.J.B. Johnston: *Endgame 1758: The Promise, the Glory, and the Despair of Louisbourg's Last Decade* (Lincoln: University of Nebraska Press, 2007); *Control and Order in French Colonial Louisbourg, 1713–1758* (East Lansing: Michigan State University Press, 2001); and *Religion in Life at Louisbourg* (Montreal: McGill-Queen's University Press, 1984). See also Johnston's article, "Fortress, Seaport, Community: Three Faces of 18th-Century Louisbourg," *Journal of the Royal Nova Scotia Historical Society* 7 (2004): 82–102. Additional perspectives are explored in Christopher Moore, *Louisbourg Portraits: Life in an Eighteenth-Century Garrison Town* (Toronto: Macmillan, 1982) and John Robert McNeil, *Atlantic Empires of France and Spain, Louisbourg and Havana, 1700–1760* (Chapel Hill: University of North Carolina Press, 1985).

7   Johnston, *Control and Order in French Colonial Louisbourg*, 11.

8   Ibid., 88.

9   Brenda Dunn, *A History of Port-Royal/Annapolis Royal, 1605–1800* (Halifax: Nimbus, 2004), 106.

10   For a detailed discussion of the origins of fishermen on the island see, A. J.B. Johnston, "The Fishermen of Eighteenth-Century Cape Breton: Numbers and Origins," *Nova Scotia Historical Review* 9, no. 1 (1989): 62–72.

11   A.J.B. Johnston, *Storied Shores: St Peter's, Isle Madame, and Chapel Island in the 17th and 18th Centuries* (Sydney: UCCB Press, 2004), 74–86, and *Control and Order in French Colonial Louisbourg*, 37, 41.

12   Johnston, *Control and Order in French Colonial Louisbourg*, 44–5.

13   Ibid., 135, 257–8.

14   Ibid., 231–2.

15   Kenneth Donovan, "Slaves and Their Owners in Île Royale, 1713–1760," *Acadiensis* 25, no. 1 (1995): 3–32, and "Female Slaves as Sexual Victims in Île Royale," *Acadiensis* 43 (Winter/Spring 2014): 147–56.

16   Johnston, *Control and Order in French Colonial Louisbourg*, 230.

17   Ibid., 142–3.

18   Ibid., 144–50, 173–222.

19   Ibid., 14.

20   Patrice Gallant, "Michel Haché Gallant," *Dictionary of Canadian Biography Online*.

21   Peter Pope, "Comparisons: Atlantic Canada," in *A Companion to Colonial America*, ed. Daniel Vickers (Oxford: Blackwell, 2003), 492–6.

22   B.A. Balcom, *The Cod Fishery of Île Royale, 1713–58* (Ottawa: Parks Canada, 1984), 50. See also Dale Miquelon, *New France, 1701–1744: "A Supplement to Europe"* (Toronto: McClelland & Stewart, 1987), 114, and Laurent Turgeron, "Le temps des pêches lointaines: permanences et transformations (vers 1500–vers 1850)," in *Historie de pêches maritime en France*, ed. M. Mallatt (Toulouse: Privat, 1987), 134–81.

23   Judith Tulloch, "The New England Fishery and Trade at Canso, 1720–1744," in *How Deep is the Ocean? Historical Essays on Canada's Atlantic Fishery*, ed. James E. Candow and Carol Corbin (Sydney: University College of Cape Breton, 1997), 65–73.

24   Dunn, *History of Port-Royal/Annapolis Royal*, 116.

25   Reid, "Imperialisms, Diplomacies, and the Conquest," in Reid et al., *"Conquest" of Acadia*, 109–10.

26   "Introduction," in Reid et al., *"Conquest" of Acadia*, ix.

27   Reid, "Imperialisms, Diplomacies, and the Conquest," in Reid et al., *"Conquest" of Acadia*, 116–17.

28   Geoffrey Plank, "New England and the Conquest," in Reid et al., *"Conquest" of Acadia*, 79–80.

29   Cited in John G. Reid, "Imperial Intrusions, 1686–1720," in *The Atlantic Region to Confederation: A History*, ed. Phillip A. Buckner and John G. Reid (Toronto; Fredericton: University of Toronto Press and Acadiensis Press, 1994), 100

30   Plank, "New England and the Conquest," 82.

31   Dunn, *History of Port-Royal/Annapolis Royal*, 124–6.

32 William C. Wicken, *Mi'kmaq Treaties on Trial: History, Land, and Donald Marshall Junior* (Toronto: University of Toronto Press, 2002).

33 Cited in ibid., 61–4. For official information on peace and friendship agreements generally, see Government of Canada, Crown-Indigenous Relations and Northern Affairs, online at https://www.rcaanc-cirnac. gc.ca/eng/1100100028599/1539609517566. Not all areas technically under British suzerainty remained safe from Mi'kmaw attacks after the treaty was signed. In the summer of 1727, the Mi'kmaq captured a New England schooner near Port aux Basques, Newfoundland, and brought it to Bras d'Or Lake. Officials at Louisbourg arranged for the Boston owner to purchase his vessel back from its captors. See Johnston, *Storied Shore*, 102.

34 John Reid, "Imperial-Aboriginal Friendship in Eighteenth-Century Mi'kma'ki/Wulstukwik," in *The Loyal Atlantic: Remaking the British Atlantic in the Revolutionary Era*, ed. Jerry Bannister and Liam Riordan (Toronto: University of Toronto Press, 2012), 75–102.

35 See Wicken, *Mi'kmaq Treaties on Trial* and Allan Greer, *Property and Dispossession: Natives, Empires and Land in Early Modern North America* (New York: Cambridge University Press, 2018).

36 Daniel Conlin, "The Golden Age of Piracy in Nova Scotia, 1720–1724," *Journal of the Royal Nova Scotia Historical Society* 12 (2009): 82–105.

37 Dunn, *History of Port-Royal/Annapolis Royal*, 133, 141–3, 147.

38 Ibid., 183.

39 Ibid., 180–1.

40 Ibid., 191–2.

41 Tulloch, "New England Fishery and Trade at Canso," 65–73.

42 Robert Ferguson et al., *Report on the 1979 Field Session at Grassy Island, Nova Scotia* (Ottawa: Parks Canada, 1981) and Gwendolyn Davies, "Researching Eighteenth-century Maritime Women Writers: Deborah How Cottnam – A Case Study," in *Working in Women's Archives: Researching Women's Private Literature and Archival Documents*, ed. Helen M. Buss and Marlene Kadar (Waterloo, ON: Wilfrid Laurier University Press, 2001), 35–50.

43 Thomas Garden Barnes, "'The Dayly Cry for Justice': The Judicial Failure of the Annapolis Royal Regime," 1713–1749," in *Essays in the History of Canadian Law*, vol. III, *Nova Scotia*, ed. Philip Gerard and Jim Phillips (Toronto: University of Toronto Press, 1990), 10–41.

44 Maurice Basque, "The Third Acadia: Political Adaptation and Societal Change," in Reid et al., *"Conquest" of Acadia*, 155–77.

45 Johnston, *Storied Shores*, 74–5. See also David Lee, "Antoine Gaulin," Gérard Finn, "Jean-Louis Le Loutre," and Micheline D. Johnston, "Pierre Maillard," *Dictionary of Canadian Biography Online*.

46 N.E.S. Griffiths, "The Golden Age: Acadian Life, 1713–1748," *Histoire Sociale* 17, no. 33 (1984): 21–34.

47 On the immigrants to Acadia, see Ronnie-Gilles LeBlanc, "Les origines français du peuple acadien avant 1714," in *Le fait acadien en France: histoire et temps présent*, ed. André Magord (La Crèche, QC: Geste Editions, 2010), 25–48, and Stephen A. White, "The True Number of Acadians," in *Du Grand Dérangement à la Déportation: nouvelles perspectives historiques*, ed. Ronnie-Gilles LeBlanc (Moncton: Université de Moncton, Chaire d'études acadiennes, 2005), 55.

48 Brenda Dunn, "Lives of Women in Ancienne Acadie," in *Looking into Acadie: Three Illustrated Lectures* (Halifax: Nova Scotia Museum, 1997), 39–40, and Dunn, *History of Port-Royal/Annapolis Royal*, 38–9.

49 Jerry Bannister, "Atlantic Canada in an Atlantic World? Northeastern North America in the Long 18th Century," *Acadiensis* 43, no. 2 (2014): 3–30.

50 W.G. Godfrey, "John Bradstreet," *Dictionary of Canadian Biography Online*. See also Godfrey's *Pursuit of Profit and Preferment in Colonial North America: John Bradstreet's Quest* (Waterloo, ON: Wilfrid Laurier University Press, 1982).

51 Dunn, *History of Port-Royal/Annapolis Royal*, 148–55.

52 Thomas Garden Barnes, "'Twelve Apostles' or a Dozen Traitors? Acadian Collaboration during King George's War, 1744–48," in *Canadian State Trials*, vol. 1, *Law, Politics, and Security Measures, 1608–1837*, ed. F. Murray Greenwood and Barry Wright (Toronto: University of Toronto Press, 1996), 98–113.

53 Dunn, *History of Port-Royal/Annapolis Royal*, 155–6.

54 George A. Rawlyk, *Yankees at Louisbourg* (Orono: University of Maine Press, 1967).

55 On the role of Mi'kmaq in the war generally and the siege of Louisbourg in particular, see B.A. Balcom, "Defending Unama'ki: Mi'kmaw Resistance in Cape Breton, 1745," *Naashwaak Review* 22/23, no. 1 (2009): 447–506.

56 Johnston, *Control and Order in French Colonial Louisbourg*, 205–12.

57 J.F. Bosher and J.-C. Dubé, "François Bigot," *Dictionary of Canadian Biography Online*.

58 James Pritchard, *Anatomy of a Naval Disaster: The 1746 French Expedition to North America* (Montreal: McGill-Queen's University Press, 1995).

59 Dunn, *History of Port-Royal/Annapolis Royal*, 165–6.

7. Reinventing Nova Scotia, 1749–1775

1 Jerry Bannister, "Atlantic Canada in an Atlantic World? Northeastern North America in the Long 18th Century," *Acadiensis* 43, no. 2 (2014):

3–30. General studies of this period include Elizabeth Mancke, Jerry Bannister, Denis B. McKim, and Scott W. See, eds., *Violence, Order, and Unrest: A History of British North America, 1749–1876* (Toronto: University of Toronto Press, 2019); John Grenier, *The Far Reaches of Empire: War in Nova Scotia, 1710–1760* (Norman: University of Oklahoma Press, 2008); Geoffrey Plank, *An Unsettled Conquest: The British Campaign Against the Peoples of Acadia* (Philadelphia: University of Pennsylvania Press, 2000); George F.G. Stanley, *New France: The Last Phase, 1744–1760* (Toronto: McClelland & Stewart, 1968); and J.B. Brebner, *New England's Outpost before the Conquest of Canada* (New York: Columbia University Press, 1927).

2 Cornwallis's expedition carried 1,174 families, 665 single men, 440 children, and 420 servants. About half the families were headed by recently discharged servicemen. Allan Everett Marble, *Surgeons, Smallpox, and the Poor: A History of Medicine and Social Conditions in Nova Scotia, 1749–1799* (Montreal: McGill-Queen's University Press, 1993), 14.

3 Andrew Beaumont, *Colonial America and the Earl of Halifax, 1748–1761* (New York: Oxford University Press, 2015).

4 A.J.B. Johnston: *Endgame 1758: The Promise, the Glory, and the Despair of Louisbourg's Last Decade* (Lincoln: University of Nebraska Press, 2007), 27, 47, 53.

5 A.J.B. Johnston, "French Attitudes toward the Acadians, ca. 1680–1756," in *Du Grand Dérangement à la Déportation: nouvelles perspectives historiques*, ed. Ronnie-Gilles LeBlanc (Moncton: Université de Moncton, Chaire d'études acadiennes, 2005), 131–66, and Phyllis E. LeBlanc, "Charles Deschamps de Boishébert et de Raffetot," *Dictionary of Canadian Biography Online*.

6 Marble, *Surgeons, Smallpox, and the Poor*, 16; Beaumont, *Colonial America and the Earl of Halifax*, 55–6.

7 John G. Reid, "The Three Lives of Edward Cornwallis," *Journal of the Royal Nova Scotia Historical Society* 16 (2013): 19–45.

8 Julian Gwyn, *Excessive Expectations: Maritime Canada and the Economic Development of Nova Scotia, 1740–1870* (Montreal: McGill-Queen's University Press, 1998), 18.

9 Sheldon J. Godfrey and Judith C. Godfrey, *Search Out the Land: The Jews and the Growth of Equality in British Colonial America, 1740–1867* (Montreal: McGill-Queen's University Press, 1995), 73–81, and Gerald Tulchinsky, *Taking Root: The Origins of the Canadian Jewish Community* (Toronto: Lester, 1992), 82.

10 Julian Gwyn, "'A slave to business all my life': Joshua Mauger, c.1712–1788: The Man and His Myth," *Journal of the Nova Scotia Historical Society* 7 (2004): 38–62, and Donald F. Chard, "Joshua Mauger," *Dictionary of Canadian Biography Online*.

11   Judith Fingard, Janet Guildford, and David Sutherland, *Halifax: The First 250 Years* (Halifax: Nimbus, 2004), 8–22. See also Thomas H. Raddall, *Halifax: Warden of the North* (Toronto: Doubleday, 1965).

12   Dean Jobb, "'The first that was ever published in the province': John Bushell's *Halifax Gazette*, 1752–1761," *Journal of the Royal Nova Scotia Historical Society* 11 (2008): 1–22.

13   Judith Fingard, "Attitudes towards the Education of the Poor in Colonial Halifax," *Acadiensis* 2, no. 2 (1973), 16.

14   Winthrop P. Bell, *The "Foreign Protestants" and the Settlement of Nova Scotia* (Toronto: University of Toronto Press, 1960).

15   Ibid., 372–8. Some two dozen families, apparently Roman Catholic in persuasion, joined discharged French soldiers living on the Mira River. See A.J.B. Johnston, *Control and Order in French Colonial Louisbourg, 1713–1758* (East Lansing: Michigan State University Press, 2001), 49.

16   The founding of the settlement is described in D.C. Harvey, ed., *Journals and Letters of Charles Lawrence*, Bulletin no. 10 (Halifax: Pubic Archives of Nova Scotia, 1953).

17   Bell, *"Foreign Protestants,"* 403.

18   William C. Wicken, *Mi'kmaq Treaties on Trial: History, Land, and Donald Marshall* (Toronto: University of Toronto Press, 2002), 176.

19   Cited in Ruth Holmes Whitehead, *The Old Man Told Us: Excerpts from Micmac History, 1500–1950* (Halifax: Nimbus, 1991), 114.

20   Gérard Finn, "Jean-Louis Le Loutre," *Dictionary of Canadian Biography Online*.

21   Thomas Aikins, ed., *Selections from the Public Documents of the Province of Nova Scotia* (Halifax: Public Archives of Nova Scotia, 1869), 582.

22   C. Alexander Pincombe, "Edward How," *Dictionary of Canadian Biography Online*.

23   Julian Gwyn, *Frigates and Foremasts: The Nova Scotia Squadron in Nova Scotia Waters, 1745–1815* (Vancouver: UBC Press, 2003), 28, and J.S. Pritchard, "Joseph-Bernard de Chabert de Cogolon," *Dictionary of Canadian Biography Online*.

24   Jeffers Lennox, *Homelands and Empires: Indigenous Spaces, Imperial Fictions, and Competition for Territory in Northeastern North America, 1690–1763* (Toronto: University of Toronto Press, 2017), chap. 5.

25   Johnston, *Endgame 1758*, 72.

26   Micheline D. Johnson, "Jean Manach," *Dictionary of Canadian Biography Online*.

27   The Acadian deportation has been addressed in several publications, including Ronnie-Gilles LeBlanc, ed., *Du Grand Dérangement à la Déportation: nouvelles perspectives historiques* (Moncton: Université de Moncton, Chaire d'études acadiennes, 2005); John Mack Faragher, *A Great and*

Noble Scheme: The Tragic Story of the Expulsion of the French Acadians from Their American Homeland (New York: W.W. Norton, 2005); Dean Jobb, *The Acadians: A People's Story of Exile and Triumph* (Mississauga, ON: Wiley and Sons, 2005); James Laxer, *The Acadians in Search of a Homeland* (Toronto: Doubleday Canada, 2006); Christopher Hodson, *The Acadian Diaspora: An Eighteenth-Century History* (Oxford: Oxford University Press, 2012); and Earle Lockerby, *Deportation of the Prince Edward Island Acadians* (Halifax: Nimbus, 2008). See also Jean-François Mouhot, *Les réfugiés acadiens en France, 1758–1785: l'impossible réintégration?* (Quebec City: Septentrion, 2009) and Ronald Rudin, *Remembering and Forgetting in Acadie: A Historian's Journey through Public Memory* (Toronto: University of Toronto Press, 2009).

28 Barry Moody, *A History of Annapolis Royal: A Town with a Memory*, vol. 2, *1749–2005* (Halifax: Historical Association of Annapolis Royal and Nimbus, 2014), 17.

29 Cited in James Moreira, "Rum in the Atlantic Provinces," in *Tempered by Rum: Rum in the History of the Maritime Provinces*, ed. James H. Morrison and James Moreira (Porters Lake, NS: Pottersfield Press, 1988), 18.

30 In addition to sources cited in note 27, see Geoffrey Plank, "King George II and the Acadian Removal," in LeBlanc, ed., *Du Grand Dérangement à la Déportation*, 83–104; Naomi Griffiths, *The Contexts of Acadian History, 1686–1784* (Montreal: McGill-Queen's University Press, 1992), chap. 3, and Sally Ross and Alphomse Deveau, *The Acadians of Nova Scotia: Past and Present* (Halifax: Nimbus, 1992), chap. 3.

31 Phyllis E. LeBlanc, "Charles Deschamps de Boishébert et de Raffetot," *Dictionary of Canadian Biography Online*.

32 Cited in Griffiths, *Contexts of Acadian History*, 91–2.

33 Linda G. Layton, *A Passion for Survival: The True Story of Marie Anne and Louis Payzant in Eighteenth-Century Nova Scotia* (Halifax: Nimbus, 2003).

34 Stephen E. Patterson, "Colonial Wars and Aboriginal Peoples, 1744–1763," in *The Atlantic Region to Confederation: A History*, ed. Phillip A. Buckner and John G. Reid (Toronto; Fredericton: University of Toronto and Acadiensis Press, 1994), 147.

35 A.J.B. Johnston, "The Acadian Deportation in Comparative Context: An Introduction," *Journal of the Royal Nova Scotia Historical Society* 10 (2007): 114–31.

36 Jerry Bannister, "Planter Studies & Atlantic Scholarship: The New History of 18th-Century Nova Scotia," in *The Nova Scotia Planters in the Atlantic World, 1759–1830*, ed. T. Stephen Henderson and Wendy G. Robichaud (Fredericton: Acadiensis Press, 2012), 21.

37 The larger context of French naval development in the wake of d'Anville's disaster in 1746 is outlined in James Pritchard, *Louis XVI's Navy,*

1748–1762: A Study of Organization and Administration (Montreal: McGill-Queen's University Press, 1987). On the British side see Gwyn, *Frigates and Foremasts*.

38 Raddall, *Halifax: Warden of the North*, 52–3.
39 Johnston, *Endgame 1758*, 172.
40 Ibid., 274.
41 M.A. MacDonald, *Rebels and Royalists: The Lives and Material Culture of New Brunswick's Early English-Speaking Settlers, 1758–1783* (Fredericton: New Ireland Press, 1990), 21. See also Andrea Bear Nicholas, "Settler Imperialism and the Dispossession of the Maliseet, 1758–1765," in *Shaping an Agenda for Atlantic Canada*, ed. John G. Reid and Donald J. Savoie (Halifax: Fernwood, 2011), 21–57, and Geoffrey Plank, "New England Soldiers in the St. John River Valley, 1758–60," in *New England and the Maritime Provinces: Connections and Comparisons*, ed. Stephen Hornsby and John G. Reid (Montreal: McGill-Queen's University Press, 2005), 59–73.
42 C.P. Stacey, "James Wolfe," *Dictionary of Canadian Biography Online*.
43 Stephen A. White, "The True Number of Acadians," in LeBlanc, *Du Grand Dérangement à la Déportation*, 21–56.
44 Earle Lockerby, *Deportation of the Prince Edward Island Acadians* (Halifax: Nimbus, 2008) and two articles by Lockerby: "The Deportation of the Acadians from Ile St.-Jean, 1758," *Acadiensis* 27, no. 2 (1998): 45–94, and "Prince Edward Island Acadians in the 1760s and Beyond, and Their Ambivalence in Taking the Oath of Allegiance," *Acadiensis* 47, no. 2 (2018): 71–92.
45 Warren Perrin, *Acadian Redemption* (Erath, LA: Acadian Heritage and Cultural Foundation, 2004); James Laxer, *The Acadians in Search of a Homeland* (Toronto: Doubleday Canada, 2006), 103–10.
46 According to a United Nations Security Council Commission Report conducted in the early 1990s, "ethnic cleansing" is defined as "a purposeful policy designed by one ethnic or religious group to remove by violent and terror-inspiring means the civilian population of another ethnic or religious group from certain geographic areas. To a large extent it is carried out in the name of misguided nationalism, historic grievances, and a powerful driving sense of revenge. The purpose seems to be the occupation of territory to the exclusion of the purged group or groups." John Mack Faragher, *A Great and Noble Scheme: The Tragic Story of the Expulsion of the French Acadians from Their American Homeland* (New York: W.W. Norton, 2005), 469.
47 See "Royal Proclamation relating to the Acadaian Deportation," *Acadian.org*, n.d., available online at https://www.acadian.org/history/royal-proclamation-relating-acadian-deportation.

48 William Wicken, *Treaty of Peace and Friendship 1760* (Ottawa: Indigenous and Northern Affairs Canada), available online at https://www.rcaanc-cirnac.gc.ca/eng/1100100028596/1539609162567. See also Stephen Patterson, "Eighteenth-Century Treaties: The Mi'kmaq, Maliseet, and Passamaquoddy Experience," *Native Studies Review* 18, no. 1 (2009): 25–52.

49 Cited in Whitehead, *The Old Man Told Us*, 156.

50 G.P. Gould and A.J. Semple, eds., *Our Land: The Maritimes* (Fredericton: Sainte Anne's Point Press, 1980), 177. See also William C. Wicken, "The Mi'kmaq and Wuastukwiuk Treaties," *University of New Brunswick Law Journal* 43 (1994): 241–53.

51 John G. Reid, "Pax Britannica or Pax Indegena? Planter Nova Scotia (1760–1782) and Competing Strategies of Pacification," *Canadian Historical Review* 85, no. 4 (2004): 669–92.

52 Ibid.

53 Stephen J. Hornsby, *Surveyors of Empire: Samuel Holland, J.F.W. DesBarres, and the Making of the Atlantic Neptune* (Montreal: McGill-Queen's University Press, 2012).

54 Phyllis R. Blakeley, "Charles Morris," *Dictionary of Canadian Biography Online* and Nicholas, "Settler Imperialism and the Dispossession of the Maliseet," 31, 37.

55 Gwyn, *Excessive Expectations*, 27.

56 On the New England Planters, see Margaret Conrad, ed., *They Planted Well: New England Planters in Maritime Canada* (Fredericton: Acadiensis Press, 1988); *Making Adjustments: Change and Continuity in Planter Nova Scotia, 1759–1800* (Fredericton: Acadiensis Press, 1991); *Intimate Relations: Family and Community in Planter Nova Scotia, 1759–1800* (Fredericton: Acadiensis Press, 1995): Margaret Conrad and Barry Moody, eds., *Planter Links: Community and Culture in Colonial Nova Scotia* (Fredericton: Acadiensis Press, 2001); T. Stephen Henderson and Wendy G. Robichaud, eds., *The Nova Scotia Planters in the Atlantic World, 1759–1830* (Fredericton: Acadiensis Press, 2012); and Carol Campbell and James Smith, *Necessities and Sufficiencies: Planter Society in Londonderry, Onslow and Truro Townships, 1761–1780* (Sydney: Cape Breton University Press, 2011).

57 Revealing details of the planning process for one township can be found in Campbell and Smith, *Necessities and Sufficiencies*, 10–20, and R.S. Longley, "The Coming of the New England Planters to the Annapolis Valley," in Conrad, *They Planted Well*, 14–28.

58 Phyllis Blakeley, "And Having a Love for People," *Nova Scotia Historical Quarterly* 5, no. 2 (1975), 172–3.

59 E. Jennifer Monaghan, "Literacy in Eighteenth-Century New England: Some Historiographical Reflections on Issues of Gender," in Conrad, *Making Adjustments*, 12–44.

60   C. Bruce Fergusson, "Simeon Perkins," *Dictionary of Canadian Biography Online*. The Champlain Society published the Perkins diary in five volumes between 1948 and 1978, available online at http://link.library.utoronto.ca/champlain/search_results.cfm?lang=eng&query=Simeon%20AND%20Perkins%20AND%20Diary&searchtype=Title&limit=All.

61   Gwendolyn Davies, "Gendered Responses: The Seccombe Diaries," in Conrad, *Intimate Relations*, 132–40.

62   A detailed exploration of the settlers from one community can be found in Robert McLaughlin, "New England Planters prior to Migration: The Case of Chatham, Massachusetts," in Conrad and Moody, *Planter Links*, 12–19.

63   Alan R. MacNeil, "The Acadian Legacy and Agricultural Development in Nova Scotia, 1860–1861," in *Farm, Factory and Fortune: New Studies in the Economic History of the Maritime Provinces*, ed. Kris Inwood (Fredericton: Acadiensis Press, 1993), 1–16.

64   Graeme Wynn, "A Region of Scattered Settlements and Bounded Possibilities: Northeastern America 1755–1800," *Canadian Geographer* 31, no. 4 (1987): 319–38.

65   J. Brian Hanington, *Every Popish Person: The Story of Roman Catholicism in Nova Scotia and the Church in Halifax, 1604–1984* (Halifax: Archdiocese of Halifax, 1984), 39, and Ross and Deveau, *Acadians of Nova Scotia*, 74–5.

66   Philip Girard, "Preacher, to Planter, to Pariah: The Vicissitudes of the Reverend James Murdoch," in Conrad and Moody, *Planter Links*, 105–18.

67   Lois Kernaghan, "A Man and His Mistress: J.F.W. DesBarres and Mary Cannon," *Acadiensis* 11, no. 1 (1981): 23–42.

68   Brebner, *Neutral Yankees of Nova Scotia*, 29.

69   Lucille H. Campey, *After the Hector: The Scottish Pioneers of Nova Scotia and Cape Breton, 1773–1852* (Toronto: Heritage Books, 2007), 23. See also Marjory Harper and Jonathan Vance, eds., *Myth, Migration, and the Making of Memory: Scotia and Nova Scotia c. 1700–1990* (Halifax: Grosebrook Institute, 1999); Donald MacKay, *Scotland Farewell: The People of the Hector* (Toronto: Natural Heritage/Natural History, 1996); and D. Campbell and R.A. MacLean, *Beyond the Atlantic Roar: A Study of Nova Scotia Scots* (Toronto: McClelland & Stewart, 1974).

70   James D. Snowdon, *Footprints in the Marsh Mud: Politics and Land Settlement in the Township of Sackville, 1760–1800* (Sackville, NB: Tantramar Heritage Trust and R.P. Bell Library Maritime Literature Reprint Series, 2000) and Lucille H. Campey, *Planters, Paupers, and Pioneers: English Settlers in Atlantic Canada* (Toronto: Natural Heritage Books, 2010), chap. 2.

71   Ronald Rompkey, "Bruin Romkes Comingo," *Dictionary of Canadian Biography Online*

72 Rusty Bittermann, *Rural Protest on Prince Edward Island: From British Colonization to the Escheat Movement* (Toronto: University of Toronto Press, 2006) and J.M. Bumsted, *Land, Settlement, and Politics on Eighteenth-Century Prince Edward Island* (Montreal: McGill-Queen's University Press, 1987).

73 Letter from Councillor Alex Grant of Halifax to the Reverend Ezra Stiles of Boston, May 1960, cited in Sutherland et al., *Halifax*, 17.

74 Julian Gwyn, *Ashore and Afloat: The British Navy and the Halifax Naval Yard Before 1820* (Ottawa: University of Ottawa Press, 2004).

75 Gwyn, *Frigates and Foremasts*, 38–40.

76 Brebner, *Neutral Yankees of Nova Scotia*, chap. 9.

77 Wendy L. Thorpe, "John Day," *Dictionary of Canadian Biography Online* and Day's *An Essay on the Present State of the Province of Nova-Scotia, with Some Strictures on the Measures Pursued by Government from its First Settlement by the English in the Years 1749* [1774].

78 J. Murray Beck, *Politics of Nova Scotia*, vol. 1, *1710–1896* (Tantallon, NS: Four East Publications, 1985), 19–41.

79 "Census of Nova Scotia, 1767," in *Censuses of Canada, 1665–1871*, vol. 4 (Ottawa: Statistics Canada, 1876), 70–2.

80 John Robinson and Thomas Rispin, *Journey through Nova Scotia Containing a Particular Account of the Country and Its Inhabitants* (1774; reprint Sackville: Ralph Pickard Bell Library, Mount Allison University, 1981).

8. The Great Divide, 1775–1792

1 This question was initially probed in great detail by J.B. Brebner, *The Neutral Yankees of Nova Scotia* (1937; Toronto: McClelland & Stewart, 1969). See also George Rawlyk, *Revolution Rejected, 1775–1776* (Scarborough, ON: Prentice-Hall, 1968) and Elizabeth Mancke, *The Fault Lines of Empire: Political Differentiation in Massachusetts and Nova Scotia, ca. 1760–1830* (London: Routledge, 2005). For the larger context of developments discussed in this chapter, see Julian Gwyn, *Excessive Expectations: Maritime Commerce and the Economic Development of Nova Scotia, 1740–1870* (Montreal: McGill-Queen's University Press, 1998); Stephen J. Hornsby, *British Atlantic, American Frontier: Spaces of Power in Early Modern British America* (Hanover, NH: University Press of New England, 2005); and Michael Meranze and Saree Makdisi, eds., *Imagining the British Atlantic After the American Revolution* (Toronto: University of Toronto Press, 2015). See also Lewis R. Fischer, "Revolution without Independence: The Canadian Colonies, 1749–1775," in *The Economy of Early America: The Revolutionary Period, 1763–1790*, ed. Ronald Hoffman et al. (Charlottesville: University of Virginia Press, 1988).

2 On the crises leading to the declaration of war, see T.H. Breen, *American Insurgents, American Patriots: The Revolution of the People* (New York: Hill and Wang, 2010).

3 Ultimately, Nova Scotians were less preoccupied with protecting their local rights than with avoiding war on their home soil. Indeed, Elizabeth Mancke goes so far as to conclude that "the American Revolution was a war against the extension of a modern bureaucratic state into the oldest colonies of British North America, while the newer colonies were willing to accept the idea of a more integrated imperial state, in part because they were products of it." Mancke, *Fault Lines of Empire*, 162.

4 Douglas Locheed, "Anthony Henry," *Dictionary of Canadian Biography Online*.

5 Harold A. Innis, ed., *The Diary of Simeon Perkins, 1766–1780* (Toronto: Champlain Society, 1948), 5.

6 Brebner, *Neutral Yankees of Nova Scotia*, 260.

7 Captain John Stanton, "A Report of the State of the Province of Nova Scotia," 4 December 1775, CO 217, vol. 52, fol. 60, cited in Carol Campbell and James F. Smith, *Necessaries and Sufficiencies: Planter Society in Londonderry, Onslow, and Truro Townships, 1761–1780* (Sydney: Cape Breton University Press, 2011), 216.

8 At least 225 vessels making for or leaving Nova Scotia ports were captured by American privateers during the war; Julian Gwyn, *Frigates and Foremasts: The North American Squadron in Nova Scotia Waters, 1745–1815* (Vancouver; UBC Press, 2003), 56. See also John Dewar Faibisy, "Privateering and Piracy: The Effects of New England Raiding upon Nova Scotia during the American Revolution, 1775–1783" (PhD diss., University of Massachusetts, 1972).

9 James S. Leamon, *Revolution Downeast: The War for American Independence in Maine* (Amherst: University of Massachusetts Press, 1993), 67–73.

10 Brebner, *Neutral Yankees of Nova Scotia*, 255.

11 Campbell and Smith, *Necessaries and Sufficiencies*, 216.

12 Ernest Clarke, *The Siege of Fort Cumberland, 1776: An Episode in the American Revolution* (Montreal: McGill-Queen's University Press, 1995), 19–31

13 Brebner, *Neutral Yankees of Nova Scotia*, 254.

14 Donald F. Chard, "Mariot Arbuthnot," *Dictionary of Canadian Biography Online*.

15 Joseph Goreham's last name is usually spelled with an "e," unlike that of his brother John. See John David Krugler, "John Gorham," and David A. Charters and Stuart R.J. Sutherland, "Joseph Goreham," *Dictionary of Canadian Biography Online*.

16 Clarke, *Siege of Fort Cumberland*, 72.

17 Hornsby, *British Atlantic, American Frontier*, chap. 6.

18 "Extracts from the Record of a Conference of the St. John and Micmac Indians with the Americans: July 10–July 17, 1776," in *Source Materials Relating to the New Brunswick Indian*, ed. W.D. Hamilton and W.A. Spray (Fredericton: Centennial Print and Litho, 1976), 40–50. The details of the negotiations relating to the treaty and the responses to it are discussed in Clarke, *Siege of Fort Cumberland*, 58–66.

19 Clarke, *Siege of Fort Cumberland*, appendix 1.

20 Ibid., 201.

21 Ernest Clarke and Jim Phillips, "Rebellion and Repression in Nova Scotia in the Era of the American Revolution," in *Canadian State Trials*, vol. 1, *Law, Politics, and Security Measures, 1608–1837*, ed. Murray Greenwood and Barry Wright (Toronto: Osgoode Society for Legal History and University of Toronto Press, 1996), 172–220.

22 Ibid., 198–9.

23 In addition to the article by Ernest Clarke and Jim Phillips, cited above, see Barry Cahill, "The Sedition Trial of Timothy Houghton: Repression in a Marginal New England Planter Township during the Revolutionary Years," *Acadiensis* 24, no. 1 (1994): 35–58, and "The Treason of the Merchants: Dissent and Repression in Halifax in the Era of the American Revolution," *Acadiensis* 26, no. 1 (1996): 52–70.

24 Daniel Conlin, "They Plundered Well: Planters as Privateers, 1793–1805," in *Planter Links: Community and Culture in Colonial Nova Scotia*, ed. Margaret Conrad and Barry Moody (Fredericton: Acadiensis Press, 2001), 20–35.

25 Leamon, *Revolution Downeast*, 90–4.

26 Unpublished manuscript, Mary [Coy] Bradley, New England Historic Genealogical Society.

27 Stephen E. Patterson, "Israel Perley," *Dictionary of Canadian Biography Online*.

28 Éloi Degrâce, "Joseph-Mathurin Bourg," *Dictionary of Canadian Biography Online*.

29 Michael Francklin to Lord George Germaine, 21 November 1780, cited in *Source Materials Relating to the New Brunswick Indian*, 58–9.

30 Keith Mercer, "Northern Exposure: Resistance to Naval Impressment in British North America, 1775–1815," *Canadian Historical Review* 91, no. 2 (2010): 199–232.

31 Gwyn, *Frigates and Foremasts*, 72.

32 Gordon T. Stewart and George A. Rawlyk, *A People Highly Favoured by God: The Nova Scotia Yankees in the American Revolution* (Hamden, CT: Archon Books, 1972).

33 G.S. French, "William Black," *Dictionary of Canadian Biography Online*.

34 J. Brian Hanington, *Every Popish Person: The Story of Roman Catholicism in Nova Scotia and the Church in Halifax, 1604–1984* (Halifax: Archdiocese of Halifax, 1984), 48–9, 52. See also Terrence Murphy, "The Emergence of Maritime Catholicism, 1781–1830," *Acadiensis* 8, no. 2 (1984): 29–49.

35 *The Modern Orator: The Speeches of the Right Hone Edmund Burke* (London: Aylott and Jones, 1847), 623.

36 Andrew Jackson O'Shaughnessy, *The Men Who Lost America: British Leadership, the American Revolution, and the Fate of Empire* (New Haven CT: Yale University Press, 2013).

37 Constitution Society, "The Last Will and Testament of Benjamin Franklin, " available online at https://www.constitution.org/primarysources /lastwill.html. See also Sheila L. Skemp, *The Making of a Patriot: Benjamin Franklin at the Cockpit* (New York: Oxford University Press, 2013), 148.

38 Ruma Chopra, *Choosing Sides: Loyalists in Revolutionary America* (Lanham, MD: Rowman & Littlefield, 2013); Maya Jasanoff, *Liberty's Exiles: American Loyalists in the Revolutionary World* (New York: Alfred Knopf, 2011); and Wallace Brown, *The Good Americans: The Loyalists in the American Revolution* (New York: William Morrow, 1969).

39 Neil MacKinnon, *This Unfriendly Soil: The Loyalist Experience in Nova Scotia, 1783–1791* (Montreal: McGill-Queen's University Press, 1986) and Margaret Ells, "Settling the Loyalists in Nova Scotia," *Canadian Historical Association Report* (Ottawa, 1934).

40 MacKinnon, *This Unfriendly Soil*, 96.

41 On Shelburne, see Marion Robertson, *King's Bounty: A History of Early Shelburne, Nova Scotia* (Halifax: Nova Scotia Museum, 1983) and Stephen Kimber, *Loyalists and Layabouts: The Rapid Rise and Faster Fall of Shelburne, Nova Scotia, 1783–1792* (Toronto: Doubleday Canada, 2008).

42 Historians have long debated who counts as a Loyalist. For the purposes of this study, I have included all "refugees," civilian and soldier alike, in the definition. See J.M. Bumsted, *Understanding the Loyalists* (Sackville, NB: Mount Allison University, 1986).

43 James B. Bell, *A War of Religion: Dissenters, Anglicans and the American Revolution* (New York: Palgrave Macmillan, 2008).

44 Julie Ross and Thomas Vincent, "Jacob Bailey," *Dictionary of Canadian Biography Online*. See also James S. Leamon, *The Reverend Jacob Bailey, Maine Loyalist: For God, King, Country, and for the Self* (Amherst: University of Massachusetts Press, 2012) and Kent Thompson, *The Man Who Said No: Reading Jacob Bailey, Loyalist* (Gaspereau, NS: Gaspereau Press, 2008).

45 Ann Gorman Condon, "Edward Winslow," *Dictionary of Canadian Biography Online*.

46 MacKinnon, *This Unfriendly Soil*, 63.

47 David Bell, *Loyalist Rebellion in New Brunswick: A Defining Conflict for Canada's Political Culture* (Halifax: Formac, 2013).

48 Beatrice Ross Buzek, "'By Fortune Wounded': Loyalist Women in Nova Scotia," *Nova Scotia Historical Review* 7, no. 2 (1987): 45–62; Beatrice Spense Ross, "Adaptation in Exile: Loyalist Women in Nova Scotia after the American Revolution" (PhD diss., Cornell University, 1981); and Mary Beth Norton, "Eighteenth-Century American Women in Peace and War: the Case of the Loyalists," *William and Mary Quarterly*, 3rd series, 33 (1976): 386–409. See also Ann Gorman Condon, "The Family in Exile: Loyalist Social Values after the American Revolution," in *Intimate Relations: Family and Community in Planter Nova Scotia, 1759–1800*, ed. Margaret Conrad (Fredericton: Acadiensis Press, 1995), 42–53.

49 Cited in Buzek, "'By Fortune Wounded,'" 56.

50 D. Campbell and R.A. MacLean, *Beyond the Atlantic Roar: A Study of the Nova Scotia Scots* (Toronto: McClelland & Stewart 1974), 33.

51 Elizabeth Lichtenstein Johnston, *Recollections of a Georgia Loyalist*, ed., Arthur Wentworth Hamilton Eaton (New York: Bankside Press, 1901).

52 René Chartrand, *American Loyalist Troops, 1775–84* (Oxford: Osprey Publishing, 2008).

53 MacKinnon, *This Unfriendly Soil*, 64.

54 Hugh Douglas, *Flora MacDonald: The Most Loyal Rebel* (Bath, UK: Sutton, 1993) and John J. Toffey, *A Woman Nobly Planned: Fact and Myth in the Legacy of Flora MacDonald* (Durham, NC: Carolina Academic Press, 1997).

55 MacKinnon, *This Unfriendly Soil*, 61.

56 Beaver Harbour, in what became the colony of New Brunswick, was founded by Quakers, who banned slave owners from settling in their community. See W.A. Spray, *The Blacks in New Brunswick* (Fredericton: Brunswick Press, 1972), 17.

57 Harvey Amani Whitfield, *North to Bondage: Loyalist Slavery in the Maritimes* (Vancouver: UBC Press, 2016), 119–20, and also Whitfield's, "The African Diaspora in Atlantic Canada: History, Historians, and Historiography," *Acadiensis* 46, no. 1 (2017): 213–32.

58 The Book of Negroes is available online at the Nova Scotia Archives, https://novascotia.ca/archives/africanns/BN.asp.

59 Cassandra Pybus, *Epic Journeys of Freedom: Runaway Slaves of the American Revolution and their Global Quest for Liberty* (Boston: Beacon Press, 2006); James W. St. G. Walker, *The Black Loyalists: The Search for a Promised Land in Nova Scotia and Sierra Leone, 1783–1870* (1976; Toronto: University of Toronto Press, 1992); and Ruth Holmes Whitehead, *Black Loyalists: Southern Settlers of Nova Scotia's First Free Black Communities* (Halifax: Nimbus, 2013). The status of Black Loyalists is debated in Barry Cahill, "The Black Loyalist Myth in Atlantic Canada," *Acadiensis* 29, no. 1 (1999): 76–87, and James W. St. G. Walker, "History and Revisionism: The Black Loyalists Revisited," *Acadiensis* 29, no. 1 (1999): 88–105.

60 Walker, *Black Loyalists*, 73.
61 Ibid., chap. 2.
62 Bridglal Pachai, *The Nova Scotia Black Experience Through the Centuries* (Halifax: Nimbus, 2007), 53.
63 MacKinnon, *This Unfriendly Soil*, 156.
64 Barry Moody, *A History of Annapolis Royal: A Town with a Memory*, vol. 2, *1749–2005* (Halifax: Nimbus, 2014), 65–6, 100. See also "Rose Fortune – a 'privileged character,'" Annapolis Heritage Society, online at http://annapolisheritagesociety.com/community-history/notable-personalities-past/rose-fortune-privileged-character/.
65 Whitfield, *North to Bondage*, 13–16.
66 John Clarkson, Nova Scotia Archives, MG 1, vol. 219, 197–201, published in C.B. Fergusson, ed., *Clarkson's Mission to America, 1791–1792* (Halifax: Public Archives of Nova Scotia Publication No. 11, 1971), 89–90.
67 Carole Watterson Troxler, "Re-enslavement of Black Loyalists: Mary Postell in South Carolina, East Florida, and Nova Scotia," *Acadiensis* 37, no. 2 (2008): 70–85.
68 G.D.N. Evans, *Uncommon Obdurate: The Several Public Careers of J.F.W. DesBarres* (Salem, MA: Peabody Essex Museum, 1969).
69 The seemingly petty squabbles can be pieced together from the biographies of Cossit, Cuyler, DesBarres, and Matthews, available in *The Dictionary of Canadian Biography Online*. See also Robert Morgan, *Early Cape Breton: From Founding to Famine, 1784–1851* (Sydney: Breton Books, 2000), 31–48.
70 Stephen J. Hornsby, *Nineteenth-Century Cape Breton: A Historical Geography* (Montreal: McGill-Queen's University Press, 1992), 25–8.
71 Ann Gorman Condon, "1783–1800: Loyalist Arrival, Acadian Return, Imperial Reform," in *The Atlantic Region to Confederation* (Toronto; Fredericton: University of Toronto and Acadiensis Press, 1994), 185.
72 Esther Clark Wright, *The Loyalists of New Brunswick* (Fredericton, 1955), 212; MacKinnon, *This Unfriendly Soil*, 158–79.
73 Carole Watterson Troxler, "Community and Cohesion in the Rawdon Loyalist Settlement." *Nova Scotia Historical Review* 12 (June 1992): 40–66; "A Loyalist Life: John Bond of South Carolina and Nova Scotia." *Acadiensis* 19, no. 2 (1990): 72–91; and "The Migration of Carolina and Georgia Loyalists to Nova Scotia and New Brunswick" (Ph.D. diss., University of North Carolina, 1974).
74 John G. Reid, "Empire, the Maritime Colonies, and the Supplanting of Mi'kma'ki/Wulstukwik, 1780–1820," *Acadiensis* 38, no. 2 (2009): 78–97; William Wicken, *The Colonization of Mi'kmaw Memory and History, 1794–1928: The King v. Gabriel Sylliboy* (Toronto: University of Toronto Press, 2012); and Micha A. Pawling, "Wəlastəkwey (Maliseet) Homeland:

Waterscapes and Continuity within the Lower St. John River Valley, 1784–1900," *Acadiensis* 66, no. 2 (2017): 5–34.

75 Reid, "Empire, the Maritime Colonies, and the Supplanting of Mi'kma'ki/Wulstuikwik," 83.

76 Julian Gwyn, "The Mi'kmaq, Poor Settlers, and the Nova Scotia Fur Trade, 1783–1853," *Journal of the Canadian Historical Association* 14 (2003): 65–91.

77 The Alexey story is detailed in Wicken, *Colonization of Mi'kmaw Memory and History*, 104–14, and the quotations are cited on pages 104, 105, and 113.

78 J. Murray Beck, *Politics of Nova Scotia*, vol. 1, *1710–1896* (Halifax: Four East Publications, 1985), 43.

79 Ibid., 47–8, and Brian Cuthbertson, *Johnny Bluenose at the Polls: Epic Nova Scotian Election Battles, 1758–1848* (Halifax: Formac, 1994), 33–5.

80 Brian Cuthbertson, *The Loyalist Governor: Biography of Sir John Wentworth* (Halifax: Petheric Press, 1983) and Judith Fingard, "Sir John Wentworth," *The Dictionary of Canadian Biography Online*.

81 Judith Fingard, *The Anglican Design in Loyalist Nova Scotia, 1783–1816* (London: SPCK, 1972) and "Charles Inglis," *Dictionary of Canadian Biography Online*.

82 Elizabeth Mancke, "At the Corner of the General Store: Women and the Economy in Eighteenth-Century Horton, Nova Scotia," in *Intimate Relations: Family and Community in Planter Nova Scotia, 1759–1800*, ed. Margaret Conrad (Fredericton: Acadiensis Press, 1995), 167–81.

83 Anthony Pagden, *The Enlightenment and Why It Still Matters* (New York: Random House, 2013).

84 Gwendolyn Davies, "Consolation to Distress: Loyalist Literary Activities in the Maritimes," *Acadiensis* 16, no. 2 (1987): 51–68.

85 See *Nova-Scotia Magazine*, Early Canadiana Online at http://eco.canadiana.ca/view/oocihm.8_06254.

86 *Nova-Scotia Magazine* 1, no. 3 (1789), 204, cited in Michael Eamon, *Imprinting Britain: Newspapers, Sociability, and the Shaping of British North America* (Montreal: McGill-Queen's University Press, 2015), 19.

87 Gwendolyn Davies, "Researching Eighteenth-Century Maritime Women Writers: Deborah How Cottnam – A Case Study," in *Working in Women's Archives: Researching Women's Private Literature and Archival Documents*, ed. Helen M. Buss and Marlene Kadar (Waterloo, ON: Wilfrid Laurier University Press, 2001), 35–50, and Lois Kernaghan, "Deborah (Cottnam) How," *Dictionary of Canadian Biography Online*.

88 Rebecca Byles to Catherine Byles, 8 November 1777, Byles Collection, MG1, vol. 163, Nova Scotia Archives, Halifax.

89 "Rebecca Byles, 1762–1853," in Margaret Conrad, Toni Laidlaw, and Donna Smyth, *No Place Like Home: The Diaries and Letters of Nova Scotia Women, 1771–1938* (Halifax: Formac, 1988), 48–58.

90 Brian C. Cuthbertson, *The Journal of John Payzant* (Windsor, NS: Lancelot Press, 1981), 44.

91 Yvan Lamonde and Andrea Rotundo, "The Book Trade and Bookstores," in *History of the Book in Canada*, vol. 1, *Beginnings to 1840*, ed. Patricia Lockhart Fleming, Gilles Gallichan, and Yvan Lamonde (Toronto: University of Toronto Press, 2004), 132.

92 D.G. Bell, ed., *Newlight Baptist Journals of James Manning and James Innis* (Saint John: Acadia Divinity College and Baptist Heritage Committee, 1984), 259.

93 Alexander D. Boutilier, *The Citadel on Stage: British Military Theatre, Sports, and Recreation in Colonial Halifax* (Halifax: New World Publishing, 2015).

94 Bonnie Huskins, "'Remarks and Rough Memorandums,' Social Sets, Sociability, and Community in the Journal of William Booth, Shelburne, 1787 and 1789," *Journal of the Royal Nova Scotia Historical Society* 13 (2010): 103–32.

95 On singing schools, both religious and secular, see Nancy Vogan, "The Musical Traditions of the Planters and 'Mary Miller Her Book,'" in *Making Adjustments in Planter Nova Scotia, 1759–1800*, ed. Margaret Conrad (Fredericton: Acadiensis Press, 1991), 247–52.

96 George Rawlyk, *New Light Letters and Spiritual Songs, 1778–1793* (Hantsport, NS: Lancelot Press, 1983).

97 See Eamon, *Imprinting Britain*, for an excellent discussion of the role of coffee houses and taverns in sustaining literacy and sociability in this period.

98 L.F.S. Upton, *Micmacs and Colonists: Indian-White Relations in the Maritimes, 1713–1867* (Vancouver: UBC Press, 1979), 81.

99 This useful distinction is summarized in the Introduction to Jasanoff, *Liberty's Exiles*.

100 Jerry Bannister, "Canada as Counter-Revolution: The Loyalist Order Framework in Canadian History, 1750–1840," in *Liberalism and Hegemony: Debating the Canadian Liberal Revolution*, ed. Jean-François Constant and Michel Ducharme (Toronto: University of Toronto Press, 2009), 98–146. David Bell offers a valuable reflection on Loyalist political sensibilities in *Loyalist Rebellion in New Brunswick: A Defining Conflict for Canada's Political Culture* (Halifax: Formac, 2013).

9. Entering the Nineteenth Century, 1792–1820

1 Julian Gwyn, *Excessive Expectations: Maritime Commerce and the Economic Development of Nova Scotia, 1740–1870* (Montreal: McGill-Queen's University Press, 1998), 28.

2 David Sutherland, "Halifax Merchants and the Pursuit of Development. 1783–1850," *Canadian Historical Review* 59, no. 1 (1978), 5.

3 N.A.M. Rodger, *The Wooden World: An Anatomy of the Georgian Navy* (Annapolis, MD: Naval Institute Press, 1986).

4 Gwyn, *Excessive Expectations*, 37–8.

5 D.A. Sutherland, "William Forsyth," and David S. Macmillan, "John Black," *Dictionary of Canadian Biography Online*.

6 Judith Fingard, Janet Guildford, and David Sutherland, *Halifax: The First 250 Years* (Halifax: Nimbus, 2004), chap. 2.

7 John N. Grant, *The Maroons in Nova Scotia* (Halifax: Formac, 2002); Brian Cuthbertson, *The Loyalist Governor: Biography of John Wentworth* (Halifax: Petheric Press, 1983), 83, and Bridglal Pachai, *The Nova Scotia Black Experience Through the Centuries* (Halifax: Nimbus 2007), 90. See also Ruma Chopra, "Maroons and Mi'kmaq in Nova Scotia, 1796–1800," *Acadiensis* 46, no. 1 (2017): 5–23.

8 Brian Cuthbertson, *Melville Prison and Deadman's Island: American and French Prisoners of War in Halifax 1794–1816* (Halifax: Formac, 2009). During the War of 1812, a few Nova Scotians were captured and incarcerated by Americans, a fate described in Joshua M. Smith, "'Find a Hell before You Leave this World': Maritimers as Prisoners of War, 1812–1815," *Journal of the Royal Nova Scotia Historical Society* 18 (2015): 65–76.

9 L.F.S. Upton, *Micmacs and Colonists: Indian-White Relations in the Maritimes, 1713–1867* (Vancouver: UBC Press, 1979), 81–7, and William C. Wicken, *The Colonization of Mi'kmaq Memory and History, 1794–1928* (Toronto: University of Toronto Press, 2012), 95–110.

10 Julian Gwyn, *Frigates and Foremasts: The Nova Scotia Squadron in Nova Scotia Waters, 1745–1815* (Vancouver: UBC Press, 2003), chaps. 4, 5, and 6. On the war in Nova Scotia, see John Boileau, *Half-Hearted Enemies: Nova Scotia, New England and the War of 1812* (Halifax: Formac, 2005). The larger context is discussed in Andrew D. Lambert, *The Challenge: Britain Against America in the Naval War of 1812* (London: Faber & Faber, 2012).

11 Spencer C. Tucker and Frank T. Reuter, *Injured Honor: The Chesapeake-Leopard Affair, June 22, 1807* (Annapolis, MD: Naval Institute Press, 1996). On the larger issue of desertion, see Martin Hubley, "Desertion, Identity and the Experience of Authority in the North American Squadron of the Royal Navy, 1745–1812" (PhD diss., University of Ottawa, 2009). See also Hubley's website: *Desertion and the North American Squadron of the Royal Navy, 1745–1812*, http://maritimemuseum.novascotia.ca/desertion-and-north-american-squadron-royal-navy-1745-1812.

12 Joshua M. Smith, "Humbert's Paradox: The Global Context of Smuggling in the Bay of Fundy," in *New England and the Maritime Provinces: Connections and Comparisons*, ed. Stephen J. Hornsby and John G. Reid (Montreal:

McGill-Queen's University Press, 2005), 111. See also Joshua M. Smith, *Battle for the Bay of Fundy: The Naval War of 1812* (Fredericton: Goose Lane Editions and the New Brunswick Military Heritage Project, 2011).

13 Walter Ronald Copp, "Nova Scotia Trade during the War of 1812," *Canadian Historical Review* 17 (June 1937): 141–55, reprinted in *Historical Essays on the Atlantic Provinces*, ed. G.A. Rawlyk (Toronto: McClelland & Stewart, 1967), 88.

14 Gwyn, *Frigates and Foremasts*, 118, 150. See also Faye Kert, *Prize and Prejudice: Privateering and Naval Prize in Atlantic Canada in the War of 1812* (St John's, NL: International Maritime Economic History Association, 1997).

15 Kert, *Prize and Prejudice*, appendix 3: Nova Scotia and New Brunswick Letter of Marque Vessels, 1812–1815, 221–4.

16 Dianne Barker and D.A. Sutherland, "Enos Collins," *Dictionary of Canadian Biography Online*.

17 Carol Anne Janzen, "Sir Alexander Croke," *Dictionary of Canadian Biography Online*.

18 Keith Mercer, "Colonial Patriotism to 'Mystical Chords of Memory': The Halifax Celebrations and Commemorations of the Shannon-Chesapeake Battle," *Acadiensis* 64, no. 1 (2015): 36–63, and Carl Christie, "Provo Wallis," *Dictionary of Canadian Biography Online*.

19 Keith Mercer, "Northern Exposure: Resistance to Naval Impressment in British North America, 1775–1815," *Canadian Historical Review* 91, no. 2 (2010): 199–232, and "Soldiers and Citizens: Press Gangs and Naval-Civilian Relations in Nova Scotia, 1756-1815," *Journal of the Royal Nova Scotia Historical Society* 10 (2007): 87–113.

20 Daniel Conlin, "A Private War in the Caribbean: Nova Scotia Privateering, 1793–1805," *Northern Mariner* 6 (1996): 29–46.

21 Keith Mercer, "Planters and Press Gangs: A Social History of Naval Impressment in Liverpool, Nova Scotia, 1759–1815, in *The Nova Scotia Planters and the Atlantic World, 1759–1830*, ed. Stephen Henderson and Wendy G. Robichaud (Fredericton: Acadiensis Press, 2010), 205–42. See also Daniel Conlin, "They Plundered Well: Planters as Privateers, 1793–1805," in *Planter Links: Community and Culture in Colonial Nova Scotia*, ed. Margaret Conrad and Barry Moody (Fredericton: Acadiensis Press, 2001), 20–35.

22 Gwyn, *Frigates and Foremasts*, 146.

23 J.S. Martell, "A Documentary Study of Provincial Finance and Currency, 1812–36," *Bulletin of the Public Archives of Nova Scotia* 2, no. 4 (1941), 7.

24 Cited in Margaret Conrad, Toni Laidlaw, and Donna Smyth, *No Place Like Home: Diaries and Letters of Nova Scotia Women, 1771–1938* (Halifax: Formac, 1988), 68–9.

25 Harvey Amani Whitfield, *Blacks on the Border: The Black Refugees in British North America, 1815–1860* (Burlington: University of Vermont Press, 2006).

26   Cited in Bridglal Pachai, *The Nova Scotia Black Experience Through the Centuries* (Halifax: Nimbus, 2007), 81.

27   Barry Moody, *A History of Annapolis Royal: A Town with a Memory*, vol. 2, *1749–2005* (Halifax: Historical Association of Annapolis Royal and Nimbus, 2014), 75.

28   Sutherland, "Halifax Merchants and the Pursuit of Development," 4

29   Martell, "Documentary Study of Provincial Finance and Currency," 5.

30   Julian Gwyn, "'A Little Province Like This': The Economy of Nova Scotia under Stress, 1812–1853," *Canadian Papers in Rural History* 6 (Gananoque, ON: Langdale Press, 1988).

31   Martell, "Documentary Study of Provincial Finance and Currency," 9.

32   John G. Reid, "Scots in Mi'kma'ki, 1760–1820," *Nashwaak Review* 22/23, no. 1 (2009): 527–57.

33   J.M. Bumsted, *The People's Clearance: Highland Emigration to British North America, 1770–1815* (Winnipeg: University of Manitoba, 1982).

34   Rusty Bittermann, "The Hierarchy of the Soil: Land and Labour in a 19th Century Cape Breton Community, *Acadiensis* 18, no. 1 (1988): 33–55, and Rusty Bittermann, Robert A. MacKinnon, and Graeme Wynn, "Of Inequality and Interdependence in the Nova Scotia Countryside, 1850–70," *Canadian Historical Review* 84, no. 1 (1993): 1–43.

35   Lucille H. Campey, *After the Hector: The Scottish Pioneers of Nova Scotia and Cape Breton, 1773–1852* (Toronto: Natural Heritage Books, 2004); Marjory Harper and Jonathan Vance, eds., *Myth, Migration, and the Making of Memory: Scotia and Nova Scotia c. 1700–1990* (Halifax: Grosebrook Institute, 1999); Stephen Hornsby, "Scottish Emigration and Settlement in Early Nineteenth-Century Cape Breton," in *The Island: New Perspectives on Cape Breton History, 1713–1990*, ed. Kenneth Donovan (Fredericton; Sydney: Acadiensis Press and University College of Cape Breton Press, 1990), 49–69; D. Campbell and R.A. MacLean, *Beyond the Atlantic Roar: A Study of Nova Scotia Scots* (Toronto: McClelland & Stewart, 1974); and J.S. Martell, *Immigration to and Emigration From Nova Scotia, 1815–1838* (Halifax: Public Archives of Nova Scotia, 1942), 8–14.

36   Cited in Margaret MacDonell, *The Emigrant Experience: Songs of Highland Emigrants in North America* (Toronto: University of Toronto Press, 1982), 73, 91, 93.

37   S. Buggy, "Edward Mortimer," *Dictionary of Canadian Biography Online*.

38   Terrence M. Punch, "Anti-Irish Prejudice in Nineteenth-Century Nova Scotia: The Literary and Statistical Evidence," in *The Irish in Atlantic Canada, 1780–1900*, ed. Thomas P. Power (Fredericton: New Ireland Press, 1991), 18.

39   Cited in Herbert Leslie Stewart, *The Irish in Nova Scotia: Annals of the Charitable Irish Society of Halifax, 1786–1836* (Kentville, NS: Kentville Publishing, 1949), 27.

40   Brian Cuthbertson, *The Old Attorney General: A Biography of Richard John Uniacke, 1753–1830* (Halifax: Nimbus, 1980), 37–8.

41   B.C. Cuthbertson, "Richard John Uniacke," *Dictionary of Canadian Biography Online.*

42   George Patterson, *A History of the County of Pictou* (1877; Belleville, ON: Mika Studio, 1972), 293–5.

43   Gillen D'Arcy Wood, *Tambora: The Eruption that Changed the World* (Princeton, NJ: Princeton University Press, 2014); C.R. Harington, ed., *The Year Without a Summer? World Climate in 1816* (Ottawa: Canadian Museum of Nature, 1992); and Teresa Devor, "The Explanatory Power of Climate History for the 19th-Century Maritimes and Newfoundland: A Prospectus," *Acadiensis* 43, no. 2 (2014): 57–78.

44   J.S. Martell, "Military Settlements in Nova Scotia after the War of 1812," *Nova Scotia Historical Society Collections* 24 (1938): 75–106.

45   Peter Thomas, *Strangers from a Secret Land: The Voyages of the Brig Albion and the Founding of the First Welsh Settlements in Canada* (Toronto: University of Toronto Press, 1986), 254.

46   Martell, *Immigration to and Emigration from Nova Scotia,* 19–21.

47   Cited in Daniel Samson, *The Spirit of Industry and Improvement: Liberal Government and Rural-Industrial Society, Nova Scotia, 1790–1862* (Montreal: McGill-Queen's University Press, 2008), 42.

48   Judith Fingard, "Sir John Wentworth," and Judith Tulloch, "William Cottnam Tonge," *Dictionary of Canadian Biography Online.* See also Samson, *Spirit of Industry and Improvement,* 93–4.

49   Peter Burroughs, "Sir George Prevost," *Dictionary of Canadian Biography Online.*

50   Judith Tulloch, "William Cottnam Tonge," *Dictionary of Canadian Biography Online.*

51   D.C. Harvey, "A Documentary Study of the Origins and Distribution of the Arms Fund," *Bulletin of the Public Archives of Nova Scotia* 2, no. 4 (1947).

52   Peter Burroughs, "Sir John Coape Sherbrooke," *Dictionary of Canadian Biography Online.*

53   Martell, "Documentary Study of Provincial Finance and Currency."

54   Peter Burroughs, "George Ramsay, 9th Earl of Dalhousie," and "Sir James Kempt," *Dictionary of Canadian Biography Online.*

55   David Bell, *The Newlight Baptist Journals of James Manning and James Innis* (Hantsport, NS: Lancelot Press and Acadia Divinity College, 1984), xiii.

56   Ibid., 19.

57   Julian Gwyn, "The Kings County World of the Reverend Edward Manning to 1846," *Journal of the Royal Nova Scotia Historical Society* 16 (2013): 1–18.

58 George Rawlyk, *Ravished by the Spirit: Religious Revivals, Baptists, and Henry Alline* (Montreal: McGill-Queen's University Press, 1984), 90. See also, G.A. Rawlyk, "From Newlight to Baptist: Harris Harding and the Second Great Awakening in Nova Scotia," in *Repent and Believe: The Baptist Experience in Maritime Canada*, ed. Barry Moody (Hantsport, NS: Lancelot Press, 1980), 1–26.

59 Burroughs, "George Ramsay."

60 Cited in Rawlyk, *Ravished by the Spirit*, 123.

61 Alan Wilson, "The Reverend James MacGregor, Highland Shepherd," in *Journal of the Royal Nova Scotia Historical Society* 17 (2014): 16–31, and his book-length biography, *Highland Shepherd: James MacGregor, Father of the Scottish Enlightenment in Nova Scotia* (Toronto: University of Toronto Press, 2015). See also Susan Buggey, "James Drummond MacGregor," *Dictionary of Canadian Biography Online*.

62 Sara Beanlands, "The Rev. Dr. Andrew Brown: Nova Scotia's Elusive Historian," *Journal of the Royal Nova Scotia Historical Society* 9 (2006): 75–99. See also Elizabeth Townsend et al., *A Sentinel on the Street: St. Matthew's United Church, Halifax 1749–1999* (Halifax: Nimbus, 1999) and Pamela Bruce, "Donald Allan Fraser," and George Shepperson, "Andrew Brown," *Dictionary of Canadian Biography Online*.

63 Susan Buggey and Gwendolyn Davies, "Thomas McCulloch," *Dictionary of Canadian Biography Online*.

64 Thomas McCulloch, "A lecture, delivered at the opening of the first theological class in the Pictou academical institution" (Glasgow, 1821), cited in Buggey and Davies, "Thomas McCulloch."

65 Phyllis C. Wagg, "Father William Phelan: An Irish Trouble-Maker in Arichat," *Nova Scotia Historical Review* 6, no. 1 (1986), 77.

66 Bernard Pothier, "Jean-Mandé Sigogne," *Dictionary of Canadian Biography Online*.

67 J. Brian Hanington, *Every Popish Person: The Story of Roman Catholicism and the Church of Halifax*, 1604–1984 (Halifax: Archdiocese of Halifax, 1984), 60–73, and R.A. MacLean, "Edmund Burke," *Dictionary of Canadian Biography Online*.

68 Cited in Sally Ross and Alphonse Deveau, *The Acadians of Nova Scotia Past and Present* (Halifax: Nimbus, 1992), 121.

69 Robert J. Morgan, *Rise Again! The Story of Cape Breton Island, Book One* (Wreck Cove, NS: Breton Books, 2008).

70 Stephen J. Hornsby, *Nineteenth-Century Cape Breton: A Historical Geography* (Montreal: McGill-Queen's University Press, 1992), chap. 3.

71 R.J. Morgan, "Sir John Despard," *Dictionary of Canadian Biography Online*.

72   Robert Morgan, "Separatism in Cape Breton, 1820–1845," in *Cape Breton at 200: Historical Essays in Honour of the Island's Bicentennial, 1785–1985*, ed. Kenneth Donovan (Sydney: University College of Cape Breton Press, 1985), 41–51.

73   Judith Fingard, "English Humanitarianism and the Colonial Mind: Walter Bromley in Nova Scotia, 1813–25," *Canadian Historical Review* 54, no. 2 (1973): 123–51, and "Walter Bromley," *Dictionary of Canadian Biography Online*.

74   Upton, *Micmacs and Colonists*, 164–5, and "Louis-Benjamin Peminuit Paul," *Dictionary of Canadian Biography Online*.

75   R.A. MacLean, "John Young," *Dictionary of Canadian Biography Online*; See also Graeme Wynn, "Exciting a Spirit of Emulation among the 'Plodholes': Agricultural Reform in Pre-Confederation Nova Scotia," *Acadiensis* 20, no. 1 (1990): 5–51.

76   Susan Buggey, "Charles Ramage Prescott," *Dictionary of Canadian Biography Online*.

77   Cited in Allan Everett Marble, *Surgeons, Smallpox, and the Poor: A History of Medical and Social Conditions in Nova Scotia, 1749–1799* (Montreal: McGill-Queen's University Press, 1993), 183.

78   Judith Fingard, "The Winter's Tale: The Seasonal Contours of Pre-Industrial Poverty in British North America, 1815–1860," *Historical Papers* 9, no. 1 (1974): 65–94.

79   Donald. C. MacKay and Sandra Paikowsky, "Joseph Brown Comingo," *Dictionary of Canadian Biography Online*.

80   "Government House," *Nova Scotia Archives Bulletin* 1 (1937–8): 5.

10. Bluenoses and Britons, 1820–1854

1   Karl Polanyi, *The Great Transformation* (New York: Farrer & Rinehart, 1944).

2   Census of Nova Scotia, 1851 and 1861, published in *Censuses of Canada, 1665 to 1871*, vol. 4 (Ottawa, 1876). See also Stephen J. Hornsby, *Nineteenth-Century Cape Breton: A Historical Geography* (Montreal: McGill-Queen's University Press, 1992), 121–2; Douglas F. Campbell and David C. Neice, *Ties that Bind: Structure and Marriage in Nova Scotia* (Port Credit, ON: Scribblers' Press, 1979), 41–3; and Ellen M. Gee, "Marriage in Nineteenth-Century Canada," *Canadian Review of Sociology and Anthropology* 19, no. 3 (1982): 311–25.

3   In this period, a "boat" was usually a small, undecked craft, while a "vessel" had at least one deck.

4   Julian Gwyn, *Excessive Expectations: Maritime Commerce and the Economic Development of Nova Scotia, 1740–1870* (Montreal: McGill-Queen's University Press, 1998), 45.

5   "The Blue Nose," in *Joseph Howe: Poems and Essays*, ed. M.G. Parkes
    (Toronto: University of Toronto Press, 1973), 145–6, and J. Murray Beck,
    Joseph Howe, 2 v. (Montreal: McGill-Queen's University Press, 1982/1983).

6   Parkes, *Joseph Howe*, 16.

7   Thomas C. Haliburton, *The Clockmaker* (1836; reprint Toronto: McClelland &
    Stewart, 1958), 50. See also Richard A. Davies, *Inventing Sam Slick:
    A Biography of Thomas Chandler Haliburton* (Toronto: University of
    Toronto Press, 2005). In Haliburton's view, the Scots were not Bluenoses:
    "'What success had you,' said I, 'in the sale of clocks among the Scotch
    in the eastern part of the Province? Do you find them as gullible as the
    Bluenoses?'" (69).

8   Phillip Buckner, "Whatever Happened to the 'British' Empire?" *Journal of
    the Canadian Historical Association* 4 (1993): 3–32.

9   Philip Girard, *Lawyers and Legal Culture in British North America: Beamish
    Murdoch of Halifax* (Toronto: University of Toronto Press, 2011), 155. See also
    K.G. Pryke, "Beamish Murdoch," *Dictionary of Canadian Biography Online*.

10 Harold Innis, *The Cod Fisheries: The History of an International Economy*,
    rev. ed. (Toronto: University of Toronto Press, 1954), 256, and Gwyn,
    Excessive Expectations, 41–89.

11 John Homer, *A Brief Sketch of the Present State of the Province of Nova-Scotia,
    with a project for its relief* (Halifax, 1834).

12 Homer, *Brief Sketch of the Present State of the Province of Nova-Scotia*, 9.

13 Haliburton, *Clockmaker*, 14, 26, 51.

14 David Sutherland, "Charles Rufus Fairbanks," *Dictionary of Canadian
    Biography Online*.

15 Marilyn Gerriets, "The Rise and Fall of a Free-Standing Company in
    Nova Scotia: The General Mining Association," *Business History* 34, no. 3
    (1992): 16–48, and "The Impact of the General Mining Association on the
    Nova Scotia Coal Industry, 1826–1850," *Acadiensis* 21, no. 1 (1991): 54–84.
    See also J.S. Martell, "Early Coal Mining in Nova Scotia," *Dalhousie
    Review* 25, no. 2 (1945): 156–72; Daniel Samson, *The Spirit of Industry and
    Improvement: Liberal Government and Rural-Industrial Society, Nova Scotia,
    1790–1862* (Montreal: McGill-Queen's University Press, 2008), chap. 5,
    and Hornsby, *Nineteenth-Century Cape Breton*, 95–107.

16 David Frank, "Richard Smith," *Dictionary of Canadian Biography Online*;
    Samson, *Spirit of Industry and Improvement*, 176–8.

17 George Patterson, *History of the County of Pictou, Nova Scotia* (Montreal:
    Dawson Brothers, 1877), 406–7.

18 John Boileau, *Samuel Cunard: Nova Scotia's Master of the North Atlantic*
    (Halifax: Formac, 2006); John G. Langley, *Steam Lion: A Biography of
    Samuel Cunard* (Halifax: Nimbus, 2006); and Phyllis Blakeley, "Sir Samuel
    Cunard," *Dictionary of Canadian Biography Online*.

19 Gwyn, *Excessive Expectations*, 165–76.
20 Rusty Bittermann, *Rural Protest on Prince Edward Island: From British Colonialism to the Escheat Movement* (Toronto: University of Toronto Press, 2006), 226–7, 251.
21 Blakeley, "Sir Samuel Cunard."
22 Richard A. Davies, "Thomas Chandler Haliburton and Steamships," *Journal of the Royal Nova Scotia Historical Society* 12 (2009), 108–9, and Charles Dickens, *American Notes* (1842), available online at https://archive.org/details/americannotesfo13dickgoog.
23 J.S. Martell, "A Documentary Study of Provincial Finance and Currency, 1812–36," *Bulletin Public Archives of Nova Scotia* 2, no. 4 (1941): 21.
24 Diane M. Barker and D.A. Sutherland, "Enos Collins," *Dictionary of Canadian Biography Online*.
25 D.A. Sutherland, "Sir Edward Kenny," *Dictionary of Canadian Biography Online*.
26 K.G. Pryke, "Alexander Keith," *Dictionary of Canadian Biography Online*.
27 Judith Fingard, Janet Guildford, and David Sutherland, *Halifax: The First Two Hundred and Fifty Years* (Halifax: Formac 1999), 67–8, and K.G. Pryke, "William Murdoch," *Dictionary of Canadian Biography Online*.
28 James D. Frost, *Merchant Princes: Halifax's First Family of Finances, Ships and Steel* (Halifax: Formac, 2003). See also David A. Sutherland, "William Machin Stairs," and J.B. Cahill, "William James Stairs," *Dictionary of Canadian Biography Online*.
29 A.A. MacKenzie, "Amos Peck Seaman," *Dictionary of Canadian Biography Online*. See also Samson, *Spirit of Industry*, 123–40.
30 Samson, *Spirit of Industry*, 226–33, 241–7, 260.
31 Mary Byers and Margaret McBurney, *Atlantic Hearth: Early Homes and Families of Nova Scotia* (Toronto: University of Toronto Press, 1994), 307, cited in Samson, *Spirit of Industry*, 233.
32 J.S. Martell, *Immigration to and Emigration from Nova Scotia, 1815–1838* (Halifax: Public Archives of Nova Scotia, 1942), 11.
33 Cited in Laurie Stanley, *The Well-Watered Garden: The Presbyterian Church in Cape Breton, 1798–1860* (Sydney: University College of Cape Breton Press, 1983), 82.
34 Ibid., 6–7, 64–84.
35 Martell, *Immigration to and Emigration from Nova Scotia*, 12–14.
36 Madeline Fowler, "From Empire to Colony: The Halifax Cholera Outbreaks of 1834 and 1866," *Acadiensis* 47, no. 2 (2018): 51.
37 Cited in Martel, *Immigration to and Emigration from Nova Scotia*, 27.
38 Fowler, "From Empire to Colony," 44–61.
39 Lucille H. Campey, *After the Hector: The Scottish Pioneers of Nova Scotia and Cape Breton, 1773–1852* (Toronto: Natural Heritage Books, 2004), 10.

40 Hornsby, *Nineteenth-Century Cape Breton*, 111–20.
41 Cited in Robert Morgan, *Early Cape Breton: From Founding to Famine, 1748–1851* (Sydney: Breton Books, 2000), 141.
42 Stanley, *Well-Watered Garden*, 150–70, and R. MacLean, "Norman McLeod," *Dictionary of Canadian Biography Online*. The quoted phrases can be found in D.C. Harvey, ed., "Letters of Rev. Norman McLeod, 1835–51," *Bulletin of the Public Archives of Nova Scotia* 2, no. 1 (1939), 22, 26.
43 "Free Church of Scotland, 1843–1900," in *Dictionary of Scottish Church History and Theology*, ed. Nigel M. de S. Cameron (Downers Grove, IL: Intervarsity Press, 1993), 337–8.
44 E. Arthur Betts, "John Stewart," *Dictionary of Canadian Biography Online*.
45 Thomas Chandler Haliburton, *The Old Judge, or, Life in a Colony* (1849, reprint Ottawa: Tecumseh Press, 1978), 304–5.
46 D.C. Harvey, "The Intellectual Awakening of Nova Scotia," *Dalhousie Review* 13 (April 1933): 1–22.
47 The best analysis of the significance of public schooling in British North America can be found in Bruce Curtis, *Building the Educational State: Canada West, 1836–1871* (London: Falmer Press, 1988)
48 [Winnifred McFatridge], "A Documentary Study of Early Education Policy," *Public Archives of Nova Scotia Bulletin* 1, no. 1 (1937).
49 Cited in Judith Fingard, "Attitudes towards the Education of the Poor in Colonial Halifax," *Acadiensis* 2, no. 2 (1973): 29, 37.
50 Charles Bruce Fergusson, *The Inauguration of the Free School System in Nova Scotia* (Halifax: Public Archives of Nova Scotia, 1964).
51 Theresa Corcoran, *Mount Saint Vincent University: A Vision Unfolding, 1873–1988* (Lanham, MD: University Press of America, 1999), 5–7.
52 James D. Cameron, *For the People: History of Saint Francis Xavier University* (Montreal: McGill-Queen's University Press, 1996) and R.A. MacLean, "Charles Francis MacKinnon," *Dictionary of Canadian Biography Online*.
53 Barry Moody, "The Maritime Baptists and Higher Education in the Early Nineteenth Century," in *Repent and Believe: The Baptist Experience in Maritime Canada*, ed. Barry Moody (Hantsport, NS: Lancelot Press, 1980), 97. See also D.A. Sutherland, "James William Johnston" and Barry Moody, "Edmund Albern Crawley," *Dictionary of Canadian Biography Online*.
54 The rivalry in higher education is summarized in P.B. Waite, *The Lives of Dalhousie University*, vol. 1, *1818–1925, Lord Dalhousie's College* (Montreal: McGill-Queen's University, 1994), 46–69.
55 Susan Buggey and Gwendolyn Davies, "Thomas McCulloch," *Dictionary of Canadian Biography Online*.
56 Peter R. Eakins and Jean Sinnamon Eakins, "Sir John William Dawson," *Dictionary of Canadian Biography Online*.

57 Karen Smith, "Community Libraries," in *History of the Book in Canada*, vol. 1, *Beginnings to 1840*, ed. Patricia Lockhart Fleming, Gilles Gallichan, and Yvan Lamond (Toronto: University of Toronto Press, 2004), 144–51.

58 Samson, *Spirit of Industry*, 247.

59 Benedict Anderson, *Imagined Communities: Reflections on the Origin and Spread of Nationalism*, rev. ed. (New York: Verso, 1991) and Michael Eamon, *Imprinting Britain: Newspapers, Sociability, and the Shaping of British North America* (Montreal: McGill-Queen's University Press, 2015).

60 Trais Decook, "The Spread of Newspapers in British North America," in Fleming, Gallichan, and Lamond, *History of the Book in Canada*, vol. 1, 229.

61 Gwendolyn Davies, "Penetrating into Scott's Field: The Covenanting Fiction of Thomas McCulloch," in *Studies in Maritime Literary History, 1760–1930* (Fredericton: Acadiensis Press, 1991), 63–70.

62 Gwendolyn Davies, "Haliburton's Literary Apprenticeship," in *Studies in Maritime Literary History*, 88–106.

63 K.G. Pryke "John Boyd," *Dictionary of Canadian Biography Online*.

64 George L. Parker, "Edmund Ward," and Gertrude Tratt, "Anthony Henry Holland," *Dictionary of Canadian Biography Online*.

65 J. Murray Beck, "Jotham Blanchard," *Dictionary of Canadian Biography Online*.

66 Janet Guildford, "Maria Morris Miller: The Many Functions of Art," *Atlantis* 20, no. 1 (1995): 113–23.

67 Terrence M. Punch, "Titus Smith," *Dictionary of Canadian Biography Online*.

68 *The Halifax Public Gardens* (Halifax: Friends of the Public Gardens, 1989).

69 Loris S. Russell, "Abraham Gesner," *Dictionary of Canadian Biography Online*.

70 Terrance M. Punch, "Charles Fenerty," *Dictionary of Canadian Biography Online*.

71 Carol Anne Janzen, "Eliza Ann Chipman," *Dictionary of Canadian Biography Online*, and James Doyle Davidson, *Eliza of Pleasant Valley* (Wolfville, NS: James Doyle Davidson, 1983).

72 Gwendolyn Davies, "'Dearer Than His Dog': Literary Women in Pre-Confederation Nova Scotia," in *Studies in Maritime Literary History*, 71–87. See also Davies, "Sarah Herbert," and "Mary Eliza Herbert," and Lois K. Kernaghan, "Mary Jane Katzmann," *Dictionary of Canadian Biography Online*.

73 Gwendolyn Davies, "William Charles M'Kinnon, Cape Breton's Sir Walter Scott," in *Studies in Maritime Literary History*, 107–29, and Minerva Tracy, "William Charles McKinnon," *Dictionary of Canadian Biography Online*.

74 Ian McKay and Robin Bates, *In the Province of History: The Making of a Public Past in Twentieth-Century Nova Scotia* (Montreal: McGill-Queen's

University Press, 2010), 71–129; Naomi Griffiths, "Longfellow's *Evangeline*: The Birth and Acceptance of a Legend," *Acadiensis* 11, no. 2 (1982): 28–41; Barbara Le Blanc, *Postcards from Acadie: Grand Pré, Evangeline & the Acadian Identity* (Kentville, NS: Gaspereau Press, 2003); and Peter Morris, *Embattled Shadows: A History of Canadian Cinema, 1895–1939* (Montreal: McGill-Queen's University Press, 1978), 50.

75 McKay and Bates, *In the Province of History*, 97–8; Brian C. Cuthbertson, "Thomas Beamish Akins: British North America's Pioneer Archivist," *Acadiensis* 7, no. 1 (1977), 88, and B.C. Cuthbertson, "Thomas Beamish Akins," *Dictionary of Canadian Biography Online*.

76 P.D. Clarke, "Beamish Murdoch: Nova Scotia's National Historian," *Acadiensis* 21, no. 1 (1991): 85–109. On Canadian historiography before Confederation, see M. Brook Taylor, *Promoters, Patriots, and Partisans: Historiography in Nineteenth-Century English Canada* (Toronto: University of Toronto Press, 1989).

77 Margaret Conrad, "'An Abiding Conviction of the Paramount Importance of Christian Education': Theodore Harding Rand as Educator, 1860–1900," in *An Abiding Conviction: Maritime Baptists and Their World*, ed. Robert S. Wilson (Saint John: Acadia Divinity College and the Baptist Historical Committee of the United Baptist Convention of the Atlantic Provinces, 1988), 155–95.

78 Janet Guildford, "Creating the Ideal Man: Middle-Class Women's Constructions of Masculinity in Nova Scotia, 1840–1880," *Acadiensis* 24, no. 2 (1995): 5–23.

79 A.J. "Sandy" Young, *Beyond Heroes: A Sport History of Nova Scotia*, vol. 2 (Hantsport, NS: Lancelot Press, 1988), 57–9.

80 Ibid., 72, 14–15, 146.

81 Anthony D. Barlow, "Heritage Recording of the Starr Manufacturing Company Factory," in *Industry and Society in Nova Scotia: An Illustrated History*, ed. James E. Candow (Halifax: Fernwood, 2001), 197–215.

82 Young, *Beyond Heroes*, vol. 1, 42.

83 L.S.F. Upton, *Micmacs and Colonists: Indian-White Relations in the Maritimes, 1713–1867* (Vancouver: UBC, 1979), 81.

84 Andrew Parnaby, "The Cultural Economy of Survival: The Mi'kmaq of Cape Breton in the mid-19th-Century," *Labour* 61 (Spring 2008): 69–96.

85 *Historical Atlas of Canada*, vol. 2, plate 33.

86 L.S.F. Upton, "Andrew James Meuse," and "Louis-Benjamin Peminuit Paul," *Dictionary of Canadian Biography Online*.

87 Cited in Ruth Holmes Whitehead, *The Old Man Told Us: Excerpts from Micmac History, 1500–1950* (Halifax: Nimbus, 1991), 218.

88 Cited in Ruth Holmes Whitehead, *The Old Man Told Us: Excerpts from Micmac History, 1500–1950* (Halifax: Nimbus, 1991), 240. See also Courtney

Mrazek, "'Our Nation is like a withering leaf on a summer's day': The Mi'kmaq and British Agricultural Policies in Colonial Nova Scotia" (MA thesis, Saint Mary's University, 2016); Jennifer Reid, *Myth, Symbol, and Colonial Encounter: British and Mi'kmaq in Acadia, 1700–1867* (Ottawa: University of Ottawa Press, 1995), 36; and Elizabeth Haigh, "They Must Cultivate the Land: Abraham Gesner as Indian Commissioner, 1847–1853," *Journal of the Royal Nova Scotia Historical Society* 3 (2000): 54–70.

89 Upton, *Micmacs and Colonists*, 140.

90 Judith Fingard, "Silas Tertius Rand," *Dictionary of Canadian Biography Online.*

91 Stephen Davidson, "John Burton," *Dictionary of Canadian Biography Online.*

92 Frank S. Boyd Jr, "Richard Preston," *Dictionary of Canadian Biography Online.*

93 Bridglal Pachai, *The Nova Scotia Black Experience through the Centuries* (Halifax: Nimbus, 2007), 97–9.

94 David A. Sutherland, "Race Relations in Halifax, Nova Scotia, during the Mid-Victorian Quest for Reform," *Journal of the Canadian Historical Association* 7 (1996): 35–54.

95 Ibid., 44–54.

96 David Sutherland, "Voluntary Societies and the Process of Middle-Class Formation in Early Victorian Halifax," *Journal of the Canadian Historical Association* 5 (1994): 237–63.

97 Judith Fingard, *Jack in Port: Sailortowns in Eastern Canada* (Toronto: University of Toronto Press, 1982) and Colin Howell and Richard Twomey, eds., *Jack Tar in History: Essays in the History of Maritime Life and Labour* (Fredericton: Acadiensis Press, 1991).

98 David Sutherland, "Violence, Sex, and Politics in Mid-Victorian Halifax: The *Winchester* Affair of 1853," *Journal of the Royal Nova Scotia Historical Society* 5 (2002): 94–105.

99 Brian Cuthbertson, *Johnny Bluenose at the Polls: Epic Nova Scotian Election Battles, 1758–1848* (Halifax: Formac, 1994), 1–27, 256, 275–80.

100 John Garner, *The Franchise and Politics in British North America, 1755–1867* (Toronto: University of Toronto Press, 1969), 56.

101 Samson, *Spirit of Industry and Improvement*, 164–86.

102 B.C. Cuthbertson, "Richard John Uniacke, [Jr]" *Dictionary of Canadian Biography Online.*

103 Robert Sedgewick, *The Proper Sphere and Influence of Woman in Christian Society: Lecture to the Young Men's Christian Society* (Halifax, 1856), available online at http://eco.canadiana.ca/view/oocihm.64166/6?r=0&s=1. See also Philip Girard, "Robert Sedgewick," *Dictionary of Canadian Biography Online.*

104 Jan Noel, *Canada Dry: Temperance Crusades Before Confederation* (Toronto: University of Toronto Press, 1995), 17–40, and James H. Morrison and James Moreira, eds., *Tempered by Rum: Rum in the History of the Maritime Provinces* (Porters Lake, NS: Pottersfield Press, 1988).

105 J. Brian Hanington, *Every Popish Person: The Story of Roman Catholicism and the Church of Halifax, 1604–1984* (Halifax: Archdiocese of Halifax, 1984), 80–1.

106 Innis, *Cod Fishery*, 273.

107 Cited in Sandra Barry, "Shades of Vice and Moral Glory: The Temperance Movement in Nova Scotia, 1828–1848" (MA thesis, University of New Brunswick, 1986), 13.

108 Barry, "Shades of Vice and Moral Glory," 270.

109 Julian Gwyn reports that the trade in rum dropped from 895,000 gallons (more than 4 million litres) in 1832–3 to 60,000 gallons (about 273,000 litres) in 1852–3 without a significant increase in local production, which stood at roughly 20,000 (91,00 litres), *Excessive Expectations*, 49.

110 Barry, "Shades of Vice and Moral Glory," 212.

11. Making Progress, 1820–1864

1 Phyllis R. Blakeley, "Sir Brenton Halliburton," *Dictionary of Canadian Biography Online*.

2 For a detailed examination of the workings of representative government in Nova Scotia, see Brian Cuthbertson, *Johnny Bluenose at the Polls: Epic Nova Scotian Election Battles, 1758–1848* (Halifax: Formac, 1994).

3 Janet Ajzenstat, "The Constitutionalism of Étienne Parent and Joseph Howe," in *Canadian Constitutionalism: 1791–1991*, ed. Janet Ajzenstat (Ottawa: Canadian Study of Parliament Group, [1992]), 159–76.

4 J. Murray Beck, *Joseph Howe*, vol. 1, *Conservative Reformer, 1804–1848* (Montreal: McGill-Queen's University Press, 1982), 109–28, and "Joseph Howe," *Dictionary of Canadian Biography Online*.

5 Beck, *Joseph Howe*, vol. 1, 133.

6 D.A. Sutherland, "William Wilkie," *Dictionary of Canadian Biography Online*.

7 Beck, *Joseph Howe*, vol. 1, 145.

8 Ibid., 161–5; Charles Bruce Fergusson, "Laurence O'Connor Doyle," *Dictionary of Canadian Biography Online*; and Terrence Murphy, "'Religion Marched Forth in All Her Majesty': The Opening of Holy Cross Cemetery and the Transformation of Halifax Catholicism," *Journal of the Royal Nova Scotia Historical Society* 18 (2015): 77–88.

9 Beck, *Joseph Howe*, vol. 1, 162.

10   "Howe's Fourth Letter to Lord John Russell," in *Joseph Howe: Opportunist? Man of Vision? Frustrated Politician?* ed. G.A. Rawlyk (Toronto: Copp Clark, n.d.), 74–5.

11   J. Murray Beck, *Politics of Nova Scotia*, vol. 1, *1710–1896* (Tantallon, NS: Four East Publications, 1985), 116–18, and A.A. Mackenzie, "Herbert Huntington," *Dictionary of Canadian Biography Online*.

12   Sutherland, "James William Johnston," and J. Murray Beck, "James Boyle Uniacke," *Dictionary of Canadian Biography Online*.

13   Beck, *Joseph Howe*, vol. 1, 274–5.

14   David A. Sutherland, "Race Relations in Halifax, Nova Scotia, during the Mid-Victorian Quest for Reform," *Journal of the Canadian Historical Association* 7 (1996): 35–54.

15   Phillip A. Buckner, *The Transition to Responsible Government: British Policy in British North America, 1815–1850* (Westport, CT: Greenwood Press, 1985), 291–306.

16   J. Murray Beck, *Joseph Howe*, vol. 2, *The Briton Becomes Canadian, 1848–1873* (Montreal: McGill-Queen's University Press, 1983), 3–25.

17   Buckner, *Transition to Responsible Government*, 304.

18   Gwynneth C.D. Jones, "Frederic Newton Gisborne," *Dictionary of Canadian Biography Online*.

19   Beck, *Joseph Howe*, vol. 2, 35.

20   Ibid., 37.

21   John Garner, *The Franchise and Politics in British North America, 1755–1867* (Toronto: University of Toronto Press, 1969), 32–3, 155–6, 160–1, and Cuthbertson, *Johnny Bluenose at the Polls*, 6; Nova Scotia Legislature, "History of Voting in Nova Scotia," available online at https://nslegislature.ca/about/history/history-voting-nova-scotia.

22   Philip Girard, "Married Women's Property, Chancery Abolition, and Insolvency Law: Law Reform in Nova Scotia, 1820–1867," and Kimberley Smith Maynard, "Divorce in Nova Scotia, 1750–1890," in *Essays in the History of Canadian Law, III, Nova Scotia*, ed. Philip Girard and Jim Phillips (Toronto: University of Toronto Press 1990), 80–127.

23   Phillip Buckner, "Charles Tupper," *Dictionary of Canadian Biography Online*

24   Beck, *Joseph Howe*, vol. 2, 145, and Terrence Punch, "Joe Howe and the Irish," *Collections of the Nova Scotia Historical Society* 41 (1982): 119–40.

25   Marilyn Gerriets, "The Impact of the General Mining Association on the Nova Scotia Coal Industry, 1826–1850," *Acadiensis* 21, no. 1 (1991): 54–84.

26   David A. Sutherland, "William Annand," and K.G. Pryke, "Sir Adams George Archibald," *Dictionary of Canadian Biography Online*.

27   Rosemary Langhout, "Developing Nova Scotia: Railways and Public Accounts, 1849–1867," *Acadiensis* 14, no. 2 (1985): 3–28.

28 Beck, *Joseph Howe*, vol. 2, 169–73, and Garner, *Franchise and Politics in British North America*, 34–6.

29 Julian Gwyn: "Golden Age or Bronze Moment? Wealth and Poverty in Nova Scotia: The 1850s and 1860s," *Canadian Papers in Rural History* 8 (1992): 195–230, and "Imports and the Changing Standard of Living in Nova Scotia, 1832–1875," *Nova Scotia Historical Review* 11 (1991): 43–64. See also Julian Gwyn and Fazley Siddiq, "Wealth Distribution in Nova Scotia during the Confederation Era, 1851 and 1871," *Canadian Historical Review* 73 (December 1992): 435–52; Robert A. MacKinnon and Graeme Wynn, "Nova Scotian Agriculture in the 'Golden Age': A New Look," in *Geographical Perspectives on the Maritime Provinces*, ed. Douglas Day et al. (Halifax: Saint Mary's University, 1988), 47–60; and Kris Inwood and James Irwin, "Canadian Regional Commodity Income Differentials at Confederation," in Kris Inwood, ed., *Farm, Factory and Fortune: New Studies in the Economic History of the Maritime Provinces* (Fredericton: Acadiensis Press, 1993), 93–120.

30 Marilyn Gerriets and Julian Gwyn, "Tariffs, Trade and Reciprocity: Nova Scotia, 1830–1866," *Acadiensis* 25, no. 2 (1996): 62–82. See also D.C. Masters, *The Reciprocity Treaty of 1854* (1937; Toronto: McClelland & Stewart, 1963); D.A. Sutherland, "Nova Scotia and the American Presence: Seeking Connections without Conquest, 1848–1854," in *New England and the Maritime Provinces: Connections and Comparisons*, ed. Stephen J. Hornsby and John G. Reid (Montreal: McGill-Queen's University Press, 2005), 144–58; R.H. McDonald, "Nova Scotia and the Reciprocity Negotiation, 1845–1854: A Re-interpretation," *Nova Scotia Historical Quarterly* (1977): 205–34; and S.A. Saunders, "The Reciprocity Treaty of 1854: A Regional Study," *Canadian Journal of Economics and Political Science* (February–November, 1936): 41–53.

31 Nova Scotia, *A Submission of its Claims with respect to Maritime Disabilities within Confederation* (Halifax, 1926), 154; Duncan Campbell, *Nova Scotia in Its Historical, Mercantile, and Industrial Relations* (Montreal: James Lovell, 1873), 319.

32 Gerriets and Gwyn, "Tariffs, Trade and Reciprocity," 79–80.

33 Greg Marquis, *In Armageddon's Shadow: The Civil War and Canada's Maritime Provinces* (Montreal: McGill-Queen's University Press, 1998), 41–2.

34 Eric W. Sager and Gerald E. Panting, *Maritime Capital: The Shipping Industry in Atlantic Canada, 1820–1914* (Montreal: McGill-Queen's University Press, 1990) and *Shipping and Shipbuilding in Atlantic Canada, 1820–1914* (Ottawa: Canadian Historical Association, 1986). See also Keith Matthews and Gerald Panting, eds., *Ships and Shipbuilding in the North Atlantic Region* (St. John's: Memorial University of Newfoundland, 1978); and *Historical Atlas of Canada, II: The Land Transformed, 1800–1891*

(Toronto: University of Toronto Press, 1993), plate 39. On individual ports, see Rosemary E. Ommer, "'Composed of all Nationalities': The Crews of Windsor Vessels, 1862–1899," and Eric Sager, "Labour Productivity in the Shipping Fleets of Halifax and Yarmouth, Nova Scotia, 1863–1900," in *Working Men Who Got Wet*, ed. Rosemary Ommer and Gerald Panting (St John's: Maritime History Group, Memorial University of Newfoundland, 1980).

35   L. Anders Sandberg, "James William Carmichael," K.G. Pryke, "Thomas Killam," and "Ezra Churchill," Charles A. Armour, "William Dawson Lawrence," and Charles Bruce Fergusson, "Thomas Dickson Archibald," *Dictionary of Canadian Biography Online*. See also Rosemary Langhout, "Alternative Opportunities: The Development of Shipping at Sydney Harbour 1842–1889," in *Cape Breton at 200: Historical Essays in Honour of the Island's Bicentennial 1785–1985*, ed. Kenneth Donovan (Sydney: University College of Cape Breton Press, 1985), 53–70, and Thomas Peace, Jim Clifford, and Judy Burns, "Maitland's Moment: Turning Nova Scotia's Forests into Ships for the Global Commodity Trade in the Mid-Nineteenth-Century," in *Moving Natures: Mobility and the Environment in Canadian History*, ed. Ben Bradley, Jay Young, and Colin M. Coates (Calgary: University of Calgary Press, 2016), 27–54.

36   Aly Thomson, "Nova Scotia 'virtually non-existent' on global business stage, report says," *Globe and Mail*, 1 July 2015.

37   Ian McKay, "Capital and Labour in the Halifax Baking and Confectionary Industry in the Second Half of the Nineteenth Century," *Labour* 3 (1978): 80–6, and "William Church Moir," *Dictionary of Canadian Biography Online*.

38   T.W. Acheson, *Saint John: The Making of a Colonial Urban Community* (Toronto: University of Toronto Press, 1985), 90.

39   Nolan Reilly, "The Rise and Fall of Industrial Amherst, 1860–1930," in *Industry and Society in Nova Scotia: An Illustrated History*, ed. James E. Candow (Halifax: Fernwood, 2001), 129–58.

40   Phillip Buckner, "An End and a Beginning," in *The Atlantic Region to Confederation: A History*, ed. Phillip A. Buckner and John G. Reid (Toronto; Fredericton: University of Toronto Press and Acadiensis Press, 1994), 360–86. See also Nova Scotia Museum, *A History of Mining Activity in Nova Scotia, 1720–1992, Time Line*, available online at https://novascotia.ca/archives/meninmines/timeline.asp?Language=English#1850. On energy politics generally, see Claire Campbell, "Privileges and Entanglements: Lessons from History for Nova Scotia's Politics of Energy," *Acadiensis* 42, no. 2 (2013): 114–37.

41   William D. Naftel, "The Iron Works of Londonderry, 1848–1910," in Candow, *Industry and Society in Nova Scotia*, 19–38. See also Nova Scotia

Archives, "Men in the Mines: A History of Mining Activity in Nova Scotia, 1720–1992, Iron Mining in Nova Scotia," available online at https://novascotia.ca/archives/meninmines/iron.asp?Language=English.

42 Gwyn, *Excessive Expectations*, 96–7. See also Jennifer L.E. Bates, *Gold in Nova Scotia* (Halifax: Department of Mines and Energy, 1987) and "Gold: A Nova Scotia Treasure," Virtual Museum of Canada, available online at http://novascotiagold.ca/index-eng.php.

43 For a glimpse of the gold rush frenzy at its height in Nova Scotia, see *A Practical Guide for Tourists, Miners, and Investors, and All Persons Interested in the Development of the Gold Fields of Nova Scotia*, published by promoter Alexander Heatherington in 1868. Nova Scotia Archives, "Gold Mining in Nova Scotia," available online at https://novascotia.ca/archives/meninmines/gold.asp?Language=English.

44 *Historical Atlas of Canada, II*, plate 37, and B.A. Balcom, "Technology Rejected: Steam Trawlers and Nova Scotia, 1897–1933," in *How Deep Is the Ocean? Historical Essays on Canada's Atlantic Fishery*, ed. James E, Candow and Carol Corbin (Sydney: University College of Cape Breton, 1997), 185–86.

45 Political economist Harold Innis underscored Nova Scotia's preoccupation with the fisheries in a chapter entitled "Mackerel and Confederation," in *The Cod Fisheries: The History of an International Economy* (New Haven, CT: Yale University Press, 1940), 324–74.

46 *Morning Journal and Commercial Advertiser*, 14 December 1859, cited in B.A. Balcom, *History of the Lunenburg Fishery* (Lunenburg, NS: Lunenburg Marine Museum Society, 1977), 15.

47 Brian Cuthburtson, *Lunenburg Then and Now* (Halifax: Formac, 2002).

48 Cited in Ruth Holmes Whitehead, *The Old Man Told Us: Excerpts from Micmac History* (Halifax: Nimbus, 1991), 266–8.

49 Gwyn, *Excessive Expectations*, 109–16; Kris Inwood and Phyllis Wagg, "Wealth and Prosperity in Nova Scotia Agriculture, 1851–71," *Canadian Historical Review* 75, no. 1 (1994): 239–64; Fazley Siddiq, "The Size Distribution of Probate Wealthholdings in Nova Scotia in the Late 19th Century," *Acadiensis* 18, no. 1 (1988): 157–83; Rusty Bittermann, Robert A. MacKinnon, and Graeme Wynn, "Of Inequality and Interdependence in the Nova Scotia Countryside, 1850–1870," *Canadian Historical Review* 74, no. 1 (1993): 1–43; Rusty Bittermann, "Farm Households and Wage Labour in the Northeastern Maritimes in the Early 19th Century," *Labour* 31 (Spring 1993): 13–45; and Alan MacNeil, "Society and Economy in Rural Nova Scotia, 1761–1861" (PhD diss., Queen's University, 1991). Cape Breton is discussed in Stephen J. Hornsby, *Nineteenth-Century Cape Breton: A Historical Geography* (Montreal: McGill-Queen's University Press, 1992), 121–51, and Rusty Bittermann, "The Hierarchy of the Soil: Land and

Labour in a 19th Century Cape Breton Community," *Acadiensis* 18, no. 1 (1988), 33–55.

50 Census of Nova Scotia, 1851 and 1861, published in *Censuses of Canada, 1665 to 1871*, vol. 4 (Ottawa, 1876).

51 Graeme Wynn, "A Region of Scattered Settlements and Bounded Possibilities: Northeastern America 1755–1800," *Canadian Geographer* 31, no. 4 (1987): 319–38.

52 Campbell, *Nova Scotia in its Historical, Mercantile, and Industrial Relations*, 418–32.

53 Margaret Conrad, "Apple Blossom Time in the Annapolis Valley, 1880–1957," *Acadiensis* 9, no. 2 (1980): 14–39.

54 Isabella Lucy Bird, *The Englishwoman in America*, ed. Andrew Hill Clark (1856; Toronto: University of Toronto Press, 1966), 16, 21.

55 Judith Fingard, Janet Guildford, and David Sutherland, *Halifax: The First Two Hundred and Fifty Years* (Halifax: Formac 1999), 75.

56 Jeffrey L. McNairn, "'Everything was new, yet familiar': British Travellers, Halifax and the Ambiguities of Empire," *Acadiensis* 36, no. 2 (2007): 28–54.

57 On the royal visit, see Ian Radforth, *Royal Spectacle: The 1860 Visit of the Prince of Wales to Canada and the United States* (Toronto: University of Toronto Press, 2004), 254–5, 255–7. These responses are contextualized in Ian McKay and Robin Bates, *In the Province of History: The Making of the Public Past in Twentieth-Century Nova Scotia* (Montreal: McGill-Queen's University Press, 2010), 60.

58 Cited in Margaret Conrad, Toni Laidlaw, and Donna Smyth, *No Place Like Home: Diaries and Letters of Nova Scotia Women, 1771–1838* (Halifax: Formac, 1988), 115.

59 The most comprehensive survey of artisans in this period focuses on Saint John, New Brunswick, See Acheson, *Saint John*, chap. 4.

60 Ian McKay, "Class Struggle and Mercantile Capitalism: Craftsmen and Labourers on the Halifax Waterfront, 1850–1902," in Ommer and Panting, *Working Men Who Got Wet*.

61 C. Bruce Fergusson, *The Labour Movement in Nova Scotia before Confederation* (Halifax: Public Archives of Nova Scotia, 1964) and K.G. Pryke, "Labour and Politics: Nova Scotia at Confederation," *Histoire Sociale* 3, no. 6 (1970): 33–55.

62 Pryke, "Labour and Politics: Nova Scotia at Confederation," 34–6.

63 McKay, "Class Struggle," 303.

64 Jennifer L.E. Bates, *Gold in Nova Scotia* (Halifax: Department of Mines and Energy, 1987); Nova Scotia Museum of Industry, "The First Gold Rush," available online at https://museumofindustry.novascotia.ca /nova-scotia-industry/gold-mining/our-gold-rushes; *Novascotian*, 28

October 1861, and "Gold: A Nova Scotia Treasure," *Virtual Museum of Canada*, available online at http://novascotiagold.ca/theme/art /cornelius-eng.php.

65 Ruth Holmes Whitehead, *Micmac Quillwork: Micmac Indian Techniques of Porcupine Quill Decoration, 1600–1950* (Halifax: Nova Scotia Museum, 1982), 201–4, and "Mary Christianne Paul," *Dictionary of Canadian Biography*.

66 G. Brenton Haliburton, *What's Brewing? Oland 1867–1971* (Tantallon, NS: Four East Publications, 1994), 10–23.

67 Janet Guildford, "'Whatever the duty of the hour demands': The Work of Middle-Class Women in Halifax, 1840–1880," *Histoire Sociale* 30, no. 59 (1997): 1–20.

68 James Doyle Davidson, *Alice of Grand Pre: Female Education in Nova Scotia and New Brunswick* (Wolfville, NS: James Doyle Davidson, 1981), 26–32.

69 Mary Ellen Wright, "Unnatural Mothers: Infanticide in Halifax, 1850–1875," *Nova Scotia Historical Review* 7, no. 2 (1987): 13–30.

70 Judith Fingard, *The Dark Side of Life in Victorian Halifax* (Porters Lake, NS: Pottersfield Press, 1989), 31–40. See also Fingard's comparative study, "The Relief of the Unemployed Poor in Saint John, Halifax, and St John's, 1815–1860, *Acadiensis* 5, no. 2 (1985): 32–50.

71 Fingard, *Dark Side of Life in Victorian Halifax*, 15–30, and [James D. Gordon, comp.] *Halifax: "Its Sins and Its Sorrows"* (Halifax: Conference Job Printing Office, 1862).

72 David W. States, "William Hall VC of Horton Bluff, Nova Scotia Nineteenth Century Naval Hero," *Collections of the Royal Nova Scotia Historical Society* 44 (1996): 71–81, and Bridgelal Pashai, "William Hall," *Dictionary of Canadian Biography Online*.

73 Greg Marquis, *In Armageddon's Shadow: The Civil War and Canada's Maritime Provinces* (Montreal: McGill-Queen's University Press, 1998), 105. See also John Boyko, *Blood and Daring: How Canada Fought the American Civil War and Forged a Nation* (Toronto: Knopf, 2013).

74 Beck, *Joseph Howe*, vol. 2, 177, 189.

75 Richard M. Reid, *African Canadians in Union Blue: Volunteering for the Cause in the Civil War* (Vancouver: UBC Press, 2014), 60, 69, 197–201, 205, 209, and Marquis, *In Armageddon's Shadow*, 80–1, 103–33.

76 William Charles Archibald, *Home-making and Its Philosophy: Illustrated by a nesting branch of the Archibalds* (Boston: William Charles Archibald, 1910).

77 Marquis, *In Armageddon's Shadow*, 98–9.

78 On Alexander "Sandy" Keith, the nephew, and other rascals involved in Civil War shenanigans, see Ann Larabee, *The Dynamite Fiend: The Chilling Tale of a Confederate Spy, Con Artist, and Mass Murderer* (London: Palgrave

Macmillan, 2005). See also Pat Lotz, *Banker, Builder, and Blockade Runner: A Victorian Embezzler and His Circle* (Gaspereau, NS: Gaspereau Press, 2002).

79 Marquis, *In Armageddon's Shadow*, 203–5, and Allan Marble, "William Johnston Almon," *Dictionary of Canadian Biography Online*.

80 Marquis, *In Armageddon's Shadow*, 23–8, 32.

81 Ibid., 96.

82 Faye Kert, *Trimming Yankee Sails: Pirates and Privateers of New Brunswick* (Fredericton: Goose Lane Editions and the New Brunswick Military Heritage Project, 2005), 70.

83 Cited in ibid., 78.

84 Marquis, *In Armageddon's Shadow*, chap. 6.

85 Ibid., 223; *New York Times*, 18–19 August 1864.

86 Marquis, *In Armageddon's Shadow*, chap. 7.

87 Phillip Buckner, "Whatever Happened to the British Empire?" *Journal of the Canadian Historical Association* 4 (1993): 3–32, and "British North America and a Continent in Dissolution: The American Civil War in the Making of Canadian Confederation," *Journal of the Civil War Era*, 7, no. 4 (2017): 512–40.

12. Confederation and Its Discontents, 1864–1873

1 David B. Flemming, "Thomas Louis Connolly" and William B. Hamilton, "Isaac LeVesconte," *Dictionary of Canadian Biography Online*. See also Robert Berard, "The End of the 'Gentlemen's Agreement': The Collapse of Catholic Education in Nova Scotia" (paper presented to the Royal Nova Scotia Historical Society, 18 October 2017).

2 P.B. Waite, *The Lives of Dalhousie University*, vol. 1, *1818–1925, Lord Dalhousie's College* (Montreal: McGill-Queen's University, 1994), 70–94.

3 The details concerning developments in London in this period are discussed in Andrew Smith, *British Businessmen and Canadian Confederation: Constitution Making in a Period of Anglo-Globalization* (Montreal: McGill-Queen's University Press, 2008). See also Paul Cornell, "John Ross," *Dictionary of Canadian Biography Online*.

4 *Rules of the British North American Association* (London, 1862), available online at https://archive.org/details/cihm_32289.

5 The details relating to Confederation are drawn from P.B. Waite, *The Life and Times of Confederation: Politicians, Newspapers, and the Union of British North America* (1962; Toronto: University of Toronto Press, 2002); Donald Creighton, *The Road to Confederation* (Toronto: Macmillan of Canada, 1964); W.L. Morton, *The Critical Years: The Union of British North America* (Toronto: McClelland & Stewart, 1964); Ged Martin, ed., *The Causes of*

Canadian Confederation (Fredericton: Acadiensis Press, 1990); Martin, *Britain and the Origins of Canadian Confederation, 1837–67* (Vancouver: UBC Press, 1995); Christopher Moore, *1867: How the Fathers Made a Deal* (Toronto: McClelland & Stewart, 1997); Moore, *Three Weeks in Quebec City: The Meeting that Made Canada* (Toronto: Allen Lane, 2015); and Ben Gilding, "The Silent Framers of British North American Union: The Colonial Office and Canadian Confederation, 1851–67," *Canadian Historical Review* 99, no. 3 (2018): 349–93.

6   J.K. Chapman, "Arthur Hamilton Gordon, 1st Baron Stanmore," *Dictionary of Canadian Biography Online.*

7   Gordon to Newcastle, 28 September 1863, cited in Creighton, *Road to Confederation*, 23. See also Moore, *1867*, chap. 2, for an extended discussion of Tupper's role in determining the nature of provincial representation at the Charlottetown meetings.

8   Martin, *Britain and the Origins of Canadian Confederation*, 230–2.

9   Kenneth G. Pryke, *Nova Scotia and Confederation, 1864–74* (Toronto: University of Toronto Press, 1979), 3–4.

10   Creighton, *Road to Confederation*, 96.

11   Cited in P.B. Waite, "Archibald Woodbury McLelan," *Dictionary of Canadian Biography Online.*

12   P.B. Waite, "Jonathan McCully," *Dictionary of Canadian Biography Online.*

13   K.G. Pryke, "Sir Adams George Archibald," *Dictionary of Canadian Biography Online.*

14   Phyllis R. Blakeney, "William Alexander Henry," *Dictionary of Canadian Biography Online.*

15   Pryke, *Nova Scotia and Confederation*, 13.

16   George G. Patterson, Judge. "Hon. Robert Barry Dickey," *Collections of the Nova Scotia Historical Society* 36 (1968): 60-64, and "Robert Barry Dickey," *Canadian Encyclopedia*, online at http://www.thecanadianencyclopedia. ca/en/article/robert-barry-dickey/. Dickey is the only Father of Confederation to be omitted from the *Dictionary of Canadian Biography* despite having served as a senator for many years.

17   Phillip Buckner, "Sir Charles Tupper," *Dictionary of Canadian Biography Online.*

18   Sir Charles Tupper, *Recollections of Sixty Years in Canada* (London: Cassell and Company, 1914), 37–8.

19   Martin, *Britain and the Origins of Canadian Confederation*, 229.

20   For reflections on the political context of Acadians, Mi'kmaq, and women in the Confederation period, see Julien Massicotte, "L'ambivalence acadienne: discours et identité à l'heure de la Confédération," *Acadiensis* 46, no. 2 (2017): 143–54; Martha Elizabeth Walls, Confederation and Maritime First Nations," *Acadiensis* 46, no. 2 (2017): 155–76; and

Heidi MacDonald, "Women's Suffrage and Confederation," *Acadiensis* 46, no. 1 (2017): 163–76.

21 Ralph C. Nelson, Walter C. Soderlund, Ronald H. Wagerberg, and C. Donald Briggs, "Canadian Confederation as a Case Study in Community Formation," in Martin, *Causes of Canadian Confederation*, 53–4, 66.

22 Moore, *1867*, 47.

23 The Quebec resolutions can be found online at https://www.collection-scanada.gc.ca/confederation/023001-7104-e.html.

24 Moore, *Three Weeks in Quebec City*, 91–2.

25 Phillip A. Buckner, "The 1860s: An End and a Beginning," in *The Atlantic Region in Confederation: A History*, ed. Phillip A. Buckner and John G. Reid (Toronto; Fredericton: University of Toronto Press and Acadiensis Press, 1994), 377.

26 George Brown to Anne Brown, 17 October 1864, cited in Moore, *Three Weeks in Quebec City*, chap. 13.

27 Diane M. Bakker and D.A. Sutherland, "Enos Collins," *Dictionary of Canadian Biography Online*.

28 Martin, *Britain and the Origins of Canadian Confederation*, 291.

29 Ibid., 244–50.

30 Pryke, *Nova Scotia and Confederation*, 27. See also Brian D. Tennyson, "Economic Nationalism and Confederation: A Case Study in Cape Breton," *Acadiensis* 2, no. 1 (1972): 39–53, and Delphin A. Muise, "The Federal Election of 1867 in Nova Scotia: An Economic Interpretation," *Collections of the Nova Scotia Historical Society* 36 (1968): 327–51.

31 James D. Frost, *Merchant Princes: Halifax's First Family of Finances, Ships and Steel* (Halifax: Formac, 2003), 88–100.

32 Pryke, *Nova Scotia and Confederation*, 25, 41–2.

33 Ibid.

34 William Garvey produced a humorous critique, *Confederation: Barney Rooney's Letters on Confederation, Botheration, and Political Transmogrification* (Halifax: Citizen, 1865), which is heavily freighted with dialect and satire.

35 Pryke, *Nova Scotia and Confederation*, 41.

36 Buckner, "Sir Charles Tupper."

37 Martin, *Britain and the Origins of Canadian Confederation*, 290.

38 Philip Girard, "The Atlantic Provinces and the Confederation Debates of 1865," *ActiveHistory*, 28 June 2016, available online at http://active-history.ca/?s=philip+girard. See also Phillip A. Buckner, "The Maritimes and Confederation: A Reassessment," and Ged Martin, "The Case Against Confederation, 1864–1867," in Martin, *Causes of Canadian Confederation*; and Buckner, "Beware the Canadian Wolf: The Maritimes and Confederation," *Acadiensis* 46, no. 2 (2017): 177–95.

39   D.A. Sutherland, "Sir Edward Kenny," *Dictionary of Canadian Biography Online.*

40   Buckner, "Sir Charles Tupper."

41   Library and Archives Canada, "Nova Scotia: Selected Newspaper Articles, July 1867," https://www.collectionscanada.gc.ca/confederation/023001-3080.01-e.html

42   Daniel Samson, "'Damn TORYISM say I': Dissent, Print Culture, and Anti-Confederation Thought in James Barry's Diary," *Acadiensis* XLVI, 1 (Winter/Spring 2017), 177.

43   Pryke, *Nova Scotia and Confederation*, 46–59.

44   Ibid., 59.

45   Ibid., 66.

46   David. A. Sutherland, "William Annand," and R.A. MacLean, "Martin Isaac Wilkins," *Dictionary of Canadian Biography Online.*

47   John A. Macdonald to Jonathan McCully, 2 January 1868, cited in Pryke, *Nova Scotia and Confederation*, 64.

48   Pryke, *Nova Scotia and Confederation*, 65.

49   Martin, *Britain and the Origins of Canadian Confederation*, 73–4.

50   Pryke, *Nova Scotia and Confederation*, 91–2.

51   Donald F. Warner, *The Idea of Continental Union: Agitation for the Annexation of Canada to the United States, 1840–1893* (Lexington: University of Kentucky Press, 1960), 81.

52   Pryke, *Nova Scotia and Confederation*, 115.

53   C.M. Wallace, "John Waterbury Cudlip," *Dictionary of Canadian Biography Online.*

54   "Order of Her Majesty in Council admitting Prince Edward Island into the Union, dated the 26th day of June 1873," available online at http://www.justice.gc.ca/eng/rp-pr/csj-sjc/constitution/lawreg-loireg/p1t61.html.

55   Robert A.J. McDonald and H. Keith Ralston, "Amor de Cosmos," *Dictionary of Canadian Biography Online.*

56   Pryke, *Nova Scotia and Confederation*, 142–4, and D.A. Muise, "Parties and Constituencies: Federal Elections in Nova Scotia, 1867–1896," *Historical Papers* (Ottawa: Canadian Historical Association, 1971): 183–202.

57   Alan A. Brookes, "Out-Migration from the Maritime Provinces, 1860–1900: Some Preliminary Considerations," *Acadiensis* 5, no. 2 (1976): 26–55, and Patricia A. Thornton, "The Problem of Out-Migration from Atlantic Canada, 1871–1921: A New Look," *Acadiensis* 15, no. 1 (1985): 3–34.

58   Cited in Margaret Conrad, Toni Laidlaw, and Donna Smyth, *No Place Like Home: Diaries and Letters of Nova Scotia Women, 1771–1838* (Halifax: Formac, 1988), 115.

Afterword

1 Margaret Conrad et al., *Canadians and Their Pasts* (Toronto: University of Toronto Press, 2013), 3–6.
2 E.R. Forbes, *Challenging the Regional Stereotype: Essays on the 20th Century Maritimes* (Fredericton: Acadiensis Press, 1989) and Raymond Blake, *Lions or Jellyfish: Newfoundland-Ottawa Relations Since 1957* (Toronto: University of Toronto Press, 2015).
3 This chapter draws upon several of my previously published articles, including Margaret Conrad, "'Nothing, of course, ever happens down there': Atlantic Canada in the National Consciousness," *Canadian Issues* (Fall 2014): 33–7; "Why I am (Sometimes) a Separatist: A View from the Margins," in *Can Canada Survive? Under What Terms and Conditions?* Transactions of the Royal Society of Canada, 1996, Sixth Series, vol. 7, ed. David Haynes (Toronto: University of Toronto Press, 1997), 91–102; and, with David Northrup, "Fail Again: Fail Better: Atlantic Canadians and Their Pasts," in *Shaping an Agenda for Atlantic Canada*, ed. John G. Reid and Donald J. Savoie (Halifax: Fernwood, 2011).
4 The Atlantic region has a deep and rich historiography, much of it published in journals such as *Acadiensis, Newfoundland and Labrador Studies, Nova Scotia Historical Review*, and *Island Magazine*, which in turn inform both the avalanche of popular histories pouring off regional presses and the public commemorations advanced to shore up a shared historical memory and attract tourist dollars. In the apt phrase employed by Ian McKay and Robin Bates, Nova Scotia (along with its Atlantic Canadian counterparts) is a "Province of History," where efforts to control the historical narrative have fuelled debates for more than two centuries. Ian McKay and Robin Bates, *In the Province of History: The Making of the Public Past in Twentieth-Century Nova Scotia* (Montreal: McGill-Queen's University Press, 2010).
5 T.W. Acheson, "The National Policy and the Industrialization of the Maritimes, 1880–1910," *Acadiensis* 1, no. 2 (1972): 3–28; L.D. McCann, "The Mercantile-Industrial Transition in Metal Towns in Pictou County, 1857–1931," *Acadiensis* 5, no. 2 (1981): 26–55; "Metropolitanism and Branch Businesses in the Maritimes, 1881–1931," *Acadiensis* 13, no. 1 (1983): 111–25; James D. Frost, "The 'Nationalization' of the Bank of Nova Scotia," *Acadiensis* 12, no. 1 (1982): 3–38; Duncan McDowall, *Quick to the Frontier: Canada's Royal Bank* (Toronto: McClelland & Stewart, 1993); and Kris Inwood, "Maritime Industrialization from 1870 to 1910: A Review of the Evidence and its Interpretation" in *Farm, Factory and Fortune: New Studies in the Economic History of the Maritime Provinces*, ed. Kris Inwood (Fredericton: Acadiensis Press, 1993), 149–70.

6 Gregory P. Marchildon, *Profit and Politics: Beaverbrook and the Gilded Age of Canadian Finance* (Toronto: University of Toronto Press, 1996) and "John F. Stairs, Max Aitken and the Scotia Group: Finance Capitalism and the Decline of the Maritimes, 1890–1914," in Inwood, *Farm, Factory and Fortune*, 197–218.

7 Colin D. Howell, "W.S. Fielding and the Repeal Elections of 1886 and 1887 in Nova Scotia," *Acadiensis* 8, no. 2 (1979): 28–46, and "Nova Scotia's Protest Tradition and the Search for a Meaningful Federalism," in *Canada and the Burden of Unity*, ed. David Jay Bercuson (Toronto: Macmillan of Canada, 1977), 169–91. See also Carman Miller, "William Stevens Fielding," in *Dictionary of Canadian Biography Online*.

8 Alan A. Brookes, "Out-Migration from the Maritime Provinces, 1860–1900: Some Preliminary Considerations," *Acadiensis* 5, no. 2 (1976): 26–55, and Patricia A. Thornton, "The Problem of Out-Migration from Atlantic Canada, 1871–1921: A New Look," *Acadiensis* 15, no. 1 (1985): 3–34.

9 "Scotia, California," *Wikipedia*, online at https://en.wikipedia.org/wiki/Scotia,_California.

10 Albert J. Kennedy, "The Provincials," introduction Alan A. Brookes, *Acadiensis* 4, no. 2 (1975), 94.

11 Edward MacDonald, *If You're Stronghearted: Prince Edward Island in the Twentieth Century* (Charlottetown: Prince Edward Island Heritage Foundation, 2000), 51–4.

12 Ibid., 26; Ernest R. Forbes, *Aspects of Maritime Regionalism, 1867–1927* (Ottawa: Canadian Historical Association, 1983) and Donald J. Savoie, *Visiting Grandchildren: Economic Development in the Maritimes* (Toronto: University of Toronto Press, 2006).

13 David Frank, "The 1920s: Class and Region, Resistance and Accommodation," in *The Atlantic Provinces in Confederation*, ed. E.R. Forbes and D.A. Musise (Toronto; Fredericton, University of Toronto Press and Acadiensis Press, 1993), 233–71, and "The Cape Breton Coal Industry and the Rise and Fall of the British Empire Steel Corporation," *Acadiensis* 7, no. 1 (1977): 3–34. See also Ken Cruikshank, "The Intercolonial Railway, Freight Rates and the Maritime Economy," in Inwood, *Farm, Factory and Fortune*, 171–96.

14 E.R. Forbes, *The Maritime Rights Movement: 1919–1927: A Study in Canadian Regionalism* (Montreal: McGill-Queens University Press, 1979); "Misguided Symmetry: The Destruction of Regional Transportation Policy for the Maritimes," in Bercuson, *Canada and the Burden of Unity*, 60–86; "Never the Twain Did Meet: Prairie-Maritime Relations, 1910–27," *Canadian Historical Review* 59, no. 1 (1978): 18–37; and Kris Inwood, "The People's Railway: The Intercolonial Railway and the Canadian Public Enterprise Experience," *Acadiensis* 16, no. 1 (1986): 78–100.

15   P.B. Waite, *In Search of R.B. Bennett* (Montreal: McGill-Queen's University Press, 2012).

16   J.L. Granatstein, *The Politics of Survival: The Conservative Party of Canada, 1939–1945* (Toronto: University of Toronto Press, 1967).

17   Carman Carroll, "The Influence of H.H. Stevens and the Reconstruction Party in Nova Scotia, 1934–35" (MA thesis, University of New Brunswick, 1972); Jim Lotz, *The Humble Giant: Moses Coady, Canada's Rural Revolutionary* (Ottawa: Novalis, 2005); Santo Dodaro and Leonard Pluta, *The Antigonish Movement in Eastern Nova Scotia* (Montreal: McGill-Queen's University Press, 2012); and Rusty Neal, *Brotherhood Economics: Women and Co-operatives in Nova Scotia* (Sydney: UCCB Press, 1998).

18   T. Stephen Henderson, *Angus L. Macdonald: A Provincial Liberal* (Toronto: University of Toronto Press, 2007), 64–6.

19   S.A. Saunders, *The Economic History of the Maritime Provinces*, ed. T.W. Acheson (1939, reprint Fredericton: Acadiensis Press, 1984), 95.

20   Sean Cadigan, *Death on Two Fronts: National Tragedies and the Fate of Democracy in Newfoundland, 1914–34* (Toronto: Allen Lane/Penguin Random House Canada, 2013) and E.R. Forbes, "Cutting the Pie into Smaller Pieces: Matching Grants and Relief in the Maritime Provinces during the1930s," *Acadiensis* 17, no. 1 (1987): 34–55.

21   E.R. Forbes, ""Consolidating Disparity: The Maritimes and the Industrialization of Canada during the Second World War," *Acadiensis* 15, no. 2 (1987): 3–27; Marc Milner, *The Battle of the Atlantic* (St Catharines, ON: Vanwell, 2003); and Roger Sarty, *The Battle of the Atlantic: The Royal Canadian Navy's Greatest Campaign, 1939–1945* (Ottawa: CEF Books, 2001).

22   Atlantic Provinces Economic Council, "Defence Expenditures and the Economy of the Atlantic Provinces," Pamphlet 9 (December 1965).

23   Raymond Blake and Melvin Baker, *Where Once We Stood: Newfoundland's Rocky Road Towards Confederation* (Regina: University of Regina Press, 2019); Raymond B. Blake, *Canadians at Last: Canada Integrates Newfoundland as a Province* (Toronto: University of Toronto Press, 1994); "Canada, Newfoundland, and Term 29: The Failure of Intergovernmentalism," *Acadiensis* 41, no. 1 (2012): 40–74; and Corey Slumkoski, *Inventing Atlantic Canada: Regionalism and the Maritime Reaction to Newfoundland's Entry into Canadian Confederation* (Toronto: University of Toronto Press, 2011).

24   W.S. MacNutt, "The Atlantic Revolution," *Atlantic Advocate* (June 1957): 11–13, and Margaret Conrad, "The Atlantic Revolution of the 1950s," in *Beyond Anger and Longing: Community and Development in Atlantic Canada*, ed. Berkeley Fleming (Fredericton: Acadiensis Press, 1988), 55–96.

25   Ralph Matthews, *The Creation of Regional Dependency* (Toronto: University of Toronto Press, 1983).

26 Margaret Conrad, *George Nowlan, Maritime Conservative in National Politics* (Toronto: University of Toronto Press, 1986), chap. 10.

27 Constitution Act, Part III, Article 36.

28 E.R Forbes, "The Atlantic Provinces, Free Trade, and the Canadian Constitution," in *Challenging the Regional Stereotype: Essays on the 20th Century Maritimes* (Fredericton: Acadiensis Press, 1989), 201, and David Alexander, "New Notions of Happiness: Nationalism, Regionalism, and Atlantic Canada," *Journal of Canadian Studies* 25, no. 2 (1980): 29–42.

29 *Maclean's*, 15 October 1926, cited in E.R. Forbes, "In Search of a Post-Confederation Maritime Historiography, 1900–1967," in *Challenging the Regional Stereotype*, 59.

30 "The best quotes from Ralph Klein's colourful public life," *Globe and Mail*, 29 March 2013. See also Margaret Conrad, "Mistaken Identities? Newfoundland and Labrador in the Atlantic Region," *Newfoundland Studies* 8, no. 2 (2002): 159–74.

31 Raymond Blake, *Lions or Jellyfish: Newfoundland-Ottawa Relations since 1957* (Toronto: University of Toronto Press, 2015), chap. 7.

32 Ibid., chap. 8.

33 "Margaret Wente says...," *Globe and Mail*, 6 January 2005. In 2016, Wente had second thoughts about her comments; see "Please forgive me and slap me with a cod," *Globe and Mail*, 24 September 2016.

34 Bertrand Marotte, "Ottawa pays AbitibiBowater $130 million for expropriation," *Globe and Mail*, 24 August 2010.

35 Blake, *Lions or Jellyfish*, chap. 2. See also Jerry Bannister, "A River Runs Through It: Churchill Falls and the End of Newfoundland History," *Acadiensis* 41, no. 1 (2012), 211–25; Jason Churchill, "Pragmatic Federalism: The Politics behind the 1969 Churchill Falls Contract," *Newfoundland Studies* 15, no. 21 (1999): 215–45; and James P. Feehan, "Smallwood, Churchill Falls, and the Power Corridor Through Quebec," *Acadiensis* 40, no. 2 (2011): 112–27.

36 Loleen Berdahl and Roger Gibbins, *Looking West: Regional Transformation and the Future of Canada* (Toronto: University of Toronto Press, 2014).

37 Mildred Schwartz, *Politics and Territory: The Sociology of Regional Persistence in Canada* (Montreal: McGill-Queen's University Press, 1974). Harper's quote is documented in the Saint John *Telegraph-Journal*, 29 May 2002. See also J. Murray Beck, "An Atlantic Region Political Culture: A Chimera," in *Eastern and Western Perspectives: Papers from the Joint Atlantic Canada/Western Canadian Studies Conference*, ed. David Jay Bercuson and Phillip A. Buckner (Toronto: University of Toronto Press, 1981), 147–68.

38 J. Murray Beck, *Joseph Howe*, vol. 2, *The Briton Becomes Canadian, 1848–1873* (Toronto: University of Toronto Press, 1983). See also Ged Martin, "Empire

Federalism and Imperial Parliamentary Union, 1820–1870," *Historical Journal* 16 (1973): 65–92.

39 Carl Berger, *The Sense of Power: Studies in the Ideas of Canadian Imperialism, 1867–1914*, 2nd ed. (Toronto: University of Toronto Press, 2013).

40 Donald Warner, *The Idea of Continental Union: Agitation for the Annexation of Canada to the United States, 1849–1893* (Lexington: University of Kentucky Press, 1960), 60–86.

41 Carman Miller, "The Restoration of Greater Nova Scotia," in Bercuson, *Canada and the Burden of Unity*, 44–59.

42 See, for example, P.B. Waite, *The Life and Times of Confederation, 1864–1867: Politicians, Newspapers, and the Union of British North America* (1962, reprint Toronto: Robin Brass Studio, 2001), 65.

43 Stephen Greene, "Why Maritime union didn't succeed in the 1970s," *Herald Opinions*, 9 March 2013, and John Reid, "The 1970s: Sharpening the Sceptical Edge," in Forbes and Muise, *Atlantic Provinces in Confederation*, 463. See also J. Murray Beck, *The History of Maritime Union: A Study in Frustration* (Fredericton: Maritime Union Study, 1969).

44 Paul McLeod, "Poll: Atlantic Canadians reject idea of Maritime merger," *Herald News*, 4 December 2012.

45 Donald J. Savoie, *Looking for Bootstraps: Economic Development in the Maritimes* (Halifax: Nimbus, 2017).

46 Heritage Newfoundland and Labrador, "Reciprocity with the United States of America," available online at http://www.heritage.nf.ca/articles/politics/reciprocity-newfoundland-united-states.php.

47 David Alexander, "Economic Growth in the Atlantic Region, 1880–1940," *Acadiensis* 8, no. 1 (1981): 47–76.

48 Sean T. Cadigan, "Regional Politics are Class Politics: A Newfoundland and Labrador Perspective on Region," *Acadiensis* 35, no. 2 (2006): 163–8.

49 I pursue this argument in *George Nowlan*, cited above. Ian McKay also argues that the Atlantic region has helped to sustain a progressive liberalism in Canada; see "A Note on "Region," in "Writing the History of Atlantic Canada," *Acadiensis* 29, no. 2 (2000): 99–101.

50 Worldometers, Iceland Population, available online at http://www.worldometers.info/world-population/iceland-population/ and *Wikipedia*, "2008–2011 Icelandic Financial Crisis," online at https://en.wikipedia.org/wiki/2008%E2%80%9311_s.

51 See, for instance, Jeff Webb, *Observing the Outports: Describing Newfoundland Culture, 1950–1980* (Toronto: University of Toronto Press, 2015). For thoughtful reflections on regionalism, see the essays in "Forum: Roundtable on Re-Imagining Regions," *Acadiensis* 35, no. 2 (2006): 127–62.

Index

The letter *f* following a page number denotes a figure; the letter *m* a map; the letter *t* a table.

STUDIES IN ATLANTIC CANADA HISTORY

Editors: John G. Reid and Peter L. Twohig